토익 Reading 목표 달성기와 함께
목표 점수를 달성해 보세요.

KB088845

나의 토익 Reading 목표 달성기

나의 목표 점수	나의 학습 플랜

□ [400점 이상] 2주 완성 학습 플랜

□ [300~395점] 3주 완성 학습 플랜

_____ 점

□ [295점 이하] 4주 완성 학습 플랜

* 일 단위의 상세 학습 플랜은 p.22에 있습니다.

각 Test를 마친 후, 해당 Test의 점수를 ● 으로 표시하여 자신의 점수 변화를 확인하세요.

495										
450							토익의 고수!			
400					고득점은 이제 시간 문제!					
350				토익 감 잡았어!						
300		토익 초보예요!								

	TEST 01	TEST 02	TEST 03	TEST 04	TEST 05	TEST 06	TEST 07	TEST 08	TEST 09	TEST 10
학습일	/	/	/	/	/	/	/	/	/	/
맞은 개수	개	개	개	개	개	개	개	개	개	개
환산점수	점	점	점	점	점	점	점	점	점	점

* 리딩 점수 환산표는 p.329에 있습니다.

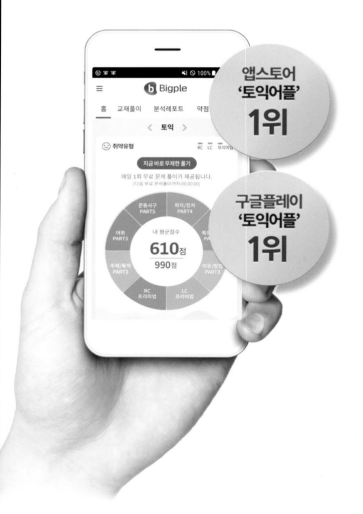

해커스
토익 RC

실전 **1000**제 **2**
READING

문제집

해커스 어학연구소

최신 토익 경향을 완벽하게 반영한
해커스 토익 실전 1000제 2 READING 문제집을 내면서

해커스 토익이 항상 독보적인 베스트셀러의 자리를 지킬 수 있는 것은 늘 **처음과 같은 마음으로** 더 좋은 책을 만들기 위해 고민하고, **최신 경향을 반영하기 위해 끊임없이 노력**하기 때문입니다.

그리고 이러한 노력 끝에 최신 토익 경향을 반영한 《해커스 토익 실전 1000제 2 Reading 문제집》(최신개정판)을 출간하게 되었습니다.

최신 출제 경향 완벽 반영!

최신 토익 출제 경향을 철저히 분석하여 실전과 가장 유사한 지문과 문제 10회분을 수록하였습니다. 수록한 모든 문제는 실전과 동일한 환경에서 풀 수 있도록 실제 토익 문제지와 동일하게 구성하였으며, Answer Sheet를 수록하여 시간 관리 연습과 더불어 실전 감각을 보다 높일 수 있도록 하였습니다.

점수를 올려주는 학습 구성과 학습 자료로 토익 고득점 달성!

모든 문제의 정답과 함께 정확한 해석을 수록하였으며, 해커스토익(Hackers.co.kr)에서 'Part 5&6 해설'을 무료로 제공합니다. 지문과 문제의 정확한 이해를 통해 토익 리딩 점수를 향상할 수 있으며, 토익 고득점 달성이 가능합니다.

《해커스 토익 실전 1000제 2 Reading 문제집》은 별매되는 해설집과 함께 학습할 때 보다 효과적으로 학습할 수 있습니다. 또한, 해커스인강(HackersIngang.com)에서 '온라인 실전모의고사 1회분'과 '단어암기 PDF&MP3'를 무료로 제공하며, 토익 스타 강사의 파트별 해설강의를 수강할 수 있습니다.

《해커스 토익 실전 1000제 2 Reading 문제집》이 여러분의 토익 목표 점수 달성에 확실한 해결책이 되고 영어 실력 향상, 나아가 여러분의 꿈을 향한 길에 믿음직한 동반자가 되기를 소망합니다.

해커스 어학연구소

CONTENTS

Part 5&6 무료 해설 바로 보기

확실하게 고득점 잡는다!

01 토익에 완벽하게 대비한다!

최신 토익 출제 경향을 반영한 실전 10회분 수록

시험 경향에 맞지 않는 문제들만 풀면, 실전에서는 연습했던 문제와 달라 당황할 수 있습니다. 《해커스 토익 실전 1000제 2 Reading 문제집》에 수록된 모든 문제는 최신 출제 경향과 난이도를 반영하여 실전에 철저하게 대비할 수 있도록 하였습니다.

실전과 동일한 구성!

《해커스 토익 실전 1000제 2 Reading 문제집》에 수록된 모든 문제는 실전 문제지와 동일하게 구성되었습니다. 또한, 교재 뒤에 수록된 Answer Sheet를 통해 답안 마킹까지 실제 시험처럼 연습해볼 수 있도록 함으로써 시간 관리 방법을 익히고, 실전 감각을 보다 극대화할 수 있도록 하였습니다.

02

한 문제를 풀어도, 정확하게 이해하고 푼다!

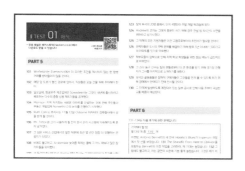

정확한 지문/문제 해석

수록된 모든 지문 및 문제에 대한 정확한 해석을 수록하였습니다. 테스트를 마친 후, 교재 뒤에 수록된 해석을 참고하여 자신의 해석과 맞는지 비교하고, 지문과 문제를 정확하게 이해할 수 있습니다.

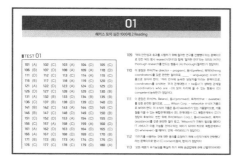

무료 해설 PDF

Part 5, 6 문제에 대한 해설을 해커스토익(Hackers.co.kr) 사이트에서 무료로 제공합니다. 이를 통해 테스트를 마친 후, 해석을 봐도 잘 이해가 되지 않는 문제를 보다 확실하게 이해하고, 몰랐던 문법 사항이나 어휘의 의미와 쓰임까지 학습할 수 있도록 하였습니다.

Self 체크 리스트

각 테스트 마지막 페이지에는 Self 체크 리스트를 수록하여 테스트를 마친 후 자신의 문제 풀이 방식과 태도를 스스로 점검할 수 있도록 하였습니다. 이를 통해 효과적인 복습과 더불어 목표 점수를 달성하기 위해 개선해야 할 습관 및 부족한 점을 찾아 보완해나갈 수 있습니다.

03 내 실력을 확실하게 파악한다!

점수 환산표

교재 부록으로 점수 환산표를 수록하여, 학습자들이 테스트를 마치고 채점을 한 후 바로 점수를 확인하여 **자신의 실력을 정확하게 파악**할 수 있도록 하였습니다. 환산 점수를 교재 첫 장의 목표 달성 그래프에 표시하여 실력의 변화를 확인하고, 학습 계획을 세울 수 있습니다.

무료 온라인 실전모의고사

교재에 수록된 테스트 외에 해커스인강(HackersIngang.com) 사이트에서 온라인 실전모의고사 1회분을 추가로 무료 제공합니다. 이를 통해 토익 시험 전, 학습자들이 자신의 실력을 마지막으로 점검해볼 수 있도록 하였습니다.

인공지능 1:1 토익어플 '빅플'

교재의 문제를 풀고 답안을 입력하기만 하면, 인공지능 어플 '해커스토익 빅플'이 **자동 채점**은 물론 성적분석표와 취약 유형 심층 분석까지 제공합니다. 이를 통해, 자신이 가장 많이 틀리는 취약 유형이 무엇인지 확인하고, 관련 문제들을 추가로 학습하며 취약 유형을 집중 공략하여 약점을 보완할 수 있습니다.

04 다양한 학습 자료를 활용한다!

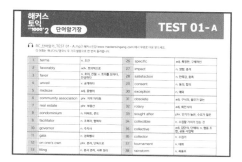

단어암기 PDF&MP3 / 정답녹음 MP3

해커스인강(HackersIngang.com) 사이트에서 단어암기 PDF와 MP3를 무료로 제공하여, 교재에 수록된 테스트의 중요 단어를 복습하고 암기할 수 있도록 하였습니다. 또한 정답녹음 MP3 파일을 제공하여 학습자들이 보다 편리하게 채점할 수 있도록 하였습니다.

방대한 무료 학습자료(Hackers.co.kr) / 동영상강의(HackersIngang.com)

해커스토익(Hackers.co.kr) 사이트에서는 토익 적중 예상특강을 비롯한 방대하고 유용한 토익 학습자료를 무료로 이용할 수 있습니다. 또한 온라인 교육 포털 사이트인 해커스인강(HackersIngang.com) 사이트에서 교재 동영상강의를 수강하면, 보다 깊이 있는 학습이 가능합니다.

해설집 미리보기

<해설집 별매>

01 정답과 오답의 이유를 확인하여 Part 5&6 완벽 정복!

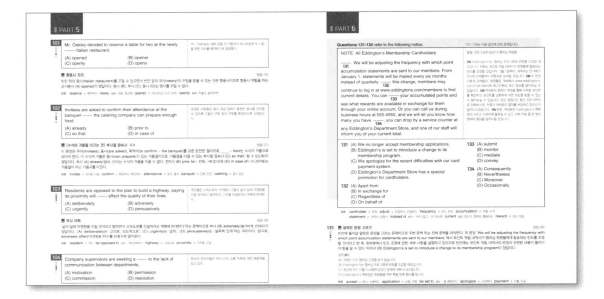

---

1 문제 및 문제 해석

최신 토익 출제 경향이 반영된 문제를 해설집에도 그대로 수록해, 해설을 보기 전 문제를 다시 한번 풀어보며 자신이 어떤 과정으로 정답을 선택했는지 되짚어 볼 수 있습니다. 함께 수록된 정확한 해석을 보며 문장 구조를 꼼꼼하게 파악하여 문제를 완벽하게 이해할 수 있습니다.

2 문제 유형 및 난이도

모든 문제마다 문제 유형을 제시하여 자주 틀리는 문제 유형을 쉽게 파악할 수 있고, 사전 테스트를 거쳐 검증된 문제별 난이도를 확인하여 자신의 실력과 학습 목표에 따라 학습할 수 있습니다. 문제 유형은 모두 《해커스 토익 Reading》의 목차 목록과 동일하여, 보완 학습이 필요할 경우 쉽게 참고할 수 있습니다.

3 상세한 해설 및 어휘

문제 유형별로 가장 효과적인 해결 방법을 제시하며, 오답 보기가 오답이 되는 이유까지 상세하게 설명하여 틀린 문제의 원인을 파악하고 보완할 수 있습니다. 또한 지문 및 문제에서 사용된 단어나 어구의 뜻을 품사 표시와 함께 수록하여, 중요 문법·어휘를 함께 학습할 수 있습니다.

02 효율적인 Part 7 문제 풀이를 통해 고득점 달성!

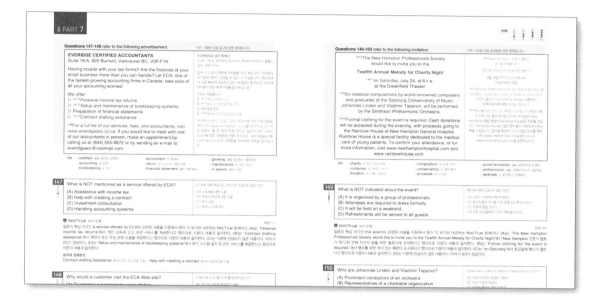

1 지문, 문제, 해석, 정답의 단서

최신 토익 출제 경향이 반영된 지문 및 문제와, 함께 수록된 정확한 해석을 보며 지문 및 문제의 내용을 완벽하게 이해할 수 있습니다. 또한, 각 문제별로 표시된 정답의 단서를 확인하여, 모든 문제에 대한 정답의 근거를 정확하게 파악하는 연습을 할 수 있습니다.

2 문제 유형별 상세한 해설 및 문제 풀이 방법

문제 유형별로 가장 효율적인 해결 방법이 적용된 문제 풀이 방법을 제시하였습니다. 질문의 핵심 어구를 파악하고, 이를 지문에서 찾아 보기와 연결하고 정답을 선택하는 과정을 읽는 것만으로도 자연스럽게 Part 7의 유형별 문제 풀이 전략을 익힐 수 있습니다.

3 바꾸어 표현하기

지문의 내용이 질문이나 보기에서 바꾸어 표현된 경우, 이를 [지문의 표현 → 보기의 표현] 또는 [질문의 표현 → 지문의 표현]으로 정리하여 한눈에 확인할 수 있도록 하였습니다. 이를 통해 Part 7 풀이 전략을 익히고 나아가 고득점 달성이 가능하도록 하였습니다.

토익 소개 및 시험장 Tips

토익이란 무엇인가?

TOEIC은 **Test Of English for International Communication**의 약자로 영어가 모국어가 아닌 사람들을 대상으로 언어 본래의 기능인 '커뮤니케이션' 능력에 중점을 두고 일상생활 또는 국제 업무 등에 필요한 실용영어 능력을 평가하는 시험입니다. 토익은 일상생활 및 비즈니스 현장에서 필요로 하는 내용을 평가하기 위해 개발되었고 다음과 같은 실용적인 주제들을 주로 다룹니다.

▌ 협력 개발: 연구, 제품 개발
▌ 재무 회계: 대출, 투자, 세금, 회계, 은행 업무
▌ 일반 업무: 계약, 협상, 마케팅, 판매
▌ 기술 영역: 전기, 공업 기술, 컴퓨터, 실험실
▌ 사무 영역: 회의, 서류 업무
▌ 물품 구입: 쇼핑, 물건 주문, 대금 지불

▌ 식사: 레스토랑, 회식, 만찬
▌ 문화: 극장, 스포츠, 피크닉
▌ 건강: 의료 보험, 병원 진료, 치과
▌ 제조: 생산 조립 라인, 공장 경영
▌ 직원: 채용, 은퇴, 급여, 진급, 고용 기회
▌ 주택: 부동산, 이사, 기업 부지

토익의 파트별 구성

구성		내용	문항 수	시간	배점
Listening Test	Part 1	사진 묘사	6문항 (1번~6번)	45분	495점
	Part 2	질의 응답	25문항 (7번~31번)		
	Part 3	짧은 대화	39문항, 13지문 (32번~70번)		
	Part 4	짧은 담화	30문항, 10지문 (71번~100번)		
Reading Test	Part 5	단문 빈칸 채우기 (문법/어휘)	30문항 (101번~130번)	75분	495점
	Part 6	장문 빈칸 채우기 (문법/어휘/문장 고르기)	16문항, 4지문 (131번~146번)		
	Part 7	지문 읽고 문제 풀기(독해) - 단일 지문 (Single Passage) - 이중 지문 (Double Passages) - 삼중 지문 (Triple Passages)	54문항, 15지문 (147번~200번) - 29문항, 10지문 (147번~175번) - 10문항, 2지문 (176번~185번) - 15문항, 3지문 (186번~200번)		
Total		7 Parts	200문항	120분	990점

토익 접수 방법 및 성적 확인

1. 접수 방법
- 접수 기간을 TOEIC위원회 인터넷 사이트(www.toeic.co.kr) 혹은 공식 애플리케이션에서 확인하고 접수합니다.
- 접수 시 jpg형식의 사진 파일이 필요하므로 미리 준비합니다.

2. 성적 확인
- 시험일로부터 약 10일 이후 TOEIC위원회 인터넷 사이트(www.toeic.co.kr) 혹은 공식 애플리케이션에서 확인합니다. (성적 발표 기간은 회차마다 상이함)
- 시험 접수 시, 우편 수령과 온라인 출력 중 성적 수령 방법을 선택할 수 있습니다.
  *온라인 출력은 성적 발표 즉시 발급 가능하나, 우편 수령은 약 7일가량의 발송 기간이 소요될 수 있습니다.

시험 당일 준비물

| 신분증 | 연필&지우개 | 시계 | 수험번호를 적어둔 메모 | 오답노트&단어암기장 |

* 시험 당일 신분증이 없으면 시험에 응시할 수 없으므로, 반드시 ETS에서 요구하는 신분증(주민등록증, 운전면허증, 공무원증 등)을 지참해야 합니다.
 ETS에서 인정하는 신분증 종류는 TOEIC 위원회 인터넷 사이트(www.toeic.co.kr)에서 확인 가능합니다.

시험 진행 순서

정기시험/추가시험(오전)	추가시험(오후)	진행내용	유의사항
AM 9:30 - 9:45	PM 2:30 - 2:45	답안지 작성 오리엔테이션	10분 전에 고사장에 도착하여, 이름과 수험번호로 고사실을 확인합니다.
AM 9:45 - 9:50	PM 2:45 - 2:50	쉬는 시간	준비해간 오답노트나 단어암기장으로 최종 정리를 합니다. 시험 중간에는 쉬는 시간이 없으므로 화장실에 꼭 다녀오도록 합니다.
AM 9:50 - 10:10	PM 2:50 - 3:10	신분 확인 및 문제지 배부	
AM 10:10 - 10:55	PM 3:10 - 3:55	Listening Test	Part 1과 Part 2는 문제를 풀면서 정답을 바로 답안지에 마킹합니다. Part 3와 Part 4는 문제의 정답 보기 옆에 살짝 표시해두고, Listening Test가 끝난 후 한꺼번에 마킹합니다.
AM 10:55 - 12:10	PM 3:55 - 5:10	Reading Test	각 문제를 풀 때 바로 정답을 마킹합니다.

* 추가시험은 토요일 오전 또는 오후에 시행되므로 이 사항도 꼼꼼히 확인합니다.
* 당일 진행 순서에 대한 더 자세한 내용은 해커스토익(Hackers.co.kr) 사이트에서 확인할 수 있습니다.

파트별 형태 및 전략

▌Part 5 단문 빈칸 채우기 (30문제)

· 한 문장의 빈칸에 알맞은 문법 사항이나 어휘를 4개의 보기 중에서 고르는 유형
· 권장 소요 시간: 11분 (문제당 풀이 시간: 20초~22초)

문제 형태

1 문법

---
101. Mr. Monroe announced his ------- to retire from the firm at a meeting last week.

    (A) decides
    (B) decisively
    (C) decision
    (D) decisive

해설 101. 빈칸 앞에 형용사 역할을 하는 소유격 인칭대명사(his)가 왔으므로 형용사의 꾸밈을 받을 수 있는 명사 (C)가 정답이다.

2 어휘

---
102. Effective on Monday, employees must start ------- a new procedure for ordering office supplies.

    (A) causing
    (B) following
    (C) excluding
    (D) informing

해설 102. '직원들은 새로운 절차를 ___하기 시작해야 한다'라는 문맥에 가장 잘 어울리는 단어는 동사 follow의 동명사 (B)이다.

문제 풀이 전략

1. 보기를 보고 문법 문제인지, 어휘 문제인지 유형을 파악합니다.

네 개의 보기를 보고 문법 사항을 묻는 문제인지, 어휘의 의미를 묻는 문제인지를 파악합니다. 보기가 첫 번째 예제의 decides, decisively, decision, decisive처럼 품사가 다른 단어들로 구성되어 있으면 문법 문제이고, 두 번째 예제의 causing, following, excluding, informing처럼 품사는 같지만 의미가 다른 단어들로 구성되어 있으면 어휘 문제입니다.

2. 문제 유형에 따라 빈칸 주변이나 문장 구조 또는 문맥을 통해 정답을 선택합니다.

문법 문제는 빈칸 주변이나 문장 구조를 통해 빈칸에 적합한 문법적 요소를 정답으로 선택합니다. 어휘 문제의 경우 문맥을 확인하여 문맥에 가장 적합한 단어를 정답으로 선택합니다.

* 실제 시험을 볼 때, Part 1과 Part 2의 디렉션이 나오는 동안 Part 5 문제를 최대한 많이 풀면 전체 시험 시간 조절에 도움이 됩니다.

▌Part 6 장문 빈칸 채우기 (16문제)

· 한 지문 내의 4개의 빈칸에 알맞은 문법 사항이나 어휘, 문장을 고르는 유형. 총 4개의 지문 출제.
· 권장 소요 시간: 8분 (문제당 풀이 시간: 25초~30초)

문제 형태

Questions 131-134 refer to the following e-mail.

Dear Ms. Swerter,

It was a treat to see your group ------- its music at the community event in Morristown. Do you think you
could do the same for us at a private gathering next month? My company ------- a welcoming
celebration for some clients. -------. We are planning a special dinner and are hoping your group can
provide the accompanying entertainment. We'd also like to book the dancers who were with you at the
concert. Their performance was quite ------- to watch. Our guests would surely enjoy seeing both acts
together. Please let me know.

Shannon Lemmick

어휘 **131.** (A) act	문장 **133.** (A) I'd like to buy tickets for the afternoon show.
(B) explain	고르기 (B) You may request their services for an additional charge.
(C) perform	(C) It will be their first time meeting with my company's staff.
(D) observe	(D) We approve of the schedule you have proposed.
문법 **132.** (A) will be hosting	
(B) hosted	어휘 **134.** (A) tough
(C) hosts	(B) thrilling
(D) to host	(C) content
	(D) punctual

해설 131. '당신의 그룹이 지역 사회 행사에서 곡을 연주하는 것을 보게 되어 좋았다'라는 문맥이므로 동사 (C)가 정답이다.

132. 앞 문장에서 다음 달에 같은 공연을 해줄 수 있는지 물었으므로 행사가 미래에 열린다는 것을 알 수 있다. 따라서 미래 시제 (A)가 정답이다.

133. 앞 문장에서 '회사는 몇몇 고객들을 위한 환영 행사를 개최할 것이다'라고 했으므로 빈칸에는 고객들과의 만남에 대한 추가적인 내용이
들어가야 함을 알 수 있다. 따라서 (C)가 정답이다.

134. '그들의 공연은 관람하기에 꽤 황홀했다'라는 문맥이므로 형용사 (B)가 정답이다.

문제 풀이 전략

1. 보기를 보고 문제 유형을 파악합니다.
보기를 먼저 보고 문법 문제, 어휘 문제, 문장 고르기 문제 가운데 어떤 유형의 문제인지를 파악합니다.

2. 문제 유형에 따라 빈칸이 포함된 문장이나, 앞뒤 문장, 또는 전체 지문의 문맥을 통해 정답을 선택합니다.
Part 6에서는 빈칸이 포함된 문장뿐만 아니라 앞뒤 문장, 전체 지문의 문맥을 통해 정답을 파악해야 하는 문제도 출제됩
니다. 그러므로 빈칸이 포함된 문장의 구조 및 문맥만으로 정답 선택이 어려울 경우 앞뒤 문맥이나 전체 문맥을 통해 정답
을 선택합니다.

▌Part 7 지문 읽고 문제 풀기 (54문제)

· 지문을 읽고 지문과 관련된 질문들에 대해 가장 적절한 보기를 정답으로 고르는 유형
· 구성: Single Passage에서 29문제, Double Passages에서 10문제, Triple Passages에서 15문제 출제
· 권장 소요 시간: 54분 (문제당 풀이 시간: 1분)

문제 형태

1 단일 지문 (Single Passage)

Questions 164-167 refer to the following advertisement.

AVALON WINDOWS
The window professionals

For over 30 years, homeowners have trusted Avalon Windows for expert window installation and repair. We offer quick and efficient service no matter what the job is. — [1] —. We ensure total customer satisfaction for a reasonable price. — [2] —. We provide accurate measurements, a complete project estimate with no hidden fees, and a 10-year warranty on all installations. We also offer a selection of window styles and sizes for you to choose from. — [3] —. Simply call us at 555-2092 to receive a free catalog in the mail or to schedule a consultation. Mention this advertisement when you call and receive 15 percent off your next window installation. — [4] —.

164. For whom is the advertisement intended?

(A) Real estate consultants
(B) Proprietors of residences
(C) Construction contractors
(D) Building supply retailers

165. What is true about Avalon Windows?

(A) It offers guarantees on installations.
(B) It also offers construction services.
(C) It plans to expand style selections.
(D) It charges a small fee for job estimates.

166. How can customers obtain discounts on a service?

(A) By ordering a specific number of windows
(B) By signing up on a Web site
(C) By mailing in a special coupon
(D) By mentioning an advertisement

167. In which of the positions marked [1], [2], [3], and [4] does the following sentence best belong?

"In fact, if you aren't pleased with our work, you'll get your money back."

(A) [1]
(B) [2]
(C) [3]
(D) [4]

해설 164. 주택 소유자들이 Avalon Windows사에 전문적인 창문 설치와 수리를 믿고 맡겨왔다고 했으므로 (B)가 정답이다.

165. Avalon Windows사가 모든 설치에 대해 10년의 보증을 제공한다고 했으므로 (A)가 정답이다.

166. 전화해서 이 광고를 언급하면 다음 창문 설치 시 15퍼센트 할인을 받는다고 했으므로 (D)가 정답이다.

167. 제시된 문장이 실제로 작업에 만족하지 않을 시에는 돈을 돌려받을 것이라고 했으므로, [2]에 제시된 문장이 들어가면 Avalon Windows사는 전면적인 고객 만족을 보장하므로 실제로 작업에 만족하지 않을 시에는 돈을 돌려받을 것이라는 자연스러운 문맥이 된다는 것을 알 수 있다. 따라서 (B)가 정답이다.

2 이중 지문 (Double Passages)

Questions 176-180 refer to the following e-mails.

To: Natalie Mercer <n.mercer@silverfield.com>
From: Robert Altieri <r.altieri@silverfield.com>
Subject: Digital Creators Conference (DCC)
Date: October 9
Attachment: DCC passes

Natalie,

I have attached four passes for you and your team to the upcoming DCC in San Francisco and would now like to go ahead and book your accommodations there. I know you stayed at the Gordon Suites and the Grand Burgess Hotel in previous years, but I think I have found some better options. Please indicate which of the following hotels you wish to stay at in response to this e-mail.

The Bismarck Hotel is close to the convention center but unfortunately does not offer access to Wi-Fi. Those who need to work from the hotel may thus be interested in the Newburg Plaza, which provides free Internet use. However, staying at this location would require the reservation of a car service, as it is a 20-minute drive from the conference venue.

Let me know which one you prefer when you have a moment. Also, please note that the passes I have attached allow entry to the event halls on all four days. Meals are not included, but there are places to purchase food at nearby restaurants. Thank you.

Robert

To: Robert Altieri <r.altieri@silverfield.com>
From: Natalie Mercer <n.mercer@silverfield.com>
Subject: Re: Digital Creators Conference (DCC)
Date: October 9

Robert,

I think it's best for us to have access to the Internet at the hotel. Some of my team members will be convening on evenings following the conference events and may want to reference information online. As for the car service, I believe we can have expenses reimbursed for that. Everyone agrees that a 20-minute ride doesn't sound like a major inconvenience.

But before you make the reservation, could you check what the rates are for parking at the hotel? Francine will be taking her own vehicle to San Francisco and will need to leave it in a lot for the duration of the conference. Thanks in advance.

Natalie

176. Why did Mr. Altieri write the e-mail?

(A) To invite a guest to speak at a conference
(B) To ask about a preference for a trip
(C) To explain a travel expense policy
(D) To ask for airline recommendations

177. What is NOT mentioned about the Digital Creators Conference?

(A) It lasts for four days.
(B) It is a short drive from the airport.
(C) It is close to dining establishments.
(D) It is being held in San Francisco.

178. In the second e-mail, the word "reference" in paragraph 1, line 2, is closest in meaning to

(A) mention
(B) supply
(C) search
(D) adapt

179. Which hotel will Mr. Altieri most likely book?

(A) The Gordon Suites
(B) The Grand Burgess Hotel
(C) The Bismarck Hotel
(D) The Newburg Plaza

180. What is indicated about Ms. Mercer?

(A) She has a team member who will bring her own car.
(B) She might change her mind about attending the DCC.
(C) She has an issue with Mr. Altieri's proposals.
(D) She is busy preparing for a series of presentations.

해설 176. 선택할 수 있는 2가지 숙박 시설 중 어느 것을 더 선호하는지 알려달라고 했으므로 (B)가 정답이다.

177. 공항에서 차로 가까운 거리에 있다는 내용은 지문에 언급되지 않았으므로 (B)가 정답이다.

178. reference를 포함하고 있는 구절 'will be convening ~ and may want to reference information online'에서 reference가 '찾아보다, 참고하다'라는 뜻으로 사용되었다. 따라서 '찾다'라는 의미의 (C)가 정답이다.

179. 두 번째 이메일에서 호텔에 인터넷 이용이 가능한 것이 좋을 것 같다고 했고, 첫 번째 이메일에서 Newburg Plaza가 무료 인터넷 이용을 제공한다고 했으므로 (D)가 정답이다.

180. 같이 회의에 가는 Francine이 자신의 차량을 샌프란시스코에 가져올 것이라고 했으므로 (A)가 정답이다.

3 삼중 지문 (Triple Passages)

Questions 186-190 refer to the following e-mail, schedule, and article.

TO: Ben Finch <ben.finch@mymail.com>
FROM: Taylor Gray <t.gray@streetmag.com>
SUBJECT: Welcome to *Street Magazine*
DATE: June 12

Hi Ben,

Congratulations on being selected as an intern for *Street Magazine*. For 25 years, the citizens of Seattle have looked to us weekly for the latest fashion, art, and music news.

Your internship will be from July 1 to December 31. You will report to me five days a week from 9:00 A.M. to 6:00 P.M. As an intern, you will not be a salaried employee, but we will provide an allowance for some expenses. If you do well, there may be a place for you here after your internship ends.

Please note that although you will have to do office work for various departments as the need arises, your responsibilities will be to research, take notes, and fact check content for me.

Taylor Gray

Personal Work Schedule: Taylor Gray
Thursday, August 7

Time	Activities	To do
09:30	Discuss budget with Mr. Robinson	
11:30	Leave for lunch appointment with photographer Stacy Larson	
13:00	Review photo submissions for "People" section	
14:30	Proofread articles for print version of lifestyle section	Send final list to Ms. McKee
16:00	Cover photo shoot at West Town Music Club	Assign to Ryan Oakley
16:30	Fact check music section for Web site	
17:30	Pick up laundry at Van's Cleaners	
18:00	Interview owner of Contempo Art Space	

Street Magazine

"Fusion In Fusion"
Opening Reception, Contempo Art Space
Thursday, August 7, 6:00 P.M. – 8:00 P.M.

This exhibit of artwork expresses an appreciation for all creative art forms, such as visual art, music, dance, film, and more. Works are representational or abstract, in 2D or 3D. All pieces exhibited in the main gallery will be for sale. This exhibit will be on display until November 6. For details, please contact gallery owner Mischa Michaels at 555-3941.

186. What is NOT true about the internship position at *Street Magazine*?

(A) It does not pay a regular salary.
(B) It involves working with different departments.
(C) It can lead to offers of a permanent job.
(D) It is available only during the summer.

187. What is suggested about *Street Magazine* in the e-mail?

(A) It is planning to relocate its office.
(B) It is published on a weekly basis.
(C) It is mainly devoted to fashion news.
(D) It has subscribers in many cities.

188. What task will Mr. Finch most likely be assigned on August 7?

(A) Proofreading lifestyle section material
(B) Collecting items from a laundry facility
(C) Reviewing photographic submissions
(D) Fact checking music section content

189. What can be inferred about Ms. Gray?

(A) She will be interviewing Ms. Michaels.
(B) She is unable to make her lunch appointment.
(C) She will be supervising a photo shoot.
(D) She is responsible for approving a budget.

190. What is mentioned about the exhibit at Contempo Art Space?

(A) It is a collection of past works by a group.
(B) Some of the artworks may be purchased on-site.
(C) It will run in conjunction with another event.
(D) Most of the participants are known artists.

해설 186. 이메일에서 *Street*지에서의 인턴직이 7월 1일부터 12월 31일까지라고 했으므로 (D)가 정답이다.

187. 지역 독자들이 *Street*지가 주간 단위로 최신 사건들을 알려줄 것이라고 기대해왔다고 했으므로 (B)가 정답이다.

188. 이메일에서 Ms. Finch가 맡을 일 중 Ms. Gray를 위해 온라인 기사의 사실 확인을 하는 것이 있다고 했고, 일정표에서 Ms. Gray의 8월 7일 일정에 웹사이트의 음악 부문에 대한 사실 확인이 포함되어 있으므로 (D)가 정답이다.

189. 일정표에서 Ms. Gray의 일정에 Contempo Art Space의 소유주와의 인터뷰가 있고, 기사에서 Contempo Art Space의 소유주가 Mischa Michaels라고 했으므로 (A)가 정답이다.

190. 기사에서 Contempo Art Space의 주요 갤러리에 전시된 모든 작품들은 판매될 것이라고 했으므로 (B)가 정답이다.

문제 풀이 전략

아래 전략 선택 TIP을 참고하여 <문제 먼저 읽고 지문 읽기> 또는 <지문 먼저 읽고 문제 읽기> 중 자신에게 맞는 전략을 택하여 빠르고 정확하게 문제를 풀 수 있도록 합니다.

전략 선택 TIP

1) 다음 주어진 글의 내용을 이해하며 읽는 데 몇 초가 걸리는지 기록해 둡니다.

Come join the annual office party on Friday, December 20th! Be sure to stop by Mr. Maschino's desk to inform him of your participation as well as the attendance of any accompanying family members. We hope to see you all there!

2) 아래 문제를 풀어봅니다.

What should employees tell Mr. Maschino about?
(A) Bringing family members to a party   (B) Planning for a celebration
(C) Catering for company events   (D) Giving cash to a charity

---

정답: (A)

글을 읽는 데 10초 이상이 걸렸거나 문제를 풀면서 다시 글의 내용을 확인했다면 → **전략 1**

글을 읽는 데 10초 미만이 걸렸고, 문제를 한번에 풀었다면 → **전략 2**

전략 1 문제 먼저 읽고 지문 읽기

1. 질문들을 빠르게 읽고 지문에서 확인할 내용을 파악합니다.
   지문을 읽기 전 먼저 질문들을 빠르게 읽어서, 어떤 내용을 지문에서 중점적으로 읽어야 하는지 확인합니다.

2. 지문을 읽으며, 미리 읽어 두었던 질문과 관련된 내용이 언급된 부분에서 정답의 단서를 확인합니다.
   미리 읽어 두었던 질문의 핵심 어구와 관련된 내용이 언급된 부분을 지문에서 찾아 정답의 단서를 확인합니다.

3. 정답의 단서를 그대로 언급했거나, 다른 말로 바꾸어 표현한 보기를 정답으로 선택합니다.

전략 2 지문 먼저 읽고 문제 읽기

1. 지문의 종류나 글의 제목을 확인하여 지문의 전반적인 내용을 추측합니다.

2. 지문을 읽으며 문제로 나올 것 같은 부분을 특히 꼼꼼히 확인합니다.
   중심 내용, 특정 인물 및 사건, 예외 및 변동 등의 사항은 문제로 나올 가능성이 크므로 이러한 부분들을 집중적으로 확인하며 지문을 읽습니다.

3. 정답의 단서를 그대로 언급했거나, 다른 말로 바꾸어 표현한 보기를 정답으로 선택합니다.

수준별 맞춤 학습 플랜

TEST 01을 마친 후 자신의 환산 점수에 맞는 학습 플랜을 선택하고 매일매일 박스에 체크하며 공부합니다. 각 TEST를 마친 후, 다양한 자료를 활용하여 각 테스트를 꼼꼼하게 리뷰합니다.

* 각 테스트를 마친 후, 해당 테스트의 점수를 교재 앞쪽에 있는 [토익 Reading 목표 달성기]에 기록하여 자신의 점수 변화를 확인할 수 있습니다.

400점 이상
2주 완성 학습 플랜

- 2주 동안 매일 테스트 1회분을 교재 뒤쪽의 Answer Sheet(p.411)를 활용하여 실전처럼 풀어본 후 꼼꼼하게 리뷰합니다.
- 리뷰 시, 틀린 문제를 다시 풀어본 후 교재 뒤의 **해석**을 활용하여 해석이 잘 되지 않았던 부분까지 완벽하게 이해합니다.
- 해커스토익(Hackers.co.kr)에서 무료로 제공되는 **Part 5&6 무료 해설**로 틀린 Part 5&6 문제를 확실하게 이해합니다.
- 해커스인강(HackersIngang.com)에서 무료로 제공되는 **단어암기장 및 단어암기 MP3**로 각 TEST의 핵심 어휘 중 모르는 어휘만 체크하여 암기합니다.

	Day 1	Day 2	Day 3	Day 4	Day 5
Week 1	☐ Test 01 풀기 및 리뷰	☐ Test 02 풀기 및 리뷰	☐ Test 03 풀기 및 리뷰	☐ Test 04 풀기 및 리뷰	☐ Test 05 풀기 및 리뷰
Week 2	☐ Test 06 풀기 및 리뷰	☐ Test 07 풀기 및 리뷰	☐ Test 08 풀기 및 리뷰	☐ Test 09 풀기 및 리뷰	☐ Test 10 풀기 및 리뷰

※ ≪해커스 토익 실전 1000제 2 Reading 해설집≫(별매)으로 리뷰하기
 - 틀린 문제와 난이도 최상 문제를 다시 한번 풀어보며 완벽하게 이해합니다.
 - 틀린 문제는 정답 및 오답 해설을 보며 오답이 왜 오답인지 그 이유까지 확실하게 파악합니다.

300~395점
3주 완성 학습 플랜

- 3주 동안 첫째 날, 둘째 날에 테스트 1회분씩을 풀어본 후 꼼꼼하게 리뷰하고, 셋째 날에는 2회분에 대한 심화 학습을 합니다.
- 리뷰 시, 틀린 문제를 다시 한번 풀어본 후 교재 뒤의 **해석**을 활용하여 해석이 잘 되지 않았던 부분까지 완벽하게 이해합니다.
- 해커스토익(Hackers.co.kr)에서 무료로 제공되는 **Part 5&6 무료 해설**로 틀린 Part 5&6 문제를 확실하게 이해합니다.
- 해커스인강(HackersIngang.com)에서 무료로 제공되는 **단어암기장 및 단어암기 MP3**로 각 TEST의 핵심 어휘를 암기합니다.

	Day 1	Day 2	Day 3	Day 4	Day 5
Week 1	☐ Test 01 풀기 및 리뷰	☐ Test 02 풀기 및 리뷰	☐ Test 01&02 심화 학습	☐ Test 03 풀기 및 리뷰	☐ Test 04 풀기 및 리뷰
Week 2	☐ Test 03&04 심화 학습	☐ Test 05 풀기 및 리뷰	☐ Test 06 풀기 및 리뷰	☐ Test 05&06 심화 학습	☐ Test 07 풀기 및 리뷰
Week 3	☐ Test 08 풀기 및 리뷰	☐ Test 07&08 심화 학습	☐ Test 09 풀기 및 리뷰	☐ Test 10 풀기 및 리뷰	☐ Test 09&10 심화 학습

※ ≪해커스 토익 실전 1000제 2 Reading 해설집≫(별매)으로 리뷰하기
 - 틀린 문제와 난이도 상 이상의 문제를 다시 한번 풀어보며 완벽하게 이해합니다.
 - 틀린 문제는 정답 및 오답 해설을 보며 오답이 왜 오답인지 그 이유까지 확실하게 파악합니다.
 - 모든 문제마다 표시된 문제 유형을 보며 자신이 자주 틀리는 문제 유형이 무엇인지 파악하고 보완합니다.
 - 지문에 파란색으로 표시된 정답의 단서를 보고 정답을 선택해보며 문제 풀이 노하우를 파악합니다.

295점 이하
4주 완성 학습 플랜

· 4주 동안 이틀에 걸쳐 테스트 1회분을 풀고 꼼꼼하게 리뷰합니다.
· 리뷰 시, 틀린 문제를 다시 풀어본 후 교재 뒤의 **해석**을 활용하여 해석이 잘 되지 않았던 부분까지 완벽하게 이해합니다.
· 해커스토익(Hackers.co.kr)에서 무료로 제공되는 **Part 5&6 무료 해설**로 틀린 Part 5&6 문제를 확실하게 이해합니다.
· 해커스인강(HackersIngang.com)에서 무료로 제공되는 **단어암기장 및 단어암기 MP3**로 각 TEST의 핵심 어휘 중 모르는 어휘만 체크하여 암기합니다.

	Day 1	Day 2	Day 3	Day 4	Day 5
Week 1	☐ Test 01 풀기	☐ Test 01 리뷰	☐ Test 02 풀기	☐ Test 02 리뷰	☐ Test 03 풀기
Week 2	☐ Test 03 리뷰	☐ Test 04 풀기	☐ Test 04 리뷰	☐ Test 05 풀기	☐ Test 05 리뷰
Week 3	☐ Test 06 풀기	☐ Test 06 리뷰	☐ Test 07 풀기	☐ Test 07 리뷰	☐ Test 08 풀기
Week 4	☐ Test 08 리뷰	☐ Test 09 풀기	☐ Test 09 리뷰	☐ Test 10 풀기	☐ Test 10 리뷰

※ **≪해커스 토익 실전 1000제 2 Reading 해설집≫**(별매)으로 리뷰하기
· 틀린 문제와 난이도 중 이상의 문제를 다시 한번 풀어보며 완벽하게 이해합니다.
· 틀린 문제는 정답 및 오답 해설을 보며 오답이 왜 오답인지 그 이유까지 확실하게 파악합니다.
· 모든 문제마다 표시된 문제 유형을 보며 자신이 자주 틀리는 문제 유형이 무엇인지 파악하고 보완합니다.
· 지문에 파란색으로 표시된 정답의 단서를 보고 정답을 선택해보며 문제 풀이 노하우를 파악합니다.
· Part 7의 중요한 바꾸어 표현하기를 정리하고 암기합니다.

해커스와 함께라면 여러분의 목표를 더 빠르게 달성할 수 있습니다!

자신의 점수에 맞춰 아래 해커스 교재로 함께 학습하시면 더욱 빠르게 여러분이 목표한 바를 달성할 수 있습니다.

400점 이상	300~395점	295점 이하
≪해커스 토익 Reading≫	≪해커스 토익 750+ RC≫	≪해커스 토익 스타트 Reading≫

▌TEST 01

PART 5
PART 6
PART 7
Self 체크 리스트

잠깐! 테스트 전 확인사항

1. 휴대 전화의 전원을 끄셨나요? □ 예
2. Answer Sheet, 연필, 지우개를 준비하셨나요? □ 예
3. 시계를 준비하셨나요? □ 예

모든 준비가 완료되었으면 목표 점수를 떠올린 후 테스트를 시작합니다.
TEST 01을 통해 본인의 실력을 평가해 본 후, 본인에게 맞는 학습 플랜(p.22~23)으로 본 교재를 효율적으로 학습해 보세요.

문제 풀이를 마치는 시간은 지금부터 75분 후인 ___시 ___분입니다.

테스트 시간은 총 75분이며, 시험 종료 전 2~3분은 정답 검토 및 답안지 마킹을 위해 사용합니다.

READING TEST

In this section, you must demonstrate your ability to read and comprehend English. You will be given a variety of texts and asked to answer questions about these texts. This section is divided into three parts and will take 75 minutes to complete.

Do not mark the answers in your test book. Use the answer sheet that is separately provided.

PART 5

Directions: In each question, you will be asked to review a statement that is missing a word or phrase. Four answer choices will be provided for each statement. Select the best answer and mark the corresponding letter (A), (B), (C), or (D) on the answer sheet.

🕐 **PART 5 권장 풀이 시간 11분**

101. Winfield Ltd. will not accept a merger deal unless ------- terms are proposed by Evertech Industries.

(A) more favorable
(B) most favorable
(C) favorably
(D) favor

102. The road in front of the store is on the parade route, ------- employees must park behind the building today.

(A) yet
(B) for
(C) so
(D) while

103. On Sunday, aerospace manufacturing firm Sowadee unveiled a number of midsize business jets that ------- aims to release next year.

(A) it
(B) theirs
(C) their
(D) its

104. The Morrison Community Association has begun ------- discussions among residents and real estate developer Norwell Co. about constructing new condominiums.

(A) facilitate
(B) facilitates
(C) facilitators
(D) to facilitate

105. Governor Ruth Collins ------- at the Osborne Academy Gala on November 13.

(A) to honor
(B) will honor
(C) will be honored
(D) has honored

106. Mr. Tritton was left on his own to get ------- with the electronic filing system he would be using.

(A) notable
(B) familiar
(C) responsive
(D) dependable

107. The island has become an ------- fashionable tourist destination in recent years thanks to improvements in the service industry.

(A) increasing
(B) increased
(C) increase
(D) increasingly

108. ------- the rain, the Amberdale End-of-Summer Festival attracted more participants than ever this year.

(A) Despite
(B) Between
(C) Although
(D) Because

109. Ahead of the launch of its new flu medication, Barlow Pharmaceuticals carried out ------- research to test the drug's safety and effectiveness.

(A) thorough
(B) presumable
(C) ritual
(D) relative

110. The director of the study abroad program much prefers hiring coordinators ------- in multiple languages.

(A) competence
(B) competently
(C) competency
(D) competent

111. Ms. Belano promised that her company's IT service would be available ------- Wilson Corp. needed assistance with its computer network.

(A) what
(B) whomever
(C) which
(D) whenever

112. Mr. Brodeur contacted the photographer to ask for ------- to use a specific image in his book.

(A) impact
(B) satisfaction
(C) consent
(D) exception

113. To ensure that all of its ingredients are 100 percent organic, the restaurant has had to be very ------- about the suppliers it works with.

(A) perceptible
(B) substantial
(C) selective
(D) constructive

114. The softball tournament last weekend was called off ------- the terrible rainstorms in the area.

(A) owing to
(B) instead of
(C) according to
(D) besides

115. California law ------- the use, sale, and production of hazardous building materials in the interest of public safety.

(A) imposes
(B) finances
(C) forbids
(D) condones

116. Quav Cola's monthly profits have nearly doubled ------- the release of its strawberry-flavored soft drink last year.

(A) along
(B) since
(C) about
(D) provided

117. The owners put up a sign indicating that the café's restrooms are for paying customers -------.

(A) apart
(B) outdoors
(C) only
(D) already

118. Mr. Zalewski has decided to stay with the company for another six months ------- retire in August as planned.

(A) rather than
(B) around
(C) as long as
(D) throughout

GO ON TO THE NEXT PAGE

119. Jabadi Motors announced that it would recall more than 4,000 vehicles due to a ------- airbag defect.

(A) suspicion
(B) suspecting
(C) suspected
(D) suspiciously

120. Like a lot of other obsolete devices, rotary dial telephones have been sought after by -------.

(A) collections
(B) collectibles
(C) collective
(D) collectors

121. ------- renovated, the old Thompson Hills Movie Theater will become a fine art gallery for local painters.

(A) Once
(B) Even though
(C) Until
(D) In case

122. Hawkins Telecom will replace its monthly paper billing statement with a digital ------- effective January 1.

(A) compilation
(B) context
(C) addition
(D) version

123. ------- 20 people in the creative department, just four came to the weekend development workshop.

(A) Out of
(B) Over
(C) Including
(D) Across

124. Andrew's coach reminded him to get eight hours of sleep the night before his race to be ------- rested.

(A) formatively
(B) distinctively
(C) sufficiently
(D) inherently

125. All applicants for the position will need a letter of ------- from a previous employer.

(A) refers
(B) references
(C) referring
(D) reference

126. Officials have committed themselves to ------- 1,500 apartment units in the next five years to resolve the city's housing issues.

(A) be building
(B) built
(C) have built
(D) building

127. The lunch menus for regional school students were ------- changed because of pressure from parents.

(A) radical
(B) radicalness
(C) radically
(D) radicals

128. The star basketball player wants the stadium host to introduce ------- last in order to get a bigger cheer from the team's fans.

(A) her
(B) herself
(C) hers
(D) she

129. The jewelry and antiques will be put on display ------- they are sold at auction to let potential buyers view them first.

(A) now that
(B) except
(C) before
(D) upon

130. Heavy traffic delays are expected beginning next week due to some ------- scheduled to occur in the area.

(A) constructs
(B) construction
(C) constructed
(D) constructing

PART 6

Directions: In this part, you will be asked to read four English texts. Each text is missing a word, phrase, or sentence. Select the answer choice that correctly completes the text and mark the corresponding letter (A), (B), (C), or (D) on the answer sheet.

PART 6 권장 풀이 시간 8분

Questions 131-134 refer to the following review.

A Night to Remember

___5___ out of 5 Stars

Last night, Antonio Bennett's new play *Horatio's Blues* debuted at the Imperium Theater.

Considering Bennett's ------- work, which includes *The Strand* and *From Here to Oblivion*, my
131.

expectations were high. -------, I was pleasantly surprised by the quality of the performance. It
132.

was one of the best things I've ever seen in a theater, with excellent work in every aspect of

the production. -------. In particular, Lucy Cartwright's heartbreaking performance as Beatrice
133.

was brilliant. At the end of the night, ------- of the audience rose and gave the play a standing
134.

ovation to salute a moving experience. Don't miss it!

---

131. (A) prior
(B) lengthy
(C) advanced
(D) collaborative

132. (A) Conversely
(B) Nonetheless
(C) For example
(D) Otherwise

133. (A) It would benefit from more professional
lighting and sound.
(B) In fact, I wouldn't be surprised if she
becomes a major star.
(C) The play features some incredibly vivid
set design.
(D) However, the acting stood out more
than anything else.

134. (A) everybody
(B) most
(C) anyone
(D) both

GO ON TO THE NEXT PAGE

Questions 135-138 refer to the following letter.

Grace Nichols
408 Glen Creek St.
New Bern, NC 28560

Dear Ms. Nichols,

I am writing with regard to your application for a -------. Based on the information you included
                                                  135.
on our online form, you could be eligible to borrow up to $20,000 for your business, to be paid

back over five years at a 7 percent interest rate.

-------. We will confirm the figures ------- above after we have verified that your information is
136.   **137.**
accurate. We ------- a background check in order to do so. If you need to make any changes
             138.
to your application, contact me at 555-3312 as soon as possible.

Sincerely,

Theo Babbit
Beasley Financial

---

135. (A) job
(B) loan
(C) visa
(D) refund

136. (A) Unfortunately, a missed payment will
impact your credit score.
(B) We are interested in knowing the
purpose of your request.
(C) Please note, however, that approval
has not yet been finalized.
(D) Your assent is needed before we
respond to the client.

137. (A) mentioning
(B) mentioned
(C) have mentioned
(D) will mention

138. (A) conducted
(B) were conducting
(C) had been conducting
(D) will be conducting

Questions 139-142 refer to the following memo.

To: All faculty and staff
From: Evelyn Perry, Vice President of Operations
Subject: Parking
Date: September 1

Over the summer, Kiefer University implemented changes to strengthen campus -------. Our
                                                                                    139.
main goal has been to make the university's parking lots safer for students and staff.

-------. We achieved this by setting up bright lights in all on-campus parking lots. We also
140.
focused on ------- some of the dense shrubbery around parking lot borders. Additionally, we
            141.
installed emergency phones in key locations.

------- these changes come at a considerable cost, we have no choice but to raise the price of
142.
monthly parking passes to $60. They are available to purchase at that price starting today.

Thank you for understanding.

---

139. (A) solidarity
(B) communication
(C) security
(D) productivity

140. (A) You may not leave your car here
overnight.
(B) This dark intersection was the site of a
serious accident.
(C) Students have complained about the
lack of parking.
(D) The first thing we did was increase
visibility.

141. (A) clearly
(B) clearing
(C) cleared
(D) clear

142. (A) Although
(B) If
(C) As
(D) Unless

GO ON TO THE NEXT PAGE

Questions 143-146 refer to the following notice.

Notice to Port Buena Restaurant Operators

All restaurants in Port Buena ------- by law to provide their staff with the skills needed to
143.
handle food hygienically. This is due to Regulation 563C, which went into effect last summer.

As it is now ------- to obtain certification to handle food in a local restaurant, the city has
144.
developed an online instructional program.

The course is free and covers the basics of food safety, with the goal of reducing the potential

for contamination. -------. Please note that participants will be tested on what they have
145.
learned once they are done. ------- who fail may retake the course at a later date.
146.

---

143. (A) are required
     (B) has been required
     (C) will be required
     (D) had been required

144. (A) straightforward
     (B) unhygienic
     (C) insufficient
     (D) obligatory

145. (A) Customer service in the restaurant
         industry is in decline.
     (B) Health inspections are carried out on a
         fairly regular basis.
     (C) It is easy to follow and can be
         completed in under an hour.
     (D) Such employment opportunities are
         becoming rare.

146. (A) Them
     (B) Those
     (C) Each
     (D) Others

PART 7

Directions: In this part, you will be asked to read several texts, such as advertisements, articles, instant messages, or examples of business correspondence. Each text is followed by several questions. Select the best answer and mark the corresponding letter (A), (B), (C), or (D) on your answer sheet.

🕐 **PART 7 권장 풀이 시간 54분**

Questions 147-148 refer to the following memo.

TO: All employees
FROM: Jim O'Connell, CEO
DATE: May 15
SUBJECT: F.Y.I.

Dear staff,

Your personal fulfillment here at O'Connell Database Software is as important to us as our bottom line. We want to ensure that you're motivated and that you feel like you're making a difference. That's why, in the next few days, we'll be sending out an online employee satisfaction survey to each of you. So, be sure to check your e-mail frequently. When taking the survey, you will be asked to rate various aspects of your experience and provide any suggestions you might have. Your responses will be totally anonymous.

147. Why was the memo written?

(A) To summarize some achievements
(B) To express appreciation for employees
(C) To notify employees about a questionnaire
(D) To announce a change in corporate benefits

148. What does the memo instruct people to do?

(A) Attend a meeting later today
(B) Leave suggestions at the HR office
(C) Finish an assignment by a given time
(D) Check their inboxes

GO ON TO THE NEXT PAGE

Questions 149-150 refer to the following advertisement.

Let Handyman Connections Do the Work for You!
Find the perfect business to take care of your home-repair needs
at handymanconnections.com!

- Browse through thousands of plumbers, carpenters, electricians, and other home-repair experts
- Search for experts in your area
- Read through reviews written by local clients, or post a review yourself of a home-repair or maintenance service
- Receive repair and maintenance discounts

Visit our Web site or download our mobile application for further details. Contact our business manager to inquire about opportunities to advertise on our site.

149. What is being advertised?

(A) A hardware store
(B) An Internet service provider
(C) A home maintenance site
(D) A job posting service

150. What is indicated about the business?

(A) It charges low membership fees.
(B) It allows customers to post comments.
(C) It offers free advertising to local businesses.
(D) It receives applications through e-mail.

Questions 151-152 refer to the following e-mail.

To: QuickShip Customer Service <support@quickship.com>
From: Peter Howard <peterhoward@yourmail.com>
Date: March 30
Subject: Missing package

To Whom It May Concern,

I recently arranged to have a package delivered by QuickShip Logistics. My package, which was given the tracking number 6519, was due to arrive on March 29 by 5 P.M.

At 4:47 P.M., I received an e-mail alert that the package had been delivered and left by my front door. But when I arrived home less than an hour later, I couldn't find it on my porch or nearby. Nor did I see it by my mailbox.

I asked my next-door neighbors if they had received my package by mistake, but they hadn't seen it. I think my package may have been delivered to the wrong address, or perhaps it was stolen from my porch.

Can you please confirm that my package was delivered to 431 Willard Avenue? I would appreciate a quick response. Please call or text me at 555-9192.

Thanks,
Peter Howard

---

151. Which information did Mr. Howard NOT receive?

(A) A delivery confirmation
(B) An arrival date
(C) A contact number
(D) A tracking code

152. What has Mr. Howard already done?

(A) Ordered a new item
(B) Processed a refund
(C) Visited a post office
(D) Checked by a mailbox

GO ON TO THE NEXT PAGE

Questions 153-154 refer to the following text-message chain.

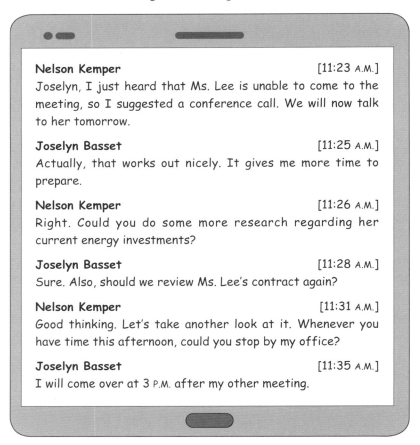

Nelson Kemper [11:23 A.M.]

Joselyn, I just heard that Ms. Lee is unable to come to the meeting, so I suggested a conference call. We will now talk to her tomorrow.

Joselyn Basset [11:25 A.M.]

Actually, that works out nicely. It gives me more time to prepare.

Nelson Kemper [11:26 A.M.]

Right. Could you do some more research regarding her current energy investments?

Joselyn Basset [11:28 A.M.]

Sure. Also, should we review Ms. Lee's contract again?

Nelson Kemper [11:31 A.M.]

Good thinking. Let's take another look at it. Whenever you have time this afternoon, could you stop by my office?

Joselyn Basset [11:35 A.M.]

I will come over at 3 P.M. after my other meeting.

153. At 11:25 A.M., what does Ms. Basset most likely mean when she writes, "Actually, that works out nicely"?

(A) She is content with a delay.
(B) She prefers to meet in person.
(C) She will change a proposal.
(D) She approves of an investment.

154. What will Ms. Basset do at 3 P.M.?

(A) Conduct some research
(B) Set up a conference call
(C) Go over a document
(D) Meet with some clients

Reviewer: Elizabeth J. Hunter

Product: TrueSure MT-1 Washer-Dryer

Rating: ★★★★☆

A few months ago, I purchased a TrueSure MT-1 washer-dryer at an appliance chain. Overall, the product has been quite satisfactory. It washes and dries clothes effectively without making much noise. The MT-1 is also very compact, and I found it easy to install under a kitchen counter. But the best thing is how little power it uses to get the job done. Over time, I think this will save a great deal of money.

Of course, you would get faster drying performance with a dedicated dryer. With the MT-1, drying clothes completely often takes a couple of hours. If you have more room in your house, I wouldn't recommend an all-in-one product like this. Yet, for many city residents, this is a decent option.

155. The word "chain" in paragraph 1, line 2, is closest in meaning to

(A) string
(B) bond
(C) series
(D) group

156. Which feature of the washer-dryer was Ms. Hunter most satisfied with?

(A) Its washing capacity
(B) Its low noise level
(C) Its energy efficiency
(D) Its drying speed

157. Whom would Ms. Hunter discourage from buying the MT-1?

(A) People with larger homes
(B) Residents of city centers
(C) Owners of laundry shops
(D) Customers with tight budgets

GO ON TO THE NEXT PAGE

Questions 158-160 refer to the following letter.

August 16

Mr. Michael Honnold
227 Miramar Boulevard
White Plains, New York

Dear Mr. Honnold,

Thank you for coming in to interview here at Goodman & Frazier. — [1] —. The other partners and I were excited to meet with you given your legal experience and the letter of recommendation that you provided. — [2] —. And indeed, we were impressed once we met you. We are therefore offering you the position of senior associate attorney.

If you're interested, you will join our banking law division, helping to provide counsel to some of the most powerful companies in the financial sector. — [3] —. You will find details about the start date and the compensation package enclosed in this letter. — [4] —. Congratulations, and I hope to hear from you soon.

Sincerely,
Nancy Frazier
Managing Partner, Goodman & Frazier

158. Why did Ms. Frazier write the letter?

(A) To arrange an interview
(B) To describe a requirement
(C) To extend a job offer
(D) To request a recommendation

159. At what type of business does Ms. Frazier work?

(A) A law office
(B) An accounting agency
(C) A bank
(D) A power company

160. In which of the positions marked [1], [2], [3], and [4] does the following sentence best belong?

"Please let me know if these terms are acceptable at your earliest convenience."

(A) [1]
(B) [2]
(C) [3]
(D) [4]

Caring for Your Randolph Farms Cheese Product

Because our farmhouse cheese is handmade and not processed with preservatives, its qualities may vary depending on the day of production and the time it has had to mature. Therefore, we recommend taking the following actions so that you consume it at its best.

First, read the storage instructions on the package. Not all of our products need to be refrigerated, and the cold, dry conditions of the fridge can cause them to quickly harden. If you do need to store a cheese this way, always allow it to come up to room temperature before serving. When eaten immediately, it will have a relatively bland flavor.

Once a piece of cheese has been cut, wipe the outer edge of the remaining cheese with a small amount of white vinegar and then rewrap it. This will limit mold growth greatly, regardless of storage location. When wrapping the cheese, only use fresh waxed paper. Wrapping it in plastic film or tin foil causes the cheese to sweat, negatively affecting its texture and appearance.

161. What is stated about Randolph Farms cheese?

(A) It may be slightly inconsistent.
(B) It needs to be processed quickly.
(C) It was made with local ingredients.
(D) It tastes better after it has matured.

162. Why does Randolph Farms encourage customers to serve cheese at room temperature?

(A) To better preserve its texture
(B) To make it easier to cut
(C) To keep it from rapidly drying out
(D) To experience its full flavor

163. According to the manual, what should customers do with cheese after cutting it?

(A) Store it in the refrigerator
(B) Wrap it in plastic foil
(C) Soak it in vinegar
(D) Keep it in waxed paper

GO ON TO THE NEXT PAGE

Questions 164-167 refer to the following information.

www.eeab.com
Eastern European Association of Builders
19th Conference and Trade Show · August 21 to 25 · Warsaw, Poland

| HOME | | COMMITTEES | | PROGRAMS | | SPONSORS | | CONTACT US |

Trade Exhibit

The trade show will be held in Building B of the Vilmos Exhibition Hall, featuring a floor plan that ensures maximum exposure to attendees. — [1] —.

Booth spaces will be allocated on a first-come, first-served basis. Submit a completed booking form to reserve your desired location. In your application, clearly indicate three alternative choices in case your first one is unavailable. — [2] —. Upon receipt of your application, a space will be reserved and an invoice sent. Full payment is required within three business days of receiving the invoice or the space will be forfeited.

All exhibitors must be registered and will receive badges displaying their company's name. A standard booth comes with two free badges, a deluxe with four, and a premium with six. If your company is a sponsor, you will be entitled to up to 12 exhibitor badges. — [3] —. For security reasons, badges must be worn by registered participants at all times.

Lastly, be reminded that all activities must be confined to the area of your exhibition booth. — [4] —. Management reserves the right to ask exhibitors to discontinue any activities it deems inappropriate.

Further details will be included in a brochure to be posted online three months before the conference starts.

164. What is stated about the trade show?

(A) The event will happen over a span of four days.
(B) It will take up the entire Vilmos Exhibition Hall.
(C) It will be the first one to be held in Warsaw.
(D) The booths will be assigned in order of application.

165. What are applicants asked to do?

(A) Submit payment with their applications
(B) Limit the number of representatives to two
(C) Make several selections for a booth space
(D) Purchase meal vouchers for their staff

166. According to the information, what will be available on a Web site?

(A) A pamphlet
(B) A floor plan
(C) A schedule
(D) A receipt

167. In which of the positions marked [1], [2], [3], and [4] does the following sentence best belong?

"Any additional exhibitors will be charged a fee."

(A) [1]
(B) [2]
(C) [3]
(D) [4]

TC Cyber Services

TC Cyber provides expert IT support for individuals and small businesses. As you probably know, we're famous for our repair services: drop off your computer with us and we'll get it up and running like new again in no time—guaranteed. However, now that TC Cyber is a part of the multinational A to Z Corporation, we have the capability to do much more. These days, we can dispatch teams to set up and optimize your new computer or server system at your home or office, and—if needed—make emergency repairs 24 hours a day. We also offer virtual appointments to help you optimize your machine or learn how to use software.

All of these services are included in a monthly TC Cyber Membership. Customers who purchase computers from A to Z Electronics are eligible for six months of TC Cyber support at no charge. We also offer competitive one-time rates. To become a member, visit our Web site or one of our Knoxville-area locations.

If you want to rest assured that your computer is always at its best, get TC Cyber on your side.

168. What is suggested about TC Cyber?

(A) It opened up a new branch in Knoxville.
(B) It sells discounted electronic devices.
(C) It mainly works with small business clients.
(D) It was acquired by another company.

169. Which is NOT offered by TC Cyber?

(A) 24-hour service
(B) Online consultations
(C) Data protection
(D) Computer installation

170. Who is eligible for free service?

(A) Purchasers of a special warranty
(B) Buyers of A to Z Electronics computers
(C) Customers whose repairs were deferred
(D) First-time clients of TC Cyber

171. What does the advertisement indicate about memberships?

(A) They have increased in price.
(B) They can be purchased in person.
(C) They last for one year at minimum.
(D) They include new server systems.

GO ON TO THE NEXT PAGE

Questions 172-175 refer to the following online chat discussion.

Henry Benson (9:42)   Alex Nigh is interested in signing a supply contract, but he wants to know if we can have everything ready by May 1. That's when he opens for business.

Jerry Trainor (9:44)   We have enough tablecloths in stock, but we will need to get more cloth napkins from our supplier. And some kitchen towels too.

Wendy Hadley (9:45)   That might be tough. I'm not sure our uniform manufacturer will be able to fulfill his order by that time. Give me a few minutes to call them and find out.

Jerry Trainor (9:45)   And the client is requesting washing services too, correct?

Henry Benson (9:47)   That's right.

Wendy Hadley (9:54)   I just got off the phone with the uniform supplier. They have the chef and kitchen staff uniforms in stock. But the client has custom requests for waiter uniforms, so they won't be ready until the end of May.

Henry Benson (10:00)   I see. That could be a problem.

Jerry Trainor (10:01)   Wendy, don't we have a supply of waiter uniforms that are plain black? We could offer those to the client until the customized ones arrive.

Wendy Hadley (10:03)   We do, actually. Lots of different sizes too.

Henry Benson (10:04)   Okay, I'll call him right now and offer him usage of the black uniforms for free until the others arrive from the supplier. I'll let you know the outcome shortly.

Send

172. What type of business does Mr. Nigh most likely own?

(A) A clothing manufacturing firm
(B) A dining establishment
(C) A uniform cleaning company
(D) A delivery service

173. At 9:45, what does Ms. Hadley mean when she writes, "That might be tough"?

(A) A deadline is tight.
(B) Supply is running out.
(C) Space is limited.
(D) A rule is too strict.

174. What is the problem with the uniforms?

(A) The supplier no longer produces some items.
(B) Some materials are too expensive to buy.
(C) A major client wants a refund for an order.
(D) Personalized items take longer to manufacture.

175. What will Mr. Benson do next?

(A) Provide a sample
(B) Ask for a custom item
(C) Place an order
(D) Contact a client

GO ON TO THE NEXT PAGE

Questions 176-180 refer to the following e-mail and review.

To: Alita Dominguez <a.dominguez@lwmail.com>
From: Frederico Matterazzi <frederico@allegratravel.com>
Subject: Re: Visiting Naples
Date: June 3

Hi Alita,

Thank you for your interest in Allegra Travel. In regard to your inquiry, I'm sorry to say that we no longer have any spaces available on the Napoli Voyager Tour. However, our company does have a few other options you might enjoy.

The first is the two-day Napoli Express Tour. On the first day, you'll explore the Naples city center on foot and then take a trip to the National Portrait Gallery. On day two, we'll take you by bus to Pompeii, where you'll see the well-preserved remains of a 2,000-year-old Roman town.

The three-day Napoli Essentials Tour follows the same itinerary but on the final day it adds a scenic boat tour of the bay of Naples. Or, if you'd like something more ambitious, we offer the four-day Napoli Extended Tour. This covers everything in the Express Tour but adds two days in the countryside, with a stop in Sorrento and a hike up Mount Vesuvius.

Let me know if you're interested soon, as demand is high.

Regards,
Frederico Matterazzi

A Perfect Way to Visit Naples: Allegra Travel

My husband and I recently had a chance to visit Naples. We'd never been to Italy before, so we decided to book with a tour company that employs only local residents. They took us on a boat trip to some beautiful islands that most tourists miss.

Vincenzo Mastroianni, who was our main guide, was witty and insightful, and that made the city and its architecture come alive. He took us to eat at a wonderful pizza restaurant, where he seemed to know all of the staff. We even got to see how the meal was made.

But the highlight of the trip was the ancient city of Pompeii. The site was awe-inspiring, and Vincenzo gave us plenty of time to wander around with our free audio guides. Highly recommended!

10 / 10
Reviewer: Alita Dominguez

176. What is one purpose of the e-mail?

(A) To provide instructions
(B) To change a timetable
(C) To suggest alternatives
(D) To offer a discount

177. What does Allegra Travel NOT provide?

(A) Transportation to Pompeii
(B) An urban walking tour
(C) Complimentary meals
(D) A visit to a museum

178. Which tour did Ms. Dominguez most likely take?

(A) The Napoli Voyager Tour
(B) The Napoli Express Tour
(C) The Napoli Essentials Tour
(D) The Napoli Extended Tour

179. What does the review suggest about Mr. Mastroianni?

(A) He is an expert on art.
(B) He replaced Mr. Matterazzi.
(C) He is an accomplished chef.
(D) He lives in Naples.

180. What did Ms. Dominguez like the most on the tour?

(A) Exploring a historical site
(B) Dining at a pizza restaurant
(C) Admiring modern architecture
(D) Shopping in Sorrento

GO ON TO THE NEXT PAGE

Clear Brook Estates – Apartments for Rent

Located in the east side of McIntyre City, Clear Brook Estates is only moments away from restaurants and shops, Castillo Subway Station, and a public library. Furthermore, the building's many amenities, such as underground parking, an on-site laundry, and a fitness facility, are included in the cost of rent.

Prices vary according to unit size and are as follows:
Studio: $1,500 per month
One bedroom: $1,700 per month
Two bedrooms: $2,100 per month
Three bedrooms: $2,500 per month

All units are freshly painted and feature ceramic tiles and new carpets, a stainless-steel refrigerator and gas range, as well as a heating and cooling system. Basement storage is available for an additional fee of $120 per month. To book a viewing of Clear Brook Estates, call 555-6721 or e-mail June Hoffman in the management office at info@clearbrookestates.com.

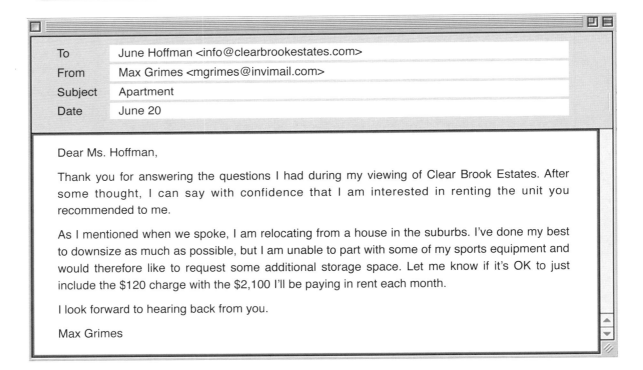

To	June Hoffman <info@clearbrookestates.com>
From	Max Grimes <mgrimes@invimail.com>
Subject	Apartment
Date	June 20

Dear Ms. Hoffman,

Thank you for answering the questions I had during my viewing of Clear Brook Estates. After some thought, I can say with confidence that I am interested in renting the unit you recommended to me.

As I mentioned when we spoke, I am relocating from a house in the suburbs. I've done my best to downsize as much as possible, but I am unable to part with some of my sports equipment and would therefore like to request some additional storage space. Let me know if it's OK to just include the $120 charge with the $2,100 I'll be paying in rent each month.

I look forward to hearing back from you.

Max Grimes

181. For whom is the advertisement most likely intended?

(A) Property developers
(B) Clear Brook tenants
(C) Maintenance personnel
(D) Prospective renters

182. What does each unit in Clear Brook Estates include?

(A) New wallpaper
(B) Kitchen equipment
(C) A washing machine
(D) A storage area

183. In the e-mail, the word "part" in paragraph 2, line 2, is closest in meaning to

(A) scrap
(B) divide
(C) separate
(D) exit

184. Which type of unit did Ms. Hoffman recommend to Mr. Grimes?

(A) A studio apartment
(B) A one-bedroom apartment
(C) A two-bedroom apartment
(D) A three-bedroom apartment

185. What is indicated about Mr. Grimes?

(A) He is on a professional sports team.
(B) He has gotten rid of some belongings.
(C) He is relocating to be closer to his job.
(D) He prefers to live near a subway station.

GO ON TO THE NEXT PAGE

www.sagetax.au/corevalues

Core Values

At Sage Tax, we are devoted to providing outstanding tax preparation solutions. Our ultimate goal is to earn each client's trust so that they return year after year. This is embodied by our core values:

- Core Value 1: Look into every way of getting the biggest possible refund; even if a client is unaware of a tax deduction, he or she may qualify for it.
- Core Value 2: Provide speedy replies to customer inquiries to show that we are working hard for them.
- Core Value 3: Explain what documents are needed in each step to make tax preparation as smooth as possible.
- Core Value 4: Above all, strive to double- and triple-check every line of each return.

To: Rachel Lim <ra_Lim@sagetax.au>
From: Jedda Purcell <Jedda91@coventrysystems.au>
Subject: Return Issue
Date: 15 October
Attachment: Updated Figures

Hi Rachel,

I'm writing again to inquire about the status of my tax return. In your last e-mail, you mentioned that you had all of my documents and would be filing my taxes soon. However, I now realise that I gave you the wrong figures for my most recent retirement contribution. I'm quite concerned that it is too late to fix this error and that the discrepancy will result in trouble with the tax office.

So, please let me know about the status of my return. As this is the third message I'm sending since hearing from you last, I'd appreciate a prompt response. A call or text message to the number I left previously would be welcome.

If I do not hear from you soon, I will have no choice but to contact Sage management.

Sincerely,
Jedda Purcell

MEMO

Date: 23 October
To: Sage Tax Client Services Team
From: Klaus Booker, Client Services Head Manager
Subject: Client Follow-Ups

Hi everyone,

Overall, I am pleased with everyone's efforts this tax season. We have attracted a record number of clients while maintaining high levels of accuracy with our tax filings. However, I believe we have room for improvement in one area: managing expectations.

This morning, I spoke with an unhappy customer. She was not sure of how long the process would take, and this feeling was only made worse by her communication with our tax agent, throughout which she received no reply to three separate messages. As a result, she felt confusion over how best to schedule meetings with her lawyer and accountant about her tax burden.

Therefore, when writing to clients, please let them know exactly when you intend to file, and then make sure to send a follow-up once you have done so.

As is stated in our employee handbook, those who receive complaints from customers will undergo extra training.

Best regards,
Klaus Booker

186. According to the Web page, what is Sage Tax's main priority?

(A) Winning repeat customers
(B) Increasing the size of returns
(C) Attracting the most clients
(D) Eliminating unnecessary processes

187. What does Ms. Purcell say about her taxes?

(A) She provided incorrect information about them.
(B) She sent them to Ms. Lim the day before.
(C) She received a smaller return than expected.
(D) She was contacted about them by the tax office.

188. Which core value did Sage Tax fail to honor?

(A) Core Value 1
(B) Core Value 2
(C) Core Value 3
(D) Core Value 4

189. What does Mr. Booker mention about this year's tax season?

(A) It has been the company's most successful so far.
(B) It has generated a record number of complaints.
(C) It has required a bigger staff than in the past.
(D) It was extended by a few additional days.

190. What is suggested about Ms. Lim?

(A) She will receive additional training.
(B) She had difficulty with a schedule.
(C) She will instruct others on follow-up calls.
(D) She did not secure further discounts.

GO ON TO THE NEXT PAGE

Questions 191-195 refer to the following notice, form, and draft of a speech.

14th Annual East Springs Chamber of Commerce
Small Business of the Year Award
Call for Nominations

The Chamber of Commerce encourages you to nominate a small business owner whose contributions greatly improved the economic and social well-being of the community. The deadline for nominations is September 15. Please note that former winners are not eligible for the award, but that past candidates may be renominated. Self-nomination is encouraged.

All nominated businesses:
- Must be a member of East Springs Chamber of Commerce
- Must have fewer than 50 employees
- Must have opened a minimum of two years before nomination

The award will be presented following a celebratory luncheon, to which the owners of all nominated businesses will be invited. For questions, contact Conrad Burroughs at cburroughs@eastspringscoc.com.

Small Business of the Year Award Nomination Form

Name of Business: Dunston Hair Academy
Business Owner: Katrina Dunston
Address: 1246 Fort Street, East Springs
Phone Number: 555-6621

Reason for Nomination: The idea of having a student stylist cut and color my hair worried me at first. However, at Dunston Hair Academy, it's clear that the training is excellent. I've been here many times and have always been satisfied. Besides, you really cannot beat the price.

In addition to being a great place to go for a haircut or to be trained, the school gives back to the community. The students also frequently donate their time and talent to help out at charity events, like the East Springs Fashion Show. For these reasons, I think Dunston Hair Academy should win the award.

Nominated by: Jessica Frappier

October 1
Jorge Ortega
Acceptance Speech: First Draft

On behalf of everyone who works with me at Go Entertainment Co., I graciously accept this award. It is a great privilege to be recognized by the Chamber of Commerce for our contributions to this town that we all love.

When I founded Go Entertainment Co., I dreamed of operating a welcoming place where people could hear great bands play. Being a small business means more than just becoming a profitable enterprise. That's why we organized a concert for the East Springs community and invited groups from the area to play last year. Thank you all so much for this award.

191. Why was the notice written?

(A) To explain the criteria for a grant
(B) To request suggestions for eligible candidates
(C) To announce the results of a recent competition
(D) To thank business owners for their community involvement

192. Why does Ms. Frappier recommend Dunston Hair Academy?

(A) Its students hold community events.
(B) Its partnerships benefit other businesses.
(C) It serves senior citizens at a discount.
(D) It offers quality service for a low cost.

193. What can be inferred about Ms. Dunston?

(A) She donates a portion of her proceeds to charity.
(B) She will receive funds from the Chamber of Commerce.
(C) She has won a local business award before.
(D) She will receive an invitation to a luncheon.

194. What is indicated about Go Entertainment Co.?

(A) It has been in business for at least two years.
(B) It was nominated by Mr. Ortega.
(C) It will soon employ more than 50 workers.
(D) It sponsors bands from East Springs.

195. What did Mr. Ortega do last year?

(A) Founded a company
(B) Planned a local event
(C) Won an award
(D) Performed on stage

GO ON TO THE NEXT PAGE

Swifty has arrived in Toronto! Effective today, the city becomes Swifty's first market outside of the United States. As people do in many other cities, Toronto residents face a growing traffic congestion problem. To address this, Swifty offers hassle-free solutions for moving groups of people, whether for a regular commute to work, a trip to the game with a group of friends, or a shuttle to and from a concert or other event. We offer four main transportation services.

Service	Who It's For	Vehicle Type	Billing Style
Point-to-Point	Single trips for small groups	Minivan (up to 7 passengers)	One-time payment, based on distance
Event	Groups in need of a temporary shuttle to and from an event venue throughout the day	Van or minibus (up to 15 passengers)	Daily
Excursion	Groups traveling long-distance to a single destination	Minibus or full-sized bus (15-40 passengers)	Hourly
Enterprise	Companies wishing to provide a daily transport option for employees	Full-sized bus (up to 40 passengers)	Monthly

As part of Swifty's Green Guarantee, all of our full-sized buses are fully electric. Service arrangements can be made with the Swifty app, but we do require up to a month of lead time for any Event or Enterprise bookings.

MEMO
BOLTON MANUFACTURING

To: Jade Robinson, Human Resources Director
From: Simon Dodd, Vice President of Human Resources
Subject: Shuttle Service
Date: April 30

I checked into Swifty, and it does appear to be a workable commuting solution. The monthly rates seem quite reasonable, and a large number of the workers I surveyed expressed interest. In fact, I think we would need to arrange for a second shuttle to meet all the demand. There are a few employees opposed to the plan. They feel that the pick-up location is a bit out of the way. Let's monitor this situation going forward, but for now I think we can go ahead and start using Swifty. If we make plans soon, we can start the service in June.

Bolton Manufacturing
Notice to Employees

Beginning in June, we will be offering a free shuttle service for all workers at our Toronto plant. It will depart from a stop at the Sheppard Station, take you straight to the factory for your shift and drop you off at the station in time to catch a train home. Trips will occur Monday through Friday at the times indicated on this notice. All shuttles will come equipped with free Wi-Fi. Parking spaces at Sheppard Station are available for a daily fee.

TO THE FACTORY	TO SHEPPARD STATION
6:10 A.M.	3:20 P.M.
6:30 A.M.	3:40 P.M.
2:10 P.M.	11:20 P.M.
2:30 P.M.	12:10 A.M.

196. What is stated about Swifty?

(A) It mainly caters to corporate clients.
(B) It will be partly funded by the city government.
(C) It offers its service in multiple countries.
(D) It will launch a new mobile application.

197. What does Swifty say about its vehicles in the advertisement?

(A) They are available 24 hours a day.
(B) They are used by professional sports teams.
(C) Some of them do not require gasoline.
(D) Most of them are intended for long distances.

198. Which vehicle will Bolton Manufacturing most likely use?

(A) A minivan
(B) A van
(C) A minibus
(D) A full-sized bus

199. What can be inferred about Sheppard Station?

(A) It is connected to Bolton's Toronto factory.
(B) Its facilities were recently expanded.
(C) Its trains are often late.
(D) It is in a remote location.

200. Which will NOT be available according to the notice?

(A) An Internet connection
(B) Transportation after midnight
(C) A weekend shuttle service
(D) Places to park a car

This is the end of the test. You may review Parts 5, 6, and 7 if you finish the test early.

정답 p.326 / 점수 환산표 p.329 / 해석 p.330 / Part 5&6 무료 해설 바로 보기(정답 및 정답 음성 포함)

* 다음 페이지에 있는 Self 체크 리스트를 통해 자신의 문제 풀이 방식과 태도를 점검해 보세요.

Self 체크 리스트

TEST 01은 무사히 잘 마치셨죠?
이제 다음의 Self 체크 리스트를 통해 자신의 테스트 진행 내용을 점검해 볼까요?

1. 나는 75분 동안 완전히 테스트에 집중하였다.

   □ 예   □ 아니오

   아니오에 답한 경우, 이유는 무엇인가요?

2. 나는 75분 동안 100문제를 모두 풀었다.

   □ 예   □ 아니오

   아니오에 답한 경우, 이유는 무엇인가요?

3. 나는 75분 동안 답안지 표시까지 완료하였다.

   □ 예   □ 아니오

   아니오에 답한 경우, 이유는 무엇인가요?

4. 나는 Part 5와 Part 6를 19분 안에 모두 풀었다.

   □ 예   □ 아니오

   아니오에 답한 경우, 이유는 무엇인가요?

5. Part 7을 풀 때 5분 이상 걸린 지문이 없었다.

   □ 예   □ 아니오

6. 개선해야 할 점 또는 나를 위한 충고를 적어보세요.

* 교재의 첫 장으로 돌아가서 자신이 적은 목표 점수를 확인하면서 목표에 대한 의지를 다지기 바랍니다. 개선해야 할 점은 반드시 다음 테스트에
  실천해야 합니다. 그것이 가장 중요하며, 그래야만 발전할 수 있습니다.

TEST **02**

PART **5**
PART **6**
PART **7**
Self 체크 리스트

잠깐! 테스트 전 확인사항

1. 휴대 전화의 전원을 끄셨나요? ☐ 예
2. Answer Sheet, 연필, 지우개를 준비하셨나요? ☐ 예
3. 시계를 준비하셨나요? ☐ 예

모든 준비가 완료되었으면 목표 점수를 떠올린 후 테스트를 시작합니다.

문제 풀이를 마치는 시간은 지금부터 75분 후인 ___시 ___분입니다.

테스트 시간은 총 75분이며, 시험 종료 전 2~3분은 정답 검토 및 답안지 마킹을 위해 사용합니다.

READING TEST

In this section, you must demonstrate your ability to read and comprehend English. You will be given a variety of texts and asked to answer questions about these texts. This section is divided into three parts and will take 75 minutes to complete.

Do not mark the answers in your test book. Use the answer sheet that is separately provided.

PART 5

Directions: In each question, you will be asked to review a statement that is missing a word or phrase. Four answer choices will be provided for each statement. Select the best answer and mark the corresponding letter (A), (B), (C), or (D) on the answer sheet.

🕐 **PART 5 권장 풀이 시간** **11분**

101. Concordia Bank may fill the vice-president's position with an executive ------- works for one of its competitors.

(A) whose
(B) whoever
(C) whom
(D) who

102. In an effort to attract more customers, Hanford Jewelers now offers ------- cleaning services for silver items at its five branches.

(A) persuaded
(B) compensated
(C) unbound
(D) complimentary

103. ------- the passengers of the overbooked flight to San Diego, only four said they would be willing to travel at a later time.

(A) Among
(B) Into
(C) Between
(D) Throughout

104. Only 25 percent of all ------- voters participated in the last election, making it one of the lowest turnouts on record.

(A) registers
(B) registered
(C) registry
(D) register

105. Multiple studies have shown that even ------- exercise can lead to marked improvements in physical health.

(A) moderate
(B) patient
(C) influential
(D) movable

106. Though the two CEOs have attended the same events, they have not yet been ------- introduced to each other.

(A) formal
(B) formality
(C) formally
(D) formalize

107. Ms. Stein decided to rent the apartment on Albright Avenue as it was the least ------- of all the ones she had seen.

(A) expend
(B) expenses
(C) expensively
(D) expensive

108. It took the work crew one week to repair the fence running along the ------- of Mr. Haskell's property.

(A) angle
(B) dimension
(C) border
(D) expression

109. The vast majority of citizens approved of the city's urban development plan, and ------- complaints were submitted to City Hall.

(A) a lot of
(B) any
(C) many
(D) few

110. Many submissions for the essay contest were ------- well-written, considering most of the participants are students.

(A) remarkably
(B) remarking
(C) remarked
(D) remarkable

111. ------- repeated reminders about economical energy consumption, more households are buying energy-efficient appliances.

(A) In response to
(B) Apart from
(C) In spite of
(D) Except for

112. Before entering the construction site, all personnel must wear appropriate ------- gear to provide them with full protection.

(A) safely
(B) safety
(C) safest
(D) safe

113. Invited guests were informed that the banquet for the sales department would start ------- at 7 P.M. at the Ogilvy Hotel.

(A) frequently
(B) promptly
(C) lately
(D) mostly

114. Ray's Automotive Center provides window coating for vehicles to keep glass clear when ------- to heavy rains or snow.

(A) exposed
(B) revealed
(C) intended
(D) deprived

115. The manager of the restaurant is considering hiring two more waiters to address complaints from diners ------- slow service.

(A) unlike
(B) regarding
(C) within
(D) because

116. Sales clerks are trained ------- customers with all product inquiries and can conduct demonstrations of store devices.

(A) aid
(B) to aid
(C) aiding
(D) aided

117. Vail Enterprises' stock price is ------- 16 percent compared to the start of the year, mostly because of an increase in its overseas revenues.

(A) behind
(B) toward
(C) up
(D) around

118. Ms. Parson received outstanding performance evaluations ------- she was employed at Keystone Developments.

(A) than
(B) where
(C) unless
(D) while

119. A new brochure from Towler Prudential provides additional information on ------- insurance coverage plans.

(A) liable
(B) various
(C) earnest
(D) cautious

GO ON TO THE NEXT PAGE

120. A large crowd is expected to attend the grand opening of the Broad Street Mall as the event ------- with a national holiday.

(A) escorts
(B) coincides
(C) corresponds
(D) substitutes

121. The Hammersmith Business Association will subsidize a new ------- of lectures to promote entrepreneurship.

(A) series
(B) trade
(C) content
(D) advance

122. Volunteers providing assistance during the Main Street Parade ------- by the bright green shirts they are wearing.

(A) distinguish
(B) distinguished
(C) are distinguished
(D) are distinguishing

123. Shopping at a farmers' market is a good way to find the ------- seasonal produce.

(A) fresher
(B) freshest
(C) freshly
(D) most freshly

124. Guests will be entitled to discounted tours and unlimited use of the resort's pool facilities ------- October 1.

(A) as of
(B) such as
(C) now that
(D) along with

125. Although the board has given its final ------- to the firm, neither party will sign the contract until a price is agreed upon.

(A) achievement
(B) contemplation
(C) approval
(D) supervision

126. A brief ------- from the newly released novel by Nigel Murphy was featured in the daily newspaper along with a glowing book review.

(A) extract
(B) extractor
(C) extractive
(D) extracting

127. ------- being able to accommodate more participants, the new event venue is more conveniently accessible from the city center.

(A) In accordance with
(B) On account of
(C) As well as
(D) With respect to

128. Customers eager to purchase the upcoming video game by Sparks Entertainment are ------- to order it in advance.

(A) urged
(B) proposed
(C) planned
(D) intended

129. Visitors are not permitted to stay overnight with patients unless arrangements have been made ------- with the hospital administration.

(A) beforehand
(B) thereby
(C) enough
(D) however

130. The plant's safety officers conduct inspections ------- throughout the year with no warning, so staff must always be prepared for such an event.

(A) alternatively
(B) approximately
(C) correctly
(D) intermittently

PART 6

Directions: In this part, you will be asked to read four English texts. Each text is missing a word, phrase, or sentence. Select the answer choice that correctly completes the text and mark the corresponding letter (A), (B), (C), or (D) on the answer sheet.

PART 6 권장 풀이 시간 **8분**

Questions 131-134 refer to the following article.

Scott Harper has been ------- to lead Canada's national sailing team in the upcoming Cannon
                          131.
Regatta. Team spokesperson Jeremy Dawes made the announcement at a press conference

earlier today. -------.
                132.

Harper, a 39-year old New Brunswick native, is a lifelong boating enthusiast who has

competed in several international events. He has won two Yachtmaster trophies for solo

sailing and will compete in a third later next month, ------- time with a crew of six.
                                                        133.

Speaking on behalf of his team in his new capacity, Mr. Harper appeared confident about

Team Canada's chances. "Most of us have worked together on previous occasions. -------,
                                                                                134.
I've been in races with at least four of the other members," he said.

131. (A) selected
(B) educated
(C) refused
(D) reserved

132. (A) No one expected the Canadian team
to lose at the Regatta.
(B) He also answered questions from
journalists at the event.
(C) This year's contest has been the
toughest in years.
(D) The media conference is scheduled for
this coming weekend.

133. (A) their
(B) which
(C) this
(D) while

134. (A) Instead
(B) In fact
(C) Despite
(D) On the other hand

GO ON TO THE NEXT PAGE

Questions 135-138 refer to the following e-mail.

TO: Randy Huffington <r.huffington@megadelta.com>
FROM: Olivia Cottrell <o_cottrell@edicare.com>
SUBJECT: Machine issues
DATE: June 20

This is my second correspondence regarding the factory equipment that ------- at our Denver
135.
plant recently. As I stated in my first e-mail, a factory worker said a machine was making a lot

of noise and shaking -------. Because there was a risk of danger, we shut the machine down
136.
to prevent it from causing serious injury to any of our workers.

The machine was delivered to our plant by your company just one week ago. -------. Could
137.
you please send an engineer to our plant to examine the equipment? Hopefully, your

technician will be able to determine why the machine failed soon after its -------.
138.

We will wait for your response and anticipate that it will be speedy.

Sincerely,

Olivia Cottrell
Senior administrator
Edicare Industrials

---

135. (A) malfunctioning
(B) to malfunction
(C) malfunctions
(D) malfunctioned

136. (A) boldly
(B) violently
(C) effortlessly
(D) instantly

137. (A) We have decided to return the
machine at your expense.
(B) However, fixing the machine may
require more time.
(C) Therefore, the equipment we
purchased is still under warranty.
(D) It was already repaired at least once in
the past year.

138. (A) modification
(B) installation
(C) appreciation
(D) restoration

DiMaggiano's Frozen Pizzas
Cooking Instructions

Remove the pizza from the packaging, but do not defrost it. If it has thawed, reduce the cooking time ------- approximately three minutes.
139.

Preheat your oven to 230 degrees Celsius. For a softer crust, put the pizza on the middle oven rack and bake it for 10 to 12 minutes. -------. For a crispier crust, bake the pizza on the
140.
top rack at a higher temperature. That is, set the dial to 280 degrees for a much ------- crust!
141.

Remove the pizza from your oven carefully so as not to burn your fingers. Allow it ------- for
142.
three to four minutes before eating. Then simply slice the pizza and enjoy a delicious DiMaggiano's meal with your favorite beverage.

139. (A) from
(B) for
(C) by
(D) until

140. (A) Store uncooked pizzas in your
refrigerator's freezer compartment.
(B) Order our pizzas online or buy them at
any supermarket.
(C) Do not cook it if the pizza is still frozen.
(D) Take it out when the crust is golden
and the cheese has melted.

141. (A) softer
(B) healthier
(C) heavier
(D) firmer

142. (A) cool
(B) cools
(C) to cool
(D) cooling

GO ON TO THE NEXT PAGE

Griffin University
MEMO

To: All faculty
From: Dale Henriksen
Subject: Journals
Date: August 24

Last year, Griffin University took steps to ------- spending on library journals. Years of inflation
                                            143.
without equivalent budget increases made it difficult to pay for many journals. Thus, it

became necessary to cancel some -------. This year, the Library Committee has chosen an
                                 144.
additional 50 journals that will be cut from the library's collection. However, we ------- to bring
                                                                                   145.
some of these titles back after the budget situation improves. -------. A complete list of
                                                               146.
retained titles has been posted on the library Web site.

143. (A) start
(B) report
(C) reduce
(D) forbid

144. (A) policies
(B) promotions
(C) benefits
(D) subscriptions

145. (A) have been tried
(B) are tried
(C) trying
(D) will try

146. (A) In the meantime, we ask for your
patience and understanding.
(B) Seating will be limited, so interested
participants are advised to call ahead.
(C) In any event, some textbooks may be
purchased at off-campus bookstores.
(D) The university budget must be
approved by the state government.

PART 7

Directions: In this part, you will be asked to read several texts, such as advertisements, articles, instant messages, or examples of business correspondence. Each text is followed by several questions. Select the best answer and mark the corresponding letter (A), (B), (C), or (D) on your answer sheet.

PART 7 권장 풀이 시간 54분

Questions 147-148 refer to the following advertisement.

EVERIDGE CERTIFIED ACCOUNTANTS

Suite 19-A, 825 Burrard, Vancouver BC, V0P-F1K

Having trouble with your tax forms? Are the finances of your small business more than you can handle? Let ECA, one of the fastest-growing accounting firms in Canada, take care of all your accounting worries!

We offer:
▷ Personal income tax returns
▷ Setup and maintenance of bookkeeping systems
▷ Preparation of financial statements
▷ Contract drafting assistance

For a full list of our services, fees, and accountants, visit www.everidgeacc.co.ca. If you would like to meet with one of our accountants in person, make an appointment by calling us at (604) 555-8872 or by sending an e-mail to everidgeacc@coolmail.com.

---

147. What is NOT mentioned as a service offered by ECA?

(A) Assistance with income tax
(B) Help with creating a contract
(C) Investment consultation
(D) Handling accounting systems

148. Why would a customer visit the ECA Web site?

(A) To arrange a personal tax consultation
(B) To read feedback from other clients
(C) To view online samples of business contracts
(D) To get information about ECA employees

GO ON TO THE NEXT PAGE

Questions 149-150 refer to the following invitation.

The New Hampton Professionals Society
would like to invite you to the

Twelfth Annual Melody for Charity Night

on Saturday, July 24, at 6 P.M.
at the Greenfield Theater

Six classical compositions by world-renowned composers and graduates of the Salzburg Conservatory of Music, Johannes Linden and Vladimir Tepanor, will be performed by the Smithson Philharmonic Orchestra.

Formal clothing for the event is required. Cash donations will be accepted during the evening, with proceeds going to the Rainbow House at New Hampton General Hospital. Rainbow House is a special facility dedicated to the medical care of young patients. To confirm your attendance, or for more information, visit www.newhamptonhospital.com and www.rainbowhouse.com.

149. What is NOT indicated about the event?

(A) It is organized by a group of professionals.
(B) Attendees are required to dress formally.
(C) It will be held on a weekend.
(D) Refreshments will be served to all guests.

150. Who are Johannes Linden and Vladimir Tepanor?

(A) Prominent conductors of an orchestra
(B) Representatives of a charitable organization
(C) Famous classical music composers
(D) Administrators at New Hampton General Hospital

Questions 151-152 refer to the following text-message chain.

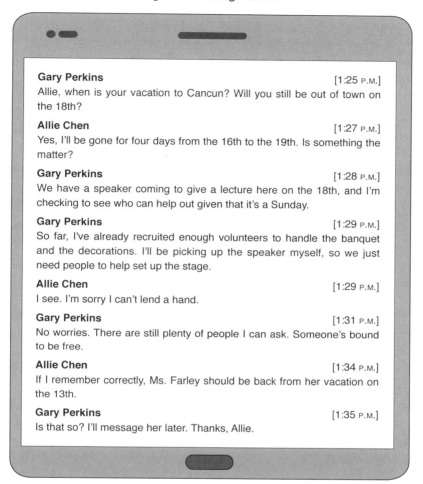

Gary Perkins [1:25 P.M.]
Allie, when is your vacation to Cancun? Will you still be out of town on the 18th?

Allie Chen [1:27 P.M.]
Yes, I'll be gone for four days from the 16th to the 19th. Is something the matter?

Gary Perkins [1:28 P.M.]
We have a speaker coming to give a lecture here on the 18th, and I'm checking to see who can help out given that it's a Sunday.

Gary Perkins [1:29 P.M.]
So far, I've already recruited enough volunteers to handle the banquet and the decorations. I'll be picking up the speaker myself, so we just need people to help set up the stage.

Allie Chen [1:29 P.M.]
I see. I'm sorry I can't lend a hand.

Gary Perkins [1:31 P.M.]
No worries. There are still plenty of people I can ask. Someone's bound to be free.

Allie Chen [1:34 P.M.]
If I remember correctly, Ms. Farley should be back from her vacation on the 13th.

Gary Perkins [1:35 P.M.]
Is that so? I'll message her later. Thanks, Allie.

151. At 1:31 P.M., what does Mr. Perkins mean when he writes, "No worries"?

(A) He is content with his plans for a holiday.
(B) He expects to hear back about an event soon.
(C) He is not stressed out about his workload.
(D) He believes he will be able to find other helpers.

152. What is suggested about Ms. Farley?

(A) She volunteered to decorate a banquet hall.
(B) She will be asked to work on the 18th.
(C) She will go to the airport on Sunday.
(D) She usually comes in to work on the weekend.

GO ON TO THE NEXT PAGE

TORONTO FISH MARKET
112 Center Plaza

Venture out to the city center waterfront on Saturdays and Sundays to sample the best in Toronto's seafood. Merchants from all across the city have stalls set up at our warehouse, where they're selling everything from fish to sushi to lobster and even exotic cuisine like squid. Not only is the food the freshest and most savory in town, it is also sold at the most affordable prices. You can get a cut of salmon or halibut for less than $25 per pound. Be sure to check our Web site, www.torontofishmarket.ca, for updates on special sales that we hold throughout the year. We also have a live camera feed of the market on our Web site, so you can see how busy it is at any given time.

153. What is stated about the Toronto Fish Market?

(A) It is only open three days a week.
(B) It is located outdoors during the summer.
(C) It is less expensive than other venues.
(D) It is frequented by tourists.

154. The word "cut" in paragraph 1, line 6, is closest in meaning to

(A) scratch
(B) reduction
(C) portion
(D) dividend

155. According to the brochure, what can people do on the Toronto Fish Market Web site?

(A) Examine a menu of fresh fish
(B) Compare the prices of various merchants
(C) Watch a video introducing the market
(D) Browse some upcoming deals

Come to the Portland Holiday Gift Fair!

The City of Portland and the Willamette Convention Center are pleased to announce the opening of the Holiday Gift Fair, which will run for two weeks, from December 1 to December 14. Open daily from 10 A.M. to 9 P.M. at the Willamette Convention Center on Naito Parkway, the fair will feature products from more than 600 vendors. The event will be held in the center's largest exhibit area, Riverside Hall.

Entrance to the fair is $5 for adults and $3 for children under 12 or senior citizens. There is no admission charge for children under five years of age. Attendees can also take part in hourly draws with more than $18,000 of merchandise to be given away! Booths include holiday gifts, decorations, cards, toys, food, and so much more! Get all your holiday supplies ahead of time by dropping by this amazing event.

For a list of vendors, please visit www.willamettecon.com/events. Tickets for the fair can be purchased on the Web site beginning November 20 or at the door to Riverside Hall.

156. For whom is the notice most likely intended?

(A) City officials
(B) Convention center employees
(C) Holiday shoppers
(D) Exhibition organizers

157. What is NOT indicated about the fair?

(A) It will include free prizes.
(B) It will exhibit a variety of products.
(C) It is free for 10-year-old children.
(D) It is scheduled to last for two weeks.

158. What is suggested about the Convention Center?

(A) It was recently constructed.
(B) It has several exhibit halls.
(C) It does not sell tickets for events.
(D) It has a seating capacity of 600.

GO ON TO THE NEXT PAGE

Questions 159-160 refer to the following e-mail.

To: Jude Feldstein <jfeldstein@lbm.com>
From: Janina Winslow <customerservice@mycel.com>
Date: December 20
Subject: Re: Poor reception

Dear Mr. Feldstein,

Thank you for informing us about the intermittent reception that you have been experiencing with our wireless phone service for the past few days. You wanted us to explain what the problem was and also asked for a discount on your service fee for this month.

First, we believe that this problem is due to the ongoing repair work on our cell phone towers in the Mountainview area, which were severely damaged during the recent snowstorm. Our maintenance crew is still working to fix the problem.

In regard to your second inquiry, I would first like to apologize for the inconvenience. Because you are a valued customer, we are deducting $40 from your next billing statement. We hope that this addresses any trouble you may have experienced.

Janina Winslow
MyCel Customer Service

159. What is the purpose of the e-mail?

(A) To inform a customer of a work date
(B) To report an Internet connection problem
(C) To respond to a customer's inquiry
(D) To persuade a client to renew a subscription

160. What does Ms. Winslow offer to provide Mr. Feldstein?

(A) An extended service contract
(B) A day's worth of free phone calls
(C) A new mobile device
(D) A reduction on a monthly charge

The City of Burbank provides a number of additional services for the benefit of its residents. These are not part of the standard municipal services provided by most city governments and are made available to residents free of charge. Below is just a sample of some of these services, but you can find out about other offerings by visiting www.burbank.ca.gov.

Energy Assessment: Residents may consult an energy advisor for some general recommendations on how to improve home energy use. It is necessary to make an appointment for this service during our regular business hours of 8:30 A.M. to 4:30 P.M., Monday through Friday. — [1] —. This service is subject to the availability of our staff.

Tree Removal: The city's Department of Environmental Management offers complimentary tree pruning and removal services for homeowners. Simply call 555-4091, extension #808, to schedule an appointment. The service is available all year round. — [2] —.

Water Analysis: Homeowners concerned about the safety of their drinking water may drop off water samples at the Department of Water for examination. — [3] —. Any water source found to be contaminated will be treated promptly.

Shuttle: The city provides complimentary shuttle services between residential and commercial areas to senior citizens who are 65 years of age or older and to those with mobility problems. — [4] —. To schedule a pickup, call the Department of Senior Welfare at 555-4091, extension #204.

161. What can be found on the city's Web site?

(A) A schedule of temporary power outages
(B) A directory of government employees
(C) Directions to City Hall
(D) Information about additional services

162. For which service is an appointment NOT required?

(A) Energy use consultations
(B) Tree removal from property
(C) Drinking water safety testing
(D) Transport to the commercial district

163. Who will most likely take a shuttle?

(A) Staff working at City Hall
(B) Youth without driver's licenses
(C) Citizens living outside of Burbank
(D) Elderly people needing to visit some stores

164. In which of the positions marked [1], [2], [3], and [4] does the following sentence best belong?

"It takes up to 10 business days for our laboratory technicians to obtain the test results."

(A) [1]
(B) [2]
(C) [3]
(D) [4]

Questions 165-168 refer to the following online chat discussion.

Julianna Lopez	10:22 A.M.	So, it's confirmed. We're presenting a marketing proposal to AEK on July 18 at their headquarters.
John Brenner	10:24 A.M.	I heard! How exciting. I went through the company profile in the brochure you gave us. They could be our biggest client to date.
Julianna Lopez	10:25 A.M.	Yes. They have 6,000 employees and manufacturing plants in Thailand, Turkey, and Mexico. They also have suppliers in China, Germany, and Korea and generated over $2 billion in sales last year.
Yvonne Bailey	10:25 A.M.	I can get to work on the marketing analysis for the presentation. I'd like to use the statistics in the brochure we were given. Do you think they're reliable?
Julianna Lopez	10:26 A.M.	That would be fine, Yvonne. I think the figures are accurate. John and Eric, I'd like you to prepare the slideshow and handouts. Start immediately if you can.
John Brenner	10:27 A.M.	Got it. It shouldn't take more than two days to finish.
Eric Zalewski	10:32 A.M.	Consider it done, Julianna. Are we going to run through the presentation before the appointment?
Julianna Lopez	10:34 A.M.	Let's do a practice session on July 15. During the presentation, I'll give the main talk, and then you three can explain your roles briefly. After that, all four of us can answer any technical or financial questions they might have. Does that sound reasonable?
Yvonne Bailey	10:34 A.M.	I think that works for all of us.

Send

165. What is true about AEK?

(A) It had a record year of profitability.
(B) It is interested in taking over another business.
(C) It is supplied by firms in at least three countries.
(D) Its customers are mostly based in Thailand.

166. What will Ms. Bailey use for her analysis?

(A) A company booklet
(B) A presentation handout
(C) A business magazine
(D) An advertising analysis

167. At 10:27 A.M., what does Mr. Brenner mean when he writes, "Got it"?

(A) He will begin doing some analyses.
(B) He will work on a presentation right away.
(C) He will confirm figures for a report.
(D) He will write staff role descriptions.

168. What will Mr. Zalewski probably do on July 18?

(A) Give the majority of the main talk
(B) Provide responses to financial inquiries
(C) Distribute copies of a company profile
(D) Conduct a session for practice

May 25

Barbara Koteva, Director of Public Relations
Ademus Petroleum, 4493 24th Avenue, New York, NY 11100

Dear Ms. Koteva,

Thank you on behalf of our organization for the support you and your company have shown to the Society for the Preservation of Earth's Environment (SPEE). As part of our standard commitment to our valuable sponsors, we have enclosed our annual report covering new developments, ongoing activities, and budget allocations for the past fiscal year. We hope that after reading our report, you will continue supporting our efforts.

In summary, let me begin by stating that the past year has been our most productive since the SPEE was established 10 years ago, but a number of challenges remain. The following are just a few of the highlights you will find inside our report.

We saw record collections in private donations, public organization support, and financial commitments from the business sector. This was aided in part by the launch of our multilingual Web site and the publicity we received from a documentary film shown during the previous year's Earth Awareness celebrations.

Joining our board of directors were two well-respected individuals from the nonprofit sector: Mr. Jonah Gelding and Ms. Heather Leach. Their combined experience working in South Asia and Eastern Europe has helped to increase membership in those regions.

Lastly, we saw the implementation of some new policies governing project administration. As you will soon find out, this has helped us to streamline our actions and produce greater efficiency in spending.

Should you have any questions or comments regarding this report, please contact me at h.grundy@spee.org.

Sincerely,

Hazel Grundy
Corporate Communications Director
Society for the Preservation of Earth's Environment

169. What is the main purpose of the letter?

(A) To introduce recently hired executives
(B) To report on the results of a survey
(C) To provide an account of an organization
(D) To project revenues for the upcoming year

170. Who most likely is Ms. Koteva?

(A) A representative of a corporate donor
(B) An employee of a nonprofit group
(C) An event organizer for Earth Awareness
(D) A founder of a charitable foundation

171. What is NOT mentioned as a recent change at the SPEE?

(A) It added a multilingual function to its Web site.
(B) Its membership increased in Eastern Europe.
(C) It implemented a policy that will reduce spending.
(D) Its board approved two upcoming projects in Asia.

Questions 172-175 refer to the following letter.

27 September

Evelyn Gray
Priory Street
Coventry CV1 5FB

Dear Ms. Gray,

I'm an English literature professor and I'm reaching out on behalf of the New Writers Project here at Coventry University. Your recent best-selling novel, *Midnight Magic*, has captivated the students and staff here on campus. The book is already assigned reading in a few courses, including my first-year writing class, and has become a part of our program's official recommended reading list.

Next year, the New Writers Project at our university will host its spring seminar and we'd like to invite you to be a guest speaker. — [1] —.

Each guest speaker is expected to deliver two 40-minute lectures during the seminar. — [2] —. Lectures can be on any topic related to writing or publishing. Each lecture will be followed by a 30-minute Q&A session. You may also receive requests to perform some additional tasks if your schedule permits. — [3] —.

As a guest speaker, you'll receive a voucher for three nights at a local hotel. We'll also cover all travel expenses, including flights and rental cars. — [4] —.

Please let me know if you'd be willing to join us for next year's seminar. We'd be honoured to have you share your expertise with our students.

Sincerely,
Vera Young
Associate Professor, New Writers Project
Coventry University

172. Why did Ms. Young write the letter?

(A) To praise a best-selling novel
(B) To ask for opinions on a reading list
(C) To make inquiries on behalf of local students
(D) To request participation in a workshop

173. What is NOT mentioned about *Midnight Magic*?

(A) It was written by Ms. Gray.
(B) It has been assigned in Ms. Young's class.
(C) It was published last year.
(D) It has sold a large number of copies.

174. The word "cover" in paragraph 4, line 2, is closest in meaning to

(A) treat
(B) contain
(C) surround
(D) fund

175. In which of the positions marked [1], [2], [3], and [4] does the following sentence best belong?

"These may include reviewing student manuscripts or providing one-on-one consultations."

(A) [1]
(B) [2]
(C) [3]
(D) [4]

GO ON TO THE NEXT PAGE

Stop and Sew
For all your dressmaking and tailoring needs

| Home | About Us | Locations | **Customer Feedback** |

Dear Stop and Sew,

Congratulations on opening the store at your new location! I have always been a fan of Stop and Sew, and I wouldn't have succeeded as a local fashion designer over the past decade if it weren't for the unique products available at your establishment. I've appreciated that you sell a variety of different cloth materials to suit every taste, as it has assisted me in creating imaginative and interesting designs.

As always, your new store is very well organized with fabrics arranged by purpose and material. On top of that, your knowledgeable salespeople are helpful and provide exceptional service. They made some fine recommendations recently when I was selecting textiles for my swimwear collection and provided me with a brochure on the basic materials you offer.

I do have a suggestion, however, regarding the wedding dress fabrics. The clients I have for wedding gowns tend to want more unique materials. Trends are changing, and customers want detailed designs rather than the simple ones you offer. I currently have all wedding dress fabrics shipped through out-of-town suppliers. You may wish to take this into consideration when ordering new stock, as it would help a lot of local dressmakers and designers.

Thank you, and I wish you continued success!

Regards,
Jenna Palmer

Stop and Sew - Basic Fabric

Cotton
- 100 percent natural
- Breathable and comfortable to wear
- Machine washable
- Recommended for making shirts

Merino Wool
- Made of the finest and softest wool from Merino sheep
- Breathable and insulating, Merino wool keeps wearers warm in the winter and cool in the summer
- Machine washable
- Recommended for making infant garments, high fashion clothing, and outdoor apparel
- Available in different colors

Silk
- 100 percent natural
- Lustrous, easy-to-dye fabric with exceptional flow
- Recommended for making evening gowns and wedding gowns

Polyester
- Lightweight and highly stretchable
- Resistant to flexing, heat, sunlight, detergent, and perspiration
- Recommended for making sportswear, such as swimsuits, ski suits, dance apparel, and skating costumes

176. According to the Web page, what does Ms. Palmer like about Stop and Sew?

(A) It arranges textiles by color.
(B) It has exceptional customer service.
(C) It has a wide selection of sewing machines.
(D) It offers helpful dressmaking tutorials.

177. On the Web page, the word "taste" in paragraph 1, line 4, is closest in meaning to

(A) preference
(B) flavor
(C) decision
(D) feeling

178. What is indicated about Ms. Palmer?

(A) She needs samples of fabrics.
(B) She has recommended the store to her associates.
(C) She is eligible for a bulk order rate.
(D) She wants to stay current with the latest fashions.

179. Which fabric did Ms. Palmer most likely buy at Stop and Sew before?

(A) Cotton
(B) Merino wool
(C) Silk
(D) Polyester

180. What is NOT mentioned about Merino wool?

(A) It can be cleaned in a washing machine.
(B) It can be worn in different seasons.
(C) It is more expensive than other fabrics.
(D) It can be purchased in a range of colors.

GO ON TO THE NEXT PAGE

Questions 181-185 refer to the following invoice and e-mail.

Date: August 12

Baja Travel, 4258 Myrtle Avenue, San Diego, California, 92105

Trip Invoice for Ostergard Tech, 6520 Beadnell Way, San Diego, California, 92117

Contact person/Position	Edith Albright/Human Resources Coordinator
General itinerary	5-Day Classic Mexico Tour
Number of travelers	10
Travel dates	September 19-23
Deposit amount/Date paid	$2,500/August 10
Remaining balance	$5,090
Due date for remaining balance	September 1

Please note that your deposit and balance include flights, bus tours and transportation fees, four nights at the Mayan Inn, museum and attraction entrance fees, five breakfasts, and five lunches. Dinners, souvenirs, and tour guide tips are not included in this price. All travelers must submit their passport numbers to Baja Travel at least one week before their departure date. Also, your remaining balance must be paid by the deadline above. Otherwise, your reservation cannot be guaranteed. We accept credit and debit cards or bank transfers.

To: Samuel Hill <shill@bajatravel.com>
From: Edith Albright <edith.albright@ostergardtech.com>
Subject: Itinerary
Date: August 15

Dear Mr. Hill,

I received the invoice for my company's upcoming employee getaway. Everything looks great, but there are a few questions I forgot to ask when we spoke a few weeks ago.

First of all, can I pay the remaining balance in two installments? Ideally, I'd like to pay half today, and half on the day before the due date. Also, are there vegetarian options at the restaurants where we will be having our included meals? Several of my colleagues would like to know soon in case they need to make other arrangements. Lastly, does your agency offer travel insurance? I think it might be good to have.

Thank you for all of your help. I'll send you our passport numbers sometime this week.

Sincerely,
Edith Albright

181. What is indicated about Ostergard Tech in the invoice?

(A) It has already submitted a deposit.
(B) It has hired a travel agency in a different state.
(C) It will pay by company credit card.
(D) It will receive a group discount.

182. What will travelers have to pay for during the trip?

(A) Air transportation
(B) Some admission fees
(C) Some meals
(D) Accommodations

183. Why was the e-mail written?

(A) To dispute a charge on an invoice
(B) To ask about a deadline extension
(C) To ask for an updated itinerary
(D) To request some further details

184. When does Ms. Albright want to make a final payment?

(A) On August 15
(B) On August 31
(C) On September 1
(D) On September 19

185. What can be inferred from the e-mail?

(A) Some of the tour participants are vegetarians.
(B) Some employees have already provided passports.
(C) Ostergard Tech requires insurance for all trips.
(D) Travel costs were higher than Ms. Albright anticipated.

GO ON TO THE NEXT PAGE

Barksdale Summer Craft Market

The Barksdale Community Organization is pleased to announce that it will be holding its annual outdoor craft market next month. The event will be held on July 7, 14, 21, and 28 at Oakville Park, on Emerson Street. This year, local restaurant owners will be setting up food booths and serving a variety of tasty treats for visitors. These will all be located in the area immediately to the left of the main gate as you enter the park. In addition, several bands have agreed to perform on the last day of the market. Visit www.bdalecommunity.com for a list of the musical acts and the times they will play. We hope to see you next month!

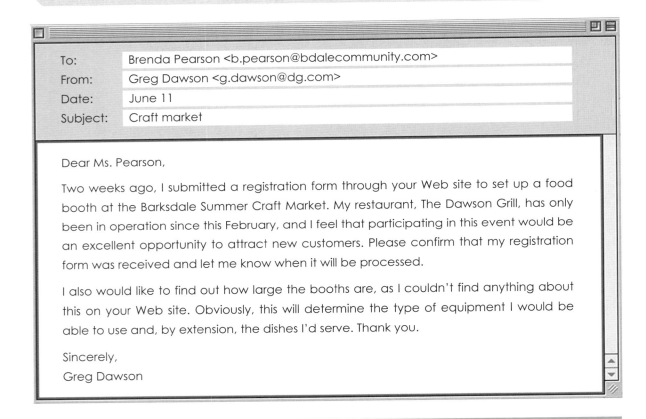

To:	Brenda Pearson <b.pearson@bdalecommunity.com>
From:	Greg Dawson <g.dawson@dg.com>
Date:	June 11
Subject:	Craft market

Dear Ms. Pearson,

Two weeks ago, I submitted a registration form through your Web site to set up a food booth at the Barksdale Summer Craft Market. My restaurant, The Dawson Grill, has only been in operation since this February, and I feel that participating in this event would be an excellent opportunity to attract new customers. Please confirm that my registration form was received and let me know when it will be processed.

I also would like to find out how large the booths are, as I couldn't find anything about this on your Web site. Obviously, this will determine the type of equipment I would be able to use and, by extension, the dishes I'd serve. Thank you.

Sincerely,
Greg Dawson

Crafts in the Summer

By Janet Gleason

The Barksdale Summer Craft Market is a community event that is always popular with city residents, and this year's was the best ever. The first thing I noticed when I visited Oakville Park was that there was delicious food being sold at a number of booths. The attendees seemed quite happy with this arrangement. Several told me that they appreciated not having to leave the premises for lunch or dinner. I was also impressed that live music had been arranged. It gave the market a festival-like atmosphere. So, if you missed the market this year, be sure to attend next year. You definitely won't regret it!

186. According to the announcement, what can be found on the Barksdale Community Organization's Web site?

(A) The name of an organizer
(B) A list of vendors
(C) A schedule of performances
(D) A map of a venue

187. What can be inferred about Mr. Dawson?

(A) He provided complimentary food to musicians.
(B) His registration form was not filled out correctly.
(C) He was required to meet with other restaurant owners.
(D) His booth was located near the park's entrance.

188. What is mentioned about the The Dawson Grill?

(A) It participated in the market previously.
(B) It opened less than a year ago.
(C) It has many regular customers.
(D) It is owned by two people.

189. What does Mr. Dawson inquire about?

(A) The cost of a booth
(B) The availability of equipment
(C) The number of attendees
(D) The size of a space

190. On which day did Ms. Gleason visit the market?

(A) July 7
(B) July 14
(C) July 21
(D) July 28

GO ON TO THE NEXT PAGE

Questions 191-195 refer to the following flyer, e-mail, and registration form.

Your Favorite Business Periodical, *Big Success Magazine*, Presents its
7th Annual Conference for Entrepreneurs

- Everything You Need to Know to Market Your Products Online -
You'll learn how to boost your Internet sales while managing your own online store.

April 5 from 10 A.M. to 5 P.M. at Traylor Hall

Featuring keynote speaker and winner of *Big Success Magazine*'s Entrepreneur of the Year Award:
Kyle Rogan, owner of Ottawa Intra Cycles

To register for this can't-miss event,
you must first complete *Big Success Magazine*'s six-week online training course.

To sign up for the course, visit www.bigsuccessmag.ca/toolsforsuccess
OR
If you have already completed the course and wish to attend the conference,
please call (519)-575-8634.

To	Harrison Marcoux <hmarcoux@skateheaven.ca>
From	Lilianne Maille <lilymaille@lmcosmetics.ca>
Subject	Entrepreneur conference
Date	February 12

Dear Mr. Marcoux,

We met at a networking event for new entrepreneurs in Toronto last month. You were telling me about the custom-made skateboard business you started last year. It hasn't been that long since I started my own line of cosmetics, so I could relate to some of the challenges you faced. Anyway, I remember that you said you were struggling a bit, so I'm writing to tell you about a conference that's coming up. I think it would be perfect for you because not only is it going to be held in your city, but it also focuses on exactly what you said you were having a hard time with. A friend of mine went to it last year when it took place in Kitchener, and she said it helped her a lot. I just registered for it. If you're interested in going, too, you can find details about it here: www.bigsuccessmag.ca.

Maybe I'll see you there.

Lilianne Maille

Big Success Magazine Leadership Course Registration Form

By registering for this invaluable course, you will receive six weeks of online training starting immediately and a DVD package in the mail. Upon completion, you will be entitled to attend Big Success Magazine events.

Contact Information		Address	
Name	Harrison Marcoux	Street	51 Fairwater Lane
E-mail	hmarcoux@skateheaven.ca	City/Province	Waterloo, Ontario
Phone	555-9368	Postal Code	N2J 1A3
Credit Card Information			
Card Type		Wixcard	
Card Number		0645-****-****-****	
Payment Plan			
1 payment of $786.00 billed now			
3 payments of $262.00 billed now and over the next two months			✓

This program has a 30-day, 100% satisfaction guarantee or your money back.

191. What is NOT true about the conference?

(A) Only those who take an online course can attend it.
(B) It is affiliated with a business-oriented publication.
(C) It will take place over a five-day period in April.
(D) The recipient of an award will be presenting at it.

192. What most likely is Mr. Marcoux having difficulty doing?

(A) Winning over its strongest competitor
(B) Completing Big Success Magazine's course
(C) Selling his skateboards over the Internet
(D) Registering for the entrepreneur conference

193. What is suggested about Ms. Maille?

(A) She has recently gone into business for herself.
(B) She was not entirely satisfied with an online course.
(C) She is in the same line of business as Mr. Marcoux.
(D) She is planning to open an office in Kitchener.

194. What is mentioned about the course?

(A) It is for invited participants only.
(B) It can be paid for in installments.
(C) It is offered at a discount to subscribers.
(D) Its fees can be refunded six weeks before a start date.

195. Where will the conference take place?

(A) Toronto
(B) Waterloo
(C) Kitchener
(D) Ottawa

GO ON TO THE NEXT PAGE

VOLO Magazine
Travel Industry News

Lessons from the AITIC

by Kate Horvath

August 20—At the recently concluded 48th Annual International Travel Industry Conference (AITIC) in Rome, delegates discussed some of the challenges that travel agencies are facing. For instance, many airlines, burdened with high fuel costs and operating losses, are reducing the commissions they pay to agencies. In addition, Web sites that allow travelers to arrange their own transportation and accommodations now account for around 60 percent of all travel bookings. Finally, the worldwide recession has caused many people to postpone or cancel planned trips.

"These developments make it necessary for agencies to promote travel products with high commission percentages," said AITIC president, Daniel Perotti. "For example, the commission fees for some products exceed 10 percent. By focusing on these, sufficient revenue can be generated even if the total sales volume declines."

Stafford Travel
MEMO

To: All sales staff
From: John Harriman
Subject: Commissions
Date: September 15

Below is an updated summary of the sales commission amounts that I negotiated for our company yesterday. Your share of any commissions earned will be deposited into your bank account with your monthly salary.

• Airline tickets	1 to 2 percent
• Car rentals	3 to 5 percent
• Hotel rooms	5 to 10 percent
• Cruises	15 to 20 percent
• Travel insurance	2 to 5 percent

To: Serena Parker <s.parker@stafford.com>
From: John Harriman <j.harriman@stafford.com>
Date: October 17
Subject: Query

Ms. Parker,

I read through the report you submitted last week, and I agree with both of your recommendations.

Developing travel packages for large groups does seem promising, especially since the major hotel chains have expressed a willingness to increase their maximum commission rates for groups of 25 or more. I also found your point about focusing on the Asian market to be very interesting. As you mentioned, there are a large number of international travelers from China, Japan, and South Korea, and it is important that we develop a better understanding of these consumers' needs.

I would like you to prepare a presentation based on your report for our senior managers. I'll provide you with more detailed instructions later this week. Thanks.

John Harriman

196. According to the article, what is NOT a challenge travel agencies are facing?

(A) Worsening economic conditions
(B) Smaller payments from airlines
(C) A greater demand for low-cost products
(D) The popularity of online services

197. Which product might Stafford Travel have to focus on promoting?

(A) Car rentals
(B) Hotel rooms
(C) Cruises
(D) Travel insurance

198. According to the memo, what did Mr. Harriman do on September 14?

(A) Reached an agreement on rates
(B) Completed salary negotiations
(C) Received a large commission
(D) Evaluated members of a team

199. What is indicated about Stafford Travel?

(A) It has opened branch offices in several countries.
(B) It sent delegates to attend a trade conference in Rome.
(C) It may receive more than 10 percent for hotel commissions.
(D) It will probably hire additional staff for its sales department.

200. According to the e-mail, what did Ms. Parker recommend that Stafford Travel do?

(A) Offer discount travel packages for groups
(B) Form partnerships with companies in Asia
(C) Avoid working with large hotel chains
(D) Learn about potential clients from a specific region

This is the end of the test. You may review Parts 5, 6, and 7 if you finish the test early.

정답 p.326 / 점수 환산표 p.329 / 해석 p.337 / Part 5&6 무료 해설 바로 보기(정답 및 정답 음성 포함)
* 다음 페이지에 있는 Self 체크 리스트를 통해 자신의 문제 풀이 방식과 태도를 점검해 보세요.

TEST 02 PART 7 83

Self 체크 리스트

TEST 02는 무사히 잘 마치셨죠?
이제 다음의 Self 체크 리스트를 통해 자신의 테스트 진행 내용을 점검해 볼까요?

1. 나는 75분 동안 완전히 테스트에 집중하였다.

   ☐ 예 ☐ 아니오

   아니오에 답한 경우, 이유는 무엇인가요?

2. 나는 75분 동안 100문제를 모두 풀었다.

   ☐ 예 ☐ 아니오

   아니오에 답한 경우, 이유는 무엇인가요?

3. 나는 75분 동안 답안지 표시까지 완료하였다.

   ☐ 예 ☐ 아니오

   아니오에 답한 경우, 이유는 무엇인가요?

4. 나는 Part 5와 Part 6를 19분 안에 모두 풀었다.

   ☐ 예 ☐ 아니오

   아니오에 답한 경우, 이유는 무엇인가요?

5. Part 7을 풀 때 5분 이상 걸린 지문이 없었다.

   ☐ 예 ☐ 아니오

6. 개선해야 할 점 또는 나를 위한 충고를 적어보세요.

* 교재의 첫 장으로 돌아가서 자신이 적은 목표 점수를 확인하면서 목표에 대한 의지를 다지기 바랍니다. 개선해야 할 점은 반드시 다음 테스트에
  실천해야 합니다. 그것이 가장 중요하며, 그래야만 발전할 수 있습니다.

TEST 03

PART 5
PART 6
PART 7
Self 체크 리스트

잠깐! 테스트 전 확인사항
1. 휴대 전화의 전원을 끄셨나요? ☐ 예
2. Answer Sheet, 연필, 지우개를 준비하셨나요? ☐ 예
3. 시계를 준비하셨나요? ☐ 예

모든 준비가 완료되었으면 목표 점수를 떠올린 후 테스트를 시작합니다.

문제 풀이를 마치는 시간은 지금부터 75분 후인 ___시 ___분입니다.

테스트 시간은 총 75분이며, 시험 종료 전 2~3분은 정답 검토 및 답안지 마킹을 위해 사용합니다.

READING TEST

In this section, you must demonstrate your ability to read and comprehend English. You will be given a variety of texts and asked to answer questions about these texts. This section is divided into three parts and will take 75 minutes to complete.

Do not mark the answers in your test book. Use the answer sheet that is separately provided.

PART 5

Directions: In each question, you will be asked to review a statement that is missing a word or phrase. Four answer choices will be provided for each statement. Select the best answer and mark the corresponding letter (A), (B), (C), or (D) on the answer sheet.

PART 5 권장 풀이 시간 **11분**

101. The food industry is governed by many regulations, which ------- at Benagra Foods keep track of carefully.

(A) we
(B) us
(C) ours
(D) ourselves

102. Museum management reminds all visitors not to leave their children ------- inside the building.

(A) unfamiliar
(B) invisible
(C) unattended
(D) inattentive

103. The inner loading dock was occupied by another vehicle, so the truck driver had to park ------- the building.

(A) through
(B) outside
(C) into
(D) about

104. The train departing from Vancouver to Calgary ------- a full day, so many travelers prefer going by plane.

(A) take
(B) takes
(C) has taken
(D) to take

105. The memorial statue in the town square was kept ------- until its unveiling during a special ceremony on May 3.

(A) detailed
(B) imaginable
(C) covered
(D) creative

106. Mr. Wilkins would like some ------- setting up the audio-visual equipment in the conference room before the seminar on Thursday.

(A) assisted
(B) assistance
(C) assistant
(D) assisting

107. For every $200 purchase of Billow Swimwear, shoppers will receive ------- a towel or a pair of slippers.

(A) also
(B) either
(C) until
(D) neither

108. Mark Hempel offered his full ------- on a project that is developing a new TV show about international cultures.

(A) cooperates
(B) cooperative
(C) cooperation
(D) cooperatively

109. The restaurant ------- the right to refuse service to customers who are not dressed appropriately.

(A) reserves
(B) relates
(C) collects
(D) allows

110. The Bolden School now offers courses for those ------- in learning a variety of pottery production methods.

(A) interesting
(B) interest
(C) interested
(D) interestingly

111. For train passengers with excess luggage, FineTrak Railways will impose a fee of $13 for every ------- bag.

(A) promising
(B) connected
(C) additional
(D) damaged

112. The charity does not accept food donations that have ------- expired because such items could be hazardous to recipients.

(A) already
(B) never
(C) more
(D) occasionally

113. Those joining the hike this weekend are advised to park ------- since there is limited space in front of the visitor's center.

(A) considered
(B) considering
(C) consideration
(D) considerately

114. The report ------- mentioned an upcoming merger between a textile company in Peru and a fashion corporation in France.

(A) intensely
(B) briefly
(C) structurally
(D) anymore

115. ------- at least five participants sign up for the seminar, it will carry on as planned next weekend.

(A) Unless
(B) Rather than
(C) Instead
(D) As long as

116. Withdrawals from Barstow Bank's automated teller machines will now be ------- to $2,500 a day per customer.

(A) assigned
(B) adhered
(C) limited
(D) enclosed

117. The financial consultant ------- Ms. Broderick to downsize the staff at the Denver branch to lower operational expenses.

(A) suggested
(B) advised
(C) commented
(D) argued

118. The forecast ------- the next 10 days indicates that going on a beach vacation would not be a good idea.

(A) from
(B) as
(C) for
(D) once

119. Being new at the job, Mr. Emmanuel struggled to keep ------- with the other assembly line workers.

(A) attention
(B) pace
(C) progress
(D) guidance

GO ON TO THE NEXT PAGE

120. Grandilla cosmetics are available ------- Harmony products are sold, including Bennington Department Stores.

(A) anytime
(B) sometime
(C) everywhere
(D) someplace

121. New assignments will be handed out after the team members ------- working on the current project.

(A) finish
(B) to finish
(C) finished
(D) will finish

122. The singer Arthur Fischman ------- his recital with a short Japanese piece that was unusual for the end of a concert.

(A) is concluding
(B) was concluded
(C) to conclude
(D) concluded

123. Wondering why the coupon had been rejected, Chester turned it over to check the ------- date.

(A) expiratory
(B) expire
(C) expired
(D) expiration

124. Mr. Aronov discovered that his hard drive was full ------- he attempted to download the file.

(A) upon
(B) when
(C) until
(D) amid

125. The interior decorator recommended a new line of furniture in order to make the room look more -------.

(A) modernity
(B) modernly
(C) modern
(D) modernize

126. Managers formerly ------- the software engineering groups for the development project will now be in charge of much larger teams.

(A) supervise
(B) supervised
(C) supervising
(D) supervisor

127. Because the cost of the ------- in the factory equipment was higher than the owner had expected, he only purchased one new machine.

(A) cover
(B) blame
(C) depth
(D) investment

128. All personnel at the factory, ------- those under contract with an outside firm, get paid time off on national holidays.

(A) excludes
(B) exclusive
(C) excluding
(D) exclusively

129. Staff attending the picnic can bring ------- food they would like to share with the group apart from burgers, which will be provided.

(A) whenever
(B) whomever
(C) whatever
(D) wherever

130. In ------- with the health department's stipulations, restaurant owners must conduct food safety sessions with kitchen staff.

(A) participating
(B) pursuing
(C) concurring
(D) keeping

PART 6

Directions: In this part, you will be asked to read four English texts. Each text is missing a word, phrase, or sentence. Select the answer choice that correctly completes the text and mark the corresponding letter (A), (B), (C), or (D) on the answer sheet.

🕐 **PART 6 권장 풀이 시간** **8분**

Questions 131-134 refer to the following letter.

September 18

Dear Ms. Murillo,

Thank you for inquiring about our services for obtaining -------.
                                                          131.

Based on the information in your letter, your daughter may have acquired citizenship by being

the child of a U.S. citizen. This will need to be ------- through documentation, which was not
                                                  132.

included with your letter. Your child's record of birth abroad is considered proof if it was

registered with a U.S. consulate or embassy. -------, the parent with citizenship must have
                                              133.

been living in the United States for at least five years before your child's birth.

For more information, feel free to visit us. Our Web site provides the address of the local

office in your area. Simply click on the state or country you presently live in. -------. Please
                                                                                  134.

bring all related documents when you visit.

Sincerely,
Sonia Esteban

---

131. (A) healthcare
(B) transportation
(C) nationality
(D) education

132. (A) decorated
(B) verified
(C) corrected
(D) postponed

133. (A) Afterward
(B) For example
(C) Additionally
(D) Henceforth

134. (A) We are sorry to hear that your documents are lost.
(B) There is no record of your child's birth in that country.
(C) You can then select the government office nearest you.
(D) The office in your area was closed only last year.

GO ON TO THE NEXT PAGE

Questions 135-138 refer to the following letter.

May 30

Cayman Interior Decorating
23 Arbor Drive
Cleveland, Ohio, 39005

Dear Mr. Maximus,

I am writing to ------- you and your crew for redecorating the interior of our lobby. The results
        135.
are even better than we had initially expected. -------. Overall, our guests appreciate the new
                                                136.
look, and they love the authentic 1920s ------- and the comfortable furniture.
                                        137.

We thought we'd mention that the hotel intends to renovate the guest rooms. If things go

according to plan, we expect to begin renovating next month. In addition, we ------- expanding
                                                                            138.
the business center on the second floor. More space will be allocated to permit the installation

of new facilities.

I would like to contact you again once our plans become more definite. We hope that your

calendar will permit you to work for us when we are ready.

I look forward to hearing from you soon.

Sincerely,
Devon Green
Manager, Nuance Hotel

135. (A) commend
     (B) persuade
     (C) invoice
     (D) encourage

136. (A) We would have preferred it if you had
         followed our original plan.
     (B) They contacted us to let us know what
         they thought about our work.
     (C) We are equally impressed by how
         quickly the job was done.
     (D) They should have informed us right
         away about these changes.

137. (A) explanation
     (B) atmosphere
     (C) combination
     (D) condition

138. (A) were
     (B) will be
     (C) are being
     (D) have been

Discover Great Deals at Dan's Hardware Store!

Dan's Hardware Store invites you to stop by for our yearly ------- sale. From September 1 to
                                                  139.
15, all of our excess inventory will be marked down to make room for new product lines. Take

advantage of reduced prices of up to 80 percent off on everything from gardening supplies to

outdoor equipment. -------.
                    140.

In addition, customers who buy $500 or more worth of merchandise will ------- to receive a
                                             141.
$50 coupon, redeemable until December 31. A limit of one coupon ------- transaction applies.
                                                                142.

For further information on the sale and directions to the store nearest you, visit our Web site

at www.danshardware.com.

139. (A) holiday
(B) loyalty
(C) clearance
(D) flash

140. (A) We have exciting offers for you in
every department.
(B) The sale is for one day only, so hurry
before it ends.
(C) This product is sold in various sizes to
suit your needs.
(D) Make sure to go online and send in
your product orders.

141. (A) be entitled
(B) be entitling
(C) entitle
(D) have entitled

142. (A) away
(B) among
(C) per
(D) next

Questions 143-146 refer to the following article.

Grimsby's *Feed* Satisfies Viewers

In the three-part miniseries *Feed*, filmmaker David Grimsby ------- explores the modern food
143.
industry. The series takes viewers behind the scenes at farms and factories to reveal

shocking details about the things we eat and how they are produced.

While there are numerous other documentaries on this -------, a combination of smart
144.
narration, intriguing interviews, and animated graphics makes *Feed* stand out. -------. It
145.
presents both the benefits and drawbacks of modern food production without endorsing any

one point of view. Richly informative and visually interesting, the series is ------- captivating
146.
that many people will want to see it twice. The first episode of *Feed* will air this month on the

Modern Film Channel.

143. (A) enthusiasm
(B) enthusiastic
(C) enthusiastically
(D) enthused

144. (A) trend
(B) level
(C) schedule
(D) topic

145. (A) The show attracted millions of viewers
when it was televised last year.
(B) What is perhaps most distinctive about
the film is its lack of bias.
(C) Mr. Grimsby plans to begin filming the
documentary next month.
(D) Ratings for the network jumped when
the final episode was aired.

146. (A) so
(B) even
(C) such
(D) right

PART 7

Directions: In this part, you will be asked to read several texts, such as advertisements, articles, instant messages, or examples of business correspondence. Each text is followed by several questions. Select the best answer and mark the corresponding letter (A), (B), (C), or (D) on your answer sheet.

PART 7 권장 풀이 시간 **54분**

Questions 147-148 refer to the following memo.

To: All staff
From: Donald Manzo
Subject: Welcome reception
Date: August 5

We are holding a reception to welcome our new regional vice president, Gertrude Crowley. Ms. Crowley previously worked as store manager of Knightland Electronics' affiliate in Charleston. After five years there, she led our office in Atlanta for two years and then transferred to New Orleans, where she has been working since as their district manager. She will now head the southeast district from our regional office here in Nashville.

The reception will be held at the Bluegrass Hotel on Friday, August 9, at 7:30 P.M. If you plan on coming, please notify my secretary at extension number 44.

Thank you.

---

147. What is the purpose of the memo?

(A) To convince staff to volunteer for an activity
(B) To appeal for help with setting up a reception
(C) To inform employees about a coming event
(D) To notify staff about a visiting client

148. Where has Ms. Crowley NOT previously worked?

(A) Charleston
(B) Atlanta
(C) New Orleans
(D) Nashville

GO ON TO THE NEXT PAGE

Questions 149-150 refer to the following text-message chain.

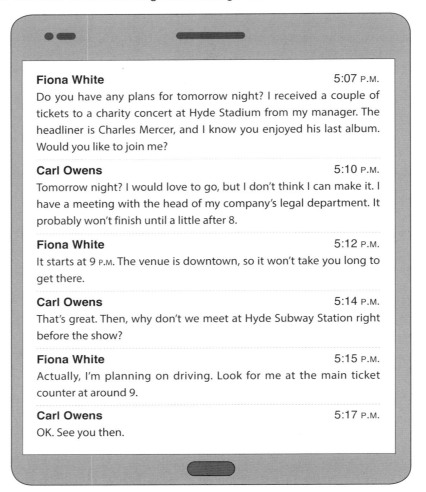

Fiona White   5:07 P.M.

Do you have any plans for tomorrow night? I received a couple of tickets to a charity concert at Hyde Stadium from my manager. The headliner is Charles Mercer, and I know you enjoyed his last album. Would you like to join me?

Carl Owens   5:10 P.M.

Tomorrow night? I would love to go, but I don't think I can make it. I have a meeting with the head of my company's legal department. It probably won't finish until a little after 8.

Fiona White   5:12 P.M.

It starts at 9 P.M. The venue is downtown, so it won't take you long to get there.

Carl Owens   5:14 P.M.

That's great. Then, why don't we meet at Hyde Subway Station right before the show?

Fiona White   5:15 P.M.

Actually, I'm planning on driving. Look for me at the main ticket counter at around 9.

Carl Owens   5:17 P.M.

OK. See you then.

149. Who is Mr. Mercer?

(A) A concert organizer
(B) A professional musician
(C) A stadium manager
(D) A corporate lawyer

150. At 5:12 P.M., what does Ms. White mean when she writes, "It starts at 9 P.M."?

(A) Mr. Owens should drive to a venue.
(B) Mr. Owens will have to end a meeting early.
(C) Mr. Owens will be able to attend an event.
(D) Mr. Owens should pick up a ticket at 8 P.M.

Questions 151-152 refer to the following e-mail.

To: Adam Webster <awebster@connex.com>
From: Caroline McElroy <services@seafront.com>
Date: April 17
Subject: Deposit

Dear Mr. Webster,

Your deposit check has been cashed, and we are pleased to confirm that you can move in to your new office at Spiral Towers on the first day of next month. As a reminder, the deposit will be kept by Seafront Realty until you choose to move out, at which time an inspection of the property will take place. The office space must be returned to the same condition it was in when your lease began. If there is any excess damage, the related costs will be taken from the deposit before it is returned to you. Note also that your deposit is being held in a bank account, and any interest earned as a result will be returned when you leave.

Please e-mail me with any further questions. Thank you.

Yours truly,
Caroline McElroy
Seafront Realty Miami

151. Who most likely is Mr. Webster?

(A) A future occupant
(B) A real estate investor
(C) A repair person
(D) A security guard

152. What is NOT stated about the deposit?

(A) It is returned when the lease ends.
(B) It is kept in a bank account.
(C) It is equivalent to one month's rent.
(D) It is used to pay for damage to the property.

GO ON TO THE NEXT PAGE

Nairobi International Marathon Draws Attention

July 28—Runners participating in this year's Nairobi International Marathon had better start getting ready for some competition. Organizers announced yesterday at a press conference that 12,000 athletes have already signed up for the race, an increase of nearly 30 percent compared to last year. Chair of the organization board, Paul Oduya, says they are expecting even more registrations. "Since the race last year, we have been working very hard to promote the marathon on social media. This allowed us to reach out more to international athletes." Oduya also said that the race's growing popularity has helped give a boost to local tourism and believes that this year's event will continue that trend.

New routes were also announced during the press conference. The full and half marathons will begin along the western edge of the National Park, while the shorter races will start on Outer Ring Road. All races will end at City Stadium. Officials have released details online at www.nairobirace.org.ke, including closures and detours for motorists along Langata, Mombasa, and other major roads. For those interested in joining, registration will remain open until the end of August. Visit www.nairobimarathon.org to learn more about entry fees and other requirements.

153. How will this year's marathon be different from the last one?

(A) It is taking place at a different time of year.
(B) It is being held in a new city.
(C) It will have a larger number of participants.
(D) It will be broadcast on local television.

154. What does the article suggest about Nairobi?

(A) Its sports programs have received more funding in recent years.
(B) Its athletes have gained increased international exposure.
(C) It has experienced an increase in tourism.
(D) Its geography is particularly well-suited to long-distance races.

155. Where will the full marathon end?

(A) At National Park
(B) At Outer Ring Road
(C) At Mombasa Road
(D) At City Stadium

Questions 156-157 refer to the following Web page.

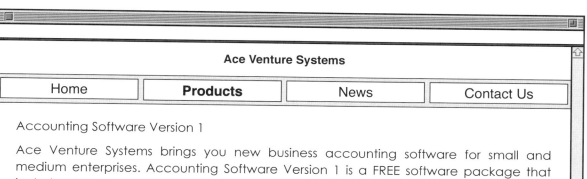

TEST | 01 | 02 | 03 | 04 | 05 | 06 | 07 | 08 | 09 | 10 | 해커스 토익 실전 1000제 2 Reading

156. What is the purpose of the Web page?

(A) To introduce accounting methods
(B) To promote a computer program
(C) To instruct users on setting up a network
(D) To gather suggestions for a new project

157. What is NOT mentioned about Ace Venture Systems?

(A) It supports the use of open-source computer programs.
(B) It asks for clients to give them feedback.
(C) It sells software on a yearly subscription basis.
(D) It provides direct downloads on its Web site.

GO ON TO THE NEXT PAGE

Questions 158-160 refer to the following article.

April 11—At a press conference yesterday, Jane Gomez, a representative of the city's public works department, unveiled plans for the installation of bicycle lanes on all major thoroughfares in the downtown core to improve safety for cyclists. Although Mayor Stevens was not in attendance, this project is important to him as it was one of his campaign promises during the election last month. According to Ms. Gomez, the bike lanes will cost the city just $1.2 million. This is significantly less than originally estimated. However, some residents are unhappy with the project. They worry that the number of lanes available for motor vehicles will be reduced, leading to worsening traffic conditions. Ms. Gomez said that the city is making a plan to address this issue and will provide additional details in May.

158. What is suggested about Mayor Stevens?

(A) He appointed a new public works manager.
(B) He attended a media event yesterday.
(C) He was recently elected.
(D) He has proposed several construction projects.

159. What are some residents concerned about?

(A) Installation costs
(B) Public safety
(C) Property taxes
(D) Traffic congestion

160. According to the article, what will happen in May?

(A) More information about a project will be given.
(B) Reporters will receive the results of a traffic study.
(C) A budget estimate will be revised.
(D) A mayor will hold a press conference.

Janice Hong	10:03 A.M.	We've run into a complication with the sales presentation we're supposed to give this afternoon to the representatives from Alliance Plastics. I was just notified that the air conditioner in the main conference room isn't working.
Devon Harris	10:06 A.M.	What about moving the presentation to the meeting room on the second floor, then?
Grace Rhodes	10:09 A.M.	Alliance Plastics is sending 11 members of its management team. The room on that floor can only seat eight people comfortably. Janice, is there any possibility of getting the air conditioner running before the meeting?
Janice Hong	10:12 A.M.	I'm afraid not. I called several repair shops, and the earliest a technician can come to our office is tomorrow at 1:00 P.M. We may have to consider postponing the presentation.
Devon Harris	10:15 A.M.	This is an important client. There must be something else we can do.
Grace Rhodes	10:16 A.M.	Why don't I contact some of the city's hotels? I'm sure that at least one of them has a suitable meeting space that we could book on short notice.
Janice Hong	10:18 A.M.	That's a great idea. Once you make a reservation, I'll call Alliance Plastics to inform them about the venue change.

Send

161. What problem does Ms. Hong mention?

(A) An appliance was installed incorrectly.
(B) A presentation needs to be shortened.
(C) A piece of equipment has stopped functioning.
(D) A representative arrived earlier than expected.

162. What is mentioned about the second-floor meeting room?

(A) It has been reserved by another team.
(B) Its capacity is insufficient for the group.
(C) It has been inspected by a technician recently.
(D) Its location is inconvenient for an event.

163. At 10:15 A.M., what does Mr. Harris mean when he writes, "This is an important client"?

(A) He hopes to make a good first impression.
(B) He does not agree with a suggestion.
(C) He wants to reschedule an event.
(D) He needs to make additional preparations.

164. What does Ms. Rhodes offer to do?

(A) Contact some businesses in the area
(B) Notify a customer of a situation
(C) Confirm a previously made booking
(D) Visit alternative meeting venues

GO ON TO THE NEXT PAGE

Questions 165-167 refer to the following flyer.

A Night of Song
A concert

On December 5, French singers Pierre Chrétien and Celine Laurier will be at the Maroon Theater for their second concert in Los Angeles, California. The event, which will begin at 7:30 P.M., will also feature French pianist Amanda Depuis as well as American soul singers Andy Red and Cindy Dawson, who will accompany Mr. Chrétien and Ms. Laurier during their performance. — [1] —. During the concert, Ms. Laurier will be introducing her inspirational album, *Crossroads*, which was released in Paris last week. — [2] —.

Witness an extraordinary fusion of French and American artists. — [3] —. Until November 20, those purchasing three or more early-bird tickets will receive complimentary backstage passes! — [4] —. Tickets are available at any Gatewing Ticketing outlet nationwide. They may also be purchased online at www.gatewing. com. Recordings from both Mr. Chrétien and Ms. Laurier will be available for purchase at the venue. Call Gatewing at 1-800-555-2541 for details.

165. What is indicated about backstage passes?

(A) They must be purchased more than a month prior to the concert.
(B) They are free for those who fulfill a certain purchasing condition.
(C) They are exclusively available to concert venue employees.
(D) They will be sold at reduced prices for all of November.

166. What is NOT mentioned about the concert?

(A) It will take place in Los Angeles.
(B) It will have items available for sale.
(C) It will promote a new recording.
(D) It will include an autograph signing session.

167. In which of the positions marked [1], [2], [3], and [4] does the following sentence best belong?

"This does not apply to regular tickets."

(A) [1]
(B) [2]
(C) [3]
(D) [4]

Questions 168-171 refer to the following e-mail.

To: Stephen Haggerty <s.haggerty@mailbag.com>
From: Customer service <cust_serv@giftlane.com>
Subject: Your order
Date: December 8

Dear Mr. Haggerty,

We received the order you placed on our online store, some details of which are below. Unfortunately, we cannot send all of the items as requested. Due to an unusually high volume of orders this holiday season, some popular items are currently unavailable for delivery before Christmas Day. We apologize for this inconvenience.

ORDER DETAILS

Quantity	Description	Status	Expected Delivery
1	Personalized bottle of rosé wine	Ready to ship	December 21
3	Chocolate gift box (assorted)	Ready to ship	December 18
1	Leather-bound journal and pen	Ready to ship	December 22
2	Decorative plant pot	Pending	December 27

To ensure at least a partial delivery of your order, we can ship the first three items to the recipients at the different addresses you provided by the dates indicated above. However, in regard to the last item on the list, the earliest that the recipient can receive it would be December 27. If this is acceptable for you, then you do not need to respond to this message, and we will proceed with the delivery to that address once we have the product in stock.

However, if it is important that all your gifts be delivered before December 25, then we recommend that you replace the pending item with another product from our store. Click here to modify your order now. For additional information, reply to this message or call us at 555-3403.

Thank you.

Sincerely,
Margaret Hill
Customer service representative
Gift Lane

168. What is the problem with Mr. Haggerty's order?

(A) A technical error occurred on a Web site.
(B) It contained the wrong products.
(C) A requested item is not readily available.
(D) It is missing important delivery details.

169. What is indicated about Mr. Haggerty?

(A) He ordered one of every item.
(B) He purchased a bottle of wine for himself.
(C) He is sending items to different recipients.
(D) He has shopped with Gift Lane in the past.

170. What will happen if Mr. Haggerty does not answer the e-mail?

(A) An order will be canceled.
(B) A delivery will proceed.
(C) An extra charge will be incurred.
(D) A special offer will be voided.

171. What should Mr. Haggerty do if he wishes to replace an item?

(A) Wait for further instructions
(B) Call the company hotline
(C) Follow a link to a Web site
(D) Send a message to customer service

GO ON TO THE NEXT PAGE

Lester Beebe Hits Stage in South Bend
By Adam Brown

A musical version of Michelle Gable's novel *The Triumph of Lester Beebe* is set to premiere next month on May 22. — [1] —. Set in South Bend, the show is the story of a teenage boy who is the son of an automobile factory worker in the 1960s. The book became a favorite of young adult readers when it was first printed in 1968. — [2] —.

Producers Todd Carlisle and Emma Wright were not even born when the book was first released but say they identified with Lester Beebe's adolescent struggles when they first read the story. "Lester Beebe isn't just a teenager from South Bend," says Carlisle, "he could be a young person from anywhere." In addition to being the show's producers, Carlisle and Wright manage the Eden Playhouse in South Bend. — [3] —. According to Wright, the area is not well-known for musical productions, but she hopes *The Triumph of Lester Beebe* will change that. "Todd and I are also counting on local interest to help in building an audience for the show," she said.

Playing the role of Beebe is actor Henry Thomas. Veteran performer Neil Chandler plays his father, while the roles of Beebe's sisters, Mandy and Corinne, will be realized by Stephanie O'Connor and Audrey Blanco. Following the run in South Bend, Carlisle and Wright will take the show to New York in August for its Broadway debut. — [4] —. Tickets for the South Bend show are on sale now through the Eden Playhouse at 555-0493.

172. What is the article mainly about?

(A) A musical performer's return to the stage
(B) An upcoming theatrical production
(C) A grand opening for a play venue
(D) An adaptation of an author's biography

173. What is NOT indicated about *The Triumph of Lester Beebe*?

(A) It had a successful run in New York.
(B) It was popular with some youth in the 1960s.
(C) It has been modified into a musical show.
(D) It is based in South Bend.

174. The word "realized" in paragraph 3, line 2, is closest in meaning to

(A) caused
(B) depicted
(C) clarified
(D) discovered

175. In which of the positions marked [1], [2], [3], and [4] does the following sentence best belong?

"Its popularity earned it widespread acclaim and, ultimately, translation into 32 languages."

(A) [1]
(B) [2]
(C) [3]
(D) [4]

GO ON TO THE NEXT PAGE

Questions 176-180 refer to the following article and advertisement.

Group Fitness Keeps Santiago Moving

By Raymond Wong

February 16

As the long winter grinds on, it is easy to forget about your New Year's resolution. But according to local gym owners, more people than ever are sticking to their fitness goals this year. The secret? Santiago residents are enrolling in group fitness classes in record numbers, and working out together is keeping them motivated.

Traditionally, the main drawback to group fitness has been its relatively high price. But this past winter, several affordable fitness centers, including Exercise Nation, greatly expanded their selection of group classes. They now offer everything from kickboxing to yoga, with varying options for people of every fitness level.

"I actually upgraded my membership so that I could go to as many classes as I wanted," said Millie Rhys, a university student and Exercise Nation gym member for the past two years. "I used to just come here to lift a few weights and ride the stationary bike, but the classes have made going to the gym exciting."

DON'T WAIT TO GET FIT!

Exercise Nation offers a wide range of group classes. All members are entitled to one free class per week. Gold and Gold-plus members get two and three free classes each week, respectively. Diamond members receive unlimited class passes and access to our advanced HIIT program. Visit us at www.exercisenation.com/classes to see which ones fit into your schedule.

Not yet a member? No problem! Join now for a low price starting at $20 a month.* Get access to our trainers, nutritionists, top-quality equipment, and more!

Sign up in March and receive a free gym bag and water bottle.
We're open 7 days a week from 5 A.M. until 10 P.M.

*A one-time $15 registration fee is applied to the first payment. Members are required to sign a 12-month contract that renews automatically.

176. According to the article, what happened last winter?

(A) A product price was lowered.
(B) A workout facility was expanded.
(C) Some new offerings became available.
(D) Some gym equipment was delivered.

177. What does the article suggest about Exercise Nation?

(A) It provides student discounts.
(B) It has received positive online reviews.
(C) It accommodates members of varying capabilities.
(D) It has been in operation for two years.

178. What can be inferred about Ms. Rhys?

(A) She has a Diamond membership.
(B) She was not charged a sign-up fee.
(C) She wants to take HIIT classes.
(D) She prefers working out alone.

179. What will take place in March?

(A) A seasonal sale
(B) A registration promotion
(C) A sporting event
(D) A gym opening

180. What is true about a gym membership?

(A) It lasts for one year.
(B) It can be upgraded for $20.
(C) It includes private training sessions.
(D) It can be renewed on a Web site.

GO ON TO THE NEXT PAGE

Questions 181-185 refer to the following brochure and e-mail.

See Bristol with City Ago!

If you're visiting Bristol, City Ago has all your transportation and logistical needs covered. Whether you are a solo traveller returning to your favourite spots or a first-time visitor arriving with a big group, we have all the vehicles and the knowledge you need.

Available types of transportation:

- Bicycle: 1 passenger each, £3 per hour(3-hour minimum)*
- Motorized scooter: up to 2 passengers each, £10 per hour(4-hour minimum)*
- Car: up to 5 passengers each, £100 per day(minimum), driver must be at least 25 years old
- Minibus: up to 15 passengers each, £550 per day(minimum), driver must be over 25 years old and have a valid commercial driver's licence

*helmet required

Each transportation option can be arranged with or without a guided tour. If you need some more help getting started, our services also include custom trip itineraries, dining and accommodation bookings, and more. To make a reservation, visit www.cityago.com/reservations and submit a request form. Please also read our terms and conditions at www.cityago.com/t&c along with information regarding accident and damage liability before completing a reservation.

To: Reservations <reservations@cityago.com>
From: Craig Black <cblack@duncanarchitects.com>
Subject: Request Update
Date: 20 June

Thank you again for confirming my reservation for Sunday, 29 June. However, I'd like to make a change to my original request. We'd actually prefer motorized scooters. We'll still be renting the vehicles for four hours. We will now require two scooters.

Also, I was wondering if you knew of a shortcut from the old quarter to the Bristol Museum of History. We're looking for a more direct route and one which won't take us onto major roads.

Regards,
Craig Black

181. In the brochure, the word "spots" in paragraph 1, line 2, is closest in meaning to

(A) locations
(B) flaws
(C) patches
(D) views

182. What does City Ago recommend that customers do?

(A) Hire transportation from an airport
(B) Check a Web site for discount deals
(C) Pack protective equipment
(D) Go over an accountability policy

183. What most likely did Mr. Black originally book?

(A) Bicycle
(B) Motorized scooter
(C) Car
(D) Minibus

184. What is true about Mr. Black?

(A) He changed the date of a booking.
(B) He made a reservation a week ago.
(C) He is waiting for a confirmation message.
(D) He will be visiting Bristol on a Sunday.

185. What does Mr. Black ask City Ago to do?

(A) Give directions to a building
(B) Repair a damaged scooter
(C) Extend the length of a rental
(D) Supply a guided tour

GO ON TO THE NEXT PAGE

Questions 186-190 refer to the following Web page, e-mail, and invoice.

http://www.stclaireeditwrite.com/about

Ruben St. Claire: Freelance Writer/Editor

ABOUT　　Contact　　Portfolio/Writing Samples

Services

I write, edit, proofread, and research materials on a wide variety of topics. If your association, business, or institution requires help creating or perfecting magazine articles, blog posts, newsletters, or press releases, do not hesitate to contact me.

Major Clients

Borton University Alumni Association, *North East Gardener*'s *Journal*, Urban Planning Association of Georgeville, Sportsworld Outfitters, Society for the Decorative Arts

Awards

National Association of Businesses Communications Award, GRB Prize for Editorial Excellence, Georgia P. Smythe Freelance Writers' Award

Education

Western Pointhead University, BA, Double Major in English Literature and Journalism

---

To: Ruben St. Claire <rstclaire@stclaireeditwrite.com>

From: Christa Gables <chgab@FineThreads.com>

Date: February 28

Subject: Inquiry

Dear Mr. St. Claire,

I am the proprietor of an online retail business, and I recently came across your Web site. I am interested in possibly hiring you to work on a series of short blog posts for my online clothing store, FineThreads.com. I went through your portfolio and noticed that you have done quite a lot of work for an athletic wear company that I know rather well. I believe you may fulfill my requirements as I retail similar types of products. Initially, I would need you to write three pages of copy to post on my Web site. If I am satisfied with your work, I will have three hours of research and about six hours of proofreading assignments for you to do as well. Please send me a list of your fees and an estimate for the total cost. Hopefully, we can get started as soon as possible.

Sincerely,

Christa Gables

St. Claire Editing and Writing Services
(805)555-3988/ rstclaire@stclaireeditwrite.com

Invoice: 001
Christa Gables, FineThreads.com
14 Lewis Crescent
West Center, OH 49242

March 6

Type of work	Quantity/Time	Price
Writing	3 pages	$225
Proofreading	6 hours	$120
Research	5 hours	$100
Subtotal Tax Total Amount Due		$445 $44.50 $489.50

The total amount is due no later than five business days from the invoice date, and online payments and bank transfers are accepted. If you are sending a check, make it payable to: Ruben St. Claire. Thank you very much for your business!

186. What is NOT indicated about Mr. St. Claire?

(A) He can do research on a variety of different subjects.
(B) He has posted selections of his work online.
(C) He has been recognized for both editorial and writing work.
(D) He is currently employed at an educational institution.

187. What is the main purpose of the e-mail?

(A) To thank a writer for previous blog posts
(B) To make a business proposition
(C) To follow up on an editing request
(D) To inquire about preferred methods of payment

188. With which of Mr. St. Claire's clients is Ms. Gables most likely familiar?

(A) Borton University Alumni Association
(B) *North East Gardener's Journal*
(C) Sportsworld Outfitters
(D) Society for the Decorative Arts

189. What does Ms. Gables ask Mr. St. Claire to do?

(A) Send her a check in the mail
(B) Provide a price quotation
(C) Create links to some blog posts
(D) E-mail her some writing samples

190. What can be inferred about Ms. Gables?

(A) She was late sending payment for some proofreading services.
(B) She underestimated the amount of time needed to do some research.
(C) She had to pay more for copywriting than she expected.
(D) She may recommend Mr. St. Claire to one of her associates.

GO ON TO THE NEXT PAGE

Questions 191-195 refer to the following notice, Web page, and text message.

NOTICE

Please be informed that subway maintenance work will commence at Ratner, Sofner, and Hambrick stations on Monday, August 15. Repairs are expected to continue for two weeks until August 28. The crews' working hours are between 7 A.M. and 6 P.M. There will be some noise in the vicinity, but workers will attempt to keep disturbances to a minimum. During this period, service at these stations will be suspended to facilitate the work. For the convenience of commuters who use these stops, the Wymore Public Transportation Office will be providing alternative transport. For more information, please visit its Web site at www.wymorepublictransport.com/announcements. We apologize for any inconvenience but are sure the renovations to the aging stations' facilities will be appreciated once complete.

Wymore Public Transportation Office

Home | About us | Online services | **Announcements** | Contact

Announcement:

Date of Issue: August 5

ALTERNATIVE TRANSPORTATION SERVICE

As announced earlier this week, repairs will be conducted at the Ratner, Sofner, and Hambrick subway stations beginning on August 15. For your convenience, buses will be serving the following routes from 5:30 A.M. to midnight:

- Ratner to and from Sofner: Bus 23
- Ratner to and from Hambrick: Bus 24
- Sofner to and from Hambrick: Bus 25
- Ratner to and from Grand Central: Bus 26

These bus routes are temporary and will be available only until the day after the maintenance work is completed. Click on "buses" above in the drop-down menu under "Online Services" to find maps that show the exact locations of bus stops at all the affected stations. For more information, call 555-1001 during office hours.

From: Jill Addis (555-2737)
To: Nick Lieb (555-0320)

Received: August 16, 3:35 P.M.

Mr. Lieb, I've made lunch reservations at Di Paolo's Italian restaurant for 1:00 P.M. When you meet me, we can go over the Cross Media contract together. I sent you the restaurant's address earlier. It's right across the street from Grand Central station, so I suggest using public transportation to get there. You'll have to take one of the temporary buses as Ratner is the station closest to you, though. You can visit the transportation office's Web site to find out which bus to take. Anyway, see you on Thursday!

191. According to the notice, what is true about the maintenance on the subway stations?

(A) It is being carried out due to residents' complaints.
(B) It is not expected to begin until August 28.
(C) It will result in noise during working hours.
(D) It will be suspended for a period of two weeks.

192. What is indicated on the Web page?

(A) Late evening bus service is usually not available.
(B) Locations of temporary bus stops are accessible online.
(C) The concluding date of the maintenance work is undecided.
(D) Passengers can use their subway passes on the bus.

193. When will the temporary bus service end?

(A) On August 15
(B) On August 16
(C) On August 28
(D) On August 29

194. Which bus will Mr. Lieb most likely take?

(A) Bus 23
(B) Bus 24
(C) Bus 25
(D) Bus 26

195. What is suggested about Mr. Lieb?

(A) He is applying for a job with Cross Media.
(B) He will meet with Ms. Addis over lunch.
(C) He notified Ms. Addis about a service interruption.
(D) He made changes to an earlier appointment.

GO ON TO THE NEXT PAGE

MOONGLOW HEALTH FOODS — TOURS AVAILABLE

On May 1, Moonglow Health Foods will open their gardens, kitchens, and packaging facilities for regular tours. Come see how your favorite foods are harvested, prepared, and packaged for sale in local grocery stores!

Tours take place each week from 10 A.M. to 12 P.M. on Mondays, Thursdays, and Fridays. Regular weekly tours are available for groups of 5 to 20 people. Call 555-4293 to make a reservation!

Larger groups can also be accommodated by special appointment. Local educators interested in school field trips are encouraged to contact us to arrange appointments. All inquiries about special appointments should be directed by e-mail to Maria Anderson at mariaanderson@moonglowhealth.com.

Special gifts and educational materials are available for students who take a Moonglow Health Foods tour! Note that students will be required to have a parent or guardian sign a facility permission slip before participating.

To: Julie Armstrong <jarmstrong@washingtonschool.edu>
From: Maria Anderson <mariaanderson@moonglowhealth.com>
Date: April 2
Subject: RE: 6th Grade Field Trip

Hi, Ms. Armstrong! Thank you for your interest in Moonglow Health Foods.
We'd love to have your 6th grade class join us for a special tour the week of May 1. We can certainly manage a group of 27 students.
Available timeslots for a student tour include:
    Tuesday, May 2, at 10 A.M.
    Wednesday, May 3, at 11:30 A.M.
    Friday, May 6, at 9 A.M.
    Friday, May 6, at 1 P.M.
Let me know which time would work best for your group. Please don't hesitate to reach out with any other questions!

Warm regards,
Maria Anderson
Marketing & Outreach Director, Moonglow Health Foods

Washington Middle School
41750 East Avenue
Toledo, Ohio 43460

Dear Ms. Anderson,

I'm writing to let you know how much my students enjoyed their tour on May 3.

The students had so much fun visiting the fields and seeing how local crops are cultivated and harvested. It was also very informative for them to see how the crops are turned into jams, sauces, and other products inside your facility's kitchens.

We were amazed by the number of products offered. I had no idea that Moonglow Health Foods had such a wide range of options.

I would also like to thank you for the souvenirs. The posters will look great in our classroom, and we'll use the seed packets to start a community garden at school.

Thanks again for your generous support!

Sincerely,
Julie Armstrong

196. What is mentioned about the tours at Moonglow Health Foods?

(A) Private tours for individuals are available on request.
(B) The schedule changes during the holiday season.
(C) The size of weekly tour groups is restricted.
(D) Special gifts can be acquired at the souvenir shop.

197. What most likely will Ms. Armstrong's group need in order to take a tour?

(A) Documents granting permission
(B) A special deposit for large groups
(C) A reservation made by phone
(D) Educational materials concerning farming

198. What is indicated about the field trip?

(A) It was arranged by the head of manufacturing.
(B) It coincided with a regular weekly tour.
(C) It was scheduled a month in advance.
(D) It took longer than originally planned.

199. At what time did the Washington Middle School students take a tour?

(A) 9 A.M.
(B) 10 A.M.
(C) 11:30 A.M.
(D) 1 P.M.

200. According to Ms. Armstrong, what was especially impressive about Moonglow Health Foods?

(A) The variety of items on sale
(B) The cost of souvenirs at the facility
(C) The quality of posters on display
(D) The number of seed packets offered

This is the end of the test. You may review Parts 5, 6, and 7 if you finish the test early.

정답 p.326 / 점수 환산표 p.329 / 해석 p.346 / Part 5&6 무료 해설 바로 보기(정답 및 정답 음성 포함)

* 다음 페이지에 있는 Self 체크 리스트를 통해 자신의 문제 풀이 방식과 태도를 점검해 보세요.

Self 체크 리스트

TEST 03은 무사히 잘 마치셨죠?
이제 다음의 **Self** 체크 리스트를 통해 자신의 테스트 진행 내용을 점검해 볼까요?

1. 나는 75분 동안 완전히 테스트에 집중하였다.
   ☐ 예   ☐ 아니오
   아니오에 답한 경우, 이유는 무엇인가요?

2. 나는 75분 동안 100문제를 모두 풀었다.
   ☐ 예   ☐ 아니오
   아니오에 답한 경우, 이유는 무엇인가요?

3. 나는 75분 동안 답안지 표시까지 완료하였다.
   ☐ 예   ☐ 아니오
   아니오에 답한 경우, 이유는 무엇인가요?

4. 나는 Part 5와 Part 6를 19분 안에 모두 풀었다.
   ☐ 예   ☐ 아니오
   아니오에 답한 경우, 이유는 무엇인가요?

5. Part 7을 풀 때 5분 이상 걸린 지문이 없었다.
   ☐ 예   ☐ 아니오

6. 개선해야 할 점 또는 나를 위한 충고를 적어보세요.

* 교재의 첫 장으로 돌아가서 자신이 적은 목표 점수를 확인하면서 목표에 대한 의지를 다지기 바랍니다. 개선해야 할 점은 반드시 다음 테스트에
  실천해야 합니다. 그것이 가장 중요하며, 그래야만 발전할 수 있습니다.

▌TEST 04

PART 5
PART 6
PART 7
Self 체크 리스트

잠깐! 테스트 전 확인사항

1. 휴대 전화의 전원을 끄셨나요? □ 예
2. Answer Sheet, 연필, 지우개를 준비하셨나요? □ 예
3. 시계를 준비하셨나요? □ 예

모든 준비가 완료되었으면 목표 점수를 떠올린 후 테스트를 시작합니다.

문제 풀이를 마치는 시간은 지금부터 75분 후인 ___시 ___분입니다.

테스트 시간은 총 75분이며, 시험 종료 전 2~3분은 정답 검토 및 답안지 마킹을 위해 사용합니다.

READING TEST

In this section, you must demonstrate your ability to read and comprehend English. You will be given a variety of texts and asked to answer questions about these texts. This section is divided into three parts and will take 75 minutes to complete.

Do not mark the answers in your test book. Use the answer sheet that is separately provided.

PART 5

Directions: In each question, you will be asked to review a statement that is missing a word or phrase. Four answer choices will be provided for each statement. Select the best answer and mark the corresponding letter (A), (B), (C), or (D) on the answer sheet.

🕒 **PART 5 권장 풀이 시간 11분**

101. Pending further notice, only members will be allowed to ------- the equipment in the fitness center.
    (A) lend
    (B) perform
    (C) utilize
    (D) assess

102. The monthly report helps analysts to stay up to date with ------- conditions in financial markets.
    (A) shift
    (B) shifts
    (C) shifting
    (D) to shift

103. The character John Greaves in the film *Silent Target* was ------- portrayed by the actor Arnold Langella.
    (A) memorial
    (B) memorable
    (C) memorably
    (D) memorizing

104. Each of the co-owners has a different opinion on ------- the company should be run.
    (A) who
    (B) how
    (C) what
    (D) which

105. Tybolt Tech uses recycled material for its -------, which consists mainly of boxes.
    (A) subscription
    (B) variable
    (C) handout
    (D) packaging

106. Professor Keating will ------- select four students to take part in a demonstration at the front of the class.
    (A) namely
    (B) concisely
    (C) randomly
    (D) narrowly

107. The Web site's advanced tracking function offers advertisers a ------- way to reach target audiences than the previous version did.
    (A) dependable
    (B) more dependable
    (C) dependably
    (D) most dependable

108. Vidiful Games has released several video games that are ------- teenage girls rather than their male counterparts.
    (A) aimed at
    (B) divided into
    (C) abided by
    (D) tracked down

109. Because Ms. Taylor ------- a remarkable ability to argue complex issues in court, she was appointed a senior partner of the law firm.

(A) shown
(B) has to show
(C) showing
(D) had shown

110. Research indicates that carrying out ------- tasks on a regular basis during middle age leads to improved cognitive function.

(A) challenge
(B) challenges
(C) challenging
(D) challengingly

111. ------- having received complaints about its lack of digital resources, Turnerfield Public Library has been criticized for failing to offer a community education program.

(A) Besides
(B) Except for
(C) In addition
(D) Throughout

112. Owing to the two phones' common design characteristics, customers have trouble distinguishing one ------- the other.

(A) to
(B) from
(C) along
(D) between

113. The fashion label is developing a new marketing ------- in line with its recent focus on online sales.

(A) disclosure
(B) installation
(C) strategy
(D) guidance

114. Individuals applying for the sales position must be ------- in their capacity to quickly acquire technical expertise.

(A) attentive
(B) familiar
(C) generic
(D) confident

115. Staff members ------- monthly paycheck issued today contains an error should seek assistance from Mr. Costa.

(A) those
(B) whose
(C) who
(D) whom

116. Only by ------- to customer expectations can companies remain competitive in today's business climate.

(A) overseeing
(B) adopting
(C) attributing
(D) responding

117. For ------- reasons that were not fully explained, the institute canceled all upcoming seminars.

(A) customary
(B) assorted
(C) studious
(D) utter

118. The city plans to replace all of its diesel buses ------- severe accumulations of airborne pollutants in the greater metropolitan area.

(A) according to
(B) seeing that
(C) far from
(D) due to

119. The funds raised through Help Hearts Foundation's annual charity event ------- the Vigneux-Dade Children's Hospital.

(A) benefiting
(B) to benefit
(C) benefits
(D) benefit

GO ON TO THE NEXT PAGE

120. Some employees were transferred to nearby branches when the Clairview location closed down, but ------- were hired by a competitor.

(A) all
(B) ones
(C) others
(D) another

121. Ms. Franklin reminded the board of its ------- to protect shareholder interests.

(A) responders
(B) responsible
(C) responsive
(D) responsibility

122. The research team undertook ------- preparations for its three-month expedition in Antarctica.

(A) elaboration
(B) elaborated
(C) elaborately
(D) elaborate

123. ------- all the stores in the mall open at 10 A.M., but Tinsel Boutiques is an exception.

(A) Highly
(B) Solely
(C) Closely
(D) Nearly

124. To prevent infection, it is necessary that medical ------- be sterilized before being used.

(A) prescriptions
(B) instruments
(C) procedures
(D) treatments

125. ------- so few people have signed up for the course on European literature, the school may decide to withdraw it from the curriculum.

(A) For
(B) Although
(C) Since
(D) While

126. In terms of fuel efficiency, the Kanon X9 is ------- Hugel Auto's most environmentally friendly vehicle to date.

(A) definitely
(B) definite
(C) define
(D) defining

127. ------- economic growth during a recession, central banks sometimes lower interest rates as this encourages spending.

(A) To stimulate
(B) Stimulate
(C) Stimulation
(D) Stimulated

128. It seems that the vast majority of employees are ------- with the salaries they receive.

(A) relaxed
(B) enthusiastic
(C) contented
(D) satisfactory

129. The students in the math class discussed some problems ------- found difficult.

(A) theirs
(B) themselves
(C) them
(D) they

130. The presentation schedule is ------- as most of the invited speakers have not committed to attending the conference yet.

(A) impulsive
(B) undecided
(C) diverse
(D) imperative

PART 6

Directions: In this part, you will be asked to read four English texts. Each text is missing a word, phrase, or sentence. Select the answer choice that correctly completes the text and mark the corresponding letter (A), (B), (C), or (D) on the answer sheet.

PART 6 권장 풀이 시간 **8분**

Questions 131-134 refer to the following announcement.

Starfire Stadium: Important Announcement

We have recently learned that several shows on The Ebbing Tide's world tour have been

------- . Unfortunately, the concert scheduled to take place at Starfire Stadium on the evening
131.

of June 6 was one of those that were called off.

Starfire Stadium would like to apologize to ticket holders for any ------- this causes them. We
132.

attempted to move the show to a date that suited the band's schedule. -------, the circumstances
133.

were beyond our control.

If you purchased tickets directly from Starfire Stadium, you will be eligible for a full refund at

our box office starting tomorrow. Please bring your ticket with you. ------- .
134.

TEST | 01 | 02 | 03 | 04 | 05 | 06 | 07 | 08 | 09 | 10

해커스 토익 실전 1000제 2 Reading

131. (A) relocated
(B) postponed
(C) combined
(D) dropped

132. (A) disappointing
(B) disappoints
(C) disappointment
(D) disappointed

133. (A) However
(B) Consequently
(C) Furthermore
(D) Specifically

134. (A) They may change the date to later this
month.
(B) You will need to present it to be
reimbursed.
(C) We anticipate that the show will sell
out quickly.
(D) It cannot be exchanged at this point.

GO ON TO THE NEXT PAGE

Questions 135-138 refer to the following letter.

July 28

Ruth Quinn
237 Spring Drive
North Augusta, SC 29841

Dear Ms. Quinn,

This letter concerns your interest in ------- Laundale Business Academy's Supervisory
                                    135.
Management class. Without a doubt, this is one of our most ------- courses. We receive a
                                                          136.
large number of requests every semester from students hoping to enroll. We are pleased to

say that you are one of the students who gained admission.

You will receive the weekly schedule and course syllabus in the coming weeks. Also, please

note that some of the course materials will only be available through Laundale Business

Academy's Web site. A username and password will be sent to you by e-mail in early August.

-------.
137.

I extend my congratulations and best wishes ------- Laundale Business Academy.
                                          138.

Sincerely,

Shaun Conway
Admissions Director
Laundale Business Academy

---

135. (A) teaching
(B) taking
(C) conducting
(D) arranging

136. (A) envious
(B) probable
(C) separate
(D) popular

137. (A) Make sure that you submit them prior
to the deadline.
(B) We plan to remove all of the online
content at that time.
(C) You always have the option of
switching majors later.
(D) They can be changed after logging into
our system for the first time.

138. (A) in honor of
(B) on behalf of
(C) by courtesy of
(D) for the sake of

(20 July)— Thanks-A-Latte is celebrating yet another year of success. Twenty-six years ago, local resident Michael Troslin opened the first Thanks-A-Latte coffee shop right here in Augusta, Maine. -------. "When I first started this business, I just wanted ------- great-tasting
139.   **140.**
coffee in a comfortable environment," said Mr. Troslin. To this day, he has stayed true to his word. Each of his stores ------- pleasant surroundings and high-quality coffee, something the
141.
diligent owner takes great care to ensure. Mr. Troslin plans to further grow the franchise over the next few years. -------, he hopes to expand internationally.
142.

139. (A) The honey cream latte is the best-selling item in his store.
(B) He fell in love with brewing coffee while traveling overseas.
(C) That's because his shop makes the best coffee in town.
(D) Now, Thanks-A-Latte has expanded to 17 stores across five states.

140. (A) to provide
(B) provides
(C) providing
(D) have provided

141. (A) compares
(B) features
(C) craves
(D) follows

142. (A) Therefore
(B) Before then
(C) Afterwards
(D) As a result

GO ON TO THE NEXT PAGE

Questions 143-146 refer to the following information.

Employee Vacation Policy

- Gemstone Multimedia grants all staff 15 paid vacation days per year. ------- adequate
  143.
  notice is given, these can be used at any point during the 12-month contract period.

  Barring an urgent situation, one week's notice is required to take a day off and two

  weeks' notice is needed to take two or more days off in a row.

- Supervisors will do their best to accommodate employees' vacation requests. However,

  they are entitled to act upon their -------. In other words, during especially busy periods
  144.
  or when urgent situations arise, they will determine whether the needs of our business

  should take priority.

- With each subsequent year of work, an employee will receive one additional day off.

  -------.
  145.

- Vacation days -------. This means that employees who fail to use their days within a year
  146.
  will lose them without being compensated.

---

143. (A) Because
(B) Provided
(C) Unless
(D) Before

144. (A) authorization
(B) delegation
(C) discretion
(D) advice

145. (A) This applies until the employee has
accrued 30 days off per year.
(B) As a result, one vacation day will have
to be deducted.
(C) In such cases, the employee will need
to present a doctor's note.
(D) Unfortunately, we believe that
productivity will begin to suffer.

146. (A) remain
(B) prevail
(C) accumulate
(D) expire

PART 7

Directions: In this part, you will be asked to read several texts, such as advertisements, articles, instant messages, or examples of business correspondence. Each text is followed by several questions. Select the best answer and mark the corresponding letter (A), (B), (C), or (D) on your answer sheet.

🕐 **PART 7** 권장 풀이 시간 **54분**

Questions 147-148 refer to the following advertisement.

Laura's Designs

448 Government Street, Victoria

End-of-Summer Discount

Drop by Laura's Designs and browse through our diverse selection of bedding, towels, and curtains, all made of the finest linen!

Print out this advertisement and show it to a salesperson to get 25 percent off on any bathroom product in our store. If you're not satisfied with a purchase, you may exchange it within seven days.

This offer is valid until September 1. It cannot be used with any other promotional offer.

147. What is being advertised?

(A) A clothing store
(B) A housewares retailer
(C) A fabric supplier
(D) A craft workshop

148. What is NOT indicated about Laura's Designs?

(A) It is offering a discount for a limited time.
(B) It is encouraging customers to bring in some promotional material.
(C) It sells products made from a variety of materials.
(D) It allows exchanges to be made within a week.

GO ON TO THE NEXT PAGE

Questions 149-150 refer to the following memo.

MEMO

To: All office staff
From: Margery Haines, HR department head
Date: October 12
Subject: Office improvements

In recent months, there have been complaints about our office's electrical system being faulty. The company has decided to address the situation by having a crew of technicians rewire our office this week. Please note that on October 13 and 14, the electricity for all of our floors will be shut off at around 6 P.M. This should not affect your work schedules as most of you finish at 5 P.M. We will also be without power while the electrical system is being tested at 11 A.M. on the first day of the work. It should be restored within 10 minutes, though. Just make sure to save any files you are working on at around 10:50 A.M. and then turn off your computer.

---

149. What is the notice mainly about?

(A) The installation of a new security system
(B) The possible causes of a malfunction
(C) Changes to normal hours of operation
(D) Some planned maintenance work

150. What are employees asked to do?

(A) Take necessary files home
(B) Clean up their desks at the end of the workday
(C) Prevent work from being lost
(D) Install a file on their computer

Questions 151-152 refer to the following text-message chain.

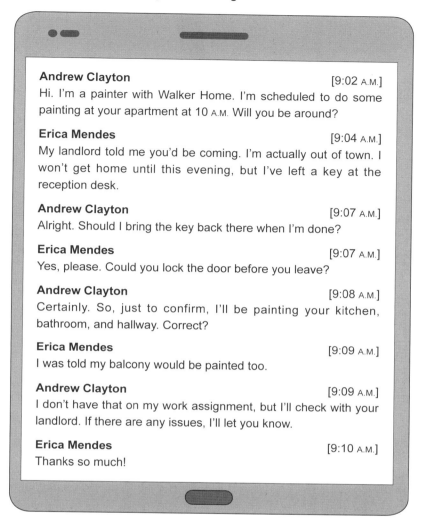

Andrew Clayton [9:02 A.M.]
Hi. I'm a painter with Walker Home. I'm scheduled to do some painting at your apartment at 10 A.M. Will you be around?

Erica Mendes [9:04 A.M.]
My landlord told me you'd be coming. I'm actually out of town. I won't get home until this evening, but I've left a key at the reception desk.

Andrew Clayton [9:07 A.M.]
Alright. Should I bring the key back there when I'm done?

Erica Mendes [9:07 A.M.]
Yes, please. Could you lock the door before you leave?

Andrew Clayton [9:08 A.M.]
Certainly. So, just to confirm, I'll be painting your kitchen, bathroom, and hallway. Correct?

Erica Mendes [9:09 A.M.]
I was told my balcony would be painted too.

Andrew Clayton [9:09 A.M.]
I don't have that on my work assignment, but I'll check with your landlord. If there are any issues, I'll let you know.

Erica Mendes [9:10 A.M.]
Thanks so much!

151. Who most likely is Ms. Mendes?

(A) A worker with a paint company
(B) A client of a real estate agency
(C) A tenant of an apartment building
(D) A security guard stationed at a housing complex

152. At 9:08 A.M., what does Mr. Clayton mean when he writes, "Certainly"?

(A) He will make some improvements to a balcony.
(B) He will repair some damage to a doorframe.
(C) He will paint an additional area of an apartment.
(D) He will secure an entrance.

GO ON TO THE NEXT PAGE

June 6

Ava Foster
Café Falu
2650 Nelmis Street
Alexandria, VA 22301

Dear Ms. Foster,

I am a reporter with the *Alexandria Record*, which recently started profiling local business owners. I think readers would be interested to learn about how you purchased Café Falu and turned it into a success, especially because the previous owner claims he was barely turning a profit. If possible, I would like to meet with you to hear your story.

Could I pay a visit to the café to speak with you sometime next week? I am available on weekday afternoons after 2:00 P.M., but I am willing to adjust my schedule if that does not work for you. Please call me at 555-4466 to let me know if you are interested.

Sincerely,

Justin Lachapelle

153. Why was the letter written?

(A) To make a reservation
(B) To discuss a business proposal
(C) To request an interview
(D) To introduce a newspaper feature

154. What does Mr. Lachapelle offer to do?

(A) Pass along a previously published article
(B) Visit a dining establishment
(C) Come up with measures for attracting customers
(D) Make special arrangements for Ms. Foster

Ideal Office Space for Lease

If you're searching for an office space downtown, you're in luck. An entire floor is now available in Trident Tower. Located across the street from Bedford Subway Station, this 38-story building has a rooftop garden and an underground parking facility equipped with charging stations for electric vehicles. As for the lobby, it contains a café, convenience store, and courier service outlet.

The available space, the 31st floor, includes:
- 25 offices of varying sizes
- Two meeting rooms
- A kitchen area and adjoining break room
- A tastefully designed bathroom

This office space is currently being offered for a five-year lease. To set up a viewing, call Claire Woolf of Pearl Real Estate at 555-4456.

155. What is NOT true about Trident Tower?

(A) It contains a delivery business.
(B) It is close to a public transportation facility.
(C) It includes a place for tenants to park.
(D) It has some residential units.

156. According to the brochure, why should some people consult with a realtor?

(A) To inquire about an annual fee
(B) To get a chance to see a building interior
(C) To receive details about leasing options
(D) To learn about sales commissions

157. The phrase "set up" in paragraph 3, line 2, is closest in meaning to

(A) practice
(B) develop
(C) schedule
(D) admit

GO ON TO THE NEXT PAGE

Questions 158-160 refer to the following review.

Hotel: Park Square Lodge

Reviewer: Lana Marcela

Date: August 25

On August 10, I arrived in Dallas to direct a three-day training session at my company's newest regional office. I chose Park Square Lodge for its proximity to the office. Also, I planned to visit several tourist attractions in the downtown area and wanted to be located right next to them. Therefore, I headed to Park Square Lodge shortly after I arrived in Dallas, but unfortunately, I was very disappointed with my accommodations. First, the room I was assigned was much smaller than advertised. Right after, I asked to be moved to a larger room at my own expense but was told that the hotel was full. This was not a great start to my stay. Second, the room service was disappointing. After checking in, late in the evening, I called the front desk to have a sandwich brought to my suite. After an hour, it still hadn't arrived, and I went down to the lobby for an explanation. Apparently, the hotel restaurant never even received my order. At this point, I decided to buy a snack from a convenience store down the street. I would not recommend staying at this hotel.

Rating: 1.5/5

158. What advantage of staying at Park Square Lodge is mentioned by Ms. Marcela?

(A) It is affiliated with her company.
(B) It is within walking distance of an airport.
(C) It is recommended for tourists.
(D) It is close to her workplace.

159. Why was the restaurant unable to meet Ms. Marcela's request?

(A) A request had not been conveyed.
(B) An ingredient had run out.
(C) A large number of guests had to be served.
(D) A phone line was busy.

160. What is NOT mentioned about the hotel?

(A) It was fully booked on August 10.
(B) It delivers food directly to guests' rooms.
(C) It contains a convenience store.
(D) It is situated in downtown Dallas.

Questions 161-164 refer to the following online chat discussion.

Gina Mansfield	2:49 P.M.	Hey, I've got 10 minutes before I have to leave. Could I get a few quick updates from everyone? Sorry, but I'm in a rush.
Sally Fadden	2:50 P.M.	Yup. I scheduled photoshoots for next week with *Klein's*, *Fashion Review*, and *Younger*. The other magazines I called haven't responded yet.
Gina Mansfield	2:51 P.M.	OK, please send the dates to my assistant, Amelia. Does Ms. Lawson need to be at any of the shoots?
Sally Fadden	2:52 P.M.	Only *Klein's* needs her to be there. For the other two, we'll just have models wearing her clothes.
Gina Mansfield	2:53 P.M.	OK. Anyone else? Have all the buyers confirmed attendance for the fashion show?
Desmond Huang	2:54 P.M.	Not all, no. But we have a good number and all the major stores are represented. There's a lot of excitement. Everyone's eager to see the new collection.
Gina Mansfield	2:55 P.M.	Great. Let's make sure the VIPs and celebrity guests get good seats. Where's Troy? I haven't heard from sales.
Troy Nazmi	2:57 P.M.	Sorry, Gina. I'm here. We're still waiting on a few prices from marketing but have settled on giving a 10 percent discount to wholesalers and 5 percent to smaller retailers.
Gina Mansfield	2:58 P.M.	All right. Well, I've got to run. I'm meeting our stage designer at the Parker Center. If anyone has anything urgent, call me on my cell phone. Otherwise, leave a message with Amelia or e-mail me.

Send

161. Who most likely is Ms. Lawson?

(A) A fashion photographer
(B) An executive assistant
(C) A clothing designer
(D) A magazine editor

162. At 2:54 P.M., what does Mr. Huang most likely mean when he writes, "There's a lot of excitement"?

(A) Shoppers are eager for a store to open.
(B) Interest in a fashion event is strong.
(C) A recent show generated good publicity.
(D) Some celebrities are attracting a lot of attention.

163. What is Mr. Nazmi responsible for?

(A) Marketing
(B) Sales
(C) Purchasing
(D) Events

164. Why is Ms. Mansfield in a hurry?

(A) She has an appointment to meet.
(B) She is trying to catch a flight.
(C) She got an urgent call from a client.
(D) She is needed at an event.

GO ON TO THE NEXT PAGE

Questions 165-167 refer to the following article.

Good News for Northpoint Mall

Northpoint Mall has announced that two new shops will be moving into the space formerly occupied by Jadean's Hardware next month. Athletic equipment retailer Haskins Sports will move into the lower level of what used to be Jadean's Hardware. Meanwhile, Knockout, a seller of contemporary apparel, accessories, and footwear, will take over the upper level.

The opening of a Haskins Sports and a Knockout outlet is expected to provide a much-needed boost to Northpoint Mall, which suffered a substantial loss when Jadean's Hardware closed in July. The athletics retailer has opened astounding 200 new locations in the last five years, while the clothing store's earnings reportedly increased by $1.5 billion in the same period.

As well as creating jobs and improving the local economy, the new stores could bring Northpoint Mall's total daily visitors to well over 5,000. With the number of mall-goers declining at a rapid rate, many shopping centers throughout the region have had no choice but to close down. However, the new additions will undoubtedly keep Northpoint Mall in business for the foreseeable future.

165. What is the topic of the article?

(A) The demolition of a shopping mall
(B) The welcoming of new retail establishments
(C) The construction of a new space
(D) The results of an economic analysis

166. What is mentioned about the new stores opening in Northpoint Mall?

(A) They have more than 200 branches each.
(B) They will together occupy two floors of a shopping center.
(C) They were both established five years ago.
(D) They will open in Northpoint Mall in July.

167. The word "well" in paragraph 3, line 2, is closest in meaning to

(A) significantly
(B) thoroughly
(C) properly
(D) generally

Tim Blake
987 West Village Lane
Southampton
SO14
UK

Dear Mr. Blake,

My name is Anne Harding, and I'm an arts teacher at Hampton Secondary School. I've long been an admirer of your sculptures, particularly the statue of the sea captain in the plaza at the city centre, and the statues of soldiers you built for the war memorial. — [1] —. I'm writing to you to ask a favour: I'd like to have a local artist come in and give a talk to my class to show students there are opportunities outside of maths and science. I want students to learn how one earns a living in today's arts environment. It would be great to hear how you got your start and how you secure your commissions. — [2] —. Many students in my class are seriously contemplating studying the arts when they go to college next year, and having someone give career guidance would be ideal. The class meets at 2:30 P.M. on Tuesdays and Thursdays. — [3] —. Are you available during any of those timeslots in the next several weeks? Yesterday I showed students the photographs which you exhibited last year, and they loved your use of colour throughout the pieces. They're excited to hear from an artist whom the critics regard so highly. — [4] —. Please let me know if you can come and give a talk.

Anne Harding
Teacher, Hampton Secondary School

168. What is the main purpose of the letter?

(A) To ask for instruction on teaching art students
(B) To offer Mr. Blake a teaching position
(C) To request that a class visit an artist's studio
(D) To invite Mr. Blake to give a speech

169. What does Ms. Harding say about her class?

(A) It only admits a small group of students.
(B) It meets twice during the week.
(C) It is focused mainly on sculpture.
(D) It will end within the next month.

170. What will Mr. Blake most likely do with Ms. Harding's class?

(A) Conduct a photography workshop
(B) Explain the history of modern art
(C) Discuss career options for artists
(D) Demonstrate sculpture techniques

171. In which of the positions marked [1], [2], [3], and [4] does the following sentence best belong?

"Their intricate stonework always fills me with wonder."

(A) [1]
(B) [2]
(C) [3]
(D) [4]

GO ON TO THE NEXT PAGE

Questions 172-175 refer to the following letter.

Docu-Drama Broadcasting
7348 Granville Street
Vancouver, BC V5K 1P3

July 19

Juan Sanchez
4332 Rancho Street
Oakland, CA 94577

Dear Mr. Sanchez,

We are so pleased that you accepted our offer and will be working with us on our new production this coming fall. As you were previously informed, your first day of work in Vancouver will be September 1, and your contract will end on December 15. — [1] —. In order to enter the country, you will have to prove that you are covered by travel insurance during the full term of your stay. You can buy this from Voyage Protector, at www.voyage-protector.com, or a provider of your choosing. — [2] —.

Visa processing will take about a week, so you'll have to submit your application at the Canadian embassy in person by August 15. Once you've obtained the visa, let me know so I can arrange a temporary apartment. — [3] —.

Enclosed you'll find two copies of your contract, which I've signed. You should sign one of them and give it to me upon arriving in Vancouver. — [4] —. Let me know your transportation details and I'll have someone meet you at the airport.

Feel free to contact me should you have any questions.

Wilma Headley
Casting director
Docu-Drama Broadcasting

Enclosure

172. What is the main purpose of the letter?

(A) To provide instructions to a new employee
(B) To respond to an inquiry about an application
(C) To make an official offer of employment
(D) To provide an overview of a benefits package

173. What must Mr. Sanchez do by August 15?

(A) Bring documents to an office
(B) Have a passport submitted
(C) Return a signed agreement
(D) File for a visa extension

174. What is implied about Docu-Drama Broadcasting?

(A) It uses the services of a recruitment firm.
(B) It offers cast members contract renewals every three months.
(C) It plans to arrange housing for an employee.
(D) It reimburses the cost of travel to and from Vancouver.

175. In which of the positions marked [1], [2], [3], and [4] does the following sentence best belong?

"The other one is for your personal records."

(A) [1]
(B) [2]
(C) [3]
(D) [4]

GO ON TO THE NEXT PAGE

Jump Fund
Support pioneering projects

Support a Project | Start a Project | FAQ | Sign In

STOPLITE
An Andy Newberg Invention

Stoplite is a high-tech bike light that lets people behind you know when you are slowing down, minimizing the risk of accidental collisions. It is battery-operated and attaches to a bicycle magnetically. It turns on when it senses movement and shuts off on its own when your bicycle is fully stopped.

Tough and compact, it operates in rainy or snowy conditions and is easy to remove and store in your pocket or bag. The Stoplite works for 20 hours on a single, one-hour charge.

- **$18,080** pledged of $100,000 goal
- **166** people support this project
- Today: **March 10** (**180** days left to complete funding)

DONATE $ _____

Donate any amount without receiving a reward, or choose a reward option below.

☐ $90	☐ $110	☐ $180	☐ $220	☐ $1,000
Early Single* Receive a Stoplite kit and a T-shirt, cost of shipping included.	**Standard Single** Receive a Stoplite kit, cost of shipping not included.	**Early Double*** Receive two Stoplite kits and a T-shirt, cost of shipping included.	**Standard Double** Receive two Stoplite kits, cost of shipping not included.	**Stoplite Hero** Receive 10 Stoplite kits with spare cases and magnets, cost of shipping not included.

*Must donate by May 5 to be eligible for Early Single or Early Double

---

To: Greg Farber <g.farber@mymail.com>
From: Michelle Lee <miclee@stoplite.com>
Subject: Thank you for your support
Date: September 20

Dear Mr. Farber,

Thank you for supporting our project on Jump Fund. As you may already know, the project has been fully funded, and you can expect to receive your shipment of two Stoplite kits very soon. We'd like to make sure that we still have the correct delivery address on file since you pledged your support a month ago. Please confirm your address by logging on to our Web site and clicking on "Update Address" or "Confirm Address." After this, you will receive an e-mail containing delivery details, including shipping costs.

Sincerely,
Michelle Lee, funding coordinator
Stoplite Innovation

176. What is true about the Stoplite?

(A) Its release date has been delayed.
(B) It is able to withstand inclement weather.
(C) It converts movement into energy.
(D) It can be used only with certain bicycle models.

177. What is mentioned about the funding campaign?

(A) It was designed by the inventor of a product.
(B) It can be participated in on an anonymous basis.
(C) It includes incentives for people who donate by a certain date.
(D) It will continue for as long as it takes to reach a targeted amount.

178. Who will receive extra containers for their Stoplite?

(A) Early Single donors
(B) Early Double donors
(C) Standard Double donors
(D) Stoplite Hero donors

179. Why did Stoplite Innovation write to Mr. Farber?

(A) To announce the launch of a product
(B) To report a shipment delay
(C) To ask that some personal details be verified
(D) To request his support for a future project

180. How much did Mr. Farber most likely donate?

(A) $90
(B) $110
(C) $180
(D) $220

GO ON TO THE NEXT PAGE

Wavelet Luxury Liners upgrades its lighting

LONDON (December 31)—Europe's leading passenger ship operator, Wavelet Luxury Liners, will soon begin installing new lighting in its vessels. This is thanks to a deal it recently signed with Serreta Lighting, a Portuguese maker of glass lights that have modern designs.

The exclusivity of Serreta Lighting's products is the main reason Wavelet Luxury Liners decided to partner with them. Products are made by a small team of craftspeople who use traditional techniques, and each one is signed by the particular worker who made it.

Wavelet Luxury Liners' newest ship *Shooting Star*, which is currently under construction, will be the first of the company's vessels to be completely equipped with Serreta Lighting products. Particularly noteworthy will be the chandelier that will be installed in the 14th-floor dining room.

"We'll be using Serreta Lighting's creations not only in our new ship but also in several of our older ships when we renovate them next year," said Wavelet Luxury Liners CEO, Zackary Jones. "We believe that these lighting elements will help differentiate us from our competitors."

Wavelet Luxury Liners
Company Memo

To: All executive staff
From: Gillian Sutcliffe, head architect
Subject: Update on construction
Date: February 29

The construction of *Shooting Star* has reached its final stages, with the exterior complete and the interior work in progress. Some good news is that the installation of carpeting in the hallways and rooms wrapped up on February 27. As for the lighting, it has been ordered and will be installed as follows:

Levels 1-4	By March 5
Levels 5-8	By March 10
Levels 9-12	By March 14
Levels 13-15	By March 20

According to the original plan, the furniture was supposed to be delivered and arranged inside the passenger ship at the same time as the lighting. Unfortunately, though, the factory has not been able to meet our request as promptly as we expected them to. I'm afraid that we may need to push back the grand unveiling of the ship from May 1 to May 15. The chief executive officer of our company, Eliza Jones, has cleared her schedule on both days to ensure that she is available to host the event.

181. What is the main topic of the article?

(A) A lighting company's business partners
(B) A strategy to conserve energy
(C) A new transportation route
(D) A company's contract with a new supplier

182. What is NOT mentioned about Serreta Lighting's products?

(A) They are contemporary in style.
(B) They are made exclusively for ships.
(C) They are marked with a signature.
(D) They are created by hand using old methods.

183. By which date will the chandelier be installed?

(A) March 5
(B) March 10
(C) March 14
(D) March 20

184. What is Ms. Sutcliffe concerned about?

(A) A manufacturing defect
(B) An unrealistic schedule
(C) A delayed order
(D) A low productivity rate

185. What can be inferred about Wavelet Luxury Liners?

(A) All of its vessels will be equipped with Serreta Lighting products.
(B) Its new ship will be shown to the public before the interior is completed.
(C) It underwent a change in leadership.
(D) It will receive financial compensation from a contractor.

GO ON TO THE NEXT PAGE

Questions 186-190 refer to the following announcement, survey, and form.

Now's the Time to Improve Your Spanish

With our continued expansion into the Latin American market, an increasing number of Glidefield Telecom workers are interacting with Spanish-speaking clients on a daily basis. Employees are also going on business trips to the region more frequently. For these reasons, Glidefield Telecom's executive team has decided to offer a free Spanish class in the evenings. This will be taught by a visiting instructor. At least one session will take place per week, from 7 to 9 P.M., and the class will last for 15 weeks. If 20 or more people want to join, though, the group will be divided according to ability, and two separate classes will be set up.

If interested, send an e-mail to Chuck Findley at findley@glidefield.ca.

Survey on Spanish instruction for Glidefield Telecom staff

Thank you for your interest in studying Spanish at our office. All the staff members who committed to joining will attend the same class, which will begin in the first week of July. Several details remain to be decided, though. So that we can best meet the needs of the group, please complete this survey and return it to HR officer Chuck Findley by June 16.

1. On which day of the week would you like the class to be held?

☐ Monday   ☑ Tuesday   ☐ Wednesday   ☐ Thursday   ☐ Friday

2. The instructor has offered a choice of textbooks. Which one would you prefer?

	Title	Focus
☐	*Speaking Spanish Effortlessly*	Daily life
☐	*Flawless Professional Spanish*	Office situations
☐	*Letters and E-Mails in Spanish*	Business correspondence
☑	*Impressing a Latin American Audience*	Speeches and presentations

Spanish Class Evaluation Form

Name: James Kitson
Position at Glidefield Telecom: Sales manager
Spanish ability level at start: Beginner
Spanish ability level at end: Intermediate

▶ **Please rate the following aspects:**

Instructor	Unsatisfactory ← ①②③❹⑤ → Excellent
Teaching materials	Unsatisfactory ← ①②❸④⑤ → Excellent
Group activities	Unsatisfactory ← ①②③④❺ → Excellent
Assignments	Unsatisfactory ← ①②③❹⑤ → Excellent
Classroom	Unsatisfactory ← ①②③④❺ → Excellent

► **Comments:**

All in all, I found this class to be beneficial. However, a few points could be improved. First, the textbook was limited in scope. It only taught us how to talk about our favorite movies, our hobbies, and other such topics. What I need to learn for my job, though, is how to communicate professionally in writing.

Also, the teacher needed to establish some rules regarding lateness. I arrived early every time, but others disrupted the lessons by entering after they'd begun.

186. What is the purpose of the announcement?

(A) To introduce an educational opportunity
(B) To request feedback on a language academy
(C) To explain the needs of a new client
(D) To announce a planned business expansion

187. What can be inferred about Mr. Findley?

(A) He is in charge of training all recently hired staff to learn Spanish.
(B) He sent a message to all the staff members of an office on June 16.
(C) He is currently working for Glidefield Telecom as a personnel director.
(D) He received requests from fewer than 20 people to take a class.

188. According to the survey, what needed to be decided?

(A) The instructor of a course
(B) The day of a session
(C) The length of a class
(D) The capacity of a space

189. According to the form, what is NOT indicated about the Spanish class?

(A) It was not always attended punctually.
(B) It was evaluated by a participant.
(C) It was taught with the help of group exercises.
(D) It was only composed of beginner-level students.

190. Which textbook was most likely used?

(A) *Speaking Spanish Effortlessly*
(B) *Flawless Professional Spanish*
(C) *Letters and E-Mails in Spanish*
(D) *Impressing a Latin American Audience*

GO ON TO THE NEXT PAGE

Questions 191-195 refer to the following Web page, booking confirmation, and schedule.

---

http://organicfoodfair.com/transport

| HOME | | PROGRAM | | EXHIBITOR INFO | | **TRANSPORT** |

The Organic Food Fair, which is held once every two years, will take place from August 16 to 18 at the Landsel Expo Center in downtown Phoenix, which is a 15-minute walk from over a dozen hotels. Most visitors and exhibitors will arrive at Phoenix Grand Airport. Upon arrival, there are several ways to reach the city center.

- Railway – This is the fastest method of reaching our venue. The 30-minute trip costs just $17. Seats are not assigned. To view a timetable of departures from the airport, visit www.phoenixrail.com.

- Shuttle Bus – A seat on an Arrow bus costs $15 one-way. Buses depart every half hour from 6 A.M. to 11 P.M. Be sure to select a seat in advance at www.arrowpho.com. In addition, Davenport Hotel runs a free shuttle bus for those with room reservations.

- Car Rental – Several agencies operate near the arrivals terminal. These include Wildcat Car Rental, Burnett Rent-A-Car, and Quincy. To ensure availability, be sure to make your booking at least 24 hours in advance.

- Taxi – The ride should cost about $40.

Booking Confirmation for Suelin Yang

Confirmation Number	27348479	**Departure Date**	August 17
Date Booked	August 3	**Departure Time**	11:30 A.M.
Payment Method	Credit card	**Seat Number**	17D
Destination	Urbano Hotel	**Pieces of Luggage**	2

Your Special Requests

"As I'm participating in the Organic Food Fair, I'll be bringing two large bags of product samples with me. They'll be heavy, and I'll need help loading them into the cargo compartment."

*If your flight arrives late, proceed to our service desk in Phoenix Grand Airport's arrivals area, between exits C and D. We will ensure that you reach your destination as soon as possible.

Organic Food Fair – Speeches for August 17

Time	Title	Speaker	Location
10:00 A.M.	New Organic Agricultural Practices in Europe	Madeline Dekker	Auditorium 2
11:15 A.M.	Why Organic Food Standards Should Be Stricter	Barry Revere	Auditorium 1
1:45 P.M.	Ways to Make Organic Food More Affordable	Heidi Schuster	Auditorium 2
3:00 P.M.	Nutritional Benefits of Organically Grown Food	Lucas Dunn	Auditorium 3
4:30 P.M.	How Organic Farming Relates to Climate Change	Suelin Yang	Auditorium 3

191. What is mentioned about the Landsel Expo Center?

(A) It operates a desk at an airport arrivals area.
(B) It hosts a food fair on a regular basis.
(C) It directly adjoins a place of accommodation.
(D) It is located in a downtown area.

192. How will Ms. Yang most likely reach her destination?

(A) By railway
(B) By shuttle bus
(C) By rental car
(D) By taxi

193. According to the booking confirmation, what should customers do if their flight is delayed?

(A) Send a notification
(B) Call a service center
(C) Head to a counter
(D) Cancel reservations

194. What is suggested about Ms. Yang?

(A) She has not yet rented out a conference booth.
(B) She will be the final speaker of the fair.
(C) She will give a talk after stopping by a hotel.
(D) She was asked to lead a question and answer session.

195. What will NOT be discussed at the Organic Food Fair on August 17?

(A) Farming methods
(B) Promotional campaigns
(C) Environmental changes
(D) Health advantages

GO ON TO THE NEXT PAGE

Questions 196-200 refer to the following e-mail, schedule, and notice.

To: Evan Langston <e.langston@cornertechsolutions.com>
From: Cindy Shelley <c.shelley@cornertechsolutions.com>
Subject: Visit
Date: July 14

Evan,

I am writing to update you on the proposed itinerary for the client visit in two weeks. I have booked accommodations for them at the Washington Grand Hotel from August 1 to 4. We are scheduled to meet with the clients on August 3, but the specific times are still being decided.

That said, it looks like they'll have some free time on the 3rd after our meeting, so it might be wise to hire a tour guide to show them around. Their hotel is located in the Loop, so there should be plenty of good options. Can you contact a tour group and arrange something? I've heard excellent things about LuxChi.

Let me know what you think.

Best,
Cindy

LuxChi
August 4 Tour Schedule for Corner Tech Solutions

8:45 A.M.	Hotel pickup
9:00 A.M.	Breakfast reception on the Coerver Building rooftop
10:30 A.M.	Architecture walking tour of the Loop
12:00 P.M.	Charter boat & lunch buffet on the Chicago River
2:00 P.M.	Fendo Chocolates factory visit

The schedule is subject to change in case of bad weather. Furthermore, our professional tour guides are free to make spontaneous adjustments if the need arises, or if something better accommodates the clients. If your group has a special request, please mention it to your guide.

Dear Washington Grand Guests

Please be notified that we will be undergoing a system relaunch. This will require our computer servers to be shut down for most of the day. As a result, we won't be able to perform regular checkouts on August 4. For guests leaving on that day, please visit the front desk on August 3. We will be finalizing all transactions then. All on-site amenities, such as our sauna and workout facilities, will remain open. We would like to offer any guests scheduled to check out on August 4 a $50 credit on items from the mini-bar or our in-house restaurant. We sincerely apologize and hope that this will make up for any inconvenience. Thank you for your understanding and patronage.

196. According to the e-mail, what does Ms. Shelley suggest for the client visit?

(A) Arranging some entertainment
(B) Presenting contract propositions
(C) Organizing daily transportation
(D) Coordinating client meetings

197. What is indicated about LuxChi?

(A) It always follows the same itinerary for every group.
(B) It will take visitors to a manufacturing facility.
(C) It requires a day's notice for special requests.
(D) It has more favorable reviews than its competitors.

198. What can be inferred about the tour?

(A) It will provide food on a charter bus.
(B) It has an arrangement with the Washington Grand.
(C) It will begin right after a meeting ends.
(D) It was moved to a different day.

199. What most likely will Ms. Shelley's clients do on August 3?

(A) Explore Chicago architecture
(B) Customize a private tour
(C) Finalize hotel transactions
(D) Sign some contracts

200. What will the Washington Grand offer to some customers?

(A) Discounts on food services
(B) Access to workout facilities
(C) Free meals at a local restaurant
(D) Entry into an in-house sauna

TEST | 01 | 02 | 03 | 04 | 05 | 06 | 07 | 08 | 09 | 10 | 해커스 토익 실전 1000제 2 Reading

This is the end of the test. You may review Parts 5, 6, and 7 if you finish the test early.

Self 체크 리스트

TEST 04는 무사히 잘 마치셨죠?
이제 다음의 Self 체크 리스트를 통해 자신의 테스트 진행 내용을 점검해 볼까요?

1. 나는 75분 동안 완전히 테스트에 집중하였다.

   □ 예   □ 아니오

   아니오에 답한 경우, 이유는 무엇인가요?

2. 나는 75분 동안 100문제를 모두 풀었다.

   □ 예   □ 아니오

   아니오에 답한 경우, 이유는 무엇인가요?

3. 나는 75분 동안 답안지 표시까지 완료하였다.

   □ 예   □ 아니오

   아니오에 답한 경우, 이유는 무엇인가요?

4. 나는 Part 5와 Part 6를 19분 안에 모두 풀었다.

   □ 예   □ 아니오

   아니오에 답한 경우, 이유는 무엇인가요?

5. Part 7을 풀 때 5분 이상 걸린 지문이 없었다.

   □ 예   □ 아니오

6. 개선해야 할 점 또는 나를 위한 충고를 적어보세요.

* 교재의 첫 장으로 돌아가서 자신이 적은 목표 점수를 확인하면서 목표에 대한 의지를 다지기 바랍니다. 개선해야 할 점은 반드시 다음 테스트에
 실천해야 합니다. 그것이 가장 중요하며, 그래야만 발전할 수 있습니다.

▍TEST 05

PART 5
PART 6
PART 7
Self 체크 리스트

잠깐! 테스트 전 확인사항

1. 휴대 전화의 전원을 끄셨나요? □ 예
2. Answer Sheet, 연필, 지우개를 준비하셨나요? □ 예
3. 시계를 준비하셨나요? □ 예

모든 준비가 완료되었으면 목표 점수를 떠올린 후 테스트를 시작합니다.

문제 풀이를 마치는 시간은 지금부터 75분 후인 ___시 ___분입니다.

테스트 시간은 총 75분이며, 시험 종료 전 2~3분은 정답 검토 및 답안지 마킹을 위해 사용합니다.

READING TEST

In this section, you must demonstrate your ability to read and comprehend English. You will be given a variety of texts and asked to answer questions about these texts. This section is divided into three parts and will take 75 minutes to complete.

Do not mark the answers in your test book. Use the answer sheet that is separately provided.

PART 5

Directions: In each question, you will be asked to review a statement that is missing a word or phrase. Four answer choices will be provided for each statement. Select the best answer and mark the corresponding letter (A), (B), (C), or (D) on the answer sheet.

PART 5 권장 풀이 시간 11분

101. Mr. Oakley decided to reserve a table for two at the newly ------- Italian restaurant.

(A) opened
(B) opener
(C) openly
(D) opens

102. Invitees are asked to confirm their attendance at the banquet ------- the catering company can prepare enough food.

(A) already
(B) prior to
(C) so that
(D) in case of

103. Residents are opposed to the plan to build a highway, saying its proximity will ------- affect the quality of their lives.

(A) deliberately
(B) adversely
(C) urgently
(D) persuasively

104. Company supervisors are seeking a ------- to the lack of communication between departments.

(A) motivation
(B) permission
(C) commission
(D) resolution

105. To avoid disputes, community concerns ------- by Everide Construction during the planning phase of projects.

(A) reviews
(B) has reviewed
(C) are reviewed
(D) reviewing

106. Mr. Harvel was told to go ------- to have a picnic since the garden was private property.

(A) leisurely
(B) simply
(C) elsewhere
(D) around

107. Please go to the circulation desk if you intend ------- a book that is currently checked out.

(A) reserved
(B) reserve
(C) to reserve
(D) reservation

108. Purchasers of flawed products made by Hulse Inc. can receive ------- as long as they have proof of purchase.

(A) solicitation
(B) recognition
(C) advancement
(D) reimbursement

109. The new model of the AutoBlade is programmed to ------- cut various shapes out of plastic.

(A) precise
(B) preciseness
(C) precision
(D) precisely

110. Ms. Elwood ------- for the position in Hong Kong because no other employee possessed fluency in Cantonese.

(A) considers
(B) has considered
(C) is considering
(D) was considered

111. Sometimes criticized for a lack of ambition, many young adults today tend to value work-life balance ------- career progression.

(A) upon
(B) above
(C) except
(D) toward

112. The Neufield History Museum's recently unveiled exhibit is full of ------- artifacts dating back to prehistoric times.

(A) authentic
(B) candid
(C) resolute
(D) widespread

113. Credit card payments are due on the first day of each month, ------- outlined in the terms and conditions.

(A) or
(B) as
(C) even
(D) so

114. By ------- handing out coupons, the café owner was able to develop a loyal customer base.

(A) statistically
(B) steadily
(C) implicitly
(D) nearly

115. The building manager has announced new ------- on where visitors are allowed to park.

(A) receptions
(B) methods
(C) restrictions
(D) characteristics

116. Mr. Venter has requested a report ------- of quarterly sales figures from each of JBD's global subsidiaries.

(A) consistently
(B) consisted
(C) consisting
(D) consistent

117. Mr. Janick ------- the auditorium if he had known that the band was going to perform an encore.

(A) is not leaving
(B) did not leave
(C) could not leave
(D) would not have left

118. Axial Inc. has terminated its business agreement with Covane ------- the recent economic upturn.

(A) given that
(B) in lieu of
(C) in spite of
(D) as if

119. Randall University is still in the process of ------- a computer engineering program.

(A) establishes
(B) established
(C) establishment
(D) establishing

120. Companies that ------- screen job applicants have a higher rate of employee retention.

(A) cares
(B) careful
(C) carefully
(D) caring

GO ON TO THE NEXT PAGE

121. A substantial section of the boarding area at Tulsa Airport is off-limits until next August due to ------- renovations.

(A) expired
(B) mutual
(C) permanent
(D) ongoing

122. Numerous ------- had to be made to the article before it was fit to appear in the newspaper.

(A) correctors
(B) corrections
(C) corrects
(D) corrected

123. Despite launching a popular new sitcom, The Fun Network was unable to ------- its position as the most-watched channel on television.

(A) shift
(B) conserve
(C) persist
(D) retain

124. Twilight Cinema does not have reserved seating, and therefore you should arrive early if you want to sit in ------- row you want.

(A) whether
(B) wherever
(C) whichever
(D) whose

125. According to the environmental standards, home appliances fall ------- one of seven groups, depending on their level of energy efficiency.

(A) on
(B) into
(C) over
(D) among

126. Having worked closely with Ms. Fielding during her internship, Mr. Rawlings was happy to ------- her as the company's new engineer.

(A) respond
(B) diagnose
(C) name
(D) renew

127. The decision to expand the Lauderdale branch was made in ------- with the regional and district managers.

(A) relation
(B) exchange
(C) operation
(D) consultation

128. As its competitors have begun focusing more on customer service, some industry experts feel that Prolina should do -------.

(A) also
(B) moreover
(C) somehow
(D) likewise

129. The guidebook lists 25 European cities that are worth visiting ------- typical destinations like Paris, London, and Rome.

(A) other than
(B) on account of
(C) regardless of
(D) whether

130. A number of tenants ------- their apartments, and the landlord has posted an advertisement for new prospective renters.

(A) estimated
(B) vacated
(C) certified
(D) obtained

PART 6

Directions: In this part, you will be asked to read four English texts. Each text is missing a word, phrase, or sentence. Select the answer choice that correctly completes the text and mark the corresponding letter (A), (B), (C), or (D) on the answer sheet.

PART 6 권장 풀이 시간 8분

Questions 131-134 refer to the following advertisement.

Throwing a Party?

------- Woldasso Party Solutions to take the stress out of planning your event. Our venue, a
131.

glamorous ballroom located at 118 Croyden Boulevard, is perfect for wedding receptions,

reunions, and other events. Large groups are welcome since we recently increased our

venue's capacity. -------.
132.

Our coordinators can help you plan every ------- of your event. From furniture and decorations,
133.

to entertainment and catering, we'll handle all the details. We also offer packages that can be

------- for you. If you just tell us what you've got in mind, we'll set up the room to meet your
134.

specifications. For reservations, call 555-9971.

131. (A) Allow
(B) Allowing
(C) To allow
(D) Allows

132. (A) The venue you choose will depend on the size of your group.
(B) The guest list has not yet been confirmed.
(C) The decision to expand our business was based on market research.
(D) It can now accommodate up to 350 people.

133. (A) form
(B) critique
(C) aspect
(D) direction

134. (A) labeled
(B) identified
(C) engaged
(D) customized

GO ON TO THE NEXT PAGE

September 17

Martin Muller
Crestfield Lumber Co.
546 Thatcher Street
Algonquin, IL 60102

Dear Mr. Muller,

We ------- over your quotation for the supply and delivery of lumber to QTE Construction
       135.
Group. Unfortunately, we have concluded that we will not be able to accept your proposal at

this time due to budget considerations. -------.
                                        136.

However, we wonder if you would be willing to consider -------. Should you lower your rate by
                                                        137.
just 10 percent, QTE Construction Group would agree to purchase lumber at that price on a

quarterly basis. Please let me know if this arrangement is possible. A ------- response would
                                                                      138.
be much appreciated, since we need all the materials for a major construction project by the

end of this month.

Sincerely,

Gina Santos
QTE Construction Group

135. (A) will go
(B) are going
(C) have gone
(D) would have gone

136. (A) Our warehouse does not have enough
space for such a large amount.
(B) You do not produce the materials we
are currently seeking.
(C) The quality of your wood was found to
be below our standards.
(D) Your prices are somewhat higher than
we anticipated.

137. (A) compromising
(B) rescheduling
(C) investing
(D) demonstrating

138. (A) subtle
(B) valid
(C) swift
(D) standing

Notice to Motorists

The upgrading of Wallace Road will start on April 8. The project, ------- will be carried out by
139.
Davis & Sons, has been deemed urgent by the city's Public Works Department because

seasonal temperature changes have severely damaged the road surface. Until the leveling

and paving work is completed, the road will be -------. Accordingly, barriers will be put up and
140.
detour signs will be placed on Fletcher Avenue to direct motorists to a side road. -------.
141.
Please note that you may encounter delays while taking the alternative route. Therefore, try

to ------- extra travel time into your schedule, particularly during rush hour. It is recommended
142.
that you leave for your destination at least 30 minutes in advance. We apologize for any

inconvenience this may cause and thank you for your understanding.

139. (A) that
(B) it
(C) some
(D) which

140. (A) monitored
(B) congested
(C) inaccessible
(D) available

141. (A) This will be attended by members of
the city council.
(B) Personnel will also be on site to help
coordinate traffic flow.
(C) The new road will make it easier to
reach the suburbs.
(D) Work may be postponed due to this
unexpected occurrence.

142. (A) budget
(B) speculate
(C) take
(D) keep

GO ON TO THE NEXT PAGE

Questions 143-146 refer to the following e-mail.

To: Blanche Patrick <b.patrick@nextnet.com>
From: David Torres <d.torres@nextnet.com>
Subject: Our start-up
Date: September 28

Dear Ms. Patrick,

I just finished reading the report written up by our business consultant on where to ------- our
143.
start-up, Nextnet. According to her, although London seems best at first glance, there are

other cities worth considering. -------, both Edinburgh and Cambridge offer some advantages.
144.
Aside from being more affordable than the capital in terms of property values, both are

offering tax incentives for technology ventures. -------. She also mentioned Brighton and
145.
Birmingham as possible options. ------- those two cities, Brighton seems like the better option
146.
because of its dynamic start-up culture, but it has some shortcomings. Anyway, we can

discuss this in depth when we meet tomorrow.

Best,
David Torres

---

143. (A) announce
(B) base
(C) release
(D) commemorate

144. (A) Similarly
(B) Additionally
(C) For instance
(D) In the meantime

145. (A) One of them might be a good
acquisition for Nextnet.
(B) The tax reduction policy may
eventually be implemented.
(C) Of course, London would be far more
advantageous in this respect.
(D) They offer free business assistance
through mentor programs as well.

146. (A) For
(B) With
(C) Between
(D) Within

PART 7

Directions: In this part, you will be asked to read several texts, such as advertisements, articles, instant messages, or examples of business correspondence. Each text is followed by several questions. Select the best answer and mark the corresponding letter (A), (B), (C), or (D) on your answer sheet.

PART 7 권장 풀이 시간 54분

Questions 147-148 refer to the following text message.

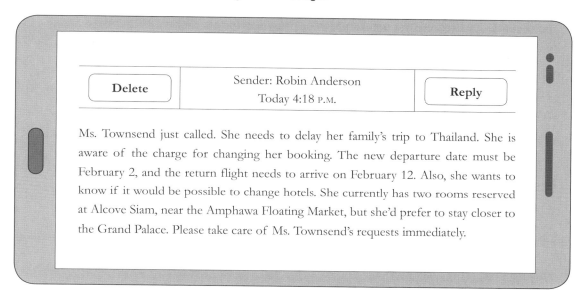

Sender: Robin Anderson
Today 4:18 P.M.

Delete

Reply

Ms. Townsend just called. She needs to delay her family's trip to Thailand. She is aware of the charge for changing her booking. The new departure date must be February 2, and the return flight needs to arrive on February 12. Also, she wants to know if it would be possible to change hotels. She currently has two rooms reserved at Alcove Siam, near the Amphawa Floating Market, but she'd prefer to stay closer to the Grand Palace. Please take care of Ms. Townsend's requests immediately.

147. Who most likely is Ms. Townsend?

(A) A hotel manager
(B) A travel agency client
(C) A trade specialist
(D) A tour group member

148. What is the recipient being asked to do?

(A) Call Ms. Anderson as soon as possible
(B) Confirm an itinerary
(C) Check the distance between two attractions
(D) Adjust some travel arrangements

GO ON TO THE NEXT PAGE

Questions 149-150 refer to the following e-mail.

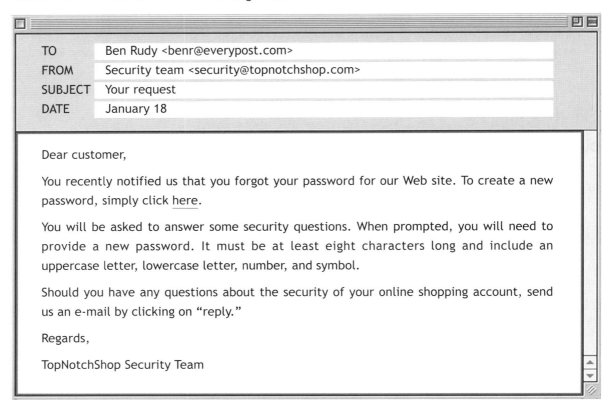

TO	Ben Rudy <benr@everypost.com>
FROM	Security team <security@topnotchshop.com>
SUBJECT	Your request
DATE	January 18

Dear customer,

You recently notified us that you forgot your password for our Web site. To create a new password, simply click here.

You will be asked to answer some security questions. When prompted, you will need to provide a new password. It must be at least eight characters long and include an uppercase letter, lowercase letter, number, and symbol.

Should you have any questions about the security of your online shopping account, send us an e-mail by clicking on "reply."

Regards,

TopNotchShop Security Team

149. Why was the e-mail written?

(A) To announce an update to account security settings
(B) To provide information about an online purchase
(C) To inform a client about a policy change
(D) To help resolve an issue involving access

150. What will Mr. Rudy have to do?

(A) Input a temporary password
(B) Reinstall some security software
(C) Provide some question responses
(D) Consult with a financial advisor

Questions 151-152 refer to the following text-message chain.

Dave Weber [9:23 A.M.]
I'm sorry to bother you while you're on leave, Tanya, but I have a problem. Steve and Emily both called in sick. So, we are very short-staffed at the clothing shop today. Would you mind coming in to work?

Tanya Parker [9:27 A.M.]
Sure. I'm always up for extra shifts. What time should I arrive at the store?

Dave Weber [9:28 A.M.]
Could you be here by 11:30 A.M.? I can handle things on my own until then.

Tanya Parker [9:30 A.M.]
I have a dentist appointment at 10:30 A.M. If I cancel it, I might have to wait a few weeks until they're able to fit me in. Could I come in at noon instead?

Dave Weber [9:32 A.M.]
I don't see why not. Thanks for agreeing to do this. I really appreciate it.

151. What problem does Mr. Weber mention?

(A) Some staff members turned down an extra shift.
(B) Some employees took a day off on short notice.
(C) A job offer was declined by a candidate.
(D) A customer was unhappy with a clothing item.

152. At 9:32 A.M., what does Mr. Weber mean when he writes, "I don't see why not"?

(A) He is willing to run a store independently today.
(B) He does not understand why there will be a delay.
(C) He thinks an alternative arrival time is suitable.
(D) He is prepared to fill out a permission form.

GO ON TO THE NEXT PAGE

Questions 153-154 refer to the following advertisement.

Plains Auto Is Always There for You!

If you're planning a trip, consider Plains Auto for all your car rental needs. We offer a wide variety of vehicles to choose from at reasonable prices. And thanks to our acquisition of Chase Car Rentals in February, we now have branches at all international airports in the country. To celebrate our expansion, we will be providing a 20 percent discount on rentals of two days or longer. This offer ends on June 30, so don't miss out! Visit www.plainsauto.com to learn more details and to reserve a vehicle.

153. What did Plains Auto do in February?

(A) Expanded some office spaces
(B) Launched foreign branches
(C) Purchased another company
(D) Hired additional employees

154. How can customers receive a discount?

(A) By making a reservation at an airport
(B) By posting feedback on a Web site
(C) By upgrading to a larger vehicle
(D) By renting a car for multiple days

www.businesslink.net/real-estate-advice

Homes in Gated Communities

Selling homes in gated communities can generate lucrative commissions and significantly raise your status in the industry. However, finding buyers for such homes can be challenging these days due to their above-average prices. — [1] —. To improve your chances of success, keep the following tips in mind:

1. Stress Safety

Let prospective buyers know that gated communities have state-of-the-art protection. Also, all entrances into the community are guarded by security officers, who deter burglars and salespeople and make sure that only homeowners' vehicles proceed past the gate. — [2] —.

2. Emphasize a Sense of Belonging

Remind buyers that because the number of homes in each community is limited, residents tend to become well acquainted with their neighbors. For this reason, neighborhood get-togethers and multifamily yard sales are common. — [3] —.

3. Mention High Property Values

Tell buyers that units in these communities are wise acquisitions because of their desirable locations, high-quality construction, and limited availability. — [4] —. That is, they are almost certain to steadily increase in value over the long term.

155. For whom is the online information most likely intended?

(A) New homeowners
(B) Real estate agents
(C) Security personnel
(D) Community developers

156. What is NOT stated about gated communities?

(A) Strangers are prevented from entering them.
(B) They often turn out to be lucrative investments.
(C) They are secured through cutting-edge means.
(D) Their residents organize events for new neighbors.

157. In which of the positions marked [1], [2], [3], and [4] does the following sentence best belong?

"This sort of familiarity can be highly appealing to some buyers, especially those with children."

(A) [1]
(B) [2]
(C) [3]
(D) [4]

Squiggle > Customer Reviews

Name: Dennis Haines

Rating: ★★★★☆

I'm a graphic designer, so I'm routinely asked to produce visuals that use a combination of elements. I used to rely on a program called Finish, but now I almost exclusively use Squiggle. It's not cheap, and you will have to own a professional-grade system to take full advantage of its features, but Squiggle represents the industry standard at the moment. The great virtue of this software is that it has such a large range of capabilities. You can create complex drawings, add any number of effects to photographs, and cut out various elements . . . the list goes on. I suppose the one problem with Squiggle is that many of its tools are hard to find on the dashboard. I think the programmers should create a toolbox that is easier to navigate. If I were a beginner, I would start with the Squiggle Essentials Edition. It provides a decent approximation of the full version and includes a tutorial to help you get started.

158. What aspect of Squiggle does Mr. Haines praise?

(A) The variety of features
(B) The inexpensive price
(C) The low system requirements
(D) The compatibility with other programs

159. What does Mr. Haines think could be improved about Squiggle?

(A) Its video-editing toolkit
(B) Its guide to using various effects
(C) Its on-screen appearance
(D) Its number of available fonts

160. What is mentioned about the Squiggle Essentials Edition?

(A) It will receive an update soon.
(B) It is more accessible for new designers.
(C) It will be available in a free version.
(D) It offers a trial period.

Barry Nolan	[4:48 P.M.]	Hi, everyone. Could you give me an update on the Jarvis Center project? We're supposed to start garden landscaping there on Wednesday. Is that going to happen?
Alison Grice	[4:49 P.M.]	I don't think it's likely. The plants and bushes we ordered won't arrive from the supplier until Friday afternoon at the very earliest.
Barry Nolan	[4:50 P.M.]	That's not good news. Did you notify Ms. Peyton at the Jarvis Center about this?
Edward Winters	[4:51 P.M.]	Yes. I handled that this morning. She said there's no rush to get the work done. We can start next week, if necessary.
Alison Grice	[4:52 P.M.]	Then I recommend we wait until Monday, after we've got everything we've ordered, to start. There's not much we'll be able to do on Friday morning without the delivery.
Edward Winters	[4:54 P.M.]	I'm just worried about the plants. Will they be safe if they're left outside over the weekend?
Alison Grice	[4:55 P.M.]	There are security guards there both Saturday and Sunday. Also, I think the plants will be fine sitting in their pots for a couple days.
Barry Nolan	[4:57 P.M.]	I agree. Let's wait until Monday. That way we can be certain we'll have the supplies needed for the project. Edward, can you communicate the schedule to Ms. Peyton today?
Edward Winters	[4:58 P.M.]	Sure thing. I was planning to call her again to discuss the sprinkler system.

Send

161. Who most likely is Mr. Nolan?

(A) A member of an outdoor design team
(B) A delivery worker at a plant supplies company
(C) A customer service agent at a landscaping firm
(D) A purchasing officer at a garden center

162. What is Mr. Winters concerned about?

(A) Failing to finish a task on time
(B) Having some plants unloaded in the right place
(C) Safeguarding some purchases
(D) Saving money for a client

163. When will garden landscaping for the Jarvis Center start?

(A) On Friday
(B) On Saturday
(C) On Sunday
(D) On Monday

164. At 4:58 P.M., what does Mr. Winters mean when he writes, "Sure thing"?

(A) He will place a call to a supplier.
(B) He will convey some information.
(C) He will check some delivered items.
(D) He will speak with a security officer.

GO ON TO THE NEXT PAGE

Questions 165-167 refer to the following e-mail.

To: Naomi Watson <nwatson@concordebank.com>
From: Ava Bradley <abradley@concordebank.com>
Date: October 28
Subject: Life insurance policy
Attachment: Life Insurance Spreadsheet, Beneficiary Signature Page

Hi, Naomi.

I hope you're settling into your new position at Concorde Bank. — [1] —. I just received your signed paperwork for the employer-sponsored health care plan. Your coverage will begin on November 1. Please don't hesitate to reach out if you have any questions about your health care policy.

— [2] —. I can also report that you have been successfully enrolled in the Concorde Bank basic life insurance plan. As we discussed previously, this is included with your other benefits, so there will be no deductions from your salary for this $50,000 policy.

— [3] —. However, employees who would like more comprehensive coverage can upgrade to a $100,000, $250,000, or $500,000 policy for an additional monthly premium. — [4] —.

If you'd like to upgrade your existing policy, please fill out the attached signature page and designate a beneficiary.

Regards,
Ava Bradley
Director of Human Resources

165. What did Ms. Watson do recently?

(A) Canceled a policy
(B) Started a new job
(C) Opened a new bank account
(D) Collected a paycheck

166. What is mentioned about Concorde Bank?

(A) It offers employees at least two types of insurance.
(B) It will send Ms. Watson a monthly bill.
(C) It will provide an improved benefits package.
(D) It deposits paychecks directly into employees' accounts.

167. In which of the positions marked [1], [2], [3], and [4] does the following sentence best belong?

"I have attached detailed information about each of these policies to this e-mail."

(A) [1]
(B) [2]
(C) [3]
(D) [4]

Attention Book Lovers

If you'd like to make new friends and read more, why not join a book club that meets right here at Patty's Pages, Hamptonville's favorite independent bookstore? We launched four different types of reading clubs this month, so you can choose the one that's right for you. All of them meet once a week at our second-floor café, are led by Patty's Pages staff members, and can be joined without registering in advance. Details are provided below.

Mystery Book Club

This group meets at 7:00 P.M. every Tuesday to discuss the best recently released detective novels. They'll keep you guessing until the end!

Sci-Fi Book Club

If you love to escape to imaginary worlds and distant planets, join this club, which meets at 8:00 P.M. every Wednesday, to chat about some of the genre's most time-honored classics.

Nonfiction Book Club

Interested in new biographies, memoirs, and literary essays? This group meets at 7:00 P.M. every Thursday.

Children's Book Club

Open to kids between the ages of 8 and 12, this club meets at 3:00 P.M. every Saturday. Parents are encouraged to sit in on discussions about the latest children's books.

All book club selections will be discounted by 10 percent at Patty's Pages during the month they are being read and talked about.

168. What is the topic of the notice?

(A) A list of recommended books
(B) Adjusted hours of operation for a store
(C) Plans for a literacy campaign
(D) A selection of weekly discussion groups

169. The word "right" in paragraph 1, line 3, is closest in meaning to

(A) ideal
(B) exact
(C) fair
(D) direct

170. Which club does NOT read new publications?

(A) Mystery Book Club
(B) Sci-Fi Book Club
(C) Nonfiction Book Club
(D) Children's Book Club

171. What is NOT mentioned about Patty's Pages?

(A) It started some book clubs this year.
(B) It contains a coffee shop on its premises.
(C) It is the most profitable bookstore in Hamptonville.
(D) It offers reading material for a reduced price.

GO ON TO THE NEXT PAGE

Questions 172-175 refer to the following memo.

To: All team leaders
From: Brad Jenkins, human resources manager
Subject: Workshops
Date: September 12

Hello, everyone. I'd like to remind you that we are holding a series of workshops to prepare for our entry into the Chinese market. These sessions will help us make the necessary adjustments for dealing with Chinese clients, which is something we have never had to do before. Please note the following information.

Workshop Name	Schedule
Overview of the Chinese Market	September 22, 2:00 P.M. — 6:00 P.M.
Chinese Business Practices	September 29, 1:00 P.M. — 5:00 P.M.
International Contract Law	October 6, 12:00 P.M. — 4:00 P.M.
Understanding Different Cultures	October 13, 3:00 P.M. — 7:00 P.M.

The first two sessions will be relevant specifically to China while the second two will have an international focus. The workshop on September 29 will be led by Brenda Hong, who will manage our Chinese division. The other three will be conducted by a visiting consultant, David Parson. His workshops have been popular among our colleagues, so I am sure you will find them worthwhile. Feel free to contact me if you have any questions.

172. Why is the company planning to hold the workshops?

(A) It is expanding into a new market.
(B) It is merging with a foreign firm.
(C) It is moving its headquarters overseas.
(D) It is hiring a number of temporary workers.

173. What is true about the workshops?

(A) They will all be conducted by management staff.
(B) They have been offered periodically for company employees.
(C) They will last for over a month.
(D) They have been scheduled to take place in the afternoon.

174. Which workshop will Ms. Hong lead?

(A) Overview of the Chinese Market
(B) Chinese Business Practices
(C) International Contract Law
(D) Understanding Different Cultures

175. What is indicated about Mr. Parson?

(A) He has worked in China for several years.
(B) He is an associate of Mr. Jenkins.
(C) He has met some of the company's employees.
(D) He plans to announce the details of a marketing campaign.

GO ON TO THE NEXT PAGE

www.lycon.com/productlist/vacuumcleaners

Lycon Vacuum Cleaners

All models come with a multiple-use dust bag.

Our Full Selection of Models		
Name	**Features**	**Price**
Speed XS	• Lightweight design — only 3.5 kilograms • Available in green, black, and gray	$125.00
Power Glide 3E	• Easily adjustable height and 35-inch cord • Ultraquiet motor	$225.00
Dual Clean 350	• Steam clean function for floors • Attachments for upholstery and curtains	$160.00
EZ Flow GD	• Rechargeable battery for cordless use • Touchpad control panel	$140.00

Each Lycon product comes with a one-year parts and service warranty. Under the terms of the warranty, products must be sent to a Lycon Service Center for repairs. To qualify for the warranty, customers must fill out and send in the registration form included with their purchase.

To: Lycon Customer Service <customersupport@lycon.com>
From: Amy Reynolds <a.reynolds@pace.com>
Date: April 13
Subject: Order #3453

To Whom It May Concern,

On April 4, I ordered a vacuum cleaner through your company's Web site. Initially, I opted for a lightweight one that would be easy to carry up and down the stairs of my home. However, I later decided that I would prefer a cordless model, so I canceled my original order and placed a new one on April 6. The vacuum cleaner was delivered on April 10, and I am quite happy with it.

Unfortunately, I just noticed today that the amount of my first order has not been charged back to my bank account. I would like this to be taken care of immediately. Please send me confirmation via e-mail once this is done. Thank you.

Sincerely,

Amy Reynolds

176. What is suggested about Lycon?

(A) It sells appliances that can be controlled with a mobile device.
(B) It replaces defective items as long as a receipt is provided.
(C) Its product lines include equipment for commercial use.
(D) Its vacuum cleaners all contain a reusable part.

177. What is NOT mentioned about the warranty?

(A) It is provided with all of Lycon's vacuum cleaners.
(B) It entitles customers to service at a repair center.
(C) It can be renewed one year after the purchase date.
(D) It is available to those who submit a completed form.

178. Which product did Ms. Reynolds most likely receive?

(A) Speed XS
(B) Power Glide 3E
(C) Dual Clean 350
(D) EZ Flow GD

179. How much will Ms. Reynolds receive as a refund?

(A) $125
(B) $140
(C) $160
(D) $225

180. In the e-mail, the word "via" in paragraph 2, line 3, is closest in meaning to

(A) in accordance with
(B) with reference to
(C) in terms of
(D) by means of

GO ON TO THE NEXT PAGE

TEST | 01 | 02 | 03 | 04 | **05** | 06 | 07 | 08 | 09 | 10 | 해커스 토익 실전 1000제 2 Reading

Mode Fashion

Enjoy 15 percent off when you sign up for a Mode Fashion Credit Card.*

The Mode Fashion Credit Card has several exciting and exclusive perks, including:

- A $10 gift card for every $200 you spend
- Invitations to members-only events
- Chances to preorder new items
- A special complimentary item on your birthday
- Free alterations on pant and skirt hems**
- An issue of Mode Fashion's monthly magazine

The Mode Fashion Credit Card has no annual fee. As a cardholder, you can authorize additional cards for family members and earn reward points every time they spend. Plus, you can manage your account and pay your bills online through card issuer Platinum Bank at www.platinumbank.com.

*Offer valid solely on the first purchase made with your Mode Fashion Credit Card. Offer cannot be applied to earlier purchases or the purchase of gift cards.

**Valid with a full-price purchase using your Mode Fashion Credit Card. Offer not valid for leather or suede products. Tailored items may not be returned or exchanged.

Mode Fashion
www.modefashion.com

May 30

Stella Helm
838 Gilbert Road
Palatine, IL 60067

Dear Ms. Helm,

Thank you for registering for a new Mode Fashion Credit Card, which has been enclosed in this letter. You will be able to take advantage of the exceptional rewards and benefits it offers as soon as it is activated. Call the card issuer at 555-0235 to do so.

Please confirm the details of your registration below:

Name: Stella P. Helm
Birthday: July 9
Card number: 4320-5387-9534-4106
Telephone: 555-5903
E-mail: s.helm@mellomail.com

For inquiries, call our dedicated customer service line at 555-9669.

Sincerely,

Anthony Marcellus
Customer Relations
Mode Fashion Credit Card Division

181. According to the flyer, what is NOT a benefit of owning the Mode Fashion Credit Card?

(A) A copy of a periodical
(B) Invitations to exclusive events
(C) Low annual interest rates
(D) Right to order new products in advance

182. What is stated about the special discount for cardholders?

(A) It is contingent upon the authorization of additional cards.
(B) It cannot be taken advantage of repeatedly.
(C) It does not apply to certain types of clothing.
(D) It is only available at a shopping Web site.

183. Why was the letter written?

(A) To emphasize the benefits of a product
(B) To state that a request is being considered
(C) To describe a customer service issue
(D) To provide information regarding a card

184. What is Ms. Helm asked to do?

(A) Confirm the details of a transaction
(B) Contact Platinum Bank
(C) Claim an earned reward points
(D) Visit the nearest location of a store

185. What can be inferred about Ms. Helm?

(A) She qualified for an upgrade to a store credit card.
(B) She shopped at Mode Fashion in May.
(C) She will receive a present from Mode Fashion in July.
(D) She will be obligated to pay a monthly credit card fee.

GO ON TO THE NEXT PAGE

Questions 186-190 refer to the following invitation, letter, and certificate.

Please join us at the 2nd Clarendon Art Auction
6:30 P.M., 19 March
Lilac Auditorium, Clarendon Art Institute
£115 per person(the same as last year)

Due to the success of Clarendon Art Institute's first-ever art auction, which took place last April, the organisers have decided to hold a second one. Once again, artwork will be donated by local artists, and audience members will be able to bid on these pieces. Even if you don't intend to buy anything, you can still show your support simply by attending. As before, all proceeds from entrance tickets and art purchases will be used to help art students who are struggling to pay their tuition fees.

Highlights from last year's event:
- A sculpture by Dana Sloan was sold to Paul Dixon.
- A set of three watercolor paintings by Otis Hidalgo was acquired by Dawn Reeves.
- A landscape painting by Blaine D'Amico was bought by a Roda Co. representative for the company's collection.

---

9 January

Dana Sloan
710 Southgate Ave.
Crawley, UK RH10 1FP

Dear Ms. Sloan,

Firstly, congratulations on your exhibition in Beijing. I read in the *British Daily News* that the show was very well attended. I expect that you're taking a much-deserved break now that it has concluded.

The reason I'm contacting you is to ask whether you'd like to contribute to the 2nd Clarendon Art Auction. The piece you gave us last year was the only sculpture among the artwork that was auctioned off.

It would be great if you could donate one of your representative wooden sculptures.

Best regards,

Neil Baker
Coordinator, Clarendon Art Auction

Certificate of Authenticity

This document guarantees that the accompanying artwork is genuine.

Name of Artist:	Dana Sloan
Title of Artwork:	*Spirit of the Grass*
Materials:	Steel
Size:	30 x 25 x 15 centimetres
Date Created:	10-15 February
Date Sold:	19 March
Location of Sale:	Clarendon Art Institute
Name of Purchaser:	Dawn Reeves

Artist's Signature: *Dana Sloan*

---

186. What is NOT mentioned about last year's auction?

(A) It featured creations by community members.
(B) It was preceded by an instructional session.
(C) It included the sale of a painting to a company.
(D) It was held on behalf of a particular group.

187. What is the main purpose of the letter?

(A) To request confirmation of attendance
(B) To ask for a work to be given
(C) To report that an event was a success
(D) To remind a sculptor about an exhibit

188. What is suggested about Mr. Dixon?

(A) He works as a reporter at the *British Daily News*.
(B) He purchases the art of Dana Sloan regularly.
(C) He paid £115 in order to attend an art auction.
(D) He spent less money than Mr. Hidalgo did.

189. What is indicated about *Spirit of the Grass*?

(A) It was created by an artist who is based in Beijing.
(B) It was signed by Ms. Sloan on February 10 to mark its completion.
(C) It is not the type of sculpture that was requested by Mr. Baker.
(D) It was shown in a documentary about the famous graduates of an academy.

190. What is suggested about Ms. Reeves?

(A) She commissioned a work of art during an event.
(B) She collects the sculptures of artist Dana Sloan.
(C) She purchased a painting on behalf of Roda Co.
(D) She attended an art auction two years in a row.

GO ON TO THE NEXT PAGE

The Hangout, Silver Lake's long-awaited retail complex, is set to open this week. It arrives just in time for the winter holiday shopping season. Construction had been delayed for two years before the ownership group was able to secure funding from a number of high-profile investors last year, saving the project from bankruptcy.

Alongside a variety of clothing stores, The Hangout will be home to the hip yoga studio Feetup, an Express Cup coffee shop, a Fabriga ice cream parlor, and more. The Hangout will most likely profit from several new residential high-rise buildings around the area as well as the newly opened Red Line subway stop one block east.

To commemorate the opening, The Hangout will host a celebration this weekend. This will include a complex-wide sale, with some stores offering prize drawings and promotional giveaways. It will also feature a concert by the legendary Harry Hill Jazz Quartet.

Celebrate the Opening of Kisak at The Hangout

Kisak is opening its first store outside of New York at The Hangout in Silver Lake. Kisak is known for eclectic styles, selling collections from some of the most well-known designers and up-and-coming talent.

The store's first day of business coincides with the grand opening event for The Hangout, which will be celebrated with fun activities throughout the complex. Kisak will participate in the action and hold some complimentary styling sessions for anyone interested. None other than celebrity stylist Tamara Kimpton will be present to provide five-minute consultations. Furthermore, many items, including our winter coats and accessories, will be discounted. And if you show this ad to a Kisak staff member, you will receive a voucher worth up to $10 in store credit.

To: Tabatha Branson <t.branson@thehangoutcomplex.com>
From: Yoshi Hondo <yoshi@silverlakeartcollective.com>
Subject: A proposal
Date: October 17

Dear Ms. Branson,

I just wanted to follow up on our recent conversation. First of all, I was really impressed that you managed to book Harry Hill. I've been a fan for years, but that was my first time seeing him perform live.

As I told you in person briefly, I am a partner in the Silver Lake Art Collective. We support local artists and often organize events to promote them. I thought you might be interested in having some of their work put on display around The Hangout. I can show you some paintings and video art pieces that would be a great addition to the complex.

If you're interested, I can put together a proposal with some pieces you might like and stop by your office on Friday.

Sincerely,
Yoshi Hondo

191. Why was the opening of a retail complex delayed?

(A) Some builders went out of business.
(B) It had difficulty raising funds.
(C) It was put off until after a peak season.
(D) Some chain stores left a business partnership.

192. What is true about the new Kisak location?

(A) It is partly owned by Tamara Kimpton.
(B) It is offering a promotion on menswear.
(C) It is between a coffee shop and a yoga studio.
(D) It is convenient to public transportation.

193. Which of the following is NOT an activity that Kisak is planning?

(A) Holding fashion consultations
(B) Distributing store coupons
(C) Launching a celebrity brand
(D) Offering a price reduction

194. What is indicated about Mr. Hondo?

(A) He worked with Ms. Branson previously.
(B) He attended an opening celebration.
(C) He manages The Hangout's art gallery.
(D) He is a renowned visual artist.

195. What is Mr. Hondo proposing?

(A) Sponsoring a gallery opening
(B) Collaborating on an exhibit
(C) Using a complex for a video shoot
(D) Holding a charity event

GO ON TO THE NEXT PAGE

UNICLOUD IS HIRING A MOBILE APPLICATION DEVELOPER

Posted October 1   Expires December 1

RESPONSIBILITIES:
- Plan user interfaces by considering target audiences and customer feedback
- Design the visual style and interface of various applications
- Develop prototypes of user interfaces
- Deliver updates on the development process at weekly progress meetings

BASIC REQUIREMENTS:
- Five years of experience as a mobile application developer
- Experience creating models of complex mobile applications
- Bachelor's degree in design or computer science
- Willingness to settle in Buenos Aires

PREFERRED QUALIFICATIONS:
- Experience designing mobile applications for cloud-based services
- Fluent English and Spanish

Along with your résumé, please submit a portfolio or samples of work demonstrating relevant experience to recruitment@unicloud.com.

ABOUT UNICLOUD

Established 10 years ago, Unicloud is the cloud computing arm of Munich-based e-commerce pioneer Unispan Group. It is among the world's top three providers of cloud services and the largest of its kind in Europe. Unicloud provides a comprehensive set of cloud computing services to clients worldwide, including start-ups, corporations, and government organizations.

Unicloud currently has offices in London, New York, and Shanghai. It has over 500 million users. It aims to attract 200 million Spanish-language users after establishing its South America office in Buenos Aires, which will open soon.

NOTICE TO UNICLOUD EMPLOYEES

Be reminded that we will be hosting a group of representatives from the electronics maker SatzCorp two weeks from now. They would like to learn about our office environment, organizational structure, and corporate culture. While here, they will be interviewing various employees. Ms. Schrader, from our parent company, will be accompanying the team during its visit. At the start of the day, she will be briefing us on what to expect. The process will be repeated at our company's two other locations, in New York and Shanghai, but not at the newly established one. Before the end of the year, we will send a delegation of our own to SatzCorp's main office. By doing so, we will hopefully learn some good practices regarding client management.

196. According to the advertisement, what will successful applicants NOT have to do?

(A) Review customer feedback
(B) Design the look of promotional material
(C) Speak to a group on a regular basis
(D) Create models of user interfaces

197. What is mentioned about Unicloud?

(A) It was the first company of its kind to be established in Europe.
(B) It works in collaboration with international organizations.
(C) It provides a specialized service as part of a larger organization.
(D) It expects to double user numbers following an upcoming expansion.

198. What can be inferred about the advertised position?

(A) It will require frequent travel.
(B) It comes with an annual bonus.
(C) It will involve working at a new branch.
(D) It must be filled before December.

199. What is the purpose of the notice?

(A) To introduce a newly hired executive
(B) To remind employees about a policy
(C) To report on the success of an event
(D) To discuss an information-gathering visit

200. What is suggested about the recipients of the notice?

(A) They will be assigned to a special project.
(B) They will be asked to participate in a survey by Ms. Schrader.
(C) They work at Unicloud's London office.
(D) They cannot be absent for the next two weeks.

This is the end of the test. You may review Parts 5, 6, and 7 if you finish the test early.

정답 p.327 / 점수 환산표 p.329 / 해석 p.362 / Part 5&6 무료 해설 바로 보기(정답 및 정답 음성 포함)
* 다음 페이지에 있는 Self 체크 리스트를 통해 자신의 문제 풀이 방식과 태도를 점검해 보세요.

TEST 05 PART 7 **173**

Self 체크 리스트

TEST 05는 무사히 잘 마치셨죠?
이제 다음의 Self 체크 리스트를 통해 자신의 테스트 진행 내용을 점검해 볼까요?

1. 나는 75분 동안 완전히 테스트에 집중하였다.
   □ 예   □ 아니오
   아니오에 답한 경우, 이유는 무엇인가요?

2. 나는 75분 동안 100문제를 모두 풀었다.
   □ 예   □ 아니오
   아니오에 답한 경우, 이유는 무엇인가요?

3. 나는 75분 동안 답안지 표시까지 완료하였다.
   □ 예   □ 아니오
   아니오에 답한 경우, 이유는 무엇인가요?

4. 나는 Part 5와 Part 6를 19분 안에 모두 풀었다.
   □ 예   □ 아니오
   아니오에 답한 경우, 이유는 무엇인가요?

5. Part 7을 풀 때 5분 이상 걸린 지문이 없었다.
   □ 예   □ 아니오

6. 개선해야 할 점 또는 나를 위한 충고를 적어보세요.

* 교재의 첫 장으로 돌아가서 자신이 적은 목표 점수를 확인하면서 목표에 대한 의지를 다지기 바랍니다. 개선해야 할 점은 반드시 다음 테스트에
  실천해야 합니다. 그것이 가장 중요하며, 그래야만 발전할 수 있습니다.

TEST 06

PART 5
PART 6
PART 7
Self 체크 리스트

잠깐! 테스트 전 확인사항

1. 휴대 전화의 전원을 끄셨나요? ☐ 예
2. Answer Sheet, 연필, 지우개를 준비하셨나요? ☐ 예
3. 시계를 준비하셨나요? ☐ 예

모든 준비가 완료되었으면 목표 점수를 떠올린 후 테스트를 시작합니다.

문제 풀이를 마치는 시간은 지금부터 75분 후인 ___시 ___분입니다.

테스트 시간은 총 75분이며, 시험 종료 전 2~3분은 정답 검토 및 답안지 마킹을 위해 사용합니다.

READING TEST

In this section, you must demonstrate your ability to read and comprehend English. You will be given a variety of texts and asked to answer questions about these texts. This section is divided into three parts and will take 75 minutes to complete.

Do not mark the answers in your test book. Use the answer sheet that is separately provided.

PART 5

Directions: In each question, you will be asked to review a statement that is missing a word or phrase. Four answer choices will be provided for each statement. Select the best answer and mark the corresponding letter (A), (B), (C), or (D) on the answer sheet.

PART 5 권장 풀이 시간 **11분**

101. The resort manager usually gives first-time visitors a tour of the property to familiarize them with the -------.

(A) surroundings
(B) surrounds
(C) surrounded
(D) surrounding

102. A former teacher, Ms. Pratt was ------- to run for office in an attempt to improve the quality of public school education.

(A) concerned
(B) connected
(C) inspired
(D) fulfilled

103. According to the engineer's ------- of the building damaged in the earthquake, it will need to be torn down.

(A) venture
(B) procedure
(C) assessment
(D) occupation

104. Ms. Bang excused ------- from the workshop in order to take an important call from a supplier.

(A) her own
(B) she
(C) herself
(D) hers

105. The chairperson of BTM Enterprise postponed Friday's board meeting, as ------- were expected to be away.

(A) few
(B) each
(C) many
(D) none

106. Vic's short film was shot so ------- that hardly anyone in the audience realized it was the work of a student.

(A) expertise
(B) expertness
(C) expert
(D) expertly

107. The new diet facilitates weight loss ------- it is paired with at least one hour of moderate exercise per day.

(A) except for
(B) even though
(C) only if
(D) such as

108. Because lots of online stores offer discounts, it is often ------- to make purchases online than to shop in person.

(A) cheap
(B) cheaply
(C) cheapest
(D) cheaper

109. The insurance investigator determined that both drivers involved in the collision had been ------- at fault.

(A) entirely
(B) busily
(C) roughly
(D) equally

110. Bolt Systems and Seer Computers announced their merger, but details ------- the agreement were kept confidential.

(A) concerning
(B) toward
(C) above
(D) since

111. Employee productivity was -------- enhanced after the company replaced all of its outdated office equipment.

(A) noticeably
(B) notice
(C) noticeable
(D) noticed

112. This coupon for free breadsticks can be redeemed at every ------- Colson Pizzeria franchise in the United States.

(A) participated
(B) participation
(C) participating
(D) participate

113. After completing the internship program, Mr. Louis was prepared to take on ------- responsibilities his new accounting job entailed.

(A) that
(B) however
(C) which
(D) whatever

114. The factory foreman decided to lease a warehouse ------- having one built because of the urgent need for the space.

(A) as opposed to
(B) in reference to
(C) so long as
(D) as far as

115. Ms. Jedlicka is this year's ------- of the Peter Vanier Award, which is presented to local entrepreneurs for outstanding community service.

(A) president
(B) descendant
(C) applicant
(D) recipient

116. Fans are speculating on what the actress will do next ------- the long-running series she starred in has ended.

(A) in case
(B) in order that
(C) for instance
(D) now that

117. The online metropolitan bus route map suggests it will take ------- 40 minutes to travel from Crawley Station to City Hall.

(A) nearer
(B) nearby
(C) nearly
(D) neared

118. Once prone to wild fluctuations, the value of the nation's currency has ------- thanks to a major change in monetary policy.

(A) elaborated
(B) stabilized
(C) alleviated
(D) clarified

119. The owner of the food truck was fined for operating his business ------- a valid permit from the city.

(A) without
(B) throughout
(C) against
(D) past

GO ON TO THE NEXT PAGE

120. If you'd care ------- us for lunch, my team is eating at a Korean restaurant around the office.

(A) to join
(B) joining
(C) join
(D) will be joining

121. Five hundred acres of ------- state land are within walking distance of the town, making it a favorite destination of outdoor enthusiasts.

(A) reconciled
(B) calculated
(C) deciphered
(D) preserved

122. Dr. Burkett's research led to a greater ------- of the human brain and helped to develop advanced surgical techniques.

(A) understands
(B) understanding
(C) understand
(D) understood

123. Even with the recent increase in the country's employment rates, the economy is ------- growing.

(A) rather
(B) barely
(C) much
(D) wholly

124. To accommodate pedestrians, parking on Fitzgerald Avenue will be ------- during the Hillfalls Music Festival.

(A) prohibit
(B) prohibited
(C) prohibition
(D) prohibiting

125. Approximately 150 jobs were ------- when the Tacchini Textiles production facility closed down.

(A) recruited
(B) collected
(C) extended
(D) eliminated

126. ------- with the ongoing delay of his shipment, Mr. Caldwell called the seller to cancel his order.

(A) Frustration
(B) Frustrating
(C) Frustrated
(D) Frustrates

127. All 12 episodes of the hit show *Quiet Predator* will air ------- during Channel 8's television marathon event.

(A) impressively
(B) generally
(C) voluntarily
(D) consecutively

128. Employees at Ruylain Co. ------- to approach their supervisors with suggestions for improving the workplace.

(A) encourage
(B) are encouraged
(C) will encourage
(D) encouraging

129. Quality is a top ------- for Karsten Manufacturing, so it takes reports of problems with its products very seriously.

(A) source
(B) direction
(C) priority
(D) reminder

130. Researchers did not expect the new medication to cause side effects, as patients in the clinical trial did not experience -------.

(A) other
(B) nothing
(C) it
(D) any

PART 6

Directions: In this part, you will be asked to read four English texts. Each text is missing a word, phrase, or sentence. Select the answer choice that correctly completes the text and mark the corresponding letter (A), (B), (C), or (D) on the answer sheet.

🕐 **PART 6 권장 풀이 시간** **8분**

Questions 131-134 refer to the following notice.

Susie's Bistro: Important Notice to Guests

-------. Although brief descriptions of all dishes can be found on our menu, some of the
131.

ingredients used to make them may not be listed. For this reason, we ask that you tell the

server about your food allergies or sensitivities ------- ordering.
132.

By letting us know about your concerns in advance, we can ensure that your meal is

prepared -------. There are plenty of ways to substitute unwanted ingredients with healthy and
133.

delicious alternatives, and we are pleased ------- your requests.
134.

---

131. (A) Delivery service is now available from
Susie's Bistro.
(B) Please review the following updated
guidelines for serving customers.
(C) We recognize that some of our guests
may have dietary restrictions.
(D) Supply cost increases have given us
no other choice but to raise prices.

132. (A) as to
(B) prior to
(C) following
(D) beyond

133. (A) quickly
(B) easily
(C) openly
(D) safely

134. (A) fulfilling
(B) fulfillment
(C) to fulfill
(D) fulfill

GO ON TO THE NEXT PAGE

Questions 135-138 refer to the following article.

The Future Is Clear for Schmidt Medical

Schmidt Medical has become a leading provider of medical ------- in recent years. The firm's
135.
research team has a reputation for working closely with doctors to produce cutting-edge tools
that make surgery less risky. But according to industry analysts, its new line of LZR-160
devices is Schmidt's most ------- product yet. The LZR-160 shortens the time it takes to
136.
perform corrective optical surgery to less than five minutes. -------. The company's stock has
137.
already jumped, but it is expected to rise ------- higher once LZR-160 units become widely
138.
available.

135. (A) diagnosis
(B) treatment
(C) eyewear
(D) equipment

136. (A) promising
(B) promised
(C) promise
(D) promises

137. (A) It has been especially popular among
family doctors.
(B) This is great news for Schmidt's
shareholders.
(C) These can include blurry vision and
headaches.
(D) The unit has many of the features of
last year's models.

138. (A) even
(B) right
(C) very
(D) almost

Call for Submissions

Photographers of all skill levels are invited to submit pictures of the downtown Walminster area for a chance to have ------- featured in City Hall's winter calendar of events. The selected
139.
photos will help showcase our beautiful city and its residents as they shop, dine, and play.

Participants may submit a maximum of three photos, all of which should be in a digital format.

-------, participants must submit a signed copyright agreement. This will grant ------- rights to
140.   **141.**
the city. In other words, the city may freely reprint participants' original photos for use in future

advertisements and other promotional materials. -------. Visit www.walminster.com/winter_
142.
photo_contest for more information.

139. (A) that
(B) them
(C) it
(D) our

140. (A) Furthermore
(B) Indeed
(C) Accordingly
(D) Likewise

141. (A) exploration
(B) modification
(C) compensation
(D) reproduction

142. (A) We hoped to draw attention to our upcoming citywide event.
(B) The photographer will still be properly credited in this case.
(C) Please enclose an envelope if you want your photo returned.
(D) Tourism to the area has improved since the contest was held.

GO ON TO THE NEXT PAGE

Questions 143-146 refer to the following e-mail.

To	Leo_Belmore@bequetteholdings.com
From	Curtis_McGovern@bequetteholdings.com
Subject	Re: A Request
Date	June 2

Good afternoon, Mr. Belmore.

You have been a valuable part of Bequette Holdings for six years now, and I have long admired your dedication. It is for this reason that I will approve your request to be -------.
143.

Your desired branch, our Nevada office, is looking for an experienced quality analyst like you. -------, you will get to keep your current position after moving. -------. However, their
144. **145.**
management team has proposed that you start on July 12. If this is ------- time to prepare, I
146.
may be able to push back your start date. Feel free to contact me if you have questions.

Best of luck,

Curtis McGovern, HR Manager

---

143. (A) promoted
(B) awarded
(C) recognized
(D) transferred

144. (A) Therefore
(B) Nevertheless
(C) Besides
(D) Though

145. (A) You should prepare an application as soon as possible.
(B) I hope we can come to a reasonable agreement.
(C) You may lack the skills needed to do the work.
(D) I know you said you wish to relocate in the fall.

146. (A) arbitrary
(B) insufficient
(C) additional
(D) unlimited

PART 7

Directions: In this part, you will be asked to read several texts, such as advertisements, articles, instant messages, or examples of business correspondence. Each text is followed by several questions. Select the best answer and mark the corresponding letter (A), (B), (C), or (D) on your answer sheet.

🕐 **PART 7 권장 풀이 시간 54분**

Questions 147-148 refer to the following announcement.

MOROCCO RAIL

We wish to thank passengers for their patience during the service interruptions on parts of our rail network earlier this week. Full service has now been restored to all stations. The interruptions were caused by multiple signal failures that posed a public safety hazard. Fortunately, our maintenance crew was shortly able to get the malfunctioning signalling equipment working again. Should similar problems occur in the future, Morocco Rail will endeavour to provide refunds for ticket holders as always.

---

147. What is mainly being announced?

(A) A work stoppage
(B) A station closure
(C) A limited-time offer
(D) A resumption of service

148. What did Morocco Rail recently do?

(A) Offered discounted tickets
(B) Extended a train line
(C) Repaired some equipment
(D) Revised emergency plans

GO ON TO THE NEXT PAGE

Questions 149-150 refer to the following Web page.

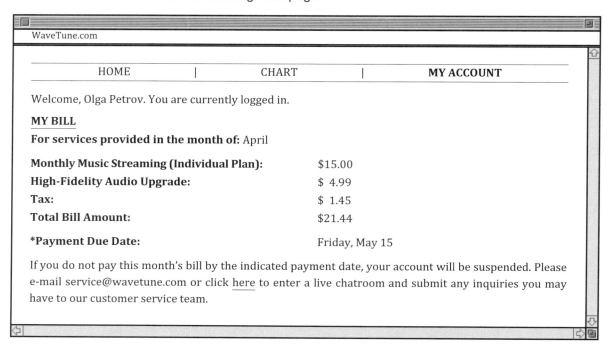

WaveTune.com

| HOME | | CHART | | **MY ACCOUNT** |

Welcome, Olga Petrov. You are currently logged in.

MY BILL

For services provided in the month of: April

Monthly Music Streaming (Individual Plan):	$15.00
High-Fidelity Audio Upgrade:	$ 4.99
Tax:	$ 1.45
Total Bill Amount:	$21.44
*Payment Due Date:	Friday, May 15

If you do not pay this month's bill by the indicated payment date, your account will be suspended. Please e-mail service@wavetune.com or click here to enter a live chatroom and submit any inquiries you may have to our customer service team.

149. What did Ms. Petrov do in April?

(A) Accessed better audio
(B) Downloaded an album
(C) Opened a family account
(D) Submitted a complaint

150. What is stated about WaveTune.com?

(A) It operates a customer service hotline.
(B) It discontinues service for missed payments.
(C) It charges subscribers' credit cards automatically.
(D) It supplies users with streaming devices.

Helping Hands

Preparing to go on a cruise this summer? Give Helping Hands a call. We collect your luggage from your home and deliver it to your cruise ship on the day of departure, so you don't have to worry about carrying heavy items yourself. Simply sign up on our Web site and fill out the form. Your luggage is picked up two to five days before your departure date and securely stored in our facility. On the day of departure, your luggage will be waiting for you in your cabin. What could be more convenient than that? A return service is also available.

Pay just $40 each way for an item weighing 25 kilograms or less, including the cost of insurance. For oversized items, call 555-8080. You may also visit our Web site at www.helpinghands.com to view detailed terms and conditions.

151. What is the main benefit of Helping Hands?

(A) It lowers the cost of summer travel.
(B) It helps customers locate lost items.
(C) It reduces travel times to a destination.
(D) It removes a personal inconvenience.

152. Why should readers of the advertisement call Helping Hands?

(A) To report problems with a service
(B) To inquire about large items
(C) To apply for a gift with purchase
(D) To obtain an additional discount

GO ON TO THE NEXT PAGE

Questions 153-155 refer to the following memo.

INTEROFFICE MEMO

To: Lauren Maguire, Vice President of Engineering, Voyar USA
From: Douglas Lima, Vice President of Operations, Voyar Brazil
Subject: Esther Castro
Date: April 10

As you know, Ms. Castro has been working with our team for the past six months and is due to return to the US very soon. — [1] —. Before that happens, I want to express my appreciation for the contributions she has made while here. Her work as a technical consultant was instrumental in allowing us to complete our factory improvements on time. — [2] —. Ms. Castro's ideas on how to enhance productivity were incredibly insightful. She approaches every problem with creativity. — [3] —. It was also very helpful that Ms. Castro learned to speak Portuguese so well because it allowed her to communicate effectively with employees at every level of the organization. — [4] —. I just wanted to be sure that her contributions to our operation here in Brazil were not overlooked. I'd also like to add that if the opportunity for a promotion ever arose, I would heartily endorse her.

---

153. Why did Mr. Lima write the memo?

(A) To commend a staff member
(B) To evaluate a team's contributions
(C) To describe a factory opening
(D) To discuss communication protocols

154. What is NOT true about Ms. Castro?

(A) She speaks a second language.
(B) She currently works in Brazil.
(C) She helped improve a factory's productivity.
(D) She is being considered for a promotion.

155. In which of the positions marked [1], [2], [3], and [4] does the following sentence best belong?

"You are probably aware of these qualities and her value as an employee."

(A) [1]
(B) [2]
(C) [3]
(D) [4]

Questions 156-157 refer to the following text-message chain.

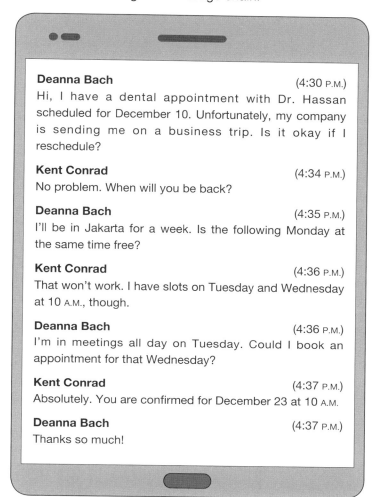

Deanna Bach (4:30 P.M.)
Hi, I have a dental appointment with Dr. Hassan scheduled for December 10. Unfortunately, my company is sending me on a business trip. Is it okay if I reschedule?

Kent Conrad (4:34 P.M.)
No problem. When will you be back?

Deanna Bach (4:35 P.M.)
I'll be in Jakarta for a week. Is the following Monday at the same time free?

Kent Conrad (4:36 P.M.)
That won't work. I have slots on Tuesday and Wednesday at 10 A.M., though.

Deanna Bach (4:36 P.M.)
I'm in meetings all day on Tuesday. Could I book an appointment for that Wednesday?

Kent Conrad (4:37 P.M.)
Absolutely. You are confirmed for December 23 at 10 A.M.

Deanna Bach (4:37 P.M.)
Thanks so much!

156. What is indicated about Ms. Bach?

(A) She is leaving on a business trip to Jakarta.
(B) She needs to see a dentist for an urgent problem.
(C) She wants to reschedule some meetings.
(D) She is running late for an appointment.

157. At 4:36 P.M., what does Mr. Conrad mean when he writes, "That won't work"?

(A) An office will be closed for a holiday.
(B) A requested time slot is already booked.
(C) A doctor will be gone for one week.
(D) An employee is scheduled to go on leave.

GO ON TO THE NEXT PAGE

Globetrotter News

By Elliot Keller, staff writer, Global Traveler Magazine

In a statement released yesterday, budget airline Columbia-Jet announced plans to launch services in the United States. The Canada-based carrier was established just nine years ago, and it has already proven popular for domestic flights. It currently operates flights to 26 destinations across Canada, and will add Seattle, New York City, and Miami starting from January 7. CEO of Columbia-Jet, Serena Hornell, said the airline also hopes to have additional routes to Los Angeles and Denver by the end of next year.

Ms. Hornell said that the carrier will be promoting the new destinations by offering a special deal. "For a limited time, we will be offering a two-for-one special. Anyone purchasing a full-price ticket on one of our new routes is eligible to receive a second one for free." Passengers should note that both check-in and carry-on luggage will incur extra charges. Full details about the offer are posted on the airline's Web site, www.columbia-jet.com.

158. What is the article mainly about?

(A) The launch of a budget airline
(B) A route expansion for an air carrier
(C) The hiring of a new CEO
(D) An increase in domestic flights

159. Which is NOT a destination that will become available on January 7?

(A) Seattle
(B) New York City
(C) Miami
(D) Denver

160. How can passengers get a free ticket to a new destination?

(A) By booking a round-trip ticket
(B) By buying a first ticket at regular price
(C) By entering an online raffle
(D) By using a promotional code

TO   Research and Development Staff
FROM   Brenda Redfield
SUBJECT   Departmental Staffing Updates
DATE   February 26

Good afternoon,

Thank you everyone for your hard work lately. I just wanted to give you all some news regarding upcoming staff appointments.

First, our new director, Kenneth Edwards, will officially take his position on March 1. Mr. Edwards was the head of research at our company's regional branch in San Diego. He will be stepping in for Muriel Bourke, who is retiring at the end of February. He was successful at his previous position and very popular with his staff. So, I'm sure you will all appreciate what he is bringing to our department.

Next, I'm pleased to announce that Helen Ing will be promoted to assistant director of the department. She will be in charge of organizing plans, implementing policies, and scheduling activities for department personnel beginning March 1.

Finally, we will be welcoming five new full-time staff members to our department on March 15. Two of them are entry-level researchers and recent graduates. They will participate in orientation sessions at first. The rest will be assigned to the P6 project and start coding right away, as each already has significant experience in the field of software development.

Brenda Redfield
Associate Director, Research and Development Department

161. The word "appointments" in paragraph 1, line 2, is closest in meaning to

(A) job placements
(B) meeting arrangements
(C) promotion nominations
(D) work responsibilities

162. What is suggested about Ms. Bourke?

(A) She is the current department director.
(B) She visited San Diego in February.
(C) She managed a hiring process.
(D) She will be given a raise soon.

163. What will Ms. Ing be responsible for?

(A) Training new hires
(B) Arranging work timetables
(C) Organizing research data
(D) Communicating with customers

164. What is mentioned about the new full-time employees?

(A) Some earned degrees in product development.
(B) They all have previous experience.
(C) Some will receive work assignments at once.
(D) They will all undergo a training session.

GO ON TO THE NEXT PAGE

Owenville High School
Fundraiser Form

Show your school spirit by supporting Owenville High School's varsity sports teams. You can choose to donate in any amount or purchase clothing featuring our school's logo. Contributions are used to fund the purchase of uniforms and equipment, hire transportation for away games, and other miscellaneous expenses.

Name: Cassandra Roberts

Date: August 9

E-mail address: c.roberts@texmail.com

Phone: 555-9325

Specify use:

_X_ General use ___ Basketball team

___ Track team ___ Baseball team

___ Swim team ___ Football team

Make a direct donation:

___ $10 ___ $20 ___ $50 ___ $100 ___ Other: _____

Or buy items of clothing:

	Small	Medium	Large	Extra Large	Unit price	Total
T-shirt	1		1		$10	$20
Tank top	1				$15	$15
Long-sleeved shirt			1		$20	$20
Varsity jacket				1	$25	$25
					TOTAL	$80

Forms may be submitted and items retrieved at the school's athletics department office. Acceptable forms of payment include cash and check(payable to Owenville High School).

165. What is implied about Owenville High School?

(A) It is building a new sports facility.
(B) It has five varsity sports teams.
(C) It recently won a championship.
(D) It aims to raise a fixed amount.

166. What is indicated about the clothes on sale?

(A) They can be shipped for a fee.
(B) They feature student-made designs.
(C) They come in multiple sizes.
(D) They can only be paid for in cash.

167. What will Ms. Roberts' contribution be used for?

(A) Funding charity work
(B) Designing new uniforms
(C) Assisting with scholarships
(D) Paying for team expenses

Questions 168-171 refer to the following online chat discussion.

Platinum Max Investments – Group Chat System

Xavier Hahn	2:43 P.M.	Janelle and Antonio, how are the income reports for the end of the year going?
Janelle Fletcher	2:44 P.M.	Sorry, but they're taking longer than expected.
Antonio Ricci	2:45 P.M.	Yeah, I'm pretty worried we won't be able to meet next Friday's deadline.
Xavier Hahn	2:46 P.M.	Why don't you ask our intern Teresa to help you out, then? She's just typing up some notes from this Tuesday's staff meeting. I'm sure she'll have time to work on the reports.
Antonio Ricci	2:47 P.M.	Oh, perfect! I should've thought of that before, since she regularly accesses the accounting database to send out weekly status updates.
Janelle Fletcher	2:48 P.M.	I'll show her how to enter the formulas we need for the report spreadsheets.
Xavier Hahn	2:49 P.M.	All right. I'm glad we got this worked out. I didn't want you two missing next Thursday's year-end party because of the reports. Our team is going to win an award for our work on the financial strategies proposal, and I'd like you both to be there.
Antonio Ricci	2:50 P.M.	I didn't realize that. Very exciting! We'll see you next Thursday at Mandarin Kitchen, then.

Send

168. When are the income reports due?

(A) By this Tuesday
(B) By this Wednesday
(C) By next Thursday
(D) By next Friday

169. According to Mr. Ricci, why is Teresa suitable for a task?

(A) She recently took a course on accounting reports.
(B) She was trained on spreadsheets.
(C) She has used a computer system on several occasions.
(D) She took notes at the staff meeting.

170. At 2:49 P.M., what does Mr. Hahn mean when he writes, "I'm glad we got this worked out"?

(A) Some employees will be able to attend an event.
(B) A technical error has been addressed.
(C) Some strategies have proven to be efficient.
(D) A report was finished earlier than anticipated.

171. What will be given out at Mandarin Kitchen next week?

(A) A prize for a group
(B) A year-end present
(C) A promotional packet
(D) A company income report

GO ON TO THE NEXT PAGE

Questions 172-175 refer to the following article.

Hilltop to Open Several New Branches

15 November—Hilltop is preparing to open seven new bookstores before the end of the year, according to managing director Lillian Jones. — [1] —. The new stores, all located in London, will bring Hilltop's total number of stores in the UK to 30. The latest openings are timed to take advantage of typically high December sales. — [2] —.

The news comes after its Swedish billionaire owner, Nicholas Holmberg, sold Hilltop to investment firm Capitalia for £140 million. Mr. Holmberg bought the company six years ago from Horizon Media for £55 million. — [3] —.

"We run a solid business," says Ms. Jones. "Unlike other retailers, our products consistently sell well. For an investor interested in holding retail assets in the UK, we make an attractive purchase. We're also obviously growing." — [4] —.

According to Ms. Jones, the secret to Hilltop's success is a management style she learned in her former life as an independent bookseller. "I urge our managers to take a "less is more" approach," she said. "Customers want a comfortable atmosphere for browsing books. All we need to do is hire staff who are passionate about books and keep the shelves well stocked."

172. What can be inferred about Mr. Holmberg?

(A) He hired Ms. Jones from Horizon Media.
(B) He plans to open additional stores in Sweden.
(C) He borrowed capital to pay for Hilltop's purchase.
(D) He more than doubled his initial investment.

173. Why is Hilltop opening its new stores in December?

(A) It is under pressure from investors.
(B) It aims to conclude a sale in January.
(C) It sells more books at the end of the year.
(D) It was able to meet its annual profitability goals.

174. To what does Ms. Jones credit Hilltop's success?

(A) Rapid expansion
(B) Smart pricing
(C) Frequent discounts
(D) Effective leadership

175. In which of the positions marked [1], [2], [3], and [4] does the following sentence best belong?

"This forms part of an aggressive development plan that includes 15 additional stores next year."

(A) [1]
(B) [2]
(C) [3]
(D) [4]

GO ON TO THE NEXT PAGE

Questions 176-180 refer to the following memo and work estimate.

To: Tara Quincy
From: Selma Hastings
Subject: Harrisburg Office Renovation Update
Date: January 16

Ms. Quincy,

The renovations to the second floor of our Harrisburg office are on track to begin next month. As discussed in our recent conference call, the architect has confirmed that the redesigned space will meet building code requirements. Also, I think I've found a qualified general contractor to oversee the remodeling. I've asked Bushong Construction's representative to make a detailed work estimate for us. This will be forwarded to your office as soon as I receive it. If everything is in order, we should be able to start soon.

Of particular concern is the glasswork for the meeting rooms, which will be crucial to achieving the modern look that we desire. I do have some out-of-town business coming up, but I've arranged my schedule so I can personally check on the day we finish that part of the project.

Give me a call if you have any questions or concerns.

Bushong Construction
Building a Brighter Future

1466 Lincoln Drive
Harrisburg, PA
17111
555-717-6443

****

Remodeling Estimate

Elmore Advertising
21 3rd Avenue, Second Floor
Harrisburg, PA
15044
555-382-0987

Note: The costs listed below reflect both material and labor costs. The final price may vary by up to 10 percent based on market prices for building materials and components.

Work Description	Dates	Labor Cost	Material Cost
Demolition: Removal of kitchen fixtures and office partitions	February 12-13	$6,000	N/A
Electrical & Plumbing: Replacing bathroom fixtures, complete rewiring	February 14-21	$30,000	$15,000
Panel Installation: Wood panel and glass pane installation	February 23-March 1	$22,500	$40,000
Décor: Painting, miscellaneous decoration	March 2-3	$2,000	$10,000
	Subtotal	$125,500	

176. Why did Ms. Hastings write the memo?

(A) To summarize conclusions from a meeting
(B) To propose a solution to an issue
(C) To provide details about an undertaking
(D) To discuss the final results of a project

177. Why does Ms. Hastings need to hire a contractor?

(A) To design a second branch
(B) To learn about building code requirements
(C) To repair damage to an office
(D) To supervise a refurbishment project

178. In the work estimate, the word "reflect" in paragraph 1, line 1, is closest in meaning to

(A) reproduce
(B) express
(C) deliberate
(D) mediate

179. Which phase of the job will probably not cost more than estimated?

(A) Demolition
(B) Electrical & Plumbing
(C) Panel Installation
(D) Décor

180. When will Ms. Hastings review some work in person?

(A) On February 13
(B) On February 21
(C) On March 1
(D) On March 3

GO ON TO THE NEXT PAGE

Questions 181-185 refer to the following advertisement and review.

Sightline Travel					You are signed in as: Jeremy Turner	
Home	Flights	Hotels	Cars	**Packages**	Cruises	Activities

Packages > Jamaican Holidays

Search
Origin: Cardiff, UK   Destination: Jamaica (all locations)
Dates: June 11- June 16   Room Type: Standard Double

Results:

Kings Hotel Montego Bay, Jamaica £1,423 per person Beautiful coastal property with over 400 luxury suites, pools and spas, on-site restaurants, and nightly live musical acts	Friendlies Resort Montego Bay, Jamaica £1,324 per person Choose from over 600 rooms and studio units with full amenities(some with ocean views), plus access to tours and activities
Spectrum Hotel and Resort Port Antonio, Jamaica £1,298 per person All-inclusive, family-friendly beach property with over 850 spacious rooms	Skywave Resort Negril, Jamaica £1,102 per person Newly built property with beach access, swimming pool, and on-site restaurant

Packages shown include flights, hotel, taxes, and fees. For concerns, contact customer service at 555-0354 or e-mail cs@sightlinetravel.com.

---

www.traveltroves.com/reviews

Agency: Sightline Travel

Rating: 3 stars

Reviewer: Jeremy Turner (Verified Traveller)

I recently took a six-day holiday in Jamaica. I used Sightline Travel, a service which, in my experience, generally provides good value on travel packages—and this trip was no exception. With prices on the rise these days, it's rare to find affordable tour accommodations at a high-end property like this, especially one that was constructed within the last year. Everything was sparkling clean. The group activities were enjoyable but also left ample time to unwind by the pool.

However, this was not a dream holiday in every respect. Our connecting flight was delayed, so we arrived at the Kingston airport late. This meant that by the time we had collected our bags, the group shuttle to our accommodations had already left. This would not have been a big issue, except when I tried to contact Sightline, I could not get in touch with anyone, despite making multiple calls and leaving several text messages. In the end, I had to pay for a taxi out of pocket. It did not ruin our trip, but I expected more from Sightline.

181. According to the advertisement, what do all of the accommodations have in common?

(A) A seaside location
(B) A swimming pool
(C) Live entertainment
(D) Nearby dining options

182. What is indicated about the packages?

(A) They require travel in June.
(B) They include air transportation.
(C) They are all in the same city.
(D) They specifically cater to families.

183. Where did Mr. Turner most likely stay during his holiday?

(A) Kings Hotel
(B) Friendlies Resort
(C) Spectrum Hotel and Resort
(D) Skywave Resort

184. What is suggested about Mr. Turner?

(A) He traveled to Jamaica by himself.
(B) He stayed in a suite for six nights.
(C) He paid the hotel for group activities.
(D) He booked with Sightline Travel previously.

185. Why was Mr. Turner dissatisfied with his trip?

(A) His check-in was delayed by an hour.
(B) Customer service was unresponsive.
(C) His luggage was lost by the airline.
(D) Shuttle service was not timely.

GO ON TO THE NEXT PAGE

Questions 186-190 refer to the following schedule and e-mails.

Lansdowne Center
Pacific Publishing Conference
Schedule of Speakers – August 2

Speaker	Seminar	Time	Room
Gary West	Changes to Copyright Laws	9:00 A.M. – 10:00 A.M.	209
Kara Adams	Self-Publishing Services	10:30 A.M. – 11:30 A.M.	105
Chad Lewis	Online Subscription Models	1:00 P.M. – 2:00 P.M.	308
Eileen Daniels	Foreign Licensing Agreements	2:30 P.M. – 3:30 P.M.	109

Space for each seminar is limited, so conference attendees must register in advance. To participate in a seminar, download the registration form here and e-mail the completed document to the conference organizer, Greta Beale, at g.beale@ppc.com.

To: Owen Williams <o.williams@eastpress.com>
From: Tara Liu <t.liu@eastpress.com>
Date: July 27
Subject: Pacific Publishing Conference

Dear Mr. Williams,

Thank you again for giving me the opportunity to represent our company at the Pacific Publishing Conference. I was able to register for all of the seminars you suggested. I signed up for them on Monday and received confirmation today.

Unfortunately, I have to change my travel itinerary for the conference. Originally, I was supposed to depart from Los Angeles on August 1. However, I now have an appointment in Portland on that day. Since the train from Portland to Seattle has a long stopover in Tacoma, I'd prefer to rent a car and drive to the seminar. Would I be able to get approval for this additional expense?

Sincerely,

Tara Liu

To: Greta Beale <g.beale@ppc.com>
From: Lloyd Green <l.green@lansdowne.com>
Date: August 1
Subject: Room Change

Dear Ms. Beale,

I'm contacting you regarding the seminars that you have scheduled for tomorrow. I just spoke with a technician who let me know that there is an electrical problem in the building that will need to be addressed right away. As a consequence of this, the power on the second floor will be shut off for much of the day tomorrow, and sessions that were to take place there will have to be moved. Luckily, Room 309, one floor up, is available during the same time period. It has a capacity of 150 people, so there should be plenty of seating for seminar participants. And, of course, I can instruct my employees to put up signs regarding the change. I apologize for any inconvenience this situation may cause.

Sincerely,

Lloyd Green
Lansdowne Center Building Services

186. What is indicated about the seminars?

(A) They will be held in rooms with the same capacity.
(B) They are led by employees from publishing companies.
(C) They will each discuss an international publishing topic.
(D) They are scheduled to last for the same duration.

187. What did Ms. Liu most likely do on Monday?

(A) Completed an assignment for Mr. Williams
(B) Updated a travel itinerary
(C) Changed a flight reservation
(D) Submitted a form to Ms. Beale

188. Where will the Pacific Publishing Conference be held?

(A) In Los Angeles
(B) In Portland
(C) In Seattle
(D) In Tacoma

189. Which seminar will be moved to a new location?

(A) Changes to Copyright Laws
(B) Self-Publishing Services
(C) Online Subscription Models
(D) Foreign Licensing Agreements

190. What does Mr. Green offer to do?

(A) Refund a room charge
(B) Confirm the size of a venue
(C) Hire additional staff for an event
(D) Arrange for notices to be posted

GO ON TO THE NEXT PAGE

For more than 10 years, Serenity has been the premier beauty salon in the New York area. Our talented stylists and beauticians offer a full range of services and treatments.

We are pleased to announce that our relocation to the Plaza Square Building in downtown Manhattan is now complete. The new space is much larger and more luxurious than our previous one. To celebrate the move, we will be offering a 15 percent discount on hair services in July and a 10 percent discount on nail and facial treatments in August.

Contact us at 555-0393 or visit our Web site to make a reservation. We hope to see you soon!

Serenity

101-1456 8th Street, New York

555-0393

www.serenitysalon.com

Date: July 25
Client: Sarah Broughton

Receipt #: 0098
Phone #: 555-9998

Service		Price
Haircut		$66.00
Nail Art		$45.00
Facial Cream		$40.00
Pedicure		$30.00
	Tax	$18.30
	Total	$199.30

Prices above include all applicable discounts.

Do you have any suggestions on how we can improve? If so, be sure to visit our Web site and submit your feedback. To show our appreciation, we'll give you a free skincare product the next time you visit the salon.

Serenity
Feel beautiful today!

| About | | Services | | Reservations | | **Feedback** |

Client Name: Sarah Broughton
Date: August 1

Overall, I was happy with my visit to your salon. The new location has a very welcoming atmosphere. The waiting area is beautifully decorated, and I loved the staff's peaceful musical selections. Everyone I interacted with was courteous and professional, especially my hair stylist, Melina. She was easy to talk to and had some great recommendations about short hairstyles. She persuaded me to try one out. It's quite a different look for me because mine usually goes past my shoulders, but I love it. However, I do have one recommendation. Many other salons in the area offer coffee and fresh juice to clients. Given that a salon session can sometimes last for several hours, it would be nice to be provided with refreshments.

191. What is NOT stated about Serenity Salon?

(A) It was established over a decade ago.
(B) It has moved to a new location.
(C) It plans to open a branch in another city.
(D) It accepts online reservations.

192. Which price listed on the receipt was discounted?

(A) $66.00
(B) $45.00
(C) $40.00
(D) $30.00

193. What will Ms. Broughton receive on her next visit to Serenity Salon?

(A) A discounted service
(B) A free treatment
(C) A personalized consultation
(D) A complimentary item

194. What can be inferred from the Web page?

(A) Ms. Broughton requested Melina as her stylist.
(B) Ms. Broughton normally has longer hair.
(C) Serenity Salon provides style tips on its Web site.
(D) Serenity Salon expanded its waiting area.

195. What does Ms. Broughton suggest for Serenity Salon?

(A) Serving beverages to customers
(B) Changing some musical selections
(C) Forming a partnership with another salon
(D) Extending the hours of operation

GO ON TO THE NEXT PAGE

Questions 196-200 refer to the following article, memo, and schedule.

Chicago Weekly Editor Stepping Down

Robert Pearl, editor-in-chief of the influential free newspaper *Chicago Weekly*, announced yesterday that he is retiring effective September 1.

A replacement has not yet been named, though a number of internal candidates are being considered. Sources have confirmed that Mr. Pearl will select one of the paper's section editors as his successor, and he will make his choice by August 15.

Mr. Pearl greatly raised the profile of *Chicago Weekly*, making the once-obscure paper one of the most talked about publications in the city. Throughout his tenure, he had a gift for attracting talented reporters, to whom he gave the freedom to pursue groundbreaking stories. In his 8 years as editor-in-chief, the newspaper's circulation grew from 15,000 to 100,000. It also won prestigious awards for its coverage of local politics and culture.

TO: All staff
FROM: Karen Levinson
SUBJECT: Introduction
DATE: August 14

Dear staff,

I'm honored to announce that Mr. Pearl has selected me to be the new editor-in-chief of *Chicago Weekly*. Starting September 1, I will be assuming all his duties, including planning future issues, assigning stories, meeting with our business team on a regular basis, and holding weekly staff meetings.

Starting now, if you have any suggestions on what direction the publication should take, please e-mail me. I welcome all new ideas. I will also be meeting with the section editors this afternoon to talk about our objectives going forward.

In addition, I will be holding an open lunch each week at a local restaurant. During the first one, I'll be sharing new potential designs for the print edition of the paper. Every employee is invited, so I look forward to seeing you there!

Best,

Karen Levinson

KAREN LEVINSON SCHEDULE: WEEK OF AUGUST 14

Mon, Aug 14	8 A.M.: Meeting with Robert Pearl 2 P.M.: Meeting with section editors
Tues, Aug 15	9 A.M.: Meeting with business team 12 P.M.: Open lunch 2 P.M.: Speech to staff writers

Wed, Aug 16	8 A.M.: Meeting with Robert Pearl 1 P.M.: Lunch with Ms. Bradford 3 P.M.: Interview with *Village Post*
Thurs, Aug 17	10 A.M.: Brunch with section editors 4 P.M.: Brainstorming session for October stories
Fri, Aug 18	11 A.M.: Meeting with board of directors 12 P.M.: Lunch at Marshall's Diner 4 P.M.: Weekly staff meeting

196. What is the main purpose of the article?

(A) To discuss the career of a resigning supervisor
(B) To critique portions of a publication
(C) To seek new writers for a newspaper
(D) To announce a newly hired editor

197. What is stated about *Chicago Weekly*?

(A) It does not have an online platform.
(B) It focuses exclusively on politics.
(C) It has attracted more readers over the years.
(D) It has increased the size of its editorial staff.

198. What can be inferred about Ms. Levinson?

(A) She was selected after a deadline passed.
(B) She edited a section of *Chicago Weekly*.
(C) She previously worked at other publications.
(D) She won a major journalism award.

199. What does Ms. Levinson invite staff members to do?

(A) Leave some anonymous comments
(B) Bid farewell to Mr. Pearl before he leaves
(C) E-mail stories to their section editors
(D) Share ideas about the future of a publication

200. On which day will new designs be disclosed?

(A) Monday
(B) Tuesday
(C) Wednesday
(D) Thursday

This is the end of the test. You may review Parts 5, 6, and 7 if you finish the test early.

Self 체크 리스트

TEST 06는 무사히 잘 마치셨죠?
이제 다음의 Self 체크 리스트를 통해 자신의 테스트 진행 내용을 점검해 볼까요?

1. 나는 75분 동안 완전히 테스트에 집중하였다.

   ☐ 예 ☐ 아니오

   아니오에 답한 경우, 이유는 무엇인가요?

2. 나는 75분 동안 100문제를 모두 풀었다.

   ☐ 예 ☐ 아니오

   아니오에 답한 경우, 이유는 무엇인가요?

3. 나는 75분 동안 답안지 표시까지 완료하였다.

   ☐ 예 ☐ 아니오

   아니오에 답한 경우, 이유는 무엇인가요?

4. 나는 Part 5와 Part 6를 19분 안에 모두 풀었다.

   ☐ 예 ☐ 아니오

   아니오에 답한 경우, 이유는 무엇인가요?

5. Part 7을 풀 때 5분 이상 걸린 지문이 없었다.

   ☐ 예 ☐ 아니오

6. 개선해야 할 점 또는 나를 위한 충고를 적어보세요.

* 교재의 첫 장으로 돌아가서 자신이 적은 목표 점수를 확인하면서 목표에 대한 의지를 다지기 바랍니다. 개선해야 할 점은 반드시 다음 테스트에
  실천해야 합니다. 그것이 가장 중요하며, 그래야만 발전할 수 있습니다.

TEST 07

PART 5
PART 6
PART 7
Self 체크 리스트

잠깐! 테스트 전 확인사항
1. 휴대 전화의 전원을 끄셨나요? ☐ 예
2. Answer Sheet, 연필, 지우개를 준비하셨나요? ☐ 예
3. 시계를 준비하셨나요? ☐ 예

모든 준비가 완료되었으면 목표 점수를 떠올린 후 테스트를 시작합니다.

문제 풀이를 마치는 시간은 지금부터 75분 후인 ___시 ___분입니다.

테스트 시간은 총 75분이며, 시험 종료 전 2~3분은 정답 검토 및 답안지 마킹을 위해 사용합니다.

READING TEST

In this section, you must demonstrate your ability to read and comprehend English. You will be given a variety of texts and asked to answer questions about these texts. This section is divided into three parts and will take 75 minutes to complete.

Do not mark the answers in your test book. Use the answer sheet that is separately provided.

PART 5

Directions: In each question, you will be asked to review a statement that is missing a word or phrase. Four answer choices will be provided for each statement. Select the best answer and mark the corresponding letter (A), (B), (C), or (D) on the answer sheet.

PART 5 권장 풀이 시간 11분

101. The organizers of the fundraiser ------- a to-do list to hand out to volunteers.

(A) compiling
(B) compiles
(C) to compile
(D) are compiling

102. Mr. Chen was surprised by the promotion because ------- had not imagined that it could happen this year.

(A) his
(B) himself
(C) he
(D) him

103. Since the report had not yet been -------, Ms. Pantel had time to correct an error she had found.

(A) distributes
(B) distributing
(C) distributed
(D) distribution

104. Inventory in the supermarket was very low, so it needed to ------- before the busy weekend.

(A) remain
(B) review
(C) restock
(D) record

105. The downtown branch of Jim's Burgers has ------- overtaken the chain's other locations in terms of profit.

(A) progressive
(B) progressively
(C) progress
(D) progressed

106. The marketing department has launched a social media campaign in an effort to reach a more ------- audience.

(A) necessary
(B) diverse
(C) deep
(D) comparable

107. Guests enjoyed the resort's new swimming pool ------- its outdoor restaurant.

(A) along
(B) due to
(C) as to
(D) in addition to

108. Employee assessments are ------- carried out in November but may be delayed until December.

(A) comparably
(B) inadvertently
(C) usually
(D) slightly

109. The ------- of the building had to find temporary accommodations during the renovation.

(A) reside
(B) residential
(C) residents
(D) residences

110. The fitness tracker is as perfectly ------- as the online advertisements say it is.

(A) accuracy
(B) accurately
(C) accurate
(D) accurateness

111. Once the account has been -------, the user will be asked to re-enter their login name and password.

(A) created
(B) composed
(C) preferred
(D) assembled

112. According to a recently commissioned study, air ------- levels in the city of Burbank are at an all-time high.

(A) polluted
(B) pollution
(C) pollutes
(D) polluting

113. The trade show convention center was ------- located right next to the subway station, making it easily accessible.

(A) currently
(B) conveniently
(C) knowingly
(D) insufficiently

114. Ms. Williams gave the graphic design team ------- May 17 to come up with ideas for a new corporate logo.

(A) within
(B) between
(C) since
(D) until

115. Applicants ------- a form for a new license should make certain that it is completely filled out.

(A) submits
(B) submitted
(C) submit
(D) submitting

116. Storing dangerous chemicals near the main factory floor creates a ------- hazardous situation for the employees who work there.

(A) potent
(B) potential
(C) potentially
(D) potentiality

117. Health One Hospice's board of directors hopes to ------- the institution with a partner that shares similar values.

(A) implement
(B) recruit
(C) affiliate
(D) denote

118. The casting director was looking for an actor with an ------- tone of voice that can persuade listeners to buy a product.

(A) occasional
(B) inviting
(C) operating
(D) apologetic

119. The company issued a statement yesterday evening in ------- to the merger agreement.

(A) relates
(B) related
(C) relate
(D) relation

GO ON TO THE NEXT PAGE

해커스 토익 실전 1000제 2 Reading

120. A banquet was held to honor five employees, all of ------- have worked at the company for more than 20 years.

(A) them
(B) us
(C) whom
(D) which

121. Company policy requires that all staff members be at their desks before 9:30 A.M., ------- unforeseen circumstances.

(A) though
(B) barring
(C) toward
(D) with

122. Hotel employees are stationed at the check-in desk ------- you have any questions during your stay.

(A) so far
(B) plus
(C) in case
(D) whereas

123. New cycling safety regulations have just been ------- by the Ministry of Transportation.

(A) constructed
(B) incorporated
(C) enacted
(D) measured

124. Author Sylvia Feldman ------- for a Publishers Guild Award for her best-selling nonfiction novel, *21 Ravens.*

(A) nominates
(B) was nominated
(C) was nominating
(D) has nominated

125. The advertisement was ------- than anyone at the firm expected, gathering millions of views within hours of being published online.

(A) popular
(B) more popular
(C) popularly
(D) most popular

126. At the end of the fundraiser, Dr. Adams thanked donors for their ------- in supporting local hospitals.

(A) value
(B) generosity
(C) gratitude
(D) comfort

127. The job comes with several significant ------- including health insurance and three weeks of paid leave.

(A) figures
(B) benefits
(C) profits
(D) values

128. ------- the deposit for the apartment has been paid, the tenant can move in immediately.

(A) So that
(B) Even though
(C) If
(D) Likewise

129. ------- the terms of his employment contract, Mr. Allen receives 1.5 times his regular pay rate for overtime hours.

(A) In front of
(B) In compliance with
(C) Instead of
(D) Out of respect for

130. The board of trustees took a ------- to decide who would replace the retiring company president.

(A) vote
(B) summary
(C) program
(D) conference

PART 6

Directions: In this part, you will be asked to read four English texts. Each text is missing a word, phrase, or sentence. Select the answer choice that correctly completes the text and mark the corresponding letter (A), (B), (C), or (D) on the answer sheet.

🕐 **PART 6 권장 풀이 시간** 8분

Questions 131-134 refer to the following notice.

NOTE: All Eddington's Membership Cardholders

-------. We will be adjusting the frequency with which point accumulation statements are sent
131.

to our members. From January 1, statements will be mailed every six months instead of

quarterly. ------- this change, members may continue to log in at www.eddingtons.com/
132.

members to find current details. You can ------- your accumulated points and see what
133.

rewards are available in exchange for them through your online account. Or you can call us

during business hours at 555-4955, and we will let you know how many you have. -------, you
134.

can drop by a service counter at any Eddington's Department Store, and one of our staff will

inform you of your current total.

---

131. (A) We no longer accept membership applications.
(B) Eddington's is set to introduce a change to its membership program.
(C) We apologize for the recent difficulties with our card payment system.
(D) Eddington's Department Store has a special promotion for cardholders.

132. (A) Apart from
(B) In exchange for
(C) Regardless of
(D) On behalf of

133. (A) submit
(B) monitor
(C) mediate
(D) convey

134. (A) Consequently
(B) Nevertheless
(C) Moreover
(D) Occasionally

GO ON TO THE NEXT PAGE

Questions 135-138 refer to the following review.

Luggage Review: Mercury Travel Pro 2 Carry-On Suitcase

The first thing I noticed about this suitcase, apart from its stylish exterior, was its weight. At just 2.9 kilograms, it is remarkably light. -------. Its hard outer shell is tough enough to
135.
withstand anything that a busy modern airport can offer.

------- the suitcase is also quite easy. The handle features a soft rubber grip that is
136.
comfortable to hold, and the bag's two silent wheels roll ------- over hard surfaces.
137.

Another feature I appreciate is the locking mechanism. It has a four-digit combination and is made from strong steel. This ensures that my belongings are ------- when I am traveling.
138.

---

135. (A) The flexible exterior compresses to fit under a seat.
(B) But I usually prefer luggage in a darker color.
(C) Yet the suitcase is also very durable.
(D) I found myself wishing it had more space.

136. (A) Bringing
(B) Moving
(C) Packing
(D) Stowing

137. (A) smooth
(B) smoothes
(C) smoothing
(D) smoothly

138. (A) invisible
(B) safe
(C) prominent
(D) cautious

Questions 139-142 refer to the following article.

City Officials Close to Selecting Developers for Downtown Building

Marinville officials have created a shortlist of developers to renovate the Halpern Building. There are now only three ------- remaining from the initial 25.
139.

As stipulated when the project first started, the firms left in the running must now add more detail to the plans they submitted at the beginning of the year. In their ------- presentations,
140.
they should demonstrate that they can meet all of the board's remodeling requirements.

-------. "If all goes well," says Brian Schmidt, director of the Marinville Downtown Authority,
141.
"We'll select the most ------- candidate, draw up an agreement, and get started before the
142.
year is out."

139. (A) obstacles
(B) agencies
(C) locations
(D) questionnaires

140. (A) preceding
(B) general
(C) forthcoming
(D) incomplete

141. (A) The candidates all came up with compelling final proposals.
(B) They hoped to develop a construction plan at that time.
(C) The deadline was extended to allow for additional projects.
(D) A complete budget must also be included in the proposal.

142. (A) impression
(B) impressionable
(C) impressed
(D) impressive

GO ON TO THE NEXT PAGE

Questions 143-146 refer to the following e-mail.

To: Anthony Lilly <anthonylilly@hotline.com>
From: Customer Service <cs@comprehensiveautoins.com>
Date: November 14
Subject: Name Change

Our records show that you ------- an automobile policy with us. We pride ourselves on keeping
143.
customers up-to-date on company business, so we are writing to ------- you that we are
144.
changing the name of our company from Comprehensive Auto Insurance to Complete Auto
and Life Insurance.

All of our communications will be labeled with the new name beginning next month. You'll find
our new name on bills, e-mails, letters, claim forms, and on our Web site. -------.
145.

At this time, you may also want to take the opportunity to renew your life insurance. ------- an
146.
appointment, please reply to this e-mail, and you will be contacted by a representative.

Best Regards,

Customer Service
Comprehensive Auto Insurance

---

143. (A) had held
(B) will hold
(C) hold
(D) were holding

144. (A) invite
(B) extend
(C) offer
(D) inform

145. (A) They have been sent to the name
provided on the form.
(B) We will mail them to your residence on
a monthly basis.
(C) They must be submitted in person to
one of our staff.
(D) We will modify our name on our policy
documents as well.

146. (A) Makes
(B) Making
(C) To make
(D) Having made

PART 7

Directions: In this part, you will be asked to read several texts, such as advertisements, articles, instant messages, or examples of business correspondence. Each text is followed by several questions. Select the best answer and mark the corresponding letter (A), (B), (C), or (D) on your answer sheet.

🕐 **PART 7** 권장 풀이 시간 **54분**

Questions 147-148 refer to the following advertisement.

It's time for the annual sale at Shoe Gold!

Buy one pair, get the next pair for 40 PERCENT OFF
Buy a third pair for 50 PERCENT OFF
Buy a fourth pair for 60 PERCENT OFF

We sell the latest designer footwear at discount prices. You won't find a better selection of styles, colors, and sizes for men and women. The sale ends August 14, so shop with us today!

Open daily from 10:00 A.M. to 8:00 P.M.
We accept cash, checks, and credit or debit cards.
Open a Shoe Gold credit card account for an extra
10 percent discount.

Shoe Gold Locations:

1223 Riverside Drive   807 Interstate 12
Minneapolis,   St. Paul,
MN 55401   MN 55519

147. What is being advertised?

(A) New locations of a store
(B) A promotional offer on footwear
(C) Extended hours for a business
(D) Refunds on canceled products

148. What is NOT indicated about Shoe Gold?

(A) It will accept payment by check.
(B) It carries its own brand of credit card.
(C) It will match competitors' prices.
(D) It operates stores in two different locations.

GO ON TO THE NEXT PAGE

Questions 149-150 refer to the following text-message chain.

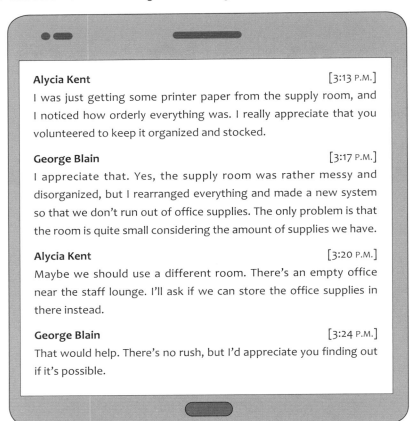

Alycia Kent [3:13 P.M.]

I was just getting some printer paper from the supply room, and I noticed how orderly everything was. I really appreciate that you volunteered to keep it organized and stocked.

George Blain [3:17 P.M.]

I appreciate that. Yes, the supply room was rather messy and disorganized, but I rearranged everything and made a new system so that we don't run out of office supplies. The only problem is that the room is quite small considering the amount of supplies we have.

Alycia Kent [3:20 P.M.]

Maybe we should use a different room. There's an empty office near the staff lounge. I'll ask if we can store the office supplies in there instead.

George Blain [3:24 P.M.]

That would help. There's no rush, but I'd appreciate you finding out if it's possible.

149. What did Mr. Blain recently do?

(A) Assigned some management duties to an employee
(B) Arranged supplies in a storage area
(C) Wrote a report on a supply system
(D) Organized furniture in the staff lounge

150. At 3:24 P.M., what does Mr. Blain suggest when he writes, "That would help"?

(A) Finding a new supplier would decrease expenses.
(B) Limiting office supplies is a helpful suggestion.
(C) Having a larger lounge would be beneficial.
(D) Relocating the supply room is a good solution.

Boardwalk Industries Employee Bulletin Board Posting

Wanted: Used car in good condition

Contact: Roy Long, extension #8113

Post Valid: June 1 - 30

I am looking for a used car in good condition for my son, who will be going to college in the fall. I would like to buy a four-door vehicle with good gas mileage. The brand of the car is not important as long as it is not in need of major repair. Minor dents and scratches are fine as I have the ability to fix them. I prefer anti-lock brakes and air bags as features for my son's safety. If you have a car that is 4-8 years old and meets the other listed criteria, please call the number above.

---

151. Why was the notice written?

(A) To sell a used vehicle
(B) To advertise repair services
(C) To find a car for sale
(D) To announce rental policies

152. What is NOT true about Mr. Long?

(A) He is concerned about safety.
(B) He prefers a particular model of car.
(C) He can perform minor fixes.
(D) He has a son who will attend university.

GO ON TO THE NEXT PAGE

CHANGES AT CCT NEWS

CCT News, the most watched cable news station in the country, has just hired Greg O'Connell to be its new 8 P.M. anchor. Mr. O'Connell is taking over for Pauline Fields, an anchor who retired last month after 20 years on the job.

Mr. O'Connell brings extensive industry experience. He began as a community news writer for the *Cork County Ledger*, and then moved on to editing headline news for five years. Following that, Mr. O'Connell took a job as the assistant news anchor at a local TV station. His broadcasts became increasingly popular, and two years later he was offered a job as the head anchor at WQZ Nightly News. After 10 years on the job, he left WQZ because of the new position at CCT News.

George McDonough, the head of CCT News, says he couldn't be happier with their new anchor. "I first met Greg while working as a producer at WQZ and have been a fan of his ever since," he says. "He is an exemplary newscaster who brings both charisma and a true investigative spirit to the job."

Mr. O'Connell's first night on the air will be May 7. Until then, Richard Marshall will be filling in as the temporary anchor.

153. What is the main topic of the article?

(A) A recently created news show
(B) A retiring cable producer
(C) A newly hired employee
(D) A change in broadcast time

154. What is indicated about Mr. McDonough?

(A) He is the head of the *Cork County Ledger*.
(B) He is serving as a temporary anchor.
(C) He will take over Ms. Fields' job.
(D) He worked with Mr. O'Connell before.

155. What was Mr. O'Connell's most recent job?

(A) Staff writer
(B) Web site editor
(C) News presenter
(D) Producer

Atkins University

Guest Speaker Request Form

This form must be completed and submitted four weeks prior to an event. Please note that a speaker's participation cannot be advertised until this form has been authorised by the Student Activities Office. The same office supplies temporary parking passes upon request.

REQUESTED BY
Name: David Coleman
Department: Atkins University Career Center
Telephone: 7946-4309
E-mail: d.coleman@atkinsu.edu/aucc

SPEAKER INFORMATION
Name: Maria Dershowitz
Organisation: Clarion Call
Telephone: 7946-9235
E-mail: m.dershowitz@clarioncall.com
Topic: Social Entrepreneurship—Developing, Funding, and Implementing Solutions to Social Problems

EVENT INFORMATION
Name: How Graduating Seniors Can Create Social Change
Date: 4 March
Time: 4:00 to 5:30 P.M.
Location: McMurdo Auditorium
Expected number of attendees: 80

SPECIAL REQUIREMENTS
Audiovisual equipment: None required
Transportation: None required
Parking: 1 temporary parking pass
Refreshments: None required

156. Why is Ms. Dershowitz visiting Atkins University?

(A) To lead a seminar for small businesses
(B) To recruit volunteers for a social cause
(C) To discuss social activism with students
(D) To authorize an activity request form

157. What will Mr. Coleman probably do before March 4?

(A) Arrange transportation for a speaker
(B) Pay for the use of an auditorium
(C) Post advertisements on a bulletin board
(D) Secure a parking pass from an office

GO ON TO THE NEXT PAGE

Questions 158-161 refer to the following information.

www.bennetthouse.org/visit

| **HOME** | VISIT | HISTORY | MAP/LOCATION | CONTACT |

Visitors and tour groups are welcome to view Bennett House from Tuesday through Saturday from 10 A.M. until 5 P.M. Groups of 10 or more are asked to make reservations a day in advance. Those who fail to do so may face significant waiting times. Admission is free, but cash boxes are located at the entrance and gift shop, where donations are gratefully accepted.

Bennett House can also arrange guided visits for students or tour groups for a flat fee of $25. — [1] —. All guests will receive informational brochures, which include history and facts about the Victorian-era home and the art and furniture contained in the rooms. — [2] —. The brochures contain pictures and short biographies of the house's former inhabitants as well. — [3] —.

A gift boutique and a tea shop are located near the exit. Postcards, souvenirs, T-shirts, tins of English teas, and teacups are available for purchase. — [4] —. The gift shop will not be open during the off-season from January through March, but the rest of our facilities will remain in operation. Bennett House closes on all national holidays.

158. What advice is included in the information?

(A) Using coupons for purchases in the gift shop
(B) Booking ahead of time for large groups
(C) Making reservations for weekend visits
(D) Following a designated path through the building

159. What is available for an additional charge?

(A) Promotional materials containing pictures
(B) Guided tours of the home
(C) Admission to a photography exhibit
(D) The shipping of purchased souvenirs

160. What is NOT indicated about Bennett House?

(A) It sells keepsakes through a retail establishment.
(B) It offers descriptive pamphlets to all guests.
(C) It closes temporarily during periods with few tourists.
(D) It accepts donations instead of charging admission.

161. In which of the positions marked [1], [2], [3], and [4] does the following sentence best belong?

"All proceeds from items sold go towards the preservation of this historic building."

(A) [1]
(B) [2]
(C) [3]
(D) [4]

To: All Staff
From: Angela Romanov, Office Manager
Subject: Building improvements

Dear all,

Please remember that the renovation of the entire headquarters building will begin two weeks from now. The work will take place one floor at a time, starting on the fifth and moving downward. Each floor is scheduled to take one week to finish. I've discussed this with the team leaders, and a solution has been reached for dealing with workspace concerns during this time.

While your floor is being renovated, space will be made available for you in the conference rooms on the third floor. When it comes time to renovate the third floor, employees who normally work there will be redistributed throughout the rest of the building. We are hoping this will not present any problems since there are only a dozen employees who permanently work on that floor. Those staff members are asked to wait for further instructions from their team leader.

I apologize in advance for any inconvenience this situation may create over the coming weeks. I am confident that we can all work together to make the process go as smoothly as possible. If you have any further queries, please contact your team leaders.

Thank you,

Angela Romanov

162. Why was the memo written?

(A) To arrange a meeting about future renovations
(B) To discuss recent employee complaints
(C) To remind employees about some construction work
(D) To ask for suggestions about a redevelopment project

163. What is indicated about the building?

(A) It is a five-story structure.
(B) It will be demolished next year.
(C) It is three decades old.
(D) It has one conference room on each floor.

164. What are the employees on the third floor asked to do?

(A) Report their concerns to the renovation crew leader
(B) Assist with presentations in the conference room
(C) Expect forthcoming details from their supervisor
(D) Distribute copies of the office manager's instructions

GO ON TO THE NEXT PAGE

Questions 165-167 refer to the following Web page.

| HOME | ABOUT | MENUS | CONTACT |

Welcome to Lunch on Demand, where the food is both on demand and in demand!

From August 8, you won't need to wait in long lines anymore to get your food. Simply browse Lunch on Demand's current menu, place an order, and pay on our Web site. We'll give you a confirmation number and the time that your food will be ready. Turn up at our location at the time we provide, tell us your number, and we'll give you back a box of the tastiest, healthiest food you'll find anywhere downtown.

Our menu changes on a weekly basis but always includes the dishes listed below:

SOUPS – We combine the freshest vegetables, beans or lentils for protein, and nutritious rice noodles to fill you up until dinner. Perfect for vegetarians.

PANINIS – Only the finest wholemeal bread is used to make our great variety of toasted sandwiches. Served with sweet potato fries.

STEWS AND CURRIES – If you're looking for something more substantial, our stews and curries are perfect! They come with rice or bread on the side.

SALADS – For those who are health-conscious, we combine crisp and crunchy greens and other vegetables with our special low-fat salad dressings.

Throughout August, we are giving our registered customers a $10 coupon for every new customer they encourage to sign up. Click here for details.

---

165. What is given to customers when they place an order?

(A) A payment receipt
(B) A time to pick up a purchase
(C) An estimated delivery fee
(D) An updated menu

166. How can customers qualify to receive a coupon?

(A) By placing a minimum order
(B) By getting others to join a Web site
(C) By registering before a deadline
(D) By ordering food from a specific location

167. What is NOT indicated about Lunch on Demand?

(A) It is suitable for those who don't eat meat.
(B) It alters its menu every week.
(C) It can customize all its menu items.
(D) It serves accompaniments with some dishes.

Helen Coulter	[July 15, 9:54 A.M.]	I hope you are all having a good break. I just heard back from the producer of *Timelight* this morning, and they would like to extend Kitchen Belle's catering contract for another two years. The studio has renewed the TV series. Shall we keep the same schedule as last year, or would you like to switch times?
Elaine Painter	[July 15, 10:00 A.M.]	That's great news! It will guarantee the business a steady income. I know Henry Lincoln usually does breakfast, but as long as he doesn't have a problem with it, can I take the morning shift instead of lunch this time?
Graham Fulton	[July 15, 10:04 A.M.]	It's fine by him. He's with me now and just told me so, Elaine. He'd actually prefer midday. As for me, I want to stick with the breakfast shift. Will there be any extra evening shoots this year?
Helen Coulter	[July 15, 10:05 A.M.]	So Elaine and Graham can do the 7:30-11:00 shift, and Henry and I will do 11:30-3:30. There will be some evening shifts for extra pay, but none that will end past midnight. In addition, the show will also be filmed outside the studio this season, so we'll have to make adjustments. Anyway, we can discuss that issue when we return from vacation next week.
Elaine Painter	[July 15, 10:07 A.M.]	Will the number of cast and crew be the same?
Graham Fulton	[July 15, 10:07 A.M.]	It sounds like more work than last year.
Helen Coulter	[July 15, 10:08 A.M.]	No, Elaine. There will be a total of 88 to feed rather than 67. As for your question, Graham, I think it will be more work. But they are paying us more, so I think we can afford to hire a couple of food preparation assistants.

Send

168. At 10:04 A.M., what does Mr. Fulton most likely mean when he writes, "It's fine by him"?

(A) He suggests Ms. Painter trade shifts with a coworker.
(B) His schedule change must be approved by Ms. Coulter.
(C) He is also interested in working during breakfast hours.
(D) His coworker finds Ms. Painter's request acceptable.

169. When will Mr. Lincoln start his regular shifts next season?

(A) At 7:30 A.M.
(B) At 11:00 A.M.
(C) At 11:30 A.M.
(D) At 3:30 P.M.

170. What is implied about *Timelight*?

(A) It will occasionally have production work at night.
(B) It reduced the size of its staff.
(C) It will film all scenes in a television studio.
(D) It will premiere on television next year.

171. What will happen next week at Kitchen Belle?

(A) A list of crew members will be finalized.
(B) A couple of new assistants will be hired.
(C) Team members will return from a holiday.
(D) Executives will be stopping by for a meeting.

GO ON TO THE NEXT PAGE

FREELANCING

We at the *Houston Portal* are always interested in hearing pitches from non-affiliated writers. — [1] —. As a small alternative weekly, we thrive off journalism from independent freelancers. If you are interested in contributing to our publication, here is what we require for story pitches:

First, please send a brief, one-page pitch for a story to editors@houstonportal.com. We will not accept previously published pieces.

If possible, please attach any previous writing you've done for newspapers, Web sites, or other general readership publications. — [2] —. We prefer to publish freelancers who have some previous experience.

We only allow our staff writers to write opinion pieces. Therefore, please limit your pitches to feature stories. We generally run articles that are between 500 and 3,000 words.

— [3] —. If you are a qualified photographer, you may also pitch a photo series. In that case, we would need to see some samples of your work.

Our newspaper is published weekly, except during our holiday and mid-summer breaks, or roughly 50 times a year. — [4] —. The paper is provided at no cost to readers, as we rely on advertisements for funding. Nonetheless, we believe strongly in supporting our writers, so we do our best to provide fair compensation for articles to be published, with rates starting at $0.30 per word.

172. What is the purpose of the information?

(A) To give guidelines on writing for a paper
(B) To provide details on a staff writer job opening
(C) To lay out the *Houston Portal*'s mission
(D) To go over some changes to a publication's rules

173. What is NOT an aspect the *Houston Portal* considers when evaluating pitches?

(A) Length
(B) Article type
(C) Experience
(D) Publishing fees

174. What is stated about the *Houston Portal*?

(A) It is not currently recruiting staff photographers.
(B) It releases new issues every week of the year.
(C) It is free of charge for all readers.
(D) It does not run articles by opinion columnists.

175. In which of the positions marked [1], [2], [3], and [4] does the following sentence best belong?

"Academic or specialized pieces are not relevant."

(A) [1]
(B) [2]
(C) [3]
(D) [4]

GO ON TO THE NEXT PAGE

Questions 176-180 refer to the following schedule and e-mail.

Gladwell Design Company

New Employee Orientation Schedule—March 18

Time	Speaker	Topic
9:00 – 10:20 A.M.	Dana Kang	Compensation and Benefits
10:30 – 11:50 A.M.	David Harris	Corporate Culture
12:00 – 1:00 P.M.		Lunch
1:00 – 2:20 P.M.	Sarah Lee	Employee Conduct
2:30 – 3:50 P.M.	Verne Peel	Performance and Evaluations
4:00 – 5:50 P.M.	Brad Murray	Professional Development Opportunities

Participants will be provided with a company handbook at the start of the first session. Employee IDs and security passes will be distributed the next morning. Parking permits will be available for new employees to pick up the following week.

To: Mike Levy <m.levy@gdc.com>
From: Lucy Sawyer <l.sawyer@gdc.com>
Date: March 14
Subject: Orientation

Mr. Levy,

I just wanted to give you some additional details about the orientation that you asked me to organize for the new employees joining us in sales. There has been a change to the schedule of speakers that I e-mailed to you last Tuesday. Bale Industries has decided to send several representatives on the morning of March 18 to discuss a contractual misunderstanding. As you know, Bale Industries is one of our most important customers, and Dana Kang is responsible for handling client contracts. Therefore, she has switched time slots with the final speaker of the day. I will update the schedule.

There is one other issue. During his session, David Harris intends to divide the trainees into groups for some team-building exercises. However, he is concerned that the reserved meeting area may be too small. Would it be possible to use the executive conference room on the seventh floor for the orientation? Please let me know if this will cause any problems. Thank you.

Lucy Sawyer

176. What will new employees receive on March 18?

(A) An employee manual
(B) An identification card
(C) A security pass
(D) A parking permit

177. What is the purpose of the e-mail?

(A) To request assistance with a project
(B) To announce the hiring of additional staff
(C) To give instructions to a subordinate
(D) To offer an update on an assignment

178. In the e-mail, the word "issue" in paragraph 2, line 1, is closest in meaning to

(A) reason
(B) matter
(C) version
(D) option

179. Whose presentation time will be changed?

(A) David Harris
(B) Sarah Lee
(C) Verne Peel
(D) Brad Murray

180. What does Ms. Sawyer ask Mr. Levy about?

(A) Using a different location
(B) Changing a training activity
(C) Rescheduling an event
(D) Meeting with a company executive

GO ON TO THE NEXT PAGE

Dakota Logistics
MEMO

To: All Staff
From: Jasmine Alexander, Chief Operations Officer
Subject: Pension scheme
Date: November 28

As you know, the company executives reviewed our pension policy at Friday's board meeting and agreed to make some changes to add more flexibility to the system. Currently, employees who have been with the company for less than five years contribute 1.8 percent of their salary to the pension fund, while those who have been here for five years or longer contribute 2.7 percent.

From January 1 of next year, this policy will change. All staff will be able to choose their level of pension payment. As well as the two existing options, employees will also be able to contribute an amount of up to 3.5 percent of their salary if they wish. In December, you will all be asked to communicate your preferences on this issue. If you would like to discuss the options and receive some advice about what might be best for your current situation, please make an appointment with the head of the human resources department.

To	Sarah Chang <schang@dlogistics.com>
From	Adam Cartwright <acartwright@dlogistics.com>
Subject	Pension appointment
Date	November 29

Hello, Sarah.

I am writing in response to yesterday's memo from Ms. Alexander. I currently contribute 1.8 percent of my salary to the pension fund. However, I received a pay raise when my contract was renewed in September, so I can now afford to contribute more. Because of that, I'm interested in increasing my contribution to 3.5 percent.

I will be available to talk about this issue all day Tuesday and Thursday and will also be free on Friday before 2 P.M. Let me know if there is a time that works best for you during those periods.

Best wishes,
Adam Cartwright

181. What is suggested about employees at Dakota Logistics?

(A) They can only change a contribution amount during contract negotiations.
(B) They have about a month to act on revised policy.
(C) They can arrange to have payments deducted automatically.
(D) They complained about a former company policy.

182. What is implied about Mr. Cartwright?

(A) He is being considered for a major promotion.
(B) He has been with the company for less than five years.
(C) He will be transferred to other department next week.
(D) He has completed a performance evaluation form.

183. Based on the memo, what will change at the beginning of next year?

(A) The sum that workers can put toward a pension
(B) The bonuses employees are given for performing well
(C) The number of years needed to qualify for a program
(D) The method by which payments must be made

184. What is Mr. Cartwright hoping to do?

(A) Increase the number of his working hours
(B) Get an extension on the deadline for a task
(C) Pay the maximum amount toward a pension scheme
(D) Take a temporary leave of absence from work

185. What is indicated about Ms. Chang?

(A) She requested a meeting with Mr. Cartwright.
(B) She schedules appointments for Ms. Alexander.
(C) She is usually unavailable in the afternoons.
(D) She is in charge of a department at Dakota Logistics.

GO ON TO THE NEXT PAGE

Association of Materials Engineers (AME)
9th Annual Eastern Regional Conference
March 10 to 11 | Clifton, New Jersey

Organized by the New Jersey chapter of AME and hosted by the Clifton University College of Materials Science and Engineering, the 9th Annual Eastern Regional Conference provides an opportunity for engineers and scientists to learn about new technologies and network with their peers. Join practical workshops, hear about the latest research, and build relationships with stakeholders and representatives from various sectors.

Additionally, the New Jersey chapter is pleased to continue supporting the High School Engineering Outreach Program as part of the conference. High school students in the area will be invited to participate in planned activities to learn about various aspects of the materials engineering profession. The program includes a special luncheon where students can interact with practicing engineers.

If your company is interested in supporting this event, please contact event coordinator Melinda Rose at m.rose@ame.org. Sponsors will be permitted to run advertisements in our program brochure or display promotional banners at the venue.

To: Melinda Rose <m.rose@ame.org>
From: Paula Vance <p.vance@hiller.com>
Date: January 22
Subject: Conference

Dear Ms. Rose,

Thank you for processing our request. A digital copy of the full-page advertisement meant for inclusion in your brochure has been attached. Other marketing materials will be sent in a separate e-mail as soon as they are finalized. I also received the four conference tickets as part of the benefits package. Incidentally, I'd like to inquire about the price of obtaining conference tickets on the day of the event. A colleague from an affiliated company in Europe is interested in attending, but he cannot be sure of his availability until a few days before the event. He is not a member of the AME but belongs to the European Society of Engineers.

I appreciate your assistance and look forward to hearing from you shortly.

Paula Vance
Senior engineer
Hiller Engineering

Association of Materials Engineers (AME)
9th Annual Eastern Regional Conference

Registration Fees

	Early	Regular	On-site
Member	$150	$230	$285
Nonmember	$175	$255	$310
Student*	$45	$75	$100

The deadline for early registration is on January 24, and February 16 is the deadline for regular registration.

*Prices shown are for both graduate and undergraduate students enrolled in any science or engineering program within the country. High school students attending as part of our outreach program may enter for free.

186. According to the announcement, what is NOT included in the 9th Annual Eastern Regional Conference?

(A) Networking opportunities
(B) A lunch with students
(C) A tour of a facility
(D) Learning sessions

187. What is indicated about Hiller Engineering?

(A) It signed up for a session through a Web site.
(B) It plans to open an exhibit booth.
(C) It registered as a conference sponsor.
(D) It is sending all of its employees to an event.

188. What can Ms. Rose expect to receive from Ms. Vance?

(A) A list of names
(B) Copies of a contract
(C) A product brochure
(D) Promotional materials

189. What is mentioned about the conference fees?

(A) They cannot be refunded after having been paid.
(B) They do not apply to individuals participating in the AME's high school program.
(C) They are lower for graduate students than for undergraduates.
(D) They may be discounted for people who register in groups.

190. How much will Ms. Vance's colleague have to pay for his ticket?

(A) $175
(B) $255
(C) $285
(D) $310

GO ON TO THE NEXT PAGE

Questions 191-195 refer to the following notice, e-mail, and form.

Attention Griffin Mobile Employees

As we make plans for our annual company convention in Chicago on March 13-17, please review the following policies for travel reimbursement:

- All employees must book their flight reservations through Thunder Airlines. No reimbursement is available for flights booked through other airlines.
- Employees flying over 300 miles to the convention site will receive a complimentary upgrade to business class. Employees traveling over 500 miles can also receive a complimentary one-day pass for the Thunder Airlines VIP airport lounge.
- Employees who need to rent a car can book their reservations through Clifford Car Rentals in Chicago. Reimbursement will only be provided for employees renting an economy vehicle.

We are expecting over 250 Griffin Mobile employees to attend the convention, so it is vital that all employees follow these regulations. Please contact Jill McGowan with any questions or concerns.

To: Laura Parker <lauraparker@griffinmobile.com>
From: Jill McGowan <jillmcgowan@griffinmobile.com>
Date: March 10
Subject: Chicago convention

Hi, Laura!

I'm so sorry to hear about your broken ankle. But I'm glad that you're recovering and still planning to join us for the Chicago convention.

Under normal circumstances, you wouldn't be eligible for a business class ticket or have access to the airport lounge. But because of your injury, I am going to upgrade your airline reservations to business class and book a day pass for the airport lounge.

Since driving a rental car isn't an option for you right now, the finance department will approve up to $150 in taxi charges. But you will need to submit a separate reimbursement request and attach your taxi receipts. Please also let me know if you need to make additional arrangements for ground transportation while you're in Chicago.

Sincerely,
Jill McGowan
Operations Coordinator, Griffin Mobile

Griffin Mobile Reimbursement Request

Employee name: Laura Parker
Employee #: 13848
Employee department: Product Development

Item	Date	Cost	Description
Taxi ride	March 13	$33.50	From airport to hotel
	March 14	$14.75	From hotel to convention center
	March 14	$15.25	From convention center to hotel
	March 15	$27.25	From hotel to restaurant
	March 15	$29.75	From restaurant to hotel
	March 17	$33.50	From hotel to airport

Total expenses: $154
Notes: Employee required taxi services during company convention due to documented medical condition. Receipts attached.

191. What can be inferred about Griffin Mobile?

(A) It has few employees located 500 miles away from Chicago.
(B) It has a business arrangement with an airline.
(C) It has been holding conventions for many years.
(D) It has a single location for its offices.

192. Why did Ms. McGowan write the e-mail?

(A) To announce a convention
(B) To confirm a flight reservation
(C) To offer an exception to a policy
(D) To inquire about an employee's condition

193. What is suggested about Ms. Parker?

(A) Her trip to the convention was less than 300 miles.
(B) She canceled a reservation with Clifford Car Rentals.
(C) She was injured a few months before the convention.
(D) Her rental car was classified as an economy car.

194. What can be concluded about Ms. Parker's taxi expenses?

(A) They were for rides taken short distances.
(B) They were incurred in multiple cities.
(C) They will not be fully reimbursed.
(D) They will be compared to rental costs.

195. On which date did Ms. Parker attend a seminar?

(A) March 13
(B) March 14
(C) March 15
(D) March 17

GO ON TO THE NEXT PAGE

Questions 196-200 refer to the following article, Web page, and announcement.

National Postal Service to Close Branches

BONDVILLE, November 1—Faced with a sharp decline in mail volume, post offices across the nation are struggling to remain viable. In fact, the National Postal Service will have a deficit of approximately $7 million by the end of the financial year despite its recent attempts to decrease expenses. So far, these efforts have involved removing hundreds of curbside mail collection boxes, reducing operating hours at thousands of branches, and raising the price of domestic stamps by two cents.

According to the chief executive officer of the National Postal Service, Myra Kane, "There is, consequently, little more the service can do but close less-used post offices." In Bondville, the following post offices will cease operating on January 1:

Neighborhood	Post Office Location
Landpiper Hills	41 Brookside Avenue
Delforte Park	5734 Livingston Street
Randall Springs	343 Medollini Drive

A nationwide list of branches slated to be closed can be viewed at www.npservice.com/actions. Members of the public may provide feedback by clicking on "Contact Us" at this site.

www.npservice.com/contactus

Name: Vincent Alvarez
Home Address: 460 Brookside Avenue, Bondville, FL 33870
Date: November 28

Comment: I believe that the plan to close three of my town's four post offices was not well considered. More people than you might think rely on them on a daily basis. I, for one, run a small business from my home and visit my neighborhood post office several times a week to mail orders. It is located a short drive away from my residence, on the same street.

In addition, my neighborhood contains a lot of small stores, and the owners use the local post office to send out orders placed online. As a large number of town residents share my sentiments, I hope you will reconsider the decision to close these branches.

SUBMIT

National Postal Service
Public Announcement for Bondville Citizens

When it was announced that three of Bondville's post offices were going to be shut down, many local residents filed complaints. They argued that the closures would result in inconvenience. It was also pointed out that the post office in Delforte Park was built in the late 19th century and is a valuable example of Renaissance Revival architecture.

Furthermore, the local government of Bondville helpfully provided us with updated figures on the number of people using each branch. We've thus decided to compromise by closing only the Randall Springs branch, which is based in a strip mall and is deemed to have little historical value. To boost the viability of the remaining postal locations, Bondville City Hall has added them to its newly launched Heritage Trail, which runs along Packard Street and other noteworthy streets. Tourists will be invited to buy National Postal Service souvenirs, including specially designed postcards, when they stop by these sites.

196. What cost-reduction strategy has the National Postal Service NOT tried?

(A) Cutting post office hours
(B) Eliminating mailboxes
(C) Hiring temporary workers
(D) Increasing the postage rate

197. What can be inferred about Landpiper Hills?

(A) It contains a lot of small-scale enterprises.
(B) It has a street that is open to pedestrians only.
(C) It is failing to attract as many tourists as it used to.
(D) It is the location of an administrative building.

198. Which street has a post office with historical value?

(A) Brookside Avenue
(B) Livingston Street
(C) Mendollini Drive
(D) Packard Street

199. What has the National Postal Service most likely done?

(A) Amended a nationwide policy
(B) Conducted a survey of some residents
(C) Inspected a historic building
(D) Partnered with a local government

200. In the announcement, the word "boost" in paragraph 2, line 3, is closest in meaning to

(A) hasten
(B) celebrate
(C) test
(D) strengthen

This is the end of the test. You may review Parts 5, 6, and 7 if you finish the test early.

정답 p.327 / 점수 환산표 p.329 / 해석 p.378 / Part 5&6 무료 해설 바로 보기(정답 및 정답 음성 포함)
* 다음 페이지에 있는 Self 체크 리스트를 통해 자신의 문제 풀이 방식과 태도를 점검해 보세요.

Self 체크 리스트

TEST 07은 무사히 잘 마치셨죠?
이제 다음의 Self 체크 리스트를 통해 자신의 테스트 진행 내용을 점검해 볼까요?

1. 나는 75분 동안 완전히 테스트에 집중하였다.

    ☐ 예   ☐ 아니오

    아니오에 답한 경우, 이유는 무엇인가요?

2. 나는 75분 동안 100문제를 모두 풀었다.

    ☐ 예   ☐ 아니오

    아니오에 답한 경우, 이유는 무엇인가요?

3. 나는 75분 동안 답안지 표시까지 완료하였다.

    ☐ 예   ☐ 아니오

    아니오에 답한 경우, 이유는 무엇인가요?

4. 나는 Part 5와 Part 6를 19분 안에 모두 풀었다.

    ☐ 예   ☐ 아니오

    아니오에 답한 경우, 이유는 무엇인가요?

5. Part 7을 풀 때 5분 이상 걸린 지문이 없었다.

    ☐ 예   ☐ 아니오

6. 개선해야 할 점 또는 나를 위한 충고를 적어보세요.

* 교재의 첫 장으로 돌아가서 자신이 적은 목표 점수를 확인하면서 목표에 대한 의지를 다지기 바랍니다. 개선해야 할 점은 반드시 다음 테스트에
  실천해야 합니다. 그것이 가장 중요하며, 그래야만 발전할 수 있습니다.

TEST 08

PART 5
PART 6
PART 7
Self 체크 리스트

잠깐! 테스트 전 확인사항

1. 휴대 전화의 전원을 끄셨나요? ☐ 예
2. Answer Sheet, 연필, 지우개를 준비하셨나요? ☐ 예
3. 시계를 준비하셨나요? ☐ 예

모든 준비가 완료되었으면 목표 점수를 떠올린 후 테스트를 시작합니다.

문제 풀이를 마치는 시간은 지금부터 75분 후인 ___시 ___분입니다.

테스트 시간은 총 75분이며, 시험 종료 전 2~3분은 정답 검토 및 답안지 마킹을 위해 사용합니다.

READING TEST

In this section, you must demonstrate your ability to read and comprehend English. You will be given a variety of texts and asked to answer questions about these texts. This section is divided into three parts and will take 75 minutes to complete.

Do not mark the answers in your test book. Use the answer sheet that is separately provided.

PART 5

Directions: In each question, you will be asked to review a statement that is missing a word or phrase. Four answer choices will be provided for each statement. Select the best answer and mark the corresponding letter (A), (B), (C), or (D) on the answer sheet.

🕐 **PART 5 권장 풀이 시간** **11분**

101. Please note that this establishment implements a time limit of 14 days for ------- non-defective and unopened purchases.

(A) return
(B) returning
(C) returns
(D) returned

102. No special seating arrangement was made for the seminar participants, but as ------- arrive, attendants will show them to the available seats.

(A) these
(B) they
(C) their
(D) them

103. Human resources will periodically ------- employees to determine if they are meeting the company's performance standards.

(A) legitimize
(B) register
(C) evaluate
(D) coordinate

104. Having studied South America for several decades, Professor Hartley ------- the preeminent authority on its civilizations.

(A) is considered
(B) considering
(C) consideration
(D) considers

105. The espresso machine comes with an easily ------- nozzle that allows users to control the amount of coffee dispensed.

(A) adjust
(B) adjusts
(C) adjustable
(D) to adjust

106. ------- the old printer is slower than the newer model, some employees still prefer using it.

(A) Because
(B) Despite
(C) Although
(D) Perhaps

107. ------- hearing the fire alarm, the students evacuated the building via the nearest exit.

(A) Upon
(B) From
(C) Within
(D) Besides

108. Citizens expressed their ------- for the mayor, who helped the city become financially solvent after 10 years of being heavily in debt.

(A) appreciation
(B) applause
(C) responsibility
(D) reluctance

109. Long Road Truck Rental posted an announcement stating that it ------- employees to wear jeans with company shirts beginning on April 2.

(A) allow
(B) would allow
(C) is allowed
(D) were allowing

110. With ------- information available on the terrain, the hikers hired a personal guide in order to ensure their safety.

(A) few
(B) little
(C) most
(D) this

111. Ms. Latta usually uses her car to get to work, but she finds it simpler to commute via bus than ------- with city traffic.

(A) deals
(B) to deal
(C) is dealing
(D) has been dealing

112. The program for the charity concert is ------- and subject to change depending on the availability of performers.

(A) exempt
(B) privileged
(C) tentative
(D) finalized

113. Students ------- for the bar exam are encouraged to review questions included on previous tests.

(A) repeating
(B) preparing
(C) accounting
(D) campaigning

114. ------- temperatures are expected to drop during the day, it might be wise to bring a warm winter coat.

(A) Unless
(B) Given that
(C) Except for
(D) As well as

115. Mr. Powers informed a customer that the special security service was not customizable, but that the payment terms were -------.

(A) negotiable
(B) probable
(C) knowledgeable
(D) profitable

116. MevTech representatives ------- arranged a press conference in order to address the sudden surge in customer complaints regarding their products.

(A) greatly
(B) noticeably
(C) severely
(D) hastily

117. ------- speculation that Whitmore Incorporated was in talks to merge with Busch & Hawley, stock prices for both companies began rising.

(A) Amid
(B) Until
(C) Since
(D) Across

118. Mr. Barton received a notice for an unpaid electricity bill and was asked to pay immediately to ensure ------- of the service.

(A) application
(B) continuation
(C) origination
(D) celebration

119. The company Web site recently underwent significant changes, making ------- who logged on confused by the modifications.

(A) all
(B) either
(C) more
(D) none

GO ON TO THE NEXT PAGE

120. Mr. Simmons is ------- in charge of keeping financial records, but he also takes care of other minor duties.

(A) steeply
(B) shortly
(C) mainly
(D) affordably

121. After closely inspecting the antique cabinet alongside the reproduction, the dealer could identify the ------- characteristics of each.

(A) distinguished
(B) distinguishing
(C) distinguishes
(D) distinguish

122. The CEO ------- resisted appeals from investors to expand the business, but he has since changed his mind.

(A) accordingly
(B) exactly
(C) ultimately
(D) initially

123. Ms. Muncy prefers investing in bonds and mutual funds rather than facing the daily ------- of individual stocks.

(A) pronunciations
(B) fluctuations
(C) experimentations
(D) installations

124. Sports commentators have been guessing ------- of the weaker teams in the league will still be eligible to participate.

(A) what
(B) which
(C) that
(D) whose

125. Crime rates have decreased considerably, thanks in part to the establishment of hotlines that people can use to ------- report suspicious behavior.

(A) anonymously
(B) anonymity
(C) anonymousness
(D) anonymous

126. ------- letting recyclable materials at the office go to waste, the Colton Company brings them to a local recycling center.

(A) After
(B) Nevertheless
(C) Instead of
(D) Not only

127. For the directors' luncheon, the administrative department reserved a ------- room away from the main dining area to discuss sensitive issues.

(A) relevant
(B) crowded
(C) decorated
(D) private

128. Dr. Marcus spoke ------- the allotted 30 minutes, leaving no time for questions after his speech.

(A) beyond
(B) about
(C) under
(D) around

129. The Nigel Art Gallery was small relative to well-known museums, but its sculptures were ------- among the best in the world.

(A) arguable
(B) arguably
(C) argument
(D) argues

130. In an attempt to make its products immediately -------, the company worked with a top advertising agency on an eye-catching logo.

(A) identifiable
(B) identifying
(C) identification
(D) identify

PART 6

Directions: In this part, you will be asked to read four English texts. Each text is missing a word, phrase, or sentence. Select the answer choice that correctly completes the text and mark the corresponding letter (A), (B), (C), or (D) on the answer sheet.

🕐 **PART 6 권장 풀이 시간** **8분**

Questions 131-134 refer to the following announcement.

Toronto Youth Orchestra (TYO) Canada Tour

In celebration of the TYO's 10th anniversary, the orchestra will tour Canada for the first time, with four performances scheduled. The tour will begin in Vancouver on November 8, include stops in Winnipeg and Quebec City, and end in Toronto on November 16. The ------- performance, in Toronto, will take place at Glenview Auditorium. Over 4,000 members of the public are expected to attend this show.
131.

Founded by Yves Guilmette, the TYO has been recognized for its ------- efforts. Its goal is to provide residents of Toronto's underserved neighborhoods with access to a musical education by offering academic assistance. -------. Many of those who have been given musical training by TYO members have gone on to join the orchestra themselves.
132. **133.**

The tour ------- by a donation from Maple Union Bank. For ticket information, visit www.tyo.org.
134.

131. (A) final
(B) outdoor
(C) exclusive
(D) initial

132. (A) budgeting
(B) outreach
(C) marketing
(D) expansion

133. (A) Several famous pop stars are expected to make an appearance.
(B) Participants also receive free instruments.
(C) The recording will later be released as an album.
(D) Some feel that the school should stick to its original objectives.

134. (A) funded
(B) will fund
(C) had funded
(D) is being funded

GO ON TO THE NEXT PAGE

Questions 135-138 refer to the following memo.

To: All Staff
From: Stephanie Johnstone
Subject: Mr. Kaur's retirement
Date: January 15

Hello everyone,

This is just a reminder that we have organized a retirement party for Mr. Kaur next Friday from 6 P.M. -------. **135.** I would appreciate it if you could all attend unless you have good reason not to. After everyone is seated, the program ------- **136.** at precisely 6:15 P.M. The CEO plans to give a congratulatory speech. -------. **137.** As our longest-serving staff member, he has certainly earned this recognition.

I have asked the supervisors of each department to ------- **138.** a book in which members of staff may write messages to Mr. Kaur wishing him well upon his retirement. The book will be passed around starting tomorrow morning. It will be given to him at the end of the ceremony, so please make the time to write something.

135. (A) around
(B) over
(C) upward
(D) onward

136. (A) has begun
(B) will begin
(C) will have begun
(D) began

137. (A) We will then ask Mr. Kaur to put off his retirement for a year.
(B) Our employees will be expected to remain loyal to the company.
(C) A board member will then present a loyalty award to Mr. Kaur.
(D) The office staff should say whether they can attend the ceremony.

138. (A) circulate
(B) retrieve
(C) determine
(D) reveal

March 31

Annika Dahl
7898 Forest Road
Boulder, CO 80301

Dear Ms. Dahl,

Thank you for your recent visit. -------. We hope that you are fully satisfied with the quality of
139.
care that you received.

We would like to know more about your experience at our medical facility through our Patient

Care Survey. Please fill out the questionnaire, and make sure that each of the five items

------- as directed. If you have additional comments, please ------- them in the space provided.
140.   **141.**

Keep in mind that the information you provide in the survey will be analyzed and used to

improve our services in the future. -------, your privacy will be protected. We will not be able to
142.
track any of your responses back to you. Thank you for your participation.

Stanley Waite
Hospital Consumer Assessment

139. (A) Please accept our sincere apologies
for the treatment you were given.
(B) We are delighted with your generous
donation to the hospital.
(C) At High Point Medical, we always
strive to meet the needs of each
patient.
(D) Our records show that you have been
missing your appointments.

140. (A) rates
(B) rating
(C) is rated
(D) to rate

141. (A) to include
(B) include
(C) included
(D) inclusion

142. (A) Likewise
(B) In other words
(C) Nonetheless
(D) For instance

GO ON TO THE NEXT PAGE

Questions 143-146 refer to the following article.

WELLINGTON (18 March)—Friday marks the beginning of the annual Wellington Literary Festival. This year's event will include presentations ------- authors from all over the world. In
143.
addition to local favourites, the festival will showcase ------- from Africa and South America. As
144.
always, the festival will be a great chance for young writers ------- publishers with their
145.
proposals. If you're passionate about literature, don't miss out. -------.
146.

143. (A) in
(B) by
(C) through
(D) since

144. (A) performers
(B) fiction
(C) films
(D) artwork

145. (A) to approach
(B) approach
(C) are approaching
(D) approached

146. (A) Some of the presentations had to be rescheduled.
(B) Most publishers would prefer you e-mail them your work.
(C) Tickets for the event are available for purchase online.
(D) To enter the raffle, call the number listed below.

PART 7

Directions: In this part, you will be asked to read several texts, such as advertisements, articles, instant messages, or examples of business correspondence. Each text is followed by several questions. Select the best answer and mark the corresponding letter (A), (B), (C), or (D) on your answer sheet.

⏱ **PART 7 권장 풀이 시간 54분**

Questions 147-148 refer to the following text message.

From: 555-2910 (unknown contact)

Thank you for patronizing Luigi's Restaurant. Please arrive 5 to 10 minutes before your booking and show this confirmation message to the host. We have received your $50 deposit, and your table for four will be ready at 7:30 P.M. on Friday evening. This amount will be subtracted from your final bill when you dine with us. Do note, however, that if you choose to cancel your booking, you will not be refunded.

147. Why was the text message sent?

(A) To confirm a reservation
(B) To provide directions to a restaurant
(C) To update a cancellation policy
(D) To mention a penalty fee

148. What is stated about a deposit payment?

(A) It can be made on Friday evening.
(B) It will be deducted from the bill.
(C) It may take 10 minutes to process.
(D) It can be refunded before dining.

GO ON TO THE NEXT PAGE

Questions 149-150 refer to the following notice.

Attention: Students with Classes in Kingsley Auditorium

All students who have classes scheduled to take place in Kingsley Auditorium should note that this facility will not be available from October 2 to 4. The biology department is using the venue for its yearly lecture series during this period, as usual. Students attending classes scheduled to be held in the auditorium on those dates are asked to go to Ward Hall instead.

In addition, please note that the October 3 session of the "Intermediate Microbiology" class that usually takes place in the auditorium at 10 A.M. has been canceled. Professor Evan Chang will hold a makeup lesson later in the semester.

Contact the department office if you have any questions.

---

149. What can be inferred about Kingsley Auditorium?

(A) It will be temporarily closed for renovations.
(B) It has a larger capacity than Ward Hall does.
(C) It has been regularly used for an academic event.
(D) It is not normally used for classes.

150. What is NOT mentioned about Intermediate Biology class?

(A) The regular location of a class
(B) The name of a class instructor
(C) The starting time of a class
(D) The duration of a class

Conference Room Reservations

If any employee of Great Files Inc. wishes to reserve a meeting room, go to the conference room reservation schedule online at: www.greatfiles.com/employee/meetings to check for available time slots. If the slot you require is not available, please send an e-mail to your respective floor administration representative listed below and include the purpose of your reservation.

Floor	Representative
2nd	Heather Greenstone
3rd	Roxanne Laddington
4th	Elissa Hunter
5th	Victor Anzelo
7th	Roxanne Laddington
8th	Jonathan Madison
9th	Ian Dexter
10th	Elissa Hunter

The representative will then follow up with you if the reservation schedule can be changed. Please do not contact any party who has already reserved the room to negotiate a scheduling change.

If the online schedule shows that your desired time is open, select the time from the drop-down menu and enter the number of attendees along with the purpose of the meeting. It is strongly suggested that reservations be made at least one week in advance as last minute reservations can be difficult to accommodate. Furthermore, please note that the large meeting rooms on the 7th and 8th floors are now available until 11 P.M. every day, including Saturday and Sunday. All others may only be reserved during regular working hours. For any questions or concerns regarding the scheduling system, contact Roxanne Laddington at extension #2968.

151. What is the main purpose of the information?

(A) To explain an office procedure to staff
(B) To clarify manager names by floor
(C) To announce meeting regulations
(D) To notify employees of room changes

152. What is NOT indicated about the floor representatives?

(A) One of them is the contact for scheduling system questions.
(B) None of them are responsible for the 6th floor.
(C) Only one of them is assigned to two floors.
(D) All of them can be contacted for room changes by floor.

153. What is suggested about the meeting rooms?

(A) They can be reserved by calling representatives directly.
(B) The hours for some of them have been extended.
(C) The ones on the 7th and 8th floors were renovated.
(D) They may be booked with the department supervisors.

GO ON TO THE NEXT PAGE

Questions 154-155 refer to the following text-message chain.

Dorothy Lee [4:15]
You're the intern in charge of booking Mr. Parker's flight to Las Vegas, right? He asked me to tell you there's been a change, and he needs to leave on June 9 and return on the 14th.

James Harter [4:18]
I haven't done it yet because I need his frequent flier number to check his points balance. I was going to ask for it earlier, but he and the other supervisors are still in a meeting.

Dorothy Lee [4:20]
I've got that information somewhere. I'm his personal assistant, so you can contact me anytime you need details like that. Let me find it.

Dorothy Lee [4:24]
It's KLJ0294SB1.

James Harter [4:25]
Got it. I'm checking now.

James Harter [4:28]
He hasn't got enough points to cover a round-trip. Should we still use them?

Dorothy Lee [4:29]
Don't bother. We can save them for a future flight.

James Harter [4:30]
OK. I'll go ahead and make the booking now.

Dorothy Lee [4:30]
Send me the confirmation by e-mail. Thanks, James.

---

154. Why was Mr. Harter unable to complete a task?

(A) He lacked some necessary information.
(B) He received two different sets of instructions.
(C) He was busy with another assignment.
(D) He misunderstood what he was supposed to do.

155. At 4:29, what does Ms. Lee mean when she writes, "Don't bother"?

(A) She wants Mr. Harter to cancel a reservation.
(B) She does not want to disturb Mr. Parker while he is busy.
(C) She prefers that Mr. Parker's flight be paid for without points.
(D) She does not think Mr. Parker will require a round-trip flight.

Capri Interiors Going Green

By Sophia Weathers

August 2—Capri Interiors' CEO Jasmine Shah revealed plans about the company's environmentally conscious future last Monday. Ms. Shah announced to crowds at the Toronto International Home Design Exposition that, starting this fall, Capri Interiors will produce furniture made entirely from domestically sourced materials. Ms. Shah stated that using local raw goods will result in a 60 percent reduction in the company's carbon emissions.

Ms. Shah also suggested at the expo that she is considering enlisting the services of Verdant Corporation to design more efficient and environmentally friendly waste management machines for Capri Interiors' production plants.

156. According to the article, what happened last week?

(A) A CEO announced a successor.
(B) A manufacturer opened new locations.
(C) A design trade show was held.
(D) A line of furniture went on sale.

157. What is Ms. Shah planning to do?

(A) Donate more money to an environmental group
(B) Import materials from countries overseas
(C) Outsource manufacturing to other companies
(D) Improve Capri's waste disposal methods

GO ON TO THE NEXT PAGE

Questions 158-160 refer to the following e-mail.

To: All Staff
From: Brendan Rogerson <b.rogerson@ellisellis.com>
Subject: Training Courses
Date: April 12

Hello all Ellis and Ellis Consulting staff,

As you know, I've been trying to find a way to improve efficiency here in the office and asked you to complete a survey providing your suggestions. — [1] —. For instance, a number of employees have expressed the desire to take more professional development classes so they can add to their skills. At the same time, I have noticed that we have had to hire graphic designers on a very regular basis. — [2] —. When it comes to very big projects, like Web site design or creating our annual report, this seems appropriate, but in many cases, we are hiring them to do an hour of work that one of our own employees could probably do with a little training. — [3] —.

Consequently, I am considering organizing a short course on basic graphic design skills for any employees who are interested. — [4] —. This would allow us to use in-house skills for smaller design projects in the future. If this sounds like something you would like to participate in, please respond to this e-mail and let me know before April 20.

Best wishes,
Brendon Rogerson
Human Resources Director, Ellis and Ellis Consulting

---

158. What is indicated about Ellis and Ellis Consulting?

(A) It provides training courses to other companies.
(B) It specializes in designing Web sites.
(C) It recently released an annual report.
(D) It has unnecessary expenditures on graphic design.

159. What does Mr. Rogerson want to do?

(A) Hire graphic designers as permanent employees
(B) Get ideas from staff about some survey questions
(C) Reduce the company's reliance on outside help
(D) Boost employees' interest in a skill-building class

160. In which of the positions marked [1], [2], [3], and [4] does the following sentence best belong?

"Going through them, a couple of trends have become very clear to me."

(A) [1]
(B) [2]
(C) [3]
(D) [4]

November 12

Cherry Valley Water District
P.O. Box 495
Cherry Valley, CA 92223

Kimberly Tompkins
47 Woodhaven Drive
Cherry Valley, CA 92223

Dear Ms. Tompkins,

This letter is to notify you that water services on Woodhaven Drive will be shut off on November 30 between the hours of 12 and 3 P.M. During this time, we will make several important repairs to the street's water pipelines.

We understand that this represents an inconvenience to local residents. We appreciate your patience as we perform the upgrades needed to provide safe, clean tap water to the Cherry Valley area.

While the tap water is shut off, residents can collect complimentary bottled water at our main office. Each resident is entitled to one free gallon of water. Please bring proof of address, such as this letter or a state-issued ID.

Our main office is located at 393 Anderson Street, Cherry Valley, CA 92223. Please call the office at 555-1311 with any questions.

Sincerely,
Candace Ludwig
Cherry Valley Director of Public Utilities

161. What is the purpose of the letter?

(A) To disclose a service interruption
(B) To warn residents about a risk
(C) To suggest alternatives for some amenities
(D) To invite residents to an event

162. The word "perform" in paragraph 2, line 2, is closest in meaning to

(A) complete
(B) entertain
(C) present
(D) function

163. What can residents receive at the Cherry Valley Water District main office?

(A) Proof of address
(B) A state-issued ID
(C) One gallon of bottled water
(D) A letter about upcoming repairs

Questions 164-167 refer to the following online chat.

Greg Fournier	9:11 A.M.	Welcome to RMP Financial Trust's live chat service. How can I help you?
Vivianne Gonyer	9:12 A.M.	I was wondering whether an account I have with your bank still works. I stopped using it when I moved overseas, but I was hoping to revive it when I return home permanently in a few weeks.
Greg Fournier	9:12 A.M.	May I have the number on your ATM card?
Vivianne Gonyer	9:13 A.M.	That's the problem. I didn't keep my ATM card because I didn't think I'd need it.
Greg Fournier	9:14 A.M.	I see. For security reasons, I need to match your name with an ATM card number. There's no other way.
Vivianne Gonyer	9:14 A.M.	I thought that might be the case. Could you tell me what your policy is regarding inactive accounts? It was a checking account, and the last time I used it must have been over two years ago.
Greg Fournier	9:15 A.M.	According to our records, you actually shut down that account.
Vivianne Gonyer	9:17 A.M.	Oh. I was hoping to send my current funds to my account before I return. Is this going to be possible?
Greg Fournier	9:18 A.M.	Well, you could use a money transfer service like PrestoDirect. There'd be a fee of about 5 percent, but you could receive the funds at any one of the company's locations, without needing to have a bank account. You can think about setting up a fresh account with us after you've arrived.

Send

164. At 9:13 A.M., what does Ms. Gonyer mean when she writes, "That's the problem"?

(A) She is unable to use an online payment system.
(B) She cannot remember her account balance.
(C) She does not have access to some information.
(D) She discovered an issue with one of her transactions.

165. What is suggested about RMP Financial Trust?

(A) It is encouraging its customers to sign up for online banking.
(B) It only accepts one method of confirming a client's identity.
(C) It runs a helpline that is open for 24 hours a day.
(D) It has established branches all over the world.

166. What does Ms. Gonyer want to do?

(A) Create an account to use overseas
(B) Open a checking account
(C) Move some money to another country
(D) Withdraw funds while abroad

167. What does Mr. Fournier advise Ms. Gonyer about?

(A) Complying with some travel restrictions
(B) Making use of a financial services provider
(C) Appointing a legal representative
(D) Avoiding a large commission fee

STRYKER AMUSEMENT PARK

October is just around the corner, and that means everyone at Stryker Amusement Park is gearing up for a month of spooky Halloween fun. Starting October 1 and continuing until October 31, we will be holding our annual Fright Nights, a series of frighteningly fun activities for visitors of all ages. Below is a schedule of some of the events we have planned.

Date	Activity	Location
October 1-31	Haunted Mansion Tour	North Pavilion
October 10-31	Evil Zombies Ride	East Pavilion
October 15-31	Corn Maze	South Parking Lot
October 25-31	Children's Zone	Food Court

Be sure to check out the following highlights:
- The Haunted Mansion Tour returns for its third run here at Stryker Amusement Park. *California Living* magazine recently ranked the mansion, which features three floors and over 100 actors, as "the third scariest haunted house on the West Coast."
- The Children's Zone features plenty of fun activities for small children, including face painting, storytelling, and pumpkin decorating.
- On October 31, the last day of Fright Nights, actor Kayla Draper from the movie *Darkness Rises* will be signing autographs in the main pavilion.
- Concession stands throughout the park will be serving our Fright Nights foods, including pumpkin spice coffee and candy apples.

Admission to Fright Nights is included with a regular ticket. For more information on these events, visit our Web site at www.strykeramusement.com/frightnights.

168. What is the notice mainly about?

(A) Renovations to a haunted house
(B) A special sale on tickets
(C) A month of festivities
(D) Amusement park admissions policies

169. Where will the pumpkin decorating take place?

(A) At the north pavilion
(B) At the east pavilion
(C) At the south parking lot
(D) At the food court

170. What is indicated about Fright Nights?

(A) It tours around the country.
(B) One of its features has been recognized by a publication.
(C) It is geared mainly towards adults.
(D) Those who attend it must pay an extra admission fee.

171. What will NOT happen during the month of October?

(A) A special screening of *Darkness Rises* will occur.
(B) Halloween-themed rides will open to the public.
(C) A parking lot will be converted into a maze.
(D) Special refreshments will be available to purchase.

Edmond Estrada Wins Albuquerque Judge's Seat

March 18—A spokesperson for the Albuquerque District Court announced that Attorney Edmond Estrada has won his bid for the judge's seat. — [1] —. He will replace current Judge Wendy Delwes, who confirmed earlier this year that she is retiring at the end of March.

In his role as an attorney for the past 25 years, Mr. Estrada has been involved in thousands of legal cases. These included both civil complaints and landlord-tenant cases. — [2] —.

"It has been my privilege to serve the citizens of Albuquerque in my capacity as a lawyer," said Estrada, "and to have witnessed the capable leadership exhibited by Judge Delwes for many years. Through her example, I have learned a great deal about how our courts work best for the people of Albuquerque. — [3] —. Indeed, I feel honored to be succeeding her."

In addition to his legal experience, Mr. Estrada is active in the local community. — [4] —. He is a member of the Rio Rancho Land Commission and has volunteered with numerous local charities.

172. What does the article mainly discuss?

(A) The process for receiving legal assistance
(B) The results of a mayoral election
(C) The selection of a candidate for a role
(D) The activities of an organization

173. Why does Mr. Estrada praise Judge Delwes?

(A) She once served as a defense lawyer in Albuquerque.
(B) She ran an effective campaign for a senate seat.
(C) She has a large amount of courtroom experience.
(D) She led an effort to change a local law.

174. What is NOT mentioned about Mr. Estrada?

(A) He represents a real estate company.
(B) He sometimes engages in unpaid work.
(C) He is frequently involved in the community.
(D) He has practiced law for over two decades.

175. In which of the positions marked [1], [2], [3], and [4] does the following sentence best belong?

"In every legal matter he has handled, he has shown a firm commitment to the pursuit of justice."

(A) [1]
(B) [2]
(C) [3]
(D) [4]

GO ON TO THE NEXT PAGE

Questions 176-180 refer to the following Web page and e-mail.

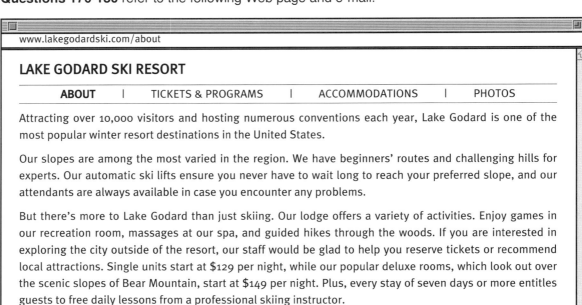

www.lakegodardski.com/about

LAKE GODARD SKI RESORT

ABOUT | TICKETS & PROGRAMS | ACCOMMODATIONS | PHOTOS

Attracting over 10,000 visitors and hosting numerous conventions each year, Lake Godard is one of the most popular winter resort destinations in the United States.

Our slopes are among the most varied in the region. We have beginners' routes and challenging hills for experts. Our automatic ski lifts ensure you never have to wait long to reach your preferred slope, and our attendants are always available in case you encounter any problems.

But there's more to Lake Godard than just skiing. Our lodge offers a variety of activities. Enjoy games in our recreation room, massages at our spa, and guided hikes through the woods. If you are interested in exploring the city outside of the resort, our staff would be glad to help you reserve tickets or recommend local attractions. Single units start at $129 per night, while our popular deluxe rooms, which look out over the scenic slopes of Bear Mountain, start at $149 per night. Plus, every stay of seven days or more entitles guests to free daily lessons from a professional skiing instructor.

If you are interested in spending your winter vacation with us, call 555-3612, or send an e-mail to booking@lakegodardski.com.

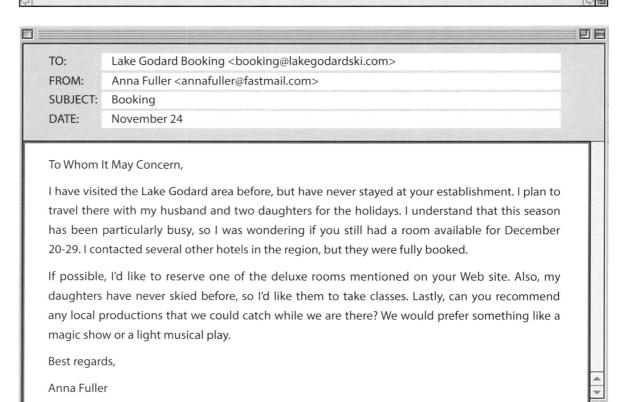

TO:	Lake Godard Booking <booking@lakegodardski.com>
FROM:	Anna Fuller <annafuller@fastmail.com>
SUBJECT:	Booking
DATE:	November 24

To Whom It May Concern,

I have visited the Lake Godard area before, but have never stayed at your establishment. I plan to travel there with my husband and two daughters for the holidays. I understand that this season has been particularly busy, so I was wondering if you still had a room available for December 20-29. I contacted several other hotels in the region, but they were fully booked.

If possible, I'd like to reserve one of the deluxe rooms mentioned on your Web site. Also, my daughters have never skied before, so I'd like them to take classes. Lastly, can you recommend any local productions that we could catch while we are there? We would prefer something like a magic show or a light musical play.

Best regards,

Anna Fuller

176. What is NOT mentioned as a service offered by Lake Godard?

(A) Tours of the nearby wilderness
(B) Transportation to the tops of slopes
(C) Activities in a game room
(D) Training for professional skiers

177. On the Web page, the word "available" in paragraph 2, line 3, is closest in meaning to

(A) for hire
(B) in reserve
(C) within reach
(D) on behalf

178. What is suggested about Ms. Fuller?

(A) She wants to change a reservation.
(B) She will cancel a booking at another hotel.
(C) She prefers accommodations with a mountain view.
(D) She would like recommendations on which slopes to ski.

179. What will Ms. Fuller's children do if her request is met?

(A) Go on a guided hike through the woods
(B) Take some days off from school
(C) Receive free lessons from an instructor
(D) Perform in a musical play

180. What does Ms. Fuller want to do?

(A) Make time to see a performance
(B) Book a room she has stayed in previously
(C) Obtain a list of local produce to try
(D) Receive a detailed skiing lesson plan by e-mail

GO ON TO THE NEXT PAGE

Questions 181-185 refer to the following e-mail and notice.

To: Angela Porter <a.porter@bigbuy.com>
From: Mason Daley <m.daley@bigbuy.com>
Subject: Managers' meeting
Date: September 21
Attachment: meeting_notes

Hi Angela,

I hope your discussion with the client went well yesterday. We missed you at the managers' meeting. To read a summary of everything we covered, please check the notes attached to this e-mail. Otherwise, the main thing you should know concerns work schedules around the upcoming holidays.

Mr. Baker wants you to compose a notice for employees to remind them of their responsibilities in this regard. Too many people were absent from work last year during this period, and he would like to make sure this doesn't happen again. He specifically mentioned planning holiday leave in advance, so that departmental supervisors can reassign work hours as needed. The final schedule will be posted on the company Intranet by November 25. This is one day before the start of our busy season, which generally lasts from November 26 to January 4. Mr. Baker added that no late requests for holiday leave will be approved, except in cases of medical or personal emergencies. The notice needs to contain all this information. Once you're done, you'll need to send it to store supervisors and have them go over it.

Let me know if you have any questions.

Thanks,
Mason
Shift Supervisor
Operations Department

BigBuy

Notice to All Employees
September 30

In preparation for the holiday shopping season, we would like to remind you to take some time to review the work schedule posted on the company Intranet. Aside from checking to make sure that you have been assigned the correct number of hours, please verify that your days off are noted on the schedule.

Please submit requests for holiday leave no later than October 30. Any requests for time off made from that date until November 25 will be approved only at the discretion of each department's supervisor who must balance employee demands with the need to have the store fully staffed.

These requests will be responded to before the final schedule is posted. Requests for holiday leave sent from November 26 to January 4 will not be granted to anyone, management included, except in the case of a personal or medical emergency. As always, documentation proving that you are eligible for an emergency leave of absence will be required in such situations.

If you have any further questions, please consult your respective departmental supervisors. Thank you for your cooperation in this matter.

181. What is one purpose of the e-mail?

(A) To modify plans for an upcoming holiday
(B) To update her on a previous request
(C) To fill her in on a recent discussion
(D) To discuss a scheduling conflict with her

182. What is stated about BigBuy?

(A) Its normal operating hours will change in the new year.
(B) It pays its employees overtime for holiday work.
(C) Its management is preparing for a restructuring.
(D) It has had issues concerning absent staff.

183. What are supervisors NOT required to do?

(A) Approve some requests for additional leave
(B) Provide training to seasonal employees
(C) Ensure there are enough workers
(D) Address inquiries from the staff

184. When can employees expect to receive confirmation of holiday leave?

(A) Between September and October
(B) No later than October 30
(C) Before November 25
(D) Between November and January

185. What did Ms. Porter most likely do at the end of September?

(A) Entrusted another employee with a duty
(B) Provided an update on her situation
(C) Sent a finished draft to some supervisors
(D) Posted an electronic notification

GO ON TO THE NEXT PAGE

Art Vibe Magazine

The remodeling of Brayman Museum of Art (BMA) has finally concluded, and the facility will reopen on Wednesday, September 26. This will be commemorated by a ceremony taking place on the front lawn of the museum, with a short speech by museum curator Jane Wellington. Ms. Wellington will talk about the progress BMA has made over its 50 years in the city of Auckland. She will also introduce the museum's new special exhibition, *France in Focus*, beginning that day, which features artifacts from Europe's ancient Gallic tribes. This traveling exhibition received terrific reviews from French publications when it first opened in Paris, and after the show at the BMA, it will go on to Sydney and then Perth. Tickets for the exhibit are $12 and may be reserved in advance at www.braymanart.org. The museum will also be offering the special admission price of $5 for children aged 10 and under instead of its regular $7 for the duration of the exhibit. Inquiries may be directed to BMA's public relations specialist, Henry Kang, at 555-1288.

Brayman Museum of Art
Confirmation of Payment

Today's Date: August 17
Guest Name: Kerry Rosales
Exhibition Description: *France in Focus*
Admission Date: September 26

Description	Amount	Unit Price	Total Price
Regular Ticket	1	$12	$12
Special Ticket	2	$5	$10
		TOTAL	$22

Payment Confirmation Number: 347792R

If you've made an advance purchase, please be sure to present this receipt to the museum official collecting tickets when entering the exhibition. Admission will be allowed daily between the hours of 8 A.M. and 3 P.M.

To: Henry Kang <h_kang@braymanart.org>
From: Jane Wellington <j_wellington@braymanart.org>
Date: September 10
Subject: Important change

Hi Henry,

I've got an urgent request. Unfortunately, I received a call this morning, and there will be a delay with the *France in Focus* exhibition. Some of the artifacts have been held up at customs. Apparently, the agents must see further documentation before they can release the items to us. We're getting the necessary paperwork, but it won't be processed in time for the show. The items should start arriving here at the museum the day after our exhibition is scheduled to open. Accordingly, the opening must be delayed by at least two weeks. I'll need you to contact those who purchased exhibition tickets in advance. Assure them that they may use the same tickets to gain admission on the new opening date but that they also have the option of getting their money back.

Let me know if you have questions.

Jane Wellington
Brayman Museum of Art, Curator

186. What is the main topic of the article?

(A) The appointment of a new curator
(B) An anniversary banquet celebrating a facility's opening
(C) A special event following a renovation
(D) The exhibition of work by a local artist

187. What is indicated about Ms. Rosales?

(A) She received a discount as she is a sponsor of the facility.
(B) She plans to accompany children to an opening exhibit.
(C) She intends to view the artifacts in the afternoon.
(D) She will pay the price of admission at the museum.

188. What are those who purchase tickets in advance asked to bring to the exhibition?

(A) Official identification
(B) Proof of purchase
(C) A discount coupon
(D) An open ticket

189. What is true about the Brayman Museum of Art?

(A) It will send artifacts to Perth immediately after the exhibit.
(B) Its curator was informed about a delay in August.
(C) Its new facility in Auckland will not be built in time for a show.
(D) It is expecting to receive some exhibit items on September 27.

190. What does Ms. Wellington ask Mr. Kang to do?

(A) Inform ticketholders of their options
(B) Send refunds to museum members
(C) Offer free admission to an exhibition
(D) Contact artists about a change of schedule

GO ON TO THE NEXT PAGE

MEMO

To: All staff
From: Tom Williams, Director
Date: August 10
Subject: New staff

As most of you are aware, Techno Tel officially bought out Regent Mobile on August 1. This is to let you know that, because of this, five staff members from Regent Mobile will be joining our offices in about a week. Three of them will be working for research and development, and the other two will be in marketing. They will start work on Monday, August 16, and will begin their training that day after fulfilling some administrative requirements. I hope that everyone will provide them with a warm welcome and answer any questions they may have so that they can adjust to their new work environment quickly.

Thank you.

From: Neil Adams <nadams@technotel.com>
To: Maude Garcia <purchasing@technotel.com>
Date: August 11
Subject: Supplies for new hires

Hi Maude,

You may have received a memo from Tom Williams in administration on August 10. In preparation for the upcoming changes, my staff and I have cubicles set up in my department that include desks, chairs, and dividers. But we are still missing a few items and I'm wondering if the purchasing department can get our regular supplier to deliver them. I want to make sure the new staff have everything they need to start working. We need to order three of each of the following: filing cabinet, personal computer, and desktop bookcase. They will also require some basic office supplies. Please let Office Interiors and Supplies know that this is a rush order. It should be delivered by August 13. The recruits start their training next week and we will need enough time to set everything up before August 16. Thanks, and sorry for the short notice.

Neil

Office Interiors and Supplies

800 Garnet Avenue
Chicago, Illinois 60615
Tel: 555-2001
E-mail: orders@officeintsup.com

Home	I	Products	I	**Your Shopping Cart**	I	Customer Service

Account holder: Techno Tel, Inc.

Your Shopping Cart

Continue Shopping

Proceed to Checkout

Search

Contact Us

ORDER #: 914579				08/12 10:45 A.M.
Product code	Description		Qty	Price
OF00928	Steel filing cabinet, gray		3	$509.97
OS1544	Ballpoint pens, black and red		6	$6.60
OF00283	Personal computers (CPU, monitor, keyboard, mouse and peripherals)		3	$1,648.50
OS1927	Notebooks		3	$15.90
OS1326	Desktop bookcase		3	$21.90
		Subtotal		$2,202.87
		Tax		$220.29
		TOTAL		$2,423.16

Refund and cancellation varies by item. Click on "Products" to learn more.
*For purchases of $3000 or more, shipping is free-of-charge.
**Delivery will be made after three days' time.

191. Why have Mr. Adams and his staff been making changes to the office?

(A) To update it with new equipment
(B) To prepare for a major project
(C) To conform to a policy change
(D) To accommodate incoming staff

192. What does Mr. Adams mention in the e-mail?

(A) A supplier has run out of some requested office furnishings.
(B) Some cubicles are missing important assembly components.
(C) Techno Tel has placed previous orders with Office Interiors and Supplies.
(D) The arriving staff members will start work on different days.

193. In what department does Mr. Adams most likely work?

(A) Research and development
(B) Purchasing
(C) Marketing
(D) Administration

194. What is inferred in the online form?

(A) Office Interiors and Supplies gave the customer a discount.
(B) Payment will be made by credit card.
(C) The filing cabinets will be delivered separately.
(D) The order is applicable for shipping charges.

195. What is implied about Office Interiors and Supplies?

(A) It will allow one of the items to be canceled within two days.
(B) It will deliver more desks and chairs to Techno Tel before August 16.
(C) It will not satisfy Mr. Adams' delivery date requirement.
(D) It will send some dividers to Techno Tel by August 14.

GO ON TO THE NEXT PAGE

Questions 196-200 refer to the following business card, e-mail, and invoice.

Neil Fitzpatrick Home Carpentry
"Adelaide's most respected carpenter"

Veteran carpenter specialising in interior carpentry, including trim and molding installation, door assembly and repairs, staircase renovations, and more.
Call or send an e-mail for a free estimate.
Phone: 5555 9743
E-mail: contact@neilfitzpatrick.au

TO: Neil Fitzpatrick <contact@neilfitzpatrick.au>
FROM: Mary-Anne Lester <maryanne.lester@webmail.com>
SUBJECT: Project
DATE: 24 October

My name is Mary-Anne Lester. I have a holiday home in Adelaide that I visit every January and February. The property has a beautiful backyard with an outdoor patio. I need a skilled carpenter to construct a wood awning to protect it from the elements. The area covered needs to be about 70 square metres. Now, given that it's already October and I'm planning on vacationing there in January, I understand that the deadline is rather tight. However, I would be willing to pay you extra if the job is finished on time. I look forward to hearing from you.

Sincerely,
Mary-Anne Lester

Neil Fitzpatrick Home Carpentry

Invoice #: 11262230
Invoice Date: 23 December
Date Beginning: 30 October
Date Ending: 22 December
Customer Name: Mary-Anne Lester
Address: 332 Fernhurst Road
Cherryville 5134
New South Wales

Description	Quantity	Total
Timber(Ironbark)	x20 posts	$860
Timber(Ash)	x4 planks	$200
Wood finish	x1 20-litre can	$25
Screws & Anchors	x40	$30
Labour	x1 worker(s), 80 total hours	$3,200
		Subtotal
		$4,315

Memo

To preserve the wood colour, a new coat of oil-based finish needs to be put on every two years. As with all of my projects, a full 5-year structural warranty is provided for any construction-related issues.

196. What is suggested about Mr. Fitzpatrick?

(A) He has been a carpenter for a decade.
(B) He runs a business based in Adelaide.
(C) He manages a company Web site.
(D) He won an award for his furniture.

197. What does Ms. Lester request for her project?

(A) A table and chairs
(B) A barbecue grill
(C) A backyard terrace
(D) An overhead cover

198. In what way does Ms. Lester's request go against Mr. Fitzpatrick's usual practice?

(A) She wants to pay him less than his usual rate.
(B) She would like him to work on a bigger property.
(C) She would like him to work on an outdoor project.
(D) She wants him to finish a job in October.

199. What can be inferred about the work at Ms. Lester's holiday home?

(A) It cost extra due to a short timeline.
(B) It delayed her planned holiday visit.
(C) It required multiple carpenters.
(D) It used more materials than expected.

200. According to the invoice, what does Neil Fitzpatrick Home Carpentry recommend?

(A) Purchasing an extended warranty
(B) Using a different type of timber
(C) Caring for a structure's appearance
(D) Replacing a damaged board

This is the end of the test. You may review Parts 5, 6, and 7 if you finish the test early.

Self 체크 리스트

TEST 08은 무사히 잘 마치셨죠?
이제 다음의 **Self** 체크 리스트를 통해 자신의 테스트 진행 내용을 점검해 볼까요?

1. 나는 75분 동안 완전히 테스트에 집중하였다.

   ☐ 예   ☐ 아니오

   아니오에 답한 경우, 이유는 무엇인가요?

2. 나는 75분 동안 100문제를 모두 풀었다.

   ☐ 예   ☐ 아니오

   아니오에 답한 경우, 이유는 무엇인가요?

3. 나는 75분 동안 답안지 표시까지 완료하였다.

   ☐ 예   ☐ 아니오

   아니오에 답한 경우, 이유는 무엇인가요?

4. 나는 Part 5와 Part 6를 19분 안에 모두 풀었다.

   ☐ 예   ☐ 아니오

   아니오에 답한 경우, 이유는 무엇인가요?

5. Part 7을 풀 때 5분 이상 걸린 지문이 없었다.

   ☐ 예   ☐ 아니오

6. 개선해야 할 점 또는 나를 위한 충고를 적어보세요.

* 교재의 첫 장으로 돌아가서 자신이 적은 목표 점수를 확인하면서 목표에 대한 의지를 다지기 바랍니다. 개선해야 할 점은 반드시 다음 테스트에
  실천해야 합니다. 그것이 가장 중요하며, 그래야만 발전할 수 있습니다.

▎TEST 09

PART 5
PART 6
PART 7
Self 체크 리스트

잠깐! 테스트 전 확인사항

1. 휴대 전화의 전원을 끄셨나요? □ 예
2. Answer Sheet, 연필, 지우개를 준비하셨나요? □ 예
3. 시계를 준비하셨나요? □ 예

모든 준비가 완료되었으면 목표 점수를 떠올린 후 테스트를 시작합니다.

문제 풀이를 마치는 시간은 지금부터 75분 후인 ___시 ___분입니다.
테스트 시간은 총 75분이며, 시험 종료 전 2~3분은 정답 검토 및 답안지 마킹을 위해 사용합니다.

READING TEST

In this section, you must demonstrate your ability to read and comprehend English. You will be given a variety of texts and asked to answer questions about these texts. This section is divided into three parts and will take 75 minutes to complete.

Do not mark the answers in your test book. Use the answer sheet that is separately provided.

PART 5

Directions: In each question, you will be asked to review a statement that is missing a word or phrase. Four answer choices will be provided for each statement. Select the best answer and mark the corresponding letter (A), (B), (C), or (D) on the answer sheet.

PART 5 권장 풀이 시간 **11분**

101. The prices in the catalog include both state and national taxes ------- not delivery charges.

(A) but
(B) neither
(C) each
(D) that

102. Cardston Corporation's fiscal records are kept in ------- boxes and are stored according to year.

(A) separate
(B) separately
(C) separates
(D) separation

103. Prior to permanently shutting down, Rebound Media thanked customers for the ------- they had shown over the years.

(A) regret
(B) support
(C) strategy
(D) comfort

104. Though hot sauce is available for free at Sam's Tacos, a portion of salsa sauce costs -------.

(A) extra
(B) less
(C) evenly
(D) also

105. Having decided to enter the Asian market, Edgeware Electronics is now seeking regional ------- for its products.

(A) distribute
(B) distributors
(C) distributive
(D) to distribute

106. ------- who wants to reserve a conference room for a meeting can simply e-mail Ms. Bloomberg in administration.

(A) Anyone
(B) Others
(C) Them
(D) Nobody

107. After ------- to build a new home in Victoria, Mr. Redmond hired an interior designer to assist him with decorating the house.

(A) decide
(B) decides
(C) decided
(D) deciding

108. First Bonneville Bank ------- 35 branches of CPG Financial Trust for $90 million, strengthening its presence in the region.

(A) explained
(B) canceled
(C) acquired
(D) committed

109. Psychologists conducted an ------- study about the negative effects of video games on young children.

(A) extent
(B) extensive
(C) extensively
(D) extend

110. Reginald Rentals ------- opened a branch in Sacramento, and after a very short time the new location became profitable.

(A) hardly
(B) recently
(C) habitually
(D) potentially

111. The city council has taken steps ------- improving air quality by introducing measures that limit factory pollution.

(A) out of
(B) toward
(C) owing to
(D) versus

112. The factory is preparing to hire ------- workers for selected manufacturing plants to meet its quarterly production goals.

(A) temporary
(B) concerned
(C) sustained
(D) instructive

113. The navigation application provides driving ------- as well as route options for walking and cycling.

(A) directly
(B) directions
(C) directors
(D) directs

114. Even experts were deceived by the forged painting, as there was barely any difference ------- it and the original.

(A) between
(B) around
(C) beside
(D) from

115. ------- ski resorts are frequently busier during peak season in the winter, they do attract hikers in the summer.

(A) Along
(B) While
(C) Once
(D) Apart

116. The organizer of the publicity convention said there is still ------- work to be done, but was not concerned about meeting the deadline.

(A) many
(B) few
(C) much
(D) a lot

117. Some of the files on Ms. Patterson's computer appear to have been ------- with a computer virus.

(A) tempered
(B) infected
(C) allocated
(D) closed

118. The executive director has asked all production supervisors to monitor the work schedule ------- in the future.

(A) most attentive
(B) attentive
(C) more attentively
(D) attention

119. Ms. Tennyson has a ------- for spotting good investments and a reputation for being bold and visionary.

(A) talent
(B) contest
(C) promise
(D) trend

GO ON TO THE NEXT PAGE

120. By the time its weeklong promotion was over, Polk Mobile ------- to sell almost its entire inventory of Kelstra smartphones.

(A) manages
(B) to manage
(C) had managed
(D) will manage

121. Mr. Jackson has ------- completed his audit of the firm's financial records, and he expects to submit his findings tomorrow.

(A) always
(B) almost
(C) enough
(D) often

122. Dr. Boyle does not generally see any patients ------- appointments, except for cases of emergency.

(A) beside
(B) without
(C) inside
(D) under

123. Turnkey's products tend to be durable, ------- items manufactured by Vania need frequent repair.

(A) than
(B) whereas
(C) because
(D) unless

124. Well attended by dozens of enthusiasts, the launch party for Fiesta Motors' newest sports car was deemed an ------- success.

(A) eligible
(B) occasional
(C) idle
(D) absolute

125. ------- the next two weeks, Star Sportswear will be conducting a customer survey on the products it offers.

(A) Near
(B) Over
(C) Since
(D) Until

126. The supervisor is skilled at managing the ------- balance between the needs of staff and those of upper management.

(A) sudden
(B) delicate
(C) lenient
(D) vague

127. Even though subscriptions to the *The Marinberg Herald*'s print edition have steadily declined, its online ------- continues to grow.

(A) definition
(B) policy
(C) readership
(D) broadcast

128. ------- the malfunctions with the Clarity Dishwasher are due to defects or low-quality materials is still being investigated.

(A) So
(B) Whether
(C) Yet
(D) Among

129. ------- those in the delivery industry had predicted, Volo-Air's new routes helped boost its quarterly earnings significantly.

(A) Instead of
(B) Up to
(C) Regardless of
(D) Just as

130. The mayor was able to ------- her plans for improving job creation through the help of local businesses.

(A) operate
(B) solidify
(C) depart
(D) prevent

PART 6

Directions: In this part, you will be asked to read four English texts. Each text is missing a word, phrase, or sentence. Select the answer choice that correctly completes the text and mark the corresponding letter (A), (B), (C), or (D) on the answer sheet.

🕐 **PART 6 권장 풀이 시간 8분**

Questions 131-134 refer to the following advertisement.

The next time you're in downtown Houston and would like a taste of Asia, visit Sensasia on the second floor of Cheviston Center. Sensasia offers authentic ------- from China, Japan, **131.** India, Thailand, Korea, and Vietnam.

-------. From Monday to Friday, enjoy handmade sushi prepared with fresh seafood, delicious **132.** Korean bibimbap, and tasty Vietnamese pho. On weekends, Hong Kong style dim sum, consisting of various bite-size portions of food, ------- along with our regular menu items. **133.** Furthermore, once a month, our chefs introduce something new for diners to try. -------, only **134.** Sensasia can give you such a wide variety of meals in one location.

For group reservations, please call 555-4272. To view our menu, please visit our Web site at www.sensasia.com.

131. (A) dishes
(B) materials
(C) components
(D) districts

132. (A) Our chefs use exotic seasonings in all of our grilled food.
(B) Some parts of our restaurant are now being refurbished.
(C) We serve a wide range of popular Asian cuisine every day.
(D) Our food is delicious but limited to seafood selections.

133. (A) prepares
(B) prepared
(C) is prepared
(D) preparing

134. (A) Conversely
(B) In short
(C) To that end
(D) Not to mention

GO ON TO THE NEXT PAGE

Questions 135-138 refer to the following e-mail.

To: Scott Douglas <sdouglas@evergladeprints.com>
From: Edward Kovac <edward.k@collinsconsulting.com>
Subject: Brochure alterations
Date: 8 May

Dear Mr. Douglas,

Please find attached a copy of the brochure you designed with our comments. Our team has

reviewed the draft, and we are ------- with the quality of the pamphlet thus far. Despite this, we
          135.

do require a few changes.

In particular, there were minor layout and color errors and some important information was

------- as well. We left notes in the brochure regarding where the omitted details should go.
136.

-------. Please send us a revised draft when it is ready. We will, of course, be happy to -------
137.   **138.**

the extra cost.

Best wishes,
Edward

---

135. (A) concerned
(B) satisfied
(C) credited
(D) troubled

136. (A) allowed
(B) asserted
(C) moving
(D) missing

137. (A) We are not sure why these details
were included.
(B) We need each correction to be
reflected precisely.
(C) We would like you to change the entire
layout.
(D) We ask that you send the invoice for
the design we chose.

138. (A) cover
(B) covered
(C) covering
(D) covers

Hartford Local

Hartford Welcomes a New Ryder's Franchise

October 12—A new Ryder's restaurant will be opening at 460 Flatbush Avenue, behind the Irving Super Center. -------. **139.** "We are just waiting for the city to issue a building permit," said owner Paul Solomon, ------- **140.** other Ryder's branch is located in Elmwood.

According to Mr. Solomon, he ------- **141.** contemplated the idea of opening a Ryder's in Hartford a few weeks after launching the Elmwood location two years ago. In fact, Mr. Solomon ------- **142.** such a high volume of customers before the Elmwood location opened for business. However, within its second week of business, that branch was already overwhelmed with orders. At that point, Mr. Solomon realized that there was sufficient demand to support a second location. After about a year of preparations, he is finally ready to expand.

139. (A) Construction will begin at the site very soon.
(B) A ceremony has been scheduled for this weekend.
(C) The business is having a sale all throughout this month.
(D) Meals at the restaurant are both delicious and affordable.

140. (A) he
(B) that
(C) whose
(D) which

141. (A) first
(B) seldom
(C) never
(D) likewise

142. (A) would not expect
(B) has not expected
(C) is not expecting
(D) had not expected

GO ON TO THE NEXT PAGE

Questions 143-146 refer to the following memo.

To: All staff
From: Susan Ward
Subject: Employee handbook
Date: April 15

Thank you to everyone who participated in the discussions with company management. Your comments about some employees being unaware of the procedures for day-to-day operations have been heard. We are now working to ------- the situation.
143.

For starters, we will be publishing the company's standard operating procedures as soon as possible. A printed guide will give management and staff an official reference on the performance of daily tasks. -------. Hopefully, it will help move us closer to our goal of having
144.
firmly ------- policies.
145.

If any revisions are required, these will be incorporated into a later version of the manual. The final version will also be ------- through the company's internal network. If you have any
146.
questions, please direct them to your departmental supervisors.

143. (A) maintain
(B) inspect
(C) address
(D) ignore

144. (A) A provisional copy of this handbook will be distributed at the next meeting.
(B) Your comments on the revised manual were very much appreciated.
(C) A copy of the article may be found in last month's company newsletter.
(D) We are glad that everyone is now up-to-date on our meeting schedule.

145. (A) establish
(B) established
(C) establishing
(D) establishment

146. (A) access
(B) accessible
(C) accesses
(D) accessing

PART 7

Directions: In this part, you will be asked to read several texts, such as advertisements, articles, instant messages, or examples of business correspondence. Each text is followed by several questions. Select the best answer and mark the corresponding letter (A), (B), (C), or (D) on your answer sheet.

PART 7 권장 풀이 시간 54분

Questions 147-148 refer to the following advertisement.

Lakewood Spa

Located in the Belmont Hotel just a 20-minute drive from downtown Portland, Lakewood Spa is the perfect place to escape for a day of relaxation. Our private treatment rooms have been carefully designed to create a soothing atmosphere. We offer a range of services, including massages, manicures, and facial treatments, all performed by our experienced therapists.

The management of Lakewood Spa is also pleased to announce that we have partnered with Décor, a renowned beauty company, to provide our clients with discounts on a variety of quality products. To celebrate, anyone who books a spa treatment in June will receive a complimentary bottle of Décor shampoo. For more information about this promotion or about our spa, please visit www.lakewoodspa. com. We hope to see you soon!

147. What is stated about Lakewood Spa?

(A) It had several private rooms redecorated recently.
(B) It will offer discounts on services to clients.
(C) It has a branch in a city's business district.
(D) It is situated in an accommodation facility.

148. What must clients do to receive a complimentary item?

(A) Purchase a product made by a beauty company
(B) Visit a branch of a spa in June
(C) Make a reservation during a designated period
(D) Complete an online questionnaire

GO ON TO THE NEXT PAGE

Tax Deductions for Telecommuters

Telecommuting employees are eligible for a number of deductions that can be applied to their income tax calculations. Those incurring home office costs related to new equipment purchases, such as computers, monitors, phones, and printers, may deduct the cost of this equipment in one of two ways. They may deduct the full cost of an item in the same year it was purchased or spread out the cost over seven years. So, for example, an item worth $70 may be fully deducted the first year or deducted by $10 each year for seven years. Employees who frequently use phones for business purposes also qualify for deductions, provided they can show documents as proof that their phones were used during office hours. Occupancy expenses, including rent, mortgage payments, and home insurance coverage, are partially tax-deductible, depending on the amount of home space used for work. For questions about this information, please contact the human resources manager for your branch of the company.

149. Where would the information most likely appear?

(A) A promotional poster
(B) An equipment manual
(C) An employee handbook
(D) An insurance policy

150. What is indicated in the information?

(A) Some expensive items require special permission to buy.
(B) Call records may be needed to subtract some charges.
(C) Expenses related to home ownership are completely tax-deductible.
(D) The cost of insuring property can be completely recovered.

Chuck Goodman   9:10 A.M.

I've been waiting at Kingston Subway Station for over 30 minutes now. I don't think I am going to be on time for my 9:30 class this morning.

Mia Jancovik   9:12 A.M.

OK, I'll see if Jodi or Victoria can cover for you. They've both taught aerobics classes before.

Chuck Goodman   9:14 A.M.

Thanks. Actually, it was just announced that train service will resume. Apparently, there was a problem with the track that has been resolved.

Mia Jancovik   9:15 A.M.

Great. When do you think you'll get here? Jodi says she can fill in for you until then, by the way.

Chuck Goodman   9:16 A.M.

Give me a few minutes. There are a lot of people waiting, so I might not get on the next train.

151. Who most likely is Mr. Goodman?

(A) A gym manager
(B) A fitness instructor
(C) A professional athlete
(D) A sports psychologist

152. At 9:16 A.M., what does Mr. Goodman mean when he writes, "Give me a few minutes"?

(A) He wants to discuss a matter with a coworker.
(B) He has not yet heard any announcements.
(C) He cannot estimate his arrival time.
(D) He is unfamiliar with a transit system.

GO ON TO THE NEXT PAGE

Questions 153-155 refer to the following announcement.

Dear participants,

Welcome to the Fifth Spatial Computing Conference (SCC). Once you have finished registering and received your name badge and program, please head downstairs to the Granville Room for coffee, tea, and a light breakfast. Today's schedule is as follows:

* **9:30 A.M.** – Welcome reception, Granville Room. Meet other participants and discuss ideas about computing trends, industry innovations, and your hopes for the conference. We ask that you please sit at the table with the number indicated on your name badge. We will seat guests from different specializations together to offer visitors a chance to interact with people working in a variety of fields.
* **11 A.M.** – Opening explanatory discussion, Gladstone Room. Join Patrizio Vincente, Michelle Bealieu, and Mark Blackwell to discuss developments in spatial computing since last year's conference.
* **12:30 P.M.** – Lunch break, Granville Room
* **1:30 P.M.** – Seminars on database technology, image processing, and mobile applications. These will be held in the Gladstone, Halifax, and Johnstone Rooms.
* **3:30 P.M.** – Seminars on location data, forest mapping, and space analysis. These will be held in the Gladstone, Halifax, and Johnstone Rooms.
* **5:30 P.M.** – SCC will conclude for the day. But for those who want to stay behind for the next hour to speak with each other and the facilitators about what they've learned, you may head to the Granville Room, where refreshments will continue to be served.

153. What is the purpose of the announcement?

(A) To provide a list of meal times
(B) To tell participants about events
(C) To inform attendees of timetable changes
(D) To propose a tentative conference schedule

154. What is NOT indicated about the welcome reception?

(A) Seating will be assigned by organizers.
(B) It will begin with an introductory speech.
(C) It will involve people from different fields.
(D) Food and beverages will be offered.

155. Which venue will be available to attendees after the seminars end?

(A) The Granville Room
(B) The Halifax Room
(C) The Johnstone Room
(D) The Gladstone Room

NOTICE

Effective September 2, the National Postal Service (NPS) will introduce a new pricing structure that better reflects the cost of serving various customer segments. The NPS consistently strives to operate as efficiently as possible. However, recent changes mandated by the government have eliminated previous subsidies, and as a result, we are required to source all of our funding from the sale of products and services. The new pricing system is therefore necessary in allowing us to continue providing essential services to our customers. Any future price adjustments will be based on national inflation.

Product	Old Price	New Price	% Increase
Domestic letter mail	$1.00	$1.20	20%
Commercial mail*	$0.70	$0.85	21%
International mail	$1.90	$2.20	16%
Metered mail**	$0.50	$0.75	50%

* Up to 30 grams by weight

** Available only by special agreement with the National Postal Service

156. What is mentioned about the National Postal Service?

(A) It raised the postage for domestic mail to $1.

(B) It recently lost government funding.

(C) It is obliged to continue offering basic services.

(D) It plans to cancel its metered mail service.

157. Why might rates be raised by the postal service in the future?

(A) To cover expenses related to an expansion

(B) To adjust for changes in inflation rate

(C) To pay for additional staff members

(D) To allow for mail heavier than 30 grams

GO ON TO THE NEXT PAGE

Questions 158-160 refer to the following e-mail.

TO: All employees <employees@xt_enterprises.com>
FROM: Audrey Hinkley <a.hinkley@xt_enterprises.com>
SUBJECT: Staffing change
DATE: February 2

Hello, everyone.

It has been my pleasure to work as the office manager here at XT-Enterprises over the past 12 years. As most of you have probably heard, I will be stepping down from my post at the end of this month. I am pleased to announce that Jennifer Harrison will be taking over my role. Many of you already know Ms. Harrison as my assistant office manager, a position she has held for four years. During this time, she has learned a lot about scheduling meetings and appointments, organizing workshops, and maintaining day-to-day office operations. The board of directors and I believe she is highly knowledgeable and qualified for the position.

I will be training Ms. Harrison during the last week of this month. During this period, Ms. Harrison will be responsible for performing my duties, but I will be present to provide her with assistance if she needs it. So, please direct any requests that would normally be handled by me to her.

Thank you all for your support and friendship during my time at this company. I am pleased with my decision to retire, but I hope to keep in touch with all of you!

Sincerely yours,

Audrey Hinkley

158. What is indicated about Ms. Hinkley?

(A) She has been working for XT-Enterprises for over a decade.
(B) She made an announcement last week.
(C) She will be on leave for 12 months.
(D) She will post a job advertisement next week.

159. What is one of Ms. Harrison's current duties?

(A) Arranging business gatherings
(B) Posting a monthly schedule
(C) Seeking potential customers
(D) Attending board meetings

160. What are employees of XT-Enterprises asked to do at the end of the month?

(A) Sign up for a workshop
(B) Send requests to Ms. Harrison
(C) Take part in a retirement party
(D) Return some company property

Questions 161-164 refer to the following online chat discussion.

Fumiko Tanaka	[2:03 P.M.]	Hello, everyone. Is everything ready for our trip tomorrow?
Connor Walsh	[2:04 P.M.]	Yes, the hotel has been confirmed. We will each receive a single room. Have we arranged transportation to get there?
Jacqueline Boulder	[2:05 P.M.]	I haven't arranged it yet, as I wanted to make sure the hotel reservations were confirmed first. I will contact the shuttle service now. Should I book transportation to the airport as well?
Fumiko Tanaka	[2:07 P.M.]	I think we should go separately to the airport. Otherwise, we'd have to meet at the office, which would take too much time.
Jacqueline Boulder	[2:08 P.M.]	That makes sense. Connor, did you tell the hotel we would need to check in early?
Connor Walsh	[2:10 P.M.]	I will call them right now. We will be landing at 10 A.M., so we all should be able to check in around 11. This will give us some time to change before we go to the meeting at 1 P.M.
Fumiko Tanaka	[2:12 P.M.]	Maybe we could have Ms. Lee come to the hotel for the lunch meeting. I heard they have a great Italian restaurant.
Jacqueline Boulder	[2:13 P.M.]	I can call her.

Send

161. What will happen tomorrow?

(A) A company retreat will take place.
(B) A conference will be organized.
(C) A business trip will commence.
(D) A team will receive some training.

162. At 2:08 P.M., what does Ms. Boulder most likely mean when she writes, "That makes sense"?

(A) She prefers to move the time of an appointment.
(B) She is pleased with a hotel's pricing.
(C) She accepts the flight arrangements.
(D) She agrees with traveling independently to an airport.

163. What is indicated about the hotel?

(A) It has not agreed to adjust a check-in time yet.
(B) It does not have an on-site dining option.
(C) It has been overbooked during high season.
(D) It is located right next to an airport.

164. By what time is the group expected to have arrived at the hotel?

(A) 10 A.M.
(B) 11 A.M.
(C) 1 P.M.
(D) 2 P.M.

GO ON TO THE NEXT PAGE

TEST 09 PART 7 **279**

Sampat Labs
Cosmetic Testing
525 Hilltop Road, New Brunswick, NJ 08901

April 14

Bethany Fulton
Little Miss Makeup
255 Greystone Avenue
Charlotte, NC 28201

Dear Ms. Fulton,

For over 30 years, Sampat Labs has helped both large and small manufacturers secure reliable test data on their cosmetic, beauty, and personal care products. Our fully equipped laboratories are staffed by experienced technicians and researchers who understand the issues that most concern consumers, researchers, and manufacturing companies like yours. — [1] —.

In addition to testing products for its effects on skin, we are able to guide you through the proper methods for mixing chemical ingredients as well as storing and transporting finished goods. — [2] —. We also test how long your products last under a variety of environmental conditions. Moreover, our access to an extensive database of test results from other providers allows us to completely avoid conducting tests on animals. — [3] —.

Please review the enclosed documentation for complete descriptions of each of our services as well as detailed information on how to submit a product sample for testing. — [4] —. To obtain estimates of specific costs and processing times, you may call me at 555-9476 or e-mail me at j.west@sampatlabs.com.

Thank you.

Sincerely,

Jacob West
Client Relations, Sampat Labs

---

165. Who most likely is Ms. Fulton?

(A) A laboratory assistant
(B) A store branch manager
(C) A client relations representative
(D) A makeup manufacturer employee

166. What is NOT indicated about Sampat Labs?

(A) It has decades of experience in the industry.
(B) It can determine how long a product will last.
(C) It will not perform tests on animals.
(D) It makes its research data available online.

167. In which of the positions marked [1], [2], [3], and [4] does the following sentence best belong?

"In this regard, you can be assured that they will be able to provide you with expert service."

(A) [1]
(B) [2]
(C) [3]
(D) [4]

Shopping for Free?

Virtual Mall is the creation of programmer Pat Gustin, who launched the free mobile game just nine months ago. To date, more than 300,000 people have downloaded the application, of which roughly 60 percent are active at any given time. Such numbers are very appealing for companies who advertise through mobile applications.

"The idea of the game is simple," says Mr. Gustin. "People rent spaces in a virtual shopping mall and select products to sell from a catalog we provide." — [1] —. He explained that if the virtual vendors are able to manage their stores correctly, they make a profit in virtual money. — [2] —.

The game offers a level of detail and customization that is appreciated by users. For instance, the customers in the game sometimes return items they bought, just as they do in real life. — [3] —.

Mr. Gustin says he is also working on another game called Virtual Farm, to which he will apply the same concepts but in an agricultural setting. — [4] —. He hopes to launch the game by early next year.

Those interested in learning more about Virtual Mall are encouraged to download the application for free. For details about Gustin's other games, go to www.virtualgamesco.com.

168. What is the main topic of the article?

(A) A new shopping center
(B) A study about online advertising
(C) A software manufacturing company
(D) A simulation game for mobile devices

169. What is NOT mentioned about Virtual Mall?

(A) It has a significant number of players.
(B) It does not charge its members for downloading.
(C) It helps to promote the products of real companies.
(D) It allows user to create multiple characters.

170. What is indicated about Mr. Gustin?

(A) He left his former job nine months ago.
(B) He profits from the sale of merchandise.
(C) He has a background in advertising.
(D) He is developing a new game.

171. In which of the positions marked [1], [2], [3], and [4] does the following sentence best belong?

"They can then use these earnings to improve their stores or purchase items from other sellers."

(A) [1]
(B) [2]
(C) [3]
(D) [4]

GO ON TO THE NEXT PAGE

Questions 172-175 refer to the following article.

Leather Store Sees Success

By Jake Lewis

August 15—Oakwood Crafts, a leather goods store owned by local artisan Judith Walker, has been attracting a lot of attention from residents and tourists alike. Although its doors first opened just three weeks ago, the shop has already become a popular destination for people looking for quality leather bags, belts, and other accessories. Ms. Walker attributes her success to the fact that all of her handcrafted items are made with the utmost care. "Leatherworking has always been a passion of mine," she said. "My grandmother taught me the basic techniques when I was young, and for the past 20 years it has been my hobby. Each product I make is an expression of my love for this craft."

Ms. Walker sold her first bag eight years ago at the Milton Summer Arts and Crafts Fair, which takes place every summer. She operated a booth at this fair for several years, developing a loyal customer base in the process. This gave her the confidence to open her own store. Six months ago, she met with a representative of the Milton Bank to arrange an advance of money, and now she is making her dream a reality. Anyone interested in visiting Oakwood Crafts is encouraged to stop by next week when all items in the store will be marked down by 10 to 20 percent as part of a special promotion. The shop is located at 14 Ferris Street, directly across from Fairway Supermarket.

172. What is the article mainly about?

(A) A newly opened retail outlet
(B) A recently expanded company
(C) A locally made product
(D) A nearly completed tourist attraction

173. The word "attributes" in paragraph 1, line 4, is closest in meaning to

(A) locates
(B) credits
(C) concedes
(D) acknowledges

174. What is stated about Ms. Walker?

(A) She relocated to Milton eight years ago.
(B) She participated in an annual event.
(C) She learned a skill at a crafts workshop.
(D) She joined a small business association.

175. According to the article, what did Ms. Walker do six months ago?

(A) She applied for a loan from a financial institution.
(B) She partnered with the owner of a local store.
(C) She organized the Milton Summer Arts and Crafts Fair.
(D) She held a promotional event at her shop.

GO ON TO THE NEXT PAGE

Questions 176-180 refer to the following e-mail and schedule.

To: Samantha Larson <s.larson@gentrydrivers.com>
From: Edwin Matthews <ematthews1965@plainsrealty.com>
Subject: April work schedule
Date: April 11

Dear Ms. Larson,

I was informed by your supervisor, Dale Blackburn, that you will be assigned to be Ms. Linda Atkins' new driver. I am Ms. Atkins' personal assistant, so I will be providing you with a regular schedule of appointments that you will be required to transport her to and from. Attached to this e-mail you will find her calendar of appointments for April. Keep in mind that you can expect changes, but I will do my best to notify you of any modifications at least 24 hours in advance.

Please read through the calendar to find details of each appointment, including the name of the person she is meeting, the time and date of the engagement, and the address or location of the meeting. Also, the individual scheduled to meet with Ms. Atkins on April 16 has yet to reply to the meeting invitation. I will notify you as soon as I know if the client is available for the appointment on that date.

Should you have any questions, please do not hesitate to reply to this e-mail.

Regards,
Edwin Matthews

Schedule For: Linda Atkins

PLAINS REALTY

From the desk of: Edwin Matthews

APRIL				
Monday	Tuesday	Wednesday	Thursday	Friday
	1	2 11 A.M. Ms. Amundsen: 32 Tucson Avenue	3	4 4 P.M. Ms. Harrow: 22-A North 33rd Street
7	8 12:30 P.M. Lunch meeting with Mr. and Mrs. Robinson, Prairie Café	9 4 P.M. Mr. Abraham, 433 Murray Street (contract signing)	10 3 P.M. Opening of Blue Star building, 285 Greenwich Street	11

14	15	16	17	18
2 P.M. Mr. Mendez: 441 Poplar Avenue		10 A.M. Mr. Choi: 907 Broadway	Leave of absence	Public holiday
21 9:30 A.M. Sales seminar (full-day), 4102 Larch Drive	22	23 9 A.M. Property inspection, 312 Poplar Avenue	24	25 7 P.M. Retirement party for Gordon, Rebecca's Grill 82 Third Street
28 1 P.M. Turn keys over to Mr. Abraham, 433 Murray Street	29 10 A.M. Annual Realtors Convention, Cole Conference Center, 12 Dodd Avenue	30		

176. Why did Mr. Matthews write the e-mail?

(A) To inquire about hiring a driving service
(B) To share ideas for a business venture
(C) To recommend a mode of transportation
(D) To inform a new employee of some job details

177. What is indicated about Mr. Matthews?

(A) He is looking to purchase a new home.
(B) He prefers traveling by car over flying.
(C) He prepares Ms. Atkins' appointment schedule.
(D) He wants to meet with Mr. Blackburn.

178. Who has not yet confirmed a meeting with Ms. Atkins?

(A) Ms. Harrow
(B) Mrs. Robinson
(C) Mr. Abraham
(D) Mr. Choi

179. On which date will Ms. Larson probably not be required to work?

(A) April 14
(B) April 16
(C) April 18
(D) April 25

180. What is NOT indicated about Ms. Atkins?

(A) She will speak at a convention.
(B) She will meet with one client twice in April.
(C) She plans to attend a retirement celebration.
(D) She plans to take a day off.

GO ON TO THE NEXT PAGE

Donnelly & Chung Publicity—Your Branding Experts!

Are you a new company having trouble increasing public awareness of your brand? Do you have a line of terrific products but don't know how to promote them? Or does your business need to change its image? Whatever your marketing problem might be, Donnelly & Chung Publicity can help! Our clients vary from local businesses, including Shasta-Clear Beverages and Deerborne Stationery, to large, international corporate customers, such as Compton Clothiers and Just-Ate Dietary Supplements.

Our experts at Donnelly & Chung can help you come up with a specific plan to promote your products or services. We offer development of advertising campaigns, corporate branding services, consumer targeting consultations, market research, and much more!

Your first consultation is completely free! One of our associates will discuss your needs and provide you with a fee estimate. Simply call 555-4951 to arrange your complimentary appointment.

July 2

Patricia Draper
Donnelly & Chung Publicity
Unit 405 C, Acres Center, 312 East 21st Avenue
Denver, CO 89110

Dear Ms. Draper,

I enjoyed our first meeting, and appreciated the opportunity to consult with someone about my branding needs. I've only just opened my business in Denver and could really use some help promoting it.

I have discussed our consultation with my business partner Walter Preston, and he remembers a promotional campaign you did for Shasta-Clear that was very successful. So, we have agreed to hire your firm to help us come up with a branding plan for our bakery. We would like to get things underway as soon as possible, so please let me know when you are free to meet with Walter and me in person. We are generally free after 11 A.M. on weekdays.

You mentioned during our meeting that your firm would require complete descriptions of all products that we sell if we decide to proceed with the branding work. I have enclosed a list of all our goods, including the ingredients they are made of. Should you require any additional information before we meet, I would be happy to supply it for you.

We look forward to working together with you and hope to hear from you soon.

Regards,

Kevin Swords
Coproprietor, PS Baked Goods

Enclosure:
Product list

181. What can Donnelly & Chung offer assistance with?

(A) Setting up a new business
(B) Designing entertaining Web sites
(C) Promoting a corporate brand
(D) Supplying event-related services

182. What is suggested about Mr. Swords?

(A) He has worked with Ms. Draper on previous projects.
(B) He was not charged a fee for his session with Ms. Draper.
(C) He plans to open additional bakery branches.
(D) He has a supply partnership with Just-Ate.

183. Who is Mr. Preston?

(A) An advertising consultant
(B) A co-owner of PS Baked Goods
(C) An ingredients supplier
(D) A Shasta-Clear executive

184. What does Mr. Swords want Ms. Draper to do?

(A) Print out a list of produce
(B) Schedule a complimentary consultation
(C) Write a promotional proposal
(D) Confirm her availability for a meeting

185. What is enclosed with the letter?

(A) Descriptions of items for sale
(B) Details about an upcoming product line
(C) Signed business contracts
(D) A completed questionnaire

GO ON TO THE NEXT PAGE

Questions 186-190 refer to the following advertisement, Web page, and e-mail.

Piedmont Limousine Company: Ride in Style!

Serving Manhattan for more than 20 years, Piedmont Limousine Company continues to provide the very best in rental vehicles as well as the most experienced and professional drivers. Whether you need a stretch limousine that can seat up to 12 passengers, a luxury minivan that holds eight, or a regular-sized sedan with a capacity of four, Piedmont Limousine can help! We provide clean and modern vehicles for any occasion, including business functions and weddings. We can even pick up important visitors from stations or airports and offer weekly or daily rental rates for those requiring the full-time services of a driver and vehicle. If you make a booking in April, you'll receive a $50 voucher that can be applied to any of our services!

For more information on our rates, location, hours of operation, and the types of vehicles we have available, visit us online at www.piedmontlimousine.com.

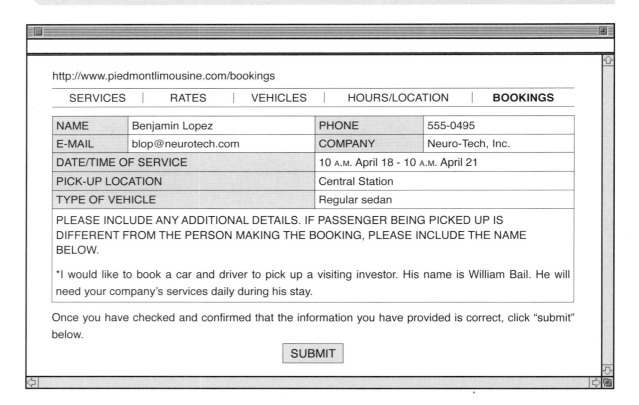

http://www.piedmontlimousine.com/bookings

| SERVICES | RATES | VEHICLES | HOURS/LOCATION | **BOOKINGS** |

NAME	Benjamin Lopez	PHONE	555-0495
E-MAIL	blop@neurotech.com	COMPANY	Neuro-Tech, Inc.
DATE/TIME OF SERVICE		10 A.M. April 18 - 10 A.M. April 21	
PICK-UP LOCATION		Central Station	
TYPE OF VEHICLE		Regular sedan	

PLEASE INCLUDE ANY ADDITIONAL DETAILS. IF PASSENGER BEING PICKED UP IS DIFFERENT FROM THE PERSON MAKING THE BOOKING, PLEASE INCLUDE THE NAME BELOW.

*I would like to book a car and driver to pick up a visiting investor. His name is William Bail. He will need your company's services daily during his stay.

Once you have checked and confirmed that the information you have provided is correct, click "submit" below.

SUBMIT

TO: Benjamin Lopez <blop@neurotech.com>
FROM: Fatima Khan <fkhan@piedmontlimousine.com>
DATE: April 6
SUBJECT: Re: Booking inquiry

Dear Mr. Lopez,

Thank you for considering Piedmont Limousine Company! We do have drivers and the type of vehicle you want for the dates and times you requested. Below is the fee breakdown.

Car Rental	$180.00
Driver Services*	$340.00
SUBTOTAL	$520.00
TAX	$52.00
DEPOSIT	$50.00
TOTAL	$622.00

*Driver will be at your disposal from 8 A.M. until 8 P.M. for daily service.

If you accept the fees, please reply to this e-mail to confirm your booking. Cancellations are allowed up to 24 hours prior to the service, but deposits will be forfeited under all circumstances. Customers canceling less than a full day in advance will not be refunded.

We also request that you provide us with the train information for your arriving guest. That way our driver, Solomon Nyongo, can be waiting for him with a sign at the platform.

Thank you, and I hope to hear from you soon.

Fatima Khan

186. What is NOT mentioned about Piedmont Limousine Company?

(A) It offers vehicles for up to 12 people.
(B) It provides services for different types of events.
(C) It has remained in business for over two decades.
(D) It has service desks at airports and train stations.

187. What will Mr. Lopez be given?

(A) A vehicle upgrade
(B) A complete refund
(C) A service coupon
(D) A train ticket

188. What is true about Mr. Lopez?

(A) He is planning to borrow money from a bank.
(B) He is using a discount coupon for a service.
(C) He is making a booking for a guest.
(D) He is meeting a visitor at Central Station.

189. What happens if a booking is canceled one day before a rental date?

(A) Customers can receive a voucher.
(B) A deposit payment must be given up.
(C) The total amount is charged to a credit card.
(D) A cancellation fee must be paid.

190. What is true about Mr. Nyongo?

(A) He will wait for William Bail on a station platform.
(B) He will drive a stretch limousine on April 18.
(C) He will meet some investors at Neuro-Tech.
(D) He will provide a passenger with a billing statement.

GO ON TO THE NEXT PAGE

Wyein Multimedia's New Office

Now that our merger is finalised, Wyein Multimedia will be combining its offices with Orio Telecom to better facilitate interdepartmental communication. In order to accommodate the increased number of employees, staff from both companies will be moving from their current offices to a single, larger location. The new building is located at 175 Duric Street, which is about a three-minute walk from Caruso Station. The move is scheduled to take place on 2 April. More details will be provided by the HR department this afternoon.

To: All Wyein Multimedia employees
From: Gerard Franco, HR manager
Date: 14 March
Subject: ID badges and parking

Hi everyone,

We will be updating company ID badges ahead of our move to Duric Street. Therefore, I've arranged for a photographer to take everyone's picture. Four departments will be photographed next Monday, 19 March, in the third-floor conference room, with others having their photos taken in the days that follow. The schedule for the departments being processed on Monday will be as follows:

Design: 9:00 A.M. – 10:00 A.M.
Sales and Marketing: 10:00 A.M. – 11:00 A.M.
Public Relations: 11:00 A.M. – 12:00 P.M.
Research: 1:00 P.M. – 2:00 P.M.

As for parking, our new building does not have spaces of its own, but there is a large car park nearby. The company is willing to rent a space for you there and withdraw the fee from your paycheck, as we do now. Please note that due to Duric Street's downtown location, car park costs are somewhat higher than they are here. You will therefore be charged £110 per month instead of the £95 you are currently paying. Please send me an e-mail by the end of the day on Friday if you have any questions or do not require a parking spot.

To: Gerard Franco <gfranco@wyeinmultimedia.com>
From: Theresa Weissert <tweissert@wyeinmultimedia.com>
Date: 16 March
Subject: ID badges and parking

Dear Mr. Franco,

I just wanted to inform you that I will no longer require a parking spot once we move to Duric Street. I live just a block from there, so it won't be necessary.

Also, I am not going to be in the office during my department's designated time to see the photographer because I have the afternoon off next Monday. Would it be OK if I joined another department's session? Please let me know.

Thank you.

Theresa Weissert

191. What will happen on April 2?

(A) Staff photographs will be taken.
(B) ID badges will be distributed.
(C) Managers will announce a merger.
(D) Two companies will relocate.

192. What information does Mr. Franco NOT provide?

(A) The cost of staff parking spots
(B) The deadline for questions
(C) The name of a photographer
(D) The date of some photo sessions

193. What can be inferred about Wyein Multimedia?

(A) It is not located in the city center.
(B) It will renovate its conference room.
(C) It is situated near public transport.
(D) It recently reduced the size of its staff.

194. What is indicated about Caruso Station?

(A) It is connected to Wyein Multimedia's headquarters.
(B) It has just reopened after an expansion project.
(C) It is within walking distance of Ms. Weissert's home.
(D) It newly increased its car park rates.

195. Which department is Ms. Weissert in?

(A) Design
(B) Sales and Marketing
(C) Public Relations
(D) Research

GO ON TO THE NEXT PAGE

LOCAL UPDATE

Until recently, the restaurants in Carpenter's Hollow could be divided into two groups: fast food chains and American-style diners. Now, however, a new Chinese restaurant, Taste of Hunan, has opened on the corner of Market and 14th Streets. It advertises "delicious Chinese dishes, prepared using family recipes." The owners, James and Nancy Chu, recently moved from New York to join their relatives in our town.

Although it only opened its doors two weeks ago, Taste of Hunan has already received a significant number of customers and garnered 50 reviews(almost all of them positive) on its Web site. One particular attraction for reviewers is the restaurant's daily $15 specials, ranging from shrimp fried rice on Mondays to Moo Shu pork on Fridays. Another major draw is the ambience of the restaurant. The interior is adorned with traditional lanterns and landscape paintings, while the dining room overlooks a garden. This creates a beautiful and relaxing environment.

TO: Alan Blake <a.blake231@webmail.com>
FROM: Food Web Online Orders <orders@foodweb.com>
SUBJECT: Order #123198
DATE: May 28

Dear Mr. Blake,

Taste of Hunan has received your order of sweet and sour chicken and Moo Shu pork. The order should be ready for pickup between 6:25 and 6:35 P.M.

Food Web now offers the Food Rewards program. To start earning points that can be used for future discounts, free orders, and more, sign up today at www.foodweb.com/foodrewards.

Method: Credit card
Order number: 123198

1 Moo Shu Pork: $15.00
1 Sweet and Sour Chicken: $19.99

Subtotal: $34.99
Tax: $2.10
Total: $37.09

Do you have any questions or concerns about your order? Please contact us by clicking <u>LINK</u>.

Sincerely,

Food Web Online Orders

CARPENTER'S HOLLOW > RESTAURANTS > TASTE OF HUNAN

Rating: 4/5 stars

Reviewer: Alan Blake

Taste of Hunan is definitely the best thing to happen to Carpenter's Hollow in a long time. Our town has been in desperate need of a Chinese restaurant, and Taste of Hunan has finally met that demand. Overall, I have little to complain about with regards to their food. They cook what may seem like typical American Chinese cuisine, but each dish has an unconventional twist. For example, their sweet and sour chicken is delicious but quite different from what readers might expect, featuring a surprisingly spicy kick. Personally, I welcome the new recipes. My one complaint is that sometimes they are unable to handle large crowds. On May 28 at 6:35 I got to their restaurant and there were at least six people at the front desk. They didn't have my food ready until 15 minutes later.

196. What is the main purpose of the article?

(A) To review a new menu item
(B) To profile Mr. and Ms. Chu
(C) To report on a new business
(D) To discuss American Chinese cuisine

197. According to the article, what do customers like about Taste of Hunan?

(A) The service
(B) The atmosphere
(C) The recipes
(D) The samples

198. What can be inferred about Mr. Blake's order?

(A) It was delivered to his house.
(B) It was eaten in the restaurant.
(C) It was paid for using a coupon.
(D) It was placed on a Friday.

199. What does Mr. Blake say about Taste of Hunan?

(A) It prepares its food in unusual ways.
(B) It often attracts large crowds for lunch.
(C) He prefers it to other Chinese restaurants.
(D) He has eaten there multiple times.

200. What information in the e-mail was inaccurate?

(A) The payment method
(B) The pickup time
(C) The items ordered
(D) The cost of the food

This is the end of the test. You may review Parts 5, 6, and 7 if you finish the test early.

정답 p.328 / 점수 환산표 p.329 / 해석 p.394 / Part 5&6 무료 해설 바로 보기(정답 및 정답 음성 포함)

* 다음 페이지에 있는 Self 체크 리스트를 통해 자신의 문제 풀이 방식과 태도를 점검해 보세요.

Self 체크 리스트

TEST 09는 무사히 잘 마치셨죠?
이제 다음의 Self 체크 리스트를 통해 자신의 테스트 진행 내용을 점검해 볼까요?

1. 나는 75분 동안 완전히 테스트에 집중하였다.

   ☐ 예　　☐ 아니오

   아니오에 답한 경우, 이유는 무엇인가요?

2. 나는 75분 동안 100문제를 모두 풀었다.

   ☐ 예　　☐ 아니오

   아니오에 답한 경우, 이유는 무엇인가요?

3. 나는 75분 동안 답안지 표시까지 완료하였다.

   ☐ 예　　☐ 아니오

   아니오에 답한 경우, 이유는 무엇인가요?

4. 나는 Part 5와 Part 6를 19분 안에 모두 풀었다.

   ☐ 예　　☐ 아니오

   아니오에 답한 경우, 이유는 무엇인가요?

5. Part 7을 풀 때 5분 이상 걸린 지문이 없었다.

   ☐ 예　　☐ 아니오

6. 개선해야 할 점 또는 나를 위한 충고를 적어보세요.

* 교재의 첫 장으로 돌아가서 자신이 적은 목표 점수를 확인하면서 목표에 대한 의지를 다지기 바랍니다. 개선해야 할 점은 반드시 다음 테스트에
  실천해야 합니다. 그것이 가장 중요하며, 그래야만 발전할 수 있습니다.

▌TEST 10

잠깐! 테스트 전 확인사항
1. 휴대 전화의 전원을 끄셨나요? □ 예
2. Answer Sheet, 연필, 지우개를 준비하셨나요? □ 예
3. 시계를 준비하셨나요? □ 예
모든 준비가 완료되었으면 목표 점수를 떠올린 후 테스트를 시작합니다.

문제 풀이를 마치는 시간은 지금부터 75분 후인 ___시 ___분입니다.
테스트 시간은 총 75분이며, 시험 종료 전 2~3분은 정답 검토 및 답안지 마킹을 위해 사용합니다.

READING TEST

In this section, you must demonstrate your ability to read and comprehend English. You will be given a variety of texts and asked to answer questions about these texts. This section is divided into three parts and will take 75 minutes to complete.

Do not mark the answers in your test book. Use the answer sheet that is separately provided.

PART 5

Directions: In each question, you will be asked to review a statement that is missing a word or phrase. Four answer choices will be provided for each statement. Select the best answer and mark the corresponding letter (A), (B), (C), or (D) on the answer sheet.

🕐 PART 5 권장 풀이 시간 **11분**

101. High-end goods sold at Barton Jewelry are rarely offered at a discount, although a few items are ------- marked down for clearance.

(A) occasionally
(B) externally
(C) previously
(D) initially

102. ------- tests must be done on all medications before they are offered for use by the general public.

(A) Rigorous
(B) Rigorousness
(C) Rigor
(D) Rigorously

103. After Jennifer Barnes ------- completed her commercial driver's license application, she was able to drive a delivery truck.

(A) successful
(B) succeeded
(C) succeeding
(D) successfully

104. Magnum Airlines began expanding its service five years ago and now ------- several daily flights throughout Eastern Europe.

(A) categorizes
(B) operates
(C) imparts
(D) multiplies

105. The train for Somerville ------- on schedule tomorrow even though bad weather is expected.

(A) left
(B) leaving
(C) will leave
(D) has left

106. Employees may not use the hotel's main entrance and must pass ------- a side door located near the back of the building.

(A) over
(B) to
(C) of
(D) through

107. The new workers had required constant ------- until they had learned how to perform their basic duties.

(A) supervises
(B) supervisory
(C) supervisor
(D) supervision

108. According to a report on work practices, people today spend ------- hours at the office than they ever did before.

(A) longest
(B) length
(C) longer
(D) lengthen

109. Pacific Cable News did not proceed with acquiring a rival network when its shareholders expressed ------- to the plan.

(A) oppose
(B) opposed
(C) opposingly
(D) opposition

110. The employee handbook states the human resources director is ------- for reviewing job applications.

(A) reasonable
(B) genuine
(C) responsible
(D) applicable

111. Visitors to Vedan Mountain are attracted by its remote location, which is ------- 25 miles away from the nearest city.

(A) approximate
(B) approximating
(C) approximation
(D) approximately

112. Additional doctors will be assigned to the Operham medical ------- next month to help run a new rehabilitation wing.

(A) territory
(B) facility
(C) exercise
(D) discussion

113. Since the cost of materials in Malaysia is relatively -------, Ms. Amarna decided to establish her factory there.

(A) affordable
(B) logical
(C) potential
(D) induced

114. The central terminal's current ticketing counters will ------- be replaced by automatic machines.

(A) gradually
(B) comparatively
(C) tragically
(D) expectantly

115. Freidrich Clinic keeps all medical details completely ------- and does not release records to any third party without prior consent.

(A) confident
(B) confidentially
(C) confidentiality
(D) confidential

116. There was ------- any merchandise left at the end of Vanita Apparel's popular annual coat sale this year.

(A) loosely
(B) hardly
(C) mostly
(D) extremely

117. Until ------- have test-driven the ARC 6000, it is hard to appreciate how driver-friendly the vehicle is.

(A) your
(B) you
(C) yours
(D) yourself

118. Hooper Incorporated is ------- its internal management structure in order to improve communication among departments.

(A) recalling
(B) representing
(C) reorganizing
(D) returning

119. The editor of *Inkdrop* Magazine contacted this month's writers to have them ------- a picture and a short biography.

(A) to submit
(B) submitting
(C) submit
(D) submitted

GO ON TO THE NEXT PAGE

해커스 토익 실전 1000제 2 Reading

120. Worker evaluation forms should be sent to Ann James in the personnel department ------- the week.

(A) just as
(B) within
(C) now that
(D) between

121. Students may make a ------- for a transfer to a different department but must provide the dean with a valid reason.

(A) distinction
(B) request
(C) formation
(D) concern

122. Starting next month, Alouette's chief accountant ------- all requests for cash expenditures of $1,000 or more.

(A) approved
(B) has approved
(C) has to approve
(D) will be approved

123. Bedford Airlines and the Concord Hotel chain have a partnership with ------- and sell holiday packages to a variety of global destinations.

(A) no
(B) each other
(C) other
(D) even

124. Management may offer permanent positions to some of the employees ------- as temporary staff on the last project.

(A) hire
(B) hires
(C) hired
(D) hiring

125. A Braun Co. spokesperson announced that the company is ------- of schedule in terms of reorganizing its structure.

(A) earlier
(B) near
(C) close
(D) ahead

126. Envelopes must be properly sealed ------- dropping them into the mailbox, as the post office is not accountable for lost documents.

(A) among
(B) before
(C) beside
(D) while

127. Speed-Ex Electronics was asked to make certain that all equipment for the new branch ------- by the end of June.

(A) will deliver
(B) is delivered
(C) delivering
(D) deliver

128. To raise ------- about environmental issues, the organization started an anti-plastic campaign.

(A) concerns
(B) awareness
(C) foundations
(D) promise

129. The city has plans to ------- local parks by planting more trees and flowers to make the areas look nicer.

(A) certify
(B) officiate
(C) revitalize
(D) aggregate

130. The CEO of Ledge Enterprises is expected to ------- the problems with the company's production facility during the press conference.

(A) break off
(B) try out
(C) bring up
(D) go for

PART 6

Directions: In this part, you will be asked to read four English texts. Each text is missing a word, phrase, or sentence. Select the answer choice that correctly completes the text and mark the corresponding letter (A), (B), (C), or (D) on the answer sheet.

⏱ **PART 6 권장 풀이 시간** 8분

Questions 131-134 refer to the following memo.

To: All advertising staff
From: Lance Cavanaugh, Project Manager
Subject: Reminder
Date: February 7

A number of you contacted me this morning to say that it will be impossible to meet your

------- this week. It seems that much of the work that is due has to be redone because the
131.

server malfunction last week resulted in irretrievable data -------.
132.

I would like to take this opportunity to remind everyone to back up important files regularly.

There are various ways to do this. -------, you can transfer files to a portable hard drive or use
133.

the company's online data-storage service.-------. Thanks.
134.

131. (A) requirements
(B) standards
(C) demands
(D) deadlines

132. (A) loss
(B) lost
(C) lose
(D) loses

133. (A) On the other hand
(B) In that case
(C) In addition
(D) For instance

134. (A) You must enter your password to access a protected computer file.
(B) These options were available for a limited period of time.
(C) Deleted data can be easily restored by a computer technician.
(D) Please do this at least once a week to avoid any future problems.

GO ON TO THE NEXT PAGE

Questions 135-138 refer to the following e-mail.

To: Denise Brooks <dbrooks@atland.com>
From: Nelson Lee <nlee@atland.com>
Subject: Acton
Date: January 18

Hello Denise,

As you know, I have an appointment with a potential client from Acton, the firm interested in purchasing our computer components on a regular basis. Since the meeting will take place in a few days, I have been hard at work trying to finalize a sales -------.
135.

However, I seem to have misplaced the copy that I printed out. Although I have the file on my hard drive, the printed one is especially important because I wrote some notes on it. -------.
136.

Could you please check whether the draft was filed away by mistake? ------- I can get that
137.

particular copy back, I'll have to go over the one I have and make notes again. It's essential that we secure the Acton as a -------, so I would really appreciate it if you could locate the
138.

missing document for me. Thank you.

Nelson Lee

135. (A) propose
(B) proposed
(C) proposal
(D) propositional

136. (A) Please make sure that the final draft is sent to the client immediately.
(B) Acton's order must be shipped out first thing in the morning.
(C) They are unwilling to agree to the deal unless we revise it.
(D) I haven't had the time to add these notes into the electronic file.

137. (A) Though
(B) Whoever
(C) Whether
(D) Unless

138. (A) developer
(B) vendor
(C) supplier
(D) customer

NOTICE TO EMPLOYEES

Effective August 10, employees who need time off for a religious or cultural observance may request a ------- change to their work schedule. -------.
139.   **140.**

Managers are instructed to accommodate such requests as long as it is ------- to do so. On **141.** occasion, work obligations must take priority. A request may also be denied if notice is provided on short notice. Employees should submit their requests at least two weeks in advance. -------, this requirement may be waived if the schedule change will not affect any **142.** ongoing projects.

139. (A) renowned
(B) separated
(C) similar
(D) brief

140. (A) Office hours are 9 A.M. to 6 P.M., Monday to Friday.
(B) Additional benefits are earned upon achieving permanent status.
(C) This option is provided as an alternative to using one's vacation days.
(D) They must notify a manager when work assignments are completed.

141. (A) mutual
(B) feasible
(C) legal
(D) profitable

142. (A) Rather
(B) Hence
(C) Likewise
(D) Nevertheless

GO ON TO THE NEXT PAGE

Questions 143-146 refer to the following advertisement.

Seattle New Light Nursing Home

We're Here to Help

Many elderly people find themselves in nursing homes far from city life and at a considerable ------- from family and friends. This is not the case at Seattle New Light Nursing Home.
143.

The physical and mental health of seniors is our number one priority. We therefore help residents to ------- a healthy degree of social interaction by keeping them occupied with a
144.
variety of stimulating activities each day including exercise classes, games, and musical performances. -------. Furthermore, because public transportation, community centers, and
145.
parks are all easily accessible from our location, residents are free to pursue their interests while also benefiting from the daily ------- and attention our staff provide.
146.

Call us at 206-665-8924 to reserve a time to tour our facilities.

143. (A) distance
(B) distant
(C) distancing
(D) distantly

144. (A) recommend
(B) maintain
(C) require
(D) evaluate

145. (A) These go a long way toward improving their quality of life.
(B) Our center is located far from the hectic urban landscape.
(C) Families may also consider alternative types of physical therapy.
(D) Some of our patients are not permitted to leave the facility.

146. (A) burden
(B) influence
(C) care
(D) caution

PART 7

Directions: In this part, you will be asked to read several texts, such as advertisements, articles, instant messages, or examples of business correspondence. Each text is followed by several questions. Select the best answer and mark the corresponding letter (A), (B), (C), or (D) on your answer sheet.

⏱ **PART 7 권장 풀이 시간** **54분**

Questions 147-148 refer to the following e-mail.

To: Frederick Montaigne <Fredm@burgundycapital.com>
From: Gina Herald <ginah6482@errmail.net>
Date: February 3
Subject: Security code

Dear Mr. Montaigne,

I cannot thank you enough for assisting me with my checking account yesterday at the Harvard Street branch of Burgundy Capital. I followed the instructions you provided me with on how to set up online banking services, and everything has gone well in that regard.

Unfortunately, I seem to be having an issue when I click on certain services for account transfers. When attempting to conduct transfers between my Burgundy Capital account and another account I hold outside of the bank, I receive a message asking me to enter my six-digit security pass number. However, I do not remember setting up such a code when we spoke yesterday. If you could please advise me as to how I can go about retrieving this code, I would appreciate your assistance greatly.

Gina Herald

147. What is the purpose of the e-mail?

(A) To ask how to set up a new account
(B) To explain a problem with an online service
(C) To request a transfer of funds
(D) To report the possibility of a security threat

148. What does Ms. Herald require from Burgundy Capital?

(A) A security code
(B) A banking card
(C) An account statement
(D) A balance confirmation

GO ON TO THE NEXT PAGE

Questions 149-150 refer to the following text-message chain.

Mitchell Roach [11:26 A.M.]

Hi, Jillian, are you free for lunch this week? I'd like to get your opinion on a new case I've been assigned.

Mitchell Roach [11:27 A.M.]

I understand you were the lead counsel when Brighton Industrials got into a patent dispute with Grant Industries. Ms. Baird has asked me to handle their latest case against Cromwell Holdings.

Jillian Barrera [11:32 A.M.]

Hi, Mitchell. Sorry to keep you waiting. I just finished a meeting with Astoria Enterprises. How does Thursday morning sound? I'm afraid I'm quite busy this week.

Mitchell Roach [11:33 A.M.]

I can meet on Thursday. We could meet for coffee or at the office whenever you're free.

Jillian Barrera [11:33 A.M.]

Why don't you come by my office at 8:30 A.M. for coffee?

Mitchell Roach [11:34 A.M.]

Sounds like a plan. I really appreciate you taking the time to do this.

Jillian Barrera [11:36 A.M.]

I'm happy to help. I'm fairly familiar with Brighton now, so I may have some good suggestions for you.

149. Which company has Mr. Roach been asked to represent?

(A) Grant Industries
(B) Brighton Industrials
(C) Cromwell Holdings
(D) Astoria Enterprises

150. At 11:34 A.M., what does Mr. Roach mean when he writes, "Sounds like a plan"?

(A) A lunchtime meeting fits into his schedule.
(B) A case can be dealt with right away.
(C) An appointment for Thursday morning is suitable.
(D) A client can drop by his office anytime in the morning.

Northeast Internet Marketers Association (NEIMA)
The Future of Internet Marketing Conference
Northeast University School of Business

Day 1: April 23

9-10 A.M.	Hawthorne Room, First Floor Registration and collection of name badges
10-11:30 A.M.	Opening Panel Discussion, Johnstone Auditorium, First Floor Important upcoming trends in Internet marketing, with time for questions Featuring James Burke (NEIMA), Andrea Harrison from Brand Solutions Limited, and Professor Ming Chao of Northeast University
11:30 A.M. -12:30 P.M.	Workshop, Washington Room, Third Floor "How To Measure Impact," with Simon Gleason from Gleason Search Analytics
12:30-1:30 P.M.	Lunch There is a cafeteria located in the Student Union building, which will be open for the event.
1:30-3:00 P.M.	Workshop, Dawson Room, Second Floor "How Interns Can Become Invaluable: What To Look For In Student Placements," with Padma Singh from Northeast University Careers Office
3:00-4:30 P.M.	Closing Panel Session, Johnstone Auditorium, First Floor NEIMA's Gwen Carter recaps lessons learned from the day's workshops. Audience members will also be asked to submit topics they would like to discuss in tomorrow's interactive sessions.

151. Which scheduled speaker will discuss student interns?

(A) Simon Gleason
(B) Ming Chao
(C) Gwen Carter
(D) Padma Singh

152. What is suggested about the conference?

(A) It includes a social event in the evening.
(B) It continues for a second day.
(C) It is held in the Student Union building.
(D) Its activities take place on four different floors.

MEMORANDUM

TO: All staff

We have come to the end of another successful year and would like to thank all our staff members for their hard work. As usual, we are organizing a special holiday evening for you all. This year, it will be held at the Cranfield Hotel on Lakeview Avenue on Dec. 22 at 7:00 P.M. Staff are free to bring their significant others.

Reservations need to be made in advance, so please contact Lionel Grimm of the personnel department at ligrimm@austel.com and let him know if you are coming and if you plan to bring a guest.

Thank you!

153. What is the memo mainly about?

(A) Work schedules for the upcoming year
(B) Taking time off for the holidays
(C) An annual company gathering
(D) Completing a project as planned

154. What are staff members asked to do?

(A) Come to a client meeting
(B) Send an e-mail to a colleague
(C) Inform the company of vacation plans
(D) Confirm a room reservation

To: Sara Brunelli <sarahb1971@easymail.ca>

From: Mitchell Harcourt <harcourt@tuton.org>

Date: January 17

Subject: Re: Tutoring

Dear Ms. Brunelli,

We recently received your e-mail regarding tutoring for your son, Jason, and would like to give you some more details about the services we offer. We currently have two history tutors available. Michael Pearson has a bachelor's degree in history from Calgary City University and is available to tutor your son either at our office in downtown Edmonton or at your home. We also have a tutor named Francine Gatineau who graduated with a master's degree in ancient history from the University of Eastern Canada. However, Ms. Gatineau only works from our office.

In the meantime, I would like to ask for a couple of extra details that you did not mention originally. For how long are you expecting Jason to need tutoring, and what school grade is he currently in? These details will help us to prepare an appropriate program that meets Jason's intellectual needs. After we have this information, we can discuss payment methods.

I look forward to hearing from you, and please do not hesitate to contact me again if you have any questions.

Yours truly,

Mitchell Harcourt
Tuton Educational Services

155. What can be inferred about Ms. Brunelli?

(A) She met with Mr. Harcourt.
(B) Her son attends a school in downtown Calgary.
(C) She contacted several tutoring companies.
(D) Her son requires assistance with studying history.

156. Where do Ms. Gatineau's tutoring sessions take place?

(A) In the student's house
(B) In an office in downtown Edmonton
(C) At the student's school
(D) At the University of Eastern Canada

157. What will Mr. Harcourt be discussing in the future?

(A) Grading systems
(B) Class schedules
(C) Tuition payment
(D) Test scores

GO ON TO THE NEXT PAGE

TEST | 01 | 02 | 03 | 04 | 05 | 06 | 07 | 08 | 09 | 10

해커스 토익 실전 1000제 2 Reading

Web-Vision: Find out what everyone else is talking about!

The future of television programming is already here! With a Web-Vision membership, you get unlimited access to thousands of television episodes. What's more, you'll be able to watch our ever-popular original content, with more than 30 different series and 24 different movies to choose from. And check out our library of movies from every genre; we have 2,200 titles to browse. All of this is available at the click of a button.

As a member, you'll get to watch our most popular television series, *Apollo Titans*. This award-winning show has three seasons available for viewing now. And our fourth season will begin on 9 September.

With memberships starting at as little as £10 per month, why spend more on cable television? Switch to Web-Vision to watch your favourite shows and movies whenever you want, without so many distracting commercials. Visit www.web-vision.com and sign up today!

158. The word "browse" in paragraph 1, line 4, is closest in meaning to

(A) shop
(B) skip
(C) observe
(D) examine

159. Why is *Apollo Titans* mentioned?

(A) To announce a change in content
(B) To emphasize a membership benefit
(C) To reveal the programming schedule
(D) To provide an example of available movies

160. What is suggested about cable television?

(A) It costs less per month.
(B) It has a larger variety of shows.
(C) It has more advertising content.
(D) It offers fewer original movies.

NOTICE

This is a notice to everyone at GlobalFerm that the cafeteria on the sixth floor of the Superion Building will be inaccessible to employees effective May 27. — [1] —. We are pleased to inform all staff, however, that the cafeteria will be renovated and converted into a Servex Modern dining establishment with an array of new food offerings. It is our hope that this cafeteria makeover will reflect the suggestions indicated in our recent survey. — [2] —. Therefore, vegetarian, vegan, and gluten-free items will also be available daily for those with dietary restrictions. Log on to the GlobalFerm intranet and click "Servex Modern" under the "Employee Benefits" tab to have a look at cafeteria menus for both breakfast and lunch. They will be updated weekly for your convenience. We are also excited to announce that seating at the Servex Modern cafeteria will be expanded to 550 seats. — [3] —. This will include ample provision for people with disabilities. We apologize for any inconveniences during this renovation period, but we are sure you will appreciate all the changes. — [4] —.

161. What is the purpose of the notice?

(A) To announce the relocation of a facility
(B) To clarify a policy concerning lunch breaks
(C) To inform employees of survey results
(D) To apprise staff of a pending renovation

162. Where can employees check food options?

(A) In the lobby of the Superion Building
(B) Next to the cafeteria's main entrance
(C) On a bulletin board on the sixth floor
(D) On the company's intranet site

163. In which of the positions marked [1], [2], [3], and [4] does the following sentence best belong?

"We agree with you that it is necessary to offer a variety of meal options to suit everyone."

(A) [1]
(B) [2]
(C) [3]
(D) [4]

First Global Expands Further

December 28

Electronics giant First Global, which makes components for smartphone manufacturers, said in a press release on Tuesday that it expects to start building its 20th overseas production plant soon. The announcement comes at the end of a successful year, with sales in the fourth quarter surpassing those in the third quarter by 15 percent. President and CEO Ms. Genevieve Durand attributes First Global's growth to its efficiency in manufacturing. — [1] —. "We find ways to do more with less," Durand claims, "producing high-quality goods at competitive prices." — [2] —.

Upon completion, the new factory will be situated near Beijing, China. It will be First Global's largest and one of six of its facilities located in the East Asian region. — [3] —. Just as First Global has done before, it is using its own earnings to fund construction rather than taking out additional loans or selling off assets. It is hoped that the new factory will boost productivity by approximately 20 percent. — [4] —. Construction on the plant will begin in spring of next year.

164. Why was the article written?

(A) To describe business trends in a region
(B) To report on sales of mobile phones
(C) To profile the goals of a CEO
(D) To announce plans for a new facility

165. How does First Global plan to finance its newest project?

(A) By selling company shares
(B) By bringing in a partner
(C) By increasing its line of credit
(D) By relying on past profits

166. What does the article suggest about First Global?

(A) Factory working conditions are below standards.
(B) Manufacturing will not grow as much as expected.
(C) Smartphone manufacturers buy their products.
(D) Expanding into Asia will be a new experience for them.

167. In which of the positions marked [1], [2], [3], and [4] does the following sentence best belong?

"This increase in output will help the company keep up with the strong demand for smartphones."

(A) [1]
(B) [2]
(C) [3]
(D) [4]

Bill Reed	9:15 A.M.	I just spoke with Deborah Lee, the CEO of Thompson Paper. She wants to know why she hasn't received an estimate for the cost of having Haydon Architects construct her company's new warehouse complex yet. I thought we sent the quote last week.
Sally Waters	9:18 A.M	I had to make some revisions to the estimate. Our supplier, Fulton Wholesale, is raising its prices for several types of building materials. We will have to charge Thompson Paper about 15 percent more than we originally planned.
David Vance	9:22 A.M	That's not good. Ms. Lee will never agree to pay that much. Aren't there other suppliers we can work with?
Sally Waters	9:25 A.M	I'm looking, but we definitely won't be able to make the transition to a new supplier in time for this project.
David Vance	9:28 A.M	We'd better figure something out. I don't want Haydon Architects to lose Thompson Paper as a client.
Sally Waters	9:30 A.M	I'll go through the estimate again. Maybe I can find some other costs we can cut to make up for the more expensive materials. It'll take a while, though.
Bill Reed	9:32 A.M	OK. Call me just before lunch to let me know if you will be able to finish today. In the meantime, I'll contact the manager of Fulton Wholesale. It's a long shot, but maybe I can convince him to give us a deal on this order.

Send

168. What is true about Mr. Reed?

(A) He revised a price estimate.
(B) He signed a contract with a supplier.
(C) He had a conversation with a client.
(D) He visited a construction site.

169. At 9:22 A.M., what does Mr. Vance mean when he writes, "That's not good"?

(A) Fulton Wholesale has made an invoice error.
(B) A client may be unwilling to pay a higher price.
(C) A building material is not available.
(D) Thompson Paper has issued a serious complaint.

170. What solution did Haydon Architects' employees NOT come up with?

(A) Using a different supplier
(B) Withholding a payment
(C) Reducing other costs
(D) Requesting a discount

171. What does Mr. Reed instruct Ms. Waters to do?

(A) Speak with a project director
(B) Provide a progress update
(C) Meet with a warehouse manager
(D) Correct a billing error

GO ON TO THE NEXT PAGE

Questions 172-175 refer to the following e-mail.

TO: Benjamin Pinkerton <benpin@ponyexpress.com>
FROM: Carol Andrews <carol@ponyexpress.com>
SUBJECT: Trip to head office
DATE: July 18

Benjamin,

I just wanted to give you a tentative summary of the itinerary for our visit to Washington, D.C. next week. A company car will pick us up at the airport when we arrive on Monday afternoon and take us to the Earthgate Hotel. I received a reservation e-mail this morning, and the hotel has confirmed us for the presidential suite, so that will be quite nice. We will have a few hours at the hotel before we meet with Linda Krakowski, the head of Recon Paper Company. She kindly offered to meet us for dinner at the hotel so that we don't have to travel anywhere after our long trip.

The next day we will have different meetings and engagements for almost the full day at the corporate headquarters. We will also have lunch with the CEO and several members of the board of directors. I estimate that we should be finished with everything by about 7 P.M.

We are booked on a return flight for Wednesday morning, but I've also been informed there's a late night flight to Los Angeles at 11:35 P.M. on Tuesday. Would you prefer returning on Tuesday or Wednesday? Either flight is fine with me. Let me know what you want to do, and I can go ahead and inform the office in D.C.

Thanks!

Carol Andrews
Sales Supervisor
Pony Express, Inc.

172. Why did Ms. Andrews write the e-mail?

(A) To inform a colleague about a schedule
(B) To request changes to a reservation
(C) To ask about hotel facilities
(D) To summarize the results of a meeting

173. What is NOT mentioned in the e-mail?

(A) A lunch has been scheduled with a superior.
(B) The hotel has already confirmed a reservation.
(C) The start of a project has been postponed.
(D) Meetings will take place at a head office.

174. Why is Ms. Krakowski coming to the hotel?

(A) It is convenient for the visitors.
(B) She will be speaking at a conference there.
(C) It is located close to her office.
(D) She wants to try a new restaurant.

175. What information does Ms. Andrews require of Mr. Pinkerton?

(A) A seat assignment
(B) A contact number
(C) A meeting agenda
(D) A preferred date

GO ON TO THE NEXT PAGE

www.sidebyside.com/kitchenappliances

Side by Side—We help you shop smarter!

Your search for drip coffee makers currently available at Wallace Appliances for between $40 and $100 has yielded the following results:

Product Description	Price	Features	Capacity	Brew Time	Ease of Cleaning
Conklin Pour 578-G	$79.99 Now on sale for $71.25*	-Adjustable temperature -Dishwasher safe	12 cups	6 minutes, 34 seconds	4.5/5
Lundi Café WDE-23V	$99.75	-Programmable; set the time you want your coffee brewed every day, and the machine will do it for you	14 cups	5 minutes, 19 seconds	5/5
Bonaveni TCD-333	$56.43 Now on sale for $43.67*	-Removable basket for paper filters -Dishwasher safe	10 cups	7 minutes, 4 seconds	2.5/5
Sandfield Velocity 1200-F	$68.92	-Comes with coffee bean grinder -Built-in filter	10 cups	4 minutes, 11 seconds	2/5

*Sale lasts from December 17 to January 31.

Click here to go back and modify your search.

Want to know about great deals on the hottest new items of the season?
Enter your e-mail address to sign up for our weekly newsletter: _____

SIGN UP

www.storereviewer.com/wallaceappliances
Latest Reviews of Wallace Appliances

Marcus Ford January 20	I visited the Wallace Appliances store in Seaward on Saturday, January 15, to purchase a new coffee maker. I was very impressed. There was ample parking available, and customers were not required to pay for it. In addition, the interior of the building was very bright and modern. The cashier mentioned that the store had been renovated last month. There was a wide selection of coffee makers to choose from, and the store clerk I dealt with was very helpful. He carefully explained the various features and recommended a model that was on sale. Overall, I am quite happy with the one he suggested, although I kind of wish it could make more than 10 cups of coffee at once.

176. What is the purpose of the Web page?

(A) To introduce newly available merchandise
(B) To describe how to use various appliances
(C) To compare some similar products
(D) To promote a store's most popular items

177. On the Web page, the word "yielded" in paragraph 1, line 2, is closest in meaning to

(A) confirmed
(B) produced
(C) described
(D) exposed

178. What is indicated about the discounts on Wallace Appliances products?

(A) They are offered for a limited time.
(B) They are only available on a Web site.
(C) They are only provided to registered customers.
(D) They are restricted to older models.

179. What is NOT mentioned about the Seaward branch of Wallace Appliances?

(A) It was recently remodeled.
(B) It hired additional cashiers.
(C) It provides free parking.
(D) It is open on Saturdays.

180. Which coffee maker did Mr. Ford most likely purchase?

(A) Conklin Pour 578-G
(B) Lundi Café WDE-23V
(C) Bonaveni TCD-333
(D) Sandfield Velocity 1200-F

GO ON TO THE NEXT PAGE

Questions 181-185 refer to the following e-mail and notice.

To: Gary Flores <gflores49@thmail.com>
From: Wendy Rhodes <w_rhodes@tarmail.net>
Date: July 10
Subject: Planning suggestions
Attachment: Guest_Pass

Dear Mr. Flores,

I hope this message finds you well. The last time we met, you had asked me to advise you on drafting a retirement plan. Below are just a few tips to get you started.

First, it is vital that you create and maintain a cash reserve for emergency purposes equal to roughly three times your typical monthly expenses. Since this amount could be quite large, it is important to start saving as early as possible.

Additionally, I recommend investigating long-term medical care options upon retiring for you, your spouse, and your parents. You should also share the details of your health-care plan with your family members.

I have attached a special guest pass so that you can attend my lecture, "Retirement for One," at a university event. The same pass also allows you to sit in on a special lunch seminar on health coverage for senior citizens conducted by Mr. Victor Rochester. The events will be free of charge to you if you present the pass at the door.

I look forward to seeing you soon.

Warmest regards,

Wendy Rhodes
Retirement Planning Specialist
Cottler Finance

The Career Development Center

Sunfield State University

The Career Development Center at Sunfield State University strives to provide high-quality, affordable education and professional development for working individuals and retirees in an open and encouraging environment.

We are pleased to announce that our Annual Center Information Event will take place on Monday, July 12, on the fifth floor of Durgan Hall. We invite you to join retirement advisor Wendy Rhodes for her lecture. On Tuesday, July 13, the first of her two-part seminar on part-time employment prospects will be held from 3 to 5 P.M. This will conclude at the same time the following day, on Wednesday, July 14. Lastly, we will also hold a special luncheon presentation by our center director, Mr. Victor Rochester, on Thursday, July 15. Entrance for each event is $10 for center members and $15 for nonmembers. Tickets for the luncheon are an additional $10 and are available for purchase from July 1 through July 15 at our main office in Durgan Hall. To learn more, call 555-2402.

181. What is the purpose of the e-mail?

(A) To extend some helpful advice
(B) To outline the details of a program
(C) To identify needs for a luncheon
(D) To discuss an upcoming lecture

182. According to the e-mail, what should Mr. Flores do with the details of his health-care plan?

(A) Keep them in a folder in his office
(B) Save them on his mobile phone
(C) Discuss them with a doctor
(D) Give them to family members

183. For whom does the Career Development Center offer courses?

(A) Small business owners
(B) Employed and retired adults
(C) University students looking for jobs
(D) Elderly volunteers

184. When will Ms. Rhodes's seminar end?

(A) On July 12
(B) On July 13
(C) On July 14
(D) On July 15

185. What is indicated about Mr. Flores?

(A) He will assist Ms. Rhodes with her lecture.
(B) He has a lunch meeting in Durgan Hall.
(C) He can attend an event on Thursday for free.
(D) He requires more than one ticket.

GO ON TO THE NEXT PAGE

Questions 186-190 refer to the following notice, advertisement, and receipt.

Notice to Customers
Partial Closure of Elm Point Shopping Center

From August 12 to 15, technicians will be installing a new security system in the shopping center. During this period, each level of the mall will be inaccessible to the public for one day according to the following schedule:

August 12 - First Floor / August 13 - Second Floor
August 14 - Third Floor / August 15 - Fourth Floor

Please note that shops will be closed on the day that their floor of the mall is being worked on. The management of Elm Point Shopping Center would like to apologize for any inconvenience this may cause our customers. We ask for your patience and understanding as we make our facility a safer place to shop.

If you have any questions about this project, please stop by the customer service desk in front of the main entrance. One of our staff members will be happy to provide any additional information you require.

 Point Sports Clearance Sale!

Point Sports is pleased to announce that a new collection of football gear will be arriving at the end of August. To make room for this exciting line of equipment, we will be holding a clearance sale from August 1 to 20. All tennis equipment will be marked down by 25 percent. In addition, members of our Point Sports Program will receive double the usual reward points when making a purchase during this promotional period. So, make sure to stop by our store! Don't forget that we have moved from the first floor of Elm Point Shopping Center to a larger space on the fourth floor. We hope to see you soon!

Point Sports

Customer: Lei Bell
Date: August 10

Cashier: Jack Lee
Receipt #: 0456

Item Description	Quantity	Price
Bonneval Tennis Racket	1	$173.00
Jones Collection Baseball Glove	1	$43.00
Zarza Running Shoes	1	$138.00
Flatlands Jump Rope	1	$9.00
Tax		$21.78
Total		$384.78

Regular-price items may be returned for any reason for up to 30 days after the date of purchase. For a refund to be issued, proof of purchase must be presented. All sales of discounted items are final. For more information about our sales policies, visit www.pointsports.com.

186. Why might some customers visit a customer service desk?

(A) To request information about an emergency procedure
(B) To pick up a schedule of a facility's operating hours
(C) To inquire about the installation of safety devices
(D) To provide feedback on an upcoming mall closure

187. On which day will Point Sports be closed?

(A) August 12
(B) August 13
(C) August 14
(D) August 15

188. What is NOT true about Point Sports?

(A) It will introduce some new gear in August.
(B) It has set up a rewards program for its customers.
(C) It will relocate to a different shopping center.
(D) It has occupied a larger commercial space.

189. On the receipt, to which price has a discount been applied?

(A) $173.00
(B) $43.00
(C) $138.00
(D) $9.00

190. What is a requirement for Point Sports to process a refund request?

(A) A discount must be verified.
(B) A transaction record must be shown.
(C) An online form must be submitted.
(D) A reason must be approved.

GO ON TO THE NEXT PAGE

The Meredith Fashion Institute (MFI) invites you to attend our annual spring fashion show featuring our graduating students:

A Breath of Fresh Air

A showcase of fashions that are light, airy, and innovative

Entertainment, Lunch, and Fashion Show
Master of ceremonies: Stylist Melvin Lee
Music by DJ Raina

$40 per Person
Saturday, May 7, Noon

Hannah Hall Banquet Room
Meredith Fashion Institute

As always, the event is being held at our campus on 1000 South Grand Avenue in Los Angeles. All proceeds benefit a start-up fund for beginning designers who need support to become established in the competitive world of fashion design.

To: Troy Seeger <t.seeger@mfi.com>
From: Anna Cruise <anna_cruise@imagephoto.com>
Date: April 4
Subject: Re: Photo services

Dear Mr. Seeger,

I received your message concerning Meredith Fashion Institute's upcoming event. I appreciate what the proceeds of the show will be used for, so I would be happy to participate as the official photographer. Moreover, I am willing to offer my services free of charge and provide you with images for the school's use. However, the costs of covering an event as large as this one are quite high, even though it will provide me with a lot of exposure. Therefore, I am asking your permission to install a photo booth by the entrance and to charge visitors a small fee for prints. All I need is space to set up my camera, table, backdrop, and printer. I can leave an assistant in charge of the table while I photograph the event. Please contact me at 555-0493 to discuss this further.

Sincerely,
Anna Cruise

Fashion Guide Magazine

LA Scene
By Beth Rowlands

As always, the Meredith Fashion Institute's annual showcase of student fashion offered an exciting glimpse into the possible future of the industry. For those who are unaware, MFI has turned out many successful graduates, including Roxy Cooper and Belle Hashimoto. The event's host, also a graduate of the institute, has done models' hair and makeup for several of *Fashion Guide Magazine*'s feature articles. The fashions in this year's show truly lived up to the theme of being "light, airy, and innovative." They featured plenty of loose tops, baggy pants, and oversized coats. The clothing was subdued, consisting mainly of neutral shades accented by the occasional hint of color. But the materials stood out the most — textured fabrics expertly cut into a variety of bold shapes. Check out some photos below. You may be able to find some of them at a local fashion retailer one day.

191. What is NOT indicated about the Meredith Fashion Institute's event?

(A) It is held yearly on school grounds.
(B) It includes a meal for participants.
(C) It coincides with the launch of a brand.
(D) It charges visitors a fee to gain entrance.

192. What does Ms. Cruise appreciate about the event?

(A) Profits from it will go toward helping aspiring designers.
(B) It will help amateur photographers gain some much-needed publicity.
(C) She will not have to bring her own equipment to it.
(D) It will provide her with an opportunity to display some work.

193. Why does Ms. Cruise want to set up a booth?

(A) To interview a potential assistant
(B) To register arriving guests
(C) To get a chance to recover some costs
(D) To have an area for taking short breaks

194. What is true about Melvin Lee?

(A) He provided entertainment for an event.
(B) He teaches a class in fashion at MFI.
(C) He attended the same school as Ms. Rowlands.
(D) He has helped style models for a magazine.

195. What does Ms. Rowlands mention about the fashions featured at MFI's event?

(A) They are more colorful than those of previous seasons.
(B) They hardly reflected the chosen theme of an event.
(C) They may be sold at clothing stores in the future.
(D) They were quickly adopted by leading fashion designers.

GO ON TO THE NEXT PAGE

NYCBikeTourist Is Taking Over Traditional Tour Companies

By Rodrigo Jimenez

NYCBikeTourist is a new tour operator guiding clients through New York City on bicycles. Bookable through an exclusive app, the program offers skilled guides and top-notch bike gear.

Each day, various tours are offered that make several stops at museums or other popular sites. NYCBikeTourist has lucrative partnerships with these local attractions and businesses to provide immediate access or special discounts. One tour takes riders to the highly popular Berkley Museum of Modern Art. The gallery has just been opened and usually has long lines outside. However, with the tour, there's no doubt that you will get in.

---

www.NYCBikeTourist.com/tours

The following tours are available on June 23:

- Tour 1 ($35 per person)
  Lady Liberty Tour. Ride across Ellis Island and visit the landmark statue. Includes appetizers and wine. You MUST be a legal adult(18 years or older) to join the tour.
  Level: Advanced, Duration: 3 hours, Start: 7 P.M.

- Tour 2 ($45 per person)
  Central Park Tour. Ride up to the park and learn about its history. Organized picnic is included.
  Level: Average, Duration: 3 hours, Start: 1 P.M.

- Tour 3 ($75 per person)
  Cross-City Tour. Ride over iconic bridges such as the Brooklyn Bridge, and ride from Uptown to Downtown. Lunch and snacks will be provided.
  Level: Advanced, Duration: 6 hours, Start: 10 A.M.

- Tour 4 ($120 per person)
  Museum Tour. Venture to several museums and receive VIP access. Museums visited during ride: Berkley Museum of Modern Art, Jester Gallery, and National History Museum Brooklyn. Includes lunch in the trendy Nolita neighborhood.
  Level: Average, Duration: 8 hours, Start: 9 A.M.

NYCBikeTourist Reviews

Posted on June 25
By Leo Reyes

As a cycling enthusiast, I was happy that the tour involved plenty of actual riding. I was interested in the museums they visit as well, but I opted to go visit those on my own time. I have walked over the Brooklyn Bridge before, but riding over it in both directions was the absolute highlight for me. Our guide's stories about its history made the experience much more special. The one downside was that we weren't able to spend much time at any of the locations we visited. But on the plus side, beverages and light snacks had been prearranged at specific points. Hope to be back soon.

196. What is true about NYCBikeTourist?

(A) It is only open from May through September.
(B) It has its own booking application.
(C) It has partnered with local authorities.
(D) It rents bikes from a famous store.

197. How is Tour 1 different from the other options?

(A) It spends time in the Nolita region.
(B) It is shorter than the other tours.
(C) Participants eat lunch in a park.
(D) Minors are not allowed to participate.

198. What is indicated about the Museum Tour?

(A) It is only recommended to advanced riders.
(B) It requires a special registration process.
(C) It includes a visit to a new attraction.
(D) It stops at more than six museums.

199. Which tour did Mr. Reyes most likely book?

(A) Tour 1
(B) Tour 2
(C) Tour 3
(D) Tour 4

200. What was Mr. Reyes disappointed about?

(A) The amount of cycling
(B) The guide's knowledge
(C) The length of visits
(D) The food and drinks

This is the end of the test. You may review Parts 5, 6, and 7 if you finish the test early.

Self 체크 리스트

TEST 10은 무사히 잘 마치셨죠?
이제 다음의 Self 체크 리스트를 통해 자신의 테스트 진행 내용을 점검해 볼까요?

1. 나는 75분 동안 완전히 테스트에 집중하였다.

    □ 예   □ 아니오

    아니오에 답한 경우, 이유는 무엇인가요?

2. 나는 75분 동안 100문제를 모두 풀었다.

    □ 예   □ 아니오

    아니오에 답한 경우, 이유는 무엇인가요?

3. 나는 75분 동안 답안지 표시까지 완료하였다.

    □ 예   □ 아니오

    아니오에 답한 경우, 이유는 무엇인가요?

4. 나는 Part 5와 Part 6를 19분 안에 모두 풀었다.

    □ 예   □ 아니오

    아니오에 답한 경우, 이유는 무엇인가요?

5. Part 7을 풀 때 5분 이상 걸린 지문이 없었다.

    □ 예   □ 아니오

6. 개선해야 할 점 또는 나를 위한 충고를 적어보세요.

* 교재의 첫 장으로 돌아가서 자신이 적은 목표 점수를 확인하면서 목표에 대한 의지를 다지기 바랍니다. 개선해야 할 점은 반드시 다음 테스트에 실천해야 합니다. 그것이 가장 중요하며, 그래야만 발전할 수 있습니다.

정답
점수 환산표
해석
Answer Sheet

TEST 01

101 (A)	102 (C)	103 (A)	104 (D)	105 (C)
106 (B)	107 (D)	108 (A)	109 (A)	110 (D)
111 (D)	112 (C)	113 (C)	114 (A)	115 (C)
116 (B)	117 (C)	118 (A)	119 (C)	120 (D)
121 (A)	122 (D)	123 (A)	124 (C)	125 (D)
126 (D)	127 (C)	128 (A)	129 (C)	130 (B)
131 (A)	132 (B)	133 (D)	134 (B)	135 (B)
136 (C)	137 (B)	138 (D)	139 (C)	140 (D)
141 (B)	142 (C)	143 (A)	144 (D)	145 (C)
146 (B)	147 (C)	148 (D)	149 (C)	150 (B)
151 (C)	152 (D)	153 (A)	154 (C)	155 (D)
156 (C)	157 (A)	158 (C)	159 (A)	160 (D)
161 (A)	162 (D)	163 (D)	164 (D)	165 (C)
166 (A)	167 (C)	168 (D)	169 (C)	170 (B)
171 (B)	172 (B)	173 (A)	174 (D)	175 (D)
176 (C)	177 (C)	178 (C)	179 (D)	180 (A)
181 (D)	182 (B)	183 (C)	184 (C)	185 (B)
186 (A)	187 (A)	188 (B)	189 (A)	190 (A)
191 (B)	192 (D)	193 (D)	194 (A)	195 (B)
196 (C)	197 (C)	198 (D)	199 (D)	200 (C)

TEST 02

101 (D)	102 (D)	103 (A)	104 (B)	105 (A)
106 (C)	107 (D)	108 (C)	109 (D)	110 (A)
111 (A)	112 (B)	113 (B)	114 (A)	115 (B)
116 (B)	117 (C)	118 (D)	119 (B)	120 (B)
121 (A)	122 (C)	123 (B)	124 (A)	125 (C)
126 (A)	127 (C)	128 (A)	129 (A)	130 (D)
131 (A)	132 (B)	133 (C)	134 (B)	135 (D)
136 (B)	137 (C)	138 (B)	139 (C)	140 (D)
141 (D)	142 (C)	143 (C)	144 (D)	145 (D)
146 (A)	147 (C)	148 (D)	149 (D)	150 (C)
151 (D)	152 (B)	153 (C)	154 (C)	155 (C)
156 (C)	157 (C)	158 (B)	159 (C)	160 (C)
161 (D)	162 (C)	163 (D)	164 (C)	165 (C)
166 (A)	167 (B)	168 (B)	169 (C)	170 (A)
171 (D)	172 (D)	173 (C)	174 (D)	175 (C)
176 (B)	177 (A)	178 (D)	179 (D)	180 (C)
181 (A)	182 (C)	183 (D)	184 (B)	185 (A)
186 (C)	187 (D)	188 (B)	189 (D)	190 (D)
191 (C)	192 (C)	193 (A)	194 (B)	195 (B)
196 (C)	197 (C)	198 (A)	199 (C)	200 (D)

TEST 03

101 (A)	102 (C)	103 (B)	104 (B)	105 (C)
106 (B)	107 (B)	108 (C)	109 (A)	110 (C)
111 (C)	112 (A)	113 (D)	114 (B)	115 (D)
116 (C)	117 (B)	118 (C)	119 (B)	120 (C)
121 (A)	122 (D)	123 (D)	124 (B)	125 (C)
126 (C)	127 (D)	128 (C)	129 (C)	130 (D)
131 (C)	132 (B)	133 (C)	134 (C)	135 (A)
136 (C)	137 (B)	138 (B)	139 (C)	140 (A)
141 (A)	142 (C)	143 (C)	144 (D)	145 (B)
146 (A)	147 (C)	148 (D)	149 (B)	150 (C)
151 (A)	152 (C)	153 (C)	154 (C)	155 (D)
156 (B)	157 (C)	158 (C)	159 (D)	160 (A)
161 (C)	162 (B)	163 (B)	164 (A)	165 (B)
166 (D)	167 (D)	168 (C)	169 (C)	170 (B)
171 (C)	172 (B)	173 (A)	174 (B)	175 (B)
176 (C)	177 (C)	178 (A)	179 (B)	180 (A)
181 (A)	182 (D)	183 (A)	184 (D)	185 (A)
186 (D)	187 (B)	188 (C)	189 (B)	190 (B)
191 (C)	192 (B)	193 (D)	194 (D)	195 (B)
196 (C)	197 (A)	198 (C)	199 (C)	200 (A)

TEST 04

101 (C)	102 (C)	103 (C)	104 (B)	105 (D)
106 (C)	107 (B)	108 (A)	109 (D)	110 (C)
111 (A)	112 (B)	113 (C)	114 (D)	115 (B)
116 (D)	117 (B)	118 (D)	119 (D)	120 (C)
121 (D)	122 (D)	123 (D)	124 (B)	125 (C)
126 (A)	127 (A)	128 (C)	129 (D)	130 (B)
131 (D)	132 (C)	133 (A)	134 (B)	135 (B)
136 (D)	137 (D)	138 (B)	139 (D)	140 (A)
141 (B)	142 (C)	143 (B)	144 (C)	145 (A)
146 (D)	147 (B)	148 (C)	149 (D)	150 (C)
151 (C)	152 (D)	153 (C)	154 (D)	155 (D)
156 (B)	157 (C)	158 (D)	159 (A)	160 (C)
161 (C)	162 (B)	163 (B)	164 (A)	165 (B)
166 (B)	167 (A)	168 (B)	169 (B)	170 (C)
171 (A)	172 (A)	173 (A)	174 (C)	175 (D)
176 (B)	177 (C)	178 (D)	179 (C)	180 (D)
181 (D)	182 (B)	183 (D)	184 (C)	185 (C)
186 (A)	187 (D)	188 (B)	189 (D)	190 (A)
191 (D)	192 (B)	193 (C)	194 (C)	195 (B)
196 (A)	197 (B)	198 (D)	199 (C)	200 (A)

▪TEST 05

101 (A)	102 (C)	103 (B)	104 (D)	105 (C)
106 (C)	107 (C)	108 (D)	109 (D)	110 (D)
111 (B)	112 (A)	113 (B)	114 (B)	115 (C)
116 (C)	117 (D)	118 (C)	119 (D)	120 (C)
121 (D)	122 (B)	123 (D)	124 (C)	125 (B)
126 (C)	127 (D)	128 (D)	129 (A)	130 (B)
131 (A)	132 (D)	133 (C)	134 (D)	135 (C)
136 (D)	137 (A)	138 (C)	139 (D)	140 (C)
141 (B)	142 (A)	143 (B)	144 (C)	145 (D)
146 (C)	147 (B)	148 (D)	149 (C)	150 (C)
151 (B)	152 (C)	153 (C)	154 (C)	155 (B)
156 (D)	157 (C)	158 (A)	159 (C)	160 (B)
161 (A)	162 (C)	163 (D)	164 (B)	165 (C)
166 (A)	167 (D)	168 (D)	169 (A)	170 (B)
171 (C)	172 (A)	173 (D)	174 (B)	175 (C)
176 (D)	177 (C)	178 (C)	179 (A)	180 (D)
181 (C)	182 (B)	183 (D)	184 (B)	185 (C)
186 (B)	187 (B)	188 (C)	189 (C)	190 (D)
191 (B)	192 (D)	193 (C)	194 (B)	195 (B)
196 (B)	197 (C)	198 (C)	199 (D)	200 (C)

▪TEST 06

101 (A)	102 (C)	103 (C)	104 (C)	105 (C)
106 (D)	107 (C)	108 (D)	109 (D)	110 (A)
111 (A)	112 (C)	113 (D)	114 (A)	115 (D)
116 (D)	117 (C)	118 (B)	119 (A)	120 (A)
121 (D)	122 (B)	123 (B)	124 (B)	125 (D)
126 (C)	127 (D)	128 (B)	129 (C)	130 (D)
131 (C)	132 (B)	133 (D)	134 (C)	135 (D)
136 (A)	137 (B)	138 (A)	139 (B)	140 (A)
141 (D)	142 (B)	143 (D)	144 (A)	145 (D)
146 (B)	147 (D)	148 (C)	149 (A)	150 (B)
151 (D)	152 (B)	153 (A)	154 (D)	155 (D)
156 (A)	157 (B)	158 (B)	159 (D)	160 (B)
161 (A)	162 (A)	163 (B)	164 (C)	165 (B)
166 (C)	167 (D)	168 (D)	169 (C)	170 (A)
171 (A)	172 (D)	173 (C)	174 (D)	175 (A)
176 (C)	177 (D)	178 (B)	179 (A)	180 (C)
181 (A)	182 (B)	183 (D)	184 (D)	185 (B)
186 (D)	187 (D)	188 (C)	189 (A)	190 (D)
191 (C)	192 (A)	193 (D)	194 (B)	195 (A)
196 (A)	197 (C)	198 (B)	199 (D)	200 (B)

▪TEST 07

101 (D)	102 (C)	103 (C)	104 (C)	105 (B)
106 (B)	107 (D)	108 (C)	109 (C)	110 (C)
111 (A)	112 (B)	113 (B)	114 (D)	115 (D)
116 (C)	117 (C)	118 (B)	119 (D)	120 (C)
121 (B)	122 (C)	123 (C)	124 (B)	125 (B)
126 (B)	127 (B)	128 (C)	129 (B)	130 (A)
131 (B)	132 (C)	133 (B)	134 (C)	135 (C)
136 (B)	137 (D)	138 (B)	139 (B)	140 (C)
141 (D)	142 (D)	143 (C)	144 (D)	145 (D)
146 (C)	147 (B)	148 (C)	149 (B)	150 (D)
151 (C)	152 (B)	153 (C)	154 (D)	155 (C)
156 (C)	157 (D)	158 (B)	159 (B)	160 (C)
161 (D)	162 (C)	163 (A)	164 (C)	165 (B)
166 (B)	167 (C)	168 (D)	169 (C)	170 (A)
171 (C)	172 (A)	173 (D)	174 (C)	175 (B)
176 (A)	177 (D)	178 (B)	179 (D)	180 (A)
181 (B)	182 (B)	183 (A)	184 (C)	185 (D)
186 (C)	187 (C)	188 (D)	189 (B)	190 (D)
191 (B)	192 (C)	193 (A)	194 (C)	195 (B)
196 (C)	197 (A)	198 (B)	199 (D)	200 (D)

▪TEST 08

101 (B)	102 (B)	103 (C)	104 (A)	105 (C)
106 (C)	107 (A)	108 (A)	109 (B)	110 (B)
111 (B)	112 (C)	113 (B)	114 (B)	115 (A)
116 (D)	117 (A)	118 (B)	119 (A)	120 (C)
121 (B)	122 (D)	123 (B)	124 (B)	125 (A)
126 (C)	127 (D)	128 (A)	129 (B)	130 (A)
131 (A)	132 (B)	133 (B)	134 (D)	135 (D)
136 (B)	137 (C)	138 (A)	139 (C)	140 (C)
141 (B)	142 (C)	143 (B)	144 (B)	145 (A)
146 (C)	147 (A)	148 (B)	149 (C)	150 (D)
151 (A)	152 (C)	153 (B)	154 (A)	155 (C)
156 (C)	157 (D)	158 (D)	159 (C)	160 (A)
161 (A)	162 (A)	163 (C)	164 (C)	165 (B)
166 (C)	167 (B)	168 (C)	169 (D)	170 (B)
171 (A)	172 (C)	173 (C)	174 (A)	175 (B)
176 (D)	177 (C)	178 (C)	179 (C)	180 (A)
181 (C)	182 (D)	183 (B)	184 (C)	185 (C)
186 (C)	187 (B)	188 (B)	189 (D)	190 (A)
191 (D)	192 (C)	193 (A)	194 (D)	195 (C)
196 (B)	197 (D)	198 (C)	199 (A)	200 (C)

▌TEST 09

101 (A)	102 (A)	103 (B)	104 (A)	105 (B)
106 (A)	107 (D)	108 (C)	109 (B)	110 (B)
111 (B)	112 (A)	113 (B)	114 (A)	115 (B)
116 (C)	117 (B)	118 (C)	119 (A)	120 (C)
121 (B)	122 (B)	123 (B)	124 (D)	125 (B)
126 (B)	127 (C)	128 (B)	129 (D)	130 (B)
131 (A)	132 (C)	133 (C)	134 (B)	135 (B)
136 (D)	137 (B)	138 (A)	139 (A)	140 (C)
141 (A)	142 (D)	143 (C)	144 (A)	145 (B)
146 (B)	147 (D)	148 (C)	149 (C)	150 (B)
151 (B)	152 (C)	153 (B)	154 (B)	155 (A)
156 (B)	157 (B)	158 (A)	159 (A)	160 (B)
161 (C)	162 (D)	163 (A)	164 (B)	165 (D)
166 (D)	167 (A)	168 (D)	169 (D)	170 (D)
171 (B)	172 (A)	173 (B)	174 (B)	175 (A)
176 (D)	177 (C)	178 (D)	179 (C)	180 (A)
181 (C)	182 (B)	183 (B)	184 (D)	185 (A)
186 (D)	187 (C)	188 (C)	189 (B)	190 (A)
191 (D)	192 (C)	193 (A)	194 (C)	195 (D)
196 (C)	197 (B)	198 (D)	199 (A)	200 (B)

▌TEST 10

101 (A)	102 (A)	103 (D)	104 (B)	105 (C)
106 (D)	107 (D)	108 (C)	109 (D)	110 (C)
111 (D)	112 (B)	113 (A)	114 (A)	115 (D)
116 (B)	117 (B)	118 (C)	119 (C)	120 (B)
121 (B)	122 (C)	123 (B)	124 (C)	125 (D)
126 (B)	127 (B)	128 (B)	129 (C)	130 (C)
131 (D)	132 (A)	133 (D)	134 (D)	135 (C)
136 (D)	137 (D)	138 (D)	139 (D)	140 (C)
141 (B)	142 (D)	143 (A)	144 (B)	145 (A)
146 (C)	147 (B)	148 (A)	149 (B)	150 (C)
151 (D)	152 (B)	153 (C)	154 (B)	155 (D)
156 (B)	157 (C)	158 (D)	159 (B)	160 (C)
161 (D)	162 (D)	163 (B)	164 (D)	165 (D)
166 (C)	167 (D)	168 (C)	169 (B)	170 (B)
171 (B)	172 (A)	173 (C)	174 (A)	175 (D)
176 (C)	177 (B)	178 (A)	179 (B)	180 (C)
181 (A)	182 (D)	183 (B)	184 (C)	185 (C)
186 (C)	187 (D)	188 (C)	189 (A)	190 (B)
191 (C)	192 (A)	193 (C)	194 (D)	195 (C)
196 (B)	197 (D)	198 (C)	199 (C)	200 (C)

* 아래 점수 환산표로 자신의 토익 리딩 점수를 예상해봅니다.

정답수	리딩 점수	정답수	리딩 점수	정답수	리딩 점수
100	495	66	305	32	125
99	495	65	300	31	120
98	495	64	295	30	115
97	485	63	290	29	110
96	480	62	280	28	105
95	475	61	275	27	100
94	470	60	270	26	95
93	465	59	265	25	90
92	460	58	260	24	85
91	450	57	255	23	80
90	445	56	250	22	75
89	440	55	245	21	70
88	435	54	240	20	70
87	430	53	235	19	65
86	420	52	230	18	60
85	415	51	220	17	60
84	410	50	215	16	55
83	405	49	210	15	50
82	400	48	205	14	45
81	390	47	200	13	40
80	385	46	195	12	35
79	380	45	190	11	30
78	375	44	185	10	30
77	370	43	180	9	25
76	360	42	175	8	20
75	355	41	170	7	20
74	350	40	165	6	15
73	345	39	160	5	15
72	340	38	155	4	10
71	335	37	150	3	5
70	330	36	145	2	5
69	320	35	140	1	5
68	315	34	135	0	5
67	310	33	130		

※ 점수 환산표는 해커스토익 사이트 유저 데이터를 근거로 제작되었으며, 주기적으로 업데이트되고 있습니다. 해커스토익(Hackers.co.kr) 사이트에서 최신 경향을 반영하여 업데이트된 점수환산기를 이용하실 수 있습니다. (토익 > 토익게시판 > 토익점수환산기)

▌TEST 01 해석

* 무료 해설은 해커스토익(Hackers.co.kr)에서
다운로드 받을 수 있습니다.

• QR 코드로
바로가기

PART 5

101 Winfield사는 Evertech사에서 더 유리한 조건을 제시하지 않는 한 합병 거래를 받아들이지 않을 것이다.

102 매장 앞 도로가 행진 경로에 있어서, 직원들은 오늘 건물 뒤에 주차해야 한다.

103 일요일에, 항공우주 제조업체인 Sowadee사는 그것이 내년에 출시하려고 목표하는 다수의 중형 상용 제트기들을 공개했다.

104 Morrison 지역 자치회는 새로운 아파트를 건설하는 것에 관해 주민들과 부동산 개발업체 Norwell사 간의 논의를 진행하기 시작했다.

105 Ruth Collins 주지사는 11월 13일 Osborne 아카데미 경축행사에서 상을 받게 될 것이다.

106 Mr. Tritton은 그가 사용하게 될 전자 문서 관리 시스템에 익숙해지도록 혼자 남겨졌다.

107 그 섬은 서비스 산업에서의 발전 덕분에 최근 몇 년간 점점 더 유행하는 관광지가 되었다.

108 비에도 불구하고, Amberdale 늦여름 축제는 올해 그 어느 때보다 많은 참가자들을 유치했다.

109 새 독감약 출시에 앞서, Barlow 제약 회사는 그 약의 안전성과 효과를 시험하기 위해 철저한 연구를 진행했다.

110 그 유학 과정의 책임자는 여러 언어에 능숙한 담당자들을 채용하는 것을 훨씬 선호한다.

111 Ms. Belano는 Wilson사가 컴퓨터 네트워크에 대한 지원이 필요할 때마다 그녀의 회사의 IT 서비스가 이용 가능할 것이라고 약속했다.

112 Mr. Brodeur는 그의 책에 특정한 이미지를 사용하는 것에 대한 동의를 요청하기 위해 그 사진작가에게 연락했다.

113 그곳의 모든 재료가 100퍼센트 유기농임을 확실히 하기 위해, 그 식당은 함께 일하는 공급업체에 관해 매우 선별적이어야만 했다.

114 지난 주말 소프트볼 대회는 그 지역의 극심한 폭풍우 때문에 취소되었다.

115 캘리포니아 법은 공중 안전을 위해 위험한 건축 자재의 사용, 판매, 그리고 생산을 금지한다.

116 Quav Cola사의 월 수익은 지난해 딸기 맛 청량음료의 출시 이래로 두 배 가까이 늘었다.

117 주인들은 카페의 화장실이 오직 돈을 지불하는 손님들만을 위한 것이라고 명시하는 팻말을 세웠다.

118 Mr. Zalewski는 계획대로 8월에 은퇴하기보다는 6개월 더 회사에 머물기로 결정했다.

119 Jabadi Motors사는 의심되는 에어백 결함으로 인해 4,000대 이상의 차량을 회수할 것이라고 발표했다.

120 다른 많은 구식 기기들처럼, 회전식 다이얼 전화기는 수집가들로부터 인기가 높아졌다.

121 일단 개조되면, 오래된 Thompson Hills 영화관은 지역 화가들을 위한 미술관이 될 것이다.

122 Hawkins Telecom사는 1월 1일부로 월간 종이 청구서를 디지털 버전으로 대체할 것이다.

123 창작 부서의 20명 중에서, 단지 4명만이 주말 개발 워크숍에 왔다.

124 Andrew의 코치는 그에게 충분히 쉬기 위해 경주 전날 밤 8시간의 수면을 취하라고 상기시켰다.

125 그 직책의 모든 지원자들은 이전 고용주로부터의 추천서가 필요할 것이다.

126 관계자들은 도시의 주택 문제를 해결하기 위해 향후 5년 이내에 1,500가구의 아파트를 짓기로 약속했다.

127 학부모들의 압력으로 인해 지역 학교 학생들을 위한 점심 메뉴가 급진적으로 바뀌었다.

128 그 스타 농구 선수는 팀의 팬들로부터 더 큰 환호를 받기 위해 경기장 진행자가 그녀를 마지막으로 소개하기를 원한다.

129 보석과 골동품들은 잠재적 구매자들이 그것들을 먼저 볼 수 있도록 하기 위해 경매에서 판매되기 전에 전시될 것이다.

130 그 지역에 발생하도록 예정되어 있는 일부 공사로 인해 다음 주부터 극심한 교통 체증이 예상된다.

PART 6

131-134는 다음 후기에 관한 문제입니다.

> 기억해야 할 밤
> 별 다섯 개 중 _다섯_ 개
>
> 어젯밤, Antonio Bennett의 새 연극 *Horatio's Blues*가 Imperium 극장에서 첫 선을 보였습니다. **131** *The Strand*와 *From Here to Oblivion*을 포함하는 Bennett의 이전 작업을 고려하여, 제 기대는 높았습니다. **132** 그럼에도 불구하고, 저는 공연의 수준에 기분 좋게 놀랐습니다. 그것은 제가 지금까지 극장에서 본 최고의 작품 중 하나였으며, 작품의 모든 측면에서 훌륭한 작업이 이루어졌습니다. **133** 그러나, 연기가 그 무엇보다 돋보였습니다. 특히, Lucy Cartwright의 Beatrice로서의 가슴 아픈 연기가 탁월했습니다. **134** 그 밤이 끝날 무렵, 대부분의 관객이 감동적인 경험에 경의를 표하기 위해 일어나서 연극에 기립 박수를 보냈습니다. 놓치지 마세요!

135-138은 다음 편지에 관한 문제입니다.

> Grace Nichols
> Glen Creek가 408번지
> New Bern, NC 28560
>
> Ms. Nichols께,
>
> **135** 귀하의 대출 신청과 관련하여 편지를 씁니다. 귀하께서 저희 온라인 양식에 포함하신 정보에 따르면, 귀하의 사업을 위해 2만 달러까지 대출받으실 자격이 있을 것이며, 7퍼센트의 금리로 5년에 걸쳐 상환하실 수 있습니다.
>
> **136** 다만, 아직 승인이 확정된 것은 아니라는 점을 유념해 주시기 바랍니다. **137** 저희는 귀하의 정보가 정확한지 확인한 후 위에 언급된 수치들을 확정할 것입니다. **138** 그렇게 하기 위해 신원 조사를 실시할 것입니다. 만약 귀하의 신청에 변경이 필요하시다면, 가능한 한 빨리 555-3312로 제게 연락 주십시오.
>
> Theo Babbit 드림
> Beasley 금융사

139-142는 다음 회람에 관한 문제입니다.

> 수신: 전 교수진 및 교직원
> 발신: Evelyn Perry 운영 부사장
> 제목: 주차
> 날짜: 9월 1일

●

139 여름 동안, Kiefer 대학교는 캠퍼스 보안을 강화하기 위해 변화를 시행했습니다. 저희의 주요 목표는 대학교 주차장을 학생과 교직원들에게 더 안전하게 만드는 것이었습니다.

140 저희가 가장 먼저 한 일은 가시성을 높이는 것이었습니다. 저희는 캠퍼스 내 모든 주차장에 밝은 조명을 설치함으로써 이것을 완수했습니다. **141** 저희는 또한 주차장 경계 주변의 빽빽한 관목을 일부 제거하는 데 주력했습니다. 추가적으로, 주요 장소에 비상 전화기를 설치했습니다.

142 이런 변화들은 상당한 비용이 들기 때문에, 저희는 월 주차권 가격을 60달러로 올릴 수밖에 없습니다. 주차권은 오늘부터 이 가격으로 구매 가능합니다.

이해해 주셔서 감사합니다.

143-146은 다음 공고에 관한 문제입니다.

Port Buena 레스토랑 운영자들에게 공고

143 Port Buena의 모든 레스토랑들은 직원들에게 식품을 위생적으로 다루는 데 필요한 기술을 제공하도록 법에 의해 요구됩니다. 이것은 지난여름부터 시행된 563C 규정으로 인한 것입니다. **144** 이제 지역 레스토랑에서 식품을 취급하기 위해 인증을 획득하는 것이 의무적임에 따라, 시에서는 온라인 교육 프로그램을 개발했습니다.

이 수업은 무료이고, 오염 가능성을 줄이기 위한 목적으로 식품 안전의 기본 사항을 다룹니다. **145** 그것은 이해하기 쉽고 한 시간 이내에 완료할 수 있습니다. 참가자들은 완료 후 학습한 내용에 대해 테스트를 받게 되는 점 참고 바랍니다. **146** 불합격자들은 나중에 재수강할 수 있습니다.

PART 7

147-148은 다음 회람에 관한 문제입니다.

수신: 전 직원
발신: Jim O'Connell 최고 경영자
날짜: 5월 15일
제목: 참고

직원 여러분께,

여기 O'Connell 데이터베이스 소프트웨어사에서 여러분의 개인적인 만족은 저희에게 수익만큼이나 중요합니다. 저희는 여러분이 의욕 있으며 변화를 창출하고 있다고 느끼도록 보장하고 싶습니다. 그렇기 때문에, 앞으로 며칠 내에 저희는 여러분 각자에게 온라인 직원 만족도 설문조사를 발송할 예정입니다. 따라서, 이메일을 꼭 자주 확인하시기 바랍니다. 설문조사에 응할 때, 여러분은 경험의 다양한 측면을 평가하고 가지고 있을 수 있는 어떤 건의 사항이든 제시하도록 요청될 것입니다. 여러분의 답변은 완전히 익명일 것입니다.

147 회람은 왜 쓰였는가?
(A) 일부 성과를 요약하기 위해
(B) 직원들에게 감사를 표하기 위해
(C) 직원들에게 설문조사에 관해 공지하기 위해
(D) 회사 복지에 관한 변경을 발표하기 위해

148 회람은 사람들에게 무엇을 하라고 지시하는가?
(A) 오늘 늦게 회의에 참석한다
(B) 인사팀에 건의 사항을 남긴다
(C) 주어진 시간까지 업무를 완료한다
(D) 수신함을 확인한다

149-150은 다음 광고에 관한 문제입니다.

Handyman Connections사가 당신을 위해 일하게 하세요!
handymanconnections.com에서 당신의 집 수리 필요 사항을 해결할·완벽한 업체를 찾으십시오!

· 수천 명의 배관공, 목수, 전기 기술자, 그리고 기타 집 수리 전문가들을 훑어보세요
· 당신의 지역에 있는 전문가들을 찾으세요
· 지역 고객들이 작성한 후기를 읽거나, 집 수리 또는 유지보수 서비스에 대한 후기를 직접 게시하세요
· 수리 및 유지보수 할인을 받으세요

더 자세한 내용을 위해서는 저희 웹사이트를 방문하거나 모바일 애플리케이션을 다운로드하십시오. 저희 사이트에서 광고할 수 있는 기회에 대해 문의하려면 사업 관리자에게 연락하십시오.

149 광고되고 있는 것은 무엇인가?
(A) 철물점
(B) 인터넷 서비스 공급업체
(C) 집 유지보수 사이트
(D) 채용 공고 서비스

150 업체에 대해 언급된 것은?
(A) 소정의 회비를 청구한다.
(B) 고객들이 의견을 게시하도록 허용한다.
(C) 지역 업체들에게 무료 광고를 제공한다.
(D) 이메일로 신청받는다.

151-152는 다음 이메일에 관한 문제입니다.

수신: QuickShip 고객 서비스 <support@quickship.com>
발신: Peter Howard <peterhoward@yourmail.com>
날짜: 3월 30일
제목: 소포 분실

담당자분께,

저는 최근에 QuickShip 물류회사로부터 소포를 배송받기로 했습니다. 추적 번호 6519를 받은 제 소포는 3월 29일 오후 5시까지 도착할 예정이었습니다.

오후 4시 47분에, 저는 소포가 배송되어 현관문 옆에 놓였다는 이메일 알림을 받았습니다. 하지만 한 시간도 되지 않아 집에 도착했을 때, 현관이나 근처에서 그것을 찾을 수 없었습니다. 제 우편함 옆에서도 보지 못했습니다.

옆집 이웃들에게 실수로 제 소포를 받았는지 물어보았지만, 그들은 그것을 보지 못했습니다. 제 소포가 잘못된 주소로 배송되었거나, 현관에서 도난당한 것 같습니다.

제 소포가 Willard로 431번지로 배송되었는지 확인해 주실 수 있나요? 빠른 답변을 주시면 감사하겠습니다. 555-9192로 전화나 메시지 주세요.

감사합니다,
Peter Howard 드림

151 Mr. Howard가 받은 정보가 아닌 것은?
(A) 배송 확인
(B) 도착일자
(C) 연락처
(D) 추적 번호

152 Mr. Howard는 이미 무엇을 했는가?
(A) 새로운 물품을 주문했다
(B) 환불을 처리했다
(C) 우체국을 방문했다
(D) 우편함 옆을 확인했다

153-154는 다음 메시지 대화문에 관한 문제입니다.

Nelson Kemper	[오전 11시 23분]

Joselyn, 방금 Ms. Lee가 회의에 올 수 없다고 들어서, 제가 전화 회담을 제안했어요. 이제 우리는 그녀와 내일 대화할 거예요.

Joselyn Basset	[오전 11시 25분]

사실, 그거 잘됐네요. 준비할 시간이 더 많아졌어요.

Nelson Kemper	[오전 11시 26분]

맞아요. 그녀의 현재 에너지 투자에 대해서 더 조사해 주실 수 있나요?

Joselyn Basset	[오전 11시 28분]

물론이죠. 또, Ms. Lee의 계약서를 재검토해야 할까요?

Nelson Kemper	[오전 11시 31분]

좋은 생각이에요. 한 번 더 봅시다. 오늘 오후에 시간 날 때 언제든, 제 사무실에 들러 주실 수 있나요?

Joselyn Basset	[오전 11시 35분]

다른 회의 후 오후 3시에 방문할게요.

153 오전 11시 25분에, Ms. Basset이 "Actually, that works out nicely"라고 썼을 때 그녀가 의도한 것 같은 것은?
(A) 지연에 대해 만족한다.
(B) 직접 만나는 것을 선호한다.
(C) 제안을 변경할 것이다.
(D) 투자에 대해 찬성한다.

154 Ms. Basset은 오후 3시에 무엇을 할 것인가?
(A) 조사를 실시한다
(B) 전화 회담을 준비한다
(C) 문서를 점검한다
(D) 고객들과 만난다

155-157은 다음 후기에 관한 문제입니다.

후기 작성자: Elizabeth J. Hunter
제품: TrueSure MT-1 세탁건조기
평점: ★★★★☆

몇 달 전, 저는 가전제품 체인점에서 TrueSure MT-1 세탁건조기를 구입했습니다. 전반적으로, 이 제품은 꽤 만족스럽습니다. 그것은 많은 소음을 내지 않으면서 효과적으로 옷을 세탁하고 건조합니다. MT-1은 또한 매우 작고, 부엌 조리대 아래에 설치하기 쉬웠습니다. 하지만 가장 좋은 것은 그것이 작업을 하기 위해 얼마나 적은 전력을 사용하는지입니다. 시간이 지남에 따라, 이것이 많은 돈을 절약할 것이라고 생각합니다.

물론, 전용 건조기가 있으면 더 빠른 건조 성능을 얻을 것입니다. MT-1을 사용하면, 옷을 완전히 건조하는 데 종종 몇 시간이 걸립니다. 만약 당신의 집에 공간이 더 많다면, 저는 이런 일체형 제품을 추천하지 않을 것입니다. 하지만, 많은 도시 주민들에게는 이것이 괜찮은 선택입니다.

155 1문단 두 번째 줄의 단어 "chain"은 의미상 ~와 가장 가깝다.
(A) 줄
(B) 연결
(C) 시리즈
(D) 그룹

156 Ms. Hunter는 세탁건조기의 어떤 특징에 가장 만족했는가?
(A) 세탁 용량
(B) 낮은 소음 수준
(C) 에너지 효율
(D) 건조 속도

157 Ms. Hunter는 누구에게 MT-1을 사는 것을 권유하지 않겠는가?
(A) 보다 넓은 집에 사는 사람들
(B) 도심 거주자들
(C) 세탁소 주인들
(D) 예산이 빠듯한 고객들

158-160은 다음 편지에 관한 문제입니다.

8월 16일

Mr. Michael Honnold
Miramar로 227번지
White Plains, New York

Mr. Honnold께,

여기 Goodman & Frazier사에 면접을 보러 와주셔서 감사합니다. ― [1] ―. 귀하의 법률적 경험과 제공하신 추천서로 인해 다른 파트너들과 저는 귀하를 만나 뵙기를 고대했습니다. ― [2] ―. 그리고 실제로, 저희는 귀하를 만났을 때 깊은 인상을 받았습니다. 따라서 저희는 귀하께 선임 변호사 직책을 제안합니다.

관심 있으시다면, 귀하는 저희 은행법 부서에 합류하셔서, 금융계에서 가장 영향력 있는 회사들 몇몇에 상담을 제공하는 것을 도우실 것입니다. ― [3] ―. 이 편지에 입사일과 보수에 대한 세부 사항이 동봉되어 있는 것을 확인하실 수 있습니다. ― [4] ―. 축하드리고, 곧 귀하로부터 연락받기를 바랍니다.

Nancy Frazier 드림
Goodman & Frazier사 대표변호사

158 Ms. Frazier는 왜 편지를 썼는가?
(A) 면접을 마련하기 위해
(B) 요구사항을 설명하기 위해
(C) 일자리를 제안하기 위해
(D) 추천서를 요청하기 위해

159 Ms. Frazier는 어떤 업종에서 일하는가?
(A) 법률사무소
(B) 회계기관
(C) 은행
(D) 전력 회사

160 [1], [2], [3], [4]로 표시된 위치 중, 다음 문장이 들어갈 곳으로 가장 적절한 것은?

"이 조건들이 만족스러우신지 가능한 한 빨리 알려주십시오."

(A) [1]
(B) [2]
(C) [3]
(D) [4]

161-163은 다음 안내서에 관한 문제입니다.

Randolph 농장 치즈 제품 관리

저희 농가 치즈는 수제이고 방부제로 가공되지 않았기 때문에, 제조일과 숙성 시간에 따라 품질이 달라질 수 있습니다. 따라서, 제품을 최상의 상태로 섭취하시도록 다음의 조치를 취하실 것을 권장합니다.

먼저, 포장지의 보관 지침을 읽으십시오. 저희의 모든 제품이 냉장 보관되어야 하는 것은 아니며, 냉장고의 차갑고 건조한 환경은 제품들이 빠르게 굳도록 할 수 있습니다. 만약 치즈를 이런 식으로 보관하셔야 한다면, 내가기 전에 항상 상온까지 올라오도록 두십시오. 바로 먹으면, 비교적 밋밋한 맛이 날 것입니다.

일단 치즈 한 조각을 자른 후에는, 남은 치즈의 바깥 가장자리를 소량의 백식초로 닦은 후 재포장하십시오. 이것은 보관 위치와 관계없이 곰팡이의 성장을 크게 제한할 것입니다. 치즈를 포장할 때는, 새 납지만을 사용하십시오. 플라스틱 필름이나 은박지로 포장하는 것은 치즈에서 물기가 스며 나오도록 하여, 식감과 외관에 부정적인 영향을 미칩니다.

161 Randolph 농장 치즈에 대해 언급된 것은?
(A) 살짝 일관되지 않을 수 있다.
(B) 빨리 가공되어야 한다.
(C) 현지 재료로 만들어졌다.
(D) 숙성된 후에 더 맛있다.

162 Randolph 농장은 왜 고객들에게 치즈를 상온으로 내가도록 권장하는가?
(A) 식감을 더 잘 보존하기 위해
(B) 더 쉽게 잘리도록 하기 위해
(C) 빠르게 마르는 것을 방지하기 위해
(D) 온전한 맛을 경험하기 위해

163 안내서에 따르면, 고객들은 치즈를 자른 후에 무엇을 해야 하는가?
(A) 냉장고에 보관한다
(B) 플라스틱 포일로 싼다
(C) 식초에 담근다
(D) 납지에 보관한다

164-167은 다음 안내문에 관한 문제입니다.

www.eeab.com
동유럽 건설업 협회
제19회 컨퍼런스 및 무역 박람회 · 8월 21일-25일 · 폴란드 바르샤바

| 홈 | 위원회 | 프로그램 | 후원자 | 연락처 |

무역 박람회

무역 박람회는 Vilmos 전시관의 B동에서 개최될 예정이며, 참가자들에게 최대의 노출을 보장하는 평면도를 특징으로 할 것입니다. — [1] —.

부스 공간은 선착순 기준으로 배정될 것입니다. 원하는 위치를 예약하기 위해서는 작성된 예약 양식을 제출하십시오. 신청서에는, 첫 번째 선택지가 불가능할 경우에 대비해서 세 가지 대안 선택지를 명확히 명시하십시오. — [2] —. 신청서가 접수되면, 공간이 예약되고 청구서가 발송될 것입니다. 청구서를 받은 후 3영업일 이내에 전액 지불이 요구되며 그렇지 않으면 공간이 박탈됩니다.

모든 참가자들은 등록되어 있어야 하며 회사명이 표시된 배지를 받게 됩니다. 일반 부스에는 2개의 무료 배지가, 디럭스 부스에는 4개가, 그리고 프리미엄 부스에는 6개가 제공됩니다. 귀사가 후원자인 경우, 최대 12개의 참가자 배지를 받을 수 있습니다. — [3] —. 보안상의 이유로, 등록된 참가자들은 항시 배지를 착용해야 합니다.

마지막으로, 모든 활동은 전시 부스 구역에만 국한되어야 한다는 것을 명심하십시오. — [4] —. 관리진은 부적절하다고 판단되는 모든 활동을 중지하도록 참가자들에게 요구할 권리를 보유합니다.

자세한 내용은 컨퍼런스 시작 3개월 전 온라인에 게시될 브로슈어에 포함될 것입니다.

164 무역 박람회에 대해 언급된 것은?
(A) 행사는 4일의 기간 동안 진행될 것이다.
(B) Vilmos 전시관 전체를 차지할 것이다.
(C) 바르샤바에서 열리는 첫 번째 박람회일 것이다.
(D) 부스는 신청 순서대로 배정될 것이다.

165 신청자들은 무엇을 하도록 요청되는가?
(A) 신청서와 함께 비용을 지불한다
(B) 대표자 수를 두 명으로 제한한다
(C) 부스 공간을 위해 몇 가지 선택을 한다
(D) 직원들을 위해 식권을 구매한다

166 안내문에 따르면, 무엇이 웹사이트에서 이용 가능할 것인가?
(A) 책자
(B) 평면도
(C) 일정표
(D) 영수증

167 [1], [2], [3], [4]로 표시된 위치 중, 다음 문장이 들어갈 곳으로 가장 적절한 것은?

"모든 추가 참가자들에게는 수수료가 부과됩니다."

(A) [1]
(B) [2]
(C) [3]
(D) [4]

168-171은 다음 광고에 관한 문제입니다.

TC Cyber사 서비스

TC Cyber사는 개인과 중소기업을 위한 전문 IT 지원을 제공합니다. 아마 아시겠지만, 저희는 수리 서비스로 유명합니다. 저희에게 컴퓨터를 맡기시면 순식간에 다시 새것처럼 제대로 작동하게 만들 것임을 보장합니다. 그런데, 이제 TC Cyber사가 다국적 기업인 A to Z사의 일부이기 때문에, 저희는 훨씬 더 많은 것을 할 수 있는 능력이 있습니다. 현재, 저희는 새 컴퓨터나 서버 시스템을 집이나 사무실에 설치 및 최적화하도록 팀을 파견할 수 있으며, 필요한 경우 24시간 응급 수리를 실시할 수 있습니다. 또한 기기를 최적화하거나 소프트웨어를 사용하는 방법을 배우시는 데 도움이 되기 위한 가상 예약을 제공합니다.

이 모든 서비스는 월간 TC Cyber사 회원권에 포함되어 있습니다. A to Z 전자회사로부터 컴퓨터를 구매하는 고객들은 6개월 동안 TC Cyber사 지원을 무료로 받을 수 있습니다. 저희는 또한 경쟁력 있는 일회성 요금도 제공합니다. 회원이 되려면, 저희 웹사이트 또는 녹스빌 지역 지점 중 한 군데를 방문하십시오.

당신의 컴퓨터가 항상 최상의 상태임을 확신하고 싶다면, TC Cyber사를 당신 편으로 만드십시오.

168 TC Cyber사에 대해 암시되는 것은?
(A) 녹스빌에 새로운 지점을 개업했다.
(B) 할인된 전자기기를 판매한다.
(C) 주로 중소기업 고객들과 거래한다.
(D) 다른 회사에 의해 인수되었다.

169 TC Cyber사에 의해 제공되지 않는 것은?
(A) 24시간 서비스
(B) 온라인 상담
(C) 데이터 보호
(D) 컴퓨터 설치

170 무료 서비스를 받을 수 있는 사람은 누구인가?
(A) 특별 보증 구매자
(B) A to Z 전자회사 컴퓨터 구매자
(C) 수리가 미루어진 고객
(D) TC Cyber사를 처음 이용하는 고객

171 광고가 회원권에 대해 암시하는 것은?
(A) 가격이 올랐다.
(B) 대면으로 구매할 수 있다.
(C) 최소 1년 동안 지속된다.
(D) 새 서버 시스템을 포함한다.

172-175는 다음 온라인 채팅 대화문에 관한 문제입니다.

Henry Benson (9시 42분)
Alex Nigh가 공급 계약을 체결하는 데 관심이 있지만, 우리가 5월 1일까지 모든 것을 준비할 수 있는지 알고 싶어 합니다. 그는 그때 영업을 시작하거든요.

Jerry Trainor (9시 44분)
식탁보 재고는 충분하지만, 천 냅킨은 우리의 공급업체로부터 더 받아야 할 거예요. 그리고 키친타월도요.

Wendy Hadley (9시 45분)

그건 빠듯할 수도 있겠는데요. 우리의 유니폼 제조업체가 그때까지 그의 주문을 이행할 수 있을지 모르겠어요. 그들에게 전화해서 알아볼 수 있도록 몇 분만 주세요.

Jerry Trainor (9시 45분)

그리고 고객은 세탁 서비스도 요청하는 거 맞죠?

Henry Benson (9시 47분)

맞아요.

Wendy Hadley (9시 54분)

방금 유니폼 공급업체와 통화했어요. 주방장과 주방 직원 유니폼은 재고가 있대요. 하지만 고객은 웨이터 유니폼에 대한 주문 제작 요청이 있어서, 그것들은 5월 말이나 돼야 준비될 거예요.

Henry Benson (10시)

그렇군요. 문제가 될 수도 있겠어요.

Jerry Trainor (10시 1분)

Wendy, 우리 무늬 없는 검정색 웨이터 유니폼 재고는 있잖아요? 맞춤 유니폼이 도착할 때까지 고객에게 그것들을 제공할 수 있어요.

Wendy Hadley (10시 3분)

네, 있어요. 다양한 치수도 많아요.

Henry Benson (10시 4분)

좋아요, 제가 지금 바로 그에게 전화해서 다른 것들이 공급업체로부터 도착할 때까지 무료로 검정색 유니폼 사용을 제안하겠습니다. 곧 결과를 알려드릴게요.

---

172 Mr. Nigh는 어떤 종류의 사업체를 소유하는 것 같은가?
   (A) 의류 제조업체
   (B) 외식업체
   (C) 유니폼 세탁 회사
   (D) 배달 서비스

173 9시 45분에, Ms. Hadley가 "That might be tough"라고 썼을 때 그녀가 의도한 것은?
   (A) 기한이 촉박하다.
   (B) 물자가 떨어지고 있다.
   (C) 공간이 한정되어 있다.
   (D) 규칙이 지나치게 엄격하다.

174 유니폼에 관한 문제는 무엇인가?
   (A) 공급업체가 몇몇 물품들을 더 이상 생산하지 않는다.
   (B) 일부 자재가 사기에 너무 비싸다.
   (C) 주요 고객이 주문에 대한 환불을 원한다.
   (D) 개인 맞춤 물품들은 제조하는 데 더 오래 걸린다.

175 Mr. Benson은 다음에 무엇을 할 것인가?
   (A) 견본을 제공한다
   (B) 주문 제작 물품을 요청한다
   (C) 주문을 한다
   (D) 고객에게 연락한다

176-180은 다음 이메일과 후기에 관한 문제입니다.

수신: Alita Dominguez <a.dominguez@lwrmail.com>
발신: Frederico Matterazzi <frederico@allegratravel.com>
제목: 회신: 나폴리 방문
날짜: 6월 3일

안녕하세요 Alita,

Allegra 여행사에 관심을 가져주셔서 감사합니다. 귀하의 문의와 관련하여, 유감스럽게도 Napoli Voyager 투어에는 더 이상 자리가 없습니다. 그러나, 저희 회사에는 귀하가 즐기실 만한 몇 가지 다른 선택지가 있습니다.

첫 번째는 이틀간의 Napoli Express 투어입니다. 첫날에는, 도보로 나폴리 도심부를 답사하고 나서 국립 초상화 미술관에 갈 것입니다. 둘째 날에는, 귀하를 버스로 폼페이에 모시고 가서, 2천 년 된 로마 마을의 잘 보존된 유적을 볼 것입니다.

3일간의 Napoli Essentials 투어는 같은 일정을 따르지만 마지막 날에 나폴리만의 경치 좋은 보트 투어를 추가합니다. 또는, 더 야심 찬 것을 원하신다면, 4일간의 Napoli Extended 투어도 제공합니다. 이것은 Express 투어의 모든 것을 포함하지만, 소렌토에 들르고 베수비어스산을 등반하는 전원에서의 이틀을 추가합니다.

수요가 높으니, 관심 있으시다면 바로 알려주십시오.

Frederico Matterazzi 드림

나폴리를 방문하는 완벽한 방법: Allegra 여행사

제 남편과 저는 최근 나폴리를 방문할 기회가 있었습니다. 저희는 전에 이탈리아에 가본 적이 없어서, 현지 주민들만을 고용하는 여행사를 통해 예약하기로 했습니다. 그들은 저희를 대부분의 관광객들이 놓치는 몇몇 아름다운 섬으로의 보트 여행에 데려가 주었습니다.

저희의 주요 가이드였던 Vincenzo Mastroianni는 재치 있고 통찰력 있었으며, 그것은 도시와 건축물에 생기를 불어넣었습니다. 그는 저희를 멋진 피자 레스토랑에 식사하러 데려갔는데, 그곳에서 그는 모든 직원을 알고 있는 것 같았습니다. 저희는 심지어 식사가 어떻게 준비되었는지도 볼 수 있었습니다.

그러나 여행의 백미는 고대 도시 폼페이였습니다. 그 장소는 경외심을 불러일으켰으며, Vincenzo는 저희에게 무료 오디오 가이드를 가지고 돌아다닐 수 있는 충분한 시간을 주었습니다. 강력히 추천합니다!

10 / 10
후기 작성자: Alita Dominguez

---

176 이메일의 한 가지 목적은 무엇인가?
   (A) 지침을 제공하기 위해
   (B) 시간표를 변경하기 위해
   (C) 대안을 제시하기 위해
   (D) 할인을 제공하기 위해

177 Allegra 여행사가 제공하지 않는 것은?
   (A) 폼페이로 가는 교통수단
   (B) 도시 도보 관광
   (C) 무료 식사
   (D) 박물관 방문

178 Ms. Dominguez는 어떤 투어를 간 것 같은가?
   (A) Napoli Voyager 투어
   (B) Napoli Express 투어
   (C) Napoli Essentials 투어
   (D) Napoli Extended 투어

179 후기가 Mr. Mastroianni에 대해 암시하는 것은?
   (A) 미술 전문가이다.
   (B) Mr. Matterazzi를 대신했다.
   (C) 뛰어난 요리사이다.
   (D) 나폴리에 거주한다.

180 Ms. Dominguez는 투어에서 무엇을 가장 좋아했는가?
   (A) 역사적 장소를 탐사하는 것
   (B) 피자 레스토랑에서 식사하는 것
   (C) 현대 건축물을 감상하는 것
   (D) 소렌토에서 쇼핑하는 것

Clear Brook 단지 - 임대 아파트

McIntyre시의 동쪽에 위치한 Clear Brook 단지는 레스토랑과 상점, Castillo 지하철역, 그리고 공공 도서관과 매우 가깝습니다. 또한, 지하 주차장, 구내 세탁실, 그리고 피트니스 시설과 같은 건물의 많은 편의 시설들이 임대료에 포함됩니다.

가격은 다음과 같이 호실 크기에 따라 다릅니다:
원룸: 월 1,500달러
침실 1개: 월 1,700달러
침실 2개: 월 2,100달러
침실 3개: 월 2,500달러

모든 호실은 새롭게 페인트칠 되었으며 도자기 타일과 새 카펫, 스테인리스강 냉장고와 가스레인지, 그리고 냉난방 시스템을 갖추고 있습니다. 지하실 창고는 월 120달러의 추가 요금으로 이용 가능합니다. Clear Brook 단지를 둘러보도록 예약하려면, 555-6721로 전화하거나 info@clearbrookestates.com으로 관리사무소의 June Hoffman에게 이메일을 보내십시오.

수신: June Hoffman <info@clearbrookestates.com>
발신: Max Grimes <mgrimes@invimail.com>
제목: 아파트
날짜: 6월 20일

Ms. Hoffman께,

제가 Clear Brook 단지를 둘러보는 동안 가졌던 질문들에 답변해 주셔서 감사합니다. 고민 끝에, 당신이 제게 추천하신 호실을 임대하는 데 관심이 있다고 확신을 가지고 말씀드릴 수 있습니다.

저희가 대화했을 때 언급했듯이, 저는 교외의 주택으로부터 이사하는 것입니다. 가능한 한 짐을 줄이려 최선을 다했지만, 일부 스포츠 용품과는 떨어질 수 없어서 추가 보관 공간을 요청하고 싶습니다. 120달러 요금을 제가 매달 임대료로 지불할 2,100달러에 그냥 포함해도 괜찮을지 알려주세요.

답장 기다리겠습니다.

Max Grimes 드림

---

181 광고는 누구를 대상으로 하는 것 같은가?
(A) 부동산 개발업자
(B) Clear Brook 세입자
(C) 유지보수 직원
(D) 예비 임대인

182 Clear Brook 단지의 각 호실은 무엇을 포함하는가?
(A) 새 벽지
(B) 부엌 장비
(C) 세탁기
(D) 창고

183 이메일에서, 2문단 두 번째 줄의 단어 "part"는 의미상 –와 가장 가깝다.
(A) 폐기하다
(B) 나누다
(C) 분리하다
(D) 나가다

184 Ms. Hoffman은 Mr. Grimes에게 어떤 종류의 호실을 추천했는가?
(A) 원룸 아파트
(B) 침실 1개짜리 아파트
(C) 침실 2개짜리 아파트
(D) 침실 3개짜리 아파트

185 Mr. Grimes에 대해 암시되는 것은?
(A) 전문 스포츠 팀에 소속되어 있다.
(B) 일부 소유물을 처분했다.
(C) 직장과 더 가까워지기 위해 이사할 것이다.

(D) 지하철역 근처에 사는 것을 선호한다.

---

www.sagetax.au/corevalues

핵심 가치

Sage Tax사에서, 우리는 뛰어난 세금 준비 해결책을 제공하는 데 헌신합니다. 우리의 궁극적인 목표는 그들이 매년 돌아오도록 각 고객의 신뢰를 얻는 것입니다. 이는 우리의 핵심 가치들에 의해 구현됩니다.

· 핵심 가치 1: 가능한 한 많은 환급을 받을 수 있는 모든 방법을 살펴봅니다. 고객이 세금 공제에 대해 알지 못하더라도, 공제받을 자격이 있을 수도 있습니다.
· 핵심 가치 2: 우리가 그들을 위해 열심히 노력하고 있다는 것을 보여주기 위해 고객 문의에 빠른 답변을 제공합니다.
· 핵심 가치 3: 세금 준비를 최대한 원활하게 하기 위해 각 단계에서 어떤 서류가 필요한지 설명합니다.
· 핵심 가치 4: 무엇보다도, 각 환급의 모든 부분을 두 번, 세 번 점검하도록 노력합니다.

수신: Rachel Lim <ra_Lim@sagetax.au>
발신: Jedda Purcell <Jedda91@coventrysystems.au>
제목: 환급 문제
날짜: 10월 15일
첨부 파일: 수치 업데이트

안녕하세요 Rachel,

제 세금 환급 현황에 대해 문의하려고 다시 연락드립니다. 지난번 당신의 이메일에서, 당신이 제 모든 서류를 가지고 있으며 곧 제 세금을 신고할 것이라고 말씀하셨습니다. 하지만, 제가 가장 최근의 퇴직연금에 대해 당신에게 잘못된 수치를 드렸다는 것을 지금 깨달았습니다. 이 오류를 고치기에 너무 늦었고 이 불일치가 세무서에서 문제를 일으킬까 봐 상당히 우려됩니다.

그러니, 제 환급 현황에 대해 알려주십시오. 이것이 당신으로부터 마지막으로 연락받은 후 제가 보내는 세 번째 메시지인 만큼, 빠른 답변을 주시면 감사하겠습니다. 전에 남겨 드린 번호로 전화나 문자 메시지를 주시면 됩니다.

곧 당신으로부터 연락받지 못하면, Sage사의 관리진에게 연락할 수밖에 없을 것입니다.

Jedda Purcell 드림

회람

날짜: 10월 23일
수신: Sage Tax사 고객 서비스 팀
발신: Klaus Booker 고객 서비스 관리자
제목: 고객 후속 조치

모두들 안녕하세요,

전반적으로, 저는 이번 세금 신고 기간 모두의 노력에 만족합니다. 우리는 세금 신고에 있어 높은 수준의 정확성을 유지하면서 기록적인 수의 고객들을 유치했습니다. 그러나, 기대치 관리라는 한 가지 영역에서는 개선의 여지가 있다고 생각합니다.

오늘 아침, 저는 불만족스러워하는 고객과 대화했습니다. 그녀는 절차가 얼마나 걸릴지 확신하지 못했고, 이 감정은 우리 세무사와의 소통으로 인해 더욱 악화되었을 뿐인데, 이 과정에서 그녀는 세 건의 별개 메시지에 대해 답을 받지 못했습니다. 결과적으로, 그녀는 변호사 및 회계사와 세금 부담에 대한 회의를 어떻게 잡는 것이 가장 좋을지 혼란을 느꼈습니다.

따라서, 고객들에게 연락할 때는, 정확히 언제 신고할 것인지 알려주시고, 신고한 후에는 반드시 후속 조치를 발송하시기 바랍니다.

직원 안내서에 명시된 대로, 고객으로부터 불만이 제기된 사람들은 추가 교육을 받을 것입니다.

Klaus Booker 드림

186 웹페이지에 따르면, 무엇이 Sage Tax사의 최우선순위인가?
(A) 재방문 고객들을 얻는 것
(B) 환급의 규모를 증가시키는 것
(C) 가장 많은 고객을 유치하는 것
(D) 불필요한 절차를 없애는 것

187 Ms. Purcell은 그녀의 세금에 대해 무엇이라고 말하는가?
(A) 세금에 대해 부정확한 정보를 제공했다.
(B) 세금을 전날 Ms. Lim에게 보냈다.
(C) 예상한 것보다 더 적은 환급을 받았다.
(D) 세무서로부터 세금에 대해 연락 받았다.

188 Sage Tax사는 어떤 핵심 가치를 지키지 못했는가?
(A) 핵심 가치 1
(B) 핵심 가치 2
(C) 핵심 가치 3
(D) 핵심 가치 4

189 Mr. Booker는 올해 세금 신고 기간에 대해 무엇을 언급하는가?
(A) 지금까지 회사의 가장 성공적인 기간이었다.
(B) 기록적인 수익 불만을 야기했다.
(C) 과거보다 더 많은 직원을 필요로 했다.
(D) 며칠 더 연장되었다.

190 Ms. Lim에 대해 암시되는 것은?
(A) 추가적인 교육을 받을 것이다.
(B) 일정에 대해 어려움을 겪었다.
(C) 다른 사람들에게 후속 전화에 대해 지시할 것이다.
(D) 추가 할인을 확보하지 않았다.

191-195는 다음 공고, 양식, 연설 초안에 관한 문제입니다.

제14회 연간 East Springs 상공회의소
올해의 중소기업상
후보 지명 공모

상공회의소는 여러분에게 지역사회의 경제적 및 사회적 안녕을 크게 향상시킨 기여를 한 영세 사업주를 지명하도록 권장합니다. 후보 지명 마감일은 9월 15일입니다. 이전 수상자들은 수상 자격이 없지만, 과거 후보자들은 재지명될 수 있는 점 참고 바랍니다. 자신을 지명하는 것도 권장됩니다.

모든 지명된 기업들은
· East Springs 상공회의소 회원이어야 합니다
· 직원이 50명 미만이어야 합니다
· 지명되기 최소 2년 전에 개업했어야 합니다

상은 지명된 모든 사업주들이 초청될 축하 오찬 후에 수여될 것입니다. 문의를 하려면, cburroughs@eastspringscoc.com으로 Conrad Burroughs에게 연락하시기 바랍니다.

올해의 중소기업상 후보 지명 양식

기업명: Dunston 미용학원
사업주: Katrina Dunston
주소: Fort로 1246번지, East Springs
전화번호: 555-6621

후보 지명 이유: 학생 미용사가 제 머리를 자르고 염색한다는 생각은 처음에는 저를 걱정스럽게 했습니다. 그러나, Dunston 미용학원에서는, 교육 수준이 훌륭하다는 것이 명백합니다. 저는 이곳을 여러 번 방문했으며 항상 만족했습니다. 게다가, 가격은 정말 이길 수가 없습니다.

머리를 자르기 위해서나 교육받기 위해 갈 좋은 장소일 뿐만 아니라, 이 학원은 사회에 환원합니다. 학생들 또한 East Springs 패션쇼와 같은 자선 행사에서 봉사하기 위해 종종 그들의 시간과 재능을 기부합니다. 이러한 이유로, 저는 Dunston 미용학원이 수상해야 한다고 생각합니다.

❍

지명자: Jessica Frappier

10월 1일
Jorge Ortega
수상 소감: 초안

저와 함께 Go Entertainment사에서 일하시는 모든 분들을 대표하여, 이 상을 감사히 받겠습니다. 우리 모두가 사랑하는 이 도시에 대한 공로를 상공회의소로부터 인정받게 되어 큰 영광입니다.

저는 Go Entertainment사를 설립했을 때, 사람들이 멋진 밴드의 연주를 들을 수 있는 따뜻한 장소를 운영하는 것을 꿈꿨습니다. 소기업이라는 것은 단순히 수익성 있는 사업체가 되는 것 이상을 의미합니다. 그것이 저희가 작년에 East Springs 지역사회를 위해 콘서트를 준비하고 지역 그룹들이 연주하도록 초대한 이유입니다. 이 상에 대해 모든 분들께 정말 감사드립니다.

---

191 공고는 왜 작성되었는가?
(A) 보조금에 대한 기준을 설명하기 위해
(B) 적합한 후보자에 대한 제안을 요청하기 위해
(C) 최근 대회의 결과를 발표하기 위해
(D) 지역사회 참여에 대해 사업주들에게 감사를 표하기 위해

192 Ms. Frappier는 왜 Dunston 미용학원을 추천하는가?
(A) 학생들이 지역사회 행사를 개최한다.
(B) 협력사업이 다른 기업들에 이익이 된다.
(C) 고령자들에게 할인을 제공한다.
(D) 낮은 비용으로 고품질의 서비스를 제공한다.

193 Ms. Dunston에 대해 추론할 수 있는 것은?
(A) 수익의 일부를 자선단체에 기부한다.
(B) 상공회의소로부터 자금을 받을 것이다.
(C) 전에 지역 사업상을 수상한 적이 있다.
(D) 오찬에 초대를 받을 것이다.

194 Go Entertainment사에 대해 암시되는 것은?
(A) 영업한 지 적어도 2년이 되었다.
(B) Mr. Ortega에 의해 지명되었다.
(C) 곧 50명 이상의 직원을 고용할 것이다.
(D) East Springs 출신 밴드들을 후원한다.

195 Mr. Ortega는 작년에 무엇을 했는가?
(A) 회사를 설립했다
(B) 지역 행사를 기획했다
(C) 상을 받았다
(D) 무대에서 공연했다

196-200은 다음 광고, 회람, 공고에 관한 문제입니다.

Swifty사가 토론토에 찾아왔습니다! 오늘부터, 이 도시는 미국 밖에서 Swifty사의 첫 번째 시장이 됩니다. 다른 많은 도시들의 사람들이 그렇듯이, 토론토 주민들은 커지는 교통 혼잡 문제에 직면해 있습니다. 이를 해결하기 위해, Swifty사는 정기적인 통근이든, 친구들 모임과 경기를 보러 가는 여행이든, 아니면 콘서트나 다른 행사로 오고 가는 셔틀이든 간에, 단체로 이동하는 사람들을 위해 편리한 해결책을 제공합니다. 저희는 네 가지 주요 교통 서비스를 제공합니다.

서비스	대상	차량 종류	청구 방식
Point-to-Point	소규모 단체를 위한 단일 이동	미니밴 (최대 7인승)	거리에 따른 일회성 지불
Event	하루 종일 행사장을 오가는 임시 셔틀이 필요한 단체	밴 또는 미니버스 (최대 15인승)	일일
Excursion	단일 목적지까지 장거리 여행을 하는 단체	미니버스 또는 일반 버스 (15-40인승)	시간당
Enterprise	직원들에게 매일 운송 수단을 제공하고자 하는 기업들	일반 버스 (최대 40인승)	월간

❍

Swifty사 친환경 보증의 일환으로, 저희의 모든 일반 버스는 전기차입니다. 서비스 준비는 Swifty 앱으로 할 수 있지만, Event 또는 Enterprise 예약을 위해서는 최대 한 달의 소요 시간이 필요합니다.

회람
Bolton 제조사

수신: Jade Robinson 인사팀장
발신: Simon Dodd 인사부팀장
제목: 셔틀 서비스
날짜: 4월 30일

제가 Swifty사를 확인해 보았는데, 실행 가능한 통근 해결책인 것 같아요. 월 비용도 꽤 합리적인 것 같고, 제가 조사한 많은 직원들이 관심을 보였습니다. 사실, 제 생각에는 모든 수요를 충족하기 위해 두 번째 셔틀을 준비해야 할 것 같아요. 계획에 반대하는 직원들이 몇 명 있긴 해요. 그들은 픽업 장소가 약간 멀다고 생각합니다. 앞으로 이 상황을 관찰해 보되, 지금으로서는 Swifty사를 사용하기 시작해도 괜찮을 것 같아요. 곧 계획을 세우면, 6월부터 서비스를 시작할 수 있습니다.

Bolton 제조사
직원들에게 공고

6월부터, 우리는 토론토 공장의 모든 직원들을 위해 무료 셔틀 서비스를 제공할 것입니다. 이것은 Sheppard역에 있는 정류장에서 출발하여, 근무를 위해 여러분을 공장으로 바로 데려다 주고 집으로 가는 기차 시간에 맞춰 역에 내려줄 것입니다. 이동은 월요일부터 금요일까지 본 공고에 명시된 시각에 진행됩니다. 모든 셔틀에는 무료 와이파이가 제공될 것입니다. Sheppard역의 주차 공간은 일일 요금으로 이용할 수 있습니다.

공장행	Sheppard역행
오전 6시 10분	오후 3시 20분
오전 6시 30분	오후 3시 40분
오후 2시 10분	오후 11시 20분
오후 2시 30분	오전 12시 10분

196 Swifty사에 대해 언급된 것은?
(A) 주로 기업 고객들을 위한 것이다.
(B) 시 정부에 의해 부분적으로 자금을 지원받을 것이다.
(C) 복수의 국가들에서 서비스를 제공한다.
(D) 새로운 모바일 애플리케이션을 출시할 것이다.

197 Swifty사는 광고에서 그것의 차량에 대해 무엇이라고 말하는가?
(A) 하루 24시간 내내 이용 가능하다.
(B) 전문 스포츠 팀에 의해 사용된다.
(C) 일부는 휘발유를 요하지 않는다.
(D) 대부분 장거리를 위해 의도되었다.

198 Bolton 제조사는 어떤 차량을 이용할 것 같은가?
(A) 미니밴
(B) 밴
(C) 미니버스
(D) 일반 버스

199 Sheppard역에 대해 추론될 수 있는 것은?
(A) Bolton사의 토론토 공장과 연결되어 있다.
(B) 시설이 최근 확장되었다.
(C) 기차가 종종 늦는다.
(D) 외진 곳에 위치해 있다.

200 공고에 따르면 이용 가능하지 않을 것은?
(A) 인터넷 연결
(B) 자정 이후 차편
(C) 주말 셔틀 서비스
(D) 주차 공간

TEST 02 해석

* 무료 해설은 해커스토익(Hackers.co.kr)에서 다운로드 받을 수 있습니다.

• QR 코드로 바로가기

PART 5

101 Concordia 은행은 부사장의 자리를 경쟁사들 중 한 곳에서 근무하는 임원으로 채울 수도 있다.

102 더 많은 고객들을 유치하려는 노력으로, Hanford Jewelers사는 현재 5개의 지점에서 은 제품의 무료 세척 서비스를 제공한다.

103 예약을 한도 이상으로 받은 샌디에이고행 항공편의 승객 중에, 오직 네 명만이 흔쾌히 나중에 이동하겠다고 말했다.

104 등록된 모든 유권자 중 오직 25퍼센트만이 지난 선거에 참여하면서, 이를 기록상 최저의 투표율 중 하나로 만들었다.

105 다수의 연구는 적당한 운동조차도 신체 건강의 뚜렷한 개선으로 이어질 수 있음을 증명해왔다.

106 비록 그 두 최고 경영자는 같은 행사들에 참석했지만, 그들은 아직 공식적으로 서로를 소개받지는 못했다.

107 그녀가 본 모든 아파트들 중에서 그것이 가장 덜 비쌌기 때문에 Ms. Stein은 Albright가의 아파트에 세 들기로 결정했다.

108 작업팀은 Mr. Haskell의 소유지의 경계를 따라 이어지는 울타리를 수리하는 데 일주일이 걸렸다.

109 대부분의 시민들은 시의 도시 개발 계획을 찬성했고, 시청에 불만이 거의 접수되지 않았다.

110 수필 대회의 많은 제출작들은 대부분의 참가자들이 학생이라는 것을 고려했을 때 매우 잘 쓰여졌다.

111 경제적인 에너지 소비에 대한 반복되는 주의에 응하여, 더 많은 가정에서 에너지 효율적인 가전제품들을 구입하고 있다.

112 공사 현장에 들어가기 전에, 모든 직원들은 완벽한 보호를 제공해줄 적절한 안전 장비를 착용해야 한다.

113 초대된 손님들은 영업부서를 위한 연회가 Ogilvy 호텔에서 정확히 오후 7시에 시작할 것이라고 통지받았다.

114 Ray's 자동차 센터는 심한 비나 눈에 노출될 때 유리를 깨끗하게 유지시켜주는 차량 창문 코팅을 제공한다.

115 식당 지배인은 느린 서비스에 대한 손님들의 불평을 처리하기 위해 웨이터를 두 명 더 고용하는 것을 고려하고 있다.

116 판매 직원들은 모든 상품에 대한 질문을 가진 고객들을 돕도록 교육받고 상점의 기기에 대해 시연을 할 수 있다.

117 Vail사의 주가는 연초에 비해 16퍼센트 상승했는데, 대부분 해외 수익의 증가 때문이다.

118 Ms. Parson이 Keystone Developments사에서 고용되었던 동안 그녀는 뛰어난 성과 평가를 받았다.

119 Towler Prudential사의 새로운 브로슈어는 다양한 보험 보장 제도에 대한 추가 정보를 제공한다.

120 행사가 국경일과 동시에 일어나므로 많은 사람들이 Broad Street 쇼핑몰 개업식에 참석할 것으로 예상된다.

121 Hammersmith 기업 연합은 기업가 정신을 장려하기 위해 새로운 일련의 강의들에 보조금을 지급할 것이다.

122 Main가 퍼레이드 동안 도움을 제공하는 자원봉사자들은 그들이 입고 있는

밝은 초록색 셔츠로 구별된다.

123 농산물 직판장에서 물건을 사는 것은 구할 수 있는 가장 신선한 제철 농작물을 찾는 좋은 방법이다.

124 투숙객들은 10월 1일부로 할인된 투어와 리조트 수영장 시설의 무제한 사용에 대한 자격이 생길 것이다.

125 위원회가 그 회사에 최종 승인을 했음에도 불구하고, 양측의 어떤 당사자들도 가격이 합의될 때까지 계약을 맺지 않을 것이다.

126 새롭게 발간된 Nigel Murphy 소설의 간략한 인용구는 극찬하는 서평과 함께 일간지에 특집으로 실렸다.

127 더 많은 참석자들을 수용할 수 있을 뿐만 아니라, 새로운 행사 장소는 도시 중심으로부터 더 편리하게 접근할 수 있다.

128 Sparks Entertainment사에서 곧 나올 비디오 게임을 구매하기를 간절히 바라는 고객들은 미리 주문하도록 강력히 권고된다.

129 병원 관리진과 미리 합의가 이루어지지 않은 이상 방문객들은 환자와 밤새 함께 있는 것이 허락되지 않는다.

130 공장의 안전 관리자들은 경고 없이 일 년 내내 간헐적으로 점검을 실시하기 때문에, 직원들은 항상 그러한 일에 대해 준비되어 있어야 한다.

PART 6

131-134는 다음 기사에 관한 문제입니다.

131 Scott Harper가 다가오는 Cannon 보트 경주에서 캐나다의 국가 대표 보트 팀을 이끌도록 선출되었다. 팀 대변인 Jeremy Dawes가 오늘 일찍 기자 회견에서 발표했다. 132 그는 또한 그 행사에서 기자들의 질문에도 답변했다.

39살의 뉴브런즈윅 출신인 Harper는 여러 국제 행사에 참가한 일평생의 보트광이다. 133 그는 혼자 보트를 타는 경주로 Yachtmaster 상을 두 번 받았고 다음 달 말에 세 번째로 경기에 참가할 것인데, 이번에는 여섯 명의 팀원들과 함께이다.

그의 새로운 지위에서 팀을 대표하여 말하는 Mr. Harper는 캐나다 팀의 가능성에 대해 자신감이 있는 것 같아 보였다. "저희 중 대부분은 이전의 경기들에서 함께 해보았습니다. 134 사실, 저는 다른 선수들 중 적어도 네 명과 함께 경주에 나간 적이 있습니다."라고 그가 말했다.

135-138은 다음 이메일에 관한 문제입니다.

수신: Randy Huffington <r.huffington@megadelta.com>
발신: Olivia Cottrell <o_cottrell@edicare.com>
제목: 기계 문제
날짜: 6월 20일

135 이것은 최근에 저희 덴버 공장에서 제대로 작동하지 않았던 공장 장비와 관련하여 보내는 두 번째 서신입니다. 136 제가 첫 번째 이메일에서 언급하였듯이, 한 공장 직원이 기계가 많은 소음을 발생시키고 있으며 거칠게 흔들리고 있다고 말했습니다. 위험할 수도 있었기 때문에, 그것이 저희 직원들 중 누구에게라도 심각한 부상을 초래하는 것을 방지하기 위해 기계를 껐습니다.

그 기계는 불과 일주일 전에 귀사로부터 저희 공장에 배달되었습니다. 137 그러므로, 저희가 구입한 장비는 아직 보증 기간 중입니다. 장비를 검사하기 위해서 저희 공장에 기술자를 보내주실 수 있습니까? 138 바라건대, 귀사의 기술자가 어째서 설치 후 얼마 지나지 않아 기계가 고장 났는지를 알아낼 수 있었으면 합니다.

귀사의 답변을 기다릴 것이며 그것이 신속하기를 기대합니다.

Olivia Cottrell 드림

상급 관리자
Edicare 산업

139-142는 다음 설명서에 관한 문제입니다.

DiMaggiano's 냉동 피자
조리 설명서

피자를 포장에서 꺼내되, 해동하지 마십시오. 139 피자가 녹았다면, 조리 시간을 약 3분만큼 줄이십시오.

오븐을 섭씨 230도로 예열하십시오. 더 부드러운 빵 껍질을 위해서는, 피자를 오븐의 중간 선반에 놓고 10분에서 12분 동안 구우십시오. 140 빵 껍질이 금색이고 치즈가 녹았을 때 피자를 꺼내십시오. 더 바삭바삭한 빵 껍질을 위해서는, 피자를 오븐의 위쪽 선반에서 더 뜨거운 온도로 구우십시오. 141 즉, 훨씬 더 단단한 빵 껍질을 위해서는 다이얼을 280도로 맞추십시오!

손가락을 데지 않도록 피자를 오븐에서 조심스럽게 꺼내십시오. 142 먹기 전에 3분에서 4분 정도 식히십시오. 그리고 나면 피자를 잘라 맛있는 DiMaggiano's의 음식을 당신이 가장 좋아하는 음료와 함께 즐기기만 하면 됩니다.

143-146은 다음 회람에 관한 문제입니다.

Griffin 대학교
회람

수신: 모든 교수진
발신: Dale Henriksen
제목: 학술지
날짜: 8월 24일

143 작년에, Griffin 대학교는 도서관 학술지에 대한 지출을 줄이기 위한 조치를 취했습니다. 몇 년간의 물가 인상에 상응하는 예산 증가가 없었던 것은 많은 학술지에 대한 비용을 지불하는 것을 어렵게 만들었습니다. 144 따라서, 일부 구독을 취소해야 했습니다. 올해, 도서관 위원회는 도서관의 소장 목록에서 삭제될 추가적인 50개의 학술지를 선정했습니다. 145 하지만, 저희는 예산 상황이 개선되고 나면 이 출판물들을 다시 되찾으려 노력할 것입니다. 146 그동안, 여러분의 인내심과 이해를 부탁드립니다. 보유하고 있는 출판물의 전체 목록은 도서관 웹사이트에 게시되어 있습니다.

PART 7

147-148은 다음 광고에 관한 문제입니다.

EVERIDGE 공인 회계사
Suite 19-A, 825번지 Burrard, 밴쿠버 브리티시 콜롬비아주, V0P-F1K

납세 신고 양식 때문에 어려움을 겪고 계십니까? 여러분의 소기업체 재무가 감당할 수 있는 그 이상입니까? 캐나다에서 가장 빠르게 성장하고 있는 회계 법인 중 하나인 ECA에 여러분의 모든 회계 걱정을 맡겨주십시오!

저희는 제공합니다:
▷ 개인 소득세 신고
▷ 부기 시스템 설치 및 관리
▷ 재무제표 준비
▷ 계약서 초안 작성 관련 도움

저희의 서비스, 요금, 그리고 회계사에 대한 전체 목록을 원하시면 www.everidgeacc.co.ca를 방문하십시오. 저희 회계사 중 한 명과 직접 만나고 싶으시다면, (604) 555-8872로 저희에게 전화 주시거나, everidgeacc@coolmail.com으로 이메일을 보내셔서 약속을 잡으십시오.

147 ECA에 의해 제공되는 서비스로 언급되지 않은 것은?
(A) 소득세에 대한 도움
(B) 계약서 작성에 대한 도움
(C) 투자 상담
(D) 회계 시스템 처리

148 고객은 왜 ECA 웹사이트를 방문하겠는가?
(A) 개인세 상담을 예약하기 위해
(B) 다른 고객들의 의견을 읽기 위해
(C) 사업 계약서의 온라인 견본을 보기 위해
(D) ECA 직원에 대한 정보를 얻기 위해

149-150은 다음 초대장에 관한 문제입니다.

New Hampton 전문가 협회가
당신을 초대합니다

제12회 연례 자선의 밤을 위한 멜로디

7월 24일 토요일 오후 6시
Greenfield 극장

세계적으로 유명한 작곡가이자 잘츠부르크 음악 학교 졸업생들인,
Johannes Linden과 Vladimir Tepanor가
작곡한 클래식 악곡 6곡이 Smithson 교향악단
오케스트라에 의해 연주될 것입니다.

행사를 위한 격식 있는 복장이 요구됩니다. 현금 기부가 저녁 시간 동안 받아
질 것이며, 수익금은 New Hampton 종합 병원의 Rainbow House로
전달될 것입니다. Rainbow House는 젊은 환자들의 의료에 헌신하는
특별 시설입니다. 참석을 확정하거나 더 많은 정보를 원하시면,
www.newhamptonhospital.com과
www.rainbowhouse.com을 방문하십시오.

---

149 행사에 대해 언급되지 않은 것은?
(A) 전문가 단체에 의해 개최된다.
(B) 참석자들은 격식을 갖춰 옷을 입도록 요구된다.
(C) 주말에 열릴 것이다.
(D) 모든 손님들에게 다과가 제공될 것이다.

150 Johannes Linden과 Vladimir Tepanor는 누구인가?
(A) 오케스트라의 유명한 지휘자
(B) 자선 기관의 대표자
(C) 유명한 클래식 음악 작곡가
(D) New Hampton 종합 병원의 관리자

151-152는 다음 메시지 대화문에 관한 문제입니다.

Gary Perkins [오후 1시 25분]
Allie, 당신의 Cancun으로의 휴가가 언제죠? 18일에도 도시를 떠나 계신가
요?

Allie Chen [오후 1시 27분]
네, 16일부터 19일까지 4일 동안 가 있을 거예요. 무슨 일 있나요?

Gary Perkins [오후 1시 28분]
18일에 연설자가 여기로 강연을 하러 오는데, 그날이 일요일이라는 점을 감
안했을 때 누가 도와줄 수 있는지 확인하고 있어요.

Gary Perkins [오후 1시 29분]
지금까지, 연회와 장식을 맡을 지원자들은 이미 충분히 모집해 놓았어요. 제
가 직접 연설자를 태워올 것이니, 무대 설치를 도울 사람만 필요해요.

Allie Chen [오후 1시 29분]
그렇군요. 도움을 주지 못해 미안해요.

Gary Perkins [오후 1시 31분]
걱정하지 마세요. 아직 부탁할 수 있는 사람들이 많이 있어요. 분명 누군가는
시간이 있을 거예요.

Allie Chen [오후 1시 34분]
만약 제가 제대로 기억한다면, Ms. Farley가 13일에 휴가에서 돌아올 거예
요.

Gary Perkins [오후 1시 35분]
그래요? 나중에 그녀에게 메시지를 보낼게요. 고마워요, Allie.

---

151 오후 1시 31분에, Mr. Perkins가 "No worries"라고 썼을 때 그가 의도한
것은?
(A) 그의 휴일 계획에 만족한다.
(B) 행사에 대해 곧 회답을 받기를 기대한다.
(C) 그의 업무량에 대해 스트레스를 받지 않는다.
(D) 도와줄 다른 사람들을 찾을 수 있을 것이라 믿는다.

152 Ms. Farley에 대해 암시되는 것은?
(A) 연회장을 장식하는 일에 자원했다.
(B) 18일에 일하도록 요청받을 것이다.
(C) 일요일에 공항에 갈 것이다.
(D) 보통 주말에 일하러 온다.

153-155는 다음 브로슈어에 관한 문제입니다.

토론토 어시장
중앙 광장 112번지

토요일과 일요일에 토론토 최고의 해산물을 맛보기 위해 도심 부둣가로 모험
을 떠나보세요. 도시 전역에서 온 상인들이 저희 창고에 가판대를 설치해 놓
았고, 그곳에서 생선부터 초밥과 바닷가재 그리고 심지어 오징어와 같은 이국
적인 요리까지 모든 것을 판매합니다. 음식은 시내에서 가장 신선하고 맛있
을 뿐만 아니라, 가장 저렴한 가격에 팔리고 있습니다. 파운드당 25달러 미만
으로 연어나 넙치 한 조각을 구할 수 있습니다. 저희 웹사이트인 www.
torontofishmarket.ca에서 저희가 연중 개최하는 특별 할인에 관한 최신
정보를 꼭 확인하십시오. 저희 웹사이트에는 시장의 생중계 영상도 있어서,
그곳이 어느 특정 시간에 얼마나 붐비는지 보실 수 있습니다.

---

153 토론토 어시장에 대해 언급된 것은?
(A) 일주일에 3일만 연다.
(B) 여름에는 야외에 위치해 있다.
(C) 다른 장소들보다 덜 비싸다.
(D) 관광객들이 자주 드나든다.

154 1문단 여섯 번째 줄의 단어 "cut"은 의미상 –와 가장 가깝다.
(A) 상처
(B) 축소
(C) 부분
(D) 배당금

155 브로슈어에 따르면, 사람들은 토론토 어시장 웹사이트에서 무엇을 할 수
있는가?
(A) 신선한 생선 메뉴를 검토한다
(B) 여러 상인들의 가격을 비교한다
(C) 시장을 소개하는 영상을 시청한다
(D) 다가오는 거래를 둘러본다

156-158은 다음 공고에 관한 문제입니다.

포틀랜드 연휴 선물 박람회로 오십시오!

포틀랜드시와 Willamette 컨벤션 센터는 12월 1일부터 12월 14일까지,
2주 동안 진행될 연휴 선물 박람회의 개막을 알리게 되어 기쁩니다. Naito
Parkway에 있는 Willamette 컨벤션 센터에서 매일 오전 10시부터 오후
9시까지 열리는 박람회는 600개가 넘는 업체의 제품들을 포함할 것입니다.
행사는 센터의 가장 큰 전시 공간인 Riverside 홀에서 열릴 것입니다.

박람회 입장권은 성인이 5달러, 12세 이하의 어린이나 고령자는 3달러입니

다. 5세 이하의 어린이들은 입장료를 받지 않습니다. 또한 참석자들은 18,000달러 이상에 달하는 상품들이 나누어지는 1시간마다의 추첨에 참여하실 수 있습니다! 부스에는 연휴 선물, 장식물, 카드, 장난감, 음식, 그리고 더 많은 것들이 있습니다! 이 놀라운 행사에 들러서 모든 연휴 선물들을 미리 구입하세요.

업체 목록을 보시려면, www.willamettecon.com/events를 방문하십시오. 박람회 티켓은 11월 20일부터 웹사이트에서 혹은 Riverside 홀의 입구에서 구매될 수 있습니다.

156 공고는 누구를 대상으로 하는 것 같은가?
(A) 시 공무원
(B) 컨벤션 센터 직원
(C) 연휴 쇼핑객
(D) 전시회 주최자

157 박람회에 대해 언급되지 않은 것은?
(A) 사은품을 포함할 것이다.
(B) 다양한 상품들을 전시할 것이다.
(C) 10살 어린이에게 무료이다.
(D) 2주간 지속되도록 예정되어 있다.

158 컨벤션 센터에 대해 암시되는 것은?
(A) 최근에 건설되었다.
(B) 몇 개의 전시관들이 있다.
(C) 행사 표를 팔지 않는다.
(D) 좌석 수가 600개이다.

159-160은 다음 이메일에 관한 문제입니다.

수신: Jude Feldstein <jfeldstein@lbm.com>
발신: Janina Winslow <customerservice@mycel.com>
날짜: 12월 20일
제목: 회신: 수신 장애

Mr. Feldstein께,

귀하께서 지난 며칠 동안 저희의 무선 전화 서비스를 사용하시면서 겪은 일시적으로 멈추는 수신 상태에 대해 알려 주셔서 감사합니다. 귀하께서는 문제가 무엇이었는지 저희가 설명해드리길 원하셨고, 이번 달 서비스 요금 할인도 요청하셨습니다.

우선, 저희는 이 문제가 Mountainview 지역의 휴대 전화 송신탑에서 진행 중인 수리 작업 때문이라고 생각하는데, 이 송신탑은 최근 폭설 중에 심하게 손상되었습니다. 저희 보수 작업 팀원이 아직 이 문제를 고치기 위해 작업 중입니다.

귀하의 두 번째 문의 사항에 대해, 우선 불편을 끼쳐 드린 점에 대해 사과드리고 싶습니다. 귀하께서는 소중한 고객이시므로, 귀하의 다음 달 대금 청구서에서 40달러를 공제하겠습니다. 이것으로 귀하께서 겪으셨을 모든 문제들이 처리되기를 바랍니다.

Janina Winslow 드림
MyCel 고객 서비스

159 이메일의 목적은 무엇인가?
(A) 고객에게 작업 날짜를 알리기 위해
(B) 인터넷 연결 문제를 보고하기 위해
(C) 고객의 문의에 응답하기 위해
(D) 고객이 서비스 사용을 연장하도록 설득하기 위해

160 Ms. Winslow는 Mr. Feldstein에게 무엇을 제공하기로 제안하는가?
(A) 서비스 계약 연장
(B) 하루 치의 무료 통화
(C) 새로운 휴대 기기
(D) 월별 청구에서의 할인

161-164는 다음 안내문에 관한 문제입니다.

Burbank시는 주민들의 이익을 위해 많은 추가 서비스를 제공합니다. 이것들은 대부분의 시 정부에 의해 제공되는 일반적인 지방 자치 서비스의 일부가 아니며 주민들에게 무료로 이용 가능하게 만들어졌습니다. 아래는 단지 이러한 몇몇 서비스들의 예시이지만, www.burbank.ca.gov를 방문하시면 다른 서비스들에 대해서도 알아보실 수 있습니다.

에너지 평가: 주민들은 가정 에너지 사용을 향상시키는 방안에 대한 몇몇 전반적인 권고를 위해 에너지 조언가와 상담할 수 있습니다. 월요일에서 금요일, 오전 8시 30분에서 오후 4시 30분까지의 정규 운영 시간 동안에 이 서비스를 예약하는 것이 필수입니다. ─ [1] ─. 이 서비스는 저희 직원들의 가능 여부에 영향을 받습니다.

나무 제거: 시의 환경관리부는 주택 소유자들에게 무료 나무 가지치기와 제거 서비스를 제공합니다. 예약 일정을 잡기 위해서는 간단히 555-4091, 내선 번호 808로 전화하시면 됩니다. 이 서비스는 일 년 내내 이용 가능합니다. ─ [2] ─.

수질 분석: 식수의 안전에 대해 걱정하는 주택 소유자들은 검사를 위해 수도부에 물 견본을 맡길 수 있습니다. ─ [3] ─. 오염된 것으로 판명된 모든 수원은 즉시 처리될 것입니다.

셔틀: 시에서는 65세 이상의 고령 주민 혹은 이동에 문제가 있는 주민들에게는 주거 지역과 상업 지역을 오가는 무료 셔틀 서비스를 제공합니다. ─ [4] ─. 픽업 예약을 하시려면, 555-4091, 내선 번호 204번으로 노인 복지부에 전화하십시오.

161 시의 웹사이트에서 무엇을 볼 수 있는가?
(A) 일시적 정전 일정
(B) 공무원들에 대한 안내 책자
(C) 시청으로 가는 길
(D) 추가 서비스에 관한 정보

162 어떤 서비스에 예약이 필요하지 않은가?
(A) 에너지 사용 상담
(B) 소유지에서의 나무 제거
(C) 식수 안전 검사
(D) 상업 지구로의 이동

163 누가 셔틀을 탈 것 같은가?
(A) 시청에서 일하는 직원들
(B) 운전면허가 없는 청년들
(C) Burbank시 외곽에 사는 시민들
(D) 상점을 방문해야 하는 노인들

164 [1], [2], [3], [4]로 표시된 위치 중, 다음 문장이 들어갈 곳으로 가장 적절한 것은?

"저희 실험실 기사들이 실험 결과를 얻는 데 최대 10일의 영업일이 걸립니다."
(A) [1]
(B) [2]
(C) [3]
(D) [4]

165-168은 다음 온라인 채팅 대화문에 관한 문제입니다.

Julianna Lopez — 오전 10시 22분
자, 확정되었어요. 우리는 7월 18일에 AEK사의 본사에서 그들에게 마케팅 제안서를 발표할 겁니다.

John Brenner — 오전 10시 24분
들었어요! 정말 신나네요. 당신이 우리에게 준 소책자 안의 회사 소개서를 살펴봤어요. 그들은 지금까지 중 우리의 가장 큰 고객이 될 수도 있어요.

Julianna Lopez 오전 10시 25분
맞아요. 그들은 6,000명의 직원이 있고 태국, 터키와 멕시코에 제조 공장들을 가지고 있어요. 그들은 또한 중국, 독일과 한국에 공급업체들이 있고 작년에 20억이 넘는 매출을 냈어요.

Yvonne Bailey 오전 10시 25분
제가 발표를 위한 마케팅 분석 작업을 시작할 수 있어요. 우리가 받았던 소책자에 있는 통계 자료들을 이용하려고 해요. 그것들이 믿을 만하다고 생각하시나요?

Julianna Lopez 오전 10시 26분
괜찮을 겁니다, Yvonne. 그 수치들은 정확한 것 같아요. John과 Eric, 여러분은 슬라이드쇼와 유인물들을 준비해 줬으면 해요. 가능하다면 바로 시작해 주세요.

John Brenner 오전 10시 27분
알겠습니다. 끝내는 데 이틀 이상 걸리진 않을 겁니다.

Eric Zalewski 오전 10시 32분
맡겨만 주세요, Julianna. 그 약속 전에 발표를 연습해 볼 건가요?

Julianna Lopez 오전 10시 34분
7월 15일에 연습 시간을 가집시다. 발표 동안에, 제가 주요 발언을 하고, 그러고 나서 여러분 세 명이 여러분이 담당한 것들을 짧게 설명할 수 있어요. 그 후에는, 우리 넷 모두가 그들이 가질 수 있는 기술적이거나 재정적인 질문에 답할 수 있습니다. 합당한 것 같나요?

Yvonne Bailey 오전 10시 34분
우리 모두 괜찮을 것 같아요.

165 AEK사에 대해 사실인 것은?
　(A) 수익성에 있어서 최고 기록의 해를 맞았다.
　(B) 다른 사업체를 인수하는 데에 관심이 있다.
　(C) 적어도 세 개 국가의 회사들에 의해 공급을 받는다.
　(D) 고객들이 대부분 태국에 있다.

166 Ms. Bailey는 분석 작업을 위해 무엇을 이용할 것인가?
　(A) 회사 소책자
　(B) 발표 유인물
　(C) 경제 잡지
　(D) 광고 분석

167 오전 10시 27분에, Mr. Brenner가 "Got it"이라고 썼을 때 그가 의도한 것은?
　(A) 몇몇 분석 작업을 시작할 것이다.
　(B) 바로 발표를 위한 작업을 할 것이다.
　(C) 보고서를 위해 수치들을 확인할 것이다.
　(D) 직원 역할에 대한 설명서를 작성할 것이다.

168 Mr. Zalewski는 7월 18일에 무엇을 할 것 같은가?
　(A) 주요 발언의 대부분을 한다
　(B) 재정 관련 문의들에 답을 제공한다
　(C) 회사 소개서 사본들을 배부한다
　(D) 연습 시간을 진행한다

169-171은 다음 편지에 관한 문제입니다.

5월 25일

Barbara Koteva, 홍보 이사
Ademus Petroleum사, 4493번지 24번가, 뉴욕, 뉴욕주 11100

Ms. Koteva께,

귀하와 귀사가 지구 환경 보호 협회(SPEE)에 보여주셨던 지지에 저희 단체를 대표하여 감사드립니다. 저희의 소중한 후원자들에게 관례적인 약속의 일환으로, 새로운 개발, 진행 중인 활동, 지난 회계 연도의 예산 배정을 다루고 있는 저희의 연례 보고서를 동봉하였습니다. 보고서를 읽으신 후에, 저희의

노력을 계속해서 지지해 주시길 바랍니다.

요약하자면, 지난해는 10년 전 SPEE가 설립된 이래로 가장 생산적인 해였지만, 많은 문제점들이 남아있다는 것을 말씀드리며 시작하겠습니다. 다음은 귀하께서 보고서에서 발견하실 몇 가지 가장 중요한 부분들입니다.

저희는 개인 기부, 공공 단체 지원, 그리고 기업 분야의 재정 기부에서 기록적인 기부금이 있었음을 확인하였습니다. 다중 언어 웹사이트의 출시와 지난해 지구에 대한 의식 고취 행사 동안 상영된 다큐멘터리 영화에서 받은 언론의 관심이 여기에 일정 부분 도움이 됐습니다.

비영리 부문에서 존경받는 Mr. Jonah Gelding과 Ms. Heather Leach 두 분께서 저희 이사회의 일원이 되셨습니다. 남아시아와 동유럽에서 일했던 그들의 결합된 경험이 해당 지역들의 회원을 증가시키는 데 도움이 되었습니다.

끝으로, 저희는 프로젝트 운영을 관리하는 몇 가지 새로운 정책이 실행된 것을 확인하였습니다. 귀하께서 곧 알게 되시겠지만, 이것은 저희의 운용을 간소화하고 지출의 효율성을 확대하는 데 기여했습니다.

이 보고서에 관한 질문이나 의견이 있으시다면, h.grundy@spee.org로 저에게 연락해 주십시오.

Hazel Grundy 드림
기업 커뮤니케이션 이사
지구 환경 보호 협회

169 편지의 주 목적은 무엇인가?
　(A) 최근에 고용된 임원들을 소개하기 위해
　(B) 설문 조사의 결과에 대해 보고하기 위해
　(C) 단체에 관한 설명을 제공하기 위해
　(D) 내년 수익을 예상하기 위해

170 Ms. Koteva는 누구일 것 같은가?
　(A) 기업 기부자의 대표
　(B) 비영리 단체의 직원
　(C) 지구에 대한 의식 고취 행사 주최자
　(D) 자선 재단의 설립자

171 SPEE의 최근 변화로 언급되지 않은 것은?
　(A) 웹사이트에 다중 언어 기능을 추가했다.
　(B) 동유럽에서 회원이 증가했다.
　(C) 지출을 줄일 정책을 실행했다.
　(D) 이사회가 아시아에서 곧 있을 두 프로젝트를 승인했다.

172-175는 다음 편지에 관한 문제입니다.

9월 27일

Evelyn Gray
Priory가
코번트리 CV1 5FB

Ms. Gray께,

저는 영문학 교수이며 여기 코번트리 대학교의 New Writers 프로젝트를 대표하여 연락드립니다. 귀하의 최근 베스트셀러 소설 *Midnight Magic*이 이곳 캠퍼스의 학생들과 교직원들의 마음을 사로잡았습니다. 그 책은 이미 제 1학년 글짓기 수업을 포함한 몇몇 과목에서 지정 도서이고, 저희 프로그램의 공식 권장 도서 목록의 일부가 되었습니다.

내년에, 저희 대학의 New Writers 프로젝트가 봄 세미나를 개최할 예정인데 귀하를 초청 연사로 초대하고자 합니다. — [1] —.

각 초청 연사는 세미나 동안 두 번의 40분짜리 강의를 할 것으로 예상됩니다. — [2] —. 강의는 글짓기나 출판과 관련된 어떤 주제든 가능합니다. 각 강의 후에는 30분간의 질의응답 시간이 이어질 것입니다. 또한 귀하의 시간이 허용할 경우 몇 가지 추가 작업을 수행하도록 요청받으실 수 있습니다. — [3] —.

초청 연사로서, 귀하는 지역 호텔에서의 3박 상품권을 받으실 것입니다. 항공편과 렌터카를 포함한 모든 여행 경비도 저희가 부담하겠습니다. — [4] —.

내년 세미나에 저희와 함께하실 의향이 있는지 알려 주십시오. 귀하의 전문성을 저희 학생들과 공유해 주신다면 영광일 것입니다.

Vera Young 드림
New Writers 프로젝트 부교수
코번트리 대학교

172 Ms. Young은 왜 편지를 썼는가?
   (A) 베스트셀러 소설을 칭찬하기 위해
   (B) 도서 목록에 관한 의견을 요청하기 위해
   (C) 지역 학생들을 대표해서 문의하기 위해
   (D) 워크숍 참여를 요청하기 위해

173 *Midnight Magic*에 대해 언급되지 않은 것은?
   (A) Ms. Gray에 의해 집필되었다.
   (B) Ms. Young의 수업에서 지정되었다.
   (C) 지난해에 출판되었다.
   (D) 대량으로 판매되었다.

174 4문단 두 번째 줄의 단어 "cover"는 의미상 -와 가장 가깝다.
   (A) 취급하다
   (B) 포함하다
   (C) 둘러싸다
   (D) 자금을 대다

175 [1], [2], [3], [4]로 표시된 위치 중, 다음 문장이 들어갈 곳으로 가장 적절한 것은?

   "여기에는 학생 원고를 검토하거나 일대일 상담을 제공하는 것이 포함될 수 있습니다."

   (A) [1]
   (B) [2]
   (C) [3]
   (D) [4]

176-180은 다음 웹페이지와 브로슈어에 관한 문제입니다.

Stop and Sew사
여러분의 모든 여성복과 남성복 제작 요구를 위해

홈	회사 소개	지점	고객 의견

Stop and Sew사께,

새로운 위치에 상점 개업을 축하드립니다! 저는 늘 Stop and Sew사의 팬이었고, 귀사의 상점에서 구매 가능한 특별한 제품들이 없었다면 저는 지난 10년간 지역 패션 디자이너로서 성공하지 못했을 것입니다. 모든 기호를 만족시키는 다양한 종류의 의류 소재들을 판매해주셔서 감사드리는 것은, 그것이 제가 창의적이고 흥미로운 디자인을 창조하는 데 도움을 주었기 때문입니다.

항상 그렇듯, 귀사의 새로운 상점은 목적과 재료에 따라 분류된 원단들로 매우 잘 정리되어 있습니다. 무엇보다도, 귀사의 박식한 판매원들은 도움이 되며 뛰어난 서비스를 제공합니다. 그들은 최근 제가 수영복 컬렉션을 위한 직물을 고를 때 좋은 추천을 해주었고, 제게 귀사가 제공하는 기본적인 재료에 관한 책자를 주었습니다.

그러나, 저는 웨딩드레스 원단에 관해 제안 사항이 있습니다. 웨딩드레스를 요청하는 제 고객은 조금 더 특별한 소재를 원하는 경향이 있습니다. 트렌드가 바뀌고 있고, 고객들은 귀사가 제공하는 단순한 디자인보다는 세밀한 디자인을 원합니다. 저는 현재 시외에 있는 공급업체를 통해 모든 웨딩드레스 원단들을 배송시키고 있습니다. 많은 지역 양재사와 디자이너들을 도울 것이기 때문에, 새 재고를 주문할 때 이것을 고려해보시는 게 좋으실 것입니다.

감사드리며 귀사가 계속해서 성공하길 바랍니다!

Jenna Palmer 드림

Stop and Sew사 - 기본 소재

면
· 100퍼센트 천연
· 통기성이 있고 입기 편안함
· 세탁기로 세탁 가능
· 셔츠를 만드는 데 추천

메리노 양모
· 메리노 양의 최고급의 가장 부드러운 양모로 만듦
· 통기성과 보온성이 있어, 메리노 양모는 착용하는 사람들을 겨울에는 따뜻하고 여름에는 시원하게 해줌
· 세탁기로 세탁 가능
· 유아 의류, 최신 유행 의류, 야외용 의류를 만드는 데 추천
· 다양한 색상 구입 가능

실크
· 100퍼센트 천연
· 광택이 나고, 특별히 잘 처지며 염색하기 쉬운 직물
· 예복과 웨딩드레스를 만드는 데 추천

폴리에스터
· 가볍고 매우 신축성 있음
· 수축, 열, 햇빛, 세제, 땀에 잘 견딤
· 수영복, 스키복, 무용복, 스케이트 의상과 같은 스포츠 의류를 만드는 데 추천

176 웹페이지에 따르면, Ms. Palmer가 Stop and Sew사에 대해 좋아하는 것은 무엇인가?
   (A) 색깔별로 직물을 정리한다.
   (B) 뛰어난 고객 서비스를 보유하고 있다.
   (C) 다양한 종류의 재봉틀을 가지고 있다.
   (D) 유용한 여성복 제작 개인 지도를 제공한다.

177 웹페이지에서 1문단 네 번째 줄의 단어 "taste"는 의미상 -와 가장 가깝다.
   (A) 선호
   (B) 풍미
   (C) 결정
   (D) 느낌

178 Ms. Palmer에 대해 암시되는 것은?
   (A) 원단 샘플이 필요하다.
   (B) 동료에게 상점을 추천했다.
   (C) 대량 주문 요금을 적용받을 자격이 있다.
   (D) 최신 패션 경향에 맞추기를 원한다.

179 Ms. Palmer는 이전에 Stop and Sew사에서 어떤 직물을 샀을 것 같은가?
   (A) 면
   (B) 메리노 양모
   (C) 실크
   (D) 폴리에스터

180 메리노 양모에 대해 언급되지 않은 것은?
   (A) 세탁기로 세탁될 수 있다.
   (B) 여러 계절에 입을 수 있다.
   (C) 다른 원단들보다 더 비싸다.
   (D) 다양한 색상으로 구매될 수 있다.

181-185는 다음 송장과 이메일에 관한 문제입니다.

날짜: 8월 12일

Baja 여행사, Myrtle로 4258번지, 샌디에이고, 캘리포니아, 92105

Ostergard 기술회사 여행 송장, Beadnell가 6520번지, 샌디에이고, 캘리포니아, 92117

담당자/직책	Edith Albright/인사팀 조정관
여행 일정 전반	5일 클래식 멕시코 투어
여행자 인원	10
여행 날짜	9월 19–23일
보증금 금액/지급일	2,500달러/8월 10일
남은 잔액	5,090달러
잔액 지급 기한일	9월 1일

보증금과 잔액에는 항공편, 버스 투어 및 교통비, Mayan 호텔에서 4박, 박물관 및 관광지 입장료, 아침 식사 5회, 그리고 점심 식사 5회가 포함되어 있는 점 참고 바랍니다. 저녁 식사, 기념품, 그리고 투어 가이드 팁은 이 금액에 포함되어 있지 않습니다. 모든 여행자들은 적어도 출발일 일주일 전까지 Baja 여행사에 여권 번호를 제출해야 합니다. 또한, 남은 잔액은 위의 기한일까지 지불되어야 합니다. 그렇지 않으면, 예약이 보장될 수 없습니다. 저희는 신용카드와 직불카드 또는 은행 송금을 받습니다.

수신: Samuel Hill <shill@bajatravel.com>
발신: Edith Albright <edith.albright@ostergardtech.com>
제목: 여행 일정
날짜: 8월 15일

Mr. Hill께,

저희 회사의 곧 있을 직원 휴가에 대한 송장을 받았습니다. 모든 것이 좋아 보이지만, 몇 주 전 저희가 대화했을 때 깜빡 잊고 하지 못한 몇 가지 질문이 있습니다.

우선, 남은 잔액을 두 번에 분할해서 지불해도 될까요? 이상적으로는, 오늘 반액을 지불하고, 기한일 전날에 반액을 지불하고 싶습니다. 또, 저희가 포함된 식사를 하게 될 식당들에 채식 선택지가 있나요? 제 동료들 중 몇 명은 다른 준비를 해야 할 경우에 대비해서 빠른 시일 내에 알고 싶어 합니다. 마지막으로, 귀사는 여행 보험을 제공하시나요? 있으면 좋을 것 같습니다.

귀하의 모든 도움에 감사드립니다. 이번 주 중에 저희의 여권 번호를 보내 드리겠습니다.

Edith Albright 드림

---

181 송장에서 Ostergard 기술회사에 대해 암시되는 것은?
(A) 이미 보증금을 지불했다.
(B) 다른 주에 있는 여행사를 고용했다.
(C) 회사 신용카드로 결제할 것이다.
(D) 단체 할인을 받을 것이다.

182 여행자들은 여행 도중 무엇을 위해 돈을 지불해야 할 것인가?
(A) 항공편
(B) 일부 입장료
(C) 일부 식사
(D) 숙박 시설

183 이메일은 왜 쓰였는가?
(A) 송장에 있는 요금에 이의를 제기하기 위해
(B) 기한 연장에 대해 문의하기 위해
(C) 업데이트된 여행 일정을 요청하기 위해
(D) 추가 세부 정보를 요청하기 위해

184 Ms. Albright는 언제 최종 지불을 하고 싶어 하는가?
(A) 8월 15일에
(B) 8월 31일에
(C) 9월 1일에
(D) 9월 19일에

185 이메일에서 추론될 수 있는 것은?
(A) 투어 참가자들 중 일부는 채식주의자이다.
(B) 일부 직원들은 이미 여권을 제공했다.
(C) Ostergard 기술회사는 모든 여행에 있어 보험을 요한다.

(D) 여행 경비는 Ms. Albright가 예상했던 것보다 비쌌다.

186~190은 다음 공고, 이메일, 기사에 관한 문제입니다.

Barksdale 여름 공예 시장

Barksdale 지역사회 단체가 다음 달에 연례 야외 공예 시장을 개최할 것임을 알리게 되어 기쁩니다. 이 행사는 Emerson가의 Oakville 공원에서 7월 7일, 14일, 21일, 그리고 28일에 개최될 것입니다. 올해는, 지역 식당 소유주들이 음식 부스를 설치하여 다양한 맛있는 요리를 방문객들에게 제공할 것입니다. 공원에 입장하면 이것들은 모두 정문의 바로 왼쪽에 위치해 있을 것입니다. 덧붙여, 여러 밴드가 시장의 마지막 날에 공연하기로 하였습니다. www.bdalecommunity.com에 방문하셔서 음악 공연자들의 목록과 그들이 공연할 시간을 확인하십시오. 다음 달에 뵙기를 바랍니다!

수신: Brenda Pearson <b.pearson@bdalecommunity.com>
발신: Greg Dawson <g.dawson@dg.com>
날짜: 6월 11일
제목: 공예 시장

Ms. Pearson께,

2주 전에, 저는 Barksdale 여름 공예 시장에서 음식 부스를 설치하기 위해 귀하의 웹사이트를 통해 신청서를 제출했습니다. 제 식당인 The Dawson Grill은 겨우 이번 2월부터 운영되어 왔어서, 저는 이 행사에 참여하는 것이 새로운 손님들을 끌어들이는 데 아주 좋은 기회가 되리라고 생각합니다. 제 신청서를 받으셨는지 확인해주시고 그것이 언제 처리가 될 것인지 알려주시기 바랍니다.

저는 또한 부스가 얼마나 큰지 알고 싶은데, 귀하의 웹사이트에서 이에 관해 아무것도 찾을 수 없었기 때문입니다. 분명히, 이는 제가 사용할 수 있는 장비의 종류를 결정할 것이고, 더 나아가, 제가 제공할 요리를 결정할 것입니다.

감사합니다.

Greg Dawson 드림

여름의 공예
Janet Gleason 작성

Barksdale 여름 공예 시장은 주민들에게 항상 인기 있는 지역사회 행사이고, 올해의 행사는 지금까지 중에서 최고였다. Oakville 공원을 방문했을 때 가장 먼저 발견한 것은 맛있는 음식들이 많은 부스에서 판매되고 있었다는 것이다. 참가자들은 이러한 준비에 대해 굉장히 만족해 하는 듯 보였다. 몇 사람들은 점심이나 저녁을 위해 그 부지를 떠나지 않아도 되었던 점을 높이 평가했다고 말했다. 또한 라이브 음악이 준비되어 있었던 점이 감명 깊었다. 그것은 시장에 축제 같은 분위기를 가져다주었다. 그러니, 만약 올해 시장을 놓쳤다면, 내년엔 반드시 참석하라. 분명 후회하지 않을 것이다!

186 공고에 따르면, Barksdale 지역사회 단체의 웹사이트에서 무엇을 찾을 수 있는가?
(A) 주최자의 이름
(B) 판매업자들의 목록
(C) 공연 시간표
(D) 장소의 지도

187 Mr. Dawson에 대해 추론될 수 있는 것은?
(A) 음악가들에게 무료 음식을 제공했다.
(B) 그의 신청서가 올바르게 작성되지 않았다.
(C) 다른 식당 소유주들을 만나도록 요구받았다.
(D) 그의 부스는 공원 입구 근처에 위치해 있었다.

188 The Dawson Grill에 대해 언급된 것은?
(A) 이전에 시장에 참가했다.
(B) 개업한 지 1년이 되지 않았다.
(C) 많은 단골손님이 있다.
(D) 두 사람이 소유하고 있다.

189 Mr. Dawson은 무엇에 대해 문의하는가?
    (A) 부스의 비용
    (B) 장비의 이용 가능성
    (C) 참석자의 수
    (D) 공간의 크기

190 Ms. Gleason은 어느 날에 시장을 방문했는가?
    (A) 7월 7일
    (B) 7월 14일
    (C) 7월 21일
    (D) 7월 28일

191-195는 다음 광고지, 이메일, 등록 양식에 관한 문제입니다.

여러분이 좋아해 주시는 비즈니스 정기간행물인
*Big Success*지가
제7회 연례 기업인 총회를 개최합니다

– 여러분의 제품들을 온라인에서 판매하기 위해 알아야 할 모든 것 –
여러분은 자신의 온라인 상점을 운영하면서 인터넷 매출을 올리는 방법을
배우게 되실 것입니다.

4월 5일 오전 10시에서 오후 5시, Traylor홀
기조 연설자이자 *Big Success*지의 올해의 기업인 상 수상자:
Ottawa Intra Cycles사의 소유주 Kyle Rogan 참석
놓칠 수 없는 이 행사에 등록하시려면,
*Big Success*지의 6주간의 온라인 교육 강좌를 먼저
이수해야 합니다.
강좌에 등록하시려면, www.bigsuccessmag.ca/toolsforsuccess를
방문하세요
혹은
이미 그 강좌를 이수하여 총회에 참석하기 원하실 경우,
(519)-575-8634로 전화 주시기 바랍니다.

수신: Harrison Marcoux <hmarcoux@skateheaven.ca>
발신: Lilianne Maille <lilymaille@lmcosmetics.ca>
제목: 기업인 총회
날짜: 2월 12일

Mr. Marcoux께,

우리는 지난달 토론토에서 신흥 기업인들을 위한 교류 행사에서 만났었습니다. 당신은 지난해에 당신이 시작한 맞춤식 스케이트보드 사업에 대해 제게 이야기했었습니다. 제 화장품 사업을 시작한 지 얼마 되지 않았기에 저는 당신이 직면한 몇몇 어려움들에 공감할 수 있었습니다. 어쨌든, 저는 당신이 다소 어려움을 겪고 있다고 말했던 것을 기억하며, 그래서 곧 있을 총회에 대해 알려드리고자 이메일을 씁니다. 그 총회는 당신이 있는 도시에서 열릴 뿐만 아니라, 당신이 어려움을 겪고 있다고 얘기한 바로 그것에 초점을 맞추고 있어서 당신에게 더할 나위 없이 좋을 것이라고 생각합니다. 제 친구 한 명도 그 총회가 작년에 키치너에서 열렸을 때 참석했었는데, 그것이 그녀에게 많이 도움이 되었다고 했습니다. 저는 그 총회에 방금 등록했습니다. 만약 당신도 가는 것에 관심이 있으시다면 www.bigsuccessmag.ca에서 총회에 대한 자세한 내용을 찾아보실 수 있습니다.

아마 그곳에서 당신을 만날지도 모르겠습니다.

Lilianne Maille 드림

---

*Big Success*지 리더십 강좌 등록 양식

매우 유용한 이 강좌에 등록함으로써, 당신은 곧바로 시작될 6주간의 온라인 교육과 DVD 패키지를 우편으로 받을 것입니다. 수료와 동시에, 당신에게는 *Big Success*지 행사들에 참석할 자격이 주어질 것입니다.

연락 정보		주소	
이름	Harrison Marcoux	도로	51번지 Fairwater로

이메일	hmarcoux@skateheaven.ca	도시/주	워털루, 온타리오주
전화	555-9368	우편번호	N2J 1A3
신용카드 정보			
카드 종류		Wixcard	
카드 번호		0645-****-****-****	
결제 방식			
786달러를 일시불로 지불			
이번과 다음 2개월에 걸쳐 262달러씩 3번 지불			✓

이 프로그램은 100퍼센트 만족을 보장하며 그렇지 않을 경우 30일 이내에 환불해드립니다.

191 총회에 대해 사실이 아닌 것은?
    (A) 온라인 강좌를 수강한 사람만 참석할 수 있다.
    (B) 비즈니스 관련 출판물과 연관되어 있다.
    (C) 4월에 5일의 기간 동안 개최될 것이다.
    (D) 수상자가 참석할 것이다.

192 Mr. Marcoux는 무엇을 하는 데에 어려움을 겪고 있는 것 같은가?
    (A) 가장 강력한 경쟁사를 이기는 것
    (B) *Big Success*지의 강좌를 이수하는 것
    (C) 스케이트보드를 인터넷상에서 판매하는 것
    (D) 기업인 총회에 등록하는 것

193 Ms. Maille에 대해 암시되는 것은?
    (A) 최근에 스스로 사업을 시작했다.
    (B) 온라인 강좌에 완전히 만족하지는 않았다.
    (C) Mr. Marcoux와 같은 계통의 사업에 종사한다.
    (D) 키치너에 사무실을 열 계획이다.

194 강좌에 대해 언급된 것은?
    (A) 초대된 참석자들만 수강할 수 있다.
    (B) 할부로 지불될 수 있다.
    (C) 구독자들에게는 할인되어 제공된다.
    (D) 시작일 6주 전에 요금이 환불될 수 있다.

195 총회는 어디에서 열릴 것인가?
    (A) 토론토
    (B) 워털루
    (C) 키치너
    (D) 오타와

196-200은 다음 기사, 회람, 이메일에 관한 문제입니다.

---

*VOLO*지
여행 산업 뉴스

AITIC으로부터의 교훈
Kate Horvath 작성

8월 20일—최근 로마에서 끝난 제48회 연례 국제 여행 산업 회의(AITIC)에서, 대표자들은 여행사들이 직면하고 있는 난제들 중 몇 가지를 논의했다. 예를 들어, 높은 연료비와 영업 손실의 부담을 지고 있는 많은 항공사들이, 그들이 여행사들에 지불하는 수수료를 삭감하고 있다. 게다가, 여행객들이 그들 자신의 교통수단과 숙박 시설을 예약하게 해주는 웹사이트는 이제 전체 여행 예약의 약 60퍼센트를 차지한다. 마지막으로, 전 세계적인 불경기는 많은 사람들이 계획된 여행을 연기하거나 취소하게 했다.

"이러한 국면은 여행사들이 높은 수수료율을 지닌 여행 상품을 판촉하는 것이 필수적이도록 만듭니다,"라고 AITIC의 회장, Daniel Perotti는 말했다. "예를 들어, 몇몇 상품의 수수료 요금은 10퍼센트를 넘습니다. 이런 것들에 집중함으로써, 총판매량은 줄어들더라도 충분한 수익이 발생할 수 있습니다."

Stafford 여행사
회람

수신: 모든 영업 사원
발신: John Harriman
제목: 수수료
날짜: 9월 15일

아래는 제가 어제 우리 회사를 위해 협상한 판매 수수료 금액에 관한 업데이트된 개요입니다. 여러분이 얻은 모든 수수료에 대한 지분은 여러분의 은행 계좌에 월급과 함께 예금될 것입니다.

· 항공권   1-2퍼센트
· 차량 대여   3-5퍼센트
· 호텔 객실   5-10퍼센트
· 유람선 여행   15-20퍼센트
· 여행 보험   2-5퍼센트

수신: Serena Parker <s.parker@stafford.com>
발신: John Harriman <j.harriman@stafford.com>
날짜: 10월 17일
제목: 문의

Ms. Parker께,

저는 지난주에 당신이 제출한 보고서를 다 읽었으며, 당신의 두 가지 제안 모두에 동의합니다. 특히 주요 호텔 체인들이 25명 이상의 단체에 대해 최대 수수료율을 높이겠다는 의사를 표현했으므로, 큰 단체를 위한 여행 상품을 개발하는 것은 전망이 좋아 보입니다. 저는 또한 아시아 시장에 집중하는 것에 대한 당신의 주장이 매우 흥미롭다고 생각했습니다. 언급하셨다시피, 중국, 일본, 그리고 한국으로부터의 많은 국제 여행객이 있고, 우리가 이러한 고객들의 요구에 대해 더 나은 이해를 발전시키는 것은 중요합니다.

고위 관리자들을 위해 당신의 보고서에 기반하여 발표를 준비해주시길 바랍니다. 이번 주 후반에 더 자세한 설명을 제공해 드리도록 하겠습니다. 감사합니다.

John Harriman 드림

---

196 기사에 따르면, 여행 대리점들이 직면하고 있는 문제가 아닌 것은?
(A) 악화되는 경제 상황
(B) 항공사로부터의 줄어든 지불금
(C) 저비용 상품에 대한 더 커진 수요
(D) 온라인 서비스의 인기

197 Stafford 여행사는 어느 상품을 판촉하는 데 집중해야 할 것 같은가?
(A) 차량 대여
(B) 호텔 객실
(C) 유람선 여행
(D) 여행 보험

198 회람에 따르면, Mr. Harriman은 9월 14일에 무엇을 했는가?
(A) 요금에 대한 합의에 도달했다
(B) 급여 협상을 완료했다
(C) 많은 수수료를 받았다
(D) 팀 구성원들을 평가했다

199 Stafford 여행사에 대해 암시되는 것은?
(A) 몇몇 국가에 지점들을 열었다.
(B) 로마의 무역 회의에 참석할 대표를 보냈다.
(C) 호텔 수수료로 10퍼센트 넘게 받을 수도 있을 것이다.
(D) 아마도 영업 부서에 추가 직원을 고용할 것이다.

200 이메일에 따르면, Ms. Parker는 Stafford 여행사에 무엇을 하라고 조언했는가?
(A) 그룹을 위한 할인된 여행 상품을 제공하는 것
(B) 아시아에 있는 회사들과 제휴를 맺는 것
(C) 큰 호텔 체인들과의 협업을 피하는 것
(D) 특정한 지역의 잠재적인 고객에 대해 배우는 것

PART 5

101 식품 산업은 많은 규정들에 의해 관리되는데, 이것들은 Benagra 식품 회사의 우리가 주의 깊게 파악하고 있는 것들입니다.

102 박물관 관리진은 모든 방문객들에게 그들의 자녀들을 건물 내에 방치하지 말 것을 상기시킨다.

103 내부의 짐 싣는 곳이 다른 차량에 의해 사용 중이었으므로, 트럭 운전사는 건물 밖에 주차해야 했다.

104 밴쿠버에서 캘거리로 떠나는 열차는 꼬박 하루가 걸리므로, 많은 여행자들은 비행기로 가는 것을 선호한다.

105 도심 광장에 있는 기념 동상은 5월 3일 특별 행사 중의 제막식까지 가려져 있었다.

106 Mr. Wilkins는 목요일의 세미나 전에 회의실에 시청각 장비를 설치하는 데 약간의 도움을 원한다.

107 Billow Swimwear사에서 200달러어치를 구매할 때마다, 쇼핑객들은 수건 한 장 또는 실내화 한 켤레 중 하나를 받을 것이다.

108 Mark Hempel은 국제 문화에 대한 새로운 TV쇼를 제작하는 프로젝트에 최대한의 협력을 제공했다.

109 그 식당은 옷을 적절하게 갖춰 입지 않은 손님들에게 서비스를 거부할 권리를 보유한다.

110 Bolden 학교는 현재 다양한 도자기 생산 방식을 배우는 것에 관심이 있는 사람들을 위한 강의를 제공한다.

111 초과 수하물이 있는 기차 승객들에게 FineTrak 철도는 모든 추가 가방마다 13달러의 요금을 부과할 것입니다.

112 수령인들에게 위험할 수 있기 때문에 자선 단체는 이미 기한이 지난 식품 기부를 받지 않는다.

113 이번 주말에 도보 여행에 참여하는 사람들은 방문객 안내소 앞에는 한정된 공간만이 있기 때문에 신중하게 주차하는 것이 권고됩니다.

114 그 보도는 페루의 직물 회사와 프랑스의 패션 기업 사이에 곧 있을 합병을 간단히 언급했다.

115 적어도 5명의 참가자들이 세미나에 등록하는 한, 세미나는 다음 주말에 예정된 대로 진행될 것이다.

116 Barstow 은행의 현금 인출기에서의 인출은 이제 고객당 하루 2,500달러로 제한될 것이다.

117 재무 컨설턴트는 Ms. Broderick에게 운영비를 줄이려면 덴버 지점의 인력을 줄여야 한다고 충고했다.

118 다음 10일 동안의 예보는 바다로 휴가를 가는 것이 좋은 생각이 아니라는 것을 시사한다.

119 그 일이 처음이어서, Mr. Emmanuel은 다른 조립 라인 직원들과 보조를 맞추려고 애썼다.

120 Grandilla 화장품은 Bennington 백화점을 포함하여 Harmony사의 제품이 팔리는 모든 곳에서 구매가 가능하다.

121 팀 구성원들이 현재의 프로젝트 작업을 완료한 후에 새로운 업무들이 주어질 것이다.

122 가수 Arthur Fischman은 연주회의 마지막에서 듣기 드문 짧은 일본 곡으로 그의 독주회를 마무리 지었다.

123 쿠폰이 왜 받아들여지지 않았는지 궁금해하며, Chester는 만료일을 확인하기 위해 그것을 뒤집었다.

124 Mr. Aronov는 파일을 다운로드 하려고 시도했을 때 그의 하드 드라이브가 가득 찼다는 것을 알게 되었다.

125 실내 장식가는 그 방이 더 현대적으로 보이게 하기 위해 새로운 종류의 가구를 추천했다.

126 이전에 개발 프로젝트를 위해 소프트웨어 공학 팀을 감독했던 담당자들은 이제 훨씬 더 큰 팀들을 담당할 것이다.

127 공장 설비의 투자 비용이 소유주가 예상했던 것보다 높아서, 그는 새로운 기계 하나만 구매했다.

128 외부 기업과의 계약하에 있는 사람들을 제외한 공장의 모든 직원들은 국가 공휴일에 유급 휴가를 받는다.

129 야유회에 참여하는 직원들은 제공될 햄버거 외에 사람들과 나누고 싶은 음식은 무엇이든 가져올 수 있다.

130 보건부의 조항에 따라, 식당 소유주들은 주방 직원들을 대상으로 식품 안전 과정을 수행해야 한다.

PART 6

131-134는 다음 편지에 관한 문제입니다.

9월 18일

Ms. Murillo께,

131 저희의 국적 획득 서비스에 대해 문의해주셔서 감사드립니다.

귀하의 편지에 있는 정보에 근거하면, 귀하의 따님은 미국 시민의 자녀가 됨으로써 시민권을 획득했을 수도 있습니다. 132 이는 서류를 통해서 확인되어야 할 텐데, 그 서류는 귀하의 편지에 포함되어있지 않았습니다. 귀하의 자녀의 해외 출생 기록은 그것이 미국 영사관이나 대사관에 등록되었을 경우 증거로 간주됩니다. 133 추가로, 시민권을 가진 부모는 귀하의 자녀의 출생 이전에 미국에서 적어도 5년은 살았어야 합니다.

더 자세한 정보를 원하시면, 언제든지 방문해 주십시오. 저희 웹사이트는 귀하의 지역에 있는 지방 사무소의 주소를 제공합니다. 귀하가 현재 살고 있는 주 또는 국가를 클릭하기만 하세요. 134 그러면 귀하와 가장 가까운 관공서를 고를 수 있습니다. 방문하실 때에는 모든 관련된 서류들을 가져와 주십시오.

Sonia Esteban 드림

135-138은 다음 편지에 관한 문제입니다.

5월 30일

Cayman 실내 장식업
23번지 Arbor로
클리블랜드, 오하이오주, 39005

Mr. Maximus께,

135 우리 로비의 실내 장식을 새로 한 것에 대해 당신과 당신의 팀에게 격찬의 말씀을 드리고자 편지를 씁니다. 결과는 우리가 처음에 예상했던 것보다 훨씬 더 좋습니다. 136 우리는 마찬가지로 작업이 얼마나 빨리 수행되었는지에 대해 깊은 인상을 받았습니다. 137 전반적으로, 우리 손님들은 이 새로운 외관을 환영하고, 진짜 1920년대 같은 분위기와 편안한 가구들을 대단히 좋아합니다.

우리가 호텔이 손님방들을 보수하려고 한다고 언급했던 것으로 압니다. 만약 일들이 계획에 따라 진행된다면, 우리는 다음 달에 보수를 시작하기를 바랍니다. 138 추가로, 우리는 2층에 비즈니스 센터를 확장할 것입니다. 더 많은 공간이 할당되어 새로운 시설들의 설치를 허용할 것입니다.

우리의 계획들이 더 확실해지면 당신과 다시 연락하고 싶습니다. 우리가 준비되었을 때 당신의 일정이 여유가 되어 당신이 우리를 위해 일할 수 있기를 바랍니다.

당신으로부터 곧 답신이 오기를 기대합니다.

Devon Green 드림
지배인, Nuance 호텔

139-142는 다음 광고에 관한 문제입니다.

Dan's 철물점에서 엄청난 거래 조건들을 찾아보세요!

139 Dan's 철물점이 연례 재고 정리 할인에 들르시도록 여러분을 초대합니다. 9월 1일부터 15일까지, 저희의 모든 초과 재고가 새로운 제품군을 위한 공간을 마련하도록 할인될 것입니다. 원예용품부터 야외 장비에 이르는 모든 것에서 최대 80퍼센트까지의 할인된 가격을 이용하십시오. **140** 모든 코너에 여러분을 위한 신나는 할인들이 있습니다.

141 게다가, 500달러 이상 상당의 제품을 구매하시는 고객들께는 12월 31일까지 사용할 수 있는 50달러짜리 쿠폰을 받을 자격이 주어질 것입니다. **142** 거래당 쿠폰 1개라는 제한이 적용됩니다.

할인이나 가장 가까운 매장 위치에 관한 추가적인 정보를 원하시면, 저희 웹사이트 www.danshardware.com을 방문해 주세요.

143-146은 다음 기사에 관한 문제입니다.

Grimsby의 *Feed*가 시청자들을 만족시키다

143 3부작 미니시리즈 *Feed*에서, 영화 제작자 David Grimsby는 현대 음식 산업을 열정적으로 탐구한다. 그 시리즈는 우리가 먹는 음식들과 그것들이 어떻게 생산되는지에 대한 충격적인 사항들을 보여주기 위해 시청자들을 농장과 공장 현장의 이면으로 이끈다.

144 이러한 주제의 수많은 다른 다큐멘터리들이 있지만, 깔끔한 내레이션, 아주 흥미로운 인터뷰, 그리고 애니메이션 그래픽의 조합이 *Feed*를 눈에 띄게 한다. **145** 아마도 이 영화의 가장 독특한 점은 편견이 없다는 점일 것이다. 이 영화는 어느 한 관점을 지지하는 것 없이 현대 음식 생산의 이로운 점과 문제점을 둘 다 보여준다. **146** 풍부한 정보를 주고 시각적으로 흥미로운 이 시리즈는 너무 매혹적이어서 많은 사람들이 그것을 두 번 보기를 원할 것이다. *Feed*의 첫 번째 에피소드는 Modern Film 채널에서 이번 달에 방영될 것이다.

PART 7

147-148은 다음 회람에 관한 문제입니다.

수신: 모든 직원
발신: Donald Manzo
제목: 환영회
날짜: 8월 5일

새로운 지역 부사장이신 Gertrude Crowley를 맞이하기 위해 환영회를 열고자 합니다. Ms. Crowley는 이전에 찰스턴에 있는 Knightland Electronics사의 계열사에서 지점장으로 근무하셨습니다. 그곳에서 5년 근무한 후에, 그녀는 우리의 애틀랜타 지점을 2년 동안 이끌고 나서 뉴올리언스로 전임하였는데, 그때부터 거기서 그녀는 지역 책임자로 근무해 왔습니다. 그녀는 이제 이곳 내슈빌에 있는 우리 지사에서 남동 구역을 총괄할 것입니다.

이 환영회는 8월 9일 금요일 저녁 7시 30분에 Bluegrass 호텔에서 열릴 ⟳

것입니다. 환영회에 오실 예정이라면, 내선 44번으로 제 비서에게 알려 주십시오.

감사합니다.

147 회람의 목적은 무엇인가?
(A) 직원들이 활동에 자원하도록 설득하기 위해
(B) 환영회를 준비하는 것에 도움을 간청하기 위해
(C) 직원들에게 곧 있을 행사에 대해 알리기 위해
(D) 직원들에게 방문 고객에 대해 알리기 위해

148 Ms. Crowley가 이전에 근무하지 않았던 곳은 어디인가?
(A) 찰스턴
(B) 애틀랜타
(C) 뉴올리언스
(D) 내슈빌

149-150은 다음 메시지 대화문에 관한 문제입니다.

Fiona White	오후 5시 7분

내일 밤에 어떤 계획이라도 있으세요? 제 관리자로부터 Hyde 경기장에서 열리는 자선 콘서트 티켓 두 장을 받았어요. 주요 출연자는 Charles Mercer인데, 당신이 그의 지난번 앨범을 좋아했던 것으로 알고 있어요. 저와 함께 가실래요?

Carl Owens	오후 5시 10분

내일 밤이요? 정말 가고 싶지만, 갈 수 없을 것 같아요. 저희 회사의 법무부서 부장님과 회의가 있어요. 아마도 8시가 조금 지나서야 끝날 거예요.

Fiona White	오후 5시 12분

그것은 오후 9시에 시작해요. 장소가 중심가이기 때문에, 그곳까지 가는 데 오래 걸리지 않을 거예요.

Carl Owens	오후 5시 14분

잘됐네요. 그러면, 공연 바로 전에 Hyde 지하철역에서 만나지 않을래요?

Fiona White	오후 5시 15분

사실, 저는 운전해서 갈 예정이에요. 9시쯤에 중앙 매표소에서 저를 찾아봐 주세요.

Carl Owens	오후 5시 17분

알겠어요. 그때 봐요.

149 Mr. Mercer는 누구인가?
(A) 콘서트 주최자
(B) 전문 음악가
(C) 경기장 관리자
(D) 회사 변호사

150 오후 5시 12분에, Ms. White가 "It starts at 9 P.M."이라고 썼을 때 그녀가 의도한 것은?
(A) Mr. Owens는 장소까지 운전을 해야 한다.
(B) Mr. Owens는 회의를 일찍 끝내야 할 것이다.
(C) Mr. Owens는 행사에 참석할 수 있을 것이다.
(D) Mr. Owens는 오후 8시에 표를 찾아야 한다.

151-152는 다음 이메일에 관한 문제입니다.

수신: Adam Webster <awebster@connex.com>
발신: Caroline McElroy <services@seafront.com>
날짜: 4월 17일
제목: 보증금

Mr. Webster께,

귀하의 보증금 수표가 현금화되었고, 우리는 귀하께서 다음 달 첫날에 Spiral 타워에 있는 새로운 사무실로 이사 올 수 있다는 것을 확정하게 되어 기쁩니다. 상기시켜드리자면, 보증금은 귀하께서 이사를 나가기로 결정하기 전 ⟳

까지 Seafront Realty사가 보관하게 될 것이고, 나가기로 결정했을 때 건물에 대한 점검이 있을 것입니다. 그 사무실 공간은 귀하의 임차가 시작되었을 때와 같은 상태로 되돌려져야 합니다. 만일 어떤 초과적인 손상이 있었을 시에는, 보증금이 귀하게 돌려지기 전에 관련된 금액이 제해질 것입니다. 또한 귀하의 보증금은 은행 계좌에 예치될 것이며 그 결과로 얻게 되는 모든 이자는 귀하께서 떠나실 때 지급된다는 것을 알아 두십시오.

추가적인 질문에 대해서는 제게 이메일을 보내주십시오. 감사합니다.

Caroline McElroy 드림
Seafront Realty사 마이애미 지점

151 Mr. Webster는 누구인 것 같은가?
   (A) 장래의 입주자
   (B) 부동산 투자자
   (C) 수리공
   (D) 안전요원

152 보증금에 대해 언급되지 않은 것은?
   (A) 임대 계약이 끝날 때 반환된다.
   (B) 은행 계좌에 보관된다.
   (C) 한 달 치 임대료와 동일하다.
   (D) 건물에 대해 손상된 비용을 치르는 데 사용된다.

153-155는 다음 기사에 관한 문제입니다.

나이로비 국제 마라톤이 관심을 끌다

7월 28일—이번 해 나이로비 국제 마라톤에 참여하는 주자들은 경쟁을 위한 준비를 시작하는 것이 좋을 것이다. 주최자들은 어제 기자회견에서 지난해에 비해 거의 30퍼센트가 증가한 1만 2천 명의 선수들이 이미 마라톤에 등록했다고 발표했다. 조직위원장 Paul Oduya는 주최자들이 심지어 더 많은 등록을 예상하고 있다고 말했다. "지난해의 경기 이후로, 우리는 소셜미디어에서 마라톤을 홍보하기 위해 매우 열심히 노력해 왔습니다. 이것은 우리가 더 많은 국제 선수들에게 다가갈 수 있도록 해줄 것입니다." Oduya는 또한 마라톤의 높아져 가는 인기가 지역 관광업에 활력을 불어넣는 것을 도왔고 이번 해의 행사가 그 경향을 지속시킬 것이라고 믿는다고 말했다.

기자회견에서 새로운 경로 또한 발표되었다. 풀 마라톤과 하프 마라톤이 국립 공원의 서쪽 가장자리를 따라서 시작될 것인 반면, 더 짧은 마라톤은 외곽 순환 도로에서 시작될 것이다. 모든 마라톤은 시립 경기장에서 끝날 것이다. 관리자들은 www.nairobirace.org.ke에 온라인으로 Langata로, Mombasa로, 그리고 다른 주요 도로들의 폐쇄와 자동차 운전자들을 위한 우회로를 포함한 세부 정보를 공개했다. 참가에 관심이 있는 사람들을 위해, 8월 말까지 등록이 계속해서 가능할 것이다. 참가비와 다른 요구 조건들에 대해 더 알기 위해서는 www.nairobimarathon.org를 방문하면 된다.

153 이번 해의 마라톤은 지난해와 어떻게 다를 것인가?
   (A) 한 해의 다른 때에 개최될 것이다.
   (B) 새로운 도시에서 열릴 것이다.
   (C) 더 많은 수의 참가자들이 있을 것이다.
   (D) 지역 TV에서 방송될 것이다.

154 기사가 나이로비에 대해 암시하는 것은?
   (A) 스포츠 프로그램이 최근 몇 년간 더 많은 재정 지원을 받았다.
   (B) 선수들이 국제적으로 더 많이 알려졌다.
   (C) 관광업의 성장을 경험했다.
   (D) 지형이 장거리 경기에 특별히 적합하다.

155 풀 마라톤은 어디서 끝날 것인가?
   (A) 국립 공원에서
   (B) 외곽 순환 도로에서
   (C) Mombasa로에서
   (D) 시립 경기장에서

156-157은 다음 웹페이지에 관한 문제입니다.

Ace Venture Systems사

홈	제품소개	소식	연락처

회계 소프트웨어 버전 1

Ace Venture Systems사는 여러분들께 새로운 중소기업용 기업 회계 소프트웨어를 제공합니다. 회계 소프트웨어 버전 1은 소규모 사업 운영에 필수적인 표준 회계 기능을 포함한 무료 소프트웨어 패키지입니다. 다른 맞춤형 소프트웨어처럼, 이 소프트웨어는 사용자들이 재고품을 관리하고, 구입 주문서와 매출 자료를 기록할 수 있도록 하는 특징을 가지고 있습니다. 이것은 재무 보고서와 다양한 계좌 정보를 정리하는 데에도 사용될 수 있습니다. 아래의 버튼을 누르셔서 회계 소프트웨어 버전 1이 귀사를 위해 무엇을 해드릴 수 있는지 찾아보십시오:

> 다운로드 하기
> 회계 소프트웨어 버전 1

Ace Venture Systems사는 개방형 소스 소프트웨어를 장려하는 기업입니다. 당사는 20만 명 이상의 사용자들을 위해 신뢰할 만한 기업용 애플리케이션을 무료로 제공합니다. 회계 소프트웨어 버전 1에 대한 의견이나 제안은 여기를 클릭하셔서 저희의 사용자 의견 설문지에 작성해 주십시오.

156 웹페이지의 목적은 무엇인가?
   (A) 회계 방식을 소개하기 위해
   (B) 컴퓨터 프로그램을 홍보하기 위해
   (C) 사용자에게 통신망을 설정하는 것을 알려주기 위해
   (D) 새로운 프로젝트를 위한 제안을 얻기 위해

157 Ace Venture Systems사에 대해 언급되지 않은 것은?
   (A) 개방형 소스 컴퓨터 프로그램의 사용을 지지한다.
   (B) 고객들에게 의견을 줄 것을 요청한다.
   (C) 소프트웨어를 연 단위 가입제로 판매한다.
   (D) 웹사이트에서 직접 다운로드할 수 있도록 한다.

158-160은 다음 기사에 관한 문제입니다.

4월 11일—어제 기자회견에서, 시 공공사업부의 대표자인 Jane Gomez는 자전거 이용자의 안전을 향상하기 위해 시내 중심부의 모든 주요 도로에 대한 자전거 도로 설치 계획을 밝혔다. 비록 Stevens 시장은 참석하지 않았지만, 이 사업은 지난달 그의 선거 동안 그의 선거 공약들 중 하나였기 때문에 그에게 중요하다. Ms. Gomez에 따르면, 자전거 도로는 시에 단지 120만 달러의 비용을 요할 것이다. 이는 처음에 추정되었던 것보다 훨씬 적다. 하지만, 일부 주민들은 이 사업에 불만족스러워한다. 그들은 자동차가 이용 가능한 도로의 수가 줄어들 것이고, 이는 더 악화되는 교통 상황으로 이어질 것이라고 우려한다. Ms. Gomez는 시에서 이 문제를 해결하기 위해 계획을 세우고 있으며 5월에 추가적인 세부 사항을 제공할 것이라고 말했다.

158 Stevens 시장에 대해 암시되는 것은?
   (A) 새로운 공공사업 관리자를 임명했다.
   (B) 어제 대중 매체 행사에 참석했다.
   (C) 최근에 당선되었다.
   (D) 몇 가지 건설 사업을 제안했다.

159 일부 주민들은 무엇에 대해 우려하는가?
   (A) 설치 비용
   (B) 공공 안전
   (C) 재산세
   (D) 교통 혼잡

160 기사에 따르면, 5월에 무슨 일이 일어날 것인가?
   (A) 사업에 대한 더 많은 정보가 주어질 것이다.
   (B) 기자들이 교통 연구의 결과를 받을 것이다.
   (C) 예산 추정안이 수정될 것이다.

(D) 시장이 기자회견을 열 것이다.

161-164는 다음 온라인 채팅 대화문에 관한 문제입니다.

Janice Hong	오전 10시 3분

우리가 오늘 오후에 Alliance Plastics사의 대표들에게 하기로 한 영업 발표와 관련해 문제에 부딪혔어요. 주 회의실에 있는 에어컨이 작동하지 않는다고 방금 통지받았어요.

| **Devon Harris** | 오전 10시 6분 |

그러면, 2층에 있는 회의실로 발표를 옮기는 것은 어때요?

| **Grace Rhodes** | 오전 10시 9분 |

Alliance Plastics사는 그곳 경영팀 중 11명을 보낼 거예요. 그 층의 방은 8명만이 편안하게 앉을 수 있어요. Janice, 회의 전에 에어컨을 작동시킬 수 있는 가능성이 있을까요?

| **Janice Hong** | 오전 10시 12분 |

안 될 것 같아요. 제가 몇몇 수리점에 전화했는데, 기술자가 우리 사무실로 올 수 있는 가장 빠른 시간이 내일 오후 1시예요. 발표를 미루는 것을 고려해야 할지도 모르겠어요.

| **Devon Harris** | 오전 10시 15분 |

중요한 고객인걸요. 뭔가 우리가 할 수 있는 다른 것이 있을 거예요.

| **Grace Rhodes** | 오전 10시 16분 |

제가 도시의 몇몇 호텔들에 연락해볼까요? 적어도 그들 중 한 곳은 우리가 예고 없이 예약할 수 있는 적당한 회의 공간을 분명히 가지고 있을 거예요.

| **Janice Hong** | 오전 10시 18분 |

좋은 생각이에요. 당신이 예약을 하면, 제가 Alliance Plastics사에 전화해서 장소 변경에 대해 알릴게요.

161 Ms. Hong은 어떤 문제를 언급하는가?
(A) 기기가 잘못 설치되었다.
(B) 발표가 단축되어야 한다.
(C) 장비가 작동을 멈췄다.
(D) 대표가 예상했던 것보다 일찍 도착했다.

162 2층 회의실에 대해 무엇이 언급되었는가?
(A) 다른 팀에 의해 예약되었다.
(B) 그 단체를 위해서는 수용력이 불충분하다.
(C) 최근에 기술자에 의해 점검되었다.
(D) 행사를 위해서는 위치가 불편하다.

163 오전 10시 15분에, Mr. Harris가 "This is an important client"라고 썼을 때 그가 의도한 것은?
(A) 좋은 첫인상을 주길 바란다.
(B) 제안에 동의하지 않는다.
(C) 행사의 일정을 변경하고 싶어 한다.
(D) 추가적인 준비를 해야 한다.

164 Ms. Rhodes는 무엇을 할 것을 제안하는가?
(A) 지역의 몇몇 사업체에 연락한다
(B) 고객에게 상황에 대해 공지한다
(C) 이전에 한 예약을 확인한다
(D) 대체 가능한 회의 장소를 방문한다

165-167은 다음 광고지에 관한 문제입니다.

A Night of Song
콘서트

12월 5일, 프랑스 가수 Pierre Chrétien과 Celine Laurier가 캘리포니아주 로스앤젤레스에서의 두 번째 콘서트를 위해 Maroon 극장에 올 것입니다. 오후 7시 30분에 시작할 이 행사에는 미국 소울 가수 Andy Red와 Cindy Dawson뿐만 아니라 프랑스 피아니스트 Amanda Depuis도 특별 출연할 것인데, Amanda Depuis는 공연 중에 Mr. Chrétien과 Ms. Laurier의 ○

반주를 할 것입니다. — [1] —. 콘서트 동안, Ms. Laurier는 영감을 주는 그녀의 앨범 *Crossroads*를 소개할 예정인데, 이 앨범은 지난주 파리에서 발매되었습니다. — [2] —.

프랑스와 미국인 예술가들의 색다른 융합을 확인해 보십시오. — [3] —. 11월 20일까지, 세 장 이상의 사전 구매 티켓을 구매하신 분들은 무료 무대 뒤 출입증을 받을 것입니다! — [4] —. 티켓은 전국의 모든 Gatewing 티켓 판매처에서 구매 가능합니다. www.gatewing.com에서 온라인으로 구매될 수 있습니다. Mr. Chrétien과 Ms. Laurier 둘 다의 앨범이 현장에서 구매 가능할 것입니다. 자세한 사항은 1-800-555-2541로 Gatewing에 전화 주세요.

165 무대 뒤 출입증에 대해 암시되는 것은?
(A) 콘서트 한 달보다 더 이전에 구매되어야 한다.
(B) 특정한 구매 조건을 만족시키는 사람들에게 무료이다.
(C) 콘서트 현장 직원들만 이용 가능하다.
(D) 11월 내내 할인된 가격에 팔릴 것이다.

166 콘서트에 대해 언급되지 않은 것은?
(A) 로스앤젤레스에서 열릴 것이다.
(B) 판매될 수 있는 상품들이 있을 것이다.
(C) 새 앨범을 홍보할 것이다.
(D) 사인회를 포함할 것이다.

167 [1], [2], [3], [4]로 표시된 위치 중, 다음 문장이 들어갈 곳으로 가장 적절한 것은?

"이는 일반 티켓에는 적용되지 않습니다."

(A) [1]
(B) [2]
(C) [3]
(D) [4]

168-171은 다음 이메일에 관한 문제입니다.

수신: Stephen Haggerty <s.haggerty@mailbag.com>
발신: 고객 서비스 <cust_serv@giftlane.com>
제목: 귀하의 주문
날짜: 12월 8일

Mr. Haggerty께,

저희는 온라인 상점에서 해주신 귀하의 주문을 받았고, 그 세부 사항이 아래에 있습니다. 안타깝게도, 저희는 요청받은 대로 모든 상품들을 보낼 수가 없습니다. 이번 연휴 기간의 유별나게 많은 주문량으로 인해, 현재 몇몇 인기 상품들이 크리스마스 이전에 배송될 수 없습니다. 저희는 이 불편에 대해 사과 드립니다.

주문 세부 사항

수량	설명	상태	예상 배송일
1	개별 맞춤 로제 와인 한 병	발송 준비됨	12월 21일
3	초콜릿 선물 상자(여러 종류)	발송 준비됨	12월 18일
1	가죽 제본 일기장과 펜	발송 준비됨	12월 22일
2	장식 식물 화분	보류됨	12월 27일

적어도 주문의 일부가 반드시 발송되도록 하기 위해, 저희는 첫 세 개의 물품들을 위에서 명시된 일자까지 귀하가 제공한 각기 다른 주소로 수취인들에게 배송할 수 있습니다. 그러나, 목록에 있는 마지막 물품과 관련해, 수취인이 그것을 받을 수 있는 가장 빠른 일자는 12월 27일입니다. 만일 귀하가 이것을 받아들인다면, 이 메시지에 답신하지 않으셔도 되며, 물품 재고가 생기면 그 주소로 배송을 진행할 것입니다.

그러나, 만일 12월 25일 이전에 귀하의 모든 선물들이 배송되는 것이 중요하다면, 보류된 상품을 저희 상점의 다른 제품으로 변경하기를 권해 드립니다. 지금 주문을 변경하려면 여기를 클릭하십시오. 추가적인 정보를 위해서는, 이 메시지에 답하거나 555-3403으로 전화해 주십시오.

○

감사합니다.

Margaret Hill 드림
고객 서비스 직원
Gift Lane사

168 Mr. Haggerty의 주문의 문제는 무엇인가?
(A) 웹사이트에서 기술적 오류가 발생했다.
(B) 잘못된 물품을 포함했다.
(C) 요청받은 물품을 쉽게 구할 수 없다.
(D) 중요한 배송 세부 사항이 누락되었다.

169 Mr. Haggerty에 대해 암시되는 것은?
(A) 모든 물품을 하나씩 주문했다.
(B) 자신을 위해 와인 한 병을 구매했다.
(C) 여러 수취인들에게 물품을 보내고 있다.
(D) 과거에 Gift Lane사에서 구매한 적이 있다.

170 Mr. Haggerty가 이메일에 답변하지 않는다면 어떤 일이 일어날 것인가?
(A) 주문이 취소될 것이다.
(B) 배송이 진행될 것이다.
(C) 추가 비용이 발생할 것이다.
(D) 특별 할인이 무효화될 것이다.

171 만일 Mr. Haggerty가 물품을 바꾸기 원한다면 무엇을 해야 하는가?
(A) 추가 설명을 기다린다
(B) 회사 상담 전화에 연락한다
(C) 웹사이트의 링크를 따라간다
(D) 고객 서비스에 메시지를 보낸다

172-175는 다음 기사에 관한 문제입니다.

Lester Beebe가 사우스벤드에서 무대에 오르다
Adam Brown 작성

Michelle Gable의 소설 *Triumph of Lester Beebe*의 뮤지컬 버전이 다음 달 5월 22일에 초연을 할 예정이다. — [1] —. 사우스벤드를 배경으로 한 그 공연은 1960년대 자동차 공장 노동자의 아들인 10대 소년의 이야기이다. 그 책은 1968년에 처음 출판되었을 때 젊은 성인 독자들 사이에서 인기를 얻게 되었다. — [2] —.

제작자인 Todd Carlisle과 Emma Wright는 책이 처음 출판되었을 때 심지어 태어나지도 않았었지만, 그들은 처음 이야기를 읽었을 때 Lester Beebe의 청소년기의 분투에 동질감을 갖게 되었다고 말한다. "Lester Beebe는 단지 사우스벤드의 10대 소년이 아닙니다," Carlisle이 말하길, "그는 모든 곳의 젊은이들이 될 수 있습니다." Carlisle과 Wright는 공연의 제작자일 뿐만 아니라 사우스벤드의 Eden 극장을 운영한다. — [3] —. Wright에 따르면, 그 지역은 뮤지컬 작품으로 잘 알려져 있지 않지만, 그녀는 *Triumph of Lester Beebe*가 그것을 변화시키길 희망한다. "Todd와 저는 또한 그 공연에 관객을 끌어모으는 것을 도울 지역의 관심을 기대하고 있습니다."라고 그녀가 말했다.

Beebe 역할을 연기하는 배우는 Henry Thomas이다. 베테랑 연기자인 Neil Chandler가 그의 아버지 역할인 반면, Beebe의 여자 형제들인 Mandy와 Corinne는 Stephanie O'Connor와 Audrey Blanco에 의해 묘사될 것이다. 사우스벤드에서의 공연 후에, Carlisle과 Wright는 8월에 뉴욕에서 브로드웨이 데뷔를 위해 그 공연을 할 것이다. — [4] —. 사우스벤드 공연을 위한 티켓은 555-0493에서 Eden 극장을 통해 지금 판매되고 있다.

---

172 기사는 주로 무엇에 관한 것인가?
(A) 뮤지컬 배우의 무대 복귀
(B) 곧 있을 공연 작품
(C) 공연 장소의 대 개장
(D) 한 작가의 자서전 각색

173 *Triumph of Lester Beebe*에 대해 언급되지 않은 것은?
(A) 뉴욕에서 성공적인 공연을 했다.
(B) 1960년대의 몇몇 젊은이들 사이에서 인기가 있었다.
(C) 뮤지컬 공연으로 각색되었다.
(D) 사우스벤드를 기반으로 한다.

174 3문단 두 번째 줄의 단어 "realized"는 의미상 -와 가장 가깝다.
(A) 초래되다
(B) 묘사되다
(C) 분명해지다
(D) 발견되다

175 [1], [2], [3], [4]로 표시된 위치 중, 다음 문장이 들어갈 곳으로 가장 적절한 것은?

"그 인기는 그것이 대폭적인 찬사를 받아 결국 32개 언어로 번역되게 했다."

(A) [1]
(B) [2]
(C) [3]
(D) [4]

176-180은 다음 기사와 광고에 관한 문제입니다.

그룹 피트니스 산티아고를 움직이게 하다
Raymond Wong 기자
2월 16일

긴 겨울이 이어지면서, 새해 다짐에 대해 잊기 쉽다. 그러나 지역 체육관 주인들에 따르면, 올해 그 어느 때보다 더 많은 사람들이 그들의 건강 목표를 고수하고 있다. 그 비결은? 산티아고 주민들은 기록적인 숫자로 그룹 피트니스 수업에 등록하고 있으며, 함께 운동하는 것이 그들에게 동기를 부여하고 있다.

통상적으로, 그룹 피트니스의 주요 단점은 상대적으로 높은 가격이었다. 그러나 지난겨울, Exercise Nation을 포함한 몇몇 저렴한 피트니스 센터들이 그룹 수업의 종류를 크게 확장했다. 그들은 이제 킥복싱에서부터 요가에 이르기까지 모든 것을 제공하며, 모든 피트니스 수준의 사람들을 위한 다양한 선택권이 있다.

"저는 사실 제가 원하는 만큼 많은 수업에 갈 수 있도록 제 회원권을 업그레이드했어요."라고 대학생이자 지난 2년 동안 Exercise Nation 체육관 회원인 Millie Rhys가 말했다. "저는 단지 역기를 몇 개 들고 실내 자전거를 타기 위해 여기에 오곤 했지만, 수업들은 체육관에 가는 것을 신나게 해주었습니다."

건강해지는 것을 미루지 마세요!

Exercise Nation은 다양한 종류의 그룹 수업을 제공합니다. 모든 회원은 일주일에 한 번 무료 수업의 자격이 있습니다. 골드 회원과 골드 플러스 회원들은 매주, 각각 2회와 3회의 무료 수업을 받습니다. 다이아몬드 회원들은 무제한 수업 이용권을 받고 저희의 고급 HIIT 프로그램을 이용할 수 있습니다. www.exercisenation.com/classes를 방문하여 어떤 수업이 일정에 맞는지 확인해 보세요.

아직 회원이 아니신가요? 문제없어요! 한 달에 20달러부터 시작하는 저렴한 가격으로 지금 가입하세요.* 저희의 트레이너들, 영양사들, 최고 품질의 장비, 그리고 더 많은 것을 이용하세요!

3월에 가입하고 무료 운동용 가방과 물통을 받으세요.
저희는 오전 5시부터 오후 10시까지 주 7일 영업합니다.

*첫 결제에는 15달러의 등록비가 1회 적용됩니다. 회원들은 자동으로 갱신되는 12개월 계약에 서명해야 합니다.

---

176 기사에 따르면, 지난겨울에 무슨 일이 있었는가?
(A) 제품의 가격이 인하되었다.
(B) 운동 시설이 확장되었다.

(C) 몇몇 새로운 상품이 이용 가능해졌다.
(D) 몇몇 체육관 장비가 배달되었다.

177 기사는 Exercise Nation에 대해 무엇을 암시하는가?
(A) 학생 할인을 제공한다.
(B) 긍정적인 온라인 후기를 받았다.
(C) 다양한 역량의 회원들을 수용한다.
(D) 2년 동안 영업해 왔다.

178 Ms. Rhys에 대해 추론될 수 있는 것은?
(A) 다이아몬드 회원권이 있다.
(B) 가입비를 청구받지 않았다.
(C) HIIT 수업을 듣고 싶어 한다.
(D) 혼자 운동하는 것을 선호한다.

179 3월에 무엇이 있을 것인가?
(A) 시즌 세일
(B) 등록 판촉행사
(C) 스포츠 경기
(D) 체육관 개관

180 체육관 회원권에 대해 사실인 것은?
(A) 1년 동안 지속된다.
(B) 20달러로 업그레이드할 수 있다.
(C) 개인 트레이닝 시간을 포함한다.
(D) 웹사이트에서 갱신할 수 있다.

181-185는 다음 브로슈어와 이메일에 관한 문제입니다.

City Ago사와 함께 브리스틀을 구경하세요!

브리스틀을 방문하신다면, City Ago사가 당신의 교통 및 수송 수요를 모두 충족시켜 드립니다. 당신이 좋아하는 장소로 돌아오는 단독 여행자이든 대규모 일행과 함께 도착하는 첫 방문객이든, 저희는 당신이 필요로 하는 모든 차량과 지식을 가지고 있습니다.

사용 가능한 교통수단 종류:

- 자전거: 각 1인승, 시간당 3파운드(최소 3시간)*
- 전동 스쿠터: 각 최대 2인승, 시간당 10파운드(최소 4시간)*
- 승용차: 각 최대 5인승, 1일(최소) 100파운드, 운전자는 적어도 25세여야 함
- 미니버스: 각 최대 15인승, 1일(최소) 550파운드, 운전자는 25세 이상이어야 하며 유효한 상용 운전 면허증을 소지해야 함

*헬멧 필수

각 교통수단 옵션은 안내 관광과 함께 또는 없이 준비될 수 있습니다. 시작하는 데 도움이 더 필요하시면, 저희 서비스는 또한 맞춤 여행 일정, 식사 및 숙박 예약, 그리고 더 많은 것을 포함합니다. 예약을 하려면, www.cityago.com/reservations를 방문하여 신청 양식을 제출하십시오. 또한 예약을 완료하기 전에 www.cityago.com/t&c에서 사고 및 손해 배상 책임에 대한 정보와 함께 저희 약관을 읽어보시길 바랍니다.

수신: 예약 <reservations@cityago.com>
발신: Craig Black <cblack@duncanarchitects.com>
제목: 신청 업데이트
날짜: 6월 20일

6월 29일 일요일을 위한 제 예약을 확정해 주셔서 다시 한번 감사드립니다. 하지만, 저는 제 기존 신청을 변경하고 싶어요. 사실 전동 스쿠터가 더 낫겠어요. 차량은 여전히 4시간 동안 대여하겠습니다. 저희는 이제 스쿠터 두 대가 필요할 것입니다.

또한, 구시가지로부터 브리스틀 역사박물관으로 가는 지름길을 아시는지 궁금합니다. 저희는 더 직행이고 주요 도로로 가지 않을 경로를 찾고 있습니다.

Craig Black 드림

---

181 브로슈어에서, 1문단 두 번째 줄의 단어 "spots"는 의미상 ~와 가장 가깝다.
(A) 위치
(B) 결함
(C) 얼룩
(D) 관점

182 City Ago사는 고객들에게 무엇을 하도록 권장하는가?
(A) 공항에서 교통수단을 빌린다
(B) 할인 거래를 위해 웹사이트를 확인한다
(C) 보호용 장비를 챙긴다
(D) 책임 정책을 검토한다

183 Mr. Black은 원래 무엇을 예약한 것 같은가?
(A) 자전거
(B) 전동 스쿠터
(C) 승용차
(D) 미니버스

184 Mr. Black에 대해 사실인 것은?
(A) 예약 날짜를 변경했다.
(B) 일주일 전에 예약했다.
(C) 확정 메시지를 기다리고 있다.
(D) 브리스틀을 일요일에 방문할 것이다.

185 Mr. Black은 City Ago사에 무엇을 해달라고 요청하는가?
(A) 건물로 가는 길을 안내한다
(B) 망가진 스쿠터를 수리한다
(C) 대여 기간을 연장한다
(D) 안내 관광을 제공한다

186-190은 다음 웹페이지, 이메일, 송장에 관한 문제입니다.

---

http://www.stclaireeditewrite.com/about

Ruben St. Claire: 프리랜서 작가/편집자

<u>소개</u>   <u>연락</u>   <u>포트폴리오/집필 샘플</u>

서비스

저는 다양한 주제들에 대해 글을 쓰고, 편집하고, 교정하며, 자료들을 조사합니다. 만약 당신의 협회, 기업, 또는 기관에서 잡지 기사, 블로그 게시글, 회보, 보도자료를 작성하거나 완벽하게 하는 데에 도움이 필요할 경우, 주저 마시고 제게 연락 주십시오.

주요 고객

Borton 대학교 동문회, *North East Gardener's*지, 조지빌 도시 계획 협회, Sportsworld 운동용품, 장식 예술 협회

수상

전국 비즈니스 커뮤니케이션 협회 상, GRB 편집 우수상, Georgia P. Smythe 프리랜서 작가상

교육

Western Pointhead 대학교, 문학 학사 학위, 영문학과 언론학 복수 전공

수신: Ruben St. Claire <rstclaire@stclaireeditwrite.com>
발신: Christa Gables <chgab@FineThreads.com>
날짜: 2월 28일
제목: 문의

Mr. St. Claire께,

저는 온라인 소매업체의 사업주로, 최근에 우연히 당신의 웹사이트를 발견했습니다. 저는 제 온라인 의류상점인 FineThreads.com을 위해 짧은 블로그 게시글들을 작업하는 데에 가능하면 당신을 고용하는 것에 관심이 있습니다. 저는 당신의 포트폴리오를 살펴보고 제가 어느 정도 잘 알고 있는 운동복 회사를 위해 당신이 꽤 많은 작업을 해왔음을 알게 되었습니다. 제가 비슷한 ➡

종류의 제품들을 소매하므로 당신이 제 요구 조건들을 충족시킬 수 있다고 생각합니다. 우선, 당신이 제 웹사이트에 게시할 3페이지 분량의 원고를 작성해 주셨으면 합니다. 만약 제가 당신의 작업에 만족한다면, 당신이 할 3시간의 조사 업무와 약 6시간의 교정 업무도 있을 것입니다. 금액 목록과 총액 견적을 보내주십시오. 우리가 가능한 한 빨리 일을 시작할 수 있기를 바랍니다.

Christa Gables 드림

St. Claire 편집 및 집필 서비스
(805)555-3988/ rstclaire@stclaireeditwrite.com

송장: 001   3월 6일
Christa Gables, FineThreads.com
14번지 Lewis Crescent가
West Center, 오하이오주 49242

업무 종류	양/시간	비용
집필	3페이지	225달러
교정	6시간	120달러
조사	5시간	100달러
소계		445달러
세금		44.50달러
총 지불액		489.50달러
총액은 송장 날짜로부터 늦어도 영업일로 5일까지는 지불되어야 하고, 온라인 지불과 은행 이체로 받습니다. 수표를 보내시려면, Ruben St. Claire를 수취인으로 해 주십시오. 거래해 주셔서 대단히 감사합니다!		

186 Mr. St. Claire에 대해 언급되지 않은 것은?
(A) 여러 가지의 다양한 주제에 대해 조사할 수 있다.
(B) 선정된 작업물들을 온라인에 게시했다.
(C) 편집과 집필 작업 모두에서 인정받았다.
(D) 현재 교육 기관에 고용되어 있다.

187 이메일의 주 목적은 무엇인가?
(A) 작가에게 이전 블로그 게시글에 대해 감사를 전하기 위해
(B) 업무 제의를 하기 위해
(C) 편집 요청에 대한 후속 조치를 하기 위해
(D) 선호되는 지불 방법에 대해 문의하기 위해

188 Ms. Gables는 Mr. St. Claire의 어떤 고객을 잘 아는 것 같은가?
(A) Borton 대학교 동문회
(B) North East Gardener's지
(C) Sportsworld 운동용품
(D) 장식 예술 협회

189 Ms. Gables는 Mr. St. Claire에게 무엇을 해달라고 요청하는가?
(A) 그녀에게 우편으로 수표를 보낸다
(B) 비용 견적을 제공한다
(C) 몇몇 블로그 게시글로 가는 링크들을 만든다
(D) 그녀에게 몇몇 집필 샘플들을 이메일로 보낸다

190 Ms. Gables에 대해 추론될 수 있는 것은?
(A) 일부 교정 서비스의 대금을 늦게 보냈다.
(B) 몇몇 조사를 하는 데 필요한 시간을 너무 적게 잡았다.
(C) 예상했던 것보다 광고 문구 작성에 더 많이 지불해야 했다.
(D) 그녀의 동료 중 한 명에게 Mr. St. Claire를 추천할 것이다.

191-195는 다음 공고, 웹페이지, 문자 메시지에 관한 문제입니다.

공고
지하철 보수 관리 작업이 8월 15일 월요일에 Ratner, Sofner, Hambrick 역에서 시작될 것임을 알아두시기 바랍니다. 보수는 8월 28일까지 2주 동안 ⊙

계속될 것으로 예상됩니다. 인부들의 작업 시간은 오전 7시부터 오후 6시까지입니다. 인근에 소음이 조금 있을 것이지만, 작업자들은 방해를 최소한으로 줄이기 위해 노력할 것입니다. 이 기간 동안, 이 역들에서의 운행은 작업을 용이하게 하기 위해 중단될 것입니다. 이 역들을 이용하는 통근자들의 편의를 위해, Wymore 대중교통국은 대체 교통수단을 제공할 것입니다. 더 많은 정보를 원하시면, 웹사이트 www.wymorepublictransport.com/announcements를 방문해 주시기 바랍니다. 불편에 대해 사과드리지만 완료되었을 때 노후화되어 가는 역 시설을 수리한 것에 대한 진가를 인정받을 것이라고 확신합니다.

Wymore 대중교통국
홈 | 소개 | 온라인 서비스 | 공지 | 연락처

공고:

발표일: 8월 5일

대체 교통수단 운행

이번 주에 미리 공지된 바와 같이, 8월 15일부터 Ratner, Sofner, Hambrick 지하철역에서 보수가 시행될 것입니다. 여러분의 편의를 위해, 버스들은 오전 5시 30분부터 자정까지 다음 경로를 운행할 것입니다:

· Ratner와 Sofner를 오가는: 23번 버스
· Ratner와 Hambrick를 오가는: 24번 버스
· Sofner와 Hambrick를 오가는: 25번 버스
· Ratner와 Grand Central을 오가는: 26번 버스

이 버스 경로들은 임시적인 것이며 보수 관리 작업이 완료되는 다음 날까지만 이용 가능할 것입니다. "온라인 서비스" 아래에 있는 위쪽 드롭다운 메뉴에서 "버스"를 클릭해서 영향을 받는 모든 역에 위치한 버스 정류장의 정확한 위치를 보여주는 지도를 확인하십시오. 더 많은 정보를 원하시면, 근무 시간 동안 555-1001로 전화해 주시기 바랍니다.

발신: Jill Addis (555-2737)
수신: Nick Lieb (555-0320)
                                  수신됨: 8월 16일, 오후 3시 35분

Mr. Lieb, 저는 오후 1시에 Di Paolo's 이탈리안 식당에서의 점심 식사를 예약했어요. 당신이 저를 만나면, Cross Media사 계약서를 함께 검토할 수 있어요. 제가 이전에 당신에게 식당 주소를 보내드렸어요. 식당은 Grand Central역의 길 바로 맞은편에 있으므로, 저는 그곳에 가기 위해 대중교통을 이용하는 것을 추천드려요. 하지만 Ratner역이 당신에게 가장 가까운 역이므로 임시 버스 중 하나를 타셔야 할 거예요. 당신은 대중교통국 웹사이트를 방문해서 어느 버스를 타야 할지 알아보실 수 있어요. 어쨌든, 목요일에 뵈어요!

191 공고에 따르면, 지하철역의 보수 관리에 대해 사실인 것은?
(A) 거주자들의 불평 때문에 실행되고 있다.
(B) 8월 28일이 되어서야 시작될 것으로 예상된다.
(C) 작업 시간 동안 소음을 발생시킬 것이다.
(D) 2주간 중단될 것이다.

192 웹페이지에서 언급된 것은?
(A) 늦은 저녁 버스 운행은 대개 이용이 불가능하다.
(B) 임시 버스 정류장의 위치는 온라인에서 찾을 수 있다.
(C) 보수 관리 작업의 완료일은 결정되지 않았다.
(D) 승객들은 버스에서 지하철 탑승권을 사용할 수 있다.

193 임시 버스 운행은 언제 끝날 것인가?
(A) 8월 15일에
(B) 8월 16일에
(C) 8월 28일에
(D) 8월 29일에

194 Mr. Lieb은 어느 버스를 탈 것 같은가?
    (A) 23번 버스
    (B) 24번 버스
    (C) 25번 버스
    (D) 26번 버스

195 Mr. Lieb에 대해 암시되는 것은?
    (A) Cross Media사의 일자리에 지원하고 있다.
    (B) Ms. Addis를 점심 식사 동안 만날 것이다.
    (C) Ms. Addis에게 서비스 중단에 대해 알렸다.
    (D) 이전의 약속을 변경했다.

196-200은 다음 안내문, 이메일, 편지에 관한 문제입니다.

MOONGLOW 건강식품사 – 투어 가능

5월 1일에, Moonglow 건강식품사는 정규 투어를 위해 정원, 주방, 그리고 포장 시설을 개방할 것입니다. 여러분이 가장 좋아하는 음식이 어떻게 수확되고, 준비되고, 지역 식료품점에서 판매될 수 있게 포장되는지 보러 오세요!

투어는 매주 월요일, 목요일, 그리고 금요일에 오전 10시부터 오후 12시까지 진행됩니다. 정규 주간 투어는 5명부터 20명의 단체에 이용 가능합니다. 555-4293으로 전화를 걸어 예약하세요!

더 큰 단체도 특별 예약으로 수용 가능합니다. 학교 현장학습에 관심 있으신 지역 교육자들은 약속을 잡기 위해 저희에게 연락하시도록 권장됩니다. 특별 예약에 대한 모든 문의는 mariaanderson@moonglowhealth.com으로 Maria Anderson에게 이메일로 보내야 합니다.

Moonglow 건강식품사 투어를 하는 학생들을 위해 특별한 선물과 교육 자료가 있습니다! 학생들은 참여하기 전에 부모나 보호자가 시설 허가서에 서명하도록 요청될 것인 점을 참고하시기 바랍니다.

수신: Julie Armstrong <jarmstrong@washingtonschool.edu>
발신: Maria Anderson <mariaanderson@moonglowhealth.com>
날짜: 4월 2일
제목: 회신: 6학년 현장학습

안녕하세요, Ms. Armstrong! Moonglow 건강식품사에 관심을 가져 주셔서 감사합니다.
5월 1일 주에 귀하의 6학년 학급이 저희와 특별 투어를 함께한다면 정말 좋겠습니다. 저희는 틀림없이 27명의 학생 단체를 관리할 수 있습니다.
학생 투어를 위해 가능한 시간대는 다음과 같습니다:
    5월 2일 화요일 오전 10시
    5월 3일 수요일 오전 11시 30분
    5월 6일 금요일 오전 9시
    5월 6일 금요일 오후 1시
귀하의 단체에 가장 적합한 시간을 알려주세요. 다른 어떤 질문이라도 있으시면 주저하지 말고 연락 주세요!

Maria Anderson 드림
Moonglow 건강식품사 마케팅 및 지원 이사

Washington 중학교
41750 East로
톨레도, 오하이오 43460

Ms. Anderson께,

제 학생들이 5월 3일 투어를 얼마나 즐겼는지 알려드리기 위해 편지를 씁니다.

학생들은 밭을 방문해서 지역 농작물이 어떻게 경작되고 수확되는지 보는 것을 매우 즐거워했습니다. 또한 농작물이 어떻게 귀사 시설의 주방에서 잼, 소스, 그리고 다른 제품들로 바뀌는지 보는 것은 그들에게 매우 유익했습니다.
저희는 판매되는 제품의 수에 정말 놀랐습니다. 저는 Moonglow 건강식품사에 이렇게 폭넓은 범위의 선택지가 있는지 전혀 몰랐습니다.

또한 기념품에 대해 감사드리고 싶습니다. 포스터는 저희 교실에 아주 잘 어울릴 것이고, 씨앗 꾸러미는 학교에서 공동 정원을 시작하기 위해 사용할 것입니다.

아낌없는 지원에 다시 한번 감사드립니다!

Julie Armstrong 드림

196 Moonglow 건강식품사의 투어에 대해 언급된 것은?
    (A) 요청 시 개인을 위한 비공개 투어가 이용 가능하다.
    (B) 휴일 기간에는 일정이 변경된다.
    (C) 주간 투어 단체의 규모는 한정되어 있다.
    (D) 기념품 가게에서 특별한 선물을 살 수 있다.

197 Ms. Armstrong의 단체는 투어를 하기 위해 무엇이 필요할 것 같은가?
    (A) 허가를 부여하는 문서
    (B) 대규모 단체를 위한 특별 보증금
    (C) 전화 예약
    (D) 농업에 관한 교육 자료

198 현장학습에 대해 암시되는 것은?
    (A) 생산 책임자에 의해 준비되었다.
    (B) 정규 주간 투어와 동시에 진행되었다.
    (C) 한 달 전에 일정이 잡혔다.
    (D) 기존에 계획된 것보다 더 오래 걸렸다.

199 Washington 중학교 학생들은 몇 시에 투어를 했는가?
    (A) 오전 9시
    (B) 오전 10시
    (C) 오전 11시 30분
    (D) 오후 1시

200 Ms. Armstrong에 따르면, Moonglow 건강식품사에 대해 무엇이 특히 인상적이었는가?
    (A) 판매되는 품목의 다양성
    (B) 시설 기념품의 가격
    (C) 전시된 포스터의 품질
    (D) 제공된 씨앗 꾸러미의 수

* 무료 해설은 해커스토익(Hackers.co.kr)에서 다운로드 받으실 수 있습니다.

* QR 코드로 바로가기

PART 5

101 추가 공지가 있을 때까지, 회원들만 피트니스 센터의 장비를 이용하도록 허용될 것이다.

102 월간 보고서는 분석가들이 금융 시장의 변화하는 상황에 대해 최신 정보를 바로 얻을 수 있도록 도와준다.

103 영화 *Silent Target*의 등장인물인 John Greaves는 영화배우 Arnold Langella에 의해 인상적으로 묘사되었다.

104 각각의 공동소유자들은 회사가 어떻게 운영되어야 하는지에 대해 다른 의견을 가지고 있다.

105 Tybolt Tech사는 재활용된 재료를 그것의 포장재에 사용하는데, 이것은 주로 상자로 구성된다.

106 Keating 교수는 교실 앞에서 시연에 참여할 네 명의 학생을 무작위로 선발할 것이다.

107 웹사이트의 향상된 추적 기능은 이전 버전이 그랬던 것보다 광고 타깃에게 다가가기 위한 더 믿을 수 있는 방법을 광고주들에게 제공한다.

108 Vidiful Games사는 10대 남자 쪽보다 10대 소녀들에 겨냥된 여러 비디오 게임을 출시했다.

109 Ms. Taylor가 법정에서 복잡한 문제를 논할 수 있는 뛰어난 능력을 보여줬기 때문에, 그녀는 법무법인의 대표 사원으로 임명되었다.

110 연구는 중년기에 정기적으로 도전적인 업무를 수행하는 것이 향상된 인지 기능으로 이어진다는 것을 보여준다.

111 Turnerfield 공공도서관은 그것의 디지털 자원 부족에 대한 불만을 받아온 것에 더해서, 지역사회 교육 프로그램을 제공하지 못했다는 비판도 받아 왔다.

112 두 전화기의 공통적인 디자인 특징들 때문에, 소비자들은 한쪽 전화기와 다른 쪽 전화기를 구별하는 데 어려움을 겪는다.

113 그 패션 상표는 최근 온라인 판매에 집중함에 따라 새로운 마케팅 전략을 개발하고 있다.

114 영업직에 지원하는 사람들은 기술 전문지식을 빨리 습득하는 능력에 대해 자신이 있어야 한다.

115 오늘 지급된 월급에 오류가 있는 직원들은 Mr. Costa에게 도움을 요청해야 한다.

116 기업들은 고객의 기대에 부응해야만 오늘날의 사업 환경에서 경쟁력을 유지할 수 있다.

117 충분히 설명되지 않은 여러 가지 이유로, 그 기관은 다가오는 모든 세미나를 취소했다.

118 그 도시는 대도시권 내에 공기로 운반되는 오염 물질의 심각한 축적으로 인해 모든 디젤 버스를 교체할 계획이다.

119 Help Hearts 재단의 연례 자선 행사를 통해 모금된 기금은 Vigneux-Dade 어린이 병원에 도움이 된다.

120 Clairview 지점이 문을 닫았을 때 일부 직원들은 인근 지점들로 이동되었지만, 다른 직원들은 경쟁사에 의해 고용되었다.

121 Ms. Franklin은 이사회에 주주 이익을 보호해야 할 책임을 상기시켰다.

122 연구팀은 3개월 간의 남극 대륙 탐험을 위해 정교한 준비를 시작했다.

123 쇼핑몰에 있는 거의 모든 상점들은 오전 10시에 문을 열지만, Tinsel 부티크는 예외이다.

124 감염을 막기 위해, 의료 기구들은 사용되기 전에 소독되는 것이 필수적이다.

125 유럽 문학 강좌에 등록한 사람이 거의 없었기 때문에, 학교는 그것을 교육 과정에서 빼기로 결정할지도 모른다.

126 연료 효율성 측면에서, 현재까지 Kanon X9은 틀림없이 Hugel 자동차사의 가장 환경친화적인 차량이다.

127 경기 침체기에 경제 성장을 자극하기 위해, 중앙은행은 가끔 금리를 낮추는데 이것이 소비를 촉진시키기 때문이다.

128 대다수의 직원들은 그들이 받는 급여에 만족하고 있는 것으로 보인다.

129 수학 수업의 학생들은 그들이 어렵다고 느낀 몇몇 문제들에 대해 의논했다.

130 대부분의 초청 연사들이 학회에 참석하는 것에 대해 아직 의사를 밝히지 않았기 때문에 발표 일정이 결정되지 않았다.

PART 6

131-134는 다음 공고에 관한 문제입니다.

Starfire 경기장: 중요 공지

131 저희는 최근에 The Ebbing Tide의 전 세계 투어 중 몇몇 공연이 취소되었다는 것을 알게 되었습니다. 안타깝게도, 6월 6일 저녁에 Starfire 경기장에서 열릴 예정이었던 콘서트가 취소된 그 공연들 중 하나였습니다.
132 Starfire 경기장은 이로 인한 티켓 구매자분들의 실망에 대해 사과드리고 싶습니다. 저희는 밴드의 일정에 맞는 날짜로 공연을 옮기려고 했습니다.
133 하지만, 상황은 저희가 통제할 수가 없었습니다.
만약 입장권을 Starfire 경기장에서 직접 구입하셨다면, 내일부터 저희 매표소에서 전액 환불을 받으실 수 있습니다. 여러분의 티켓을 가져와 주십시오.
134 환불받기 위해서는 그것을 제시하셔야 할 것입니다.

135-138은 다음 편지에 관한 문제입니다.

7월 28일
Ruth Quinn
237번지 Spring로
노스 오거스타, 사우스캐롤라이나주 29841

Ms. Quinn께,

135 이 편지는 Laundale 비즈니스 아카데미의 감독 관리 수업을 수강하는 것에 대한 귀하의 관심에 관한 것입니다. 136 의심할 여지 없이, 이것은 저희의 가장 인기 있는 수업들 중 하나입니다. 저희는 매 학기 등록하기를 희망하는 학생들로부터 수많은 신청서를 받습니다. 귀하께서 참가하게 된 학생들 중 한 명이라고 전하게 되어 기쁩니다.

귀하께서는 주간 시간표와 강의 개요를 돌아오는 주에 받게 될 것입니다. 또한, 수업 자료 중 일부는 Laundale 비즈니스 아카데미의 웹사이트에서만 구할 수 있다는 점을 유의해 주십시오. 8월 초에 사용자명과 비밀번호가 귀하께 이메일로 보내질 것입니다. 137 그것들은 저희 시스템에 처음 로그인한 뒤 변경될 수 있습니다.

138 Laundale 비즈니스 아카데미를 대표하여 축하 인사를 드리며 행운을 빕니다.

Shaun Conway 드림
입학부장
Laundale 비즈니스 아카데미

139-142는 다음 기사에 관한 문제입니다.

(7월 20일)— Thanks-A-Latte가 또 한 번의 성공적인 해를 기념하고 있다. 26년 전, 지역 주민 Michael Troslin은 바로 여기 메인주 오거스타에 첫 번째 Thanks-A-Latte 커피숍을 열었다. **139** 이제, Thanks-A-Latte는 5개 주에 걸친 17개의 매장으로 확장되었다. **140** "제가 이 사업을 처음 시작했을 때, 저는 그저 편안한 환경에서 맛있는 커피를 제공하고 싶었습니다."라고 Mr. Troslin은 말했다. 오늘날까지도, 그는 그 약속을 지켰다. **141** 그의 각 매장은 쾌적한 환경과 고품질의 커피를 특징으로 하며, 이 부지런한 소유주는 그것을 보장하기 위해 매우 신경 쓴다. Mr. Troslin은 향후 몇 년 동안 프랜차이즈를 더욱 성장시킬 계획이다. **142** 그 후에, 그는 국제적으로 확장하기를 희망한다.

143-146은 다음 안내문에 관한 문제입니다.

직원 휴가 규정

· Gemstone Multimedia사는 전 직원에게 1년에 15일의 유급 휴가를 부여합니다. **143** 적절한 통지가 주어진다면, 이것들은 12개월의 계약 기간 중 어느 시점에서든 사용될 수 있습니다. 긴급한 상황을 제외하고, 하루 휴가를 내기 위해서는 1주일 전의 통지가 요구되며 이틀 이상 연이어 휴가를 내기 위해서는 2주 전의 통지가 필요합니다.

· 관리자들은 직원들의 휴가 요청을 수용하기 위해 최선을 다할 것입니다. **144** 하지만, 그들은 그들의 재량에 따라 행동할 자격이 있습니다. 다시 말해서, 특히 바쁜 시기나 긴급한 상황이 발생할 때는, 그들이 회사의 요구가 우선 사항이 되어야 할지를 결정할 것입니다.

· 각각의 다음 근무 연도에, 직원들은 하루의 추가 휴가를 받을 것입니다. **145** 이는 직원이 연 30일의 휴가를 누적할 때까지 적용됩니다.

· **146** 휴가 일수는 만료됩니다. 이것은 1년 내에 휴가를 사용하지 못한 직원들은 보상을 받지 못한 채 그것들을 잃게 된다는 것을 의미합니다.

PART 7

147-148은 다음 광고에 관한 문제입니다.

Laura's Designs
448번지 Government가, 빅토리아주

늦여름 할인

Laura's Designs에 들러서 모두 최고급 린넨으로 만들어진, 저희의 다양한 침구, 수건, 그리고 커튼들을 둘러보세요!

저희 가게의 모든 욕실용품에 대해 25퍼센트 할인을 받기 위해 이 광고를 인쇄해서 판매원에게 보여주세요. 구매한 제품에 만족하지 않으면, 7일 이내에 교환할 수 있습니다.

이 할인은 9월 1일까지 유효합니다. 이것은 어떤 다른 판촉 할인과도 함께 사용될 수 없습니다.

147 무엇이 광고되고 있는가?
(A) 옷 가게
(B) 가정용품 소매업체
(C) 직물 공급업체
(D) 수공예 워크숍

148 Laura's Designs에 대해 언급되지 않은 것은?
(A) 한정된 기간 동안 할인을 제공하고 있다.
(B) 고객들에게 판촉물을 가져올 것을 권장하고 있다.
(C) 각종 직물로 만들어진 제품들을 판매한다.
(D) 일주일 이내에 교환이 이루어지는 것을 허용한다.

149-150은 다음 회람에 관한 문제입니다.

회람

수신: 사무실 전 직원
발신: Margery Haines, 인사부장
날짜: 10월 12일
제목: 사무실 개선사항

최근 몇 달 동안, 우리 사무실의 전기 시스템에 결함이 있다는 항의가 있었습니다. 회사는 이번 주에 일단의 기술자들이 사무실의 배선을 바꾸도록 함으로써 이 사태에 대처하기로 결정했습니다. 10월 13일과 14일, 오후 6시경에 모든 층의 전기가 차단될 것이라는 점을 유의해주십시오. 여러분 대부분이 오후 5시에 일을 마무리하기 때문에 이것이 여러분의 업무 일정에 영향을 미치지는 않을 것입니다. 또한 작업 첫날 오전 11시에 전기 시스템이 테스트되는 동안에도 전원이 공급되지 않을 것입니다. 하지만, 이는 10분 이내로 복구될 것입니다. 그저 오전 10시 50분쯤에 반드시 작업 중인 모든 파일을 저장하고 나서 컴퓨터를 종료하도록 하십시오.

149 회람은 주로 무엇에 대한 것인가?
(A) 새 보안 시스템의 설치
(B) 오작동에 대한 가능한 원인
(C) 정상 운영 시간의 변경
(D) 계획된 몇몇 보수 작업

150 직원들은 무엇을 해달라고 요청받는가?
(A) 중요한 파일을 집으로 가져간다
(B) 근무가 끝날 때 책상을 정리한다
(C) 작업물이 손실되는 것을 방지한다
(D) 컴퓨터에 파일을 설치한다

151-152는 다음 메시지 대화문에 관한 문제입니다.

Andrew Clayton [오전 9시 2분]
안녕하세요. 저는 Walker Home의 페인트공입니다. 제가 오전 10시에 귀하의 아파트에서 페인트 작업을 좀 하기로 예정되어 있습니다. 그때 근처에 계실 건가요?

Erica Mendes [오전 9시 4분]
집주인이 제게 당신이 올 거라고 말해주었어요. 사실 제가 도시 밖에 있어요. 오늘 저녁이 되어서야 집에 갈 것이지만, 프런트에 열쇠를 맡겨두었어요.

Andrew Clayton [오전 9시 7분]
알겠습니다. 제가 일을 마치면 다시 그곳에 열쇠를 돌려주어야 하나요?

Erica Mendes [오전 9시 7분]
네, 부탁드려요. 가시기 전에 문을 잠가주시겠어요?

Andrew Clayton [오전 9시 8분]
그럼요. 그러면, 확인을 좀 하려고 하는데, 제가 귀하의 주방, 욕실, 그리고 현관을 칠하는 거죠. 맞나요?

Erica Mendes [오전 9시 9분]
저는 발코니도 칠해질 거라고 들었어요.

Andrew Clayton [오전 9시 9분]
제 업무 배정에 그건 없는데, 귀하의 집주인과 확인해보겠습니다. 문제가 있으면, 알려드리겠습니다.

Erica Mendes [오전 9시 10분]
정말 감사해요!

151 Ms. Mendes는 누구인 것 같은가?
(A) 페인트 회사의 직원
(B) 부동산 중개소의 고객
(C) 아파트 건물의 세입자
(D) 주택 단지에 배치된 경비원

152 오전 9시 8분에, Mr. Clayton이 "Certainly"라고 썼을 때 그가 의도한 것은?
(A) 발코니에 개량 공사를 할 것이다.
(B) 문틀의 손상된 부분을 수리할 것이다.
(C) 아파트의 추가적인 부분을 칠할 것이다.
(D) 문을 잠글 것이다.

153-154는 다음 편지에 관한 문제입니다.

6월 6일

Ava Foster
Falu 카페
2650번지 Nelmis가
알렉산드리아, 버지니아주 22301

Ms. Foster께,

저는 최근에 지역 사업주들을 소개하는 것을 시작한 *Alexandria Record*지의 기자입니다. 저는 귀하가 어떻게 Falu 카페를 매입하여 그것을 성공적으로 바꾸어 놓았는지에 대해 알게 되는 데에 독자들이 관심을 가질 것이라고 생각하는데, 특히 이전 주인이 자신은 거의 이익을 내지 못했었다고 주장하기 때문입니다. 가능하다면, 저는 귀하의 이야기를 듣기 위해 귀하를 만나고 싶습니다.

다음 주 중 언젠가 귀하와 이야기를 나누기 위해 카페를 방문해도 될까요? 저는 평일 오후 2시 이후에 시간이 나지만, 만약 귀하께서 그 시간이 가능하지 않다면 기꺼이 제 일정을 조정하겠습니다. 555-4466으로 전화 주셔서 관심이 있으신지 알려주십시오.

Justin Lachapelle 드림

---

153 편지는 왜 쓰였는가?
(A) 예약을 하기 위해
(B) 사업 제안을 논의하기 위해
(C) 인터뷰를 요청하기 위해
(D) 신문 특집을 소개하기 위해

154 Mr. Lachapelle은 무엇을 하겠다고 제안하는가?
(A) 이전에 출판된 기사를 전달한다
(B) 음식점에 방문한다
(C) 고객을 끌어들이기 위한 방안을 제시한다
(D) Ms. Foster를 위해 특별 조정을 한다

155-157은 다음 브로슈어에 관한 문제입니다.

임차 가능한 이상적인 사무실 공간

만약 시내에서 사무실 공간을 찾고 계신다면, 여러분은 운이 좋으신 겁니다. Trident Tower의 한 층 전체가 현재 이용 가능합니다. Bedford 지하철역의 길 건너에 위치한, 이 38층 건물에는 옥상 정원과 전기 자동차를 위한 충전소가 설치된 지하 주차 시설이 있습니다. 로비에는, 카페, 편의점, 그리고 택배 회사 대리점이 있습니다.

이용 가능한 공간인, 31층은 다음을 포함합니다:
· 다양한 크기의 25개의 사무실
· 두 개의 회의실
· 주방 공간 및 인접해 있는 휴게실
· 멋지게 디자인된 화장실

이 사무실 공간은 현재 5년 임대차 계약으로 내놓아져 있습니다. 둘러볼 기회를 마련하기 위해서는, 555-4456으로 Pearl 부동산의 Claire Woolf에게 전화하세요.

---

155 Trident Tower에 대해 사실이 아닌 것은?
(A) 배송 업체가 들어가 있다.
(B) 대중교통 시설과 가깝다.
(C) 세입자들이 주차할 수 있는 공간을 포함한다.
(D) 몇몇 주거용 방이 있다.

156 브로슈어에 따르면, 몇몇 사람들은 왜 부동산 중개인과 의논해야 하는가?
(A) 연간 비용에 대해 문의하기 위해서
(B) 건물 내부를 볼 기회를 얻기 위해
(C) 임차 옵션에 대한 세부정보를 받기 위해
(D) 매매 수수료에 대해 알기 위해

157 3문단의 두 번째 줄의 표현 "set up"은 의미상 -와 가장 가깝다.
(A) 실행하다
(B) 발달하다
(C) 일정을 잡다
(D) 인정하다

158-160은 다음 후기에 관한 문제입니다.

호텔: Park Square Lodge
후기 작성자: Lana Marcela
날짜: 8월 25일

8월 10일에, 저는 제 회사의 신규 지사에서 열린 3일간의 연수 과정을 총괄하기 위해 댈러스에 도착했습니다. 저는 사무실과의 근접성 때문에 Park Square Lodge를 선택했습니다. 또한, 저는 시내 구역에 있는 몇몇 관광 명소들을 방문할 계획이었고 제가 그곳들 바로 옆에 위치해 있기를 원했습니다. 따라서, 댈러스에 도착한 직후 저는 Park Square Lodge로 향했지만, 유감스럽게도 저는 제 숙소에 대해 매우 실망했습니다. 먼저, 제게 배정된 방은 광고된 것보다 훨씬 작았습니다. 곧바로, 저는 제 돈으로 더 큰 방으로 옮겨줄 것을 요청했으나 호텔이 꽉 찼다는 말을 들었습니다. 제 숙박의 좋지 않은 시작이었습니다. 두 번째로, 룸서비스가 실망스러웠습니다. 체크인한 후, 늦은 저녁에, 저는 샌드위치를 제 스위트룸에 가져오도록 하기 위해 프런트에 전화했습니다. 한 시간 후, 그것은 여전히 도착하지 않았고, 저는 이유를 듣기 위해 로비에 내려갔습니다. 듣자 하니, 호텔 식당은 심지어 제 주문을 접수한 적조차 없었습니다. 그 시점에, 저는 길 아래편에 있는 편의점에서 군것질거리를 사기로 했습니다. 저는 이 호텔에서 머무르는 것을 추천하지 않을 것입니다.

평점: 1.5/5

---

158 Park Square Lodge에 머무는 것의 어떤 장점이 Ms. Marcela에 의해 언급되었는가?
(A) 그녀의 회사와 제휴가 되어 있다.
(B) 공항에서 도보 거리 내에 있다.
(C) 관광객들에게 추천할 만하다.
(D) 그녀의 직장에서 가깝다.

159 식당은 왜 Ms. Marcela의 요청을 충족시킬 수 없었는가?
(A) 요청이 전달되지 않았다.
(B) 재료가 다 떨어졌었다.
(C) 많은 손님들에게 음식이 제공되어야 했다.
(D) 전화가 통화 중이었다.

160 호텔에 대해 언급되지 않은 것은?
(A) 8월 10일에 모든 방이 예약되어 있었다.
(B) 투숙객의 방으로 음식을 직접 배달해준다.
(C) 편의점이 있다.
(D) 댈러스 시내에 위치해 있다.

161-164는 다음 온라인 채팅 대화문에 관한 문제입니다.

Gina Mansfield   오후 2시 49분
안녕하세요, 제가 가야 하기 전까지 10분이 있어요. 모두에게서 몇 가지 빠른 업데이트를 받을 수 있을까요? 미안하지만, 제가 급해서요.

Sally Fadden   오후 2시 50분
네. 저는 다음 주에 *Klein's*지, *Fashion Review*지, 그리고 *Younger*지와 사진 촬영을 잡았어요. 제가 전화한 다른 잡지사들은 아직 응답이 없어요.

Gina Mansfield 오후 2시 51분
알았어요, 제 비서인 Amelia에게 날짜를 보내주세요. Ms. Lawson이 어느 촬영장에든 있어야 하나요?

Sally Fadden 오후 2시 52분
*Klein's*지에서만 그녀를 필요로 해요. 다른 두 잡지에서는, 모델들에게 그녀의 옷을 입도록 하기만 할 거예요.

Gina Mansfield 오후 2시 53분
좋아요. 다른 분은요? 모든 바이어들이 패션쇼 참석을 확정했나요?

Desmond Huang 오후 2시 54분
아뇨, 전부는 아니에요. 하지만 괜찮은 인원이 있고 모든 주요 상점들이 대변되었어요. 기대감이 상당해요. 모두들 새 컬렉션을 보고 싶어 해요.

Gina Mansfield 오후 2시 55분
잘됐네요. VIP들과 유명 인사 손님들이 좋은 자리를 얻을 수 있도록 합시다. Troy는 어디 있죠? 영업팀 소식은 못 들었어요.

Troy Nazmi 오후 2시 57분
죄송해요, Gina. 저 여기 있어요. 저희는 아직 마케팅팀으로부터 몇 가지 가격에 관해 대기하고 있지만 도매업체에는 10퍼센트 그리고 더 소규모의 소매업체에는 5퍼센트 할인을 제공하기로 결정했어요.

Gina Mansfield 오후 2시 58분
알겠어요. 자, 저는 가봐야겠네요. Parker 센터에서 우리 무대 디자이너를 만날 거예요. 급한 일이 있으시면, 제 휴대폰으로 전화 주세요. 그렇지 않으면, Amelia에게 메시지를 남기거나 저에게 이메일을 보내세요.

161 Ms. Lawson은 누구인 것 같은가?
(A) 패션 사진작가
(B) 임원 비서
(C) 의류 디자이너
(D) 잡지 편집장

162 오후 2시 54분에, Mr. Huang이 "There's a lot of excitement"라고 썼을 때 그가 의도한 것 같은 것은?
(A) 쇼핑객들은 상점이 열기를 갈망하고 있다.
(B) 패션 행사에 대한 관심이 높다.
(C) 최근 쇼가 긍정적인 관심을 불러일으켰다.
(D) 몇몇 유명 인사들이 많은 주의를 끌고 있다.

163 Mr. Nazmi는 무엇을 담당하는가?
(A) 마케팅
(B) 영업
(C) 구매
(D) 행사

164 Ms. Mansfield는 왜 서두르는가?
(A) 지킬 약속이 있다.
(B) 비행기를 타려고 하고 있다.
(C) 고객으로부터 급한 전화를 받았다.
(D) 행사에 필요하다.

165-167은 다음 기사에 관한 문제입니다.

Northpoint 쇼핑몰의 좋은 소식

Northpoint 쇼핑몰은 이전에 Jadean's Hardware에 의해 사용되었던 자리에 새로운 두 개의 상점이 다음 달에 들어설 것이라고 발표했다. 운동 기구 소매업체인 Haskins Sports는 Jadean's Hardware였던 곳의 아래층에 들어설 것이다. 한편, 컨템퍼러리 의류, 액세서리, 그리고 신발 판매업체인 Knockout은 그 위층을 차지할 것이다.

Haskins Sports와 Knockout 매장의 개점은 Jadean's Hardware가 7월에 문을 닫았을 때 상당한 손실을 겪었던 Northpoint 쇼핑몰이 매우 필요로 했던 부양책을 제공할 것으로 예상된다. 스포츠 소매업체는 지난 5년 동안

200개라는 놀라운 수의 새로운 지점을 열었고, 한편 의류 상점의 수익은 전하는 바에 따르면 같은 기간에 15억이 증가했다.

일자리를 창출하고 지역 경제를 향상시키는 것만이 아니라, 이 새로운 상점들은 Northpoint 쇼핑몰의 일일 총 방문객을 5000명이 상당히 넘도록 이끌 수 있다. 쇼핑몰에 가는 사람들의 수가 빠른 속도로 감소함에 따라, 이 지역 곳곳의 많은 쇼핑센터들은 문을 닫을 수밖에 없었다. 그러나, 새롭게 추가된 것들은 확실히 Northpoint 쇼핑몰이 당분간 장사를 계속할 수 있게 해줄 것이다.

165 기사의 주제는 무엇인가?
(A) 쇼핑몰의 철거
(B) 새로운 소매업체에 대한 환영
(C) 새로운 장소의 공사
(D) 경제 분석의 결과

166 Northpoint 쇼핑몰에 개점하는 새로운 상점들에 대해 언급된 것은?
(A) 200개가 넘는 지점을 각각 가지고 있다.
(B) 함께 쇼핑센터의 2개의 층을 차지할 것이다.
(C) 둘 다 5년 전에 설립되었다.
(D) 7월에 Northpoint 쇼핑몰에 개점할 것이다.

167 3문단의 두 번째 줄의 단어 "well"은 의미상 ―와 가장 가깝다.
(A) 상당히
(B) 철저히
(C) 제대로
(D) 일반적으로

168-171은 다음 편지에 관한 문제입니다.

Tim Blake
West Village로 987번지
사우샘프턴
SO14
영국

Mr. Blake께,

제 이름은 Anne Harding이고, Hampton 중고등학교의 미술 교사입니다. 저는 오랫동안 당신의 조각품들, 특히 도심 광장에 있는 해군 대령의 동상과 전쟁 기념관을 위해 만드신 군인 동상들의 팬이었습니다. ― [1] ―. 저는 부탁을 드리기 위해 편지를 씁니다. 학생들에게 수학과 과학 외에도 기회가 있다는 것을 보여주기 위해 지역 예술가가 오셔서 제 수업에 강연해 주시면 좋겠습니다. 저는 학생들이 오늘날 예술계에서 어떻게 생계를 꾸리는지 배웠으면 합니다. 당신이 어떻게 시작하게 되었는지 그리고 작업 의뢰를 어떻게 확보하시는지 들을 수 있다면 좋을 것입니다. ― [2] ―. 제 수업의 많은 학생들은 내년에 대학에 가면 미술을 전공하는 것을 진지하게 고민하고 있는데, 진로 지도를 제공하는 사람이 있다면 이상적일 것입니다. 수업은 화요일과 목요일 오후 2시 30분에 있습니다. ― [3] ―. 다음 몇 주 동안 이 시간대에 가능하신 때가 있으신가요? 어제 학생들에게 당신이 작년에 전시하신 사진들을 보여주었는데, 그들은 그 작품들을 통틀어 당신의 색 활용을 매우 좋아했습니다. 그들은 평론가들이 매우 높이 평가하는 예술가로부터 강연을 듣는 것에 대해 들떠 있습니다. ― [4] ―. 오셔서 강연해 주실 수 있는지 알려주세요.

Anne Harding
Hampton 중고등학교 교사

---

168 편지의 주 목적은 무엇인가?
(A) 미술 학생들을 가르치는 것에 대한 지도를 요청하기 위해
(B) Mr. Blake에게 교직을 제안하기 위해
(C) 학급이 예술가의 작업실을 방문하게 해달라고 요청하기 위해
(D) Mr. Blake에게 연설하도록 초청하기 위해

169 Ms. Harding은 그녀의 수업에 대해 무엇이라고 말하는가?
(A) 소수의 학생들만 받는다.

(B) 주 2회 진행된다.
(C) 주로 조각에 초점을 맞추고 있다.
(D) 다음 달 안에 끝날 것이다.

170 Mr. Blake는 Ms. Harding의 수업에서 무엇을 할 것 같은가?
(A) 사진 워크숍을 진행한다
(B) 현대미술의 역사를 설명한다
(C) 예술가들의 진로 선택안을 논의한다
(D) 조각 기술을 보여준다

171 [1], [2], [3], [4]로 표시된 위치 중, 다음 문장이 들어갈 곳으로 가장 적절한 것은?

"그것들의 정교한 석조 세공은 항상 저를 경탄하게 합니다."

(A) [1]
(B) [2]
(C) [3]
(D) [4]

172-175는 다음 편지에 관한 문제입니다.

Docu-Drama 방송사
7348번지 Granville가
밴쿠버, 브리티시컬럼비아주 V5K 1P3

7월 19일

Juan Sanchez
4332번지 Rancho가
오클랜드, 캘리포니아주 94577

Mr. Sanchez께,

귀하께서 저희의 제의를 받아들여 다가오는 가을에 저희와 함께 새로운 작품을 작업하게 되어 매우 기쁩니다. 전에 통지받으신 대로, 귀하의 밴쿠버에서의 첫 출근일은 9월 1일이며, 귀하의 계약은 12월 15일에 종료될 것입니다. ─ [1] ─. 입국하시려면, 귀하께서 체류하는 총 기간 동안 여행 보험에 의해 보장된다는 것을 증명해야 할 것입니다. 이것은 Voyage Protector사로부터 www. voyage-protector.com에서 가입하거나, 귀하께서 선택한 서비스 업체로부터 가입할 수 있습니다. ─ [2] ─.

비자 심사가 일주일 정도 소요될 것이므로, 신청서를 8월 15일까지 캐나다 대사관에 직접 제출해야 할 것입니다. 비자를 얻게 되면, 제가 귀하의 임시 아파트를 마련할 수 있도록 제게 알려주십시오. ─ [3] ─.

동봉된 것에서 제가 서명한 귀하의 계약서 사본 두 장을 보실 것입니다. 그중 하나에 서명하시고 밴쿠버에 도착하자마자 그것을 제게 주십시오. ─ [4] ─. 귀하의 이동 수단 세부사항을 제게 알려주시면 공항에 마중을 나갈 사람을 보내겠습니다.

문의 사항이 있으시면 언제든지 저에게 연락해 주십시오.

Wilma Headley 드림
캐스팅 담당자
Docu-Drama 방송사

동봉물

172 편지의 주 목적은 무엇인가?
(A) 새 직원에게 지침을 제공하기 위해
(B) 지원서에 대한 문의 사항에 답변하기 위해
(C) 정식 채용 제의를 하기 위해
(D) 복리 후생 제도의 개요를 설명하기 위해

173 Mr. Sanchez는 8월 15일까지 무엇을 해야 하는가?
(A) 서류를 사무실에 가져간다
(B) 여권이 제출되도록 한다
(C) 서명된 계약서를 돌려준다
(D) 비자 연장을 신청한다

174 Docu-Drama 방송사에 대해 암시되는 것은?
(A) 채용 회사의 서비스를 이용한다.
(B) 3개월마다 배역들에게 계약 갱신을 제안한다.
(C) 직원에게 숙소를 마련해줄 계획이다.
(D) 밴쿠버로 오고 가는 이동 경비를 상환해준다.

175 [1], [2], [3], [4]로 표시된 위치 중, 다음 문장이 들어갈 곳으로 가장 적절한 것은?

"다른 하나는 귀하의 개인 기록을 위한 것입니다."

(A) [1]
(B) [2]
(C) [3]
(D) [4]

176-180은 다음 웹페이지와 이메일에 관한 문제입니다.

Jump 기금

선구적인 프로젝트들을 후원하세요

프로젝트 후원 | 프로젝트 시작 | 자주 묻는 질문 | 로그인

STOPLITE Andy Newberg의 발명품	· 100,000달러 목표 중 18,080달러가 기부 약속됨
Stoplite는 당신이 속도를 낮출 때 당신의 뒤에 있는 사람들에게 이를 알려주어, 우발적인 충돌의 위험을 최소화하는 첨단 기술 자전거 조명입니다. 이것은 배터리로 작동되며 자전거에 자석으로 부착됩니다. 이것은 움직임을 감지하면 켜지고 자전거가 완전히 정지하면 저절로 꺼집니다.	· 166명의 사람들이 이 프로젝트를 후원함 · 오늘: 3월 10일 (기금 지원 완료까지 180일 남음) _____ 달러 기부
튼튼하면서 소형인 이것은 비가 오거나 눈이 오는 환경에서도 작동하며, 떼어내서 주머니나 가방에 보관하기 쉽습니다. Stoplite는 단 한 번, 1시간의 충전으로 20시간 동안 작동합니다.	보상을 받지 않고 어떤 금액이든 기부하시거나, 아래에서 보상 옵션을 선택하십시오.

□ 90달러* **빠른 싱글**	□ 110달러 **일반 싱글**	□ 180달러 **빠른 더블***	□ 220달러 **일반 더블**	□ 1,000달러 **Stoplite 영웅**
Stoplite 키트 1개와 티셔츠 1장을 받으며, 배송비가 포함되어 있습니다.	Stoplite 키트 1개를 받으며, 배송비가 포함되어 있지 않습니다.	Stoplite 키트 2개와 티셔츠 1장을 받으며, 배송비가 포함되어 있지 않습니다.	Stoplite 키트 2개를 받으며, 배송비가 포함되어 있지 않습니다.	여분 케이스와 자석과 함께 Stoplite 키트 10개를 받으며, 배송비가 포함되어 있지 않습니다.

*빠른 싱글과 빠른 더블의 자격이 되려면 5월 5일까지 기부해야 함

수신: Greg Farber <g.farber@mymail.com>
발신: Michelle Lee <miclee@stoplite.com>
제목: 귀하의 후원에 감사드립니다
날짜: 9월 20일

Mr. Farber께,

Jump 기금에서 저희 프로젝트를 후원해주셔서 감사드립니다. 이미 알고 계실지도 모르겠지만, 프로젝트는 기금이 전액 지원되었으며, 귀하께서 곧 Stoplite 키트 2개의 배송을 받게 될 것이라고 예상하시면 됩니다. 귀하께서 한 달 전에 후원을 약속해주셨기 때문에 저희에게 여전히 정확한 배송 주소가 기록되어 있는지 확인하고자 합니다. 저희 웹사이트에 로그인하신 뒤 "주소 업데이트" 혹은 "주소 확정"을 눌러서 귀하의 주소를 확정해주시기 바랍니다. 그 후에, 배송비를 포함하여, 배송 세부 사항이 포함된 이메일을 받게 되실 것입니다.

기금 관리자 Michelle Lee 드림
Stoplite Innovation사

176 Stoplite에 대해 사실인 것은?
(A) 출시일이 연기되었다.
(B) 궂은 날씨를 견뎌낼 수 있다.
(C) 움직임을 에너지로 전환시킨다.
(D) 특정 자전거 모델과만 함께 사용될 수 있다.

177 기금 캠페인에 대해 언급된 것은?
(A) 제품의 발명자에 의해 계획되었다.
(B) 익명으로 참여할 수 있다.
(C) 특정 날짜까지 기부하는 사람들을 위한 우대책을 포함한다.
(D) 목표된 금액을 달성할 때까지 지속될 것이다.

178 누가 Stoplite를 위한 여분의 보관함을 받을 것인가?
(A) 빠른 싱글 기부자
(B) 빠른 더블 기부자
(C) 일반 더블 기부자
(D) Stoplite 영웅 기부자

179 Stoplite Innovation사는 왜 Mr. Farber에게 편지를 썼는가?
(A) 제품 출시를 알리기 위해
(B) 배송 지연을 알리기 위해
(C) 개인 정보가 정확한지 확인해달라고 요청하기 위해
(D) 추후 프로젝트에 대한 지원을 요청하기 위해

180 Mr. Farber는 얼마를 기부한 것 같은가?
(A) 90달러
(B) 110달러
(C) 180달러
(D) 220달러

181-185는 다음 기사와 회람에 관한 문제입니다.

Wavelet Luxury Liners사가 조명을 업그레이드하다

런던 (12월 31일)—유럽의 선도적인 여객선 회사인, Wavelet Luxury Liners사는 곧 그것의 선박들 내부에 새 조명을 설치하기 시작할 것이다. 이는 최근에 현대적인 디자인을 지닌 유리 조명을 만드는 포르투갈 회사, Serreta Lighting사와 체결한 계약 덕분이다.

Serreta Lighting사 제품들의 고급스러움은 Wavelet Luxury Liners사가 그들과 파트너 관계를 맺기로 결정한 주요한 이유이다. 제품들은 전통 기술을 사용하는 장인들로 이뤄진 소규모 팀에 의해 만들어지며, 각각의 제품은 그것을 완성한 각 작업자에 의해 서명된다.

현재 공사 중인 Wavelet Luxury Liners사의 최신형 선박, *Shooting Star*는 완전히 Serreta Lighting사의 제품들로만 갖춰질 그 회사의 첫 번째 선박이 된다. 특히 주목할 만한 것은 14층 식당에 설치될 샹들리에일 것이다.

"저희는 새 선박의 내부뿐만 아니라 내년에 몇몇 낡은 선박들을 개조할 때 그것들의 내부에도 Serreta Lighting사의 창작물을 사용할 것입니다."라고 Wavelet Luxury Liners사의 최고 경영자인 Zackary Jones는 말했다. "저희는 이러한 조명 요소들이 저희를 경쟁사들과 차별화하는 데 도움이 될 것이라고 생각합니다."

Wavelet Luxury Liners사
회사 회람

수신: 전 임원진
발신: Gillian Sutcliffe, 수석 건축가
제목: 공사에 관한 최신 정보
날짜: 2월 29일

*Shooting Star*의 공사는 외부가 완성되고 내부 작업이 진행 중인 상태로,

마지막 단계에 이르렀습니다. 좋은 소식은 복도와 객실의 카펫 설치가 2월 27일에 마무리되었다는 것입니다. 조명에 대해 말하자면, 그것은 주문되었으며 다음과 같이 설치될 것입니다:

1-4층	3월 5일까지
5-8층	3월 10일까지
9-12층	3월 14일까지
13-15층	3월 20일까지

원래 계획에 따르면, 가구들이 배송되어 조명과 동시에 여객선 내부에 설치되었어야 했습니다. 하지만, 유감스럽게도, 공장은 저희가 그들에게 기대했던 만큼 신속히 저희의 요구에 부응하지 못했습니다. 저는 저희가 선박의 공개일을 5월 1일에서 5월 15일로 미뤄야 할지도 몰라서 걱정입니다. 우리 회사의 최고 경영자인 Eliza Jones는 그녀가 행사를 주최할 수 있도록 이틀 모두 일정을 비워두었습니다.

181 기사의 주요 주제는 무엇인가?
(A) 조명 회사의 사업 파트너들
(B) 에너지를 절약할 방안
(C) 새로운 교통 경로
(D) 회사의 새로운 공급업체와의 계약

182 Serreta Lighting사의 제품에 관해 언급되지 않은 것은?
(A) 스타일이 현대적이다.
(B) 오직 선박을 위해서 만들어진다.
(C) 서명이 표시되어 있다.
(D) 오래된 방법을 사용하여 사람 손으로 만들어진다.

183 샹들리에는 어느 날짜까지 설치될 것인가?
(A) 3월 5일
(B) 3월 10일
(C) 3월 14일
(D) 3월 20일

184 Ms. Sutcliffe는 무엇에 대해 걱정하는가?
(A) 제조 결함
(B) 비현실적인 일정
(C) 지연된 주문
(D) 낮은 생산성

185 Wavelet Luxury Liners사에 관해 추론될 수 있는 것은?
(A) 모든 선박들이 Serreta Lighting사 제품들로 갖춰질 것이다.
(B) 새 선박은 그것의 내부가 완성되기 전에 대중에게 공개될 것이다.
(C) 대표직의 변화를 겪었다.
(D) 계약자로부터 재정적인 보상을 받을 것이다.

186-190은 다음 공고, 설문 조사, 양식에 관한 문제입니다.

지금이 당신의 스페인어를 향상시킬 때입니다

우리의 지속적인 라틴 아메리카 시장으로의 확장에 따라, 점점 더 많은 Glidefield 통신사 직원들이 스페인어를 사용하는 고객들과 매일 소통하고 있습니다. 직원들은 또한 더 자주 그 지역으로 출장을 가고 있습니다. 이러한 이유로, Glidefield 통신사의 경영진은 저녁에 무료 스페인어 강의를 제공하기로 결정했습니다. 이것은 방문 강사에 의해 가르쳐질 것입니다. 오후 7시부터 9시까지, 매주 최소 하나의 수업이 열릴 것이며, 수업은 15주 동안 계속될 것입니다. 그렇지만 만약 20명 이상의 사람들이 참여하길 원하는 경우, 능력에 따라 그룹이 나눠질 것이고, 두 개의 개별적인 수업이 개설될 것입니다.

관심이 있으시다면, Chuck Findley에게 findley@glidefield.ca로 이메일을 보내 주십시오.

Glidefield 통신사 직원들을 위한 스페인어 교육에 대한 설문 조사

우리 사무실에서 스페인어를 공부하는 것에 관심을 가져주셔서 감사합니다. 참여하겠다고 의사를 밝힌 모든 직원들은 같은 수업에 참석하게 될 것이며,

이것은 7월 첫째 주에 시작될 것입니다. 하지만, 몇 가지 세부 사항들은 아직 정해져야 합니다. 단체의 요구를 가장 잘 충족시킬 수 있도록, 이 설문 조사를 완료하여 6월 16일까지 인사부 직원 Chuck Findley에게 반납해주시길 바랍니다.

1. 주중 어느 요일에 수업이 열리길 원하십니까?

☐ 월요일 ☑ 화요일 ☐ 수요일 ☐ 목요일 ☐ 금요일

2. 강사가 교재 선택권을 제시하였습니다. 어느 것을 선호하십니까?

	제목	중심내용
☐	스페인어 어려움 없이 말하기	일상생활
☐	완벽한 전문 스페인어	회사 상황
☐	스페인어 편지와 이메일	업무상의 서신
☑	라틴 아메리카 청중에게 깊은 인상 주기	연설과 발표

스페인어 수업 평가 양식

이름: James Kitson
Glidefield 통신사에서의 직책: 판매부장
시작 시 스페인어 능력 수준: 초보자
종료 시 스페인어 능력 수준: 중급자

▶ 다음 측면들을 평가해주십시오:

강사	불만족스러운 ← ①②③④❺ → 훌륭한
교육 자료	불만족스러운 ← ①②③❹⑤ → 훌륭한
그룹 활동	불만족스러운 ← ①②③④❺ → 훌륭한
과제	불만족스러운 ← ①②③❹⑤ → 훌륭한
교실	불만족스러운 ← ①②③④❺ → 훌륭한

▶ 의견:

전반적으로, 저는 이 수업이 유익하다고 생각했습니다. 하지만, 몇몇 사항들은 개선될 수 있습니다. 먼저, 교재의 범위가 제한적이었습니다. 그것은 저희에게 좋아하는 영화, 취미, 그리고 이런 다른 주제들에 대해 이야기하는 방법만을 가르쳐주었습니다. 하지만, 제가 제 일을 위해 배워야 하는 것은 서면으로 전문적으로 소통하는 방법입니다.

또한, 선생님은 지각에 관한 규칙들을 세울 필요가 있었습니다. 저는 매번 일찍 도착했지만, 다른 사람들은 수업이 시작된 후에 들어와 수업에 지장을 주었습니다.

186 공고의 목적은 무엇인가?
(A) 교육 기회를 소개하기 위해
(B) 어학원에 대한 의견을 요청하기 위해
(C) 새로운 고객의 요구를 설명하기 위해
(D) 계획된 사업 확장을 알리기 위해

187 Mr. Findley에 대해 추론될 수 있는 것은?
(A) 그는 최근에 고용된 모든 직원들이 스페인어를 배우도록 교육시키는 것을 담당한다.
(B) 그는 6월 16일에 사무실의 모든 직원에게 메시지를 보냈다.
(C) 그는 현재 Glidefield 통신사에서 인사부장으로 일하고 있다.
(D) 그는 20명 미만의 사람들로부터 수업 수강 요청을 받았다.

188 설문 조사에 따르면, 무엇이 결정되어야 했는가?
(A) 수업 강사
(B) 수업 요일
(C) 수업 시간
(D) 공간 수용력

189 양식에 따르면, 스페인어 수업에 관해 언급되지 않은 것은?
(A) 항상 정각에 출석 되지는 않았다.
(B) 참가자에 의해 평가되었다.
(C) 그룹 활동에 도움을 받아 가르쳐졌다.
(D) 초보자 수준의 학생들로만 구성되었다.

190 어떤 교재가 사용된 것 같은가?
(A) 스페인어 어려움 없이 말하기
(B) 완벽한 전문 스페인어
(C) 스페인어 편지와 이메일
(D) 라틴 아메리카 청중에게 깊은 인상 주기

191-195는 다음 웹페이지, 예약 확인서, 일정표에 관한 문제입니다.

http://organicfoodfair.com/transport

| 홈 | 프로그램 | 출품자 정보 | 이동 수단 |

2년에 한 번씩 개최되는 유기농 식품 박람회는 8월 16일부터 18일까지 Phoenix 시내에 있는 Landsel 박람회장에서 열릴 예정이며, 이곳은 12개 이상의 호텔들로부터 도보 15분 거리 내에 있습니다. 대부분의 방문객과 출품자들은 Phoenix Grand 공항에 도착할 것입니다. 도착 후, 도심에 닿을 수 있는 몇 가지 방법이 있습니다.

• 기차 – 이는 저희 장소에 도달하는 가장 빠른 방법입니다. 이 30분의 이동에는 단 17달러가 듭니다. 좌석은 지정되지 않습니다. 공항에서 출발하는 열차의 시간표를 보시려면, www.phoenixrail.com을 방문하십시오.

• 셔틀 버스 – Arrow 버스의 좌석은 편도 15달러입니다. 버스는 오전 6시부터 오후 11시까지 30분마다 출발합니다. 반드시 www.arrowpho.com에서 좌석을 미리 선택하십시오. 덧붙여, Davenport 호텔은 방을 예약한 손님들을 위해 무료 셔틀버스를 운영합니다.

• 자동차 대여 – 여러 회사가 도착 터미널 주변에서 영업을 합니다. 이것에는 Wildcat Car Rental사, Burnett Rent-A-Car사, 그리고 Quincy사가 포함됩니다. 이용 가능성을 보장받기 위해, 최소 24시간 전에 사전에 예약을 하십시오.

• 택시 – 이 차량을 타고 가는 것은 40달러 정도가 들 것입니다.

Suelin Yang의 예약 확인서

확인 번호	27348479	출발 날짜	8월 17일
예약 날짜	8월 3일	출발 시간	오전 11시 30분
결제 수단	신용카드	좌석 번호	17D
목적지	Urbano 호텔	수하물 개수	2

귀하의 특별 요청사항

"저는 유기농 식품 박람회에 참석할 것이기 때문에, 제품 샘플이 든 큰 가방 2개를 가지고 갈 것입니다. 그것들은 무거울 것이고, 저는 그것들을 화물칸에 싣는 데 도움이 필요할 것입니다."

*비행기가 연착될 경우, Phoenix Grand 공항의 도착 구역의, 출구 C와 D 사이에 있는 저희 서비스 데스크로 가십시오. 저희가 귀하께서 목적지에 가능한 한 빨리 도달하실 수 있도록 보장하겠습니다.

유기농 식품 박람회 – 8월 17일 연설

시간	제목	연설가	장소
오전 10시	유럽의 새로운 유기농 농경 관행	Madeline Dekker	2강당
오전 11시 15분	유기농 식품의 기준이 더 엄격해져야 하는 이유	Barry Revere	1강당
오후 1시 45분	유기농 식품을 더 저렴하게 만드는 방법	Heidi Schuster	2강당
오후 3시	유기농 식품의 영양적 이점	Lucas Dunn	3강당
오후 4시 30분	유기 농업이 어떻게 기후 변화와 연관되는가	Suelin Yang	3강당

191 Landsel 박람회장에 대해 언급된 것은?
(A) 공항 도착 구역에서 데스크를 운영한다.
(B) 정기적으로 식품 박람회를 주최한다.
(C) 숙박 장소와 바로 붙어 있다.
(D) 시내에 위치한다.

192 Ms. Yang은 어떻게 목적지에 갈 것 같은가?
    (A) 기차로
    (B) 셔틀버스로
    (C) 대여한 자동차로
    (D) 택시로

193 예약 확인서에 따르면, 비행기가 연착될 경우 고객은 무엇을 해야 하는가?
    (A) 통지를 보낸다
    (B) 서비스 센터에 전화한다
    (C) 카운터로 향한다
    (D) 예약을 취소한다

194 Ms. Yang에 대해 암시되는 것은?
    (A) 아직 회의 부스를 빌리지 않았다.
    (B) 박람회의 마지막 연설자일 것이다.
    (C) 호텔에 들른 뒤에 연설할 것이다.
    (D) 질의응답 시간을 이끌어달라는 요청을 받았다.

195 8월 17일의 유기농 식품 박람회에서 논의되지 않을 것은 무엇인가?
    (A) 농경 방식
    (B) 홍보 캠페인
    (C) 환경 변화
    (D) 건강상의 이점

196-200은 다음 이메일, 일정표, 공고에 관한 문제입니다.

수신: Evan Langston <e.langston@cornertechsolutions.com>
발신: Cindy Shelley <c.shelley@cornertechsolutions.com>
제목: 방문
날짜: 7월 14일

Evan,

2주 후 있을 고객 방문을 위해 제안된 일정에 대한 업데이트를 제공하기 위해 이메일을 보냅니다. 저는 8월 1일부터 4일까지 Washington Grand 호텔에 그들을 위한 숙소를 예약했습니다. 우리는 8월 3일에 고객들과 만날 예정이지만, 구체적인 시간은 아직 결정 중입니다.

그렇긴 하지만, 그들이 3일에 우리 회의 후에는 여유 시간이 있을 것으로 보이니, 그들을 구경시켜 줄 수 있도록 관광 가이드를 고용하는 것이 좋을 것 같습니다. 그들의 호텔은 루프에 위치해 있어서, 좋은 선택지가 충분할 것입니다. 관광 대행사에 연락해서 무언가를 준비해 주실 수 있나요? 저는 LuxChi 사에 대해 훌륭한 이야기를 들었습니다.

어떻게 생각하는지 알려주세요.

Cindy 드림

────────────────────────

LuxChi사
Corner Tech Solutions사 8월 4일 관광 일정

오전 8시 45분	호텔 픽업
오전 9시	Coerver 건물 옥상에서 조찬 연회
오전 10시 30분	루프의 건축물 도보 관광
오후 12시	시카고강에서 전세 보트 및 점심 뷔페
오후 2시	Fendo 초콜릿 공장 방문

악천후의 경우 일정이 변경될 수 있습니다. 또한, 저희의 전문 관광 가이드들은 필요한 경우, 또는 고객을 수용할 더 나은 것이 있다면 즉흥적인 조정을 실시할 수 있습니다. 일행에 특수 요청이 있다면, 가이드에게 말씀해 주세요.

────────────────────────

Washington Grand 손님 여러분께

저희가 시스템 재개시 작업을 진행할 것임을 알려드립니다. 이것은 하루 중 대부분의 시간 동안 저희의 컴퓨터 서버가 차단되도록 요구할 것입니다. 따라서, 저희는 8월 4일에 일반 체크아웃을 실행할 수 없을 것입니다. 그날 떠나시는 손님들은 8월 3일에 프런트를 방문해 주세요. 저희는 그때 모든 거래를

마무리할 것입니다. 저희 사우나와 운동 시설 등 모든 구내 편의시설은 개방된 상태로 유지될 것입니다. 저희는 8월 4일에 체크아웃하기로 예정되어 있는 모든 손님들께 미니바의 물품 또는 호텔 내의 식당에서 50달러의 할인을 제공하고자 합니다. 진심으로 사과드리며 이것이 불편을 만회하기를 바랍니다. 여러분의 이해와 애용에 감사드립니다.

196 이메일에 따르면, Ms. Shelley는 고객 방문을 위해 무엇을 제안하는가?
    (A) 손님대접을 준비하는 것
    (B) 계약 제안을 제시하는 것
    (C) 일일 교통편을 준비하는 것
    (D) 고객 회의를 조정하는 것

197 LuxChi사에 대해 언급된 것은?
    (A) 모든 일행을 위해 항상 같은 일정을 따른다.
    (B) 방문객들을 제조 시설로 데려갈 것이다.
    (C) 특수 요청을 위해서는 하루의 예고를 요한다.
    (D) 경쟁사들보다 더 호의적인 후기를 가지고 있다.

198 관광에 대해 추론될 수 있는 것은?
    (A) 전세 버스에서 음식을 제공할 것이다.
    (B) Washington Grand와 협의가 되었다.
    (C) 회의가 끝난 직후에 시작할 것이다.
    (D) 다른 날로 옮겨졌다.

199 Ms. Shelley의 고객들은 8월 3일에 무엇을 할 것 같은가?
    (A) 시카고의 건축물을 둘러본다
    (B) 개인 관광을 맞춤화한다
    (C) 호텔 거래를 마무리한다
    (D) 일부 계약서에 서명한다

200 Washington Grand는 일부 고객들에게 무엇을 제공할 것인가?
    (A) 음식 서비스 할인
    (B) 운동 시설 이용
    (C) 지역 식당에서 무료 식사
    (D) 호텔 내 사우나 입장

TEST 05 해석

* 무료 해설은 해커스토익(Hackers.co.kr)에서
다운로드 받으실 수 있습니다.

• QR 코드로
바로가기

PART 5

101 Mr. Oakley는 새로 문을 연 이탈리아 레스토랑에 두 사람을 위한 자리를 예약하기로 결정했다.

102 초대된 사람들은 음식 공급 업체가 충분한 음식을 준비할 수 있도록 그들의 연회 참석 여부를 확정하도록 요청받는다.

103 주민들은 고속도로의 가까움이 그들의 삶의 질에 악영향을 미칠 것이라고 말하면서, 그것을 건설하려는 계획에 반대한다.

104 회사의 관리자들은 부서 간의 소통 부족에 대한 해결책을 찾고 있다.

105 분쟁을 피하기 위해, 주민 우려 사항은 프로젝트 계획 단계 동안 Everide 건설사에 의해 검토된다.

106 Mr. Harvel은 그 정원이 개인 소유지이므로 소풍을 즐기기 위해서는 다른 곳으로 가라는 말을 들었다.

107 현재 대출된 상태인 서적을 예약하려고 한다면 대출 데스크로 가세요.

108 Hulse사에 의해 제조된 결함 있는 제품을 구입한 사람들은 구입 증명서가 있는 한 환불을 받을 수 있다.

109 AutoBlade사의 새로운 모델은 플라스틱을 다양한 모양으로 정밀하게 자르도록 설정되어 있다.

110 다른 그 어떤 직원도 광둥어에 유창성을 갖추고 있지 않았기 때문에 Ms. Elwood가 홍콩에 있는 직책에 고려되었다.

111 때때로 야망이 부족한 것으로 비판받는 오늘날의 많은 젊은이들은 일과 삶의 균형을 직장에서의 승진보다 중요하게 여기는 경향이 있다.

112 Neufield 역사박물관의 최근에 공개된 전시회는 선사시대까지 역사가 거슬러 올라가는 진짜 유물들로 가득 차 있다.

113 약관에 약술된 것처럼, 신용카드 대금은 매월 첫째 날에 지급되어야 한다.

114 쿠폰을 꾸준히 나누어 줌으로써, 카페 주인은 단골 고객층을 키울 수 있었다.

115 건물 관리인은 방문객들이 주차하도록 허용되는 장소에 대한 새로운 규제를 고지했다.

116 Mr. Venter는 JBD사의 세계 자회사들 각각에게 분기별 매출액으로 이루어져 있는 보고서를 요청했다.

117 만약 그 밴드가 앵코르 공연을 할 것이었음을 알았다면 Mr. Janick은 객석을 떠나지 않았을 것이다.

118 Axial사는 최근 경기 상승에도 불구하고 Covane사와의 사업 계약을 종료했다.

119 Randall 대학교는 아직 컴퓨터 공학 과정을 설립하는 중이다.

120 취업 지원자들을 신중히 심사하는 회사들은 더 높은 직원 유지 비율을 지닌다.

121 Tulsa 공항의 탑승 구역 중 상당 부분은 계속 진행 중인 보수 공사로 인해 내년 8월까지 출입이 금지되어 있다.

122 기사가 신문에 나오기 적합해지기까지 그것에는 많은 수정이 이루어져야만 했다.

123 인기 있는 새 시트콤을 시작했음에도 불구하고, The Fun Network사는 텔레비전에서 가장 많이 시청되는 채널로서의 그것의 지위를 유지할 수 없었다.

124 Twilight 영화관은 예약석이 없으며, 따라서 당신이 원하는 어느 줄이든 앉고 싶다면 일찍 도착해야 한다.

125 환경 기준에 따르면, 가정용 전기제품들은 그것들의 에너지 효율 수준에 따라 일곱 개의 그룹 중 하나로 분류된다.

126 Ms. Fielding의 인턴십 동안 그녀와 함께 밀접하게 일해 보았으므로, Mr. Rawlings는 기꺼이 그녀를 회사의 신입 엔지니어로 임명했다.

127 Lauderdale 지사를 확장하기로 한 결정은 지역 및 구역 관리자들과 협의하여 내려졌다.

128 Prolina사의 경쟁사들이 고객 서비스에 더 집중하기 시작했기 때문에, 일부 업계 전문가들은 Prolina사도 똑같이 해야 한다고 생각한다.

129 그 여행안내서는 파리, 런던, 그리고 로마와 같은 전형적인 목적지들 이외에 방문할 가치가 있는 25개의 유럽 도시들을 열거한다.

130 많은 세입자들이 그들의 아파트를 비웠고, 집주인은 새로운 예비 임차인들을 구하는 광고를 게시했다.

PART 6

131-134는 다음 광고에 관한 문제입니다.

> 파티를 여시나요?
>
> 131 Woldasso Party Solutions가 행사를 계획하는 것에 대한 스트레스를 없앨 수 있도록 하세요. 118번지 Croyden대로에 위치한 화려한 연회장인 저희 장소는 결혼 피로연, 동창회, 그리고 그 밖의 다른 행사들에 적합합니다. 저희는 최근에 장소의 수용력을 늘렸기 때문에 규모가 큰 모임도 환영합니다. 132 그것은 이제 최대 350명의 사람들을 수용할 수 있습니다.
>
> 133 저희 코디네이터들은 당신의 행사의 모든 측면을 계획하는 것을 도와드릴 수 있습니다. 가구와 장식부터, 오락과 음식 공급까지, 저희가 모든 세부 사항을 처리할 것입니다. 134 저희는 또한 당신에게 알맞게 주문 제작될 수 있는 패키지를 제공합니다. 당신이 생각하고 있는 것을 저희에게 알려주기만 하면, 당신의 기준을 만족시킬 방을 준비해 놓을 것입니다. 예약을 위해서는, 555-9971로 전화 주세요.

135-138은 다음 편지에 관한 문제입니다.

> 9월 17일
>
> Martin Muller
> Crestfield 목재사
> Thatcher가 546번지
> 알곤킨, 일리노이주 60102
>
> Mr. Muller께,
>
> 135 저희는 QTE 건설사로의 목재 공급 및 인도에 대한 귀사의 견적서를 검토해 보았습니다. 유감스럽게도, 저희가 고려해야 할 예산 문제로 인해 현재는 귀사의 제안을 받아들일 수 없을 것이라는 결론을 내렸습니다. 136 귀사의 가격은 저희가 예상했던 것보다 다소 더 높습니다.
>
> 137 하지만, 저희는 귀사가 타협하는 것을 고려해 볼 의향이 있는지 궁금합니다. 귀사가 가격을 단 10퍼센트만 낮춰준다면, QTE 건설사는 분기별로 그 가격에 목재를 구입하는 것에 동의할 것입니다. 이 조정이 가능한지 제게 알려주십시오. 138 저희는 이달 말까지 주요 건설 프로젝트를 위한 모든 자재가 필요하므로, 신속한 답변을 주시면 매우 감사하겠습니다.
>
> Gina Santos 드림
> QTE 건설사

362 무료 토익 학습자료 및 취업정보 Hackers.co.kr

139-142는 다음 공고에 관한 문제입니다.

> **운전자들께 드리는 공고**
>
> Wallace로의 개선이 4월 8일에 시작될 것입니다. **139** Davis & Sons사에 의해 수행될 이 프로젝트는, 계절의 온도 변화가 도로 표면을 심하게 손상시켰기 때문에 시의 공공 사업부에 의해 긴급하다고 여겨졌습니다. **140** 표면을 평평하게 하고 도로를 포장하는 작업이 완료될 때까지, 그 도로는 접근할 수 없을 것입니다. 이에 따라, 장벽이 세워질 것이고 운전자들을 옆길로 안내하기 위해 Fletcher가에 우회 표지판이 설치될 것입니다. **141** 직원들도 차량 흐름 조정을 돕기 위해 현장에 있을 것입니다. 이 대체 도로를 이용하는 동안 지연을 겪을 수도 있다는 점을 유의해 주십시오. **142** 따라서, 특히 출퇴근 혼잡 시간대에는 일정에 추가적인 이동 시간을 배분하도록 해 주십시오. 적어도 30분 앞서 목적지로 출발하는 것이 권장됩니다. 이것이 초래할 수 있는 불편에 대해 사과드리며 이해해 주셔서 감사합니다.

143-146은 다음 이메일에 관한 문제입니다.

> 수신: Blanche Patrick <b.patrick@nextnet.com>
> 발신: David Torres <d.torres@nextnet.com>
> 제목: 우리의 신생 기업
> 날짜: 9월 28일
>
> Ms. Patrick께,
>
> **143** 저는 방금 우리의 사업 컨설턴트가 상세히 작성한 우리 신생 기업, Nextnet사의 본사를 둘 장소에 대한 보고서를 읽는 것을 끝냈습니다. 그녀에 따르면, 비록 런던이 언뜻 보기에는 최적인 것처럼 보이지만, 고려해 볼 가치가 있는 다른 도시들이 있습니다. **144** 예를 들어, 에든버러와 케임브리지 둘 다 몇 가지 이점을 제공합니다. 부동산 가격 면에서 수도보다 더 저렴하다는 것 이외에도, 둘 다 기술 벤처 사업에 세금 감면을 제공하고 있습니다. **145** 그들은 멘토링 프로그램을 통해 무료 사업 지원도 제공합니다. 그녀는 또한 브라이턴과 버밍엄을 가능한 선택으로 언급했습니다. **146** 이 두 도시 사이에서는, 역동적인 신생 기업 문화 때문에 브라이턴이 더 나은 선택으로 보이지만, 그것은 몇 가지 단점이 있습니다. 어쨌든, 내일 우리가 만날 때 이것에 대해 상세히 논의할 수 있습니다.
>
> David Torres 드림

PART 7

147-148은 다음 문자 메시지에 관한 문제입니다.

> | 삭제 | 발신자: Robin Anderson
오늘 오후 4시 18분 | 답장 |
>
> Ms. Townsend가 방금 전화했어요. 그녀는 태국으로 가는 가족여행을 연기해야 해요. 그녀는 예약 변경 요금에 대해서 알고 있어요. 새 출발 날짜는 2월 2일이어야 하고, 돌아오는 비행기는 2월 12일에 도착해야 해요. 또한, 그녀는 호텔을 바꾸는 것이 가능할지 알고 싶어 해요. 그녀는 현재 Amphawa 수상 시장 근처에 있는 Alcove Siam에 두 개의 방을 예약해 두었지만, 타이왕궁에 더 가까이 숙박하기를 원해요. Ms. Townsend의 요청 사항을 즉시 처리해주세요.

147 Ms. Townsend는 누구일 것 같은가?
(A) 호텔 지배인
(B) 여행사 고객
(C) 무역 전문가
(D) 관광 단체 일원

148 수신자는 무엇을 해달라고 요청받고 있는가?
(A) 가능한 한 빨리 Ms. Anderson에게 전화한다

(B) 여행 일정표를 확인해 준다
(C) 두 명소 간의 거리를 확인한다
(D) 일부 여행 계획을 조정한다

149-150은 다음 이메일에 관한 문제입니다.

> 수신 Ben Rudy <benr@everypost.com>
> 발신 보안팀 <security@topnotchshop.com>
> 제목 귀하의 요청
> 날짜 1월 18일
>
> 고객님께,
>
> 귀하께서는 최근 저희에게 저희 웹사이트의 비밀번호를 잊어버렸다고 알려주셨습니다. 새로운 비밀번호를 만드시려면, 여기를 클릭하시기만 하면 됩니다.
>
> 귀하께서는 몇 가지 보안 질문에 답변해달라는 요청을 받으실 것입니다. 그렇게 되면, 새로운 비밀번호를 제공해주셔야 할 것입니다. 그것은 최소 8자 길이여야 하며 대문자, 소문자, 숫자, 그리고 기호를 포함해야 합니다.
>
> 귀하의 온라인 쇼핑 계정의 보안과 관련하여 무엇이든 질문이 있으시면, "답신"을 클릭하여 저희에게 이메일을 보내 주십시오.
>
> TopNotchShop 보안팀 드림

149 이메일은 왜 쓰였는가?
(A) 계정 보안 설정에 대한 최신 정보를 알리기 위해
(B) 온라인 구매에 대한 정보를 제공하기 위해
(C) 고객에게 정책 변경에 대해 알리기 위해
(D) 접속과 관련된 문제를 해결하는 것을 돕기 위해

150 Mr. Rudy는 무엇을 해야 할 것인가?
(A) 임시 비밀번호를 입력한다
(B) 일부 보안 소프트웨어를 재설치한다
(C) 몇몇 질문에 답변을 제공한다
(D) 재정 자문 위원과 상담한다

151-152는 다음 메시지 대화문에 관한 문제입니다.

> **Dave Weber** [오전 9시 23분]
> Tanya, 휴가 중에 귀찮게 해서 미안하지만, 문제가 생겼어요. Steve와 Emily 둘 다 아파서 결근한다고 전화로 알렸어요. 그래서, 오늘 옷가게에 직원이 아주 부족해요. 당신이 나와서 일해줄 수 있을까요?
>
> **Tanya Parker** [오전 9시 27분]
> 물론이죠. 전 언제나 추가 교대 근무를 할 준비가 되어 있어요. 제가 몇 시에 가게에 도착해야 하나요?
>
> **Dave Weber** [오전 9시 28분]
> 오전 11시 30분까지 여기로 올 수 있나요? 그때까지는 제가 혼자서 일을 처리할 수 있어요.
>
> **Tanya Parker** [오전 9시 30분]
> 오전 10시 30분에 치과 예약이 있어요. 만약에 그걸 취소하면, 그들이 시간을 내어 저를 만나줄 수 있을 때까지 몇 주 기다려야 할지도 몰라요. 대신 정오에 도착해도 될까요?
>
> **Dave Weber** [오전 9시 32분]
> 되고말고요. 이렇게 하는 데 동의해줘서 고마워요. 정말 고마워요.

151 Mr. Weber는 어떤 문제를 언급하는가?
(A) 일부 직원들이 추가 교대 근무를 거절했다.
(B) 일부 직원들이 갑자기 하루를 쉬었다.
(C) 지원자가 일자리 제의를 거절하였다.
(D) 고객이 의류 제품에 대해 불만족스러워했다.

152 오전 9시 32분에, Mr. Weber가 "I don't see why not"이라고 썼을 때 그가 의도한 것은?
(A) 오늘 단독으로 가게를 운영할 의향이 있다.

(B) 왜 지연이 생길 것인지 이해할 수 없다.
(C) 대체 도착 시각이 적당하다고 생각한다.
(D) 그는 허가서를 작성할 준비가 되었다.

153-154는 다음 광고에 관한 문제입니다.

Plains Auto사는 항상 당신 곁에 있습니다!

여행을 계획하고 있다면, 당신의 자동차 대여에 필요한 모든 것을 위해 Plains Auto사를 고려해보세요. 저희는 선택할 수 있는 매우 다양한 차량을 합리적인 가격으로 제공합니다. 그리고 저희가 2월에 Chase Car Rentals 사를 인수한 덕분에, 저희는 현재 전국의 모든 국제공항에 지점을 가지고 있습니다. 저희의 확장을 기념하기 위해, 이틀 이상의 대여에 대해 20퍼센트 할인을 제공할 것입니다. 이 할인은 6월 30일에 끝나므로, 기회를 놓치지 마세요! 더 많은 세부 사항을 얻고 차량을 예약하기 위해서는 www.plains auto.com을 방문하세요.

---

153 Plains Auto사는 2월에 무엇을 했는가?
(A) 일부 사무실 공간을 확장했다
(B) 해외 지점을 개시했다
(C) 다른 회사를 매입했다
(D) 추가 직원을 고용했다

154 고객들은 어떻게 할인을 받을 수 있는가?
(A) 공항에서 예약함으로써
(B) 웹사이트에 의견을 게시함으로써
(C) 더 큰 차량으로 업그레이드함으로써
(D) 며칠 동안 차를 대여함으로써

155-157은 다음 온라인 안내문에 관한 문제입니다.

---

www.businesslink.net/real-estate-advice

외부인 출입 통제 단지에 있는 집들

외부인 출입 통제 단지에 있는 집들을 매각하는 것은 수익성이 높은 수수료를 발생시키며 업계에서 당신의 입지를 상당히 높여줄 수 있습니다. 하지만, 그것들의 평균보다 높은 가격 때문에 요즘 그러한 집의 구매자들을 찾는 것은 어려울 수 있습니다. ─ [1] ─. 당신의 성공 확률을 향상시키기 위해서는, 다음 조언들을 유념하십시오:

1. 안전을 강조하세요
예상 구매자들에게 외부인 출입 통제 단지들은 최신 기술의 보호 기능을 가지고 있다는 것을 알리십시오. 또한, 이 단지로 들어가는 모든 입구는 강도나 상인들을 저지하고 반드시 집주인들의 차량만 출입구를 지나가도록 하는 경비원들의 보호를 받습니다. ─ [2] ─.

2. 소속감을 강조하세요
각 단지 내에 있는 주택의 수가 제한되어 있기 때문에, 주민들은 이웃을 잘 알게 되는 경향이 있다는 것을 구매자들에게 상기시키십시오. 이러한 이유로, 이웃 모임 및 여러 가족이 함께하는 야드 세일이 흔히 있습니다. ─ [3] ─.

3. 높은 부동산 가치에 대해 언급하세요
바람직한 위치, 고품질의 건축, 그리고 한정된 입수 가능성 때문에 이러한 단지에 있는 가구들은 현명한 매입이라고 구매자들에게 말씀하십시오. ─ [4] ─. 즉, 그것들은 거의 확실히 장기적으로 가치가 꾸준히 상승할 것입니다.

---

155 온라인 안내문은 누구를 대상으로 하는 것 같은가?
(A) 새로운 주택 소유주
(B) 부동산 중개업자
(C) 보안 요원
(D) 지역사회 개발자

156 외부인 출입 통제 단지에 대해 언급되지 않은 것은?
(A) 낯선 사람들은 들어가지 못한다.
(B) 보통 수익성이 있는 투자가 된다.

(C) 최첨단 수단을 통해 안전하게 보호된다.
(D) 주민들은 새 이웃을 위한 행사를 준비한다.

157 [1], [2], [3], [4]로 표시된 위치 중, 다음 문장이 들어갈 곳으로 가장 적절한 것은?

"이러한 친밀감은 일부 구매자들, 특히 아이들이 있는 구매자들에게 매우 매력적일 수 있습니다."

(A) [1]
(B) [2]
(C) [3]
(D) [4]

158-160은 다음 후기에 관한 문제입니다.

Squiggle > 고객 후기

이름: Dennis Haines
평점: ★★★★☆

저는 그래픽 디자이너이기 때문에, 일상적으로 여러 요소를 조합한 시각 자료를 제작해 달라는 요청을 받습니다. 예전에는 Finish라는 프로그램에 의존했지만, 지금은 거의 오로지 Squiggle만을 사용합니다. 저렴하지는 않고, 기능을 최대한 활용하려면 전문가급 시스템을 보유해야 할 것이지만, Squiggle은 현재 업계 표준을 대표합니다. 이 소프트웨어의 큰 장점은 매우 다양한 종류의 기능을 가지고 있다는 것입니다. 복잡한 그림을 만들고, 사진에 많은 효과를 추가하고, 다양한 요소를 잘라낼 수 있는 등 . . . 이 목록은 계속 이어집니다. Squiggle의 한 가지 문제는 많은 도구들이 계기판에서 찾기 어렵다는 점일 것입니다. 프로그래머들이 탐색하기 더 쉬운 도구판을 만들어야 한다고 생각합니다. 만약 제가 초보자라면, 저는 Squiggle Essentials 판으로 시작할 것입니다. 이것은 전체 버전과 적당히 비슷한 것이며 시작하는 데 돕기 위한 사용 지침서를 포함합니다.

---

158 Mr. Haines는 Squiggle의 어떤 점을 칭찬하는가?
(A) 다양한 기능
(B) 저렴한 가격
(C) 적은 시스템 요구사항
(D) 다른 프로그램과의 호환성

159 Mr. Haines는 Squiggle에 관해 무엇이 개선될 수 있다고 생각하는가?
(A) 영상 편집 도구세트
(B) 다양한 효과 활용에 대한 안내
(C) 화면상의 모습
(D) 사용 가능한 폰트의 수

160 Squiggle Essentials 판에 관해 언급된 것은?
(A) 곧 업데이트를 받을 것이다.
(B) 신규 디자이너들이 더 쉽게 이용 가능하다.
(C) 무료 버전으로 제공될 것이다.
(D) 체험 기간을 제공한다.

161-164는 다음 온라인 채팅 대화문에 관한 문제입니다.

Barry Nolan [오후 4시 48분]
안녕하세요, 여러분. 제게 Jarvis 센터 프로젝트에 대한 최신 정보를 제공해 주겠어요? 우리가 수요일에 그곳에서 정원 조경 작업을 시작하기로 되어 있는데요. 그게 가능할까요?

Alison Grice [오후 4시 49분]
그럴 것 같지 않아요. 우리가 주문한 초목과 관목은 아무리 일러도 금요일 오후가 되어서야 공급업체로부터 배달될 거예요.

Barry Nolan [오후 4시 50분]
좋지 않은 소식이네요. Jarvis 센터의 Ms. Peyton에게 이것에 대해 통지했나요?

Edward Winters [오후 4시 51분]
네. 제가 오늘 아침에 그것을 처리했어요. 그녀는 작업을 끝내기 위해 서두를 필요가 없다고 말했어요. 필요한 경우, 우리는 다음 주에 시작해도 돼요.

Alison Grice [오후 4시 52분]
그렇다면 저는 우리가 주문한 모든 것을 받은 후인 월요일이 될 때까지 기다려서 시작할 것을 권해요. 배달이 되지 않은 채로 금요일 아침에 우리가 할 수 있을 일은 별로 없어요.

Edward Winters [오후 4시 54분]
저는 단지 그 식물들이 걱정돼요. 주말 동안 밖에 놓여 있어도 안전할까요?

Alison Grice [오후 4시 55분]
토요일과 일요일에 모두 경비원이 거기 있어요. 또한, 식물들이 며칠 동안은 화분 안에 있어도 괜찮을 것 같아요.

Barry Nolan [오후 4시 57분]
동의해요. 월요일이 될 때까지 기다립니다. 그렇게 하면 우리는 확실히 프로젝트에 필요한 물품들을 갖고 있을 수 있을 거예요. Edward, 오늘 Ms. Peyton에게 이 일정을 전달해줄 수 있나요?

Edward Winters [오후 4시 58분]
그럼요. 저는 스프링클러 시스템에 대해 논의하려고 그녀에게 다시 전화할 계획이었어요.

161 Mr. Nolan은 누구일 것 같은가?
(A) 야외 장식 팀의 일원
(B) 식물 공급 업체의 배달 직원
(C) 조경 회사의 고객 서비스 직원
(D) 원예용품점의 구매 관리자

162 Mr. Winters는 무엇에 대해 걱정하는가?
(A) 제시간에 작업을 완료하지 못하는 것
(B) 식물들이 정확한 장소에 내려지도록 하는 것
(C) 구매품을 보호하는 것
(D) 고객을 위해 비용 절감하는 것

163 Jarvis 센터를 위한 정원 조경 작업은 언제 시작될 것인가?
(A) 금요일에
(B) 토요일에
(C) 일요일에
(D) 월요일에

164 오후 4시 58분에, Mr. Winters가 "Sure thing"이라고 썼을 때 그가 의도한 것은?
(A) 공급 업체에 전화할 것이다.
(B) 정보를 전달할 것이다.
(C) 배달된 물품을 확인할 것이다.
(D) 경비원과 이야기를 나눌 것이다.

165-167은 다음 이메일에 관한 문제입니다.

수신: Naomi Watson <nwatson@concordebank.com>
발신: Ava Bradley <abradley@concordebank.com>
날짜: 10월 28일
제목: 생명보험 정책
첨부파일: 생명보험 스프레드시트, 수익자 서명 페이지

안녕하세요, Naomi.

Concorde 은행에서의 새 일자리에 적응하고 있기를 바랍니다. ― [1] ―. 방금 고용주가 지원하는 의료보험 정책을 위한 당신의 서명된 서류를 받았습니다. 당신의 보험 보장은 11월 1일부터 시작됩니다. 의료보험 정책에 대해 질문이 있으시면 주저하지 말고 연락 주세요.

― [2] ―. 또한 당신이 Concorde 은행 기본 생명보험 정책에 성공적으로 가입되신 것을 알려드립니다. 이전에 논의한 바와 같이, 이것은 당신의 다른

혜택과 함께 포함되어 있으므로, 이 5만 달러 보험 정책을 위한 급여 공제액은 없을 것입니다.

― [3] ―. 그러나, 더 포괄적인 보장을 원하는 직원은 추가 월 보험료를 내고 10만 달러, 25만 달러, 또는 50만 달러 정책으로 업그레이드할 수 있습니다. ― [4] ―.

기존 정책을 업그레이드하고 싶다면, 첨부된 서명 페이지를 작성하고 수익자를 지정해 주세요.

Ava Bradley 드림
인사부장

165 Ms. Watson은 최근에 무엇을 했는가?
(A) 정책을 취소했다
(B) 새로운 일을 시작했다
(C) 새로운 은행 계좌를 개설했다
(D) 급여를 수령했다

166 Concorde 은행에 대해 언급된 것은?
(A) 직원들에게 적어도 두 가지 종류의 보험을 제공한다.
(B) Ms. Watson에게 매달 청구서를 보낼 것이다.
(C) 개선된 복지 혜택을 제공할 것이다.
(D) 급여를 직원들의 계좌에 바로 입금한다.

167 [1], [2], [3], [4]로 표시된 위치 중, 다음 문장이 들어갈 곳으로 가장 적절한 것은?

"이 이메일에 각 정책들에 대한 자세한 정보를 첨부했습니다."

(A) [1]
(B) [2]
(C) [3]
(D) [4]

168-171은 다음 공고에 관한 문제입니다.

책을 좋아하시는 분들은 주목해주십시오

새로운 친구들을 사귀고 책을 더 많이 읽고 싶다면, 바로 여기 Hamptonville의 인기 있는 자영 서점인 Patty's Pages에서 모이는 독서 클럽에 가입하는 것은 어떠신가요? 이번 달에 저희가 네 개의 서로 다른 종류의 독서 클럽을 시작했으므로, 여러분에게 알맞은 것을 선택하실 수 있습니다. 그것들 모두 저희의 2층에 있는 카페에서 일주일에 한 번 모이고, Patty's Pages의 직원에 의해 인솔되며, 사전 등록 없이 참여하실 수 있습니다. 세부 내용은 아래에 있습니다.

추리 소설 독서 클럽
이 모임은 매주 화요일 오후 7시에 만나 최근에 발간된 최고의 탐정 소설에 대해 논합니다. 그것들은 마지막까지 당신을 추측하게 만들 것입니다!

공상 과학 소설 독서 클럽
상상의 세계 및 멀리 떨어져 있는 행성으로 탈출하는 것을 좋아한다면, 매주 수요일 오후 8시에 만나는 이 클럽에 가입하여, 이 장르의 가장 오래된 고전들에 대해 이야기를 나눠보세요.

논픽션 독서 클럽
새로 나온 전기, 회고록, 그리고 문학 에세이에 관심이 있으신가요? 이 모임은 매주 목요일 오후 7시에 모입니다.

아동 도서 독서 클럽
8세에서 12세 사이의 아이들이 참여할 수 있는 이 클럽은 매주 토요일 오후 3시에 모입니다. 부모들은 최신 아동 도서에 대한 토론에 참관하도록 권장됩니다.

독서 클럽이 선정한 모든 책들은 그것들이 읽히고 논의되는 달 동안 Patty's Pages에서 10퍼센트 할인될 것입니다.

168 공고의 주제는 무엇인가?
(A) 추천 도서 목록

(B) 조정된 상점 영업시간
(C) 문맹 퇴치 캠페인을 위한 계획
(D) 엄선된 주간 토론 모임

169 1문단 세 번째 줄의 단어 "right"는 의미상 -와 가장 가깝다.
(A) 가장 알맞은
(B) 정확한
(C) 공정한
(D) 직접적인

170 신간 도서를 읽는 클럽이 아닌 것은?
(A) 추리 소설 독서 클럽
(B) 공상 과학 소설 독서 클럽
(C) 논픽션 독서 클럽
(D) 아동 도서 독서 클럽

171 Patty's Pages에 대해 언급되지 않은 것은?
(A) 올해 몇몇 독서 클럽을 시작했다.
(B) 건물 내에 커피숍을 포함하고 있다.
(C) Hamptonville에서 가장 수익성 있는 서점이다.
(D) 할인된 가격으로 독서 자료를 제공한다.

172-175는 다음 회람에 관한 문제입니다.

수신: 팀장 전체
발신: Brad Jenkins, 인사부장
제목: 워크숍
날짜: 9월 12일

안녕하세요, 여러분. 우리의 중국 시장 진출을 준비하기 위해 일련의 워크숍을 개최할 것임을 여러분께 상기시켜 드리고 싶습니다. 이 수업들은 우리가 이전에는 전혀 할 필요가 없었던 일인 중국 고객들을 상대하는 데 필요한 조정을 할 수 있도록 도와줄 것입니다. 다음 정보를 유념해 주십시오.

워크숍 명칭	일정
중국 시장에 대한 개요	9월 22일, 오후 2시 - 오후 6시
중국의 사업 관행	9월 29일, 오후 1시 - 오후 5시
국제 계약법	10월 6일, 오후 12시 - 오후 4시
다른 문화의 이해	10월 13일, 오후 3시 - 오후 7시

첫 두 수업은 중국과 구체적으로 연관될 것이지만 다른 두 수업은 국제적인 부분에 초점을 둘 것입니다. 9월 29일에 있는 워크숍은 우리의 중국 부서를 총괄할 Brenda Hong에 의해 진행될 것입니다. 나머지 세 개는 방문 컨설턴트인 David Parson에 의해 시행될 것입니다. 그의 워크숍은 우리 회사의 동료 직원들 사이에서 인기가 있었기 때문에, 저는 여러분이 그것들을 가치 있다고 생각할 것이라고 확신합니다. 무엇이든 질문이 있으시면 주저 말고 언제든 제게 연락해 주십시오.

---

172 회사는 왜 워크숍을 개최하는 것을 계획하고 있는가?
(A) 새로운 시장으로 확장하고 있다.
(B) 외국 회사와 합병하고 있다.
(C) 본사를 해외로 이전하고 있다.
(D) 다수의 임시 직원들을 고용하고 있다.

173 워크숍에 대해 사실인 것은?
(A) 모두 경영진에 의해서 시행될 것이다.
(B) 회사 직원들을 위해 정기적으로 제공되어 왔다.
(C) 한 달이 넘도록 지속될 것이다.
(D) 오후에 열리도록 예정되었다.

174 Ms. Hong은 어느 워크숍을 이끌 것인가?
(A) 중국 시장에 대한 개요
(B) 중국의 사업 관행
(C) 국제 계약법
(D) 다른 문화의 이해

175 Mr. Parson에 대해 암시되는 것은?
(A) 중국에서 수년간 일했었다.
(B) Mr. Jenkins의 동료이다.
(C) 회사의 몇몇 직원들을 만났었다.
(D) 마케팅 캠페인의 세부 사항을 발표할 예정이다.

176-180은 다음 웹페이지와 이메일에 관한 문제입니다.

---

www.lycon.com/productlist/vacuumcleaners

Lycon사 진공청소기

모든 모델에는 여러 번 사용할 수 있는 먼지 주머니가 딸려 있습니다.

선택 가능한 모든 모델		
이름	특징	가격
Speed XS	· 가벼운 디자인 — 단 3.5킬로그램 · 녹색, 검은색, 그리고 회색으로 구매 가능	125달러
Power Glide 3E	· 쉽게 조절할 수 있는 높이와 35인치의 선 · 초 저소음 모터	225달러
Dual Clean 350	· 바닥 스팀 청소 기능 · 덮개 및 커튼을 위한 부가 장치	160달러
EZ Flow GD	· 무선 사용을 위한 재충전할 수 있는 배터리 · 터치패드 형태의 조작 패널	140달러

Lycon사의 각 제품에는 1년간의 부품 및 서비스 보증이 딸려 있습니다. 보증 조항에 따라, 수리를 위해서는 제품들이 Lycon사 서비스 센터로 보내져야 합니다. 보증을 받을 자격을 얻으려면, 고객들은 신청서를 작성하여 그들의 구입품과 함께 발송해야 합니다.

수신: Lycon사 고객 서비스 <customersupport@lycon.com>
발신: Amy Reynolds <a.reynolds@pace.com>
날짜: 4월 13일
제목: 주문번호 3453번

관계자분께,

4월 4일에, 저는 귀사의 웹사이트를 통해 진공청소기를 주문했습니다. 처음에, 저는 집의 계단에서 들고 오르내리기 쉬운 가벼운 것을 선택했습니다. 하지만, 이후에 저는 무선 모델을 더 선호할 것 같다고 결정해서, 원래의 주문을 취소하고 4월 6일에 새 주문을 했습니다. 그 진공청소기는 4월 10일에 배달되었고, 저는 그것에 매우 만족합니다.

유감스럽게도, 오늘 저는 제 첫 주문 금액이 은행 계좌로 환불 처리가 되지 않았다는 것을 알게 되었습니다. 저는 이것이 즉시 처리되길 원합니다. 이것이 완료되면 이메일을 통해 제게 확인서를 보내주십시오. 감사합니다.

Amy Reynolds 드림

---

176 Lycon사에 대해 암시되는 것은?
(A) 모바일 기기로 조작할 수 있는 가전제품을 판매한다.
(B) 영수증이 제시되는 한 결함이 있는 제품을 교체해 준다.
(C) 제품 라인은 상업적 용도를 위한 장비를 포함한다.
(D) 진공청소기는 모두 재사용할 수 있는 부분을 포함한다.

177 보증에 대해 언급되지 않은 것은?
(A) Lycon사의 모든 진공청소기에 제공된다.
(B) 고객에게 수리 센터에서 서비스를 받을 권리를 준다.
(C) 구매일로부터 1년 후에 갱신될 수 있다.
(D) 작성된 양식을 제출하는 사람들이 이용할 수 있다.

178 Ms. Reynolds는 어느 제품을 받았을 것 같은가?
(A) Speed XS
(B) Power Glide 3E
(C) Dual Clean 350
(D) EZ Flow GD

179 Ms. Reynolds는 얼마를 환불금으로 받을 것인가?
  (A) 125달러
  (B) 140달러
  (C) 160달러
  (D) 225달러

180 이메일에서, 2문단 세 번째 줄의 단어 "via"는 의미상 ~와 가장 가깝다.
  (A) ~에 부합하여
  (B) ~에 관하여
  (C) ~ 면에서는
  (D) ~을 이용해서

181-185는 다음 광고지와 편지에 관한 문제입니다.

Mode Fashion

Mode Fashion 신용카드에 가입할 때 15퍼센트 할인을 누리세요.*

Mode Fashion 신용카드는 여러 가지의 놀라운 전용 특전들을 가지고 있으며, 다음을 포함합니다:

- 200달러의 소비마다 10달러 상품권 제공
- 회원 전용 행사 초대
- 신제품 선주문 기회
- 생일에 제공되는 특별 무료 상품
- 바지와 치마단 무료 수선**
- Mode Fashion의 월간지 한 부

Mode Fashion 신용카드는 연회비가 없습니다. 카드 소지자로서, 당신은 가족 구성원을 위해 추가적인 카드 권한을 부여하고, 매번 그들이 소비할 때마다 보상 포인트를 얻을 수 있습니다. 또한, www.platinumbank.com에서 카드 발급사인 Platinum 은행을 통해 온라인으로 당신의 계좌를 관리하고 대금을 지불할 수 있습니다.

*할인은 오로지 Mode Fashion 신용카드로 구매한 첫 구매에만 유효합니다. 할인은 이전 구매나 기프트 카드 구매에는 적용될 수 없습니다.

**Mode Fashion 신용카드를 사용해 전액을 구매하는 경우 유효합니다. 가죽 또는 스웨이드 제품에는 혜택 제공이 유효하지 않습니다. 주문에 따라 맞춰진 제품은 반품 또는 교환될 수 없습니다.

Mode Fashion
www.modefashion.com

5월 30일

Stella Helm
838번지 Gilbert가
팰러타인, 일리노이주 60067

Ms. Helm께,

새로운 Mode Fashion 신용카드를 신청해주셔서 감사 드리며, 신용카드는 이 편지에 동봉되어 있습니다. 이것이 활성화되는 대로 카드가 제공하는 특별한 보상과 혜택을 이용하실 수 있을 것입니다. 그렇게 하기 위해서는 555-0235로 카드 발급사에 전화하십시오.

아래에 있는 귀하의 세부 신청 사항을 확인해 주십시오:

이름: Stella P. Helm
생일: 7월 9일
카드 번호: 4320-5387-9534-4106
전화번호: 555-5903
이메일: s.helm@mellomail.com

문의 사항이 있으시면, 555-9669로 저희 고객 서비스 전용 번호로 전화해 주십시오.

Anthony Marcellus 드림
고객 관리부
Mode Fashion 신용카드 부서

---

181 광고지에 따르면, Mode Fashion 신용카드를 소유하는 것의 혜택이 아닌 것은?
  (A) 정기 간행물 한 부
  (B) 전용 행사 초대
  (C) 낮은 연이율
  (D) 신제품을 미리 주문할 권리

182 카드 소지자를 위한 특별 할인에 대해 언급된 것은?
  (A) 추가적인 카드 권한 부여를 조건으로 한다.
  (B) 반복적으로 이용될 수 없다.
  (C) 특정 종류의 옷에는 적용되지 않는다.
  (D) 쇼핑 웹사이트에서만 이용할 수 있다.

183 편지는 왜 쓰였는가?
  (A) 제품의 혜택을 강조하기 위해
  (B) 요청이 고려되고 있음을 명시하기 위해
  (C) 고객 서비스 문제에 대해 설명하기 위해
  (D) 카드 관련 정보를 제공하기 위해

184 Ms. Helm은 무엇을 해달라고 요청받는가?
  (A) 거래의 세부 사항을 확인한다
  (B) Platinum 은행에 연락한다
  (C) 얻은 보상 포인트를 청구한다
  (D) 가장 가까운 위치의 매장을 방문한다

185 Ms. Helm에 대해 추론될 수 있는 것은?
  (A) 상점 신용카드를 업그레이드 받을 자격을 얻었다.
  (B) 5월에 Mode Fashion에서 쇼핑을 했다.
  (C) 7월에 Mode Fashion으로부터 선물을 받을 것이다.
  (D) 매월 신용 카드 수수료를 반드시 지불해야 한다.

186-190은 다음 초대장, 편지, 보증서에 관한 문제입니다.

제2회 Clarendon 미술품 경매에 참여하세요
3월 19일, 오후 6시 30분
Lilac 강당, Clarendon 미술회관
인당 115파운드(작년과 동일)

지난 4월에 열린 Clarendon 미술회관의 첫 번째 미술품 경매의 성공 때문에, 주최자들은 두 번째 경매를 열기로 결정했습니다. 또다시, 미술품은 지역 예술가들에 의해 기증될 것이고, 관람객들은 이 작품들에 입찰할 수 있을 것입니다. 비록 여러분이 아무것도 구매할 생각이 없더라도, 그저 참석하는 것만으로도 여전히 여러분의 지지를 보여줄 수 있습니다. 이전처럼, 입장권과 미술품 구입으로부터 나오는 모든 수익금은 수업료를 내는 데 어려움을 겪고 있는 미술 전공 학생들을 돕는 데 사용될 것입니다.

작년 행사의 주요 부분:
- Dana Sloan의 조각상이 Paul Dixon에게 판매되었음.
- Otis Hidalgo의 수채화 세 점이 Dawn Reeves에 의해 취득되었음.
- Blaine D'Amico의 풍경화 한 점이 Roda사의 대표에 의해 회사의 소장품으로 구입되었음.

1월 9일

Dana Sloan
710번지 Southgate가
크롤리, 영국 RH10 1FP

Ms. Sloan께,

먼저, 베이징에서 열린 귀하의 전시회에 대해 축하드립니다. 저는 *British Daily News*지에서 그 전시회에 아주 많은 사람들이 참석했다는 것을 읽었습니다. 이제 그것이 끝났으니 저는 귀하께서 받으셔야 마땅할 휴식을 취하시고 계시리라고 생각합니다.

제가 귀하께 연락을 드리는 이유는 귀하께서 제2회 Clarendon 미술품 경매에 기증할 의향이 있으신지 여쭤보기 위함입니다. 작년에 귀하께서 저희에 ❍

게 주신 작품은 경매된 작품들 중 유일한 조각상이었습니다.

귀하의 대표적인 목재 조각상들 중 하나를 기증해주실 수 있다면 정말 좋을 것입니다.

Neil Baker 드림
책임자, Clarendon 미술품 경매

진품 보증서

이 문서는 동봉한 작품이 진품임을 보증합니다.

예술가명:	Dana Sloan
예술품명:	*Spirit of the Grass*
재료:	강철
크기:	30 x 25 x 15센티미터
창작일:	2월 10일~15일
판매일:	3월 19일
판매처:	Clarendon 미술회관
구매자명:	Dawn Reeves

예술가 서명: _Dana Sloan_

---

186 작년의 경매에 대해 언급되지 않은 것은?
(A) 지역사회 구성원의 창작물을 포함하였다.
(B) 교육 시간이 선행되었다.
(C) 한 회사에 그림 한 점을 판매한 것을 포함하였다.
(D) 특정 그룹을 위해 개최되었다.

187 편지의 주 목적은 무엇인가?
(A) 참석 확정을 요청하기 위해
(B) 작품을 기부해 달라고 요청하기 위해
(C) 행사가 성공적이었다고 알리기 위해
(D) 조각가에게 전시회에 대해 상기시키기 위해

188 Mr. Dixon에 대해 암시되는 것은?
(A) *British Daily News*지에서 기자로 일한다.
(B) Dana Sloan의 작품을 정기적으로 구입한다.
(C) 예술품 경매에 참여하기 위해 115파운드를 지불했다.
(D) 그는 Mr. Hidalgo보다 더 적은 돈을 지출했다.

189 *Spirit of the Grass*에 대해 언급된 것은?
(A) 베이징에 본거지를 둔 예술가에 의해 만들어졌다.
(B) 완성을 나타내기 위해 2월 10일에 Ms. Sloan에 의해 서명되었다.
(C) Mr. Baker가 요청했던 종류의 조각상이 아니다.
(D) 예술원의 유명한 졸업생들에 대한 다큐멘터리에서 보였다.

190 Ms. Reeves에 대해 암시되는 것은?
(A) 행사 동안에 예술 작품을 의뢰했다.
(B) 예술가 Dana Sloan의 조각품들을 수집한다.
(C) Roda사를 대표하여 그림을 구입했다.
(D) 2년 연속으로 미술품 경매에 참가했다.

191-195는 다음 기사, 광고, 이메일에 관한 문제입니다.

실버레이크의 대망의 쇼핑 복합단지 The Hangout이 이번 주 문을 열 예정이다. 이는 겨울 휴일 쇼핑 시즌에 딱 맞춰 찾아온다. 소유 그룹이 작년 여러 유명 투자자들로부터 자금을 확보할 수 있어서 이 프로젝트를 파산으로부터 구제하기 전, 건설이 2년 동안 지연된 바 있다.

다양한 의류 매장들과 함께, The Hangout에는 최신 유행하는 요가 스튜디오 Feetup, Express Cup 커피숍, Fabriga 아이스크림 상점 등이 들어설 것이다. The Hangout은 동쪽으로 한 블록 거리에 새로 생긴 Red선 지하철 역뿐만 아니라 근방의 몇몇 새로운 주거용 고층 건물 덕분에 이익을 볼 가능성이 높다.

개점을 기념하기 위해, The Hangout은 이번 주말 축하 행사를 개최할 것 ◐

이다. 이는 경품 추첨과 홍보용 증정품을 제공하는 일부 상점과 더불어, 복합단지 전체 세일을 포함할 것이다. 또한 전설적인 Harry Hill 재즈 사중주단의 콘서트를 특징으로 할 것이다.

The Hangout에서 Kisak의 개업을 축하해 주세요

Kisak이 실버레이크의 The Hangout에서 뉴욕 바깥의 첫 매장을 열 예정입니다. Kisak은 가장 잘 알려진 디자이너들 중 몇몇과 떠오르는 신인들의 컬렉션을 판매하는 절충적인 스타일로 알려져 있습니다.

매장 첫 영업일은 The Hangout의 개점 행사와 겹치는데, 이는 복합단지 곳곳에서 재미있는 활동으로 기념될 것입니다. Kisak도 행사에 참여하여 관심 있는 분들을 위해 무료 스타일링 시간을 가질 것입니다. 다름 아닌 유명 인사 스타일리스트 Tamara Kimpton이 참석해서 5분 상담을 제공할 예정입니다. 게다가, 저희의 겨울 코트와 액세서리를 포함한 많은 품목들이 할인될 것입니다. 그리고 이 광고를 Kisak 직원에게 보여주시면, 최대 10달러의 매장 적립금 쿠폰을 받으실 것입니다.

수신: Tabatha Branson <t.branson@thehangoutcomplex.com>
발신: Yoshi Hondo <yoshi@silverlakeartcollective.com>
제목: 제안
날짜: 10월 17일

Ms. Branson께,

최근 저희의 대화를 끝까지 하고 싶어요. 우선, 당신이 Harry Hill을 예약하는 데 성공하신 것이 매우 인상 깊었습니다. 저는 수년간 팬이었지만, 그가 라이브로 공연하는 것을 보는 건 처음이었어요.

제가 직접 간략히 말씀드린 대로, 저는 실버레이크 예술 협동조합의 파트너입니다. 저희는 지역 예술가들을 지원하고 종종 그들을 홍보하기 위한 행사를 조직합니다. 당신이 The Hangout 곳곳에 그들의 작품 몇 점을 전시하는 데 관심 있으실 것 같아서요. 복합단지에 훌륭한 보탬이 될 그림들과 비디오 예술 작품들을 몇 점 보여드릴 수 있습니다.

관심 있으시다면, 좋아하실 만한 작품 몇 점으로 제안서를 준비해서 금요일에 당신 사무실에 들를 수 있습니다.

Yoshi Hondo 드림

---

191 쇼핑 복합단지의 개점이 왜 지연되었는가?
(A) 일부 건축업자들이 폐업했다.
(B) 자금 조달에 어려움을 겪었다.
(C) 성수기 이후로 연기되었다.
(D) 일부 체인점들이 사업제휴를 해지했다.

192 새로운 Kisak 지점에 대해 사실인 것은?
(A) 부분적으로 Tamara Kimpton의 소유이다.
(B) 남성복에 대한 판촉행사를 진행하고 있다.
(C) 커피숍과 요가 스튜디오 사이에 있다.
(D) 대중교통에 편리하다.

193 다음 중 Kisak이 계획하고 있는 활동이 아닌 것은?
(A) 패션 상담을 진행하는 것
(B) 매장 쿠폰을 나눠주는 것
(C) 유명 인사의 브랜드를 출시하는 것
(D) 가격 할인을 제공하는 것

194 Mr. Hondo에 대해 암시된 것은?
(A) 이전에 Ms. Branson과 일했다.
(B) 개점 축하 행사에 참석했다.
(C) The Hangout의 미술관을 관리한다.
(D) 명망 있는 시각 예술가이다.

195 Mr. Hondo는 무엇을 제안하는가?
(A) 갤러리 개관을 후원하는 것
(B) 전시에 협력하는 것

(C) 영상 촬영을 위해 복합단지를 사용하는 것
(D) 자선행사를 개최하는 것

196-200은 다음 광고, 안내문, 공고에 관한 문제입니다.

UNICLOUD사에서 모바일 애플리케이션 개발자를 구인합니다

10월 1일 게시   12월 1일 만료

직무:
· 타깃층과 고객 의견을 고려하여 사용자 인터페이스 구상
· 다양한 애플리케이션의 시각적 스타일과 인터페이스 설계
· 사용자 인터페이스 견본 개발
· 주간 진행 상황 회의에서 개발 진행 과정에 대한 최신 정보 전달

기본 요건:
· 모바일 애플리케이션 개발자로서 5년의 경력
· 복잡한 모바일 애플리케이션 모델 제작 경력
· 디자인 또는 컴퓨터 공학 학사 학위
· 부에노스아이레스에 정착하려는 의사

선호되는 자질:
· 클라우드 기반의 서비스를 위한 모바일 애플리케이션 설계 경력
· 유창한 영어와 스페인어

당신의 이력서와 함께, 관련 경력을 보여주는 포트폴리오 또는 작업물 샘플을 recruitment@unicloud.com으로 제출해 주십시오.

UNICLOUD사에 대해

10년 전에 설립된 Unicloud사는 뮌헨에 본사를 둔 전자 상거래의 선구자 Unispan사의 클라우드 컴퓨팅 지부입니다. 이것은 세계 3대 클라우드 서비스 공급업체 중 하나이며 유럽에서는 동종 업체 중에서 가장 큰 업체입니다. Unicloud사는 신생 기업, 큰 규모의 회사, 그리고 정부 기관을 포함하여, 전 세계의 고객들에게 일련의 종합적인 클라우드 컴퓨팅 서비스를 제공합니다.

Unicloud사는 현재 런던, 뉴욕, 그리고 상하이에 지사를 두고 있습니다. 그것은 5억 명이 넘는 사용자를 가지고 있습니다. 그것은 부에노스아이레스에 조만간 문을 열 남미 지사를 세운 후 2억 명의 스페인어 사용자를 끌어들이는 것을 목표로 하고 있습니다.

UNICLOUD 직원들에게 알림

지금으로부터 2주 후에 우리가 전자제품 제조업체인 SatzCorp사의 대표단을 접대할 것임을 기억해 주십시오. 그들은 우리의 사무 환경, 조직 구조, 그리고 기업 문화에 대해 배우고 싶어 합니다. 여기에 있는 동안, 그들은 다양한 직원들을 인터뷰할 것입니다. 우리의 모기업에서 온 Ms. Schrader가 그 팀이 방문하는 동안 동행할 것입니다. 그날 시작할 때, 그녀는 우리에게 무엇을 예상해야 하는지에 대해 간단히 알려줄 것입니다. 그 절차는 우리 회사의 다른 두 곳, 뉴욕과 상하이에서도 반복될 것이지만, 새로 설립된 곳에서는 그렇지 않을 것입니다. 연말 전에, 우리는 우리 대표단을 SatzCorp사의 본사에 파견할 것입니다. 그렇게 함으로써, 우리가 고객 관리에 관한 몇몇 모범적인 관행을 배울 수 있기를 바랍니다.

---

196 광고에 따르면, 합격자들이 해야 하는 것이 아닌 것은?
(A) 고객 의견을 검토한다
(B) 홍보물의 외관을 디자인한다
(C) 정기적으로 모임에 이야기한다
(D) 사용자 인터페이스 견본을 만든다

197 Unicloud에 대해 언급된 것은?
(A) 동종 업체 중에서 유럽에 설립된 첫 번째 회사였다.
(B) 국제기관들과 협력하여 일한다.
(C) 더 큰 조직의 일부로서 전문화된 서비스를 제공한다.
(D) 다가오는 확장에 이어 사용자 수를 두 배로 늘릴 것으로 기대한다.

198 광고된 직책에 대해 추론될 수 있는 것은?
(A) 잦은 출장을 요구할 것이다.
(B) 연례 상여금이 나온다.
(C) 새로운 지사에서 일하는 것을 수반할 것이다.
(D) 12월 전에 자리가 채워져야 한다.

199 공고의 목적은 무엇인가?
(A) 새롭게 채용된 임원을 소개하기 위해
(B) 규정에 대해 직원들에게 상기시키기 위해
(C) 행사의 성공을 알리기 위해
(D) 정보 수집을 위한 방문에 대해 논의하기 위해

200 공고 수신자들에 대해 암시되는 것은?
(A) 특별 프로젝트에 배정될 것이다.
(B) Ms. Schrader에 의해 설문 조사에 참여하도록 요청받을 것이다.
(C) Unicloud의 런던 사무실에서 근무한다.
(D) 다음 2주 동안 결근할 수 없다.

PART 5

101 리조트 관리자는 보통 첫 방문자들이 환경에 익숙해지도록 숙박시설을 구경시켜 준다.

102 전직 교사였던 Ms. Pratt은 공립학교 교육의 질을 향상하기 위한 시도로 공직에 출마하도록 영감을 받았다.

103 지진으로 손상된 건물에 관한 기술자의 평가에 따르면, 그것은 철거되어야 할 것이다.

104 Ms. Bang은 공급업체로부터 중요한 전화를 받기 위해 워크숍에 불참했다.

105 많은 사람들이 자리를 비울 것으로 예상되었기 때문에, BTM사의 의장은 금요일 이사 회의를 연기했다.

106 Vic의 단편 영화는 너무 전문적으로 촬영되어서 관객들 중 거의 아무도 그것이 학생의 작품이라는 것을 알아차리지 못했다.

107 이 새로운 식단은 오직 적어도 하루에 한 시간의 적당한 운동과 병행된 경우에만 체중 감량을 용이하게 한다.

108 많은 온라인 상점들이 할인을 제공하기 때문에, 직접 쇼핑하는 것보다 온라인에서 구매하는 것이 종종 더 저렴하다.

109 보험 조사원은 충돌에 연루된 두 운전자 모두가 동등하게 책임이 있다고 판단했다.

110 Bolt Systems사와 Seer 컴퓨터사가 합병을 발표했지만, 합의에 관한 세부 사항은 비밀에 부쳐졌다.

111 회사가 오래된 사무 장비를 모두 교체한 후 직원 생산성이 눈에 띄게 향상되었다.

112 이 무료 막대 빵 쿠폰은 미국 내 모든 참여하는 Colson Pizzeria 가맹점에서 사용될 수 있다.

113 인턴십 과정을 마친 후, Mr. Louis는 그의 새로운 회계 업무가 수반하는 어떤 책임이든 간에 맡을 준비가 되어 있었다.

114 그 공장 감독은 공간에 대한 시급한 필요로 인해 창고를 짓는 것이 아니라 임대하기로 결정했다.

115 Ms. Jedlicka가 올해 Peter Vanier 상의 수상자인데, 이것은 뛰어난 지역 사회 봉사활동을 한 지역 기업인들에게 수여된다.

116 그녀가 주연을 맡았던 장기 시리즈가 끝났기 때문에 팬들은 다음에 그 배우가 무엇을 할지 추측하고 있다.

117 온라인 광역버스 노선도는 Crawley역에서 시청까지 이동하는 데 거의 40분이 걸릴 것이라고 나타낸다.

118 한때 극심하게 변동하는 경향이 있었던 그 국가의 화폐 가치는 통화 정책의 대대적인 변경 덕분에 안정되었다.

119 그 푸드 트럭 주인은 유효한 시 허가증 없이 사업을 운영하여 벌금형을 받았다.

120 혹시 저희와 점심을 함께할 의향이 있으시다면, 저희 팀은 사무실 주변에 있는 한식당에서 식사할 거예요.

121 500에이커의 보존된 주립 토지가 마을에서 걸어갈 수 있는 거리에 있어서, 그곳은 야외 애호가들에게 가장 인기 있는 목적지가 되었다.

122 Dr. Burkett의 연구는 인간의 뇌에 대한 더 발전된 이해로 이어졌고 진보된 수술 기술을 개발하는 데 도움을 주었다.

123 최근 국가의 취업률이 증가했음에도 불구하고, 경제는 거의 성장하지 않고 있다.

124 보행자들을 수용하기 위해, Fitzgerald가에 주차하는 것은 Hillfalls 음악 축제 동안 금지될 것이다.

125 Tacchini 섬유회사 생산 공장이 문을 닫았을 때 약 150개의 일자리가 사라졌다.

126 그의 출고가 계속 지연되는 것에 불만스러워서, Mr. Caldwell은 판매자에게 전화해서 주문을 취소했다.

127 히트 쇼 Quiet Predator의 12화 모두 8번 채널의 텔레비전 마라톤 행사 동안 연속으로 방송될 것이다.

128 Ruylain사의 직원들은 업무 현장을 개선하기 위한 제안을 가지고 그들의 관리자들에게 다가가도록 권장된다.

129 Karsten 제조사에게는 품질이 최우선 사항이기 때문에, 제품의 문제에 대한 보고를 매우 심각하게 받아들인다.

130 임상 시험의 환자들이 아무것도 경험하지 않았기 때문에, 연구원들은 새로운 약이 부작용을 일으킬 것이라고 예상하지 않았다.

PART 6

131-134는 다음 공고에 관한 문제입니다.

> Susie's 식당: 손님들께 중요한 공고
>
> 131 저희는 일부 손님들께서 식단 제한이 있으실 수 있는 점을 인지하고 있습니다. 저희 메뉴에는 모든 요리에 관한 간단한 설명이 있지만, 그것들을 만드는 데 사용되는 일부 재료는 나와있지 않을 수 있습니다. 132 이러한 이유로, 저희는 여러분이 주문하기 전에 음식 알레르기나 민감성에 관해 서버에게 말씀하실 것을 요청드립니다.
>
> 133 여러분의 우려사항에 관해 미리 알려주시면, 저희는 여러분의 식사가 안전하게 준비되도록 보장할 수 있습니다. 134 원치 않는 재료를 건강하고 맛있는 대안으로 대체할 방법은 많고, 저희는 여러분의 요청을 기꺼이 이행하겠습니다.

135-138은 다음 기사에 관한 문제입니다.

> Schmidt Medical사의 밝은 미래
>
> 135 Schmidt Medical사는 최근 몇 년간 의료 장비의 선두적인 공급자가 되었다. 이 회사의 연구팀은 수술을 덜 위험하게 만드는 최첨단 도구를 생산하기 위해 의사들과 긴밀히 협력하는 것으로 정평이 나 있다. 136 그러나 업계 분석가들에 따르면, 새로운 LZR-160 기기 라인은 Schmidt사의 역대 가장 유망한 제품이다. LZR-160은 시력 교정 수술에 걸리는 시간을 5분 이내로 단축한다. 137 이것은 Schmidt사의 주주들에게 매우 좋은 소식이다. 138 회사의 주가는 이미 뛰어올랐지만, LZR-160 기기들이 널리 보급되면 훨씬 더 높이 오를 것으로 예상된다.

139-142는 다음 공고에 관한 문제입니다.

> 제출 공모
>
> 139 모든 수준의 사진작가들은 시청의 겨울 행사 달력에 실릴 수 있는 기회를 위해 Walminster 지역 시내의 사진을 제출하도록 초청됩니다. 선정된 사진들은 우리의 아름다운 도시와 주민들이 쇼핑하고, 식사하고, 즐기는 것을 소개하도록 도울 것입니다.
>
> 참가자들은 최대 3장의 사진을 제출할 수 있으며, 이는 모두 디지털 형식이어야 합니다. 140 뿐만 아니라, 참가자들은 서명한 저작권 동의서를 제출해야 합니다. 141 이것은 시에 복제권을 부여할 것입니다. 즉, 시는 향후 광고 및 ➲

기타 홍보자료에 사용하기 위해 참가자들의 원본 사진을 자유롭게 재인쇄할 수 있습니다. **142** 이 경우에도 사진작가는 적절히 저작 표기를 받을 것입니다. 더 많은 정보를 원하시면 www.walminster.com/winter_photo_contest를 방문하세요.

143-146은 다음 이메일에 관한 문제입니다.

수신 Leo_Belmore@bequetteholdings.com
발신 Curtis_McGovern@bequetteholdings.com
제목 회신: 요청
날짜 6월 2일

좋은 오후입니다, Mr. Belmore.

당신은 이제 6년 동안 Bequette Holdings사의 귀중한 일원이었고, 저는 당신의 헌신에 오랫동안 감탄해 왔습니다. **143** 이러한 이유로 저는 당신의 전근 요청을 승인하겠습니다.

당신이 원하는 지점인 우리의 네바다 지사에서는 당신처럼 경험 있는 품질 분석가를 찾고 있습니다. **144** 그러므로, 당신은 옮긴 후에도 현재의 직책을 유지할 수 있을 것입니다. **145** 당신이 가을에 이전하고 싶다고 하신 것을 알고 있습니다. 그러나, 그들의 관리팀은 당신이 7월 12일부터 시작할 것을 제안했습니다. **146** 만약 준비할 시간이 부족하다면, 제가 당신의 시작일을 미룰 수 있을지도 모릅니다. 질문이 있으시면 언제든지 연락 주세요.

행운을 빕니다,
Curtis McGovern 인사부장 드림

PART 7

147-148은 다음 공고에 관한 문제입니다.

모로코 철도회사

이번 주 초 저희 철도망 일부분에서 운행이 중단된 동안 승객들의 인내심에 감사를 표하고자 합니다. 이제 모든 역에 운행이 완전히 복구되었습니다. 이 중단은 공공 안전 위험을 야기한 다수의 신호 장애로 인해 발생했습니다. 다행히도, 저희 정비사들이 오작동하는 신호 장비를 곧 다시 작동시킬 수 있었습니다. 앞으로 유사한 문제가 발생할 경우, 모로코 철도회사는 언제나처럼 티켓 소지자들께 환불을 제공하도록 노력할 것입니다.

147 주로 공지되고 있는 것은 무엇인가?
(A) 작업 중단
(B) 역사 폐쇄
(C) 기간 한정 상품
(D) 서비스 재개

148 모로코 철도회사는 최근에 무엇을 했는가?
(A) 할인 티켓을 제공했다
(B) 기차 선로를 연장했다
(C) 일부 장비를 수리했다
(D) 비상 계획을 수정했다

149-150은 다음 웹페이지에 관한 문제입니다.

WaveTune.com

홈	차트	내 계정

환영합니다, Olga Petrov. 귀하는 현재 로그인되어 있습니다.

내 청구서
서비스가 제공된 달: 4월

월간 음악 스트리밍 (개인 요금제):	15.00달러
고성능 오디오 업그레이드:	4.99달러
세금:	1.45달러
총 청구액:	21.44달러
*납부기한:	5월 15일 금요일

명시된 납부일까지 이번 달 청구액을 지불하지 않으시면, 귀하의 계정이 정지될 것입니다. service@wavetune.com으로 이메일을 보내거나 여기를 클릭하여 실시간 채팅방에 접속하고 가지고 계실 수 있는 문의 사항을 저희 고객 서비스팀에 제출하십시오.

149 Ms. Petrov는 4월에 무엇을 했는가?
(A) 더 나은 오디오를 이용했다
(B) 앨범을 다운로드했다
(C) 가족 계정을 개설했다
(D) 항의를 제출했다

150 WaveTune.com에 대해 언급된 것은?
(A) 고객 서비스 직통 전화를 운영한다.
(B) 결제가 누락되면 서비스를 중단한다.
(C) 자동으로 구독자 신용카드에 청구한다.
(D) 사용자들에게 스트리밍 기기를 제공한다.

151-152는 다음 광고에 관한 문제입니다.

Helping Hands사

올여름에 유람선 여행을 갈 준비를 하고 있으신가요? Helping Hands사에 전화 주세요. 저희는 고객님의 집에서 짐을 가져와서 출발 당일 유람선으로 배송해 드리기 때문에, 무거운 물건을 직접 들고 가실 걱정을 하지 않으셔도 됩니다. 그저 저희 웹사이트에서 가입하고 양식만 작성하세요. 고객님의 짐은 출발일 2일에서 5일 전에 수령되어 저희 시설에 안전하게 보관됩니다. 출발 당일, 짐은 고객님의 객실에서 기다리고 있을 것입니다. 이보다 더 편리한 것이 있을까요? 귀가 서비스도 이용 가능합니다.

보험료를 포함하여, 25킬로그램 이하의 물건에 편도 40달러만 지불하세요. 특대 물품에 관해서는, 555-8080으로 전화 주세요. 또한 저희 웹사이트 www.helpinghands.com을 방문하여 자세한 이용 약관을 보실 수 있습니다.

151 Helping Hands사의 주요 이점은 무엇인가?
(A) 여름 여행의 비용을 낮춘다.
(B) 고객들이 분실된 물품을 찾는 것을 돕는다.
(C) 목적지로의 이동 시간을 줄인다.
(D) 개인적인 불편을 없앤다.

152 광고의 독자들은 왜 Helping Hands사에 전화해야 하는가?
(A) 서비스에 대한 문제를 신고하기 위해
(B) 대형 물품에 대해 문의하기 위해
(C) 구매와 함께 선물을 신청하기 위해
(D) 추가 할인을 얻기 위해

153-155는 다음 회람에 관한 문제입니다.

사내 회람

수신: Lauren Maguire Voyar 미국지사 공학부 부사장
발신: Douglas Lima Voyar 브라질지사 운영 부사장
제목: Esther Castro
날짜: 4월 10일

아시다시피, Ms. Castro는 지난 6개월 동안 저희 팀과 일해왔고 곧 미국으로 돌아갈 예정입니다. ㅡ [1] ㅡ. 그 전에, 저는 그녀가 여기 있는 동안 기여한 것에 대해 제 감사를 표하고 싶습니다. 기술 자문 위원으로서 그녀의 작업은 저희가 제시간에 공장 개선을 완료할 수 있도록 하는 데 중요했습니다.

— [2] —. 생산성을 향상하기 위한 Ms. Castro의 아이디어는 놀라울 만큼 통찰력 있었습니다. 그녀는 모든 문제에 창의적으로 접근합니다. — [3] —. 그녀가 조직 내 모든 직급의 직원들과 효과적으로 소통할 수 있도록 했기 때문에 Ms. Castro가 포르투갈어를 아주 잘 배운 것도 큰 도움이 되었습니다. — [4] —. 저는 단지 여기 브라질에서 저희의 운영에 그녀가 기여한 바가 간과되지 않도록 확실히 하고 싶었습니다. 또한 만약 언제든 승진의 기회가 생긴다면, 제가 그녀를 진심으로 추천할 것이라고 덧붙이고 싶습니다.

153 Mr. Lima는 왜 회람을 작성했는가?
(A) 직원을 칭찬하기 위해
(B) 팀의 공로를 평가하기 위해
(C) 공장 개업에 대해 설명하기 위해
(D) 소통 규약을 논의하기 위해

154 Ms. Castro에 대해 사실이 아닌 것은?
(A) 제2외국어를 한다.
(B) 현재 브라질에서 일한다.
(C) 공장의 생산성을 개선하는 것을 도왔다.
(D) 승진 대상으로 고려되고 있다.

155 [1], [2], [3], [4]로 표시된 위치 중, 다음 문장이 들어갈 곳으로 가장 적절한 것은?

"당신은 아마 이러한 자질과 직원으로서 그녀의 가치에 관해 알고 계실 것입니다."

(A) [1]
(B) [2]
(C) [3]
(D) [4]

156-157은 다음 메시지 대화문에 관한 문제입니다.

Deanna Bach	(오후 4시 30분)
안녕하세요, 저는 12월 10일에 Dr. Hassan과 치과 예약이 있어요. 유감스럽지만, 제가 회사에서 출장을 가게 되었습니다. 일정을 변경해도 괜찮을까요?	
Kent Conrad	(오후 4시 34분)
문제없습니다. 언제 돌아오시나요?	
Deanna Bach	(오후 4시 35분)
저는 일주일 동안 자카르타에 있을 거예요. 그 다음 주 월요일 같은 시간에 가능한가요?	
Kent Conrad	(오후 4시 36분)
그건 안 되겠는데요. 하지만 화요일과 수요일 오전 10시에는 시간이 있어요.	
Deanna Bach	(오후 4시 36분)
화요일에는 하루 종일 회의가 있어요. 그 주 수요일에 예약을 잡을 수 있을까요?	
Kent Conrad	(오후 4시 37분)
물론이죠. 12월 23일 오전 10시 확인되셨습니다.	
Deanna Bach	(오후 4시 37분)
정말 감사합니다!	

156 Ms. Bach에 대해 암시되는 것은?
(A) 자카르타로 출장을 떠난다.
(B) 긴급한 문제로 치과에 가야 한다.
(C) 일부 회의 일정을 변경하고 싶어 한다.
(D) 약속 시간에 늦고 있다.

157 오후 4시 36분에, Mr. Conrad가 "That won't work"이라고 썼을 때 그가 의도한 것은?
(A) 사무실이 휴일로 문을 닫을 것이다.
(B) 요청된 시간대가 이미 예약되어 있다.

(C) 의사가 일주일 동안 자리를 비울 것이다.
(D) 직원이 휴가를 갈 예정이다.

158-160은 다음 기사에 관한 문제입니다.

세계여행자 소식
*Global Traveler*지 전속 기자 *Elliot Keller* 작성

어제 공개된 성명에서, 저가 항공사 Columbia-Jet사가 미국에서 서비스를 개시할 계획을 발표했다. 캐나다에 본사를 둔 이 항공사는 불과 9년 전에 창립되었고, 이미 국내 항공편으로 인기가 있다는 것이 입증되었다. 그것은 현재 캐나다 전역에서 26군데의 목적지로 항공편을 운항하고 있으며, 1월 7일부터 시애틀, 뉴욕시, 그리고 마이애미를 추가할 것이다. Columbia-Jet사의 최고 경영자 Serena Hornell은 항공사가 또한 내년 말까지 로스앤젤레스와 덴버로 가는 추가 노선을 갖기를 희망한다고 말했다.

Ms. Hornell은 항공사가 특별 거래를 제공하여 새로운 목적지들을 홍보할 것이라고 했다. "한정된 기간 동안, 저희는 한 개의 가격으로 두 개를 드리는 특가를 제공할 것입니다. 저희의 신규 노선 중 하나에서 정가 항공권을 구매하시는 누구나 무료로 두 번째 항공권을 받으실 자격이 있습니다." 탑승객들은 위탁 및 기내 수하물 모두 추가 요금이 발생할 것임에 유의해야 한다. 할인에 대한 자세한 내용은 항공사 웹사이트 www.columbia-jet.com에 게시되어 있다.

158 기사는 주로 무엇에 대한 것인가?
(A) 저가 항공사의 창립
(B) 항공사의 노선 확장
(C) 새로운 최고 경영자의 채용
(D) 국내 항공편의 증가

159 1월 7일에 이용 가능해질 목적지가 아닌 것은?
(A) 시애틀
(B) 뉴욕시
(C) 마이애미
(D) 덴버

160 탑승객들은 어떻게 새로운 목적지로 가는 무료 항공권을 받을 수 있는가?
(A) 왕복 항공권을 예약함으로써
(B) 첫 번째 항공권을 정가에 구매함으로써
(C) 온라인 추첨에 참여함으로써
(D) 쿠폰 번호를 사용함으로써

161-164는 다음 회람에 관한 문제입니다.

수신 연구개발팀 직원들
발신 Brenda Redfield
제목 부서 직원 채용 업데이트
날짜 2월 26일

좋은 오후입니다,

최근 모두의 노고에 감사드립니다. 곧 있을 직원 임명에 관해 모두에게 몇 가지 소식을 전달하려고 합니다.

먼저, 우리의 신임 이사인 Kenneth Edwards가 3월 1일에 공식적으로 취임할 예정입니다. Mr. Edwards는 샌디에이고에 있는 우리 회사의 지방 지사에서 연구 책임자였습니다. 그는 2월 말에 은퇴할 Muriel Bourke를 대신할 것입니다. 그는 이전 직책에서 성공적이었고 직원들에게 매우 인기 있었습니다. 그래서, 저는 여러분 모두 그가 우리 부서에 기여할 것을 환영하리라고 확신합니다.

다음으로, Helen Ing이 부서 차장으로 승진할 것이라고 발표하게 되어 기쁩니다. 그녀는 3월 1일부터 계획 수립, 규정 시행, 그리고 부서 직원들을 위한 활동 일정 수립을 담당할 것입니다.

마지막으로, 3월 15일에 다섯 명의 신입 정규 직원들을 우리 부서에 맞이할 것입니다. 이들 중 두 명은 초임 연구원이자 최근 졸업생입니다. 그들은 우선

교육 과정에 참여할 것입니다. 나머지는 각각 이미 소프트웨어 개발 분야에서 상당한 경험이 있는 만큼, P6 프로젝트에 배정되어 바로 코딩을 시작할 것입니다.

Brenda Redfield
연구개발팀 부이사

161 1문단 두 번째 줄의 단어 "appointments"는 의미상 ~와 가장 가깝다.
(A) 직무 배치
(B) 회의 준비
(C) 승진 추천
(D) 업무 책임

162 Ms. Bourke에 대해 암시되는 것은?
(A) 현재 부서 이사이다.
(B) 2월에 샌디에이고를 방문했다.
(C) 채용 절차를 관리했다.
(D) 곧 임금 인상을 받을 것이다.

163 Ms. Ing은 무엇을 담당할 것인가?
(A) 신입사원을 교육하는 것
(B) 업무 시간표를 수립하는 것
(C) 연구 데이터를 정리하는 것
(D) 고객들과 소통하는 것

164 신입 정규 직원들에 대해 언급된 것은?
(A) 일부는 제품 개발 학위를 받았다.
(B) 모두 사전 경력이 있다.
(C) 일부는 즉시 업무 배정을 받을 것이다.
(D) 모두 교육을 받을 것이다.

165-167은 다음 양식에 관한 문제입니다.

Owenville 고등학교
모금 양식

Owenville 고등학교의 대표 스포츠 팀을 응원함으로써 여러분의 애교심을 보여주세요. 어떤 액수이든 기부하시거나 우리 학교의 로고가 새겨진 옷을 구매하실 수 있습니다. 기여금은 유니폼과 장비 구입, 원정 경기용 교통수단 대여, 그리고 그 외 기타 비용의 자금을 대기 위해 사용됩니다.

이름: Cassandra Roberts
날짜: 8월 9일
이메일 주소: c.roberts@texmail.com
전화번호: 555-9325

용도 지정:
  X 일반 사용   ___ 농구팀
___ 육상팀   ___ 야구팀
___ 수영팀   ___ 축구팀

직접 기부:
__ 10달러 __ 20달러 __ 50달러 __ 100달러 __ 기타: ___

또는 의류 품목 구매:

	소형	중형	대형	초대형	단가	총액
티셔츠	1		1		10달러	20달러
민소매 티셔츠	1				15달러	15달러
긴 소매 셔츠			1		20달러	20달러
대표팀 재킷				1	25달러	25달러
					합계	80달러

학교 체육부 사무실에 양식을 제출하고 물품을 회수할 수 있습니다. 가능한 지불 방식은 현금과 수표(수취인 Owenville 고등학교)를 포함합니다.

---

165 Owenville 고등학교에 대해 암시되는 것은?
(A) 새로운 스포츠 시설을 짓고 있다.
(B) 다섯 개의 대표 스포츠 팀이 있다.
(C) 최근 선수권 대회에서 우승했다.
(D) 정해진 액수를 모금하는 것을 목표로 한다.

166 판매되는 옷에 대해 언급된 것은?
(A) 요금을 지불하면 배송될 수 있다.
(B) 학생들이 만든 디자인을 특징으로 한다.
(C) 다양한 크기로 나온다.
(D) 현금으로만 값을 지불할 수 있다.

167 Ms. Roberts의 기여금은 무엇을 위해 사용될 것인가?
(A) 자선사업에 자금을 대는 것
(B) 새로운 유니폼을 디자인하는 것
(C) 장학금을 지원하는 것
(D) 팀 경비를 지불하는 것

168-171은 다음 온라인 채팅 대화문에 관한 문제입니다.

Platinum Max 투자사 – 단체 채팅 시스템

Xavier Hahn 오후 2시 43분
Janelle과 Antonio, 연말 손익 보고서는 어떻게 진행되고 있나요?

Janelle Fletcher 오후 2시 44분
죄송하지만, 예상보다 오래 걸리고 있어요.

Antonio Ricci 오후 2시 45분
맞아요, 저희가 다음 주 금요일 기한을 맞추지 못할까 봐 꽤 걱정스러워요.

Xavier Hahn 오후 2시 46분
그렇다면, 우리 인턴 Teresa에게 도움을 요청하는 건 어때요? 그녀는 이번 주 화요일 직원회의 기록만 작성하고 있어요. 그 보고서를 작업할 시간이 있을 거라고 확신해요.

Antonio Ricci 오후 2시 47분
아, 완벽하네요! 그녀는 주간 현황 업데이트를 발송하기 위해 정기적으로 회계 데이터베이스에 접속하는 만큼, 제가 그 방법을 진작에 떠올렸어야 해요.

Janelle Fletcher 오후 2시 48분
제가 그녀에게 보고서 스프레드시트에 우리가 필요한 수식을 입력하는 방법을 알려줄게요.

Xavier Hahn 오후 2시 49분
좋아요. 이 일이 해결되어서 다행이에요. 보고서 때문에 두 분이 다음 주 목요일 송년회를 놓치는 일은 없었으면 했거든요. 우리 팀이 재정 전략 제안서 업무로 상을 받을 예정인데, 두 분 다 거기에 계셨으면 좋겠어요.

Antonio Ricci 오후 2시 50분
그건 몰랐어요. 매우 신나네요! 그럼 다음 주 목요일 Mandarin Kitchen에서 뵐게요.

---

168 손익 보고서는 언제까지 마감되어야 하는가?
(A) 이번 주 화요일까지
(B) 이번 주 수요일까지
(C) 다음 주 목요일까지
(D) 다음 주 금요일까지

169 Mr. Ricci에 따르면, Teresa는 왜 업무에 적합한가?
(A) 최근에 회계 보고서에 관한 강의를 들었다.
(B) 스프레드시트에 관한 교육을 받았다.
(C) 몇 차례 컴퓨터 시스템을 사용해 왔다.
(D) 직원회의에서 기록을 작성했다.

170 오후 2시 49분에, Mr. Hahn이 "I'm glad we got this worked out"이라고 썼을 때 그가 의도한 것은?
(A) 몇몇 직원들이 행사에 참석할 수 있을 것이다.
(B) 기술적 오류가 해결되었다.
(C) 몇몇 전략이 효율적인 것으로 드러났다.
(D) 보고서가 예상보다 빨리 완성되었다.

171 다음 주 Mandarin Kitchen에서 무엇이 주어질 것인가?
(A) 단체를 위한 상
(B) 연말 선물
(C) 홍보 패키지
(D) 회사 손익 보고서

172-175는 다음 기사에 관한 문제입니다.

Hilltop사, 몇몇 새로운 지점 개점 예정

11월 15일—Lillian Jones 전무이사에 따르면, Hilltop사는 올해가 끝나기 전에 일곱 군데의 신규 서점을 열 준비를 하고 있다. — [1] —. 모두 런던에 위치한 이 새로운 매장들은 영국 내 Hilltop사의 총 매장 수를 30개로 만들 것이다. 최신 개점은 12월의 일반적으로 높은 매출을 활용하도록 시기를 맞추었다. — [2] —.

이 소식은 스웨덴인 억만장자 소유주 Nicholas Holmberg가 Hilltop사를 Capitalia 투자사에 1억 4천만 파운드로 매각한 후 전해졌다. Mr. Holmberg는 6년 전 Horizon Media사로부터 5천 5백만 파운드에 그 회사를 인수했다. — [3] —.

"저희는 탄탄한 사업을 하고 있습니다."라고 Ms. Jones는 말한다. "다른 소매업체와 달리, 저희 제품은 한결같이 잘 팔립니다. 영국에서 소매 자산을 보유하는 데 관심이 있는 투자자에게 있어, 저희는 매력적인 매물입니다. 저희는 또한 명백히 성장하고 있습니다." — [4] —.

Ms. Jones에 따르면, Hilltop사의 성공 비결은 그녀가 이전에 독립 서적상으로서 배운 경영 방식이다. "저는 저희 관리자들이 '적을수록 좋다'는 접근 방식을 취하도록 권고합니다."라고 그녀는 말했다. "고객들은 책을 둘러볼 수 있는 편안한 분위기를 원합니다. 저희가 해야 할 일은 책에 열정적인 직원을 고용하고 책장을 잘 채워 두는 것뿐입니다."

---

172 Mr. Holmberg에 대해 추론될 수 있는 것은?
(A) Ms. Jones를 Horizon Media사로부터 고용했다.
(B) 스웨덴에 추가적인 매장을 개점할 계획이다.
(C) Hilltop사 인수 비용을 위해 자금을 대출받았다.
(D) 초기 투자금액을 두 배 이상 늘렸다.

173 Hilltop사는 왜 12월에 새로운 매장을 개점하는가?
(A) 투자자들로부터 압력을 받고 있다.
(B) 1월에 매각을 마무리하려고 목표한다.
(C) 연말에 책을 더 많이 판매한다.
(D) 연간 수익성 목표를 달성할 수 있었다.

174 Ms. Jones는 Hilltop사의 성공이 무엇 덕분이라고 하는가?
(A) 빠른 확장
(B) 현명한 가격 책정
(C) 잦은 할인
(D) 효과적인 리더십

175 [1], [2], [3], [4]로 표시된 위치 중, 다음 문장이 들어갈 곳으로 가장 적절한 것은?

"이는 내년에 15군데의 추가적인 매장을 포함하는 적극적인 성장 계획의 일환이다."

(A) [1]
(B) [2]
(C) [3]
(D) [4]

176-180은 다음 회람과 작업 견적서에 관한 문제입니다.

수신: Tara Quincy
발신: Selma Hastings
제목: 해리스버그 사무실 보수 공사 업데이트
날짜: 1월 16일

Ms. Quincy께,

저희 해리스버그 사무실의 2층 보수 공사가 다음 달에 시작되도록 진행 중입니다. 최근 전화 회담에서 논의한 대로, 건축가는 재설계된 공간이 건축 법규 요구사항을 충족할 것임을 확인했습니다. 또한, 리모델링 공사를 감독할 자격을 갖춘 종합 시공사를 찾은 것 같습니다. 저는 Bushong 건설사의 담당자에게 저희를 위해 자세한 작업 견적을 내 달라고 요청해 두었습니다. 이것은 제가 받는 대로 당신의 사무실에 전달될 것입니다. 모든 것이 제대로 되어 있다면, 저희는 곧 시작할 수 있을 것입니다.

특히 우려되는 것은 회의실을 위한 유리 세공인데, 이것은 저희가 원하는 현대적 외관을 실현하는 데 결정적일 것입니다. 저는 곧 시외에서 일이 있긴 하지만, 프로젝트의 그 부분을 마치는 날 제가 직접 확인할 수 있도록 일정을 조정했습니다.

문의사항이나 우려가 있으시다면 저에게 전화 주세요.

Bushong 건설사
더 밝은 미래를 짓습니다

Lincoln로 1466번지
해리스버그, 펜실베이니아
17111
555-717-6443

****

리모델링 견적서

Elmore 광고회사
3번가 21번지, 2층
해리스버그, 펜실베이니아
15044
555-382-0987

참고: 아래 나열된 비용은 재료비와 인건비를 모두 반영합니다. 최종 비용은 건축 자재 및 부품의 시장 가격에 따라 최대 10퍼센트까지 변동될 수 있습니다.

작업 설명	날짜	인건비	재료비
철거: 주방 붙박이 설비 및 사무실 칸막이 제거	2월 12-13일	6,000달러	해당 없음
전기 및 배관: 욕실 붙박이 설비 교체, 전체 배선	2월 14-21일	30,000달러	15,000달러
판 설치: 목재 판 및 창유리 설치	2월 23일-3월 1일	22,500달러	40,000달러
장식: 페인트칠, 기타 장식	3월 2-3일	2,000달러	10,000달러
		소계	125,500달러

176 Ms. Hastings는 왜 회람을 작성했는가?
(A) 회의의 결론을 요약하기 위해
(B) 문제에 대한 해결책을 제시하기 위해
(C) 일에 관한 세부 사항을 제공하기 위해
(D) 프로젝트의 최종 결과를 논의하기 위해

177 Ms. Hastings는 왜 시공사를 고용해야 하는가?
(A) 두 번째 지점을 설계하기 위해
(B) 건축 법규 요구사항을 배우기 위해
(C) 사무실에 대한 손상을 수리하기 위해
(D) 재정비 프로젝트를 감독하기 위해

178 작업 견적서에서, 1문단 첫 번째 줄의 단어 "reflect"는 의미상 –와 가장 가깝다.
(A) 재생산하다
(B) 나타내다
(C) 숙고하다
(D) 중재하다

179 작업의 어떤 단계가 예상 비용보다 더 많이 들지 않을 것 같은가?
(A) 철거
(B) 전기 및 배관
(C) 판 설치
(D) 장식

180 Ms. Hastings는 언제 작업을 직접 점검할 것인가?
(A) 2월 13일에
(B) 2월 21일에
(C) 3월 1일에
(D) 3월 3일에

181-185는 다음 광고와 후기에 관한 문제입니다.

Sightline 여행사				로그인 정보: Jeremy Turner

홈 │ 항공편 │ 호텔 │ 차량 │ **패키지** │ 크루즈 │ 활동

패키지 > 자메이카 휴가

검색

출발: Cardiff, 영국	목적지: 자메이카 (전 지역)
날짜: 6월 11일-6월 16일	객실 종류: 일반 더블

결과:

Kings 호텔 Montego Bay, 자메이카 인당 1,423파운드 400개 이상의 고급 스위트룸, 수영장 및 스파, 호텔 내 식당, 그리고 야간 라이브 음악 공연이 있는 해안가의 아름다운 건물	Friendlies 리조트 Montego Bay, 자메이카 인당 1,324파운드 모든 편의 시설을 갖춘 600개 이상의 객실 및 원룸(일부는 바다 경치를 볼 수 있음) 중에서 선택, 그리고 투어 및 활동 이용 가능
Spectrum 호텔 및 리조트 Port Antonio, 자메이카 인당 1,298파운드 850개 이상의 넓은 객실을 갖추고 여행 통상경비가 전체 포함된, 가족 친화적인 해변 건물	Skywave 리조트 Negril, 자메이카 인당 1,102파운드 해변에 접근성이 좋고, 수영장, 그리고 호텔 내 식당이 있는 신축 건물

표시된 패키지에는 항공편, 호텔, 세금, 그리고 수수료가 포함됩니다. 우려 사항이 있으시면, 555-0354로 고객 서비스에 연락하시거나 cs@sightlinetravel.com으로 이메일을 보내십시오.

www.traveltroves.com/reviews

대행사: Sightline 여행사
평가: 별 세 개
후기 작성자: Jeremy Turner (검증된 여행자)

저는 최근 자메이카로 6일간 휴가를 다녀왔습니다. 제 경험상 일반적으로 여행 패키지 품질이 좋은 서비스 회사인 Sightline 여행사를 이용했고, 이번 여행도 예외는 아니었습니다. 최근 물가가 상승하여, 이런 고급 건물, 특히 지난 해 안에 지어진 곳에서 저렴한 관광 숙소를 찾는 것은 드문 일입니다. 모든 것이 반짝이도록 깨끗했습니다. 그룹 활동은 즐거우면서도 수영장 근처에서 휴식을 취할 충분한 시간 또한 남겨 두었습니다.

그러나, 모든 면에서 완벽한 휴가는 아니었습니다. 연결 항공편이 지연되어서, 저희는 킹스턴의 공항에 늦게 도착했습니다. 이는 저희가 짐을 챙겼을 때쯤에, 숙소로 가는 단체 셔틀이 이미 떠났다는 것을 의미했습니다. 제가 Sightline사에 연락하려고 했을 때, 여러 번 전화하고 몇 개의 문자 메시지를 남겼음에도 불구하고 누구와도 연락이 닿지 않았다는 것을 제외하면, 이것은 큰 문제가 되지 않았을 것입니다. 결국, 저는 사비로 택시를 타야 했습니다. 이것이 저희의 여행을 망치지는 않았지만, 저는 Sightline사로부터 더 많은 것을 기대했습니다.

181 광고에 따르면, 모든 숙소의 공통점은 무엇인가?
(A) 해변가의 위치
(B) 수영장
(C) 라이브 공연
(D) 가까운 식사 선택지

182 패키지들에 대해 언급된 것은?
(A) 6월에 여행해야 한다.
(B) 비행편을 포함한다.
(C) 모두 같은 도시에 있다.
(D) 특별히 가족을 위한 것이다.

183 Mr. Turner는 휴가 동안 어디에서 묵은 것 같은가?
(A) Kings 호텔
(B) Friendlies 리조트
(C) Spectrum 호텔 및 리조트
(D) Skywave 리조트

184 Mr. Turner에 대해 암시된 것은?
(A) 혼자서 자메이카로 여행했다.
(B) 스위트룸에서 6박 묵었다.
(C) 그룹 활동을 위해 호텔에 돈을 지불했다.
(D) 이전에 Sightline 여행사에서 예약했다.

185 Mr. Turner는 왜 그의 여행에 불만족했는가?
(A) 체크인이 한 시간 지연되었다.
(B) 고객 서비스가 응답하지 않았다.
(C) 그의 짐이 항공사에 의해 분실되었다.
(D) 셔틀 서비스가 시간을 지키지 않았다.

186-190은 다음 일정표와 두 이메일에 관한 문제입니다.

Lansdowne 센터
Pacific 출판 컨퍼런스
연사 일정 – 8월 2일

연사	세미나	시간	강의실
Gary West	저작권법 개정	오전 9시 – 오전 10시	209
Kara Adams	자체 출판 서비스	오전 10시 30분 – 오전 11시 30분	105
Chad Lewis	온라인 구독 모델	오후 1시 – 오후 2시	308
Eileen Daniels	해외 라이선스 계약	오후 2시 30분 – 오후 3시 30분	109

각 세미나를 위한 공간이 한정되어 있으므로, 컨퍼런스 참석자들은 사전에 등록해야 합니다. 세미나에 참가하려면, 여기에서 등록 양식을 다운로드하고 작성한 문서를 g.beale@ppc.com으로 컨퍼런스 담당자 Greta Beale에게 이메일로 보내십시오.

수신: Owen Williams <o.williams@eastpress.com>
발신: Tara Liu <t.liu@eastpress.com>
날짜: 7월 27일
제목: Pacific 출판 컨퍼런스

Mr. Williams께,

Pacific 출판 컨퍼런스에서 우리 회사를 대표할 기회를 주셔서 다시 한번 감사드립니다. 제안하신 모든 세미나에 등록할 수 있었어요. 월요일에 신청했고 오늘 확인을 받았습니다.

유감스럽게도, 저는 컨퍼런스를 위한 이동 일정을 변경해야 합니다. 원래, 저는 8월 1일에 로스앤젤레스에서 출발하기로 되어 있었습니다. 그러나, 저는 이제 그날 포틀랜드에서 일정이 있습니다. 포틀랜드에서 시애틀로 가는 기차는 터코마에서 오랫동안 경유하기 때문에, 차를 빌려서 세미나로 운전해서 가고 싶습니다. 이 추가 비용을 승인받을 수 있을까요?

Tara Liu 드림

수신: Greta Beale <g.beale@ppc.com>
발신: Lloyd Green <l.green@lansdowne.com>
날짜: 8월 1일
제목: 강의실 변경

Ms. Beale께,

내일 예정된 세미나와 관련해서 연락드립니다. 방금 기술자와 대화했는데 건물에 즉시 해결되어야 하는 전기 문제가 있다고 알려주었습니다. 이에 따라, 내일 하루 중 상당 기간 동안 2층의 전원이 차단될 것이고, 그곳에서 진행될 예정이었던 세미나는 옮겨져야 합니다. 다행히, 한 층 위의 309호가 같은 시간대에 이용 가능합니다. 수용 인원이 150명이므로, 세미나 참가자들을 위한 좌석은 충분할 것입니다. 그리고 물론, 저희 직원들에게 변경과 관련한 표지판을 게시하도록 지시할 수 있습니다. 이 상황이 야기할 수 있는 불편에 대해 사과드립니다.

Lloyd Green 드림
Lansdowne 센터 건물 서비스 담당자

186 세미나에 대해 언급된 것은?
(A) 수용 인원이 같은 강의실에서 열릴 것이다.
(B) 출판사 직원들에 의해 안내된다.
(C) 각각 국제적 출판 주제를 다룰 것이다.
(D) 같은 기간 동안 지속하도록 예정되었다.

187 Ms. Liu는 월요일에 무엇을 한 것 같은가?
(A) Mr. Williams를 위한 업무를 완료했다
(B) 여행 일정표를 업데이트했다
(C) 항공권 예약을 변경했다
(D) Ms. Beale에게 양식을 제출했다

188 Pacific 출판 컨퍼런스는 어디에서 개최될 것인가?
(A) 로스앤젤레스에서
(B) 포틀랜드에서
(C) 시애틀에서
(D) 터코마에서

189 어떤 세미나가 새로운 장소로 옮겨질 것인가?
(A) 저작권법 개정
(B) 자체 출판 서비스
(C) 온라인 구독 모델
(D) 해외 라이선스 계약

190 Mr. Green은 무엇을 해주겠다고 제안하는가?
(A) 강의실 요금을 환불한다
(B) 행사장의 크기를 확인한다
(C) 행사를 위한 추가적인 직원을 고용한다
(D) 공고가 게시되도록 준비한다

191-195는 다음 광고, 영수증, 웹페이지에 관한 문제입니다.

10년이 넘도록, Serenity는 뉴욕 지역에서 최고의 미용실이었습니다. 저희의 재능 있는 스타일리스트들과 미용사들은 모든 범위의 서비스와 시술을 제공합니다.

저희는 맨해튼 시내에 있는 Plaza Square 건물로의 이전이 이제 완료되었음을 알려드리게 되어 기쁩니다. 새로운 공간은 저희의 이전 공간보다 훨씬 더 넓고 고급스럽습니다. 이사를 축하하기 위해, 7월에는 헤어 서비스에 15퍼센트 할인을 제공하고 8월에는 네일과 얼굴 시술에 10퍼센트 할인을 제공할 것입니다.

555-0393으로 연락하시거나 저희 웹사이트를 방문하여 예약하세요. 곧 뵙길 바랍니다!

Serenity
8번가 101-1456번지, 뉴욕

555-0393
www.serenitysalon.com

날짜: 7월 25일 · 영수증 번호: 0098
고객: Sarah Broughton · 전화번호: 555-9998

헤어 커트		66.00달러
네일 아트		45.00달러
얼굴 크림		40.00달러
페디큐어		30.00달러
	세금	18.30달러
	총액	199.30달러

위 가격에는 해당되는 모든 할인이 포함됩니다.

저희가 개선할 수 있는 제안사항이 있으신가요? 그렇다면, 꼭 저희 웹사이트를 방문하여 의견을 남겨 주세요. 감사의 표시로, 다음에 미용실을 방문하시면 무료 스킨케어 제품을 드립니다!

Serenity
오늘 아름다운 기분을 느껴보세요!

소개	서비스	예약	의견

고객 이름: Sarah Broughton
날짜: 8월 1일

전반적으로, 저는 미용실 방문에 만족했습니다. 새로운 장소는 매우 따뜻한 분위기입니다. 대기실은 아름답게 꾸며져 있고, 직원들의 평온한 음악 선곡이 매우 좋았습니다. 제가 교류했던 모두가 정중하고 전문적이었는데, 특히 제 헤어 스타일리스트였던 Melina가 그랬습니다. 그녀는 대화하기 편했고 짧은 헤어 스타일에 대해 좋은 추천을 해주었습니다. 그녀는 저에게 그런 스타일을 시도해 보도록 설득했습니다. 보통 제 머리는 어깨 아래까지 오기 때문에 저에겐 꽤 다른 모습이지만, 아주 맘에 듭니다. 그런데, 한 가지 추천이 있습니다. 지역의 많은 다른 미용실은 고객들에게 커피와 신선한 주스를 제공합니다. 미용실 방문은 때때로 몇 시간 동안 지속될 수도 있으니, 다과를 제공받을 수 있다면 좋을 것입니다.

191 Serenity 미용실에 대해 언급되지 않은 것은?
(A) 10년도 더 전에 개업했다.
(B) 새로운 위치로 이동했다.
(C) 다른 도시에 지점을 열 계획이다.
(D) 온라인 예약을 받는다.

192 영수증에 기재된 가격 중 어떤 것이 할인되었는가?
(A) 66.00달러
(B) 45.00달러
(C) 40.00달러
(D) 30.00달러

193 Ms. Broughton은 다음 Serenity 미용실 방문 때 무엇을 받을 것인가?
(A) 서비스 할인
(B) 무료 시술
(C) 개인 맞춤형 상담
(D) 무료 상품

194 웹페이지에서 추론될 수 있는 것은?
(A) Ms. Broughton은 Melina를 스타일리스트로 요청했다.
(B) Ms. Broughton은 보통 머리가 더 길다.
(C) Serenity 미용실은 웹사이트에서 스타일 팁을 제공한다.
(D) Serenity 미용실은 대기실을 확장했다.

195 Ms. Broughton은 Serenity 미용실에 무엇을 제안하는가?
(A) 고객들에게 음료를 제공하는 것
(B) 일부 음악 선곡을 변경하는 것
(C) 다른 미용실과 제휴하는 것
(D) 영업 시간을 연장하는 것

196-200은 다음 기사, 회람, 일정표에 관한 문제입니다.

---

*Chicago Weekly*지 편집장 퇴임

영향력 있는 무료 신문 *Chicago Weekly*지의 편집장 Robert Pearl이 9월 1일부로 은퇴할 것이라고 어제 발표했다.

아직 후임자는 지명되지 않았지만, 다수의 내부 후보들이 고려되고 있다. 소식통에 따르면 Mr. Pearl은 신문의 섹션 편집자들 중 한 명을 후임으로 선발할 것이며, 8월 15일까지 결정을 내릴 것이라고 한다.

Mr. Pearl은 *Chicago Weekly*지의 인지도를 크게 높여, 한때 잘 알려져 있지 않았던 이 신문을 시에서 가장 널리 회자되는 간행물 중 하나로 만들었다. 재임 기간 내내, 그는 능력 있는 기자들을 유치하는 재능이 있었고, 그들에게 획기적인 소재를 추적하도록 자유를 주었다. 그가 편집장으로 있었던 8년 동안, 신문의 발행 부수는 1만 5천 부에서 10만 부로 증가했다. 그것은 또한 지역 정치와 문화에 대한 보도로 권위 있는 상을 수상했다.

수신: 전 직원
발신: Karen Levinson
제목: 소개
날짜: 8월 14일

직원들께,

Mr. Pearl이 *Chicago Weekly*지의 새 편집장으로 저를 선택했다는 것을 발표하게 되어 영광입니다. 9월 1일부터, 저는 향후 간행물 기획, 기사 배정, 우리 사업팀과의 정기적인 회의, 그리고 주간 직원회의 주관을 포함하여 그의 모든 업무를 맡게 될 것입니다.

지금부터, 신문이 어떤 방향으로 나아가야 할지에 대한 제안이 있다면, 제게 이메일을 보내 주십시오. 모든 새로운 아이디어를 환영합니다. 또한 오늘 오후에는 섹션 편집자들과 만나 앞으로 우리의 목표에 대해 이야기할 것입니다.

추가로, 저는 매주 근처 식당에서 공개 점심을 진행할 것입니다. 첫 번째 시간에는, 신문의 인쇄판을 위한 새로운 잠재적 디자인을 공유할 것입니다. 모든 직원들이 초대되었으니, 거기서 뵙길 기대하겠습니다!

Karen Levinson 드림

KAREN LEVINSON 일정표: 8월 14일 주

8월 14일 월요일	오전 8시: Robert Pearl과 회의
	오후 2시: 섹션 편집자들과 회의
8월 15일 화요일	오전 9시: 사업팀과 회의
	오후 12시: 공개 점심
	오후 2시: 전속 기자들에게 연설
8월 16일 수요일	오전 8시: Robert Pearl과 회의
	오후 1시: Ms. Bradford와 점심
	오후 3시: *Village Post*지와 인터뷰
8월 17일 목요일	오전 10시: 섹션 편집자들과 브런치
	오후 4시: 10월호 기사 브레인스토밍 회의
8월 18일 금요일	오전 11시: 이사회와 회의
	오후 12시: Marshall's 식당에서 점심
	오후 4시: 주간 직원회의

196 기사의 주 목적은 무엇인가?
(A) 사임하는 관리자의 경력을 논의하기 위해
(B) 간행물의 일부를 비평하기 위해
(C) 신문을 위한 새로운 기자들을 구하기 위해
(D) 새로 고용된 편집자를 발표하기 위해

197 *Chicago Weekly*지에 대해 언급된 것은?
(A) 온라인 플랫폼이 없다.
(B) 오로지 정치에만 집중한다.
(C) 수년간 더 많은 독자들을 유치했다.
(D) 편집진의 규모를 늘렸다.

198 Ms. Levinson에 대해 추론될 수 있는 것은?
(A) 기한이 지난 후에 선발되었다.
(B) *Chicago Weekly*지의 한 섹션을 편집했다.
(C) 이전에 다른 간행물에서 일했다.
(D) 주요 언론상을 수상했다.

199 Ms. Levinson은 직원들에게 무엇을 하도록 권유하는가?
(A) 익명의 댓글을 남긴다
(B) Mr. Pearl이 떠나기 전에 작별을 고한다
(C) 그들의 섹션 편집자에게 이메일로 기사를 보낸다
(D) 간행물의 미래에 대한 아이디어를 공유한다

200 새로운 디자인은 무슨 요일에 공개될 것인가?
(A) 월요일
(B) 화요일
(C) 수요일
(D) 목요일

* 무료 해설은 해커스토익(Hackers.co.kr)에서
다운로드 받을 수 있습니다.

* QR 코드로
바로가기

PART 5

101 모금 행사의 주최자들은 자원봉사자들에게 배부하기 위한 해야 할 일을 적은 목록을 편집하고 있다.

102 Mr. Chen은 올해에 승진이 있을 것이라고 생각하지 않았기 때문에 승진을 해서 놀랐다.

103 보고서가 아직 배부되지 않았기 때문에, Ms. Pantel은 그녀가 찾은 오류를 수정할 시간이 있었다.

104 슈퍼마켓의 재고가 매우 적어서, 바쁜 주말 전에 물건들을 다시 채워 넣어야 했다.

105 Jim's Burgers의 시내 지점은 수익 면에서 이 체인의 다른 지점들을 꾸준히 능가해 왔다.

106 마케팅 부서는 더 다양한 독자층에 영향을 주기 위한 노력으로 소셜 미디어 캠페인을 시작했다.

107 투숙객들은 야외 식당뿐만 아니라 리조트의 새로운 수영장을 즐겼다.

108 직원 평가는 보통 11월에 실행되지만 12월까지 연기될 수도 있다.

109 그 건물의 거주자들은 수리 기간 동안 임시 거처를 찾아야만 했다.

110 그 운용성 거리 추적 장치는 온라인 광고가 그렇다고 하는 만큼 더할 나위 없이 정밀하다.

111 일단 계정이 만들어지면, 사용자들은 로그인 이름과 비밀번호를 재입력하는 것이 요구될 것이다.

112 최근 의뢰된 연구에 따르면, 버뱅크시의 대기 오염 수준은 사상 최고치다.

113 무역 박람회 컨벤션 센터는 지하철역 바로 옆에 편리하게 위치해 있어서, 쉽게 접근할 수 있게 한다.

114 Ms. Williams는 그래픽 디자인 팀에게 새로운 회사 로고에 대한 아이디어를 제안하도록 5월 17일까지 시간을 주었다.

115 새 면허증을 위해 양식을 제출하는 신청자들은 양식이 완전히 작성되었는지 확인해야 한다.

116 주요한 작업 현장 근처에 위험한 화학 물질을 보관하는 것은 그곳에서 근무하는 직원들에게 잠재적으로 위험한 상황을 일으킨다.

117 Health One Hospice의 이사회는 그 기관이 비슷한 가치관을 공유하는 협력 단체와 합병하기를 바란다.

118 캐스팅 감독은 청자들이 제품을 구매하도록 설득할 수 있는 매력적인 목소리 톤을 가진 배우를 찾고 있었다.

119 회사는 어제저녁에 합병 합의와 관련하여 성명을 발표했다.

120 연회는 다섯 명의 직원들에게 영예를 주기 위해 열렸는데, 그들 모두는 회사에서 20년 이상 근무했다.

121 회사 규정은 예기치 않은 상황이 없다면 모든 직원들이 오전 9시 30분 전에 그들의 자리에 있을 것을 요구한다.

122 귀하께서 머무시는 동안 어떠한 문의라도 있을 경우를 대비하여 호텔 직원들이 체크인 데스크에 배치되어 있습니다.

123 새로운 자전거 안전 규정은 교통부에 의해 막 제정되었다.

124 작가 Sylvia Feldman은 그녀의 베스트셀러 논픽션 소설인 *21 Ravens*로 인해 출판사 협회상 후보로 지명되었다.

125 그 광고는 회사의 그 누가 예상한 것보다 더 인기 있어서, 온라인에 게시된 지 몇 시간 만에 수백만 조회 수를 모았다.

126 모금 행사의 말미에, Dr. Adams는 기부자들에게 지역 병원 지원에 대한 그들의 관대함에 감사를 표했다.

127 그 일자리는 건강 보험과 3주의 유급 휴가를 포함하여 여러 가지의 상당한 혜택을 수반한다.

128 아파트의 보증금이 지불되면, 세입자는 즉시 이사 올 수 있다.

129 그의 고용 계약 조건에 따라, Mr. Allen은 초과 근무 시간에 대해 정규 임금의 1.5배를 받는다.

130 이사회는 은퇴하는 회사 회장을 누가 대신할 것인지 결정하기 위해 투표를 했다.

PART 6

131-134는 다음 공고에 관한 문제입니다.

> 알림: 모든 Eddington's 멤버십 회원들
>
> 131 Eddington's는 멤버십 프로그램에 변화를 도입할 예정입니다. 저희는 포인트 적립 내역서가 회원들께 발송되는 빈도를 조정할 것입니다. 1월 1일부터, 내역서는 연 4회가 아니라 6개월마다 우편으로 보내질 것입니다. 132 이 변경 사항과 관계없이, 회원들은 계속해서 www.eddingtons.com/members에 로그인해서 최신 정보를 알아보실 수 있습니다. 133 여러분의 온라인 계정을 통해 누적된 포인트를 확인하고 포인트를 교환하여 어떤 보상을 받을 수 있는지 알아보실 수 있습니다. 또는 영업시간 동안 555-4955로 전화하시면, 저희가 여러분이 얼마를 보유하고 있으신지 알려드리겠습니다. 134 또한, 여러분은 Eddington's 백화점의 서비스 카운터에 들르실 수 있고, 저희 직원 중 한 명이 현재의 총점을 알려드릴 것입니다.

135-138은 다음 후기에 관한 문제입니다.

> 여행 가방 후기: Mercury Travel Pro 2 휴대용 여행 가방
>
> 멋진 외관 이외에, 이 여행 가방에 대해 제가 가장 먼저 주목한 것은 이것의 무게였습니다. 겨우 2.9킬로그램으로, 이것은 놀랍도록 가볍습니다. 135 그런데도 이 여행 가방은 또한 매우 튼튼하기까지 합니다. 가방의 단단한 바깥면은 붐비는 현대의 공항이 가할 수 있는 그 어떤 것도 견딜 만큼 충분히 튼튼합니다.
>
> 136 여행 가방을 이동시키는 것도 상당히 쉽습니다. 137 손잡이는 잡기 편한 부드러운 고무 그립을 특징으로 하며, 가방의 두 개의 조용한 바퀴는 단단한 지면 위를 부드럽게 굴러갑니다.
>
> 제가 높이 평가하는 또 다른 기능은 잠금장치입니다. 그것은 네 자릿수 조합으로 이루어져 있으며 튼튼한 강철로 만들어져 있습니다. 138 이것은 제가 여행하고 있을 때 제 소지품이 안전하도록 보장해줍니다.

139-142는 다음 기사에 관한 문제입니다.

> 시 공무원들이 시내 건물의 개발업체 선정에 거의 다다르다
>
> Marinville시 공무원들은 Halpern 건물을 개조할 개발업체들의 최종 명단을 만들었다. 139 최초 25개에서 이제는 단 세 회사만이 남았다.
>
> 사업이 처음 시작되었을 때 규정된 대로, 경쟁에 남겨진 회사들은 이제 그들이 연초에 제출했던 계획에 더 많은 세부 사항을 추가해야 한다. 140 곧 있을 발표에서, 그들은 이사회의 모든 리모델링 요구 사항을 만족시킬 수 있다는 것을 보여주어야 한다. 141 제안서에는 전체 예산도 포함되어야만 한다. 142 "만약 모든 일이 순조롭게 진행된다면," Marinville시 당국의 책임자인 Brian Schmidt가 말하기를, "저희는 가장 인상적인 후보자를 선정하여, 계약서를 작성하고, 연내에 작업을 시작할 것입니다."

143-146은 다음 이메일에 관한 문제입니다.

수신: Anthony Lilly <anthonylilly@hotline.com>
발신: 고객 서비스 <cs@comprehensiveautoins.com>
날짜: 11월 14일
제목: 이름 변경

143 저희 기록은 귀하께서 저희의 자동차 보험 증권을 보유하고 계신다는 것을 보여주고 있습니다. **144** 저희는 고객들에게 지속적으로 회사 사업에 대한 최신 정보를 알게 한다는 점을 자랑스럽게 여기고 있으며, 이에 따라 회사 이름을 Comprehensive Auto Insurance사에서 Complete Auto and Life Insurance사로 변경할 것임을 알려드리기 위해 이메일을 씁니다.

다음 달부터 저희의 모든 소통 수단에는 새로운 이름으로 라벨이 붙을 것입니다. 귀하께서는 청구서, 이메일, 편지, 신청 양식, 그리고 웹사이트에서 저희의 새로운 이름을 보시게 될 것입니다. **145** 저희는 보험 증권 문서에 있는 저희 회사명도 수정할 것입니다.

이번에, 귀하께서는 생명 보험을 갱신할 기회를 가지기를 원하실 수도 있습니다. **146** 약속을 잡기 위해 이 이메일에 답장을 해주시면, 직원으로부터 연락을 받으실 것입니다.

고객 서비스 드림
Comprehensive Auto Insurance사

PART 7

147-148은 다음 광고에 관한 문제입니다.

Shoe Gold에서 연례 세일을 합니다!

신발 한 켤레를 사고, 다음 한 켤레는 40퍼센트 할인을 받으세요
세 번째 신발은 50퍼센트 할인을 받아 구매하세요
네 번째 신발은 60퍼센트 할인을 받아 구매하세요

저희는 최신 유명 브랜드 신발을 할인가에 판매합니다. 당신은 남성과 여성을 위한 더 나은 종류의 스타일, 색상, 그리고 사이즈를 찾을 수 없을 것입니다. 세일은 8월 14일에 끝나므로, 오늘 쇼핑을 하러 오십시오!

매일 오전 10시부터 오후 8시까지 엽니다.
현금, 수표, 신용카드나 직불카드를 받습니다.
추가 10퍼센트 할인을 받기 위해 Shoe Gold 신용카드 계좌를 개설하세요.

Shoe Gold 지점:

1223번지 Riverside로	807번지 12번 주간 고속도로
미니애폴리스,	세인트폴,
미네소타주 55401	미네소타주 55519

147 광고되고 있는 것은 무엇인가?
(A) 상점의 새로운 장소
(B) 신발에 대한 판촉 할인
(C) 가게의 연장된 영업시간
(D) 취소된 상품에 대한 환불

148 Shoe Gold에 대해 언급되지 않은 것은?
(A) 수표로 지불하는 것을 허용할 것이다.
(B) 자체 브랜드의 신용카드를 가지고 있다.
(C) 경쟁사의 가격에 맞출 것이다.
(D) 두 개의 다른 지점에서 상점을 운영한다.

149-150은 다음 메시지 대화문에 관한 문제입니다.

Alycia Kent [오후 3시 13분]
방금 제가 비품실에서 인쇄용지를 좀 가져오던 중이었는데, 모든 것이 잘 정돈되어 있다는 것을 알아차렸어요. 자원해서 비품실이 정리되고 재고가 채워져 있도록 유지해줘서 정말 고마워요.

George Blain [오후 3시 17분]
감사해요. 네, 비품실이 다소 지저분하고 체계적이지 못했지만, 사무용품이 떨어지지 않도록 제가 모든 것을 재배치하고 새로운 시스템을 만들었어요. 유일한 문제는 저희가 가지고 있는 비품의 수량을 고려했을 때 비품실이 꽤 좁다는 거예요.

Alycia Kent [오후 3시 20분]
아마 다른 방을 사용해야 하겠네요. 직원 휴게실 근처에 비어 있는 사무실이 하나 있어요. 거기에 사무용품을 대신 보관해도 될지 제가 물어볼게요.

George Blain [오후 3시 24분]
그건 도움이 되겠네요. 서두를 건 없지만, 혹시 그게 가능할지 알아봐 주시면 감사하겠어요.

149 Mr. Blain은 최근에 무엇을 했는가?
(A) 직원에게 몇 가지 관리 업무를 배정했다
(B) 보관 구역에 있는 비품을 정리했다
(C) 재고 시스템에 관한 보고서를 작성했다
(D) 직원 휴게실의 가구를 정리했다

150 오후 3시 24분에, Mr. Blain이 "That would help"라고 썼을 때 그가 의도한 것은?
(A) 새로운 공급업체를 찾는 것은 비용을 줄여줄 것이다.
(B) 사무용품 수량을 제한하는 것은 도움이 되는 제안이다.
(C) 더 큰 휴게실을 가지는 것은 이로울 것이다.
(D) 비품실을 이전하는 것은 좋은 해결책이다.

151-152는 다음 공고에 관한 문제입니다.

Boardwalk Industries사의 직원 게시판 메시지

구합니다: 상태가 좋은 중고차
연락처: Roy Long, 내선 8113번
게시글은 유효합니다: 6월 1일 – 30일

저는 가을에 대학교에 가게 될 제 아들을 위해 상태가 좋은 중고차를 찾고 있습니다. 저는 연비가 좋은 문이 4개인 차량을 구매하고 싶습니다. 큰 수리를 필요로 하지 않는 한 차량의 브랜드는 중요하지 않습니다. 별로 심각하지 않은 찌그러진 곳과 긁힌 자국은 제가 수리할 수 있는 능력이 있기 때문에 괜찮습니다. 제 아들의 안전을 위한 주안점으로 잠금 방지 장치가 된 브레이크와 에어백이 있는 것을 선호합니다. 만약 4년에서 8년 정도가 되고 나열된 다른 기준을 충족하는 차량이 있으시다면, 위의 번호로 전화 주십시오.

151 공고는 왜 쓰였는가?
(A) 중고 차량을 팔기 위해
(B) 수리 서비스를 광고하기 위해
(C) 팔려고 내놓은 차량을 찾기 위해
(D) 임대 규정을 알리기 위해

152 Mr. Long에 대해 사실이 아닌 것은?
(A) 안전에 대해 염려한다.
(B) 특정 모델의 차량을 선호한다.
(C) 가벼운 수리를 할 수 있다.
(D) 대학교에 다닐 아들이 있다.

153-155는 다음 기사에 관한 문제입니다.

CCT NEWS사의 변화

국내에서 가장 많이 보는 케이블 뉴스 방송국인 CCT News사가 막 Greg O'Connell을 새로운 오후 8시 앵커로 고용했습니다. Mr. O'Connell은 20년간 근무한 후 지난달에 퇴직한 앵커 Pauline Fields를 대신해서 인계받을 것이다.

Mr. O'Connell은 폭넓은 업계 경력을 가지고 있다. 그는 *Cork County*

*Ledger*지의 지역 신문 기자로 시작했고, 그러고 나서 5년간 헤드라인 뉴스를 편집하는 것으로 나아갔다. 그 이후에, Mr. O'Connell은 지역 텔레비전 방송국에서 보조 뉴스 앵커로서의 일자리를 구했다. 그의 방송은 점점 더 인기 있어졌고, 2년 후에 그는 WQZ Nightly News의 메인 앵커 자리를 제안받았다. 그는 10년간 근무 후, CCT News사에서의 새 일자리를 위해 WQZ를 떠났다.

CCT News사의 사장인 George McDonough는 그들의 새로운 앵커로 인해 기쁘지 않을 수가 없다고 말한다. "저는 WQZ사에서 제작자로 일하는 동안 Greg를 처음 만났고 그 이후로 계속 그의 팬이었습니다,"라고 그는 말한다. "그는 일에 있어서 카리스마와 부정을 철저히 파헤치는 참된 정신 둘 다를 갖춘 본보기가 되는 뉴스 프로 진행자입니다."

Mr. O'Connell이 첫 번째로 방송하는 밤은 5월 7일이 될 것이다. 그때까지는, Richard Marshall이 임시 앵커로서 대신할 것이다.

153 기사의 주요 주제는 무엇인가?
(A) 최근에 제작된 뉴스 쇼
(B) 퇴직하는 케이블 방송 제작자
(C) 새로 고용된 직원
(D) 방송 시간의 변화

154 Mr. McDonough에 대해 암시되는 것은?
(A) *Cork County Ledger*지의 사장이다.
(B) 임시 앵커로 일하고 있다.
(C) Ms. Fields의 자리를 인계받을 것이다.
(D) 이전에 Mr. O'Connell과 일했다.

155 Mr. O'Connell의 가장 최근 직업은 무엇이었는가?
(A) 전속 기자
(B) 웹사이트 편집자
(C) 뉴스 진행자
(D) 제작자

156-157은 다음 양식에 관한 문제입니다.

Atkins 대학교
초청 연사 신청 양식

이 양식은 행사 4주 전에 작성하여 제출되어야 합니다. 이 양식이 학생 활동 사무실에 의해 승인된 후에야 연사 참여가 홍보될 수 있는 점 참고 바랍니다. 요청 시 같은 사무실에서 임시 주차권을 지급합니다.

신청인
이름: David Coleman
부서: Atkins 대학교 진로 센터
전화번호: 7946-4309
이메일: d.coleman@atkinsu.edu/aucc

연사 정보
이름: Maria Dershowitz
단체: Clarion Call사
전화번호: 7946-09235
이메일: m.dershowitz@clarioncall.com
주제: 사회적 기업가 활동―사회 문제의 해결책에 대한 개발, 자금 조달, 그리고 실행

행사 정보
이름: 졸업하는 4학년 학생들이 사회적 변화를 창출할 수 있는 방법
날짜: 3월 4일
시간: 오후 4시부터 5시 30분까지
장소: McMurdo 강당
예상 참석자 수: 80명

특별 요청사항
시청각 장비: 필요 없음

교통수단: 필요 없음
주차: 임시 주차권 1매
다과: 필요 없음

156 Ms. Dershowitz는 왜 Atkins 대학교를 방문하는가?
(A) 소기업들을 위한 세미나를 주도하기 위해
(B) 사회적 대의를 위한 자원봉사자를 모집하기 위해
(C) 학생들과 사회 행동을 논의하기 위해
(D) 활동 신청 양식을 승인하기 위해

157 Mr. Coleman은 3월 4일 전에 무엇을 할 것 같은가?
(A) 연사를 위해 교통수단을 준비한다
(B) 강당 사용을 위해 돈을 지불한다
(C) 게시판에 광고를 게시한다
(D) 사무실에서 주차권을 확보한다

158-161은 다음 안내문에 관한 문제입니다.

www.bennetthouse.org/visit

홈	방문	이력	지도/위치	연락처

방문객과 단체 여행객들은 화요일부터 토요일 오전 10시에서 오후 5시 사이에 Bennett 저택을 관람하실 수 있습니다. 열 명 이상의 단체는 하루 전에 예약하는 것이 요구됩니다. 그렇게 하지 못한 분들은 상당한 대기 시간이 있을 가능성이 있습니다. 입장은 무료이지만 입구와 선물 가게에 현금함이 있으며, 그곳에서 기부금이 매우 감사히 받아들여질 것입니다.

Bennett 저택은 25달러의 균일 요금으로 학생들과 단체 여행객들을 위한 가이드 견학도 준비할 수 있습니다. ― [1] ―. 모든 방문객들은 정보를 제공하는 책자를 받게 될 것이며, 그것은 빅토리아 시대의 주택과 방 안에 포함된 미술품 및 가구에 대한 역사와 정보를 포함하고 있습니다. ― [2] ―. 책자는 저택의 이전 거주자들의 사진과 짧은 약력도 포함합니다. ― [3] ―.

선물 가게와 찻집이 출구 근처에 위치해 있습니다. 엽서, 기념품, 티셔츠, 통에 담긴 영국 차, 그리고 찻잔이 구매 가능합니다. ― [4] ―. 선물 가게는 비수기인 1월부터 3월까지는 열지 않으나, 시설의 다른 곳들은 계속 운영 중일 것입니다. Bennett 저택은 모든 법정 공휴일에 문을 닫습니다.

158 안내문에 어떤 조언이 포함되어 있는가?
(A) 선물 가게 내 구매를 위해 쿠폰을 사용하는 것
(B) 규모가 큰 단체를 위해 미리 예약하는 것
(C) 주말 견학을 위해 예약하는 것
(D) 건물 내의 지정된 길을 따라가는 것

159 추가 요금으로 무엇이 이용 가능한가?
(A) 사진을 포함한 홍보 자료
(B) 저택의 가이드 견학
(C) 사진 전시회 입장
(D) 구매한 기념품 배송

160 Bennett 저택에 대해 언급되지 않은 것은?
(A) 소매 시설을 통해 기념품을 판매한다.
(B) 모든 방문객들에게 설명 책자를 제공한다.
(C) 방문객이 적은 기간에 일시적으로 문을 닫는다.
(D) 입장료를 청구하는 것 대신에 기부금을 받는다.

161 [1], [2], [3], [4]로 표시된 위치 중, 다음 문장이 들어갈 곳으로 가장 적절한 것은?

"판매된 물품으로 인한 모든 수익금은 이 역사적인 건물의 보존 비용으로 쓰입니다."

(A) [1]
(B) [2]
(C) [3]
(D) [4]

162-164는 다음 회람에 관한 문제입니다.

수신: 전 직원

발신: Angela Romanov, 사무장

제목: 건물 개선

모든 분들께,

본사 건물 전체의 수리가 오늘부터 2주 후에 시작될 것임을 기억해 주십시오. 작업은 한 번에 한 층씩 이루어질 것이고, 5층부터 시작해서 아래로 내려갈 것입니다. 각 층은 완료하는 데 일주일이 걸릴 예정입니다. 저는 이와 관련하여 팀장들과 논의했고, 이 기간 동안의 작업 공간 문제를 처리하기 위한 해결 방안이 도출되었습니다.

여러분의 층이 수리되고 있는 동안, 3층 회의실 내 여러분이 이용 가능하도록 공간이 마련될 것입니다. 3층을 수리할 때가 되면, 원래 그곳에서 근무하는 직원들은 건물 나머지 곳곳으로 재배치될 것입니다. 그 층에서 상시로 근무하는 직원은 12명뿐이기 때문에 이것이 어떠한 문제도 발생시키지 않기를 바라고 있습니다. 그 직원들은 팀장으로부터 추가 지시를 기다릴 것이 요청됩니다.

앞으로 몇 주간 이 상황이 야기할 수 있는 불편에 대해 미리 사과드립니다. 저는 이 과정이 가능한 한 순조롭게 진행되도록 우리 모두가 함께 협력할 수 있다고 확신합니다. 만약 추가 문의가 있으시다면, 여러분의 팀장에게 연락해 주십시오.

감사합니다,

Angela Romanov 드림

---

162 회람은 왜 쓰였는가?
(A) 앞으로 있을 수리와 관련된 회의를 준비하기 위해
(B) 최근의 직원 불평에 대해 논의하기 위해
(C) 직원들에게 몇몇 공사 작업을 상기시키기 위해
(D) 재개발 프로젝트에 대한 제안을 요청하기 위해

163 건물에 대해 암시되는 것은?
(A) 5층 건물이다.
(B) 내년에 철거될 것이다.
(C) 30년이 되었다.
(D) 각 층에 한 개의 회의실이 있다.

164 3층의 직원들은 무엇을 하도록 요청되는가?
(A) 수리팀 팀장에게 우려 사항을 알린다
(B) 회의실에서 발표 준비를 돕는다
(C) 관리자로부터 곧 있을 세부 사항들을 기다린다
(D) 사무장의 지시 사항 사본을 배부한다

165-167은 다음 웹페이지에 관한 문제입니다.

| 홈 | 소개 | 메뉴 | 연락처 |

음식이 언제든지 만들어지고 또 인기 있는 곳, Lunch on Demand에 오신 것을 환영합니다!

8월 8일부터는, 음식을 받기 위해 긴 줄을 기다릴 필요가 없습니다. 간단히 Lunch on Demand의 현재 메뉴를 훑어보시고, 주문을 하시고, 저희 웹사이트에서 돈을 지불하시기만 하면 됩니다. 저희는 확인 번호와 음식이 준비될 시간을 알려드릴 것입니다. 알려드린 시간에 이곳에 도착하셔서, 번호를 말씀해 주시면, 시내에서 찾을 수 있는 가장 맛있고 건강한 음식이 있는 상자를 드릴 것입니다.

저희 메뉴는 주 단위로 바뀌지만 항상 아래 나열된 요리를 포함합니다:

수프 – 가장 신선한 채소, 단백질을 위한 콩이나 렌즈콩, 저녁까지 배를 채워줄 영양가 높은 쌀국수를 섞습니다. 채식주의자들에게 더할 나위 없이 좋습니다.

파니니 – 저희의 매우 다양한 노릇노릇한 샌드위치를 만드는 데에는 오로지 최고급 통밀로 된 빵만이 사용됩니다. 고구마튀김과 함께 제공됩니다.

스튜와 카레 – 만약 좀 더 많은 양의 것을 찾고 있으시다면, 저희 스튜와 카레가 딱 좋습니다! 곁들여 나오는 요리로 밥이나 빵이 함께 나옵니다.

샐러드 – 건강을 항상 의식하는 분들을 위해, 저희는 신선하고 아삭아삭한 푸른색 채소와 다른 채소들을 저희의 특별 저지방 샐러드드레싱과 같이 섞습니다.

8월 내내, 저희는 등록된 고객들이 새로운 고객을 등록하게 할 때마다 10달러 쿠폰을 드리고 있습니다. 자세한 내용은 여기를 클릭하세요.

---

165 주문을 할 때 고객들에게 무엇이 주어지는가?
(A) 지불 영수증
(B) 구입한 것을 가지러 갈 시간
(C) 예상되는 배송료
(D) 업데이트된 메뉴

166 고객들은 어떻게 쿠폰을 받을 자격을 얻을 수 있는가?
(A) 최소한의 주문을 함으로써
(B) 다른 사람들이 웹사이트에 가입하게 함으로써
(C) 마감 기한 전에 등록함으로써
(D) 특정 지역에서 음식을 주문함으로써

167 Lunch on Demand에 대해 언급되지 않은 것은?
(A) 고기를 먹지 않는 사람들에게 적합하다.
(B) 메뉴를 매주 바꾼다.
(C) 모든 메뉴를 주문 제작할 수 있다.
(D) 몇몇 요리에 곁들인 음식을 제공한다.

168-171은 다음 메시지 대화문에 관한 문제입니다.

Helen Coulter [7월 15일, 오전 9시 54분]
여러분 모두 즐거운 휴가를 보내고 있길 바랍니다. 저는 오늘 오전에 막 *Timelight* 제작자로부터 답을 들었고, 그들은 앞으로 또 다른 2년 동안 Kitchen Belle사의 음식 공급 계약을 연장하기를 원해요. 그 스튜디오는 TV 시리즈를 다시 시작했어요. 작년과 동일한 일정을 유지할까요, 아니면 시간을 변경하기를 원하시나요?

Elaine Painter [7월 15일, 오전 10시]
좋은 소식이네요! 회사에 꾸준한 수입을 보장해 주겠네요. 저는 Henry Lincoln이 주로 아침에 근무한다는 것을 알지만, 그만 문제가 없다면, 이번에는 제가 점심 대신에 아침 교대 근무를 맡아도 될까요?

Graham Fulton [7월 15일, 오전 10시 4분]
그는 괜찮아요. 그는 지금 저와 함께 있고 방금 제게 그렇게 얘기했어요, Elaine. 사실 그는 점심때를 선호해요. 저는 계속해서 아침 교대 근무를 하고 싶어요. 올해에 추가 저녁 촬영이 있을 건가요?

Helen Coulter [7월 15일, 오전 10시 5분]
그럼 Elaine과 Graham이 7시 30분부터 11시까지의 교대 근무를 할 수 있고, Henry와 제가 11시 30분부터 3시 30분까지 할게요. 추가 수당을 받는 저녁 교대 근무도 어느 정도 있을 것이지만, 자정을 넘겨서 끝나는 것은 없을 거예요. 게다가, 쇼는 이번 시즌에 스튜디오 외부에서도 촬영될 것이므로, 우리는 조정을 해야 할 거예요. 어쨌든, 우리는 다음 주에 휴가에서 돌아왔을 때 그 문제에 대해 논의할 수 있어요.

Elaine Painter [7월 15일, 오전 10시 7분]
출연자와 팀 수는 동일할 건가요?

Graham Fulton [7월 15일, 오전 10시 7분]
작년보다 일이 많을 것 같네요.

Helen Coulter [7월 15일, 오전 10시 8분]
아뇨, Elaine. 음식을 제공할 사람이 67명이 아니라 총 88명이 될 거예요. 당신의 질문에 대해서는, Graham, 제 생각에는 일이 더 많을 것 같아요. 하지만 그들이 우리에게 더 많이 지불할 것이라, 제 생각에는 음식 준비 보조원 몇 명을 고용할 수 있을 것 같아요.

168 오전 10시 4분에, Mr. Fulton이 "It's fine by him"이라고 썼을 때 그가 의도한 것 같은 것은?
(A) 그는 Ms. Painter가 동료와 교대 근무를 바꾸는 것을 제안한다.
(B) 그의 일정 변경은 Ms. Coulter에 의해 승인되어야 한다.
(C) 그도 아침 시간 동안 근무하는 것에 관심이 있다.
(D) 그의 동료는 Ms. Painter의 요청을 받아들일 수 있다고 생각한다.

169 Mr. Lincoln은 다음 시즌에 언제 정규 교대 근무를 시작할 것인가?
(A) 오전 7시 30분에
(B) 오전 11시에
(C) 오전 11시 30분에
(D) 오후 3시 30분에

170 *Timelight*에 대해 암시되는 것은?
(A) 때때로 밤에 제작 업무가 있을 것이다.
(B) 직원의 규모를 줄였다.
(C) 텔레비전 스튜디오에서 모든 장면을 촬영할 것이다.
(D) 내년에 텔레비전에서 첫 방송을 할 것이다.

171 다음 주에 Kitchen Belle사에서 무슨 일이 일어날 것인가?
(A) 팀의 명단이 확정될 것이다.
(B) 새로운 보조원 몇 명이 고용될 것이다.
(C) 팀들이 휴가에서 돌아올 것이다.
(D) 임원들이 회의를 위해 들를 것이다.

172-175는 다음 안내문에 관한 문제입니다.

프리랜서 작업

저희 *Houston Portal*지는 무소속 기자들로부터 아이디어를 듣는 것에 늘 관심 있습니다. — [1] —. 소규모 대안 주간지로서, 저희는 독립 프리랜서들의 보도를 통해 번창하고 있습니다. 만약 저희 간행물에 기고하는 데 관심이 있으시다면, 저희가 기사 아이디어에 대해 요하는 사항은 다음과 같습니다:

먼저, editors@houstonportal.com으로 간략한, 한 페이지 분량의 기사 아이디어를 보내 주십시오. 이전에 발행된 글은 받지 않습니다.

가능하다면, 신문, 웹사이트, 혹은 다른 일반 독자층을 대상으로 하는 출판물을 위해 이전에 쓰신 어떤 글이라도 첨부해 주십시오. — [2] —. 저희는 이전 경력이 좀 있는 프리랜서의 글을 발행하는 것을 선호합니다.

저희는 전속 기자들만이 사설을 집필하도록 허용합니다. 그러므로, 아이디어는 특집 기사로 제한해 주십시오. 저희는 보통 500에서 3,000단어 사이의 기사를 발행합니다.

— [3] —. 만약 자격 있는 사진작가이시라면, 사진 시리즈 아이디어를 제안하셔도 됩니다. 그럴 경우, 저희가 작업의 일부 예시를 봐야 할 것입니다.

저희 신문은 명절 및 한여름 휴가를 제외하고 매주 발행되어, 1년에 약 50회 발행됩니다. — [4] —. 저희는 자금을 위해 광고에 의존하기 때문에, 신문은 독자들에게 무료로 제공됩니다. 그럼에도 불구하고, 저희는 기자들을 지원하는 것에 대한 강한 신념을 가지고 있으므로, 단어당 0.30달러부터 시작하는 임금으로, 발행될 기사에 대한 공정한 보상을 제공하기 위해 최선을 다합니다.

---

172 안내문의 목적은 무엇인가?
(A) 신문에 글을 쓰는 것에 대한 지침을 제공하기 위해
(B) 전속 기자 구인에 대한 세부 사항을 제공하기 위해
(C) *Houston Portal*지의 사명을 제시하기 위해
(D) 간행물의 규정에 대한 변경을 검토하기 위해

173 *Houston Portal*지가 아이디어를 평가할 때 고려하는 요소가 아닌 것은?
(A) 길이
(B) 기사 종류
(C) 경력
(D) 출판료

174 *Houston Portal*지에 대해 언급된 것은?
(A) 현재 전속 사진작가를 모집하지 않고 있다.
(B) 한 해의 모든 주에 새로운 호를 발간한다.
(C) 모든 독자들에게 무료이다.
(D) 사설 칼럼니스트의 기사는 싣지 않는다.

175 [1], [2], [3], [4]로 표시된 위치 중, 다음 문장이 들어갈 곳으로 가장 적절한 것은?

"학술적이거나 전문적인 글은 관련 없습니다."

(A) [1]
(B) [2]
(C) [3]
(D) [4]

176-180은 다음 일정표와 이메일에 관한 문제입니다.

Gladwell 디자인 회사

신입사원 오리엔테이션 일정표—3월 18일

시간	발표자	주제
오전 9시 – 10시 20분	Dana Kang	보상과 혜택
오전 10시 30분 – 11시 50분	David Harris	기업 문화
오후 12시 – 1시	점심시간	
오후 1시 – 2시 20분	Sarah Lee	직원 행동
오후 2시 30분 – 3시 50분	Verne Peel	성과와 평가
오후 4시 – 5시 50분	Brad Murray	전문성 개발 기회

참가자들에게는 첫 번째 세션 시작 시 회사 안내 책자가 제공될 것입니다. 직원 신분증과 보안 출입증은 그다음 날 오전에 배부될 것입니다. 주차증은 그다음 주에 신입사원들이 가져갈 수 있도록 이용 가능할 것입니다.

수신: Mike Levy <m.levy@gdc.com>
발신: Lucy Sawyer <l.sawyer@gdc.com>
날짜: 3월 14일
제목: 오리엔테이션

Mr. Levy께,

당신이 우리 영업부에 합류할 신입사원들을 대상으로 준비해달라고 제게 요청한 오리엔테이션과 관련하여 몇 가지 추가적인 세부 사항을 전달하고자 합니다. 제가 지난 화요일에 당신에게 이메일로 보낸 발표자들의 일정에서 변동이 있었습니다. Bale Industries사가 계약상의 오해를 논의하기 위해 3월 18일 오전에 몇몇 대표들을 보내기로 결정했습니다. 아시다시피, Bale Industries사는 우리의 가장 중요한 고객 중 하나이며, Dana Kang이 고객 계약을 처리하는 일을 담당하고 있습니다. 따라서, 그녀는 그날의 마지막 발표자와 시간대를 바꿨습니다. 제가 그 일정을 업데이트할 것입니다.

또 다른 사안이 하나 있습니다. David Harris의 세션 동안, 그는 몇 가지 팀워크 구축 훈련을 위해 교육생들을 그룹으로 나누려고 합니다. 하지만, 그는 예약된 모임 장소가 너무 작을까 봐 걱정하고 있습니다. 7층의 임원 회의실을 오리엔테이션을 위해 사용해도 될까요? 이것이 어떤 문제를 야기할 것이라면 제게 알려주십시오. 감사합니다.

Lucy Sawyer 드림

176 신입사원들은 3월 18일에 무엇을 받을 것인가?
(A) 직원 안내서
(B) 신분증
(C) 보안 출입증
(D) 주차증

177 이메일의 목적은 무엇인가?
(A) 프로젝트에 대한 도움을 요청하기 위해
(B) 추가 직원의 채용을 공지하기 위해
(C) 부하 직원에게 지시를 내리기 위해

(D) 업무에 대한 최신 정보를 제공하기 위해

178 이메일에서, 2문단 첫 번째 줄의 단어 "issue"는 의미상 ~와 가장 가깝다.
(A) 이유
(B) 사안
(C) 버전
(D) 선택권

179 누구의 발표 시간이 변경될 것인가?
(A) David Harris
(B) Sarah Lee
(C) Verne Peel
(D) Brad Murray

180 Ms. Sawyer는 Mr. Levy에게 무엇에 대해 묻는가?
(A) 다른 장소를 이용하는 것
(B) 훈련 활동을 변경하는 것
(C) 행사 일정을 변경하는 것
(D) 회사 임원과 만나는 것

181-185는 다음 회람과 이메일에 관한 문제입니다.

Dakota Logistics사
회람

수신: 전 직원
발신: Jasmine Alexander, 최고 운영 책임자
제목: 연금 제도
날짜: 11월 28일

여러분도 아시다시피, 회사 경영진들은 금요일 이사회에서 연금 정책을 검토하였고 제도에 유연성을 더하도록 몇 가지를 변경하는 것에 동의했습니다. 현재, 회사와 5년 미만 동안 함께해 온 직원들은 연금 기금에 급여의 1.8퍼센트를 내는 반면, 5년 이상 함께해 온 직원들은 2.7퍼센트를 내고 있습니다.

내년 1월 1일부터, 이 정책은 변경될 것입니다. 모든 직원들은 그들의 연금 지불 정도를 선택할 수 있을 것입니다. 기존의 두 개의 선택권뿐만 아니라, 직원들은 원한다면 급여의 3.5퍼센트까지의 액수를 낼 수도 있을 것입니다. 12월에, 여러분 모두는 이 사안에 대해 여러분이 선호하는 것을 알리도록 요청받을 것입니다. 선택권에 대해 논의하고 여러분의 현재 상황에 어느 것이 가장 적합할지에 대해 조언을 받고 싶다면, 인사부장과 약속을 잡으십시오.

수신: Sarah Chang <schang@dlogistics.com>
발신: Adam Cartwright <acartwright@dlogistics.com>
제목: 연금 약속
날짜: 11월 29일

안녕하세요, Sarah.

Ms. Alexander가 보낸 어제의 회람에 대한 답변으로 이메일을 씁니다. 저는 현재 연금 기금에 제 급여의 1.8퍼센트를 내고 있습니다. 하지만, 저는 9월에 계약이 갱신되었을 때 임금 인상을 받게 되어, 지금은 더 낼 여유가 있습니다. 이 때문에, 저는 3.5퍼센트로 개인 부담금을 늘리는 데 관심이 있습니다.

저는 화요일과 목요일에 온종일 이 사안에 대해 논의할 시간이 있으며 금요일에도 오후 2시 전까지 시간이 있을 것입니다. 이 기간 동안 당신에게 가장 좋은 때가 있는지 알려 주십시오.

Adam Cartwright 드림

181 Dakota Logistics사의 직원들에 대해 암시되는 것은?
(A) 계약 협상 중에만 개인 부담금 액수를 변경할 수 있다.
(B) 변경된 정책이 시행되기까지 약 한 달이 있다.
(C) 지불금이 자동으로 공제되도록 정할 수 있다.
(D) 이전의 회사 정책에 대해 불평했다.

182 Mr. Cartwright에 대해 암시되는 것은?
(A) 주요 승진에 고려되고 있다.

(B) 5년 미만 동안 회사와 함께해 왔다.
(C) 다음 주에 다른 부서로 옮길 것이다.
(D) 실적 평가서를 작성했다.

183 회람에 따르면, 내년 초에 무엇이 변경될 것인가?
(A) 직원들이 연금에 낼 수 있는 액수
(B) 직원들이 일을 잘 수행하여 받게 되는 상여금
(C) 프로그램의 자격을 얻기 위해 요구되는 햇수
(D) 지불금이 납부되어야 하는 방식

184 Mr. Cartwright는 무엇을 하기를 바라고 있는가?
(A) 근무 시간을 늘린다
(B) 업무 기한을 연장한다
(C) 연금 제도에 최대 액수를 지불한다
(D) 직장에서 떠나 임시 휴가를 간다

185 Ms. Chang에 대해 암시되는 것은?
(A) Mr. Cartwright와의 회의를 요청했다.
(B) Ms. Alexander를 위해 약속 일정을 잡는다.
(C) 주로 오후에 시간이 없다.
(D) Dakota Logistics사의 한 부서를 담당하고 있다.

186-190은 다음 공고, 이메일, 안내문에 관한 문제입니다.

재료 공학자 협회 (AME)
제9회 연례 동부 지역 학회
3월 10일부터 11일까지 | 클리프턴, 뉴저지주

AME의 뉴저지 지부가 준비하고 클리프턴 재료 과학 및 공학 대학이 주최하는 제9회 연례 동부 지역 학회는 공학자들과 과학자들이 새로운 기술에 대해 배우고 동료들과 교류할 기회를 제공합니다. 유용한 워크숍에 참석해서, 최근의 연구에 대해 듣고, 투자자들 그리고 다양한 분야의 대표들과 관계를 형성하십시오.

또한, 뉴저지 지부는 학회의 일부로서 고등학교 공학 봉사 프로그램을 계속해서 지원하게 되어 기쁩니다. 지역의 고등학교 학생들은 재료 공학 직종의 다양한 측면에 대해 배울 수 있는 계획된 활동들에 참여하도록 초대될 것입니다. 이 프로그램은 학생들이 현직 공학자들과 교류할 수 있는 특별 오찬을 포함합니다.

만약 여러분의 회사가 이 행사를 후원하는 것에 관심이 있다면, 행사 진행자인 Melinda Rose에게 m.rose@ame.org로 연락해 주십시오. 후원자들은 저희 프로그램 소책자에 광고를 게재하거나 행사 장소에 홍보용 현수막을 전시하는 것이 허용될 것입니다.

수신: Melinda Rose <m.rose@ame.org>
발신: Paula Vance <p.vance@hiller.com>
날짜: 1월 22일
제목: 학회

Ms. Rose께,

저희 요청을 처리해 주셔서 감사합니다. 소책자에 포함하기로 예정된 전면 광고의 디지털 사본을 첨부하였습니다. 다른 마케팅 자료들은 마무리되는 대로 별도의 이메일로 보내질 것입니다. 또한 저는 복지 혜택의 하나로써 네 장의 학회 입장권을 받았습니다. 그런데, 저는 행사 당일에 학회 입장권을 구매하는 데 드는 비용에 대해 문의하고 싶습니다. 유럽에 있는 계열사의 동료가 참석하는 데 관심이 있지만, 행사 며칠 전까지 참석 여부를 확신할 수 없습니다. 그는 AME의 회원은 아니지만 유럽 공학자 협회에 속해 있습니다.

도와주셔서 감사하고 곧 귀하의 답을 듣게 되기를 기다리겠습니다.

Paula Vance 드림
선임 공학자
Hiller Engineering사

재료 공학자 협회 (AME)
제9회 연례 동부 지역 학회
등록비

	사전	일반	당일
회원	150달러	230달러	285달러
비회원	175달러	255달러	310달러
학생*	45달러	75달러	100달러

사전 등록 마감일은 1월 24일이고, 2월 16일은 일반 등록 마감일입니다.

*제시된 가격은 국내의 과학 또는 공학 프로그램에 등록한 대학원생과 학부생 모두에게 해당됩니다. 저희 봉사 프로그램의 일부로 참석하는 고등학생들은 무료로 입장할 수 있습니다.

186 공고에 따르면, 제9회 연례 동부 지역 학회에 포함되지 않은 것은?
(A) 교류 기회
(B) 학생들과의 점심
(C) 시설 둘러보기
(D) 학습 시간

187 Hiller Engineering사에 대해 암시되는 것은?
(A) 웹사이트를 통해 회의에 등록했다.
(B) 전시 부스를 열 계획이다.
(C) 학회 후원자로 등록했다.
(D) 행사에 모든 직원을 보낼 것이다.

188 Ms. Rose는 Ms. Vance로부터 무엇을 받을 것으로 예상할 수 있는가?
(A) 명단
(B) 계약서 사본
(C) 제품 소책자
(D) 홍보용 자료

189 학회 입장료에 대해 언급된 것은?
(A) 지불된 후에는 환불될 수 없다.
(B) AME의 고등학교 프로그램에 참여하는 사람들에게는 적용되지 않는다.
(C) 학부생보다 대학원생들에게 더 저렴하다.
(D) 단체로 등록하는 사람들에게는 할인될 수 있다.

190 Ms. Vance의 동료는 입장권에 얼마를 지불해야 할 것인가?
(A) 175달러
(B) 255달러
(C) 285달러
(D) 310달러

191-195는 다음 공고, 이메일, 양식에 관한 문제입니다.

Griffin Mobile사 직원들에게 안내

3월 13일부터 17일까지 시카고에서 열리는 우리의 연례 회사 컨벤션을 위한 계획을 세울 때, 출장비 상환에 관한 다음 규정을 검토하십시오:

- 모든 직원은 Thunder 항공사를 통해 비행편을 예약해야 합니다. 다른 항공사를 통해 예약한 비행편에 대해서는 상환이 불가능합니다.
- 컨벤션 장소까지 300마일 이상 비행하는 직원들은 비즈니스 클래스로 무료 업그레이드를 받을 것입니다. 500마일 이상 이동하는 직원들은 Thunder 항공사 VIP 공항 라운지 1일 무료 이용권도 받을 수 있습니다.
- 차를 대여해야 하는 직원들은 시카고의 Clifford 렌터카 회사를 통해 예약할 수 있습니다. 일반 차량을 대여하는 직원들에게만 상환이 제공될 것입니다.

우리는 250명 이상의 Griffin Mobile사 직원들이 컨벤션에 참석할 것으로 예상하기 때문에, 모든 직원들이 이 규정을 따르는 것이 필수적입니다. 질문이나 우려 사항이 있으시면 Jill McGowan에게 연락하십시오.

수신: Laura Parker <lauraparker@griffinmobile.com>
발신: Jill McGowan <jillmcgowan@griffinmobile.com>
날짜: 3월 10일
제목: 시카고 컨벤션

안녕하세요, Laura!

발목이 부러졌다니 정말 안타깝네요. 하지만 당신이 회복하고 있고 여전히 시카고 컨벤션에서 우리와 함께할 계획이라니 다행이에요.

일반적인 상황에서는, 당신은 비즈니스 클래스 항공권을 받거나 공항 라운지를 이용할 수 없었을 거예요. 하지만 당신의 부상으로 인해, 당신의 항공편 예약을 비즈니스 클래스로 업그레이드하고 공항 라운지 일일 이용권을 예약할게요.

당신은 지금 렌터카를 운전할 수 없으니, 재무팀이 최대 150달러의 택시 요금을 승인할 거예요. 하지만 별도의 상환 요청서를 제출하고 택시 영수증을 첨부하셔야 합니다. 시카고에 계시는 동안 추가로 지상 교통을 위한 준비가 필요하시면 또 말씀해 주세요.

Jill McGowan 드림
Griffin Mobile사 운영 담당자

Griffin Mobile사 상환 요청서
사원 이름: Laura Parker
사원 번호: 13848
사원 부서: 제품 개발

항목	날짜	비용	설명
택시	3월 13일	33.50달러	공항에서 호텔로
	3월 14일	14.75달러	호텔에서 컨벤션 센터로
	3월 14일	15.25달러	컨벤션 센터에서 호텔로
	3월 15일	27.25달러	호텔에서 식당으로
	3월 15일	29.75달러	식당에서 호텔로
	3월 17일	33.50달러	호텔에서 공항으로

총 비용: 154달러
비고: 사원은 증빙된 질병으로 인해 회사 컨벤션 도중 택시 서비스가 필요했습니다. 영수증을 첨부했습니다.

191 Griffin Mobile사에 대해 추론될 수 있는 것은?
(A) 시카고에서 500마일 거리에 위치한 직원들이 거의 없다.
(B) 항공사와 업무 협약을 맺고 있다.
(C) 수년 동안 컨벤션을 개최해 왔다.
(D) 사무실을 위한 장소가 한 군데이다.

192 Ms. McGowan은 왜 이메일을 썼는가?
(A) 컨벤션을 공지하기 위해
(B) 비행편 예약을 확정하기 위해
(C) 규정에 대한 예외를 제공하기 위해
(D) 직원의 상태에 대해 묻기 위해

193 Ms. Parker에 대해 암시된 것은?
(A) 컨벤션까지의 이동이 300마일보다 짧았다.
(B) Clifford 렌터카 회사 예약을 취소했다.
(C) 컨벤션 몇 달 전에 부상을 당했다.
(D) 렌터카가 일반 차량으로 분류되었다.

194 Ms. Parker의 택시 비용에 대해 결론지을 수 있는 것은?
(A) 단거리 이동을 위한 것이었다.
(B) 여러 도시에서 발생했다.
(C) 전체 상환되지 않을 것이다.
(D) 대여 비용과 비교될 것이다.

195 Ms. Parker는 며칠에 세미나에 참석했는가?
(A) 3월 13일
(B) 3월 14일

(C) 3월 15일
(D) 3월 17일

196-200은 다음 기사, 웹페이지, 공고에 관한 문제입니다.

국영 우정공사가 지점들을 폐쇄할 것이다

BONDVILLE시, 11월 1일—우편물 양의 급격한 감소에 직면하여, 전국의 우체국들은 생존을 유지하기 위해 애쓰고 있다. 사실, 국영 우정공사는 비용을 절감하기 위한 최근의 시도에도 불구하고 이번 회계연도 말까지 약 7백만 달러의 적자가 생길 것이다. 지금까지, 이러한 노력은 수백 개의 거리 우체통을 없애는 것, 수천 개 지점의 영업시간을 줄이는 것, 그리고 국내 우표 가격을 2센트 올리는 것을 포함했다.

국영 우정공사의 최고 경영자인 Myra Kane에 따르면, "결과적으로, 이용이 적은 우체국들을 닫는 것 외에 공사가 할 수 있는 것이 거의 없다." Bondville시에서는, 아래의 우체국들이 1월 1일에 운영을 중단할 것이다:

구역	우체국 위치
Landpiper Hills	41번지 Brookside가
Delforte Park	5734번지 Livingston가
Randall Springs	343번지 Medollini로

폐쇄될 예정인 전국 지점들의 목록은 www.npservice.com/actions에서 볼 수 있다. 대중들은 이 사이트에서 "연락"을 클릭해 의견을 제공할 수 있다.

---

www.npservice.com/contactus

이름: Vincent Alvarez
집 주소: 460번지 Brookside가, Bondville시, 플로리다주 33870
날짜: 11월 28일

의견: 저는 저희 동네의 우체국 네 곳 중 세 곳을 폐쇄하는 계획은 충분히 숙고되지 않았다고 생각합니다. 생각보다 더 많은 사람들이 매일 그것들에 의존합니다. 한 예로, 저는 집에서 작은 사업을 운영하며 주문품을 우편으로 보내기 위해 한 주에 여러 번 저희 동네 우체국을 방문합니다. 이곳은 제 집과 같은 도로, 자동차로 가까운 거리에 위치해 있습니다.

또한, 저희 동네에는 많은 소규모의 가게들이 있고, 그 주인들은 온라인으로 주문된 상품들을 보내기 위해 지역 우체국을 이용합니다. 많은 동네 주민들이 저와 같은 의견을 가지고 있으므로, 이 지점들을 폐쇄하려는 결정을 재고해주시길 바랍니다.

[제출]

국영 우정공사
Bondville시 시민들에게 공고

Bondville시의 우체국 중 세 곳이 폐쇄될 것이라고 공지되었을 때, 많은 지역 주민들이 이의를 제기했습니다. 그들은 이 폐쇄가 불편을 야기할 것이라고 주장했습니다. 또한 Delforte Park에 있는 우체국 건물은 19세기 말에 지어졌으며 르네상스 부흥 양식 건축물의 귀중한 사례라는 점도 지적되었습니다.

그뿐만 아니라, Bondville시 지방 정부에서 저희에게 도움이 되도록 각 지점을 이용하는 사람들의 수에 대한 최신 수치를 제공하였습니다. 따라서 저희는 소규모 쇼핑몰에 위치하며 역사적 가치가 거의 없다고 여겨지는 Randall Springs 지점만 폐쇄하는 것으로 타협하기로 했습니다. 남아있는 우체국 지점들의 생존 가능성을 증진시키기 위해, Bondville 시청은 그것들을 새롭게 개시된 문화유산 탐방로에 추가했으며, 이것은 Packard가와 다른 주목할 만한 거리들을 따라 이어집니다. 여행객들은 이 장소들을 들를 때, 특별히 디자인된 엽서를 포함하여 국영 우정공사 기념품들을 사도록 권유될 것입니다.

196 국영 우정공사가 시도하지 않은 비용 절감 전략은?
(A) 우체국 시간 단축
(B) 우체통 제거
(C) 임시 근로자 고용
(D) 우편 요금 인상

197 Landpiper Hills에 대해 추론될 수 있는 것은?
(A) 많은 소규모 사업체들이 있다.
(B) 보행자들에게만 개방된 도로가 있다.
(C) 예전만큼 많은 관광객들을 끌어들이지 못하고 있다.
(D) 행정 건물이 있는 곳이다.

198 어느 거리에 역사적 가치를 지닌 우체국이 있는가?
(A) Brookside가
(B) Livingston가
(C) Mendollini로
(D) Packard가

199 국영 우정공사는 무엇을 했을 것 같은가?
(A) 전국적인 정책을 개정했다
(B) 일부 주민들에게 설문 조사를 시행했다
(C) 역사적인 건물을 점검했다
(D) 지역 정부와 협력했다

200 공고에서, 2문단 세 번째 줄의 단어 "boost"는 의미상 –와 가장 가깝다.
(A) 재촉하다
(B) 축하하다
(C) 시험하다
(D) 강화하다

• 무료 해설은 해커스토익(Hackers.co.kr)에서
다운로드 받으실 수 있습니다.

• QR 코드로
바로가기

PART 5

101 이 시설이 결함이 없고 개봉되지 않은 구매품들을 반품하는 데에 14일의 기한 제한을 실시함을 알아 두십시오.

102 세미나 참가자들을 위한 특별 좌석 배정이 되어 있지는 않았지만, 그들이 도착하는 대로 안내원들은 그들을 가능한 자리로 안내할 것이다.

103 인사부는 직원들이 회사의 수행 기준을 충족시키는지 산정하기 위해 주기적으로 직원들을 평가할 것이다.

104 몇십 년 동안 남미를 연구해 와서, Hartley 교수는 그 문명에 대해 탁월한 권위자로 여겨진다.

105 그 에스프레소 기계는 사용자들이 나오는 커피의 양을 조절하도록 하는, 쉽게 조정 가능한 노즐이 달려 있다.

106 비록 그 오래된 프린터는 더 신형인 모델보다 느리지만, 몇몇 직원들은 여전히 그것을 사용하는 것을 선호한다.

107 화재경보음을 듣자마자, 학생들은 가장 가까운 출구를 통해 건물에서 빠져나갔다.

108 시민들은 시가 빚이 많았던 10년 끝에 재정적으로 상환 능력이 생기도록 시를 도운 시장에게 감사를 표했다.

109 Long Road Truck Rental사는 4월 2일부터 직원들이 회사 셔츠와 함께 청바지를 입는 것을 허용할 것임을 명시하는 공고를 게시했다.

110 지형에 대해 얻을 수 있는 정보가 거의 없어서, 도보 여행자들은 그들의 안전을 보장하기 위해 개인 가이드를 고용했다.

111 Ms. Latta는 보통 직장에 가기 위해 그녀의 차를 이용하지만, 도시 교통을 상대하는 것보다 버스를 이용하여 통근하는 것이 더 간단하다고 생각한다.

112 자선 콘서트의 프로그램은 잠정적이고 공연자들의 섭외 가능성에 따라 변경될 수 있다.

113 변호사 시험을 준비하는 학생들은 이전 시험에 포함된 문제들을 검토하도록 권장된다.

114 낮 동안에 기온이 떨어질 것으로 예상되기 때문에, 따뜻한 겨울 코트를 가져오는 것이 현명할 것이다.

115 Mr. Powers는 고객에게 특수 보안 서비스는 주문에 따라 제공될 수 없지만, 납부 조건은 절충 가능하다고 알렸다.

116 MevTech사 대표들은 그들의 제품들과 관련된 고객 불만의 갑작스러운 급증에 대해 다루기 위하여 급히 기자 회견을 준비했다.

117 Whitmore사가 Busch & Hawley사와 합병하기 위해 논의하고 있다는 추측 가운데, 두 회사 모두의 주가가 오르기 시작했다.

118 Mr. Barton은 미납된 전기 요금에 대한 통지를 받았고, 서비스의 지속을 보장하려면 즉시 납부할 것을 요구받았다.

119 회사 웹사이트는 최근에 상당한 변화를 겪었고, 로그인했던 모든 사람들을 변경으로 인해 혼란스럽게 만들었다.

120 Mr. Simmons는 주로 재정 기록 문서를 보관하는 것을 담당하지만, 그는 또한 다른 사소한 업무들도 처리한다.

121 골동품 장식장을 복제품과 함께 면밀히 살펴본 후, 중개인은 각각의 구별되는 특징을 찾을 수 있었다.

122 최고 경영자는 처음에는 사업을 확장하자는 투자자들의 요청을 반대했지만, 그 이후에 마음을 바꿨다.

123 Ms. Muncy는 개별주가가 매일 변동하는 것을 보는 것보다 채권과 계약형 투자 신탁에 투자하는 것을 선호한다.

124 스포츠 해설자들은 리그에서 더 약세에 있는 팀들 중 그래도 어느 팀이 참가할 수 있을지를 추측해왔다.

125 범죄율이 상당히 감소해왔는데, 이는 부분적으로 사람들이 수상한 행동을 익명으로 신고하는 데 사용할 수 있는 긴급 직통 전화의 설치 덕분이다.

126 사무실에 있는 재활용 가능한 용품들이 낭비되게 하는 것 대신에, Colton 사는 그것들을 지역의 재활용 센터에 가지고 간다.

127 이사들의 오찬을 위해, 관리부는 민감한 사안을 논의하려고 중앙의 식사 구역에서 떨어진 개인실을 예약했다.

128 Dr. Marcus는 할당된 30분을 넘겨 연설을 했고, 연설 이후 질문을 위한 시간을 남겨놓지 않았다.

129 Nigel 미술관은 유명한 박물관들에 비하면 규모가 작았지만, 그 조각품들은 거의 틀림없이 세계 최고들 중에 있었다.

130 제품들이 바로 눈에 띄게 만들기 위해서, 회사는 눈길을 끄는 로고와 관련하여 일류 광고 대행업체와 작업했다.

PART 6

135-138은 다음 회람에 관한 문제입니다.

131-134는 다음 공고에 관한 문제입니다.

토론토 청소년 오케스트라(TYO) 캐나다 순회공연

TYO의 10주년을 기념하여 오케스트라는 처음으로 캐나다 순회공연을 할 것이며, 4개의 공연이 예정되어 있습니다. 순회공연은 11월 8일에 밴쿠버에서 시작될 것이며, 위니펙과 퀘벡시에서 머무는 것을 포함하고, 11월 16일에 토론토에서 끝날 것입니다. 131 토론토에서 열리는 마지막 공연은 Glenview 강당에서 열릴 것입니다. 4,000명 이상의 대중들이 이 공연에 참석할 것으로 예상됩니다.

132 Yves Guilmette에 의해 설립되어, TYO는 봉사활동 노력으로 알려져 있습니다. 그것의 목표는 학업 지원을 제공함으로써 지원을 충분히 받지 못한 토론토의 지역 주민들에게 음악 교육에 대한 접근을 제공하는 것입니다. 133 참가자들은 또한 무료 악기를 받습니다. TYO의 일원들로부터 음악 교육을 받은 많은 사람들은 직접 오케스트라에 합류하기까지 했습니다.

134 이 순회공연은 Maple Union 은행으로부터의 기부금으로 자금을 제공받을 것입니다. 티켓 정보를 얻으시려면, www.tyo.org를 방문하십시오.

135-138은 다음 회람에 관한 문제입니다.

수신: 전 직원
발신: Stephanie Johnstone
제목: Mr. Kaur의 은퇴
날짜: 1월 15일

안녕하세요 여러분,

135 이 회람은 우리가 다음 주 금요일 오후 6시부터 그 이후로 있을 Mr. Kaur를 위한 은퇴 기념 파티를 준비해 두었다는 것을 상기시키기 위한 것입니다. 참석하지 않을 타당한 이유가 없는 한 여러분 모두가 참석해주시면 감사하겠습니다. 136 모두가 착석하고 난 후, 일정은 정확히 오후 6시 15분에 시작할 것입니다. 대표이사님이 축사를 할 계획입니다. 137 그다음에 임원이 Mr. Kaur에게 장기근속 표창을 수여할 것입니다. 최장기간 근무한 우리 직원으로서, 그는 확실히 이러한 인정을 받을 만합니다.

138 저는 각 부서의 관리자들에게 직원들이 Mr. Kaur에게 은퇴 이후 잘 지내기를 바라는 메시지를 적을 수 있는 책자를 돌리도록 요청했습니다. 그 책

자는 내일 아침부터 돌려질 것입니다. 책자는 식의 마지막에 그에게 전달될 것이니, 무언가를 쓰기 위한 시간을 내주시기 바랍니다.

139-142는 다음 편지에 관한 문제입니다.

3월 31일

Annika Dahl
7898번지 Forest로
볼더, 콜로라도주 80301

Ms. Dahl께,

귀하의 최근 방문에 감사드립니다. **139** High Point Medical에서 저희는 각 환자의 필요를 충족시키기 위해 항상 노력합니다. 저희는 귀하께서 받으신 치료의 질에 충분히 만족하시기를 희망합니다.

저희는 환자 치료 설문 조사를 통하여 저희 의료 시설에서의 귀하의 경험에 대해 더 알고 싶습니다. **140** 설문지를 작성해 주시고, 각 5개의 항목이 지시된 대로 평가되었는지 확인해 주십시오. **141** 만약 추가적인 의견이 있으시면, 마련된 빈 공간에 그것들을 포함시켜 주십시오.

설문 조사에 귀하가 제공하는 정보는 검토되어 향후에 저희 서비스를 개선하는 데에 이용될 것이라는 점을 유념해 주십시오. **142** 그렇더라도, 귀하의 개인 정보는 보호될 것입니다. 저희는 귀하의 어떤 응답이라도 추적하여 귀하를 찾을 수 없을 것입니다. 참여해 주셔서 감사드립니다.

Stanley Waite 드림
병원 고객 평가부

143-146은 다음 기사에 관한 문제입니다.

웰링턴 (3월 18일)—금요일은 연례 웰링턴 문학 축제의 시작을 알린다. **143** 올해 행사는 전 세계의 작가들에 의한 발표를 포함할 것이다. **144** 지역에서 인기 있는 것들뿐만 아니라, 축제는 아프리카와 남아메리카의 소설을 선보일 예정이다. **145** 언제나처럼, 이 축제는 젊은 작가들이 제안을 가지고 출판사들에 다가갈 좋은 기회가 될 것이다. 당신이 문학에 대해 열정적이라면, 놓치지 말아야 한다. **146** 행사 티켓은 온라인에서 구매 가능하다.

PART 7

147-148은 다음 문자 메시지에 관한 문제입니다.

발신: 555-2910 (알 수 없는 연락처)

Luigi's 레스토랑을 애용해 주셔서 감사합니다. 예약 5분에서 10분 전에 도착하시면 이 확인 메시지를 호스트에게 보여주십시오. 저희는 귀하의 보증금 50달러를 받았으며, 귀하의 4인석 테이블은 금요일 저녁 7시 30분에 준비될 것입니다. 이 금액은 귀하께서 저희 식당에서 식사하실 때 최종 청구서에서 공제될 것입니다. 그러나, 예약을 취소하시는 경우에는 환불되지 않을 것임을 참고해주세요.

147 문자 메시지는 왜 보내졌는가?
(A) 예약을 확정하기 위해
(B) 레스토랑으로 가는 길을 제공하기 위해
(C) 취소 규정을 업데이트하기 위해
(D) 위약금을 언급하기 위해

148 보증금 지불에 대해 언급된 것은?
(A) 금요일 저녁에 지불할 수 있다.
(B) 청구서에서 차감될 것이다.
(C) 처리하는 데 10분이 걸릴 수 있다.
(D) 식사하기 전에 환불될 수 있다.

149-150은 다음 공고에 관한 문제입니다.

주목해주십시오: Kingsley 강당에서 수업이 있는 학생들

Kingsley 강당에서 열리기로 예정된 수업을 듣는 모든 학생들은 10월 2일부터 4일까지 그 시설을 이용할 수 없을 것이라는 점을 유의해야 합니다. 여느 때와 같이, 생물학부가 이 기간 동안 연례 강연 시리즈를 위해 이 장소를 사용할 것입니다. 이 날짜들에 이 강당에서 열리기로 예정된 수업에 참석하는 학생들은 대신에 Ward 홀로 가도록 요청됩니다.

덧붙여, 보통 오전 10시에 이 강당에서 열리는 "중급 미생물학" 수업의 10월 3일 강의가 취소되었음을 유의해주시기 바랍니다. Evan Chang 교수님은 이번 학기 말에 보충 수업을 여실 것입니다.

무엇이든 질문이 있으시면 부서 사무실로 연락하십시오.

149 Kingsley 강당에 대해 추론될 수 있는 것은?
(A) 보수를 위해 일시적으로 폐쇄될 것이다.
(B) Ward 홀보다 수용력이 더 크다.
(C) 정기적으로 학술 행사를 위해 사용되어 왔다.
(D) 일반적으로는 수업을 위해 사용되지 않는다.

150 중급 미생물학 수업에 대해 언급되지 않은 것은?
(A) 평소 수업 장소
(B) 수업의 강사 이름
(C) 수업 시작 시간
(D) 수업 지속 시간

151-153은 다음 안내문에 관한 문제입니다.

회의실 예약

Great Files사의 직원 누구든지 회의실을 예약하길 원하면, 온라인 www.greatfiles.com/employee/meetings에 있는 회의실 예약 일정표에 가서 예약 가능한 시간대를 확인하십시오. 만약 필요로 하는 시간대가 예약 불가일 경우, 아래에 나열된 각 층의 행정 대리 직원에게 이메일을 보내고 예약 목적을 포함하십시오.

층	대리 직원
2층	Heather Greenstone
3층	Roxanne Laddington
4층	Elissa Hunter
5층	Victor Anzelo
7층	Roxanne Laddington
8층	Jonathan Madison
9층	Ian Dexter
10층	Elissa Hunter

대리 직원은 예약 일정이 변경될 수 있으면 그때 연락을 드릴 것입니다. 일정 변경을 협의하기 위해 이미 회의실을 예약한 어떤 당사자에게도 연락하지 마십시오.

만약 온라인 일정표가 여러분이 원하는 시간이 비어있다고 보여줄 경우, 드롭다운 메뉴에서 시간을 선택하고 회의 목적과 함께 참석자 수를 입력하십시오. 임박한 예약에는 회의실을 제공하기 어려울 수 있으므로 최소한 일주일 전에 예약하는 것이 강력히 권고됩니다. 또한, 7층과 8층의 대회의실들은 이제 토요일과 일요일을 포함하여 매일 오후 11시까지 이용 가능함을 알아 두십시오. 다른 모든 회의실들은 정규 근무 시간 동안에만 예약될 수 있습니다. 일정 관리 시스템과 관련하여 어떠한 문의나 우려 사항이 있으면, 내선 번호 2968번으로 Roxanne Laddington에게 연락하십시오.

151 안내문의 주 목적은 무엇인가?
(A) 직원들에게 사무 절차를 설명하기 위해
(B) 층별 관리자 이름을 분명히 알리기 위해
(C) 회의 규정을 공지하기 위해
(D) 직원들에게 회의실 변경을 알리기 위해

152 층의 대리 직원들에 대해 언급되지 않은 것은?
(A) 그들 중 한 명은 일정 관리 시스템 문의를 위한 중개자이다.
(B) 그들 중 누구도 6층에 대해서는 책임이 없다.
(C) 그들 중 한 명만이 2개의 층에 배정된다.
(D) 그들 모두는 회의실 변경에 대해 층별로 연락을 받을 수 있다.

153 회의실들에 대해 암시되는 것은?
(A) 대리 직원에게 직접 전화해서 예약될 수 있다.
(B) 일부 회의실들의 시간이 연장되었다.
(C) 7층과 8층의 회의실은 개조되었다.
(D) 부서 관리자들로부터 예약될 수 있다.

154-155는 다음 메시지 대화문에 관한 문제입니다.

Dorothy Lee	[4시 15분]

당신이 Mr. Parker의 라스베이거스행 항공편 예약을 맡은 인턴이죠? 그가 변경 사항이 있다고 당신에게 말해줄 것을 저에게 부탁했는데, 그는 6월 9일에 떠나서 14일에 돌아와야 해요.

James Harter	[4시 18분]

포인트 잔액을 확인하려면 그의 상용 고객 번호가 필요해서 아직 하지 않았어요. 그것에 관해 일찍이 물어보려고 했었는데, 그와 다른 관리자들이 아직 회의 중이에요.

Dorothy Lee	[4시 20분]

제가 그 정보를 어딘가에 가지고 있어요. 제가 그의 개인비서이니, 그러한 세부 사항들이 필요할 때면 언제든 저에게 연락하시면 됩니다. 제가 그것을 찾아볼게요.

Dorothy Lee	[4시 24분]

KLJ0294SB1이에요.

James Harter	[4시 25분]

알겠어요. 지금 확인하고 있어요.

James Harter	[4시 28분]

그는 왕복 여행 비용을 댈 만큼 충분한 포인트를 가지고 있지 않네요. 그래도 포인트를 사용해야 할까요?

Dorothy Lee	[4시 29분]

신경 쓰지 마세요. 그것들은 앞으로의 비행을 위해 아껴두죠.

James Harter	[4시 30분]

알겠어요. 그럼 제가 지금 예약할게요.

Dorothy Lee	[4시 30분]

이메일로 제게 확인서를 보내주세요. 고마워요, James.

154 Mr. Harter는 왜 업무를 완료할 수 없었는가?
(A) 필요한 정보가 없었다.
(B) 두 가지의 다른 지시를 받았다.
(C) 다른 업무로 바빴다.
(D) 해야 하는 것을 잘못 이해했다.

155 4시 29분에, Ms. Lee가 "Don't bother"라고 썼을 때 그녀가 의도한 것은?
(A) Mr. Harter가 예약을 취소하기를 원한다.
(B) Mr. Parker가 바쁜 동안 그를 방해하고 싶지 않아 한다.
(C) Mr. Parker의 항공편이 포인트를 사용하지 않고 결제되는 것을 선호한다.
(D) Mr. Parker가 왕복 항공편이 필요할 것이라고 생각하지 않는다.

156-157은 다음 기사에 관한 문제입니다.

Capri 인테리어 회사 친환경적이 되다
Sophia Weathers 기자

8월 2일—Capri 인테리어 회사의 최고 경영자 Jasmine Shah가 지난 월요일 회사의 환경친화적인 미래에 대한 계획을 공개했다. Ms. Shah는 토론토 국제 홈 디자인 박람회에서 관중들에게 올가을부터, Capri 인테리어 회사 ◐

는 전체 국내 출처의 자재로 만든 가구를 생산할 것이라고 발표했다. Ms. Shah는 현지 원자재 사용이 회사 탄소 배출량의 60퍼센트 감소로 이어질 것이라고 말했다.

Ms. Shah는 또한 박람회에서 Capri 인테리어 회사의 생산 공장을 위해 더 효율적이고 친환경적인 폐기물 관리 기계를 설계하도록 Verdant사의 서비스를 요청하여 얻는 것을 고려하고 있다고 암시했다.

156 기사에 따르면, 지난주에 무슨 일이 일어났는가?
(A) 최고 경영자가 후임자를 발표했다.
(B) 제조업체가 새로운 지점을 열었다.
(C) 디자인 무역 박람회가 개최되었다.
(D) 가구 제품군이 할인되었다.

157 Ms. Shah는 무엇을 하려고 계획하는가?
(A) 환경 단체에 더 많은 돈을 기부한다
(B) 해외 국가들로부터 자재를 수입한다
(C) 제조를 다른 회사들에 위탁한다
(D) Capri사의 폐기물 처리 방식을 개선한다

158-160은 다음 이메일에 관한 문제입니다.

수신: 전 직원
발신: Brendan Rogerson <b.rogerson@ellisellis.com>
제목: 교육 과정
날짜: 4월 12일

안녕하세요 Ellis and Ellis Consulting사의 전 직원 여러분,

아시다시피, 저는 사무실에서 효율성을 높이기 위한 방안을 찾기 위해 노력해 왔고 여러분들의 제안 사항들을 제공하는 설문 조사를 작성해줄 것을 요청했었습니다. ― [1] ―. 예를 들어, 많은 직원들이 그들의 기술들을 늘릴 수 있도록 더 많은 전문성 개발 강의를 듣고 싶다는 바람을 표현해왔습니다. 동시에, 저는 우리가 매우 정기적으로 그래픽 디자이너들을 고용했어야 했음을 알게 되었습니다. ― [2] ―. 웹사이트 디자인이나 우리의 연례 보고서 작성과 같은 아주 큰 프로젝트에 관한 한 이것은 적절해 보이지만, 많은 경우에서 우리는 우리 직원들 중 한 명이 약간의 교육을 통해 할 수 있을 듯한 한 시간 분량의 업무를 하도록 그들을 고용하고 있습니다. ― [3] ―.

결과적으로, 저는 관심 있는 직원 누구나를 위해 기본적인 그래픽 디자인 기술에 관한 짧은 강좌를 계획하는 것을 고려하고 있습니다. ― [4] ―. 이는 우리가 앞으로 더 작은 디자인 프로젝트에 사내 기술을 이용하도록 할 것입니다. 만약 여러분들이 참여하고 싶으신 것 같다면, 4월 20일 전에 이 이메일에 회신하셔서 제게 알려 주십시오.

Brendon Rogerson 드림
인사부장, Ellis and Ellis Consulting사

158 Ellis and Ellis Consulting사에 대해 암시되는 것은?
(A) 다른 기업들에게 교육 과정을 제공한다.
(B) 웹사이트 디자인을 전문으로 한다.
(C) 최근에 연례 보고서를 발표했다.
(D) 그래픽 디자인과 관련된 불필요한 지출이 있다.

159 Mr. Rogerson은 무엇을 하고 싶어 하는가?
(A) 그래픽 디자이너들을 정규직 사원으로 고용한다
(B) 몇 가지 설문 조사 질문에 대해 직원들에게서 아이디어를 얻는다
(C) 외부 지원에 대한 회사의 의존을 줄인다
(D) 기술 개발 강의에 대한 직원들의 관심을 북돋운다

160 [1], [2], [3], [4]로 표시된 위치 중, 다음 문장이 들어갈 곳으로 가장 적절한 것은?

"그것들을 살펴보면서, 제게 두 가지 추세들이 매우 분명해졌습니다."

(A) [1]
(B) [2]

(C) [3]

(D) [4]

161-163은 다음 편지에 관한 문제입니다.

11월 12일

체리밸리 상수 지구

495번 사서함

체리밸리, 캘리포니아 92223

Kimberly Tompkins

Woodhaven로 47번지

체리밸리, 캘리포니아 92223

Ms. Tompkins께,

이 편지는 Woodhaven로의 수도 서비스가 11월 30일 오후 12시와 3시 사이에 차단될 것임을 알리기 위한 것입니다. 이 시간 동안, 저희는 거리의 관수로에 몇 가지 중요한 수리를 진행할 것입니다.

저희는 이것이 지역 주민들에게 불편을 의미한다는 것을 이해합니다. 체리밸리 지역에 안전하고 깨끗한 수돗물을 공급하기 위해 필요한 개선을 실시하는 동안 여러분의 인내심에 감사드립니다.

수돗물이 차단되는 동안, 주민들은 저희 본사에서 병에 든 물을 무료로 수령할 수 있습니다. 각 주민은 무료로 물 1갤런을 받을 수 있습니다. 이 편지 또는 주에서 발급한 신분증 등, 주소 증빙자료를 가져오시기 바랍니다.

저희 본사는 Anderson가 393번지, 체리밸리, 캘리포니아 92223에 위치해 있습니다. 문의 사항이 있으시면 555-1311로 사무실에 전화 주십시오.

Candace Ludwig 드림

체리밸리 공공사업국장

161 편지의 목적은 무엇인가?

(A) 서비스 중단을 알리기 위해

(B) 주민들에게 위험을 경고하기 위해

(C) 일부 편의시설에 대한 대안을 제시하기 위해

(D) 주민들을 행사에 초대하기 위해

162 2문단 두 번째 줄의 단어 "perform"은 의미상 -와 가장 가깝다.

(A) 완료하다

(B) 접대하다

(C) 제시하다

(D) 기능하다

163 주민들은 체리밸리 상수 지구 본사에서 무엇을 받을 수 있는가?

(A) 주소 증빙자료

(B) 주에서 발급한 신분증

(C) 병에 든 물 1갤런

(D) 곧 있을 수리에 대한 편지

164-167은 다음 온라인 채팅 대화문에 관한 문제입니다.

Greg Fournier   오전 9시 11분

RMP 금융 신탁의 실시간 채팅 서비스에 오신 것을 환영합니다. 어떻게 도와드릴까요?

Vivianne Gonyer   오전 9시 12분

귀사의 은행에 제가 가지고 있는 계좌가 아직도 유효한지 궁금합니다. 제가 외국으로 이주할 때 계좌 사용을 중단했었는데, 몇 주 내에 영구적으로 귀국했을 때 그것을 되살리고 싶어요.

Greg Fournier   오전 9시 12분

귀하의 ATM 카드에 있는 번호를 알 수 있을까요?

Vivianne Gonyer   오전 9시 13분

그게 문제예요. 제 ATM 카드가 필요할 것이라고 생각하지 않았기 때문에 그것을 보관하지 않았어요.

Greg Fournier   오전 9시 14분

알겠습니다. 보안상의 이유로, 저는 귀하의 성함과 ATM 카드 번호를 맞추어 보아야 합니다. 다른 방법이 없어요.

Vivianne Gonyer   오전 9시 14분

그럴 거라고 생각했어요. 휴면계좌에 관한 귀사의 방침이 무엇인지 말해주실 수 있나요? 그건 당좌 예금 계좌였고, 제가 마지막으로 그걸 사용한 게 분명 2년도 더 넘었을 거예요.

Greg Fournier   오전 9시 15분

저희 기록에 따르면, 귀하께서 사실 그 계좌를 닫으셨습니다.

Vivianne Gonyer   오전 9시 17분

아. 저는 귀국하기 전에 제 계좌로 현재 자금을 보내고 싶었는데요. 이것이 가능할까요?

Greg Fournier   오전 9시 18분

음, PrestoDirect와 같은 송금 서비스를 이용하실 수 있어요. 약 5퍼센트의 수수료가 있을 것이지만, 은행 계좌를 갖고 있을 필요 없이, 그 기업의 어느 지점에서든지 돈을 받으실 수 있습니다. 새로운 계좌를 만드는 것은 도착하신 후 저희와 함께 생각해 보셔도 됩니다.

164 오전 9시 13분에, Ms. Gonyer가 "That's the problem"이라고 썼을 때 그녀가 의도한 것은?

(A) 온라인 결제 시스템을 사용할 수 없다.

(B) 그녀의 계좌 잔액을 기억할 수 없다.

(C) 어떤 정보에 접근할 수 없다.

(D) 그녀의 거래들 중 하나와 관련된 문제를 발견했다.

165 RMP 금융 신탁에 대해 암시되는 것은?

(A) 고객이 온라인 뱅킹을 신청하도록 장려하고 있다.

(B) 고객의 신분을 확인하는 한 가지 방법만을 인정한다.

(C) 하루 24시간 열려 있는 전화 상담 서비스를 운영한다.

(D) 전 세계에 지점을 설립했다.

166 Ms. Gonyer는 무엇을 하고 싶어 하는가?

(A) 해외에서 사용할 계좌를 만든다

(B) 당좌 예금 계좌를 개설한다

(C) 다른 나라로 돈을 옮긴다

(D) 해외에 있는 동안 자금을 인출한다

167 Mr. Fournier는 Ms. Gonyer에게 무엇에 대해 조언하는가?

(A) 여행 규제를 준수하는 것

(B) 금융 서비스 제공업체를 이용하는 것

(C) 법정 대리인을 지명하는 것

(D) 높은 수수료를 피하는 것

168-171은 다음 공고에 관한 문제입니다.

STRYKER 놀이공원

10월이 아주 가까이 왔고, 이는 Stryker 놀이공원의 모두가 무시무시한 핼러윈 재미의 달을 준비하고 있다는 것을 의미합니다. 10월 1일부터 10월 31일까지 계속해서, 저희는 모든 연령대의 방문객들을 위한 깜짝 놀랄 정도로 재미있는 행사 시리즈인 연례 Fright Nights를 열 것입니다. 아래는 저희가 계획한 몇 가지 행사들의 일정입니다.

날짜	행사	장소
10월 1-31일	귀신의 집 투어	북쪽 파빌리온
10월 10-31일	사악한 좀비 놀이기구	동쪽 파빌리온
10월 15-31일	옥수수밭 미로	남쪽 주차장
10월 25-31일	어린이 구역	푸드 코트

다음의 주요 볼거리들을 꼭 확인하세요:

- 귀신의 집 투어가 여기 Stryker 놀이공원에 세 번째 연속으로 돌아옵니다. *California Living*지는 최근 삼 층짜리로 100명 이상의 배우를 포함하는

이 저택을 "서부 해안에서 세 번째로 가장 무서운 귀신의 집"으로 평가했습니다.
- 어린이 구역은 페이스 페인팅, 스토리텔링, 호박 장식을 포함하여 어린아이들을 위한 많은 재미있는 활동들을 포함합니다.
- Fright Nights의 마지막 날인 10월 31일에는 영화 *Darkness Rises*의 배우 Kayla Draper가 중앙 파빌리온에서 사인을 해줄 것입니다.
- 공원 곳곳의 매점들은 호박 맛 커피와 캔디 애플을 포함하는 Fright Nights 음식을 제공할 것입니다.

Fright Nights의 입장료는 일반 입장권에 포함됩니다. 이 행사들에 대한 더 많은 정보를 원하시면 저희 웹사이트 www.strykeramusement.com/frightnights를 방문하세요.

168 공고는 주로 무엇에 대한 것인가?
(A) 귀신의 집 수리
(B) 입장권의 특별 할인
(C) 축제 행사의 달
(D) 놀이공원 입장 규정

169 호박 장식은 어디에서 열릴 것인가?
(A) 북쪽 파빌리온에서
(B) 동쪽 파빌리온에서
(C) 남쪽 주차장에서
(D) 푸드 코트에서

170 Fright Nights에 대해 언급된 것은?
(A) 전국을 순회한다.
(B) 볼거리들 중 하나가 한 출판물에 의해 인정받았다.
(C) 주로 성인들에게 적합하도록 맞춰져 있다.
(D) 참여하는 사람들은 추가 입장료를 내야 한다.

171 10월 동안에 일어나지 않을 것은?
(A) *Darkness Rises*의 특별 상영이 있을 것이다.
(B) 핼러윈을 테마로 한 놀이기구가 대중에게 개방될 것이다.
(C) 주차장이 미로로 바뀔 것이다.
(D) 특별한 다과가 구매 가능할 것이다.

172-175는 다음 기사에 관한 문제입니다.

Edmond Estrada가 앨버커키 판사직을 차지하다

3월 18일—앨버커키 지방법원의 대변인이 Edmond Estrada 변호사가 판사직을 위한 출마에서 이겼다고 발표했다. — [1] —. 그는 3월 말에 퇴임할 것이라고 올해 초에 공식화한 현직 판사 Wendy Delwes의 후임자가 될 것이다.

지난 25년 동안 변호사로서의 그의 역할에 있어서, Mr. Estrada는 수천 건의 법률 소송들에 관여해왔다. 이 소송들은 민원들과 임대차 관계 소송들을 모두 포함했다. — [2] —.

"변호사로서 앨버커키 시민들을 위해 일한 것", Estrada가 말하길, "그리고 수년 동안 Delwes 판사가 보여주었던 유능한 리더십을 직접 보아온 것은 저의 특권이었습니다. 그녀의 선례를 통해, 저는 앨버커키 시민들을 위해 저희 법원이 최선을 다해 일하는 방법에 대해 많이 배워왔습니다. — [3] —. 진심으로, 그녀의 뒤를 잇게 되어 영광스럽습니다."

그의 법적 경험 외에도, Mr. Estrada는 지역 공동체에서도 적극적이다. — [4] —. 그는 Rio Rancho 토지 위원회의 일원이며 수많은 지역 자선단체들과 봉사를 해왔다.

172 기사는 주로 무엇에 대한 것인가?
(A) 법적 지원을 받기 위한 절차
(B) 시장 선거의 결과
(C) 직책으로 선발된 후보자
(D) 기관의 활동들

173 Mr. Estrada는 왜 Delwes 판사를 칭찬하는가?
(A) 한때 앨버커키에서 피고측 변호인으로 일했다.

(B) 상원 의석을 위한 효과적인 선거 유세를 펼쳤다.
(C) 많은 법정 경험을 가지고 있다.
(D) 지역 법을 바꾸기 위한 노력을 주도했다.

174 Mr. Estrada에 대해 언급되지 않은 것은?
(A) 부동산 회사를 변호한다.
(B) 때때로 무보수 일에 관여한다.
(C) 지역 공동체에 자주 참여한다.
(D) 20년 이상 동안 변호사 일을 해왔다.

175 [1], [2], [3], [4]로 표시된 위치 중, 다음 문장이 들어갈 곳으로 가장 적절한 것은?

"그가 다뤘던 모든 법적 사안에서, 그는 정의의 추구에 대한 변함없는 헌신을 보여주었다."

(A) [1]
(B) [2]
(C) [3]
(D) [4]

176-180은 다음 웹페이지와 이메일에 관한 문제입니다.

www.lakegodardski.com/about

LAKE GODARD 스키 리조트

소개	표와 프로그램	숙박	사진

매년 만 명 이상의 방문객들을 유치하고 많은 협의회를 주최하는 Lake Godard는 미국에서 가장 인기 있는 겨울 휴양지들 중 하나입니다.

저희 스키 슬로프는 지역 내에서 가장 다양한 축에 속합니다. 저희는 초보자 코스들과 숙련자들을 위한 어려운 경사로들을 보유하고 있습니다. 저희의 자동 스키 리프트는 여러분이 원하는 슬로프에 도착하는 데에 절대 오래 기다리지 않아도 된다는 것을 보장하고, 여러분이 문제에 맞닥뜨릴 경우를 대비하여 저희 안내원들은 항상 이용 가능합니다.

하지만 Lake Godard에는 단순히 스키 타기 이상의 것이 있습니다. 저희 산장은 다양한 활동들을 제공합니다. 저희 오락실에서 게임을, 스파에서 마사지를, 그리고 안내원을 동반한 숲 하이킹을 즐겨보십시오. 만약 리조트 밖의 도시를 탐험하는 데에 관심이 있으시면, 저희 직원들이 기꺼이 표를 예매하는 것을 도와 드리거나 지역 명소들을 추천해 드릴 것입니다. 객실 하나는 1박에 129달러부터이지만, 경치 좋은 Bear산의 언덕들이 내다보이는, 저희의 인기 있는 고급 객실은 1박에 149달러부터입니다. 게다가, 7박 이상의 숙박을 할 때마다 손님들께 전문 스키 강사로부터 무료 일일 강습을 받을 자격을 드립니다.

저희와 함께 겨울 휴가를 보내는 것에 관심이 있으시면, 555-3612로 전화주시거나 booking@lakegodardski.com으로 이메일을 보내주십시오.

수신: Lake Godard 예약 <booking@lakegodardski.com>
발신: Anna Fuller <annafuller@fastmail.com>
제목: 예약
날짜: 11월 24일

담당자분께,

저는 이전에 Lake Godard 지역을 방문한 적이 있지만, 그쪽 시설에서 숙박한 적은 없습니다. 휴일에 저는 제 남편과 두 딸과 함께 그곳으로 여행을 갈 계획입니다. 이번 시즌이 특히 붐빈다는 것을 알기에, 12월 20일에서 29일에 투숙 가능한 방이 아직 있는지 궁금합니다. 그 지역의 다른 몇몇 호텔에도 연락해 보았지만, 예약이 꽉 차 있었습니다.

가능하다면, 저는 리조트의 웹사이트에서 언급된 고급 객실 중 하나를 예약하고 싶습니다. 또한, 제 딸들은 이전에 스키를 타본 적이 없어서, 그들이 강습을 받았으면 합니다. 마지막으로, 저희가 거기에 머무는 동안 볼 수 있는 지역 공연을 추천해 주실 수 있으신가요? 저희는 마술쇼나 가벼운 뮤지컬 같은 것을 선호합니다.

Anna Fuller 드림

176 Lake Godard가 제공하는 서비스로 언급되지 않은 것은?
　　(A) 근처 자연의 관광
　　(B) 슬로프 정상까지의 운송
　　(C) 오락실에서의 활동
　　(D) 프로 스키 선수들을 위한 강습

177 웹페이지에서, 2문단 세 번째 줄의 단어 "available"은 의미상 ~와 가장 가깝다.
　　(A) 고용되어
　　(B) 예비로 마련해 둔
　　(C) 손이 닿는 곳에
　　(D) 대신하여

178 Ms. Fuller에 대해 암시되는 것은?
　　(A) 예약을 변경하기를 원한다.
　　(B) 다른 호텔에서의 예약을 취소할 것이다.
　　(C) 산이 보이는 전망을 가진 숙소를 원한다.
　　(D) 어느 슬로프에서 스키를 탈지에 대한 추천을 원한다.

179 요청이 충족되면 Ms. Fuller의 아이들은 무엇을 할 것인가?
　　(A) 안내원을 동반한 숲 하이킹을 하러 간다
　　(B) 학교를 며칠 쉰다
　　(C) 강사로부터 무료 강습을 받는다
　　(D) 뮤지컬 공연을 한다

180 Ms. Fuller는 무엇을 하고 싶어 하는가?
　　(A) 공연을 볼 시간을 마련한다
　　(B) 이전에 숙박했던 방을 예약한다
　　(C) 시도해보는 지역 농산물의 목록을 얻는다
　　(D) 이메일로 상세한 스키 강습 계획안을 받는다

181-185는 다음 이메일과 공고에 관한 문제입니다.

수신: Angela Porter <a.porter@bigbuy.com>
발신: Mason Daley <m.daley@bigbuy.com>
제목: 관리자 회의
날짜: 9월 21일
첨부: 회의록

안녕하세요 Angela,

어제 고객과의 논의가 잘 진행되었기를 바랍니다. 우리는 관리자 회의에 당신이 참석하지 않아 아쉬웠습니다. 우리가 다루었던 모든 것의 요약본을 읽어보려면, 이 이메일에 첨부된 기록을 확인해 보십시오. 그 밖에, 당신이 알아야 할 가장 중요한 것은 다가오는 연휴 즈음의 업무 일정과 관련된 것입니다.

Mr. Baker는 당신이 이것과 관련하여 직원들에게 그들의 책무에 대해 상기시키는 공고를 작성해주기를 원합니다. 작년 이 기간 동안 너무 많은 사람들이 결근했고, 그는 이런 일이 다시 일어나지 않도록 확실히 하기를 바랍니다. 그는 특별히 부서 감독들이 필요에 따라 근무 시간을 다시 배정할 수 있도록 연휴 휴가를 미리 계획하는 것에 대해 언급했습니다. 최종 일정은 11월 25일까지 회사 인트라넷에 게시될 것입니다. 이는 우리의 성수기 시작 하루 전이고, 성수기는 일반적으로 11월 26일부터 1월 4일까지입니다. Mr. Baker는 의료적 또는 개인적인 응급 상황의 경우들을 제외하고 늦은 휴가 신청은 승인되지 않을 것이라고 덧붙였습니다. 공고는 이 모든 정보를 포함하여야 합니다. 작업이 완료되면, 점포 관리자들에게 그것을 보내서 그들이 이것을 검토할 수 있게 해야 할 것입니다.

질문이 있으면 제게 알려 주십시오.

감사합니다,
Mason 드림
교대근무 관리자
운영 부서

BigBuy사
전 직원 대상 공고
9월 30일

휴일 쇼핑 시즌에 대비하여, 저희는 여러분이 시간을 내서 회사 인트라넷에 게시된 근무 일정표를 확인할 것을 상기시켜 드리고자 합니다. 정확한 근무 시간이 배정되었는지 확실히 하기 위해 확인하는 것 외에, 여러분의 휴가들이 일정표에 기재되어 있는지 확인해 주시기 바랍니다.

휴가 신청은 늦어도 10월 30일까지 제출해주시기 바랍니다. 그 날짜부터 11월 25일까지 이루어진 휴가 신청은 오직 각 부서 감독의 재량으로 승인될 것이며, 각 부서 감독은 상점에 직원들이 충분히 배치되어야 하는 필요와 직원 요구의 균형을 맞춰야 합니다.

이 신청들은 최종 일정이 게시되기 전에 답을 받을 것입니다. 11월 26일에서 1월 4일에 이루어진 휴가 신청들은 개인적 또는 의료적 응급 상황의 경우를 제외하고 관리자를 포함하여 누구에게든 승인되지 않을 것입니다. 항상 그렇듯이, 이러한 상황의 경우에는 응급 휴가에 대한 자격이 있음을 증명하는 서류가 요구될 것입니다.

만약 추가 질문이 있으면, 여러분 각자의 부서 감독들과 논의하십시오. 이 사안에 대해 협조해 주셔서 감사합니다.

---

181 이메일의 한 가지 목적은 무엇인가?
　　(A) 곧 있을 휴가 계획을 수정하기 위해
　　(B) 이전 요청에 대해 그녀에게 최신 정보를 알리기 위해
　　(C) 최근 논의에 대해 그녀에게 최신 정보를 주기 위해
　　(D) 그녀와 일정 충돌에 대해 논의하기 위해

182 BigBuy사에 대해 언급된 것은?
　　(A) 새해에 정규 영업시간이 바뀔 것이다.
　　(B) 직원들에게 휴일 근무에 대한 초과 근무 수당을 제공한다.
　　(C) 경영진이 구조조정을 준비하고 있다.
　　(D) 결근한 직원들과 관련된 문제가 있었다.

183 부서 감독들이 하도록 요구되는 것이 아닌 것은?
　　(A) 추가적인 휴가에 대한 일부 신청을 승인한다
　　(B) 계절 근로자 직원들에게 교육을 제공한다
　　(C) 충분한 직원들이 있도록 한다
　　(D) 직원들의 문의를 처리한다

184 직원들은 언제 휴가에 대한 승인을 받을 것으로 예상할 수 있는가?
　　(A) 9월과 10월 사이에
　　(B) 늦어도 10월 30일까지
　　(C) 11월 25일 전에
　　(D) 12월과 1월 사이에

185 Ms. Porter는 9월 말에 무엇을 했을 것 같은가?
　　(A) 다른 직원에게 업무를 맡겼다
　　(B) 그녀의 상황에 대한 최신 정보를 제공했다
　　(C) 완성된 원고를 몇몇 관리자에게 보냈다
　　(D) 전자 공지를 게시했다

186-190은 다음 기사, 영수증, 이메일에 관한 문제입니다.

Art Vibe지

Brayman 미술관(BMA)의 리모델링이 마침내 완료되었고, 그 시설은 9월 26일 수요일에 재개장할 것이다. 이는 미술관 큐레이터 Jane Wellington의 짧은 연설과 함께, 미술관의 앞쪽 잔디밭에서 개최되는 행사로 기념될 것이다. Ms. Wellington은 BMA가 오클랜드시에서 50년이 넘게 이뤄온 발전에 대해 이야기할 것이다. 그녀는 또한 미술관의 새로운 특별 전시 *France in Focus*를 소개할 것이고, 이 전시는 그날 시작하며, 유럽의 고대 Gallic 부족들의 유물들을 포함한다. 이 순회 전시는 파리에서 처음 개장했을 때 프랑스 출판물들로부터 아주 좋은 평가를 받았고, BMA에서의 전시 이후 시드니로,

그 후 퍼스로 옮겨갈 것이다. 전시 티켓은 12달러이며 www.braymanart.org에서 사전에 예매될 수 있다. 미술관은 또한 전시 기간 동안 10세 이하의 어린이에게는 정가 7달러 대신 5달러의 특별 입장료를 제공할 것이다. 문의는 555-1288로 BMA의 홍보 전문가인 Henry Kang에게 하면 된다.

Brayman 미술관
지불 확인서

오늘 일자: 8월 17일
손님 성함: Kerry Rosales
전시 종류: *France in Focus*
입장 일자: 9월 26일

종류	장수	장당 가격	총 가격
일반 티켓	1	12달러	12달러
특별 티켓	2	5달러	10달러
		전체	22달러

지불 확인 번호: 347792R

사전 예매를 했을 시에는, 전시에 입장할 때 티켓을 받는 미술관 직원에게 이 영수증을 반드시 보여주십시오. 입장은 매일 오전 8시에서 오후 3시 사이에 허용될 것입니다.

수신: Henry Kang <h_kang@braymanart.org>
발신: Jane Wellington <j_wellington@braymanart.org>
날짜: 9월 10일
제목: 중요한 변경 사항

안녕하세요 Henry,

긴급한 요청이 있습니다. 안타깝게도, 저는 오늘 아침에 전화를 받았는데, *France in Focus* 전시에 지연이 있을 것입니다. 몇몇 유물들이 세관에서 통과하지 못하고 있습니다. 보아하니, 세관 직원들이 우리에게 물품들을 보내주기 전에 반드시 추가 서류를 확인해야 한다고 합니다. 우리는 필요한 서류 작업을 하고 있지만, 전시 일정에 맞춰 처리되지는 않을 것입니다. 물품들은 전시를 개장하기로 예정된 그다음 날부터 이곳 미술관에 도착하기 시작할 것입니다. 따라서, 개장은 최소 2주 연기되어야 합니다. 저는 미리 전시 티켓을 구매한 사람들에게 당신이 연락해줬으면 합니다. 그들에게 새로운 개장일에 동일한 티켓을 사용해서 입장할 수 있지만, 돈을 돌려받는 선택 사항도 있다는 것을 확실히 알려주시기 바랍니다.

질문이 있으면 제게 알려주세요.

Jane Wellington 드림
Brayman 미술관, 큐레이터

---

186 기사의 주제는 무엇인가?
(A) 새로운 큐레이터의 임명
(B) 시설의 개장을 축하하는 기념일 연회
(C) 보수 이후의 특별 행사
(D) 지역 예술가의 작품 전시

187 Ms. Rosales에 대해 암시되는 것은?
(A) 시설의 후원자여서 할인을 받았다.
(B) 개장하는 전시에 아이들과 함께 갈 계획이다.
(C) 오후에 유물들을 관람할 계획이다.
(D) 미술관에서 입장료를 지불할 것이다.

188 티켓을 미리 구매한 사람들은 전시에 무엇을 가지고 오도록 요구되는가?
(A) 공인 신분증
(B) 구매 증명서
(C) 할인 쿠폰
(D) 오픈 티켓

189 Brayman 미술관에 대해 사실인 것은?
(A) 전시 후에 바로 퍼스로 유물들을 보낼 것이다.

(B) 큐레이터가 8월에 지연에 대해 통지받았다.
(C) 오클랜드의 새로운 시설이 전시 기간에 맞춰 건설되지 않을 것이다.
(D) 9월 27일에 몇 가지 전시품을 받을 것으로 예상하고 있다.

190 Ms. Wellington은 Mr. Kang에게 무엇을 해달라고 요청하는가?
(A) 티켓 소지자들에게 그들의 선택권에 관해 알린다
(B) 박물관 회원들에게 환불금을 전달한다
(C) 전시회에 무료 입장을 제공한다
(D) 예술가들에게 일정 변경에 관해 연락한다

191-195는 다음 회람, 이메일, 온라인 양식에 관한 문제입니다.

회람

수신: 전 직원
발신: Tom Williams, 이사
날짜: 8월 10일
제목: 신입사원들

여러분들 대부분이 아시다시피, Techno Tel사는 8월 1일에 Regent Mobile사를 공식적으로 인수했습니다. 이 회람은 이로 인해 Regent Mobile사로부터 다섯 명의 직원들이 약 일주일 내로 우리 사무실에 합류할 것임을 여러분들에게 알려드리기 위한 것입니다. 그들 중 세 명은 연구개발팀에서 근무할 것이고, 다른 두 명은 마케팅팀에서 일할 것입니다. 그들은 8월 16일 월요일에 근무를 시작할 것이고, 몇 가지 행정상 필요한 일들을 수행한 후 그날 교육을 받기 시작할 것입니다. 저는 모든 직원들이 그들을 따뜻하게 맞아주고 그들이 가질 수 있는 어떠한 질문에라도 답변해주어 그들이 새로운 업무 환경에 빠르게 적응할 수 있기를 바랍니다.

감사합니다.

발신: Neil Adams <nadams@technotel.com>
수신: Maude Garcia <purchasing@technotel.com>
날짜: 8월 11일
제목: 신입사원들을 위한 물품

안녕하세요 Maude,

당신은 아마 8월 10일에 관리부의 Tom Williams로부터 회람을 받았을 것입니다. 이번 변화들에 대한 준비로, 직원들과 저는 저희 부서에 책상, 의자, 가리개를 포함하는 칸막이가 있는 자리를 마련해 두었습니다. 하지만 저희는 아직 몇 가지 물품들이 없으며, 구매부서가 저희의 고정 공급업체로 하여금 그것들을 배달하도록 할 수 있는지 알고 싶습니다. 저는 신규 직원들이 근무를 시작하는 데 필요한 모든 것을 확실히 갖추도록 하고 싶습니다. 저희는 서류 정리함, 개인용 컴퓨터, 탁상용 책꽂이가 각각 3개씩을 주문해야 합니다. 또한 그들은 몇 가지의 기본적인 사무용품들도 필요할 것입니다. 이것이 급한 주문이라는 것을 Office Interiors and Supplies사에 알려 주십시오. 이는 8월 13일까지 배송되어야 합니다. 신입사원들이 다음 주에 그들의 교육을 시작하니 저희는 8월 16일 전에 모든 것을 준비할 충분한 시간이 필요할 것입니다. 감사드리며, 촉박하게 통보하게 되어 죄송합니다.

Neil 드림

Office Interiors and Supplies사
800번지 Garnet가
시카고, 일리노이주 60615
전화: 555-2001
이메일: orders@officeintsup.com

	홈 | 제품 | **귀하의 쇼핑 카트** | 고객 서비스		

계정 보유자: Techno Tel사

주문 번호: 914579		08/12 오전 10시 45분	
제품 코드	종류	수량	가격
OF00928	철제 서류 정리함, 회색	3	509.97달러
OS1544	볼펜, 검정과 빨강	6	6.60달러
OF00283	개인용 컴퓨터 (중앙처리 장치, 모니터, 키보드, 마우스와 주변장치)	3	1,648.50달러
OS1927	노트	3	15.90달러
OS1326	탁상용 책꽂이	3	21.90달러
	소계		2,202.87달러
	세금		220.29달러
	합계		2,423.16달러

귀하의 쇼핑 카트

쇼핑 계속하기

결제하기

[검색]

연락처

환불과 취소는 제품마다 다릅니다. 더 알아보려면 "제품"을 클릭하십시오.

*3000달러 이상의 구매에 대해서는 배송이 무료입니다.

**배송은 3일 후에 될 것입니다.

---

191. Mr. Adams와 직원들은 왜 사무실에 변화를 주고 있는가?
(A) 새로운 장비로 최신화하기 위해
(B) 중요한 프로젝트를 준비하기 위해
(C) 정책 변화에 따르기 위해
(D) 들어오는 직원들에게 공간을 제공하기 위해

192. Mr. Adams가 이메일에서 무엇을 언급하는가?
(A) 공급업체에 요청된 사무 가구들이 다 떨어졌다.
(B) 몇몇 칸막이가 있는 자리에 중요한 조립 부품들이 빠졌다.
(C) Techno Tel사는 이전에 Office Interiors and Supplies사에 주문을 했었다.
(D) 들어올 직원들은 각각 다른 날에 업무를 시작할 것이다.

193. Mr. Adams는 어떤 부서에서 일할 것 같은가?
(A) 연구개발
(B) 구매
(C) 마케팅
(D) 관리

194. 온라인 양식에서 추론될 수 있는 것은?
(A) Office Interiors and Supplies사가 고객에게 할인을 해주었다.
(B) 지불은 신용카드로 이루어질 것이다.
(C) 서류 정리함은 따로 배달될 것이다.
(D) 주문에는 배송비가 적용된다.

195. Office Interiors and Supplies사에 대해 암시되는 것은?
(A) 제품들 중 하나가 이틀 내에 취소되는 것을 허용할 것이다.
(B) 8월 16일 이전에 Techno Tel사에 더 많은 책상과 의자를 배달할 것이다.
(C) Mr. Adams의 배송일 조건을 만족시킬 수 없을 것이다.
(D) 8월 14일까지 Techno Tel사에 가리개 몇 개를 보낼 것이다.

196-200은 다음 명함, 이메일, 송장에 관한 문제입니다.

Neil Fitzpatrick 주택 목공소
"애들레이드에서 가장 존경받는 목수"

테두리 및 몰딩 설치, 문 조립 및 수리, 계단 보수 등 실내 목공 작업 전문 베테랑 목수입니다.
전화하거나 이메일을 보내서 무료 견적을 받으십시오.
전화: 5555 9743
이메일: contact@neilfitzpatrick.au

수신: Neil Fitzpatrick <contact@neilfitzpatrick.au>
발신: Mary-Anne Lester <maryanne.lester@webmail.com>
제목: 프로젝트
날짜: 10월 24일

제 이름은 Mary-Anne Lester입니다. 저는 애들레이드에 매년 1월과 2월에 방문하는 별장을 가지고 있습니다. 그 건물에는 야외 테라스가 딸린 아름다운 뒷마당이 있습니다. 저는 그것을 비바람으로부터 보호하기 위한 나무 차양을 만들 숙련된 목수가 필요합니다. 덮인 면적은 약 70평방미터가 되어야 합니다. 이제, 이미 10월이고 제가 1월에 그곳으로 휴가를 갈 계획임을 감안하면, 마감일이 다소 촉박한 것을 알고 있습니다. 그러나, 작업이 제시간에 끝난다면 추가 비용을 지불할 용의가 있습니다. 당신의 연락을 기다리겠습니다.

Mary-Anne Lester 드림

Neil Fitzpatrick 주택 목공소

송장 번호: 11262230
송장일자: 12월 23일
시작일자: 10월 30일
종료일자: 12월 22일
고객 이름: Mary-Anne Lester
주소: Fernhurst길 332번지
Cherryville 5134
뉴사우스웨일스

설명	수량	합계
목재(유칼리나무)	20포스트	860달러
목재(물푸레나무)	4플랭크	200달러
목재 마감재	20리터 캔 1개	25달러
나사 및 앵커 볼트	40개	30달러
인건비	근로자 1명, 총 80시간	3,200달러
		소계
		4,315달러

참고

목재 색상을 보존하기 위해, 2년마다 새롭게 유성 마감재 코팅을 입혀야 합니다. 제 모든 프로젝트가 그렇듯이, 어떤 공사 관련 문제에 대해서든 5년간의 전체 구조물 보증이 제공됩니다.

---

196. Mr. Fitzpatrick에 대해 암시되는 것은?
(A) 10년 동안 목수로 일해왔다.
(B) 애들레이드에 기반을 둔 사업을 운영한다.
(C) 회사 웹사이트를 관리한다.
(D) 가구로 상을 받았다.

197. Ms. Lester는 그녀의 프로젝트를 위해 무엇을 요청하는가?
(A) 탁자와 의자들
(B) 바비큐 그릴
(C) 뒷마당 테라스
(D) 머리 위 덮개

198. Ms. Lester의 요청은 Mr. Fitzpatrick의 평소 관행에 어떤 식으로 어긋나는가?
(A) 그에게 평소보다 적은 임금을 지불하고 싶어한다.
(B) 그가 더 큰 건물을 작업하기를 원한다.
(C) 그가 야외 프로젝트를 진행하기를 원한다.
(D) 그가 10월에 작업을 마치기를 원한다.

199. Ms. Lester의 별장에서의 작업에 대해 추론될 수 있는 것은?
(A) 짧은 일정으로 인해 추가 비용이 들었다.
(B) 그녀가 계획한 휴일 방문을 지연시켰다.
(C) 여러 명의 목수가 필요했다.
(D) 예상보다 더 많은 재료를 사용했다.

200 송장에 따르면, Neil Fitzpatrick 주택 목공소는 무엇을 권장하는가?
(A) 연장된 보증을 구매하는 것
(B) 다른 종류의 목재를 사용하는 것
(C) 구조물의 외관을 관리하는 것
(D) 손상된 판자를 교체하는 것

PART 5

101 카탈로그에 있는 가격은 주세와 국세 둘 다를 포함하지만 배송비는 포함하지 않는다.

102 Cardston사의 회계 기록은 별도의 상자에 담겨서 연도에 따라 보관된다.

103 영구히 폐업하기 전, Rebound Media사는 수년 동안 보여준 지지에 대해 고객들에게 감사를 표했다.

104 Sam's Tacos에서 매운 소스는 무료로 이용할 수 있지만, 약간의 살사 소스는 추가로 비용이 든다.

105 아시아 시장에 진출하기로 결정한 후, Edgeware Electronics사는 지금 그들 제품의 지역 판매업체를 찾고 있다.

106 회의를 위해 회의실을 예약하고자 하는 누구든지 행정과 Ms. Bloomberg에게 이메일을 보내기만 하면 된다.

107 빅토리아에 새 집을 짓기로 결정한 후, Mr. Redmond는 그가 집을 장식하는 것을 도울 인테리어 디자이너를 고용했다.

108 First Bonneville 은행은 9천만 달러에 CPG Financial Trust사의 35개 지점을 인수했고, 지역 내에서 영향력을 강화했다.

109 심리학자들은 어린아이들에게 미치는 비디오 게임의 부정적인 영향에 대한 광범위한 연구를 실시했다.

110 Reginald Rentals사는 최근 새크라멘토에 지점을 열었고, 매우 짧은 기간 후에 그 새로운 지점은 이윤을 내게 되었다.

111 시 의회는 공장의 공해를 제한하는 기준을 도입함으로써 공기의 질을 개선하는 것에 대해 조치를 취해왔다.

112 그 공장은 분기별 생산 목표를 달성하기 위해 지정된 제조 공장들에 임시 근로자를 고용할 준비를 하고 있다.

113 내비게이션 애플리케이션은 걷기와 자전거 타기를 위한 경로 선택권뿐만 아니라 주행 안내도 제공한다.

114 그것과 원작 사이에 거의 차이가 없어서, 전문가들조차 위조된 그림에 속았다.

115 스키 리조트는 흔히 겨울 성수기 동안 더 바쁜 반면에, 여름에는 도보 여행자들을 끌어모은다.

116 홍보 협의회 주최자는 아직 끝내야 할 일이 많다고 했지만, 마감일을 맞추는 것에 대해 걱정하지 않았다.

117 Ms. Patterson의 컴퓨터에 있는 몇몇 파일들은 컴퓨터 바이러스에 감염된 것으로 보인다.

118 전무 이사는 모든 생산 관리자들에게 앞으로는 작업 일정을 더 주의 깊게 관찰할 것을 요구했다.

119 Ms. Tennyson은 좋은 투자 대상을 발견하는 재능과 대담하고 선견지명이 있다는 평판을 가지고 있다.

120 일주일에 걸친 판촉 행사가 끝날 때쯤, Polk Mobile사는 Kelstra사 스마트폰의 거의 모든 재고를 판매할 수 있었다.

121 Mr. Jackson은 회사의 재무 기록에 대한 회계 감사를 거의 완료했고, 조사 결과를 내일 제출할 것으로 예상한다.

122 Dr. Boyle은 응급 상황을 제외하고는, 보통 예약 없이 환자들을 보지 않는다.

123 Turnkey's 제품들은 오래가는 경향이 있는 반면, Vania에서 제작된 제품들은 빈번한 수리가 필요하다.

124 수십 명의 열성 팬들이 많이 참석하여, Fiesta Motors사의 최신 스포츠카 출시 파티는 완전한 성공으로 여겨졌다.

125 다음 2주 동안, Star Sportswear사는 그곳에서 제공하는 제품들에 대한 고객 설문 조사를 실시할 것이다.

126 그 관리자는 직원들의 요구들과 고위 경영진의 요구들 사이에 미묘한 균형을 관리하는 데 노련하다.

127 비록 *Marinberg Herald*지의 인쇄판 구독은 꾸준히 감소했지만, 온라인 독자 수는 계속해서 증가하고 있다.

128 Clarity 식기세척기의 오작동이 결함 때문인지 저급 자재 때문인지는 아직 조사되고 있다.

129 배송업에 종사하는 사람들이 예상했던 것처럼, Volo-Air사의 새로운 노선은 분기별 수입을 크게 신장시키는 것에 도움이 되었다.

130 시장은 지역 기업들의 원조를 통해 일자리 창출을 개선시키기 위한 그녀의 계획을 확고히 할 수 있었다.

PART 6

131-134는 다음 광고에 관한 문제입니다.

다음번에 당신이 휴스턴 시내에 있고 아시아의 풍미를 원한다면, Cheviston 센터 2층에 있는 Sensasia를 방문하세요. 131 Sensasia는 중국, 일본, 인도, 태국, 한국, 그리고 베트남의 정통 요리를 제공합니다.

132 저희는 인기 있는 다양한 아시아 요리를 매일 제공합니다. 월요일부터 금요일까지, 신선한 해산물로 만들어진 수제 초밥, 맛있는 한국식 비빔밥, 그리고 맛있는 베트남식 쌀국수를 즐기세요. 133 주말에는, 다양한 한입 크기의 1인분 요리로 구성되어 있는 홍콩식 딤섬이 일반 메뉴와 함께 준비됩니다. 게다가, 한 달에 한 번, 저희 요리사들은 손님들께서 시도해보실 만한 새로운 것을 소개합니다. 134 요컨대, 오직 Sensasia만이 그토록 다양한 음식을 한 장소에서 선사할 수 있습니다.

단체 예약을 하시려면, 555-4272로 전화하십시오. 메뉴를 보시려면, www.sensasia.com으로 저희 웹사이트를 방문해 주십시오.

135-138은 다음 이메일에 관한 문제입니다.

수신: Scott Douglas <sdouglas@evergladeprints.com>
발신: Edward Kovac <edward.k@collinsconsulting.com>
제목: 브로슈어 수정
날짜: 5월 8일

Mr. Douglas께,

귀하께서 디자인하신 브로슈어에 저희의 의견을 포함한 사본이 첨부된 것을 확인하여 주시기 바랍니다. 135 저희 팀에서는 초안을 검토하였고, 여태까지의 팸플릿의 질에 만족합니다. 이러한 상황에도 불구하고, 몇 가지 변경을 요청 드립니다.

136 특히, 작은 레이아웃과 색상 오류가 있었고 몇몇 중요한 정보 또한 누락되어 있었습니다. 저희는 누락된 세부 정보가 어디에 포함되어야 하는지에 대해 브로슈어에 메모를 남겨두었습니다. 137 저희는 각각의 수정 사항이 정확히 반영되기를 원합니다. 수정된 초안이 준비되면 저희에게 보내주시기 바랍니다. 138 저희는 당연히, 기꺼이 추가 비용을 부담할 것입니다.

Edward 드림

139-142는 다음 기사에 관한 문제입니다.

Hartford 지방 기사

Hartford는 새로운 Ryder's 체인점을 환영한다

10월 12일—새로운 Ryder's 레스토랑이 Irving Super 센터 뒤편인 460번지 Flatbush가에 개점할 것이다. 139 그 부지에서 공사가 곧 시작될 것이다. 140 "저희는 그저 시에서 건축 허가를 발부하기를 기다리고 있습니다."라고 소유주 Paul Solomon은 말했으며, 그의 다른 Ryder's 지점은 Elmwood 지역에 위치해 있다.

141 Mr. Solomon에 따르면, 그는 2년 전 Elmwood 지점을 개시하고 나서 몇 주 후에 Hartford에 Ryder's를 개점한다는 발상을 처음으로 고려해보았다. 142 사실, Mr. Solomon은 Elmwood 지점이 영업을 시작하기 전에는 그렇게 많은 고객을 예상하지 않았었다. 그러나, 영업 두 번째 주 이내에, 그 지점은 이미 너무 많은 주문으로 어쩔 줄 모르게 되었다. 그 시점에, Mr. Solomon은 두 번째 지점을 뒷받침할 충분한 수요가 있음을 알아차렸다. 약 1년 정도의 준비과정 후에, 그는 마침내 확장할 준비가 되었다.

143-146은 다음 회람에 관한 문제입니다.

수신: 전 직원
발신: Susan Ward
제목: 직원 안내서
날짜: 4월 15일

회사 경영진과의 논의에 참여해주신 모든 분들께 감사 드립니다. 몇몇 직원들이 일일 작업 절차를 모르고 있다는 것에 대한 여러분의 의견은 수렴되었습니다. 143 저희는 현재 그 상황을 처리하기 위해 노력하고 있습니다.

우선, 저희는 가능한 한 빨리 회사의 표준 작업 절차를 출판할 것입니다. 인쇄된 안내서는 경영진과 직원들에게 매일의 업무 수행에 대해 공식적인 기준을 제공할 것입니다. 144 이 안내서의 임시 복사본은 다음 회의에서 배부될 것입니다. 145 아마, 이것은 저희의 목표인 확고히 확립된 정책에 좀 더 가까이 다가가는 것을 도울 것입니다.

만약 수정이 필요하다면, 이것들은 안내서의 다음 버전에 포함될 것입니다. 146 최종 버전은 회사 내부 네트워크를 통해서도 이용할 수 있을 것입니다. 질문이 있으시다면, 부서 관리자에게 보내주십시오.

PART 7

147-148은 다음 광고에 관한 문제입니다.

Lakewood 스파

포틀랜드 도심에서 차로 20분밖에 걸리지 않는 Belmont 호텔에 위치한 Lakewood 스파는 하루의 휴식을 위해 도피하기에 완벽한 장소입니다. 저희의 개인 관리실은 편안한 분위기를 조성하기 위해 신중하게 설계되었습니다. 저희는 마사지, 손톱 손질, 그리고 얼굴 관리를 포함해, 모두 저희의 숙련된 관리사들에 의해 행해지는 다양한 서비스를 제공합니다.

Lakewood 스파의 경영진은 또한 고객들에게 다양한 고급 상품에 대한 할인을 제공해드릴 수 있도록, 저희가 유명한 미용 회사인 Décor와 제휴했다는 것을 알려드리게 되어 기쁩니다. 축하하기 위해, 누구든 6월에 스파 관리를 예약하시는 분은 무료 Décor 샴푸 한 통을 받게 될 것입니다. 이 판촉 활동이나 저희 스파에 대한 더 많은 정보를 위해서는, www.lakewoodspa.com을 방문해주시기 바랍니다. 여러분을 곧 뵙기를 바랍니다!

147 Lakewood 스파에 대해 언급된 것은?
(A) 최근 몇몇 개인실을 개조했다.
(B) 고객들에게 서비스에 대한 할인을 제공할 것이다.

(C) 도시의 상업 지역에 지점이 있다.
(D) 숙박 시설 안에 위치해 있다.

148 고객들은 무료 물품을 받기 위해서 무엇을 해야 하는가?
(A) 미용 회사에서 만들어진 제품을 구매한다
(B) 6월에 스파의 한 지점을 방문한다
(C) 지정된 기간 동안에 예약한다
(D) 온라인 설문지를 작성한다

149-150는 다음 안내문에 관한 문제입니다.

재택근무자를 위한 세금 공제

재택근무를 하는 직원들은 소득세 계산에 적용될 수 있는 여러 가지 공제를 받을 자격이 있습니다. 컴퓨터, 모니터, 전화기, 그리고 프린터와 같은 새로운 장비 구입과 관련된 재택 사무 비용을 물게 되는 사람들은 둘 중에 한 가지 방법으로 이 장비의 비용을 공제할 수 있습니다. 그들은 항목이 구입된 같은 해에 총금액을 공제하거나 금액을 7년에 걸쳐 나눌 수 있습니다. 그래서, 예를 들어, 70달러 상당의 항목은 첫해에 완전히 공제되거나 7년 동안 매년 10달러씩 공제될 수 있습니다. 업무 목적으로 전화를 자주 사용하는 직원들은 또한 전화가 업무 시간 중에 사용되었다는 증명으로서 서류를 제시할 수 있다면 공제를 받을 자격이 있습니다. 임대료, 융자금, 그리고 주택 보험 보상을 포함한 주거 비용은 근무를 위해 사용되는 주택 공간 크기에 따라서 부분적으로 세금에서 공제될 수 있습니다. 이 정보에 대해 문의가 있으시다면, 회사의 본인 지점 인사 담당자에게 연락하십시오.

---

149 안내문은 어디에서 볼 수 있을 것 같은가?
(A) 홍보 포스터
(B) 장비 사용 설명서
(C) 직원 안내서
(D) 보험 정책

150 안내문에서 암시되는 것은?
(A) 몇몇 비싼 항목들은 구매하기 위해 특별 허가가 필요하다.
(B) 일부 비용을 공제하려면 전화 기록이 필요할 것이다.
(C) 주택 소유와 관련된 비용은 완전히 세금 공제될 수 있다.
(D) 부동산을 보험에 든 비용은 완전히 되찾아질 수 있다.

151-152는 다음 메시지 대화문에 관한 문제입니다.

Chuck Goodman — 오전 9시 10분
저는 지금 Kingston 전철역에서 30분 넘게 기다리고 있어요. 저의 오늘 오전 9시 30분 수업에 제때 도착하지 못할 것 같아요.

Mia Jancovik — 오전 9시 12분
알겠어요, Jodi나 Victoria가 당신을 대신해줄 수 있는지 알아볼게요. 그들 둘 다 전에 에어로빅 수업을 가르쳐봤어요.

Chuck Goodman — 오전 9시 14분
고마워요. 사실, 방금 열차 운행이 재개될 것이라고 공지되었어요. 보아하니, 선로에 문제가 있었고 해결되었어요.

Mia Jancovik — 오전 9시 15분
좋네요. 언제 여기에 도착할 수 있을 것 같아요? 그나저나, Jodi가 그때까지 당신을 대신해줄 수 있다고 해요.

Chuck Goodman — 오전 9시 16분
잠시만 기다려주세요. 많은 사람들이 기다리고 있어서, 다음 열차를 타지 못할 수도 있어요.

---

151 Mr. Goodman은 누구인 것 같은가?
(A) 체육관 관리자
(B) 운동 강사
(C) 전문 운동선수
(D) 스포츠 심리학자

152 오전 9시 16분에, Mr. Goodman이 "Give me a few minutes"라고 썼을 때 그가 의도한 것은?
(A) 문제에 대해 동료와 논의하고 싶어 한다.
(B) 아직 어떠한 공지도 듣지 못했다.
(C) 그의 도착 시각을 추정할 수 없다.
(D) 교통 체계에 익숙하지 않다.

153-155는 다음 공고에 관한 문제입니다.

참석자분들께,

제5회 공간 연산 학회(SCC)에 오신 것을 환영합니다. 등록을 마치고 명찰과 일정표를 받고 나면 커피, 차, 그리고 간단한 아침 식사를 위해 Granville실로 내려가십시오. 오늘 일정은 다음과 같습니다:

* **오전 9시 30분** – 환영회, Granville실. 다른 참가자들을 만나 연산 동향과 업계 혁신에 관한 의견 및 학회에 바라는 바에 대해 논의합니다. 명찰에 적혀 있는 번호의 테이블에 착석하시기를 요청합니다. 내방객들에게 다양한 분야에서 일하고 있는 사람들과 소통할 기회를 제공하기 위해 다른 전문 분야의 손님들과 함께 앉게 할 것입니다.
* **오전 11시** – 개막 설명회, Gladstone실. Patrizio Vincente, Michelle Bealieu, Mark Blackwell과 함께하여 작년 학회 이후의 공간 연산 분야의 발전에 대해 논의합니다.
* **오후 12시 30분** – 점심 식사, Granville실
* **오후 1시 30분** – 데이터베이스 기술, 영상 처리, 휴대 전화 애플리케이션에 대한 세미나. 이는 Gladstone, Halifax, Johnstone실에서 개최됩니다.
* **오후 3시 30분** – 위치 정보, 산림 지도 제작, 공간 분석에 대한 세미나. 이는 Gladstone, Halifax, Johnstone실에서 개최됩니다.
* **오후 5시 30분** – 오늘의 SCC를 마칩니다. 하지만 남아서 앞으로 한 시간 동안 배운 것에 대해 서로 그리고 협력자분들과 이야기하고 싶은 분들은 다과가 계속해서 제공되는 Granville실로 가시면 됩니다.

---

153 공고의 목적은 무엇인가?
(A) 식사 시간 목록을 제공하기 위해
(B) 참가자들에게 행사에 대해 말하기 위해
(C) 참석자들에게 시간표 변경을 알리기 위해
(D) 잠정적인 회의 일정을 제안하기 위해

154 환영회에 대해 언급되지 않은 것은?
(A) 좌석은 주최자들에 의해 배정될 것이다.
(B) 소개 연설로 시작할 것이다.
(C) 다른 분야의 사람들을 포함할 것이다.
(D) 음식과 음료가 제공될 것이다.

155 세미나가 끝난 후 참가자들에게 어떤 장소가 이용 가능할 것인가?
(A) Granville실
(B) Halifax실
(C) Johnstone실
(D) Gladstone실

156-157은 다음 공고에 관한 문제입니다.

공고

9월 2일부터, 우체국(NPS)은 다양한 고객군에게 서비스를 제공하는 비용을 더 잘 반영하는 새로운 가격 책정 체계를 도입할 것입니다. 우체국은 최대한 효율적으로 운영하려고 끊임없이 노력하고 있습니다. 그러나, 정부에 의해 지시된 최근의 변화들은 이전 보조금을 없앴고, 결과적으로, 저희는 모든 자금을 상품과 서비스의 판매로부터 얻으라고 요구받았습니다. 그러므로 새로운 가격 책정 시스템은 저희가 고객들께 필수적인 서비스를 계속해서 제공하도록 하는 데 있어 불가피합니다. 차후의 모든 가격 조정은 국가 물가 상승률에 근거할 것입니다.

상품	기존 가격	새로운 가격	퍼센트 인상
국내 우편	1.00달러	1.20달러	20퍼센트
상업 우편*	0.70달러	0.85달러	21퍼센트
국제 우편	1.90달러	2.20달러	16퍼센트
요금 별납 우편**	0.50달러	0.75달러	50퍼센트

* 무게는 최대 30그램까지

** 우체국과의 특별 계약에 의해서만 가능함

156 우체국에 대해 언급된 것은?
(A) 국내 우편에 대한 우편 요금을 1달러로 올렸다.
(B) 최근 정부의 재정 지원을 잃었다.
(C) 기본 서비스를 계속해서 제공할 의무가 있다.
(D) 요금 별납 우편 서비스를 취소할 계획이다.

157 차후에 왜 우체국에 의해 요금이 인상될 수도 있는가?
(A) 확장과 관련된 비용을 부담하기 위해
(B) 물가 상승률 변화에 따라 조정하기 위해
(C) 추가 직원들에게 임금을 지불하기 위해
(D) 30그램보다 무거운 우편을 허용하기 위해

158-160은 다음 이메일에 관한 문제입니다.

수신: 전 직원 <employees@xt_enterprises.com>
발신: Audrey Hinkley <a.hinkley@xt_enterprises.com>
제목: 직원 변동
날짜: 2월 2일

안녕하세요, 여러분.

저는 지난 12년간 여기 XT-Enterprises에서 사무장으로 근무하게 되어 영광이었습니다. 여러분 대부분이 아마 들으셨듯이, 저는 이번 달 말에 제 자리에서 물러날 것입니다. Jennifer Harrison이 제 역할을 인계받게 될 것을 발표하게 되어 기쁩니다. 여러분 중 많은 분이 4년간 그녀가 맡아 온 직무인 저의 보조 사무장으로 Ms. Harrison을 이미 알고 있습니다. 이 시간 동안, 그녀는 회의와 약속 일정을 잡고, 워크숍을 준비하고, 그날그날의 사무실 운영을 유지하는 일에 대해 많은 것을 배웠습니다. 이사회와 저는 그녀가 일에 매우 정통하며 이 자리에 적임이라고 생각합니다.

이번 달의 마지막 주 동안 저는 Ms. Harrison을 교육할 것입니다. 이 기간 동안, Ms. Harrison은 제 직무를 수행할 책임을 지게 될 것이지만, 저는 그녀가 필요로 한다면 도움을 줄 수 있도록 여기 있을 것입니다. 따라서, 보통 제가 다루던 요청 사항은 무엇이든 그녀에게 보내주십시오.

이 회사에서의 시간 동안 여러분의 지지와 친선에 모두 감사드립니다. 저는 은퇴하기로 한 제 결정에 만족하지만, 여러분 모두와 연락을 취하며 지내면 좋겠습니다!

Audrey Hinkley 드림

158 Ms. Hinkley에 대해 언급된 것은?
(A) XT-Enterprises에서 10년 넘게 일해 왔다.
(B) 지난주에 발표를 했다.
(C) 12개월 동안 휴가를 갈 것이다.
(D) 다음 주에 구인 광고를 게시할 것이다.

159 Ms. Harrison의 현재 직무 중 하나는 무엇인가?
(A) 기업 모임을 준비하는 것
(B) 월간 일정표를 게시하는 것
(C) 잠재적인 고객들을 찾는 것
(D) 이사회에 참석하는 것

160 이번 달 말에 XT-Enterprises의 직원들은 무엇을 하도록 요청받는가?
(A) 워크숍에 등록한다
(B) Ms. Harrison에게 요청을 보낸다
(C) 은퇴 기념 파티에 참석한다
(D) 회사 자산을 반납한다

161-164는 다음 온라인 채팅 대화문에 관한 문제입니다.

Fumiko Tanaka [오후 2시 3분]
안녕하세요, 여러분. 내일 여행 준비가 다 되었나요?

Connor Walsh [오후 2시 4분]
네, 호텔은 확정되었어요. 우리는 각자 싱글 룸을 받을 거예요. 거기까지 갈 교통편은 마련했나요?

Jacqueline Boulder [오후 2시 5분]
호텔 예약이 확정되었는지 먼저 확인하고 싶어서, 아직 마련하지 않았어요. 지금 셔틀 서비스에 연락할게요. 공항까지 가는 교통편도 예약할까요?

Fumiko Tanaka [오후 2시 7분]
공항까지는 따로 가는 게 좋을 것 같아요. 그렇지 않으면, 사무실에서 만나야 할 텐데, 그건 시간이 너무 많이 걸릴 거예요.

Jacqueline Boulder [오후 2시 8분]
일리가 있네요. Connor, 호텔에 우리가 일찍 체크인해야 할 것이라고 말했나요?

Connor Walsh [오후 2시 10분]
지금 바로 호텔에 전화할게요. 우리는 오전 10시에 착륙할 것이니, 11시쯤에는 모두 체크인할 수 있을 거예요. 그러면 우리가 오후 1시 회의에 가기 전에 옷을 갈아입을 시간이 좀 있을 거예요.

Fumiko Tanaka [오후 2시 12분]
점심 회의를 위해 Ms. Lee를 호텔로 오시도록 할 수도 있을 것 같아요. 호텔에 훌륭한 이탈리안 레스토랑이 있다고 들었어요.

Jacqueline Boulder [오후 2시 13분]
제가 그녀에게 전화할 수 있어요.

161 내일 무슨 일이 일어날 것인가?
(A) 회사 야유회가 진행될 것이다.
(B) 회의가 준비될 것이다.
(C) 출장이 시작될 것이다.
(D) 팀이 교육을 받을 것이다.

162 오후 2시 8분에, Ms. Boulder가 "That makes sense"라고 썼을 때 그녀가 의도한 것 같은 것은?
(A) 약속 시간을 옮기는 것을 선호한다.
(B) 호텔 가격에 만족한다.
(C) 항공편 준비를 받아들인다.
(D) 공항까지 단독으로 이동하는 것에 동의한다.

163 호텔에 대해 암시된 것은?
(A) 아직 체크인 시간을 조정하기로 동의하지 않았다.
(B) 건물 내 식사 선택안이 없다.
(C) 성수기에 예약을 한도 이상으로 받았다.
(D) 공항 바로 옆에 위치해 있다.

164 일행은 호텔에 몇 시까지 도착해 있을 예정인가?
(A) 오전 10시
(B) 오전 11시
(C) 오후 1시
(D) 오후 2시

165-167은 다음 편지에 관한 문제입니다.

Sampat 연구소
화장품 실험 부서
525번지 Hilltop로, 뉴브런즈윅, 뉴저지주 08901

4월 14일

Bethany Fulton
Little Miss Makeup사
255번지 Greystone가

샬럿, 노스캐롤라이나주 28201

Ms. Fulton께,

30년 이상 동안, Sampat 연구소는 크고 작은 제조사 모두가 그들의 화장품, 미용 및 개인 관리 용품들에 대해 믿을만한 실험 결과를 얻을 수 있도록 도와왔습니다. 모든 설비를 갖추고 있는 저희 실험실은 소비자, 연구원, 그리고 귀사와 같은 제조업체들에게 가장 많은 영향을 주는 사안들에 대해 알고 있는 숙련된 기술자와 연구원들로 구성되어 있습니다. ─ [1] ─.

피부의 효과에 대해 제품을 검사하는 것에 더하여, 저희는 완제품을 저장하고 수송하는 것뿐만 아니라 화학 성분들을 섞는 적절한 방법에 대해서도 설명해 드릴 수 있습니다. ─ [2] ─. 저희는 다양한 환경 조건에서 제품이 얼마나 지속되는지를 검사하기도 합니다. 게다가, 다른 제조사들의 광범위한 실험 결과 데이터베이스로의 접근은 저희가 동물들에게 실험하는 것을 완전히 피하도록 합니다. ─ [3] ─.

검사를 위해 제품의 견본을 제출하는 방법에 대한 상세한 정보뿐만 아니라 저희의 서비스를 각각에 대한 모든 설명을 위해 동봉된 서류를 확인해 주시기 바랍니다. ─ [4] ─. 상세 비용과 처리 시간에 대해 견적을 받고 싶으시면, 제게 555-9476으로 전화 주시거나 j.west@sampatlabs.com으로 이메일을 보내 주십시오.

감사합니다.

Jacob West 드림
고객 관리 부서, Sampat 연구소

165 Ms. Fulton은 누구일 것 같은가?
(A) 실험실 조수
(B) 상점 지사 관리자
(C) 고객 관리 직원
(D) 화장품 제조업체 직원

166 Sampat 연구소에 대해 언급되지 않은 것은?
(A) 업계에서 수십 년의 경력을 갖고 있다.
(B) 제품이 얼마나 오랫동안 지속될지 알아낼 수 있다.
(C) 동물에게 실험을 하지 않을 것이다.
(D) 연구 결과를 온라인에서 볼 수 있게 한다.

167 [1], [2], [3], [4]로 표시된 위치 중, 다음 문장이 들어갈 곳으로 가장 적절한 것은?

"이 점과 관련해, 그들이 귀사에 전문적인 서비스를 제공하는 것이 가능하다는 것을 보장받으실 수 있습니다."

(A) [1]
(B) [2]
(C) [3]
(D) [4]

168-171은 다음 기사에 관한 문제입니다.

무료로 쇼핑하기?

Virtual Mall은 불과 9개월 전에 무료 모바일 게임을 출시한 프로그래머 Pat Gustin의 창작물이다. 지금까지, 30만 명 이상의 사람들이 이 애플리케이션을 다운로드 했고, 그중 대략 60퍼센트가 언제든지 활발히 사용하고 있다. 이러한 수치는 모바일 애플리케이션을 통해 광고를 하는 회사들에게 굉장히 매력적이다.

"게임의 발상은 간단합니다."라고 Mr. Gustin은 말한다. "사람들이 가상의 쇼핑몰에 자리를 빌리고 저희가 제공하는 카탈로그에서 판매할 상품들을 선택합니다." ─ [1] ─. 가상의 판매자가 올바르게 상점을 운영할 수 있다면 가상의 돈으로 수익을 얻는다고 그는 설명했다. ─ [2] ─.

게임은 사용자들이 이해하는 수준의 세부 사항과 사용자 자체 설정을 제공한다. 예를 들어, 실생활에서 그러는 것처럼, 게임 내의 고객들은 때때로 그들이 샀던 물건들을 반환한다. ─ [3] ─.

Mr. Gustin은 Virtual Farm이라고 불리는 또 다른 게임도 작업하고 있다고 말하는데, 이 게임에 그는 동일한 컨셉을 적용하지만 농업을 배경으로 할 것이다. ─ [4] ─. 그는 이 게임을 내년 초에 출시하길 바라고 있다.

Virtual Mall에 관해 더 많이 알고 싶은 사람은 애플리케이션을 무료로 다운로드하는 것이 권장된다. Gustin의 다른 게임에 대한 세부 정보를 원하면, www.virtualgamesco.com을 방문하면 된다.

168 기사의 주요 주제는 무엇인가?
(A) 새로운 쇼핑센터
(B) 온라인 광고에 관한 연구
(C) 소프트웨어 제작 회사
(D) 휴대 기기용 시뮬레이션 게임

169 Virtual Mall에 대해 언급되지 않은 것은?
(A) 많은 수의 사용자가 있다.
(B) 다운로드에 대해 회원들에게 요금을 부과하지 않는다.
(C) 실제 회사의 상품을 홍보하는 데 도움을 준다.
(D) 사용자들이 복수의 캐릭터를 만들 수 있도록 한다.

170 Mr. Gustin에 대해 언급된 것은?
(A) 9개월 전에 이전 직장을 그만두었다.
(B) 제품의 판매로부터 수익을 얻는다.
(C) 광고에 경력이 있다.
(D) 새로운 게임을 개발하고 있는 중이다.

171 [1], [2], [3], [4]로 표시된 위치 중, 다음 문장이 들어갈 곳으로 가장 적절한 것은?

"그들은 이 수익을 이용해 자신들의 가게를 개선하거나 다른 판매자들로부터 아이템들을 구매할 수 있습니다."

(A) [1]
(B) [2]
(C) [3]
(D) [4]

172-175는 다음 기사에 관한 문제입니다.

가죽 상점이 성공을 거두다
Jake Lewis 작성

8월 15일─지역 공예가인 Judith Walker 소유의 가죽 제품 가게 Oakwood 공예점이 주민들과 관광객 양쪽 모두에게서 많은 관심을 끌고 있다. 단 3주 전에 처음 문을 열었음에도, 이 가게는 벌써 고급 가죽 가방, 벨트, 그리고 다른 장신구를 찾는 사람들에게 인기 있는 목적지가 되었다. Ms. Walker는 그녀의 성공은 모든 수공예품이 극도의 주의를 들여서 만들어진다는 사실 덕분이라고 말했다. "가죽 세공은 항상 제 열정의 대상이었어요."라고 그녀는 말했다. "제가 어렸을 때 할머니께서 기본 기술들을 가르쳐 주셨고, 지난 20년 동안 그것은 제 취미였어요. 제가 만드는 각각의 제품이 이 공예에 대한 제 사랑의 표현이죠."

Ms. Walker는 8년 전 매년 여름에 열리는 Milton 여름 공예 박람회에서 그녀의 첫 가방을 판매했다. 그녀는 몇 년 동안 이 박람회에서 부스를 운영했고, 그 과정에서 단골 고객층을 형성했다. 이것은 그녀만의 가게를 여는 데 용기를 주었다. 6일 전, 그녀는 대출을 마련하기 위해 Milton 은행의 대표를 만났고, 이제 그녀의 꿈을 현실로 만들고 있다. 누구든 Oakwood 공예점을 방문하는 데 관심이 있는 사람은 특별 판촉 행사의 일환으로 가게의 모든 물품이 10퍼센트에서 20퍼센트까지 가격이 인하될 예정인 다음 주에 들르는 것이 권장된다. 이 가게는 Fairway 슈퍼마켓의 바로 맞은편인, 14번지 Ferris가에 위치해 있다.

172 기사는 주로 무엇에 대한 것인가?
(A) 새로 개업한 소매 판매점
(B) 최근에 확장한 회사
(C) 지역에서 생산된 제품

(D) 거의 완성된 관광 명소

173 1문단 네 번째 줄의 단어 "attributes"는 의미상 –와 가장 가깝다.
(A) ~에 두다
(B) ~의 덕분으로 돌리다
(C) 수긍하다
(D) 인정하다

174 Ms. Walker에 대해 언급된 것은?
(A) 8년 전 Milton으로 이사했다.
(B) 연례행사에 참여했다.
(C) 수공예 워크숍에서 기술을 배웠다.
(D) 중소기업협회에 가입했다.

175 기사에 따르면, Ms. Walker는 여섯 달 전에 무엇을 했는가?
(A) 금융 기관으로부터 대출을 신청했다.
(B) 지역 상점의 소유주와 협력했다.
(C) Milton 여름 공예 박람회를 준비했다.
(D) 그녀의 가게에서 판촉 행사를 열었다.

176-180은 다음 이메일과 일정표에 관한 문제입니다.

수신: Samantha Larson <s.larson@gentrydrivers.com>
발신: Edwin Matthews <ematthews1965@plainsrealty.com>
제목: 4월 업무 일정
날짜: 4월 11일

Ms. Larson께,

저는 당신의 상사인 Dale Blackburn으로부터 당신이 Ms. Linda Atkins의 새로운 운전기사로 배정될 것이라고 들었습니다. 저는 Ms. Atkins의 개인 비서이므로 그녀를 오고 가도록 이동시켜야 할 정기적인 약속 스케줄을 당신에게 제공할 것입니다. 이 이메일에 첨부된 것에서 당신은 그녀의 4월 약속 일정표를 확인할 수 있을 것입니다. 변동 사항이 있을 수 있지만, 저는 최소한 24시간 전에 변경에 대해 당신에게 통지할 수 있도록 최선을 다할 것임을 알아두십시오.

일정표를 꼼꼼히 읽으셔서 그녀가 만날 사람의 이름, 약속 시간 및 날짜, 그리고 약속이 있을 주소나 장소를 포함하는 각 약속의 세부 사항을 확인하시기 바랍니다. 또한, Ms. Atkins와 4월 16일에 만나기로 예정되어 있는 사람은 아직 만나자는 요청에 답하지 않았습니다. 그 고객이 그날 약속에 가능한지 제가 알게 되는 즉시 당신에게 알려 드리겠습니다.

어떠한 질문이라도 있으시다면, 망설이지 마시고 이 이메일로 답장해 주십시오.

Edwin Matthews 드림

일정표: Linda Atkins

PLAINS 부동산

담당: Edwin Matthews

4월				
월요일	화요일	수요일	목요일	금요일
	1	2 오전 11시 Ms. Amundsen: 32번지 Tucson가	3	4 오후 4시 Ms. Harrow: 22–A North 33번가
7	8 오후 12시 30분 Robinson 부부와 Prairie Café에서 점심 모임	9 오후 4시 Mr. Abraham: 433번지 Murray가 (계약서 서명)	10 오후 3시 Blue Star건물 개관: 285번지 Greenwich가	11

14 오후 2시 Mr. Mendez: 441번지 Poplar가	15	16 오전 10시 Mr. Choi: 907번지 브로드웨이	17 휴가	18 공휴일
21 오전 9시 30분 영업 세미나 (온종일), 4102번지 Larch로	22	23 오전 9시 부동산 점검, 312번지 Poplar가	24	25 오후 7시 Gordon 은퇴 기념 파티 Rebecca's Grill 82번지 3번가
28 오후 1시 Mr. Abraham에게 열쇠 넘겨주기, 433번지 Murray가	29 오전 10시 연례 부동산업자 총회, Cole 회의장, 12번지 Dodd가	30		

176 Mr. Matthews는 왜 이메일을 썼는가?
(A) 운전 서비스를 이용하는 것에 대해 문의하기 위해
(B) 벤처 사업에 대한 생각을 공유하기 위해
(C) 교통수단을 추천하기 위해
(D) 신규 직원에게 직무 세부 사항에 대해 알려주기 위해

177 Mr. Matthews에 대해 언급된 것은?
(A) 새로운 집 구입을 고려하고 있다.
(B) 비행기보다 차로 여행하는 것을 선호한다.
(C) Ms. Atkins의 약속 스케줄을 준비한다.
(D) Mr. Blackburn을 만나고 싶어 한다.

178 누가 Ms. Atkins와의 만남을 아직 확정하지 않았는가?
(A) Ms. Harrow
(B) Mrs. Robinson
(C) Mr. Abraham
(D) Mr. Choi

179 Ms. Larson은 어떤 날짜에 일하도록 요구되지 않을 것 같은가?
(A) 4월 14일
(B) 4월 16일
(C) 4월 18일
(D) 4월 25일

180 Ms. Atkins에 대해 언급되지 않은 것은?
(A) 회의에서 연설을 할 것이다.
(B) 4월에 한 고객을 두 번 만날 것이다.
(C) 은퇴 기념식에 참석할 예정이다.
(D) 하루 휴가를 낼 예정이다.

181-185는 다음 광고와 편지에 관한 문제입니다.

Donnelly & Chung 광고 회사—당신의 브랜딩 전문가!

당신 회사는 브랜드에 대한 대중 관심을 높이는 데 어려움을 겪고 있는 신생 기업입니까? 아주 좋은 제품 라인을 가지고 있지만 어떻게 홍보하는지 모르십니까? 아니면 당신의 사업체가 이미지 변화가 필요합니까? 당신의 마케팅 문제가 무엇이든 간에, Donnelly & Chung 광고 회사는 도울 수 있습니다! 저희 고객들은 Shasta-Clear 음료 회사와 Deerborne 문구사를 포함한 지역 회사에서부터 Compton 의류 회사와 Just-Ate 식이 보충제 회사와 같이 크고 국제적인 기업까지 다양합니다.

Donnelly & Chung사의 저희 전문가들은 당신의 제품이나 서비스를 홍보하기 위한 구체적인 계획을 찾는 것을 도울 수 있습니다. 저희는 광고 캠페

인 개발, 기업 브랜딩 서비스, 소비자 타깃 상담, 시장 조사, 그리고 더 많은 것을 제공합니다!

당신의 첫 상담은 완전히 무료입니다! 저희 직원 중 한 명이 당신이 필요한 것을 논의하고 비용 견적을 제공해 드릴 것입니다. 무료 예약을 잡으시려면 555-4951로 전화하기만 하시면 됩니다.

7월 2일

Patricia Draper
Donnelly & Chung 광고 회사
405 C호, Acres 센터, 312번지 East 21번가
덴버, 콜로라도주 89110

Ms. Draper께,

우리의 첫 만남은 즐거웠으며, 제 브랜딩 필요성에 대해 누군가와 함께 의논할 수 있는 기회에 감사했습니다. 저는 이제 막 덴버에 저의 사업체를 개업했고 홍보를 하는 데 정말 도움을 받고 싶습니다.

우리 상담에 대해 저는 제 사업 동료인 Walter Preston과 논의했고, 그는 귀사가 Shasta-Clear사를 위해 진행했던 매우 성공적인 홍보 캠페인을 기억합니다. 그래서, 저희는 제과점을 위한 브랜딩 계획을 찾는 데 도움을 줄 귀사를 고용하는 것에 동의했습니다. 저희는 가능한 한 빠르게 진행하고 싶으니, 언제 Walter와 저를 직접 만날 시간이 있는지 알려주시기 바랍니다. 저희는 보통 평일 오전 11시 이후에 한가합니다.

만약 브랜딩 작업을 진행하기로 결정한다면 저희가 파는 모든 제품들의 전체적인 설명이 필요하다고 우리의 회의 동안 귀하께서 언급하셨습니다. 사용되는 재료를 포함하여, 저희의 모든 제품 목록을 동봉했습니다. 우리가 만나기 전에 추가적인 정보를 요구하신다면, 귀하를 위해 기꺼이 제공해드리겠습니다.

저희는 귀하와 함께 일하기를 고대하며 곧 답변을 듣게 되기를 바랍니다.

Kevin Swords 드림
공동소유주, PS 제빵 회사

동봉물:
제품 목록

---

181 Donnelly & Chung사는 무엇에 도움을 제공할 수 있는가?
(A) 새로운 사업체를 설립하는 것
(B) 재미있는 웹사이트를 디자인하는 것
(C) 기업 브랜드를 홍보하는 것
(D) 행사 관련 서비스를 제공하는 것

182 Mr. Swords에 대해 암시되는 것은?
(A) 이전 프로젝트들에서 Ms. Draper와 함께 일했다.
(B) Ms. Draper와의 상담에 대해 비용을 청구받지 않았다.
(C) 추가적인 제과점 지점을 열려고 계획한다.
(D) Just-Ate사와 공급 제휴 관계이다.

183 Mr. Preston은 누구인가?
(A) 광고 컨설턴트
(B) PS 제빵 회사의 공동소유주
(C) 재료 공급자
(D) Shasta-Clear사 임원

184 Mr. Swords는 Ms. Draper가 무엇을 하기를 원하는가?
(A) 생산품의 목록을 출력한다
(B) 무료 상담을 예약한다
(C) 홍보 제안서를 작성한다
(D) 회의 가능 여부를 확인한다

185 무엇이 편지에 동봉되었는가?
(A) 판매되는 제품에 대한 명세서
(B) 새로 나올 제품 라인에 관한 세부 사항

(C) 서명된 사업 계약서
(D) 작성 완료된 설문지

186-190은 다음 광고, 웹페이지, 이메일에 관한 문제입니다.

Piedmont Limousine사: 멋지게 타세요!

맨해튼에서 20년 넘게 서비스를 제공하고 있는 Piedmont Limousine사는 가장 경험이 많고 전문적인 기사뿐만 아니라 대여 차량에 있어서 최고의 차량을 계속해서 제공합니다. 12명의 승객까지 앉을 수 있는 스트레치 리무진이나, 8명을 태울 수 있는 고급 미니밴, 혹은 4명을 수용할 수 있는 일반 크기의 세단을 필요로 하든 Piedmont Limousine사가 도와드릴 수 있습니다! 저희는 기업 행사와 결혼을 포함한 모든 특별한 행사에 깨끗하고 현대적인 차량을 제공합니다. 저희는 역이나 공항으로 중요한 방문객을 마중 나갈 수 있고 기사와 차량 서비스를 하루 종일 필요로 하시는 분들을 위해 주 단위 혹은 일 단위의 대여 비용을 제공해드릴 수 있습니다. 4월에 예약하시면, 저희의 모든 서비스에 적용될 수 있는 50달러 상품권을 받으실 것입니다!

가격, 위치, 영업시간, 그리고 저희가 보유하고 있는 이용 가능한 차종에 대해 더 자세한 정보를 원하시면, 온라인 www.piedmontlimousine.com으로 저희에게 방문해 주시기 바랍니다.

http://www.piedmontlimousine.com/bookings

서비스	가격	차량	시간/장소	**예약**

이름	Benjamin Lopez	전화번호	555-0495
이메일	blop@neurotech.com	회사	Neuro-Tech사
서비스 이용 날짜/시간		4월 18일 오전 10시-4월 21일 오전 10시	
마중 나갈 장소		중앙역	
차종		일반 세단	

추가 세부 사항을 적어주십시오. 차에 타실 승객분과 예약하시는 분이 다르다면, 아래에 이름을 적어 주십시오.

*저는 방문하시는 투자자를 마중 나갈 차와 기사를 예약하고 싶습니다. 그분의 이름은 William Bail입니다. 그가 머무는 동안 귀사의 서비스가 매일 필요할 것입니다.

제공하신 정보가 정확한지 확인하시고 확정하셨다면, 아래의 "제출하기"를 클릭해 주십시오.

제출하기

수신: Benjamin Lopez <blop@neurotech.com>
발신: Fatima Khan <fkhan@piedmontlimousine.com>
날짜: 4월 6일
제목: 회신: 예약 문의

Mr. Lopez께,

Piedmont Limousine사를 고려해주셔서 감사합니다! 저희는 귀하께서 요청하신 날짜와 시간에 기사와 원하시는 차종을 보유하고 있습니다. 아래는 비용 명세서입니다.

차량 대여	180.00달러
기사 서비스*	340.00달러
소계	520.00달러
세금	52.00달러
보증금	50.00달러
총계	622.00달러

*일일 서비스의 경우 기사는 오전 8시부터 오후 8시까지 마음대로 이용하실 수 있을 것입니다.

비용을 받아들이신다면, 예약 확정을 위해 이 이메일에 답장해 주시기 바랍니다. 취소는 서비스 24시간 전까지 허용되지만, 보증금은 어떠한 상황에서도 돌려받으실 수 없을 것입니다. 하루를 채 남겨 놓지 않고 취소하시는 손님들은 환불을 받지 못할 것입니다.

또한 저희는 도착하시는 손님의 열차 정보를 제공해 주시기를 요청드립니다. 그러면 저희 기사인 Solomon Nyongo가 승강장에서 표지판을 들고 그를 기다릴 수 있을 것입니다.

감사드리며, 곧 귀하께 답을 듣기를 바랍니다.

Fatima Khan 드림

186 Piedmont Limousine사에 대해 언급되지 않은 것은?
(A) 12명까지 수용 가능한 차량을 제공한다.
(B) 다양한 종류의 행사를 위한 서비스를 제공한다.
(C) 20년이 넘는 동안 계속 사업을 유지하고 있다.
(D) 공항과 기차역에 서비스 창구가 있다.

187 Mr. Lopez는 무엇을 받을 것인가?
(A) 차량 업그레이드
(B) 전액 환불
(C) 서비스 쿠폰
(D) 기차표

188 Mr. Lopez에 대해 사실인 것은?
(A) 은행에서 돈을 빌릴 계획이다.
(B) 서비스를 위해 할인 쿠폰을 사용하고 있다.
(C) 손님을 위해 예약을 하고 있다.
(D) 중앙역에서 방문객을 만날 것이다.

189 예약이 대여일 하루 전에 취소되면 무슨 일이 일어나는가?
(A) 고객들은 상품권을 받을 수 있다.
(B) 보증금을 포기해야 한다.
(C) 신용카드로 전액이 청구된다.
(D) 취소 수수료를 지불해야 한다.

190 Mr. Nyongo에 대해 사실인 것은?
(A) 역 승강장에서 William Bail을 기다릴 것이다.
(B) 4월 18일에 스트레치 리무진을 운전할 것이다.
(C) Neuro-Tech사에서 몇몇 투자자들을 만날 것이다.
(D) 승객에게 대금 청구서를 제공할 것이다.

191-195는 다음 공고, 회람, 이메일에 관한 문제입니다.

Wyein Multimedia사의 새로운 사무실

이제 우리의 합병이 확정되었으므로, Wyein Multimedia사는 Orio Telecom사와 사무실을 합쳐서 부서간 소통을 더욱 용이하게 할 것입니다. 늘어난 수의 직원들을 수용하기 위해, 양사의 직원들은 현재의 사무실에서 한 군데의 더 넓은 장소로 이전할 것입니다. 새 건물은 Duric가 175번지에 위치해 있는데, 이는 Caruso역에서 도보 3분 정도 거리입니다. 이사는 4월 2일에 진행될 예정입니다. 오늘 오후 인사팀에서 더 많은 세부 정보를 제공할 것입니다.

수신: Wyein Multimedia사 전 직원
발신: Gerard Franco 인사과장
날짜: 3월 14일
제목: 사원증 배지와 주차

안녕하세요 여러분,

우리는 Duric가로 이사하기 전에 회사 사원증 배지를 갱신할 것입니다. 따라서, 사진사가 모두의 사진을 찍도록 준비했습니다. 다음 주 월요일인 3월 19일 3층 회의실에서 4개 부서가 사진을 찍을 예정이며, 그다음 며칠 동안 다른 부서들도 사진을 찍을 것입니다. 월요일에 처리되는 부서들의 일정은 다음과 같습니다:

디자인: 오전 9시 - 오전 10시
영업 및 마케팅: 오전 10시 - 오전 11시
홍보: 오전 11시 - 오후 12시

연구: 오후 1시 - 오후 2시

주차에 관해서는, 우리의 새 건물에는 자체 공간이 없지만, 근처에 넓은 주차장이 있습니다. 회사는 지금과 마찬가지로, 여러분을 위해 그곳에 공간을 대여하고 급여에서 요금을 인출할 용의가 있습니다. Duric가의 시내 위치로 인해, 주차장 비용이 여기보다 다소 높다는 점을 참고하시기 바랍니다. 따라서 여러분은 현재 지불하고 있는 95파운드 대신 월 110파운드를 청구받으실 것입니다. 문의 사항이 있거나 주차 공간이 필요 없는 경우 금요일 퇴근 시간까지 이메일을 보내 주세요.

수신: Gerard Franco <gfranco@wyeinmultimedia.com>
발신: Theresa Weissert <tweissert@wyeinmultimedia.com>
날짜: 3월 16일
제목: 사원증 배지와 주차

Mr. Franco께,

우리가 Duric가로 이사가면 저는 더 이상 주차 공간이 필요 없을 것임을 알려드리려고요. 저는 그곳에서 한 블록 거리에 살아서, 필요 없을 거예요.

또한, 저는 다음 주 월요일 오후에 휴무이기 때문에 사진사와 만나도록 지정된 제 부서의 시간에 사무실에 없을 거예요. 다른 부서 시간에 합류해도 괜찮을까요? 알려주시길 부탁드려요.

감사합니다.

Theresa Weissert 드림

191 4월 2일에 무슨 일이 일어날 것인가?
(A) 직원들의 사진이 촬영될 것이다.
(B) 사원증 배지가 배포될 것이다.
(C) 관리자들이 합병을 발표할 것이다.
(D) 두 회사가 이전할 것이다.

192 Mr. Franco가 제공하는 정보가 아닌 것은?
(A) 직원 주차 공간의 비용
(B) 질문을 위한 기한
(C) 사진사의 이름
(D) 일부 사진촬영 시간의 날짜

193 Wyein Multimedia사에 대해 추론될 수 있는 것은?
(A) 도심에 위치해 있지 않다.
(B) 회의실을 개조할 것이다.
(C) 대중교통 수단 근처에 위치해 있다.
(D) 최근 직원 규모를 줄였다.

194 Caruso역에 대해 암시된 것은?
(A) Wyein Multimedia사의 본사와 연결되어 있다.
(B) 확장 프로젝트 후에 막 재개장했다.
(C) Ms. Weissert의 집에서 걸어갈 수 있는 거리에 있다.
(D) 주차장 요금을 새로 인상했다.

195 Ms. Weissert는 어떤 부서에 소속되어 있는가?
(A) 디자인
(B) 영업 및 마케팅
(C) 홍보
(D) 연구

196-200은 다음 기사, 이메일, 후기에 관한 문제입니다.

지역 소식

최근까지, Carpenter's Hollow의 식당은 두 종류로 나눌 수 있었다: 바로 패스트푸드 체인점과 미국식 식당이다. 하지만 이제, Market가와 14번가의 모퉁이에 새로운 중국 음식점인 Taste of Hunan이 문을 열었다. 그곳은 "가족 레시피를 사용하여 만든 맛있는 중국 요리"를 광고한다. 주인인 James와 Nancy Chu는 우리 도시에 있는 친척들과 합류하기 위해 최근 New York

에서 이사 왔다.

불과 2주 전에 문을 열었지만, Taste of Hunan은 이미 상당한 수의 고객을 받았고 웹사이트에 50개의 후기(거의 모두 긍정적이다)를 얻었다. 후기 작성자들에게 한 가지 특별한 매력은 식당의 일일 15달러 특별 메뉴로, 월요일의 새우 볶음밥부터 금요일의 무슈포크까지 있다. 또 다른 주요 묘미는 식당의 분위기이다. 내부는 전통 등불과 풍경화로 꾸며져 있으며, 식사 공간은 정원을 내려다본다. 이는 아름답고 편안한 환경을 조성한다.

수신: Alan Blake <a.blake231@webmail.com>
발신: Food Web 온라인 주문팀 <orders@foodweb.com>
제목: 123198번 주문
날짜: 5월 28일

Mr. Blake께,

Taste of Hunan이 귀하의 깐풍기와 무슈포크 주문을 받았습니다. 주문은 오후 6시 25분에서 6시 35분 사이에 수령할 준비가 될 것입니다.

Food Web은 이제 Food Rewards 프로그램을 제공합니다. 향후 할인, 무료 주문, 그리고 더 많은 것을 위해 사용될 수 있는 포인트 획득을 시작하려면, 오늘 www.foodweb.com/foodrewards에서 가입하세요.

결제 방식: 신용카드
주문 번호: 123198

무슈포크 1: 15.00달러
깐풍기 1: 19.99달러

소계: 34.99달러
세금: 2.10달러
총액: 37.09달러

주문에 대해 질문이나 우려 사항이 있으신가요? 링크를 클릭하여 연락 주세요.

Food Web 온라인 주문팀 드림

CARPENTER'S HOLLOW > 식당 > TASTE OF HUNAN
점수: 별 5개 중 4개
후기 작성자: Alan Blake

Taste of Hunan은 확실히 오랜만에 Carpenter's Hollow에서 일어난 최고의 일입니다. 우리 도시는 중국 음식점이 절실히 필요했고, Taste of Hunan이 마침내 그 수요를 충족시켰습니다. 전반적으로, 저는 그들의 음식에 대해 불평할 것이 거의 없습니다. 그들은 전형적인 미국식 중식처럼 보일지 모르는 음식을 요리하지만, 각 요리에는 독특한 반전이 있습니다. 예를 들어, 그들의 깐풍기는 맛있지만 뜻밖의 매운맛을 포함하여, 독자들이 예상할 만한 것과는 상당히 다릅니다. 개인적으로, 저는 새로운 조리법을 환영합니다. 한 가지 불만은 때때로 그들이 많은 손님을 감당하지 못한다는 것입니다. 5월 28일 6시 35분에 제가 그들의 식당에 도착해 보니 프런트에 적어도 여섯 명의 사람들이 있었습니다. 그들은 15분 후에야 제 음식 준비를 마쳤습니다.

196. 기사의 주 목적은 무엇인가?
(A) 새로운 메뉴 품목을 평론하기 위해
(B) Mr. Chu와 Ms. Chu의 약력을 제공하기 위해
(C) 새로운 업체에 관해 보도하기 위해
(D) 미국식 중식을 논의하기 위해

197. 기사에 따르면, 고객들이 Taste of Hunan에 관해 좋아하는 것은 무엇인가?
(A) 서비스
(B) 분위기
(C) 조리법
(D) 샘플

198. Mr. Blake의 주문에 대해 추론될 수 있는 것은?
(A) 그의 집으로 배달되었다.
(B) 식당에서 먹었다.
(C) 쿠폰을 사용하여 결제되었다.
(D) 금요일에 이루어졌다.

199. Mr. Blake는 Taste of Hunan에 대해 무엇이라고 말하는가?
(A) 그곳은 색다른 방식으로 음식을 준비한다.
(B) 그곳은 점심 시간에 종종 많은 사람들을 유치한다.
(C) 그는 그곳을 다른 중국 음식점들보다 선호한다.
(D) 그는 그곳에서 여러 번 식사했다.

200. 이메일의 어떤 정보가 부정확했는가?
(A) 결제 방식
(B) 수령 시간
(C) 주문 품목
(D) 음식의 가격

* 무료 해설은 해커스토익(Hackers.co.kr)에서
  다운로드 받으실 수 있습니다.

* QR 코드로
  바로가기

PART 5

101 Barton Jewelry에서 판매되는 최고급 제품들은 재고 정리 판매를 위해 가끔 몇 가지 항목이 가격이 인하되긴 하지만, 거의 할인된 가격으로 판매되지 않는다.

102 일반 대중들에게 사용하도록 제공되기 전에 엄격한 검사가 모든 약물에 반드시 행해져야 한다.

103 Jennifer Barnes가 성공적으로 그녀의 1종 운전면허 신청을 완료한 뒤, 그녀는 배달용 트럭을 운전할 수 있었다.

104 Magnum 항공사는 5년 전 서비스를 확대하기 시작했고 현재 동유럽 전역에서 몇 개의 일일 항공편을 운항하고 있다.

105 비록 궂은 날씨가 예상되지만 서머빌행 기차는 일정대로 내일 떠날 것이다.

106 직원들은 호텔의 정문을 이용하지 말고 건물 뒤쪽에 위치한 옆문을 통해 지나가야 한다.

107 신입 사원들은 기본 업무를 수행하는 법을 익힐 때까지 지속적인 감독이 필요했다.

108 업무 관행에 대한 보고서에 따르면, 오늘날의 사람들은 이전 어느 때보다 더 오랜 시간을 직장에서 보낸다.

109 Pacific 케이블 방송사는 주주들이 계획에 반대를 표명하자 경쟁 방송사를 인수하는 것을 진행하지 않았다.

110 직원 수칙서에는 인사부 관리자가 입사 지원서들을 검토할 책임이 있다고 명시한다.

111 Vedan산의 방문객들은 가장 가까운 도시로부터 대략 25마일 떨어진 외딴 위치에 이끌린다.

112 새로운 재활 별관을 운영하는 것을 돕기 위해 추가 의사들이 다음 달에 Operham 의료 시설에 배치될 것이다.

113 말레이시아의 재료 가격이 비교적 저렴하기 때문에, Ms. Amarna는 그녀의 공장을 그곳에 설립하기로 결정했다.

114 중앙 터미널의 현재 매표소들은 점차 자동 기기로 교체될 것이다.

115 Freidrich 진료소는 모든 의료 정보들을 전적으로 기밀로 유지하고 사전 동의 없이 제3자에게 기록을 공개하지 않는다.

116 올해 Vanita Apparel사의 인기 있는 연례 코트 세일의 마지막에는 거의 상품이 남아 있지 않았다.

117 당신이 ARC 6000을 시운전해 볼 때까지는, 그 차량이 얼마나 운전자 친화적인지 인식하기 어렵다.

118 Hooper사는 부서들 간의 소통을 향상시키기 위해 내부 운영 구조를 재정비하고 있다.

119 *Inkdrop*지의 편집자는 이달의 작가들이 사진과 짧은 전기를 제출하도록 하기 위해 그들에게 연락했다.

120 직원 평가서는 인사부서의 Ann James에게 이번 주 이내에 보내져야 한다.

121 학생들은 다른 학과로의 이동을 요청할 수 있지만 학과장에게 타당한 이유를 제시해야 한다.

122 다음 달부터, Alouette사의 수석 회계사는 1,000달러 이상의 모든 현금 지출 요청을 승인해야 한다.

123 Bedford 항공사와 Concord 호텔 체인은 서로 제휴를 맺어 세계의 다양한 목적지로의 휴가 패키지를 판매한다.

124 경영진은 지난 프로젝트에서 임시직으로 고용된 직원들 중 일부에게 정규직을 제의할 수도 있다.

125 Braun사 대변인은 회사 구조를 재편성하는 데 있어서 회사가 예정보다 앞서 있다고 발표했다.

126 우체국에서는 분실 서류에 대해 책임을 지지 않으므로, 봉투들은 우편함에 넣어지기 전에 제대로 봉해져야 한다.

127 Speed-Ex Electronics사는 6월 말까지 새로운 지점에 필요한 모든 장비가 배달되는 것을 확실히 하도록 요청받았다.

128 환경 문제에 대한 인식을 높이기 위해, 그 단체는 플라스틱 반대 운동을 시작했다.

129 시에서는 더 많은 나무와 꽃을 심어서 지역이 더 좋아 보이도록 만듦으로써 지역 공원을 다시 활성화할 계획이 있다.

130 Ledge Enterprises사의 최고 경영자는 기자회견 동안 회사의 생산 시설이 지닌 문제점에 대해 얘기할 것으로 예상된다.

PART 6

131-134는 다음 회람에 관한 문제입니다.

수신: 광고 직원 전체
발신: Lance Cavanaugh, 프로젝트 관리자
제목: 알림
날짜: 2월 7일

131 오늘 아침에 여러분 중 다수가 이번 주 여러분의 마감 일자를 맞추는 것이 불가능할 것이라고 이야기하기 위해 제게 연락했습니다. 132 지난주 서버 오작동이 복구할 수 없는 데이터 손실을 야기했기 때문에 제출 기한이 된 많은 업무들이 다시 되어야만 하는 것 같습니다.

이 기회를 빌려 중요한 파일들을 정기적으로 백업해 둘 것을 모두에게 상기시키고 싶습니다. 이것을 하는 데에는 다양한 방법이 있습니다. 133 예를 들어, 휴대용 하드 드라이브로 파일을 옮기거나 회사의 온라인 데이터 보관 서비스를 사용할 수 있습니다. 134 추후의 어떤 문제라도 방지하기 위해 적어도 일주일에 한 번 이것을 해 주십시오. 감사합니다.

135-138은 다음 이메일에 관한 문제입니다.

수신: Denise Brooks <dbrooks@atland.com>
발신: Nelson Lee <nlee@atland.com>
제목: Acton사
날짜: 1월 18일

안녕하세요 Denise,

아시다시피, 저는 우리의 컴퓨터 부품들을 정기적으로 구매하는 데 관심이 있는 회사인 Acton사의 잠재 고객분과 약속이 있습니다. 135 회의가 며칠 뒤에 있을 것이기 때문에, 저는 판매 제안서를 마무리 짓기 위해 노력하며 열심히 일했습니다.

그러나, 제가 인쇄해 놓은 사본을 잃어버린 것 같습니다. 비록 그 파일을 제 하드 드라이브에 가지고 있긴 하지만, 인쇄된 사본은 제가 그 위에 몇몇 메모를 써 놓았기 때문에 특히 중요합니다. 136 저는 이 메모들을 전자 파일에 추가할 시간이 없었습니다. 그 초안이 실수로 다른 곳에 보관되지 않았는지 확인해 줄 수 있으신가요? 137 만약 바로 그 사본을 되찾지 못한다면, 제가 가지고 있는 서류를 검토하고 다시 메모를 해야 할 것입니다. 138 Acton사를 고객으로 확보하는 것이 매우 중요하기에, 저를 위하여 잃어버린 서류를 찾아주신다면 정말 감사드리겠습니다. 감사합니다.

Nelson Lee 드림

139-142는 다음 공고에 관한 문제입니다.

직원 공고

139 8월 10일부터 시행되어, 종교 혹은 문화 의식을 위해 시간을 빼야 하는 직원들은 그들의 근무 일정에 잠시 동안의 변경을 요청할 수 있습니다. **140** 이 선택권은 개인의 휴가를 사용하는 것에 대한 대체 수단으로서 제공됩니다.

141 관리자는 그렇게 하는 것이 가능하기만 하면 이러한 요청을 수용하도록 지시받습니다. 때에 따라서는, 업무상의 의무가 우선시되어야 합니다. 또한 통지가 충분한 예고 없이 제공될 경우 요청은 거부될 수 있습니다. 직원들은 그들의 요청을 적어도 2주 앞서 제출해야 합니다. **142** 그렇지만, 진행 중인 그 어떤 프로젝트에도 일정 변경이 영향을 미치지 않을 경우 이 요건은 적용되지 않을 수 있습니다.

143-146은 다음 광고에 관한 문제입니다.

시애틀 New Light 요양원

저희는 도움을 드리기 위해 여기에 있습니다

143 많은 어르신들께서 가족과 친구들로부터 상당히 멀리 떨어져서 도시 생활과 먼 양로원에 계시고는 합니다. 시애틀 New Light 요양원에서는 그렇지 않습니다.

어르신들의 신체적, 정신적 건강이 저희의 최우선 순위입니다. **144** 그러므로 저희는 거주자들이 날마다 운동 교실, 게임, 음악 공연들을 포함하는 다양한 고무적인 활동들에 계속 열중하게 함으로써 그들이 건강한 수준의 사회적 상호 작용을 유지하도록 돕습니다. **145** 이것들은 그들의 삶의 질을 향상시키는 데에 크게 도움이 됩니다. **146** 게다가, 대중 교통, 시민 문화회관들과 공원들이 모두 저희 위치로부터 접근하기 쉽기 때문에, 거주자들은 저희 직원이 제공하는 매일의 보살핌과 관심으로부터 혜택을 받으면서도 그들의 흥미를 마음껏 추구할 수 있습니다.

저희 시설을 둘러보기 위한 시간을 예약하시려면 206-665-8924로 저희에게 전화 주십시오.

PART 7

147-148은 다음 이메일에 관한 문제입니다.

수신: Frederick Montaigne <fredm@burgundycapital.com>
발신: Gina Herald <ginah6482@errmail.net>
날짜: 2월 3일
제목: 보안 코드

Mr. Montaigne께,

어제 Burgundy 금융의 Harvard가 지점에서 예금 계좌와 관련해서 저를 도와주신 것에 대해 아무리 감사를 드려도 부족합니다. 온라인 뱅킹 서비스를 설정하는 법에 대해 제게 제공해주신 설명을 따랐고, 그 점과 관련해서는 모든 것이 잘 되었습니다.

유감스럽게도, 계좌 이체를 위한 특정 서비스를 클릭할 때 문제가 있는 것 같습니다. Burgundy 금융 계좌와 제가 타 은행에서 보유하고 있는 다른 계좌 사이에 이체를 실행하려고 시도할 때, 제 여섯 자리 보안 번호를 입력하라는 메시지를 받습니다. 그러나, 어제 저희가 이야기했을 때 코드를 만든 기억이 없습니다. 이 접근 코드를 찾는 방법에 대해 조언해주신다면, 당신의 도움에 매우 감사드리겠습니다.

Gina Herald 드림

---

147 이메일의 목적은 무엇인가?
(A) 새로운 계좌를 만드는 방법을 묻기 위해
(B) 온라인 서비스에 대한 문제를 설명하기 위해
(C) 자금 이체를 요청하기 위해
(D) 보안상 위험의 가능성을 보고하기 위해

148 Ms. Herald가 Burgundy 금융으로부터 무엇을 필요로 하는가?
(A) 보안 코드
(B) 은행 카드
(C) 계좌 명세서
(D) 잔액 확인서

149-150은 다음 메시지 대화문에 관한 문제입니다.

Mitchell Roach [오전 11시 26분]
안녕하세요, Jillian, 이번 주 점심에 시간 있어요? 제가 맡은 새로운 소송건에 대해 당신의 의견을 얻고 싶어요.

Mitchell Roach [오전 11시 27분]
Brighton Industrials사가 Grant Industries사와의 특허 분쟁에 휘말렸을 때 당신이 수석 변호인이었다고 알고 있어요. Ms. Baird가 저에게 그 회사의 Cromwell Holdings사를 상대로 한 최근 소송건을 맡아 달라고 요청했어요.

Jillian Barrera [오전 11시 32분]
안녕하세요, Mitchell. 기다리게 해서 죄송해요. Astoria Enterprises사와의 회의를 이제 막 끝냈어요. 목요일 아침 어때요? 제가 이번 주엔 꽤 바쁠 것 같아요.

Mitchell Roach [오전 11시 33분]
목요일에 만날 수 있어요. 당신이 시간 될 때 언제든지 커피를 마시거나 사무실에서 만날 수 있어요.

Jillian Barrera [오전 11시 33분]
오전 8시 30분에 커피를 마시러 제 사무실에 들르는 건 어때요?

Mitchell Roach [오전 11시 34분]
좋은 계획인 것 같아요. 이 일을 하는 데 시간을 내주어서 정말 감사해요.

Jillian Barrera [오전 11시 36분]
도와드릴 수 있어 기쁘네요. 저는 이제 Brighton사에 대해 꽤 잘 알고 있어서, 당신에게 몇몇 좋은 제안을 줄 수 있을 거예요.

---

149 Mr. Roach는 어떤 회사를 대변하도록 요청되었는가?
(A) Grant Industries사
(B) Brighton Industrials사
(C) Cromwell Holdings사
(D) Astoria Enterprises사

150 오전 11시 34분에, Mr. Roach가 "Sounds like a plan"이라고 썼을 때 그가 의도한 것은?
(A) 점심 회의가 그의 일정에 맞는다.
(B) 소송이 즉시 다뤄질 수 있다.
(C) 목요일 아침 약속이 알맞다.
(D) 고객이 아침에 언제든지 그의 사무실에 들를 수 있다.

151-152는 다음 일정표에 관한 문제입니다.

Northeast 인터넷 마케터 협회 (NEIMA)
인터넷 마케팅의 미래 학회
Northeast 경영대학교

첫째 날: 4월 23일

오전 9시-10시	Hawthorne실, 1층 등록 및 이름표 수령

오전 10시- 11시 30분	개막 패널 토론회, Johnstone 강당, 1층 인터넷 마케팅의 앞으로의 중요한 경향, 질의 시간 있음 NEIMA의 James Burke, Brand Solutions사의 Andrea Harrison, 그리고 Northeast 대학교의 Ming Chao 교수가 함께함
오전 11시 30분- 오후 12시 30분	워크숍, Washington실, 3층 "영향을 측정하는 방법," Gleason 검색 분석 기관의 Simon Gleason과 함께함
오후 12시 30분- 1시 30분	점심 식사 구내식당이 학생회관 건물에 위치해 있으며, 행사를 위 해 개방될 예정임.
오후 1시 30분- 3시	워크숍, Dawson실, 2층 "인턴들이 어떻게 유용해질 수 있는가: 학생 현장 실습 에서 기대해야 할 것들," Northeast 진로 센터의 Padma Singh과 함께함
오후 3시- 4시 30분	폐막 패널 토론, Johnstone 강당, 1층 NEIMA의 Gwen Carter가 오늘 워크숍에서 배운 것들 을 요약함. 청중들은 또한 내일의 상호 회의 시간에 토론 하고 싶은 주제를 제출할 것을 요청받을 것임.

151 어떤 예정된 연설자가 학생 인턴에 대해 논할 것인가?
(A) Simon Gleason
(B) Ming Chao
(C) Gwen Carter
(D) Padma Singh

152 학회에 대해 암시되는 것은?
(A) 저녁에 사교 행사를 포함한다.
(B) 두 번째 날도 계속된다.
(C) 학생회관 건물에서 개최된다.
(D) 활동들은 4개의 서로 다른 층에서 열린다.

153-154는 다음 회람에 관한 문제입니다.

회람

수신: 모든 직원들

우리는 또 다른 성공적인 해의 끝에 도달했고, 모든 직원 여러분들의 노고에 감사드리고 싶습니다. 여느 때처럼, 저희는 여러분 모두를 위한 특별 축제의 밤을 준비하고 있습니다. 올해에는, 12월 22일 오후 7시에 Lakeview가에 있는 Cranfield 호텔에서 개최될 것입니다. 직원분들은 배우자를 모셔와도 됩니다.

사전에 예약이 되어야 하므로, 인사부의 Lionel Grimm에게 ligrimm@austel.com으로 연락하셔서 참석할 것인지 그리고 손님을 모시고 올 것인지를 알려주시기 바랍니다.

감사합니다!

---

153 회람은 주로 무엇에 대한 것인가?
(A) 다가오는 해의 업무 일정
(B) 휴가를 위해 시간을 내는 것
(C) 회사 연례 모임
(D) 계획대로 프로젝트를 끝내는 것

154 직원들은 무엇을 하도록 요청되는가?
(A) 고객과의 회의에 참석한다
(B) 동료에게 이메일을 보낸다
(C) 회사에 휴가 계획을 알린다
(D) 객실 예약을 확정한다

155-157은 다음 이메일에 관한 문제입니다.

수신: Sara Brunelli <sarahb1971@easymail.ca>
발신: Mitchell Harcourt <harcourt@tuton.org>
날짜: 1월 17일
제목: 회신: 개인 교습

Ms. Brunelli께,

저희는 최근에 귀하의 아드님인 Jason의 개인 교습에 관한 귀하의 이메일을 받았고, 저희가 제공하는 서비스에 대해 귀하께 더 많은 세부 사항을 알려드리고자 합니다. 저희에게는 현재 수업할 수 있는 두 명의 역사 선생님이 있습니다. Michael Pearson은 Calgary 시립 대학교에서 역사학 학사 학위를 받았고 귀하의 아드님을 Edmonton 시내에 있는 저희 사무실이나 귀하의 댁에서 가르칠 수 있습니다. 저희에게는 또한 Eastern Canada 대학교에서 고대사 석사 학위를 받은 Francine Gatineau라는 선생님도 있습니다. 그러나, Ms. Gatineau는 저희 사무실에서만 일합니다.

한편, 귀하께서 처음에 언급하지 않으신 몇 가지 추가 세부 사항을 문의드리고 싶습니다. Jason이 얼마 동안 개인 교습을 받아야 한다고 예상하시며, 현재 그는 몇 학년입니까? 이러한 세부 사항들은 저희가 Jason의 지적 필요 사항을 충족시키는 적절한 프로그램을 준비하는 데 도움이 될 것입니다. 저희가 이 정보를 받고 난 후에, 지불 방식에 대해 논의할 수 있습니다.

귀하로부터 답장을 받기를 기대하며, 질문이 있으시다면 주저하지 마시고 다시 연락해 주십시오.

Mitchell Harcourt 드림
Tuton 교육 서비스

---

155 Ms. Brunelli에 대해 추론될 수 있는 것은?
(A) Mr. Harcourt와 만났다.
(B) 아들이 캘거리 시내에 있는 학교에 다닌다.
(C) 몇몇 개인 교습 회사에 연락했다.
(D) 아들이 역사 공부에 도움이 필요하다.

156 Ms. Gatineau의 개인 교습은 어디에서 열리는가?
(A) 학생의 집에서
(B) Edmonton 시내의 사무실에서
(C) 학생의 학교에서
(D) Eastern Canada 대학교에서

157 Mr. Harcourt는 추후에 무엇에 대해 논의할 것인가?
(A) 성적 시스템
(B) 수업 일정
(C) 수업료 지불
(D) 시험 성적

158-160은 다음 광고에 관한 문제입니다.

Web-Vision: 모두가 무슨 이야기를 하는지 알아보세요!

텔레비전 프로그램의 미래는 이미 여기 있습니다! Web-Vision 회원권이 있으면, 수천 편의 텔레비전 에피소드에 무제한으로 접근할 수 있습니다. 게다가, 30가지 이상의 다양한 시리즈와 24편 이상의 다양한 영화 중에서 고를 수 있는, 저희의 늘 인기 있는 오리지널 콘텐츠를 볼 수 있을 것입니다. 그리고 모든 장르의 저희 영화 자료를 확인해 보세요. 둘러볼 2,200편의 작품이 있습니다. 이 모든 것이 버튼 클릭 한 번으로 이용 가능합니다.

회원으로서, 여러분은 저희의 가장 인기 있는 텔레비전 시리즈인 *Apollo Titans*를 볼 수 있습니다. 수상 경력이 있는 이 쇼는 현재 세 시즌이 시청 가능합니다. 그리고 네 번째 시즌이 9월 9일에 시작할 것입니다.

회원권이 월 10파운드만큼이나 적은 가격부터 시작하는데, 왜 케이블 텔레비전에 더 많은 돈을 쓰시나요? Web-Vision으로 바꿔서 그만큼의 방해되는 광고 없이, 원하는 언제든지 가장 좋아하는 쇼와 영화를 보세요. www.web-vision.com을 방문하여 오늘 등록하세요!

---

158 1문단 네 번째 줄의 단어 "browse"는 의미상 −와 가장 가깝다.
(A) 쇼핑하다
(B) 건너뛰다
(C) 관찰하다
(D) 살펴보다

159 *Apollo Titans*는 왜 언급되는가?
(A) 콘텐츠의 변경을 발표하기 위해
(B) 회원권 혜택을 강조하기 위해
(C) 프로그램 일정을 공개하기 위해
(D) 이용 가능한 영화의 예시를 제공하기 위해

160 케이블 텔레비전에 대해 암시된 것은?
(A) 한 달에 비용이 덜 든다.
(B) 더 다양한 종류의 쇼가 있다.
(C) 광고 콘텐츠가 더 많다.
(D) 더 적은 오리지널 영화를 제공한다.

161-163은 다음 공고에 관한 문제입니다.

공고

이것은 Superion 건물 6층에 있는 구내식당에 5월 27일부터 직원들의 접근이 불가능하다는 것을 GlobalFerm사의 전 직원에게 알리는 공고입니다. — [1] —. 그러나, 구내식당이 개조되어 다수의 새로운 음식을 제공하는 Servex Modern 식당 시설로 바뀌게 될 것임을 모든 직원들께 알리게 되어 기쁩니다. 이러한 구내식당의 개조가 저희의 최근 설문 조사에서 나타난 제안들을 반영하는 것이 저희의 바람입니다. — [2] —. 따라서, 채식주의, 엄격한 채식주의, 그리고 글루텐을 함유하지 않은 항목들 또한 식단 제한이 있는 분들을 위해 매일 이용 가능할 것입니다. GlobalFerm사 인트라넷에 로그인하여 "직원 복지" 탭 아래에 있는 "Servex Modern"을 클릭하셔서 구내식당의 아침 및 점심 메뉴 모두를 확인하십시오. 그 메뉴들은 여러분의 편의상 매주 업데이트될 것입니다. Servex Modern 구내식당의 좌석이 550석으로 확장될 것이라는 점 또한 알리게 되어 기쁩니다. — [3] —. 이것은 장애가 있는 사람들을 위한 충분한 설비를 포함할 것입니다. 개조 기간 동안의 불편함에 대해 사과드리나, 저희는 여러분이 모든 변화의 진가를 인정할 것이라고 확신합니다. — [4] —.

---

161 공고의 목적은 무엇인가?
(A) 시설의 이전을 알리기 위해
(B) 점심시간에 관련된 정책을 명백하게 설명하기 위해
(C) 설문 조사 결과를 직원들에게 알리기 위해
(D) 직원들에게 곧 있을 개조에 대해 알리기 위해

162 직원들은 어디에서 음식 선택 사항을 확인할 수 있는가?
(A) Superion 건물의 로비에서
(B) 구내식당의 정문 옆에서
(C) 6층의 게시판에서
(D) 회사 인트라넷 사이트에서

163 [1], [2], [3], [4]로 표시된 위치 중, 다음 문장이 들어갈 곳으로 가장 적절한 것은?

"저희는 모든 사람들을 만족시키기 위해 다양한 식사 선택권을 제공할 필요가 있다는 여러분들에 동의합니다."

(A) [1]
(B) [2]
(C) [3]
(D) [4]

164-167은 다음 기사에 관한 문제입니다.

First Global사가 더 확장하다
12월 28일

스마트폰 제조사를 위한 부품을 만드는 전자 기술 거대 기업인 First Global사는 화요일의 기자 회견에서 곧 20번째 해외 생산 공장 건설을 시작할 것으로 기대한다고 말했다. 이 발표는 4분기의 매출액이 3분기 매출액을 15퍼센트 초과한 성공적인 한 해의 마지막에 나온 것이다. 회장이자 최고 경영자인 Ms. Genevieve Durand는 First Global사의 성장을 제조상의 효율성 덕분으로 보고 있다. — [1] —. "저희는 더 적은 것으로 더 많은 것을 할 방법들을 찾습니다"라고 Durand은 주장한다. "높은 품질의 제품을 경쟁력 있는 가격에 생산하는 것이죠." — [2] —.

완료되면, 새로운 공장은 중국의 베이징 가까이에 위치할 것이다. 이것은 First Global사의 가장 큰 공장이자 동아시아 지역에 위치한 여섯 개의 시설 중 하나가 될 것이다. — [3] —. 전에 해왔던 것처럼, First Global사는 건설 자금을 모으기 위해 추가 대출을 받거나 자산을 파는 것보다는 자사 수입을 이용할 것이다. 새로운 시설이 생산성을 약 20퍼센트 높일 것으로 기대된다. — [4] —. 공장 건설은 내년 봄에 시작될 것이다.

164 기사는 왜 쓰였는가?
(A) 한 지역의 사업 경향을 설명하기 위해
(B) 휴대폰 판매액을 보고하기 위해
(C) 최고 경영자의 목표를 알려주기 위해
(D) 새로운 시설을 위한 계획을 알리기 위해

165 First Global사는 어떻게 최신 프로젝트에 자금을 댈 계획인가?
(A) 회사의 주식을 팔아서
(B) 공동 경영자를 데려옴으로써
(C) 대출 한도를 높여서
(D) 지난 수익에 의존해서

166 기사가 First Global사에 대해 암시하는 것은?
(A) 공장 근무 환경이 표준에 미치지 않는다.
(B) 생산이 기대되는 것만큼 늘지 않을 것이다.
(C) 스마트폰 제조사들이 그들의 제품을 구매한다.
(D) 아시아로 확장하는 것은 그들에게 새로운 경험이 될 것이다.

167 [1], [2], [3], [4]로 표시된 위치 중, 다음 문장이 들어갈 곳으로 가장 적절한 것은?

"이러한 생산량의 증가는 회사가 스마트폰의 높은 수요를 따라가는 데 도움이 될 것이다."

(A) [1]
(B) [2]
(C) [3]
(D) [4]

168-171은 다음 온라인 채팅 대화문에 관한 문제입니다.

Bill Reed   오전 9시 15분
저는 방금 Thompson 제지사의 최고 경영자인 Deborah Lee와 이야기했어요. 그녀는 Haydon 건설사가 그녀의 회사의 새로운 창고 단지를 건설하게 하는 비용에 대한 견적서를 왜 아직 받지 못했는지 알고 싶어 해요. 저는 우리가 지난주에 견적을 보냈다고 생각했어요.

Sally Waters   오전 9시 18분
견적서에 수정을 좀 해야 했어요. 우리의 공급업체인 Fulton Wholesale사가 여러 종류의 건축 자재들에 대해 가격을 인상하고 있어요. 우리는 Thompson 제지사에 우리가 원래 계획했던 것보다 약 15퍼센트를 더 청구해야 할 거예요.

David Vance   오전 9시 22분
그건 좋지 않은데요. Ms. Lee는 그만큼을 지불하는 것에 절대 동의하지 않을 거예요. 우리가 함께 일할 수 있는 다른 공급업체는 없나요?

Sally Waters   오전 9시 25분
찾아보고 있는 중이지만, 우리는 절대 이 프로젝트 기한에 맞춰서 새로운 공급업체로 전환할 수는 없을 거예요.

David Vance 오전 9시 28분
무엇이든 생각해내는 것이 좋겠어요. 저는 Haydon 건설사가 고객인 Thompson 제지사를 잃는 것을 원치 않아요.

Sally Waters 오전 9시 30분
견적서를 다시 검토해볼게요. 어쩌면 더 비싸진 자재를 상쇄하기 위해 우리가 줄일 수 있는 다른 비용을 좀 찾을 수 있을지도 몰라요. 하지만, 시간이 조금 걸릴 거예요.

Bill Reed 오전 9시 32분
알겠어요. 점심시간 바로 전에 저에게 전화해서 당신이 오늘 일을 끝낼 수 있을지 알려주세요. 그동안, 저는 Fulton Wholesale사의 관리자에게 연락할게요. 가능성은 희박하지만, 어쩌면 이 주문에 대해 우리에게 할인을 해달라고 그를 설득할 수 있을지도 몰라요.

168 Mr. Reed에 대해 사실인 것은?
(A) 비용 견적서를 수정했다.
(B) 공급업체와 계약을 맺었다.
(C) 고객과 대화를 나눴다.
(D) 공사 현장을 방문했다.

169 오전 9시 22분에, Mr. Vance가 "That's not good"이라고 썼을 때 그가 의도한 것은?
(A) Fulton Wholesale사가 송장 오류를 냈다.
(B) 고객이 더 높은 가격을 지불하기를 꺼릴 수도 있다.
(C) 한 건축 자재를 구할 수 없다.
(D) Thompson 제지사가 심각한 불만을 제기했다.

170 Haydon 건설사의 직원들이 제시한 해결책이 아닌 것은?
(A) 다른 공급업체의 사용
(B) 지급 보류
(C) 기타 비용 절감
(D) 할인 요청

171 Mr. Reed는 Ms. Waters에게 무엇을 지시하는가?
(A) 프로젝트 감독과 이야기한다
(B) 진행 상황에 대한 최신 정보를 제공한다
(C) 창고 관리자와 만난다
(D) 계산서 청구 오류를 바로잡는다

172-175는 다음 이메일에 관한 문제입니다.

수신: Benjamin Pinkerton <benpin@ponyexpress.com>
발신: Carol Andrews <carol@ponyexpress.com>
제목: 본사로의 출장
날짜: 7월 18일

Benjamin,

다음 주 워싱턴 D.C.로의 우리의 방문 일정에 대한 잠정적인 개요를 당신께 전달하고 싶었습니다. 우리가 월요일 오후에 도착하면 회사 차가 공항에서 우리를 태워 Earthgate 호텔로 데려다줄 것입니다. 저는 오늘 아침에 예약 이메일을 받았고 호텔이 우리에게 귀빈실로 예약을 확정해 주었는데, 그것은 꽤 괜찮을 것 같습니다. 우리는 Recon 제지 회사의 사장인 Linda Krakowski를 만나기 전에 호텔에서 몇 시간을 보낼 것입니다. 그녀는 친절하게도 우리가 긴 여행 후 다른 곳으로 이동하지 않아도 되도록 저녁 식사를 위해 호텔에서 만나자고 제안하였습니다.

다음 날 우리는 회사 본사에서 거의 온종일 여러 회의와 약속이 있을 것입니다. 또한 최고 경영자 및 몇몇 이사회 회원들과 오찬을 가질 것입니다. 우리는 모든 일을 저녁 7시 무렵까지는 마칠 것으로 예상합니다.

우리는 수요일 아침에 돌아오는 항공편으로 예약이 되어 있지만, 화요일 오후 11시 35분에 로스앤젤레스행 늦은 밤 항공편도 있다고도 들었습니다. 화요일과 수요일 중 언제 돌아오는 것이 더 좋습니까? 저는 어느 항공편이든 좋습니다. 어떻게 하고 싶으신지 알려주시면, 제가 진행해서 D.C.의 사무실에

알리도록 하겠습니다.

감사합니다!

Carol Andrews 드림
판매 관리자
Pony Express사

172 Ms. Andrews는 왜 이메일을 썼는가?
(A) 동료에게 일정에 대해 알려주기 위해
(B) 예약에 대한 변경을 요청하기 위해
(C) 호텔 시설들에 대해 문의하기 위해
(D) 회의 결과를 요약하기 위해

173 이메일에서 언급되지 않은 것은?
(A) 상사와의 점심 식사 일정이 잡혀 있다.
(B) 호텔이 이미 예약을 확정했다.
(C) 프로젝트의 시작이 연기되었다.
(D) 회의들은 본사에서 열릴 것이다.

174 Ms. Krakowski는 왜 호텔로 올 것인가?
(A) 그곳이 방문객들에게 편리하다.
(B) 그녀는 그곳에서 열리는 회의에서 연설을 할 것이다.
(C) 그곳이 그녀의 사무실과 가까이 위치한다.
(D) 그녀는 새로운 식당에 가보고 싶어 한다.

175 Ms. Andrews는 Mr. Pinkerton에게 어떤 정보를 요구하는가?
(A) 좌석 배정
(B) 연락처
(C) 회의 안건
(D) 선호하는 날짜

176-180은 다음 웹페이지와 온라인 후기에 관한 문제입니다.

www.sidebyside.com/kitchenappliances
Side by Side—저희는 여러분이 더 현명하게 쇼핑하도록 도와드립니다!

현재 Wallace Appliances 에서 40달러 에서 100달러 사이로 구매 가능한 드립 커피 제조기 에 대한 당신의 검색은 다음의 결과를 산출했습니다:

제품 설명	가격	특징	용량	추출 시간	청소의 용이함
Conklin Pour 578-G	~~79.99달러~~ 현재 71.25 달러로 할인 중*	-온도 조절 가능 -식기세척기 사용 가능	12잔	6분, 34초	4.5/5
Lundi Café WDE-23V	99.75달러	-프로그램 설정 가능; 매일 커피가 추출되기를 원하는 시간을 설정하면 기계가 당신을 위해 그렇게 해줄 것임	14잔	5분, 19초	5/5
Bonaveni TCD-333	~~56.43달러~~ 현재 43.67 달러로 할인 중*	-탈부착할 수 있는 종이 필터 바구니 -식기세척기 사용 가능	10잔	7분, 4초	2.5/5
Sandfield Velocity 1200-F	68.92 달러	-커피 콩 분쇄기가 딸려 있음 -필터 내장	10잔	4분, 11초	2/5

*할인은 12월 17일부터 1월 31일까지 계속됩니다.

다시 돌아가서 검색을 변경하려면 여기를 클릭하십시오.

이번 시즌 가장 인기 있는 신제품의 매우 좋은 가격에 관해 알고 싶으십니까? 저희의 주간 소식지를 신청하기 위해 당신의 이메일 주소를 입력해주십시오: _____

[등록]

www.storereviewer.com/wallaceappliances
Wallace Appliances의 최신 후기들

| Marcus Ford 1월 20일 | 저는 1월 15일, 토요일에 새 커피 제조기를 구입하기 위해 Seaward에 있는 Wallace Appliances 매장을 방문했습니다. 저는 매우 깊은 인상을 받았습니다. 이용할 수 있는 넓은 주차 공간이 있었고, 고객들은 그것에 대해 돈을 지불할 필요가 없었습니다. 게다가, 건물의 내부는 매우 밝고 현대적이었습니다. 계산원은 그 매장이 지난달에 개조되었다고 언급했습니다. 선택할 수 있는 커피 제조기의 선택권도 넓었고, 제가 상대한 매장 점원도 매우 도움이 되었습니다. 그는 다양한 특징들을 자세하게 설명했고 할인 중이었던 모델을 추천해주었습니다. 전반적으로, 저는 그가 제안해준 것에 꽤 만족하지만, 그것이 한 번에 10잔보다 많은 커피를 만들 수 있었으면 좋겠다고 약간은 생각합니다. |

176 웹페이지의 목적은 무엇인가?
(A) 새롭게 이용 가능한 제품을 소개하기 위해
(B) 다양한 가전제품을 사용하는 방법을 설명하기 위해
(C) 몇몇 비슷한 제품들을 비교하기 위해
(D) 가게의 가장 인기 있는 제품을 홍보하기 위해

177 웹페이지에서, 1문단 두 번째 줄의 단어 "yielded"는 의미상 –와 가장 가깝다.
(A) 확인했다
(B) 산출했다
(C) 묘사했다
(D) 드러냈다

178 Wallace Appliances의 제품들에 대한 할인에 대해 언급된 것은?
(A) 한정된 기간 동안 제공된다.
(B) 웹사이트에서만 구매할 수 있다.
(C) 등록된 고객들에게만 제공된다.
(D) 구형 모델로 제한된다.

179 Wallace Appliances의 Seaward 지점에 대해 언급되지 않은 것은?
(A) 최근에 개조되었다.
(B) 추가 점원을 고용했다.
(C) 무료 주차를 제공한다.
(D) 토요일에 문을 연다.

180 Mr. Ford는 어떤 커피 제조기를 구매했을 것 같은가?
(A) Conklin Pour 578-G
(B) Lundi Café WDE-23V
(C) Bonaveni TCD-333
(D) Sandfield Velocity 1200-F

181-185는 다음 이메일과 공고에 관한 문제입니다.

수신: Gary Flores <gflores49@thmail.com>
발신: Wendy Rhodes <w_rhodes@tarmail.net>
날짜: 7월 10일
제목: 계획에 대한 제안
첨부: 초대권

Mr. Flores께,

이 메시지가 당신이 잘 지내고 있음을 확인해주기 바랍니다. 지난번에 우리가 만났을 때, 당신은 은퇴 계획의 초안을 작성하는 데 조언을 해달라고 제게 부탁했었습니다. 아래는 당신이 시작할 수 있는 몇 가지 조언입니다.

첫째로, 보통의 월 지출의 대략 세 배에 상응하는 현금 예비금을 비상시의 목적을 위해 만들고 유지하는 것이 필수적입니다. 이 액수는 꽤 클 수 있기 때문에, 가능한 한 빨리 저축을 시작하는 것이 중요합니다.

추가로, 당신, 당신의 배우자, 그리고 당신의 부모님을 위한, 은퇴 이후의 장기적인 의료 선택 사항들을 살펴볼 것을 권장합니다. 당신은 또한 당신의 건강 관리 계획의 세부 사항도 가족 구성원들과 공유해야 합니다.

대학 행사에서 제가 할 강의인 "하나를 위한 은퇴"에 참석하실 수 있도록 특별 초대권을 첨부하였습니다. 같은 초대권은 또한 당신이 Mr. Victor Rochester에 의해 진행되는 노인을 위한 건강 보험에 대한 특별 오찬 세미나에 참석하실 수 있도록 합니다. 이 행사들은 당신이 입구에서 초대권을 보여주면 무료입니다.

곧 뵙게 되기를 기대합니다.

Wendy Rhodes 드림
은퇴 계획 전문가
Cottler 금융

경력 개발 센터
Sunfield 주립 대학

Sunfield 주립 대학의 경력 개발 센터는 개방적이고 고무적인 환경 내에서 일하는 사람들과 퇴직자들에게 높은 품질의, 적당한 가격의 교육 및 전문성 개발을 제공하기 위해 노력합니다.

저희의 연간 센터 정보 행사가 7월 12일 월요일에 Durgan홀 5층에서 열리게 됨을 공고하게 되어 기쁩니다. 여러분이 은퇴 조언가 Wendy Rhodes의 강의에 참석하도록 초대합니다. 7월 13일 화요일에는, 시간제 채용의 전망에 대한 그녀의 2부로 이루어진 세미나 중 첫 번째가 오후 3시부터 5시까지 열릴 것입니다. 이것은 다음 날인 7월 14일 수요일, 같은 시간에 마무리될 것입니다. 마지막으로, 7월 15일 목요일에는, 저희의 센터장이신 Mr. Victor Rochester의 특별 오찬 발표회를 또한 열 것입니다. 각 행사의 입장권은 센터 회원들은 10달러이며 비회원에게는 15달러입니다. 오찬 티켓은 추가 10달러이며, Durgan 홀에 있는 저희의 본사 사무실에서 7월 1일부터 15일까지 구매할 수 있습니다. 더 알고 싶으시면, 555-2402로 전화하십시오.

181 이메일의 목적은 무엇인가?
(A) 몇 가지 도움이 되는 조언을 주기 위해
(B) 프로그램에 대한 세부 사항의 개요를 서술하기 위해
(C) 오찬의 필요성을 확인하기 위해
(D) 다가오는 강의에 대해 논의하기 위해

182 이메일에 따르면, Mr. Flores는 그의 건강 관리 계획의 세부 사항으로 무엇을 해야 하는가?
(A) 그의 사무실의 폴더에 보관한다
(B) 그의 핸드폰에 저장한다
(C) 의사와 함께 논의한다
(D) 가족 구성원들에게 전한다

183 경력 개발 센터는 누구에게 강좌를 제공하는가?
(A) 소기업 소유주들
(B) 일하고 있거나 퇴직한 성인들
(C) 구직 중인 대학생들
(D) 노인 자원봉사자들

184 Ms. Rhodes의 세미나는 언제 끝날 것인가?
(A) 7월 12일에
(B) 7월 13일에
(C) 7월 14일에
(D) 7월 15일에

185 Mr. Flores에 대해 암시되는 것은?
(A) Ms. Rhodes의 강의를 도와줄 것이다.
(B) Durgan 홀에서 점심 회의가 있다.
(C) 목요일의 행사에 무료로 참석할 수 있다.
(D) 한 장보다 많은 표가 필요하다.

186-190은 다음 공고, 광고, 영수증에 관한 문제입니다.

고객 대상 공고
Elm Point 쇼핑센터의 부분 폐쇄

8월 12일부터 15일까지, 기술자들이 쇼핑센터에 새로운 보안 시스템을 설치할 것입니다. 이 기간 동안, 쇼핑몰의 각 층은 다음 일정에 따라 하루 동안 일반 대중이 접근할 수 없을 것입니다:

8월 12일 - 1층 / 8월 13일 - 2층
8월 14일 - 3층 / 8월 15일 - 4층

쇼핑몰의 상점이 위치한 층에 작업이 진행되는 날에는 상점이 문을 닫을 것이라는 점을 유념해 주십시오. Elm Point 쇼핑센터 경영진은 이것이 저희 고객분들께 야기할 수 있는 불편에 대해 사과드리고자 합니다. 저희 시설을 쇼핑하기에 더 안전한 곳으로 만들고자 하니 여러분의 인내와 이해를 부탁드립니다.

이 계획에 관해 어떤 것이든 질문이 있으시다면, 정문 앞에 있는 고객 서비스 창구에 들러 주십시오. 저희 직원 중 한 명이 기꺼이 귀하께서 요구하시는 추가 정보를 제공해 드릴 것입니다.

Point Sports 재고 정리 할인!

Point Sports는 새로운 축구 장비 컬렉션이 8월 말에 나올 것이라고 발표하게 되어 기쁩니다. 이 가을을 설레게 하는 장비 제품 라인을 위한 공간을 만들기 위해, 저희는 8월 1일부터 20일까지 재고 정리 할인을 열 것입니다. 모든 테니스 장비는 가격이 25퍼센트 인하될 것입니다. 덧붙여, 저희 Point Sports 프로그램의 회원들은 이 판촉 기간 동안 구매하시면 평소 보상 포인트의 두 배를 받으실 것입니다. 그러니, 저희 가게에 꼭 들르세요! 저희가 Elm Point 쇼핑 센터 1층에서 4층의 더 넓은 공간으로 옮겼다는 것을 잊지 마세요. 곧 뵙기를 바랍니다!

Point Sports

고객: Lei Bell		**계산원:** Jack Lee
날짜: 8월 10일		**영수증 #:** 0456

상품 설명	수량	가격
Bonneval 테니스 라켓	1	173.00달러
Jones Collection 야구 글러브	1	43.00달러
Zarza 러닝화	1	138.00달러
Flatlands 줄넘기	1	9.00달러
	세금	21.78달러
	합계	384.78달러

정가 물품은 구입일 이후 30일까지 어떤 이유로든 반품할 수 있습니다. 환불금이 지급되려면, 구매 증거가 반드시 제시되어야 합니다. 모든 할인 품목의 판매는 변경될 수 없습니다. 할인 정책에 대한 더 많은 정보를 원하신다면, www.pointsports.com을 방문하세요.

186 일부 고객들은 왜 고객 서비스 창구를 방문할 것 같은가?
(A) 비상조치에 대한 정보를 요청하기 위해
(B) 시설의 운영 시간에 대한 시간표를 가지러 가기 위해
(C) 안전 장비의 설치에 대해 문의하기 위해
(D) 다가오는 쇼핑몰 폐쇄에 대한 의견을 제공하기 위해

187 Point Sports는 어느 날에 문을 닫을 것인가?
(A) 8월 12일
(B) 8월 13일
(C) 8월 14일
(D) 8월 15일

188 Point Sports에 대해 사실이 아닌 것은?
(A) 8월에 몇몇 새로운 장비를 소개할 것이다.
(B) 고객을 위한 보상 프로그램을 마련했다.
(C) 다른 쇼핑센터로 이전할 것이다.
(D) 더 큰 상업 공간을 차지했다.

189 영수증에서, 어느 가격에 할인이 적용되었는가?
(A) 173.00달러
(B) 43.00달러
(C) 138.00달러
(D) 9.00달러

190 Point Sports에서 환불 요청을 처리하기 위해 요구되는 것은 무엇인가?
(A) 할인이 입증되어야 한다.
(B) 거래 기록이 제시되어야 한다.
(C) 온라인 양식이 제출되어야 한다.
(D) 사유가 승인되어야 한다.

191-195는 다음 공고, 이메일, 후기에 관한 문제입니다.

Meredith 패션 학교(MFI)가 저희 졸업 예정 학생들이 참여하는 연례 봄 패션쇼에 여러분을 초대합니다:

신선한 바람의 숨결
가볍고 경쾌하고 혁신적인 패션 행사

오락, 점심, 패션쇼
사회자: 스타일리스트 Melvin Lee
DJ Raina의 음악

1인당 40달러
5월 7일 토요일, 정오

Hannah 홀 연회장
Meredith 패션 학교

언제나처럼, 이 행사는 로스앤젤레스의 South Grand가 1000번지의 저희 캠퍼스에서 열립니다. 모든 수익금은 경쟁이 치열한 패션 디자인계에서 확실히 자리 잡기 위해 지원이 필요한 신규 디자이너들의 초기 자금에 도움이 됩니다.

수신: Troy Seeger <t.seeger@mfi.com>
발신: Anna Cruise <anna_cruise@imagephoto.com>
날짜: 4월 4일
제목: 회신: 사진 서비스

Mr. Seeger께,

저는 곧 있을 Meredith 패션 학교의 행사와 관련한 귀하의 메시지를 받았습니다. 저는 쇼의 수익금이 어디에 쓰일지에 대해 높이 평가하기에, 공식 사진 작가로서 참석하게 되면 기쁠 것입니다. 또한, 저는 기꺼이 무료로 서비스를 제공해드리고 학교가 사용할 수 있도록 사진들을 드리겠습니다. 그러나, 이 행사가 비록 저를 많이 알려지게 할 것이기는 하지만 이렇게 큰 행사를 담당하는 비용이 꽤 많이 듭니다. 따라서, 입구 옆에 포토 부스를 설치해서 방문객들에게 소정의 출력 비용을 부과해도 되는지 허가를 받으려고 합니다. 필요한 것은 제 카메라, 테이블, 배경 막, 프린터를 설치할 공간이면 됩니다. 제가 행사 사진을 찍는 동안 제 조수가 테이블을 담당하도록 할 수 있습니다. 이것에 대해 더 논의하시려면 제게 555-0493으로 연락 주십시오.

Anna Cruise 드림

---

*Fashion Guide*지

LA 현장
Beth Rowlands 작성

늘 그렇듯, Meredith 패션 학교의 연례 학생 패션 행사는 업계의 가능성 있는 미래에 대한 흥미로운 짧은 경험을 제공했다. 모르는 사람들을 위해 말하자면, MFI는 Roxy Cooper와 Belle Hashimoto를 포함하여 많은 성공한 졸업생들을 배출시켜왔다. 이 학교의 졸업생이기도 한 행사의 진행자는 *Fashion Guide*지의 몇몇 특집 기사를 위해 모델들의 머리 손질과 화장을 했었다. 올해 쇼에서의 패션들은 "가볍고 경쾌하고 혁신적인"이라는 주제를 정확히 실현했다. 다수의 헐렁한 상의, 배기바지, 오버사이즈 코트가 특징

이었다. 옷은 차분했고, 가끔 약간의 색상을 통해 강조되는 중간색의 색조로 주로 이루어져 있었다. 하지만 가장 눈에 띈 것은 소재였는데, 그것들은 여러 가지의 과감한 형태들로 훌륭하게 재단된, 특별한 질감이 나게 만든 직물이었다. 몇몇 사진들을 아래에서 확인해보기 바란다. 당신은 언젠가 그것들 중 일부를 지역 패션 소매업체에서 볼 수도 있다.

191 Meredith 패션 학교의 행사에 대해 언급되지 않은 것은?
(A) 학교 부지에서 매년 열린다.
(B) 참석자들을 위한 식사를 포함한다.
(C) 브랜드 출시와 함께 열린다.
(D) 방문객들에게 입장료를 부과한다.

192 Ms. Cruise는 행사에 대해 무엇을 높이 평가하는가?
(A) 수익금이 신예 디자이너들을 돕는 데 쓰일 것이다.
(B) 아마추어 사진작가들이 대중의 관심을 얻는 데 도움이 될 것이다.
(C) 그녀가 자신의 장비를 가져오지 않아도 될 것이다.
(D) 그녀에게 몇몇 작품을 전시할 기회를 제공할 것이다.

193 Ms. Cruise는 왜 부스를 설치하고 싶어 하는가?
(A) 잠재적 조수를 면접 보기 위해
(B) 오는 손님들을 기록하기 위해
(C) 일부 비용을 만회할 기회를 얻기 위해
(D) 짧은 휴식을 가질 공간을 갖기 위해

194 Melvin Lee에 대해 사실인 것은?
(A) 행사에 오락을 제공했다.
(B) MFI에서 패션 수업을 가르친다.
(C) Ms. Rowlands와 같은 학교에 다녔다.
(D) 잡지를 위해 모델들을 스타일링하는 것을 도왔다.

195 Ms. Rowlands가 MFI의 행사에 포함된 패션들에 대해 언급하는 것은?
(A) 이전 시즌의 옷들보다 색상이 다채롭다.
(B) 행사의 정해진 주제를 거의 반영하지 않았다.
(C) 향후 의류 상점들에서 판매될 수도 있다.
(D) 주요 패션 디자이너들에 의해 빠르게 차용되었다.

196-200은 다음 기사, 웹페이지, 후기에 관한 문제입니다.

NYCBikeTourist사, 전통적인 관광업체들을 대체하다

Rodrigo Jimenez 작성

NYCBikeTourist사는 고객들을 자전거로 뉴욕시에 안내하는 새로운 관광 회사이다. 전용 앱을 통해 예약할 수 있는 이 프로그램은 숙련된 가이드와 최고의 자전거 장비를 제공한다.

매일, 박물관이나 다른 인기 있는 장소에서 몇 차례 정차하는 다양한 투어가 제공된다. NYCBikeTourist사는 이러한 지역 명소 및 업체들과 수익성 높은 제휴를 맺어 즉시 입장 또는 특별 할인을 제공한다. 한 투어는 자전거 이용자들을 매우 인기 있는 Berkley 현대 미술관으로 데려간다. 이 미술관은 막 문을 열었고 보통 바깥에 긴 줄이 있다. 그러나, 투어를 한다면, 틀림없이 들어갈 수 있을 것이다.

---

www.NYCBikeTourist.com/tours

6월 23일에 이용할 수 있는 투어는 다음과 같습니다:

- **1번 투어 (인당 35달러)**
  자유의 여신상 투어. Ellis섬을 가로질러 자전거를 타고 역사적인 동상을 방문하세요. 전채 요리와 와인을 포함합니다. 이 투어에 참여하려면 반드시 법적 성인(18세 이상)이어야 합니다.
  수준: 고급, 소요 시간: 3시간, 시작: 오후 7시

- **2번 투어 (인당 45달러)**
  센트럴파크 투어. 공원으로 자전거를 타고 가서 그곳의 역사에 대해 배워보세요. 준비된 소풍이 포함됩니다.

수준: 평균, 소요 시간: 3시간, 시작: 오후 1시

- **3번 투어 (인당 75달러)**
  도시 횡단 투어. 브루클린 다리와 같은 상징적인 다리들을 건너고, 외곽부터 시내까지 자전거를 타세요. 점심과 간식이 제공됩니다.
  수준: 고급, 소요 시간: 6시간, 시작: 오전 10시

- **4번 투어 (인당 120달러)**
  박물관 투어. 여러 박물관에 가서 VIP 입장권을 받으세요. 투어 중 방문하는 박물관들: Berkley 현대 미술관, Jester 미술관, 그리고 브루클린 국립 역사 박물관. 트렌디한 Nolita 동네에서의 점심식사를 포함합니다.
  수준: 평균, 소요 시간: 8시간, 시작: 오전 9시

NYCBikeTourist사 후기

6월 25일 게시
Leo Reyes 작성

자전거 애호가로서, 저는 투어가 실제 자전거 탑승을 충분히 포함해서 기뻤습니다. 저는 그들이 방문하는 박물관들에도 관심 있었지만, 그곳들은 제 개인 시간에 방문하기로 선택했습니다. 저는 이전에 브루클린 다리를 걸어본 적은 있지만, 자전거를 타고 양방향으로 건너는 것은 정말이지 저에게 가장 좋은 부분이었습니다. 그것의 역사에 대한 저희 가이드의 이야기들은 이 경험을 훨씬 더 특별하게 만들어 주었습니다. 한 가지 단점은 저희가 방문한 어떤 장소에서도 많은 시간을 보낼 수 없었다는 것이었습니다. 하지만 좋은 점은, 특정 지점들에 음료와 가벼운 간식이 미리 준비되어 있었다는 것입니다. 곧 다시 이용하고 싶습니다.

196 NYCBikeTourist사에 대해 사실인 것은?
(A) 5월부터 9월까지만 문을 연다.
(B) 자체 예약 애플리케이션이 있다.
(C) 지역 정부 관계자들과 제휴를 맺었다.
(D) 유명한 가게로부터 자전거를 대여한다.

197 1번 투어는 다른 선택지들로부터 어떻게 다른가?
(A) Nolita 지역에서 시간을 보낸다.
(B) 다른 투어들보다 더 짧다.
(C) 참가자들은 공원에서 점심식사를 한다.
(D) 미성년자들은 참가할 수 없다.

198 박물관 투어에 대해 언급된 것은?
(A) 고급 자전거 이용자들에게만 권장된다.
(B) 특별한 등록 절차를 요구한다.
(C) 새로운 명소 방문을 포함한다.
(D) 여섯 군데 이상의 박물관에서 정차한다.

199 Mr. Reyes는 어떤 투어를 예약한 것 같은가?
(A) 1번 투어
(B) 2번 투어
(C) 3번 투어
(D) 4번 투어

200 Mr. Reyes는 무엇에 실망했는가?
(A) 자전거를 타는 양
(B) 가이드의 지식
(C) 방문의 시간
(D) 음식과 음료

Answer Sheet

TEST 01

READING (Part V~VII)

101	A B C D	121	A B C D	141	A B C D	161	A B C D	181	A B C D
102	A B C D	122	A B C D	142	A B C D	162	A B C D	182	A B C D
103	A B C D	123	A B C D	143	A B C D	163	A B C D	183	A B C D
104	A B C D	124	A B C D	144	A B C D	164	A B C D	184	A B C D
105	A B C D	125	A B C D	145	A B C D	165	A B C D	185	A B C D
106	A B C D	126	A B C D	146	A B C D	166	A B C D	186	A B C D
107	A B C D	127	A B C D	147	A B C D	167	A B C D	187	A B C D
108	A B C D	128	A B C D	148	A B C D	168	A B C D	188	A B C D
109	A B C D	129	A B C D	149	A B C D	169	A B C D	189	A B C D
110	A B C D	130	A B C D	150	A B C D	170	A B C D	190	A B C D
111	A B C D	131	A B C D	151	A B C D	171	A B C D	191	A B C D
112	A B C D	132	A B C D	152	A B C D	172	A B C D	192	A B C D
113	A B C D	133	A B C D	153	A B C D	173	A B C D	193	A B C D
114	A B C D	134	A B C D	154	A B C D	174	A B C D	194	A B C D
115	A B C D	135	A B C D	155	A B C D	175	A B C D	195	A B C D
116	A B C D	136	A B C D	156	A B C D	176	A B C D	196	A B C D
117	A B C D	137	A B C D	157	A B C D	177	A B C D	197	A B C D
118	A B C D	138	A B C D	158	A B C D	178	A B C D	198	A B C D
119	A B C D	139	A B C D	159	A B C D	179	A B C D	199	A B C D
120	A B C D	140	A B C D	160	A B C D	180	A B C D	200	A B C D

맞은 문제 개수: ___/100

TEST 01의 점수를 환산한 후 목표 달성기에 TEST 01의 점수를 표시합니다.
점수 환산표는 문제집 329페이지, 목표 달성기는 교재의 첫 장에 있습니다.

Answer Sheet

TEST 02

READING (Part V~VII)

101	A B C D	121	A B C D	141	A B C D	161	A B C D	181	A B C D
102	A B C D	122	A B C D	142	A B C D	162	A B C D	182	A B C D
103	A B C D	123	A B C D	143	A B C D	163	A B C D	183	A B C D
104	A B C D	124	A B C D	144	A B C D	164	A B C D	184	A B C D
105	A B C D	125	A B C D	145	A B C D	165	A B C D	185	A B C D
106	A B C D	126	A B C D	146	A B C D	166	A B C D	186	A B C D
107	A B C D	127	A B C D	147	A B C D	167	A B C D	187	A B C D
108	A B C D	128	A B C D	148	A B C D	168	A B C D	188	A B C D
109	A B C D	129	A B C D	149	A B C D	169	A B C D	189	A B C D
110	A B C D	130	A B C D	150	A B C D	170	A B C D	190	A B C D
111	A B C D	131	A B C D	151	A B C D	171	A B C D	191	A B C D
112	A B C D	132	A B C D	152	A B C D	172	A B C D	192	A B C D
113	A B C D	133	A B C D	153	A B C D	173	A B C D	193	A B C D
114	A B C D	134	A B C D	154	A B C D	174	A B C D	194	A B C D
115	A B C D	135	A B C D	155	A B C D	175	A B C D	195	A B C D
116	A B C D	136	A B C D	156	A B C D	176	A B C D	196	A B C D
117	A B C D	137	A B C D	157	A B C D	177	A B C D	197	A B C D
118	A B C D	138	A B C D	158	A B C D	178	A B C D	198	A B C D
119	A B C D	139	A B C D	159	A B C D	179	A B C D	199	A B C D
120	A B C D	140	A B C D	160	A B C D	180	A B C D	200	A B C D

맞은 문제 개수: ___/100

TEST 02의 점수를 환산한 후 목표 달성기에 TEST 02의 점수를 표시합니다.
점수 환산표는 문제집 329페이지, 목표 달성기는 교재의 첫 장에 있습니다.

무료 토익·토스·오픽·지텔프 자료 제공
Hackers.co.kr

Answer Sheet

TEST 04

READING (Part V~VII)

#		#		#		#	
101	Ⓐ Ⓑ Ⓒ Ⓓ	121	Ⓐ Ⓑ Ⓒ Ⓓ	141	Ⓐ Ⓑ Ⓒ Ⓓ	161	Ⓐ Ⓑ Ⓒ Ⓓ	181	Ⓐ Ⓑ Ⓒ Ⓓ
102	Ⓐ Ⓑ Ⓒ Ⓓ	122	Ⓐ Ⓑ Ⓒ Ⓓ	142	Ⓐ Ⓑ Ⓒ Ⓓ	162	Ⓐ Ⓑ Ⓒ Ⓓ	182	Ⓐ Ⓑ Ⓒ Ⓓ
103	Ⓐ Ⓑ Ⓒ Ⓓ	123	Ⓐ Ⓑ Ⓒ Ⓓ	143	Ⓐ Ⓑ Ⓒ Ⓓ	163	Ⓐ Ⓑ Ⓒ Ⓓ	183	Ⓐ Ⓑ Ⓒ Ⓓ
104	Ⓐ Ⓑ Ⓒ Ⓓ	124	Ⓐ Ⓑ Ⓒ Ⓓ	144	Ⓐ Ⓑ Ⓒ Ⓓ	164	Ⓐ Ⓑ Ⓒ Ⓓ	184	Ⓐ Ⓑ Ⓒ Ⓓ
105	Ⓐ Ⓑ Ⓒ Ⓓ	125	Ⓐ Ⓑ Ⓒ Ⓓ	145	Ⓐ Ⓑ Ⓒ Ⓓ	165	Ⓐ Ⓑ Ⓒ Ⓓ	185	Ⓐ Ⓑ Ⓒ Ⓓ
106	Ⓐ Ⓑ Ⓒ Ⓓ	126	Ⓐ Ⓑ Ⓒ Ⓓ	146	Ⓐ Ⓑ Ⓒ Ⓓ	166	Ⓐ Ⓑ Ⓒ Ⓓ	186	Ⓐ Ⓑ Ⓒ Ⓓ
107	Ⓐ Ⓑ Ⓒ Ⓓ	127	Ⓐ Ⓑ Ⓒ Ⓓ	147	Ⓐ Ⓑ Ⓒ Ⓓ	167	Ⓐ Ⓑ Ⓒ Ⓓ	187	Ⓐ Ⓑ Ⓒ Ⓓ
108	Ⓐ Ⓑ Ⓒ Ⓓ	128	Ⓐ Ⓑ Ⓒ Ⓓ	148	Ⓐ Ⓑ Ⓒ Ⓓ	168	Ⓐ Ⓑ Ⓒ Ⓓ	188	Ⓐ Ⓑ Ⓒ Ⓓ
109	Ⓐ Ⓑ Ⓒ Ⓓ	129	Ⓐ Ⓑ Ⓒ Ⓓ	149	Ⓐ Ⓑ Ⓒ Ⓓ	169	Ⓐ Ⓑ Ⓒ Ⓓ	189	Ⓐ Ⓑ Ⓒ Ⓓ
110	Ⓐ Ⓑ Ⓒ Ⓓ	130	Ⓐ Ⓑ Ⓒ Ⓓ	150	Ⓐ Ⓑ Ⓒ Ⓓ	170	Ⓐ Ⓑ Ⓒ Ⓓ	190	Ⓐ Ⓑ Ⓒ Ⓓ
111	Ⓐ Ⓑ Ⓒ Ⓓ	131	Ⓐ Ⓑ Ⓒ Ⓓ	151	Ⓐ Ⓑ Ⓒ Ⓓ	171	Ⓐ Ⓑ Ⓒ Ⓓ	191	Ⓐ Ⓑ Ⓒ Ⓓ
112	Ⓐ Ⓑ Ⓒ Ⓓ	132	Ⓐ Ⓑ Ⓒ Ⓓ	152	Ⓐ Ⓑ Ⓒ Ⓓ	172	Ⓐ Ⓑ Ⓒ Ⓓ	192	Ⓐ Ⓑ Ⓒ Ⓓ
113	Ⓐ Ⓑ Ⓒ Ⓓ	133	Ⓐ Ⓑ Ⓒ Ⓓ	153	Ⓐ Ⓑ Ⓒ Ⓓ	173	Ⓐ Ⓑ Ⓒ Ⓓ	193	Ⓐ Ⓑ Ⓒ Ⓓ
114	Ⓐ Ⓑ Ⓒ Ⓓ	134	Ⓐ Ⓑ Ⓒ Ⓓ	154	Ⓐ Ⓑ Ⓒ Ⓓ	174	Ⓐ Ⓑ Ⓒ Ⓓ	194	Ⓐ Ⓑ Ⓒ Ⓓ
115	Ⓐ Ⓑ Ⓒ Ⓓ	135	Ⓐ Ⓑ Ⓒ Ⓓ	155	Ⓐ Ⓑ Ⓒ Ⓓ	175	Ⓐ Ⓑ Ⓒ Ⓓ	195	Ⓐ Ⓑ Ⓒ Ⓓ
116	Ⓐ Ⓑ Ⓒ Ⓓ	136	Ⓐ Ⓑ Ⓒ Ⓓ	156	Ⓐ Ⓑ Ⓒ Ⓓ	176	Ⓐ Ⓑ Ⓒ Ⓓ	196	Ⓐ Ⓑ Ⓒ Ⓓ
117	Ⓐ Ⓑ Ⓒ Ⓓ	137	Ⓐ Ⓑ Ⓒ Ⓓ	157	Ⓐ Ⓑ Ⓒ Ⓓ	177	Ⓐ Ⓑ Ⓒ Ⓓ	197	Ⓐ Ⓑ Ⓒ Ⓓ
118	Ⓐ Ⓑ Ⓒ Ⓓ	138	Ⓐ Ⓑ Ⓒ Ⓓ	158	Ⓐ Ⓑ Ⓒ Ⓓ	178	Ⓐ Ⓑ Ⓒ Ⓓ	198	Ⓐ Ⓑ Ⓒ Ⓓ
119	Ⓐ Ⓑ Ⓒ Ⓓ	139	Ⓐ Ⓑ Ⓒ Ⓓ	159	Ⓐ Ⓑ Ⓒ Ⓓ	179	Ⓐ Ⓑ Ⓒ Ⓓ	199	Ⓐ Ⓑ Ⓒ Ⓓ
120	Ⓐ Ⓑ Ⓒ Ⓓ	140	Ⓐ Ⓑ Ⓒ Ⓓ	160	Ⓐ Ⓑ Ⓒ Ⓓ	180	Ⓐ Ⓑ Ⓒ Ⓓ	200	Ⓐ Ⓑ Ⓒ Ⓓ

TEST 04의 점수를 환산한 후 목표 달성기에 TEST 04의 점수를 표시합니다.
점수 환산표는 문제집 329페이지, 목표 달성기는 교재의 첫 페이지에 정해 있습니다.

맞은 문제 개수: ___/100

자르는 선 ✂

Answer Sheet

TEST 03

READING (Part V~VII)

#		#		#		#	
101	Ⓐ Ⓑ Ⓒ Ⓓ	121	Ⓐ Ⓑ Ⓒ Ⓓ	141	Ⓐ Ⓑ Ⓒ Ⓓ	161	Ⓐ Ⓑ Ⓒ Ⓓ	181	Ⓐ Ⓑ Ⓒ Ⓓ
102	Ⓐ Ⓑ Ⓒ Ⓓ	122	Ⓐ Ⓑ Ⓒ Ⓓ	142	Ⓐ Ⓑ Ⓒ Ⓓ	162	Ⓐ Ⓑ Ⓒ Ⓓ	182	Ⓐ Ⓑ Ⓒ Ⓓ
103	Ⓐ Ⓑ Ⓒ Ⓓ	123	Ⓐ Ⓑ Ⓒ Ⓓ	143	Ⓐ Ⓑ Ⓒ Ⓓ	163	Ⓐ Ⓑ Ⓒ Ⓓ	183	Ⓐ Ⓑ Ⓒ Ⓓ
104	Ⓐ Ⓑ Ⓒ Ⓓ	124	Ⓐ Ⓑ Ⓒ Ⓓ	144	Ⓐ Ⓑ Ⓒ Ⓓ	164	Ⓐ Ⓑ Ⓒ Ⓓ	184	Ⓐ Ⓑ Ⓒ Ⓓ
105	Ⓐ Ⓑ Ⓒ Ⓓ	125	Ⓐ Ⓑ Ⓒ Ⓓ	145	Ⓐ Ⓑ Ⓒ Ⓓ	165	Ⓐ Ⓑ Ⓒ Ⓓ	185	Ⓐ Ⓑ Ⓒ Ⓓ
106	Ⓐ Ⓑ Ⓒ Ⓓ	126	Ⓐ Ⓑ Ⓒ Ⓓ	146	Ⓐ Ⓑ Ⓒ Ⓓ	166	Ⓐ Ⓑ Ⓒ Ⓓ	186	Ⓐ Ⓑ Ⓒ Ⓓ
107	Ⓐ Ⓑ Ⓒ Ⓓ	127	Ⓐ Ⓑ Ⓒ Ⓓ	147	Ⓐ Ⓑ Ⓒ Ⓓ	167	Ⓐ Ⓑ Ⓒ Ⓓ	187	Ⓐ Ⓑ Ⓒ Ⓓ
108	Ⓐ Ⓑ Ⓒ Ⓓ	128	Ⓐ Ⓑ Ⓒ Ⓓ	148	Ⓐ Ⓑ Ⓒ Ⓓ	168	Ⓐ Ⓑ Ⓒ Ⓓ	188	Ⓐ Ⓑ Ⓒ Ⓓ
109	Ⓐ Ⓑ Ⓒ Ⓓ	129	Ⓐ Ⓑ Ⓒ Ⓓ	149	Ⓐ Ⓑ Ⓒ Ⓓ	169	Ⓐ Ⓑ Ⓒ Ⓓ	189	Ⓐ Ⓑ Ⓒ Ⓓ
110	Ⓐ Ⓑ Ⓒ Ⓓ	130	Ⓐ Ⓑ Ⓒ Ⓓ	150	Ⓐ Ⓑ Ⓒ Ⓓ	170	Ⓐ Ⓑ Ⓒ Ⓓ	190	Ⓐ Ⓑ Ⓒ Ⓓ
111	Ⓐ Ⓑ Ⓒ Ⓓ	131	Ⓐ Ⓑ Ⓒ Ⓓ	151	Ⓐ Ⓑ Ⓒ Ⓓ	171	Ⓐ Ⓑ Ⓒ Ⓓ	191	Ⓐ Ⓑ Ⓒ Ⓓ
112	Ⓐ Ⓑ Ⓒ Ⓓ	132	Ⓐ Ⓑ Ⓒ Ⓓ	152	Ⓐ Ⓑ Ⓒ Ⓓ	172	Ⓐ Ⓑ Ⓒ Ⓓ	192	Ⓐ Ⓑ Ⓒ Ⓓ
113	Ⓐ Ⓑ Ⓒ Ⓓ	133	Ⓐ Ⓑ Ⓒ Ⓓ	153	Ⓐ Ⓑ Ⓒ Ⓓ	173	Ⓐ Ⓑ Ⓒ Ⓓ	193	Ⓐ Ⓑ Ⓒ Ⓓ
114	Ⓐ Ⓑ Ⓒ Ⓓ	134	Ⓐ Ⓑ Ⓒ Ⓓ	154	Ⓐ Ⓑ Ⓒ Ⓓ	174	Ⓐ Ⓑ Ⓒ Ⓓ	194	Ⓐ Ⓑ Ⓒ Ⓓ
115	Ⓐ Ⓑ Ⓒ Ⓓ	135	Ⓐ Ⓑ Ⓒ Ⓓ	155	Ⓐ Ⓑ Ⓒ Ⓓ	175	Ⓐ Ⓑ Ⓒ Ⓓ	195	Ⓐ Ⓑ Ⓒ Ⓓ
116	Ⓐ Ⓑ Ⓒ Ⓓ	136	Ⓐ Ⓑ Ⓒ Ⓓ	156	Ⓐ Ⓑ Ⓒ Ⓓ	176	Ⓐ Ⓑ Ⓒ Ⓓ	196	Ⓐ Ⓑ Ⓒ Ⓓ
117	Ⓐ Ⓑ Ⓒ Ⓓ	137	Ⓐ Ⓑ Ⓒ Ⓓ	157	Ⓐ Ⓑ Ⓒ Ⓓ	177	Ⓐ Ⓑ Ⓒ Ⓓ	197	Ⓐ Ⓑ Ⓒ Ⓓ
118	Ⓐ Ⓑ Ⓒ Ⓓ	138	Ⓐ Ⓑ Ⓒ Ⓓ	158	Ⓐ Ⓑ Ⓒ Ⓓ	178	Ⓐ Ⓑ Ⓒ Ⓓ	198	Ⓐ Ⓑ Ⓒ Ⓓ
119	Ⓐ Ⓑ Ⓒ Ⓓ	139	Ⓐ Ⓑ Ⓒ Ⓓ	159	Ⓐ Ⓑ Ⓒ Ⓓ	179	Ⓐ Ⓑ Ⓒ Ⓓ	199	Ⓐ Ⓑ Ⓒ Ⓓ
120	Ⓐ Ⓑ Ⓒ Ⓓ	140	Ⓐ Ⓑ Ⓒ Ⓓ	160	Ⓐ Ⓑ Ⓒ Ⓓ	180	Ⓐ Ⓑ Ⓒ Ⓓ	200	Ⓐ Ⓑ Ⓒ Ⓓ

TEST 03의 점수를 환산한 후 목표 달성기에 TEST 03의 점수를 표시합니다.
점수 환산표는 문제집 329페이지, 목표 달성기는 교재의 첫 페이지에 정해 있습니다.

맞은 문제 개수: ___/100

무료 토익·토스·오픽·지텔프 자료 제공
Hackers.co.kr

READING (Part V~VII)

101	102	103	104	105	106	107	108	109	110	111	112	113	114	115	116	117	118	119	120
121	122	123	124	125	126	127	128	129	130	131	132	133	134	135	136	137	138	139	140
141	142	143	144	145	146	147	148	149	150	151	152	153	154	155	156	157	158	159	160
161	162	163	164	165	166	167	168	169	170	171	172	173	174	175	176	177	178	179	180
181	182	183	184	185	186	187	188	189	190	191	192	193	194	195	196	197	198	199	200

맞은 문제 개수: ___ /100

TEST 06의 점수를 환산한 후 목표 달성기에 TEST 06의 점수를 표시합니다.
점수 환산표는 문제집 329페이지, 목표 달성기는 교재의 첫 장에 있습니다.

✂ 자르는 선

Answer Sheet

TEST 05

READING (Part V~VII)

101	102	103	104	105	106	107	108	109	110	111	112	113	114	115	116	117	118	119	120
121	122	123	124	125	126	127	128	129	130	131	132	133	134	135	136	137	138	139	140
141	142	143	144	145	146	147	148	149	150	151	152	153	154	155	156	157	158	159	160
161	162	163	164	165	166	167	168	169	170	171	172	173	174	175	176	177	178	179	180
181	182	183	184	185	186	187	188	189	190	191	192	193	194	195	196	197	198	199	200

맞은 문제 개수: ___ /100

TEST 05의 점수를 환산한 후 목표 달성기에 TEST 05의 점수를 표시합니다.
점수 환산표는 문제집 329페이지, 목표 달성기는 교재의 첫 장에 있습니다.

✂ 자르는 선

무료 토익·토스·오픽·지텔프 자료 제공
Hackers.co.kr

Answer Sheet

TEST 08

READING (Part V~VII)

101	102	103	104	105	106	107	108	109	110	111	112	113	114	115	116	117	118	119	120
121	122	123	124	125	126	127	128	129	130	131	132	133	134	135	136	137	138	139	140
141	142	143	144	145	146	147	148	149	150	151	152	153	154	155	156	157	158	159	160
161	162	163	164	165	166	167	168	169	170	171	172	173	174	175	176	177	178	179	180
181	182	183	184	185	186	187	188	189	190	191	192	193	194	195	196	197	198	199	200

맞은 문제 개수: ___/100

TEST 08의 점수를 환산한 후 목표 달성기에 TEST 08의 점수를 표시합니다.
점수 환산표는 문제집 329페이지, 목표 달성기는 교재의 첫 장에 있습니다.

자르는 선 ✂

Answer Sheet

TEST 07

READING (Part V~VII)

101	102	103	104	105	106	107	108	109	110	111	112	113	114	115	116	117	118	119	120
121	122	123	124	125	126	127	128	129	130	131	132	133	134	135	136	137	138	139	140
141	142	143	144	145	146	147	148	149	150	151	152	153	154	155	156	157	158	159	160
161	162	163	164	165	166	167	168	169	170	171	172	173	174	175	176	177	178	179	180
181	182	183	184	185	186	187	188	189	190	191	192	193	194	195	196	197	198	199	200

맞은 문제 개수: ___/100

TEST 07의 점수를 환산한 후 목표 달성기에 TEST 07의 점수를 표시합니다.
점수 환산표는 문제집 329페이지, 목표 달성기는 교재의 첫 장에 있습니다.

자르는 선 ✂

무료 토익·토스·오픽·지텔프 자료 제공
Hackers.co.kr

Answer Sheet

TEST 10

READING (Part V~VII)

101 Ⓐ Ⓑ Ⓒ Ⓓ	121 Ⓐ Ⓑ Ⓒ Ⓓ	141 Ⓐ Ⓑ Ⓒ Ⓓ	161 Ⓐ Ⓑ Ⓒ Ⓓ	181 Ⓐ Ⓑ Ⓒ Ⓓ
102 Ⓐ Ⓑ Ⓒ Ⓓ	122 Ⓐ Ⓑ Ⓒ Ⓓ	142 Ⓐ Ⓑ Ⓒ Ⓓ	162 Ⓐ Ⓑ Ⓒ Ⓓ	182 Ⓐ Ⓑ Ⓒ Ⓓ
103 Ⓐ Ⓑ Ⓒ Ⓓ	123 Ⓐ Ⓑ Ⓒ Ⓓ	143 Ⓐ Ⓑ Ⓒ Ⓓ	163 Ⓐ Ⓑ Ⓒ Ⓓ	183 Ⓐ Ⓑ Ⓒ Ⓓ
104 Ⓐ Ⓑ Ⓒ Ⓓ	124 Ⓐ Ⓑ Ⓒ Ⓓ	144 Ⓐ Ⓑ Ⓒ Ⓓ	164 Ⓐ Ⓑ Ⓒ Ⓓ	184 Ⓐ Ⓑ Ⓒ Ⓓ
105 Ⓐ Ⓑ Ⓒ Ⓓ	125 Ⓐ Ⓑ Ⓒ Ⓓ	145 Ⓐ Ⓑ Ⓒ Ⓓ	165 Ⓐ Ⓑ Ⓒ Ⓓ	185 Ⓐ Ⓑ Ⓒ Ⓓ
106 Ⓐ Ⓑ Ⓒ Ⓓ	126 Ⓐ Ⓑ Ⓒ Ⓓ	146 Ⓐ Ⓑ Ⓒ Ⓓ	166 Ⓐ Ⓑ Ⓒ Ⓓ	186 Ⓐ Ⓑ Ⓒ Ⓓ
107 Ⓐ Ⓑ Ⓒ Ⓓ	127 Ⓐ Ⓑ Ⓒ Ⓓ	147 Ⓐ Ⓑ Ⓒ Ⓓ	167 Ⓐ Ⓑ Ⓒ Ⓓ	187 Ⓐ Ⓑ Ⓒ Ⓓ
108 Ⓐ Ⓑ Ⓒ Ⓓ	128 Ⓐ Ⓑ Ⓒ Ⓓ	148 Ⓐ Ⓑ Ⓒ Ⓓ	168 Ⓐ Ⓑ Ⓒ Ⓓ	188 Ⓐ Ⓑ Ⓒ Ⓓ
109 Ⓐ Ⓑ Ⓒ Ⓓ	129 Ⓐ Ⓑ Ⓒ Ⓓ	149 Ⓐ Ⓑ Ⓒ Ⓓ	169 Ⓐ Ⓑ Ⓒ Ⓓ	189 Ⓐ Ⓑ Ⓒ Ⓓ
110 Ⓐ Ⓑ Ⓒ Ⓓ	130 Ⓐ Ⓑ Ⓒ Ⓓ	150 Ⓐ Ⓑ Ⓒ Ⓓ	170 Ⓐ Ⓑ Ⓒ Ⓓ	190 Ⓐ Ⓑ Ⓒ Ⓓ
111 Ⓐ Ⓑ Ⓒ Ⓓ	131 Ⓐ Ⓑ Ⓒ Ⓓ	151 Ⓐ Ⓑ Ⓒ Ⓓ	171 Ⓐ Ⓑ Ⓒ Ⓓ	191 Ⓐ Ⓑ Ⓒ Ⓓ
112 Ⓐ Ⓑ Ⓒ Ⓓ	132 Ⓐ Ⓑ Ⓒ Ⓓ	152 Ⓐ Ⓑ Ⓒ Ⓓ	172 Ⓐ Ⓑ Ⓒ Ⓓ	192 Ⓐ Ⓑ Ⓒ Ⓓ
113 Ⓐ Ⓑ Ⓒ Ⓓ	133 Ⓐ Ⓑ Ⓒ Ⓓ	153 Ⓐ Ⓑ Ⓒ Ⓓ	173 Ⓐ Ⓑ Ⓒ Ⓓ	193 Ⓐ Ⓑ Ⓒ Ⓓ
114 Ⓐ Ⓑ Ⓒ Ⓓ	134 Ⓐ Ⓑ Ⓒ Ⓓ	154 Ⓐ Ⓑ Ⓒ Ⓓ	174 Ⓐ Ⓑ Ⓒ Ⓓ	194 Ⓐ Ⓑ Ⓒ Ⓓ
115 Ⓐ Ⓑ Ⓒ Ⓓ	135 Ⓐ Ⓑ Ⓒ Ⓓ	155 Ⓐ Ⓑ Ⓒ Ⓓ	175 Ⓐ Ⓑ Ⓒ Ⓓ	195 Ⓐ Ⓑ Ⓒ Ⓓ
116 Ⓐ Ⓑ Ⓒ Ⓓ	136 Ⓐ Ⓑ Ⓒ Ⓓ	156 Ⓐ Ⓑ Ⓒ Ⓓ	176 Ⓐ Ⓑ Ⓒ Ⓓ	196 Ⓐ Ⓑ Ⓒ Ⓓ
117 Ⓐ Ⓑ Ⓒ Ⓓ	137 Ⓐ Ⓑ Ⓒ Ⓓ	157 Ⓐ Ⓑ Ⓒ Ⓓ	177 Ⓐ Ⓑ Ⓒ Ⓓ	197 Ⓐ Ⓑ Ⓒ Ⓓ
118 Ⓐ Ⓑ Ⓒ Ⓓ	138 Ⓐ Ⓑ Ⓒ Ⓓ	158 Ⓐ Ⓑ Ⓒ Ⓓ	178 Ⓐ Ⓑ Ⓒ Ⓓ	198 Ⓐ Ⓑ Ⓒ Ⓓ
119 Ⓐ Ⓑ Ⓒ Ⓓ	139 Ⓐ Ⓑ Ⓒ Ⓓ	159 Ⓐ Ⓑ Ⓒ Ⓓ	179 Ⓐ Ⓑ Ⓒ Ⓓ	199 Ⓐ Ⓑ Ⓒ Ⓓ
120 Ⓐ Ⓑ Ⓒ Ⓓ	140 Ⓐ Ⓑ Ⓒ Ⓓ	160 Ⓐ Ⓑ Ⓒ Ⓓ	180 Ⓐ Ⓑ Ⓒ Ⓓ	200 Ⓐ Ⓑ Ⓒ Ⓓ

맞은 문제 개수: ___ /100

TEST 10의 점수를 환산한 후 목표 달성기에 TEST 10의 점수를 표시합니다.
점수 환산표는 문제집 329페이지, 목표 달성기는 교재의 첫 장에 있습니다.

✂ 자르는 선

Answer Sheet

TEST 09

READING (Part V~VII)

101 Ⓐ Ⓑ Ⓒ Ⓓ	121 Ⓐ Ⓑ Ⓒ Ⓓ	141 Ⓐ Ⓑ Ⓒ Ⓓ	161 Ⓐ Ⓑ Ⓒ Ⓓ	181 Ⓐ Ⓑ Ⓒ Ⓓ
102 Ⓐ Ⓑ Ⓒ Ⓓ	122 Ⓐ Ⓑ Ⓒ Ⓓ	142 Ⓐ Ⓑ Ⓒ Ⓓ	162 Ⓐ Ⓑ Ⓒ Ⓓ	182 Ⓐ Ⓑ Ⓒ Ⓓ
103 Ⓐ Ⓑ Ⓒ Ⓓ	123 Ⓐ Ⓑ Ⓒ Ⓓ	143 Ⓐ Ⓑ Ⓒ Ⓓ	163 Ⓐ Ⓑ Ⓒ Ⓓ	183 Ⓐ Ⓑ Ⓒ Ⓓ
104 Ⓐ Ⓑ Ⓒ Ⓓ	124 Ⓐ Ⓑ Ⓒ Ⓓ	144 Ⓐ Ⓑ Ⓒ Ⓓ	164 Ⓐ Ⓑ Ⓒ Ⓓ	184 Ⓐ Ⓑ Ⓒ Ⓓ
105 Ⓐ Ⓑ Ⓒ Ⓓ	125 Ⓐ Ⓑ Ⓒ Ⓓ	145 Ⓐ Ⓑ Ⓒ Ⓓ	165 Ⓐ Ⓑ Ⓒ Ⓓ	185 Ⓐ Ⓑ Ⓒ Ⓓ
106 Ⓐ Ⓑ Ⓒ Ⓓ	126 Ⓐ Ⓑ Ⓒ Ⓓ	146 Ⓐ Ⓑ Ⓒ Ⓓ	166 Ⓐ Ⓑ Ⓒ Ⓓ	186 Ⓐ Ⓑ Ⓒ Ⓓ
107 Ⓐ Ⓑ Ⓒ Ⓓ	127 Ⓐ Ⓑ Ⓒ Ⓓ	147 Ⓐ Ⓑ Ⓒ Ⓓ	167 Ⓐ Ⓑ Ⓒ Ⓓ	187 Ⓐ Ⓑ Ⓒ Ⓓ
108 Ⓐ Ⓑ Ⓒ Ⓓ	128 Ⓐ Ⓑ Ⓒ Ⓓ	148 Ⓐ Ⓑ Ⓒ Ⓓ	168 Ⓐ Ⓑ Ⓒ Ⓓ	188 Ⓐ Ⓑ Ⓒ Ⓓ
109 Ⓐ Ⓑ Ⓒ Ⓓ	129 Ⓐ Ⓑ Ⓒ Ⓓ	149 Ⓐ Ⓑ Ⓒ Ⓓ	169 Ⓐ Ⓑ Ⓒ Ⓓ	189 Ⓐ Ⓑ Ⓒ Ⓓ
110 Ⓐ Ⓑ Ⓒ Ⓓ	130 Ⓐ Ⓑ Ⓒ Ⓓ	150 Ⓐ Ⓑ Ⓒ Ⓓ	170 Ⓐ Ⓑ Ⓒ Ⓓ	190 Ⓐ Ⓑ Ⓒ Ⓓ
111 Ⓐ Ⓑ Ⓒ Ⓓ	131 Ⓐ Ⓑ Ⓒ Ⓓ	151 Ⓐ Ⓑ Ⓒ Ⓓ	171 Ⓐ Ⓑ Ⓒ Ⓓ	191 Ⓐ Ⓑ Ⓒ Ⓓ
112 Ⓐ Ⓑ Ⓒ Ⓓ	132 Ⓐ Ⓑ Ⓒ Ⓓ	152 Ⓐ Ⓑ Ⓒ Ⓓ	172 Ⓐ Ⓑ Ⓒ Ⓓ	192 Ⓐ Ⓑ Ⓒ Ⓓ
113 Ⓐ Ⓑ Ⓒ Ⓓ	133 Ⓐ Ⓑ Ⓒ Ⓓ	153 Ⓐ Ⓑ Ⓒ Ⓓ	173 Ⓐ Ⓑ Ⓒ Ⓓ	193 Ⓐ Ⓑ Ⓒ Ⓓ
114 Ⓐ Ⓑ Ⓒ Ⓓ	134 Ⓐ Ⓑ Ⓒ Ⓓ	154 Ⓐ Ⓑ Ⓒ Ⓓ	174 Ⓐ Ⓑ Ⓒ Ⓓ	194 Ⓐ Ⓑ Ⓒ Ⓓ
115 Ⓐ Ⓑ Ⓒ Ⓓ	135 Ⓐ Ⓑ Ⓒ Ⓓ	155 Ⓐ Ⓑ Ⓒ Ⓓ	175 Ⓐ Ⓑ Ⓒ Ⓓ	195 Ⓐ Ⓑ Ⓒ Ⓓ
116 Ⓐ Ⓑ Ⓒ Ⓓ	136 Ⓐ Ⓑ Ⓒ Ⓓ	156 Ⓐ Ⓑ Ⓒ Ⓓ	176 Ⓐ Ⓑ Ⓒ Ⓓ	196 Ⓐ Ⓑ Ⓒ Ⓓ
117 Ⓐ Ⓑ Ⓒ Ⓓ	137 Ⓐ Ⓑ Ⓒ Ⓓ	157 Ⓐ Ⓑ Ⓒ Ⓓ	177 Ⓐ Ⓑ Ⓒ Ⓓ	197 Ⓐ Ⓑ Ⓒ Ⓓ
118 Ⓐ Ⓑ Ⓒ Ⓓ	138 Ⓐ Ⓑ Ⓒ Ⓓ	158 Ⓐ Ⓑ Ⓒ Ⓓ	178 Ⓐ Ⓑ Ⓒ Ⓓ	198 Ⓐ Ⓑ Ⓒ Ⓓ
119 Ⓐ Ⓑ Ⓒ Ⓓ	139 Ⓐ Ⓑ Ⓒ Ⓓ	159 Ⓐ Ⓑ Ⓒ Ⓓ	179 Ⓐ Ⓑ Ⓒ Ⓓ	199 Ⓐ Ⓑ Ⓒ Ⓓ
120 Ⓐ Ⓑ Ⓒ Ⓓ	140 Ⓐ Ⓑ Ⓒ Ⓓ	160 Ⓐ Ⓑ Ⓒ Ⓓ	180 Ⓐ Ⓑ Ⓒ Ⓓ	200 Ⓐ Ⓑ Ⓒ Ⓓ

맞은 문제 개수: ___ /100

TEST 09의 점수를 환산한 후 목표 달성기에 TEST 09의 점수를 표시합니다.
점수 환산표는 문제집 329페이지, 목표 달성기는 교재의 첫 장에 있습니다.

✂ 자르는 선

무료 토익·토스·오픽·지텔프 자료 제공
Hackers.co.kr

최신 기출유형으로 실전 완벽 마무리

해커스 토익 RC

실전 1000제 READING 2 문제집

개정 3판 4쇄 발행 2024년 12월 9일

개정 3판 1쇄 발행 2023년 1월 2일

지은이	해커스 어학연구소
펴낸곳	㈜해커스 어학연구소
펴낸이	해커스 어학연구소 출판팀

주소	서울특별시 서초구 강남대로61길 23 ㈜해커스 어학연구소
고객센터	02-537-5000
교재 관련 문의	publishing@hackers.com
동영상강의	HackersIngang.com

ISBN	978-89-6542-538-0 (13740)
Serial Number	03-04-01

외국어인강 1위, 해커스인강
HackersIngang.com

해커스인강

· 해커스 토익 스타강사의 **본 교재 인강**
· 최신 출제경향이 반영된 **무료 온라인 실전모의고사**
· 들으면서 외우는 **무료 단어암기장 및 단어암기 MP3**
· 빠르고 편리하게 채점하는 **무료 정답녹음 MP3**

영어 전문 포털, 해커스토익
Hackers.co.kr

해커스토익

· 본 교재 무료 **Part 5&6 해설**
· **무료 매월 적중예상특강 및 실시간 토익시험 정답확인/해설강의**
· 매일 실전 RC/LC 문제 및 토익 기출보카 TEST, 토익기출 100단어 등 다양한 무료 학습 콘텐츠

헤럴드 선정 2018 대학생 선호브랜드 대상 '대학생이 선정한 외국어인강' 부문 1위

5천 개가 넘는
해커스토익 무료 자료!

대한민국에서 공짜로 토익 공부하고 싶으면 | 해커스영어 Hackers.co.kr ▾ | 검색

강의도 무료

베스트셀러 1위 토익 강의 150강 무료 서비스,
누적 시청 1,900만 돌파!

문제도 무료

토익 RC/LC 풀기, 모의토익 등
실전토익 대비 문제 3,730제 무료!

최신 특강도 무료

2,400만뷰 스타강사의
압도적 적중예상특강 매달 업데이트!

공부법도 무료

토익 고득점 달성팁, 비법노트,
점수대별 공부법 무료 확인

가장 빠른 정답까지!

615만이 선택한 해커스 토익 정답!
시험 직후 가장 빠른 정답 확인

*미션 달성 시

더 많은
토익무료자료 보기 ▶